9/30/97

To Ric [barcode] 's

ole pal — a real

crystal Champagne

type guy ~

Charlie Keally

Legal Extortion

The War against Lincoln Savings and Charlie Keating

Legal Extortion

The War against Lincoln Savings and Charlie Keating

Jack D. Atchison

Northwest Publishing, Inc.
Salt Lake City, Utah

Legal Extortion

For information address: Northwest Publishing, Inc.
6906 South 300 West, Salt Lake City, Utah 84047

SCM 02 17 95

PRINTING HISTORY
First Printing 1995

ISBN: 0-7610-0151-4

NPI books are published by Northwest Publishing, Incorporated,
6906 South 300 West, Salt Lake City, Utah 84047.
The name "NPI" and the "NPI" logo are trademarks belonging to
Northwest Publishing, Incorporated.

PRINTED IN THE UNITED STATES OF AMERICA.
10 9 8 7 6 5 4 3 2 1

To the survivors and victims of the Lincoln Savings War
particularly
Andy Ligget, Bob Wurzelbacher, and Charles H. Keating III
and to
the warriors who protected my interests in the battles:
John Munger, Philip Kimble, Mark Chadwick, Wrenn Chais,
Paul Murphy, and Ed Meier

Table of Contents

Acknowledgments ix
Introduction xi
1. Deregulation Brings ACC to the Battlefield 1
2. Re-regulation Sets Stage for War 13
3. The First Shot: 1986 Examination of Lincoln 33
4. Keating Meets the FHLBB's Field Troops 49
5. FHLBB's Line of Attack 73
6. Tightening the Screws on Lincoln 111
7. The Keating Five 135
8. Dirty Tricks and the Regulators' Report 169
9. San Francisco Rejects Peace Overture 197
10. Negotiating a Peaceful Solution 217
11. Cease-Fire Agreement 251
12. FHLBB Violates Peace Accord 267
13. Lincoln's Largest Transaction Produces Fallout 287
14. FHLBB Launches Vicious Attack 295

15. FHLBB Moves in for the Kill 329
16. ACC Raises White Flag 377
17. FHLBB Rejects ACC's Surrender 409
18. Congress Covers Its Tracks 427
19. Keating and Wall Cast as Scapegoats 449
20. Federal Judge Seals Keating's Fate 493
21. Legal Extortion 523
Epilogue: Has the Truth Been Told? 563
Characters 569
Abbreviations 575

Acknowledgments

I am very indebted to the following people for their support and assistance in bringing this book to print: Amy, Douglas, and Michael Atchison, Fr. Joseph Fessio, S.J., Anne Englund Nash, Dean Dwyer, Larry Kornegay, William C. Brown, Elaine Boland, and Carol Kassick. You each know your individual contributions, and I trust that you know how grateful I am for them.

Introduction

This is a story about a war. It started in 1984 as a philosophical disagreement. In 1986, a series of skirmishes broke out which later escalated to a full-scale conflagration that lasted for over three years.

The combatants were: the United States government, the victor; and American Continental Corporation (ACC) and its chairman, Charles H Keating, Jr., the vanquished. The object of the war was Lincoln Savings and Loan Association of Irvine, California (Lincoln). It died in the conflict.

The forces of the United States government were led by the Federal Home Loan Bank Board (FHLBB), a troika whose members changed several times during the war. Its troops consisted of examiners and regulators employed by the FHLBB, most notably those stationed in Washington, D.C., and San Francisco. Its allies were numerous and ranged from the Securities and Exchange Commission and the United States Department of Justice to the United States Congress. It also engaged mercenaries—consultants, accountants, and lawyers.

The forces of ACC were commanded by Charlie Keating. His troops consisted of the officers, directors, and employees of ACC and Lincoln. They too engaged mercenaries—consultants, accountants, and lawyers. They were outgunned.

The government forces fought many similar wars. And won them all. Since 1980, government victories have resulted in the deaths of nearly two thousand savings and loans and banks; the most bank failures and seizures since the Great Depression. More wars will be fought in the future—government forces will win those too.

During the Lincoln Savings war, the most publicized the government has engaged in, government forces did not display their customary discipline. The troops in San Francisco did not follow the FHLBB's established order of battle. They rebelled against Washington's authority and later, when under the scrutiny of Congress, mutinied and turned on their generals.

Mid-level leaders in both San Francisco and Washington violated the rules of the game. They leaked confidential documents to the press with the conscious intent to damage their opponent. Their plans, in part, backfired. In an attempt to make amends to the opposition, and in search of a peaceful solution to the conflict, the FHLBB stripped San Francisco of its command.

But San Francisco had sympathizers among the lower ranks in Washington. They carried on San Francisco's cause and utilized its tactics. They continued to leak information. They violated the terms of the cease-fire and launched a new and more vigorous attack against the enemy. They deceived their superiors by withholding information and distorting other important data. They created numerous diversions which occupied the enemy forces and drained the enemy's resources.

With the enemy weakened, the Washington troops encouraged a retreat with honor. If ACC would surrender Lincoln to a party acceptable to the FHLBB, ACC would be allowed to live. So, ACC tried to negotiate a surrender. It learned too late that the FHLBB's offer was nothing more than a ruse. The FHLBB's troops had no intention of allowing ACC to live. While ACC was negotiating in good faith, the Washington troops put in place plans for the final and decisive attack.

With ACC's defeat, the government did what all victors do; it wrote the history of the war. There is established precedent for how the government writes history. It has been doing so for decades and is very skilled at inculcating its citizens with its version of the facts. The events of the war, as described to the press and which the press later reported to the public, conformed to the spin put on them by the government.

In the official story presented to the American public, the government's forces were honored as heroes. The enemy was accused of heinous deeds, and its forces were labeled criminals.

The enemy and parties who were allied with it were forced to pay extortionate reparations to the government as well as to citizens who claimed they were injured in the conflict. Politicians who supported the enemy's cause, or who intervened in trying to resolve the conflict, were excoriated by their colleagues in government.

But, as in all wars, we have learned there are two sides to the story. The official version and eyewitness versions. This is an eyewitness account of the Lincoln Savings War. It does not conform to the government's official version that you have read in the press.

This is what really happened.

One

Deregulation Brings ACC to the Battlefield

War is a strange phenomenon. Circumstances draw two parties onto the same turf. Each believes it is in control of all that happens within the domain. Differences emerge between the two factions, sowing the seeds of conflict. Seemingly innocuous events are converted into grievous transgressions. The parties' emotions become overheated. Tempers flare. A point is reached where one party decides that in order to preserve its own self-interests, it must attack and destroy the other. When all is over, nobody, including historians using twenty-twenty hindsight, can say with absolute certainty what caused the first shot to be fired.

Thus was the nature of this war.

The contested turf was a Southern California financial institution—Lincoln Savings and Loan Association of Irvine. The warring factions were brought together on February 22, 1984, when Lincoln, which was subject to the regulatory supervision of the Federal Home Loan Bank Board (FHLBB), was purchased by American Continental Corporation (ACC), a Phoenix, Arizona-based, home-building company. ACC's purchase of Lincoln set the stage for a series of bitterly fought battles between ACC and the United States government and its agent, the FHLBB.

As in virtually all other wars, the parties were drawn onto the battlefield by the convergence of events whose origins lay in the past. So, to understand this war, it is necessary first briefly to review the history of the savings-and-loan industry in the United States and ACC's entry into that industry.

For the decades prior to the 1970s, most savings and loan associations (S&Ls) were traditional. Their primary business was accepting monies in the form of savings deposits and using such monies to fund loans to buyers of single-family homes. The S&Ls held the loans, secured by first mortgages on the purchased homes, for collection. The mortgage loans generally called for repayment by the borrower over a term of thirty years and bore a fixed rate of interest. The S&L's income was the difference between the interest it collected from borrowers and the interest it paid depositors plus its operating expenses.

Operating a traditional savings and loan was a relatively simple business—a no-brainer—requiring limited managerial talent to produce a modest profit. The rate an S&L paid to depositors was fixed by the government. In effect, so was the rate charged to borrowers for mortgage loans. The difference between the two rates, known as the interest-rate spread, was about 2 percent. To make money, an S&L simply had to control its operating expenses, such as salaries and rents, relative to its level of deposits and loans.

In the 1970s, this simple business began to change. New competition for savings deposits emerged. National stock brokerages, such as Merrill Lynch and Paine Webber, offered their customers the chance to invest in money-market funds. These funds accepted monies from customers and invested such monies by buying government securities, usually bonds or notes issued by the U.S. Treasury. The fund passed through to its investors the interest it collected from the government securities, less a relatively small management fee. The yield to the investor from these funds was greater than the rate savings and loans were permitted to pay. Because the securities held by the funds were backed by the full faith and credit of the U.S. government, the investor's risk was nominal. Fueled by the higher yields, money was driven out of the S&Ls and into the funds.

The exodus of deposits from the S&Ls increased in the late 1970s, when inflation raised its ugly head. Inflation caused general interest rates to soar into double digits. As a consequence, the rates offered by the money-market funds skyrocketed. But the rate offered by S&Ls was still pegged by the government at 5.5 percent for most deposits.

The outflow of funds caused horrendous problems for the savings and loans. At first, they didn't have enough funds to make new loans, stopping the S&Ls' growth rates, individually and as an industry. Then, S&Ls had to borrow funds or sell assets to have sufficient monies to cover deposit withdrawals. Their income began to decline as their assets shrank and, unable to reduce expenses, they started to incur losses. By 1980, hundreds of S&Ls were reporting big losses, and some were nearing capital deficits. Regulators and S&L owners alike began to fear that the entire industry would fail.

Realizing limits on rates had to be removed, Congress passed the Depository Institutions Deregulation and Monetary Control Act. The Act provided for the phasing out of all interest-rate caps on deposits over a period of six years. This freed S&Ls to compete with the money-market funds for new deposits by allowing S&Ls to offer depositors rates established by market forces rather than by government fiat.

The Act also began to liberalize, or deregulate, the types of investments an S&L could make. It allowed an S&L to invest up to 20 percent of its assets in any combination of consumer loans, corporate bonds, or commercial paper. Because of intense lobbying efforts by the S&L industry, the Act also permitted S&Ls to offer their customers a form of checking account, called NOW Accounts, standing for "negotiable order of withdrawal accounts," closing the gap between commercial banks and S&Ls.

The Act had one other very significant provision. Deposits in S&Ls, up to a specified dollar limit, were insured by the Federal Savings and Loan Insurance Corporation (FSLIC), an entity created and backed by the U.S. government. The insurance was designed solely to protect depositors— not the S&L or its shareholders. If an insured S&L was unable to repay a depositor, the FSLIC would. Prior to the passage of the Act, amounts up to $40,000 had been covered by federal insurance. The Act increased the covered amount to $100,000. This let S&Ls attract larger deposits.

Armed with the ability to offer market interest rates, S&Ls stemmed the outflow of monies, and new deposits replenished their depleted coffers. Just as the S&Ls thought the crisis had passed, a new problem arose. Inflation continued to drive up interest rates, and interest expense was climbing at an increasing rate. In 1981, the prime rate, a rate that influenced what S&Ls paid their depositors, hit 21.5 percent, an all-time high. When certificates of deposits matured, they were replaced by new certificates at higher rates.

Meanwhile, the bulk of the S&Ls' assets continued to earn their lower fixed rates. The assets, consisting primarily of mortgage loans, many of which had been originated years earlier when rates were very low (generally less than 8 percent), did not reprice like the liabilities. Moreover, because the interest rates on the loans were low, borrowers were not anxious to pay these debts off early. Instead, borrowers took advantage of assumption options and, when they sold the property securing the loan, the new buyer was permitted to assume the existing loan. These mortgage assumptions allowed S&Ls only to collect a modest fee and make a minor increase in the interest rate.

The combination of increasing interest costs and static interest income rapidly eroded the interest-rate spread. With huge inventories of fixed-rate mortgages bearing low interest rates, and with rates on deposits inexorably moving up as each day passed, the spread turned negative. Interest expense exceeded interest income. Losses mounted, and the S&Ls were awash in red ink.

The S&Ls had no way to cure their earnings problem. Market forces would not allow them to sell their inventories of mortgage loans. When interest rates rise, the market value of fixed-rate securities falls. It did not take long for the market value of the mortgages which the S&Ls held to be far, far below the value at which the mortgages were recorded on the S&Ls' books. If the S&Ls opted to relieve themselves of their burdensome inventories, they would suffer losses. It was a "Catch-22" situation. If the S&Ls held their inventories, they lost money. If they sold the inventories, they lost money. There was no way out of the trap that had ensnared them.

In early 1981, nearly 90 percent of the S&Ls in the country were losing money, and the number of dying S&Ls was increasing at an alarming rate. The Reagan administration, under the direction of Secretary of the Treasury Donald Regan, started to consider various plans to stem the impending disaster that would result if all of the country's S&Ls continued on their path toward failure. If the troubled S&Ls were all to fail and were liquidated, it could cost the government in excess of $100 billion.

Regan, who ran Merrill Lynch prior to joining the government, viewed S&Ls with disdain. He believed the S&Ls had been unduly insulated from competition by protective regulations. Moreover, Regan appeared to believe that the majority of S&L managers were not as competent as their counterparts in commercial banks. Under Regan's direction, the Reagan administration began to espouse the idea that distinctions between S&Ls and commercial banks, which were created and perpetuated by government regulations, should be eliminated. In effect, Regan wanted free-market forces to replace government regulations, thus allowing S&Ls to pursue lines of business other than residential lending.

As the government started to explore alternatives for dealing with the S&L crisis, the industry presented its own ideas. The U.S. League of Savings Institutions, the industry's largest trade and lobby organization, proposed that the government buy low-rate mortgages from the S&Ls and hold them until rates decreased and values rebounded; at which time, the government could sell the mortgages to investors or hold them for collection. Further, the League suggested that the government provide assistance to home buyers by granting direct subsidies or tax credits. The logic behind the League's proposal was that the S&Ls would be relieved of the old, low-yielding assets that were causing the negative spread, and, through the subsidies, the S&Ls could generate new mortgages, yielding higher rates. The rub was that the proposal would cost the government well over $10 billion in the first year and billions more in later years.

The Reagan administration viewed the League's proposal as a bailout of the industry—a bailout that would increase the federal deficit and frustrate Reagan's campaign pledge to balance the budget—and rejected it out of hand. The administration continued to offer deregulation as the solution for the earnings problem of the S&Ls—allowing them to diversify into lines of business comparable to those conducted by commercial banks.

As for those S&Ls that were already under water, or on the verge of drowning in a sea of red ink, the administration proposed that they be merged into or be purchased by healthy S&Ls and commercial banks.

The regulations governing banks prohibited interstate banking, so the banks viewed this proposal favorably. It gave them an opportunity to expand geographically, something they had been actively seeking for years. This proposal provided a vehicle for bypassing the restrictions in the banking regulations.

The larger S&Ls also supported the general concept; however, they wanted banks excluded from the proposal. The smaller S&Ls were generally opposed. They feared the competition that interstate expansion by larger S&Ls or banks would bring to their local markets.

The administration also had another idea. It believed that, if the S&Ls could be kept afloat until rates started coming down, the use of any government funds could be avoided. The problem was that the law required the government to close any S&L or bank that was considered to be insolvent—and there were plenty of institutions that were insolvent or were rapidly approaching insolvency. If the underwater S&Ls were taken over and closed, it would surely require government funds. So, the administration's solution was simply to have the FSLIC issue notes— notes qualifying as capital—to the S&Ls, thereby shoring up their capital and erasing the possibility of insolvency. When interest rates came down, and the S&Ls were able to generate capital through actual earnings, the notes would be canceled.

The proposed notes were called Net Worth Certificates. Once the proposal was announced, it was greeted with skepticism by both Wall Street and certified public accountants serving the industry, who viewed these certificates as nothing more than bookkeeping gimmickry. They cited, and quite appropriately, that the FSLIC did not have the resources to back up the notes. The Net Worth Certificates were worthless. Nevertheless, the idea was implemented, and Net Worth Certificates were issued to a number of S&Ls, keeping them afloat and avoiding, or at least postponing, a government bailout.

During 1981, the Reagan administration and the FHLBB also tried other tactics to keep S&Ls solvent. The FHLBB liberalized accounting rules and allowed the deferral of losses on the sale of certain assets. These measures were designed to buy time for the industry in the hope that interest rates would come down and the institutions' negative-spread problem would be eliminated. But it wasn't enough. Further action by Congress was required truly to deregulate the industry.

In late 1982, the Garn-St. Germain Depository Institutions Act was passed into law. Garn-St. Germain completed the deregulation of deposits by allowing S&Ls to offer a variety of new accounts, including regular checking accounts that replaced the more restrictive NOW accounts. But more significantly, it allowed institutions with federal charters to invest up to 40 percent of their assets in nonresidential or commercial real estate loans. Other investments also became permissible.

Additionally, Garn-St. Germain included a provision, known as the due-on-sale provision, which overrode the state laws allowing homeowners to transfer their mortgages on the sale of their homes. This ended the mortgage-assumption problem that had kept low-rated mortgages on the S&Ls' books, even when the borrower changed. It was a provision that the industry had been seeking for several years.

In 1982, less than half of the S&Ls insured by the Federal Savings and Loan Insurance Corporation held federal charters. The others were chartered by the various states. Following the lead of Garn-St. Germain, the states amended their laws, expanding the investment options of institutions holding their charters. Some states, most notably, Texas, California, and Arizona, permitted a very broad range of investments with virtually no restrictions. S&Ls in these states could invest their funds in almost anything as long as their respective boards of directors approved the investment.

The earnings crisis of the early 1980s caused other regulatory changes that eased restrictions on S&Ls. Stockholder requirements were changed to permit a single person to own all of an S&L's voting common stock. Prior to this change, the regulations required at least four hundred shareholders. As a consequence, S&Ls became acquisition targets of wealthy individuals and nonbank corporations, such as Ford Motor and American Continental Corporation. In fact, regulators encouraged—hell, they damn near begged—healthy S&Ls, nonbank corporations, and others to buy ailing S&Ls whose capital had become depleted. A new breed of S&L owners and managers, attracted by the regulators' urging and the new deregulated environment, entered the industry.

Federally chartered S&Ls were mutual associations. Mutual associations did not have stockholders. Instead, they were owned by their depositors. New rules allowed mutuals to convert to stock associations by selling newly issued shares to the public. Beginning in 1983, many associations took advantage of the new conversion rules in order to raise badly needed capital, so they could grow out of the reduced, or negative, spread conditions they suffered.

The conversion of a mutual association to a stock company produced an interesting side effect. As a mutual, the pressure on management to produce profits was minimal. There were no stockholders clamoring for earnings, increased share values, and dividends. But once the association took on shareholders, management felt the pressure experienced by all publicly held companies' executives to generate ever-increasing earnings.

This need for profit provided the impetus for newly converted associations to pursue aggressively the expanded lines of business permitted by Garn-St. Germain.

With the deregulation of deposits, S&Ls did not have to rely on branch networks to attract new deposits. Rather, they could use national brokers to find customers for their certificates of deposit. Branches became a relatively expensive source of deposits when compared to brokered accounts.

The relaxed regulations also made it easier to start up an S&L. Without the need for branches, and with new investment options, an entrepreneur could capitalize a new association, raise deposits through brokers, and invest the monies in all kinds of assets. The new S&L, depending on where it was chartered, did not have to make a single, home-mortgage loan.

Prior to Garn-St. Germain, S&Ls generally were required to restrict the amount they lent to 80 percent, or less, of the value of the collateral pledged by the borrower. Garn-St. Germain permitted an S&L to lend a borrower up to 100 percent of the value of the borrower's collateral. These loans could also be made on a non-recourse basis. If the borrower defaulted on the loan, the S&L could look only to the collateral for repayment. With a non-recourse loan, the S&L could not go after the borrower's other assets to make up any deficiency between the loan amount and the value of the collateral.

Finally, the changed regulations permitted an S&L to own subsidiaries that could conduct a wide range of businesses. S&Ls, hungry for new sources of income, created subsidiary companies to engage in insurance, leasing, real-estate development and management, hotel operations, mortgage banking, property syndication, data processing, and so on.

Thus, in the short period of time between late-1979 and 1983, the Reagan administration and Congress, through two pieces of legislation and relaxed regulations, converted an industry that for decades had been characterized by institutions with severely restricted business options and profit potentials into an industry with virtually no restrictions on the business opportunities those institutions could pursue and unlimited profit potential. S&Ls now had the highly desirable combination of broad investment powers and insured deposits—a combination unequaled by any other type of financial institution.

The deregulated environment caught the eye of many corporations and entrepreneurs who saw owning and operating a savings and loan association as an unparalleled opportunity. Through the use of deposits—deposits insured by the U.S. government—they could raise unlimited funds. These funds could be invested directly by the S&L, or through a network of subsidiaries, in virtually any line of business they chose.

They could easily enter the industry by purchasing an existing association or by forming a new one.

At the same time, regulators were actively appealing to these new potential owners to enter the industry. The regulators were faced with a huge number of institutions that were suffering from mounting operating losses and disappearing capital. Some had already failed. New owners could pump badly needed capital into the walking-wounded and rescue them from certain death, thereby relieving the regulators from having to close them down.

Entrepreneurs and nonbank corporations responded rapidly to the beckoning opportunity and the regulators' entreaties. In late 1983 and 1984, hundreds of new S&Ls were formed by investor groups, many of whom had little or no prior experience in the industry. Mutual associations stampeded to convert into stock companies, and the stock they offered was gobbled up by investors anxious to participate in the industry's promised revitalization and new profitability. And many existing associations, particularly those in states offering liberal charters, were acquired by new owners. Literally overnight, the ownership and management of the industry changed.

One of the companies that was intrigued by the opportunities offered by deregulation was American Continental Corporation. ACC was led by Charlie Keating (Charles H Keating, Jr.), the chairman of its board and its largest shareholder.

From 1959 to 1976, Keating, a lawyer by training, worked for a large, diversified, Cincinnati-based company, American Financial Corporation, which owned ACC. In 1976, Keating was able to acquire ACC from American Financial and took over its management. ACC was engaged primarily in the construction, sale, and financing of residential housing in Arizona and other western and mountain states. Under Keating's direction, ACC became one of the largest builders of single-family, detached homes in the country.

ACC's business started with acquiring relatively large parcels of land and developing them into residential-housing subdivisions or master-planned (also called mixed-use) communities. ACC prepared detailed plans, including engineering studies, for the project, designating portions of the land for residential usage and other portions for commercial, school, church, multifamily, and other uses. Then, ACC obtained the necessary governmental planning and zoning approvals and construction permits. In some instances, ACC got the project annexed into an existing city or municipality.

After the planning was approved, ACC constructed the major off-site improvements, such as streets, utilities, and amenities. ACC's projects were characterized by man-made lakes (a rarity in a state like Arizona), parks, and recreational features. These attributes separated ACC's projects from those of its competitors and enhanced the value ACC was able to bring to its customers.

With the off-sites completed, ACC retained an inventory of residential lots for its own use and sold the remaining lots, residential and commercial, to other builders and developers. Many builders followed ACC from one project to another, acquiring lots and building homes which complemented ACC's products. Thus, ACC was not only a significant builder in its own right, but it emerged as a primary source of improved lots for others.

ACC also financed its customers' home purchases. Through finance subsidiaries, ACC accepted and processed mortgage-loan applications. Mortgage loans extended by ACC met the standards of the Government National Mortgage Association (GNMA), a U.S. government-sponsored insurer of home mortgages. After ACC extended the mortgages to its customers, it conveyed the mortgages, in pools, to GNMA in exchange for GNMA certificates, which are securities backed by a pool of mortgages and the full faith and credit of the United States. ACC then issued bonds, which were secured by the GNMA certificates, to the public for cash. ACC claimed it was one of the first to use this financing process which later became widely adopted by other builders throughout the country. It provided a means of financing housing and yielded favorable tax advantages to ACC.

Home building is a complicated business fraught with economic peril. It is highly susceptible to shifts in the national economy. During upswings in the economy, sales of new homes are usually robust. But in recessionary periods, home sales can, and often do, dry up and virtually disappear, severely punishing the income statements of many in the industry.

Inflation, which was rampant during the period from 1979 to 1984, is particularly devastating to builders. Potential buyers, unable to afford prices and interest rates which are driven higher by inflationary pressures, postpone the purchase of big-ticket items, such as homes, and sales plunge. At the same time that sales are sinking and revenues are waning, costs escalate, catching the builder in a painful profit squeeze.

As ACC analyzed the roller-coaster track on which its home-building business had been propelled, it realized that the vast majority of its profits had been generated by its land-development activities and not by the more cyclical construction of homes per se. The process of converting raw land into buildable lots could, and did, create large increases in the value of the developed land, producing healthy profits to the developer. On the other hand, the profit margins generated by the construction and sale of homes were much less and, more importantly, were more vulnerable to the vicissitudes of the swings in the economy.

The only drawback to the land-development business was that it required a great deal of capital. Large sums of cash could be, and often were, required to acquire the raw land and install the improvements leading to finished lots. During periods when builders were unable or unwilling to buy lots, the developer had to be able to hold its inventory of raw land and lots. If lenders (providers of debt capital) got nervous, the developer could lose through foreclosure the value created by its development activities.

ACC saw the deregulated S&L as, among other things, a vehicle for conducting land-development activities. Funding through long-term certificates of deposit would provide ACC with immunity to a land developer's economic roller-coaster ride. The subsidiaries could use the capital provided by the S&L to acquire and develop land into finished lots. As the lots were sold, the S&L would receive repayments of debt and dividends on capital investments from the subsidiaries.

S&Ls had been created to facilitate the "American Dream" of home ownership. Their initial mission had been to provide financing at a reasonable interest rate to home buyers. ACC believed that its idea to use subsidiaries to develop lots was consistent with the spirit of the S&Ls' original mission. After all, it's not possible to build homes unless there are first lots on which to construct them. Further, these plans were completely consistent with the types of business contemplated in the Garn-St. Germain legislation.

So, ACC began to look for an S&L to acquire. It centered its search on associations holding California charters, as these charters granted an institution wide latitude in the types of businesses it could conduct. The search ultimately focused on Lincoln Savings and Loan Association of Irvine, California.

From ACC's perspective, Lincoln was an excellent candidate. Its stock was held by a small number of shareholders, and they were willing, for the right price, to sell their stock. Lincoln's branches were located in desirable areas of Southern California. And with about $1 billion in assets, it was an ideal size—neither too big nor too small.

Keating and his staff determined that it would be reasonable to pay between $40 million and $50 million for Lincoln's stock, particularly after considering the location of Lincoln's branches and the opportunities its broad charter offered. Following an exploratory phone call, during which an opening offer of about $40 million was made, Keating met with Lincoln's president and upped ACC's offer to about $50 million. Once ACC offered the higher price, Lincoln's shareholders opted to sell their stock. At the time, both parties believed they had struck a favorable deal. Lincoln's shareholders received a generous price for their stock, and ACC purchased an institution that it believed was ideally situated to take appropriate advantage of the deregulated environment.

In order to purchase an S&L, a buyer has to file an application for a change in control with the FHLBB. The application, among other things, sets out the terms of the transaction, discloses pertinent facts about the buyer, discusses the accounting the buyer will use for the transaction, and contains a brief business plan that the buyer intends to follow. After a short period, during which it applied various due-diligence procedures looking into Lincoln's assets, liabilities and operations, ACC filed its application for a change in control with the FHLBB.

The business plan which accompanies an application for a change in control was viewed by most purchasers as a somewhat innocuous document. The due-diligence procedures a buyer performs are limited in nature. They are designed to ferret out contingent liabilities and to identify conditions which might negate any decision to buy the target company. They are not generally sufficient to allow a buyer to formulate a comprehensive business plan for operating the acquired business; that comes later, when the buyer is in full possession of the target company and is able to analyze thoroughly all of its operating characteristics, including the adequacy of existing personnel.

After the normal delays and red tape inherent in all dealings with government bureaucrats, the FHLBB granted its approval of ACC's application. On February 22, 1984, ACC bought Lincoln for approximately $51 million. Again, the price paid reflected the value of being able to use the franchise granted by Lincoln's charter, not the present worth of its net assets.

Within months of ACC's assumption of control over Lincoln, the first seeds of conflict were planted. Initially, ACC believed it could retain Lincoln's management and could continue its single-family lending program—and had said so in its application for a change in control. But as ACC's people became more familiar with Lincoln's operations and systems, it became apparent that problems existed in Lincoln's operations—problems which were not and could not have been discovered through the limited due-diligence procedures applied in connection with the acquisition. Major changes were needed. So, a massive restructuring of Lincoln's operations and business activities was undertaken.

As the changes in Lincoln started to occur, the FHLBB formed the belief that by not spelling out each and every element of this restructuring in its initial business plan—a document which ACC did not believe was very significant when it filed the application for a change in control—ACC had made misrepresentations. The regulators felt they had been intentionally lied to and became incensed.

Lincoln and ACC did not know about the FHLBB's beliefs regarding

alleged misrepresentations, because the FHLBB did not share its concerns
over the changes in Lincoln's business plans with Lincoln's management
until years later. So, Lincoln continued with its restructuring efforts,
unaware of the negative feelings which were developing within the
regulators' ranks. So far as Lincoln knew, it was conforming to the
deregulation strategy that the FHLBB and the Reagan administration
encouraged and endorsed.

But the FHLBB now viewed Lincoln as an institution that could not
be trusted. Further, as a consequence of the dramatic changes which
Lincoln continued to make in its operations, the FHLBB felt Lincoln was
defying its authority and started placing obstacles in Lincoln's path—
obstacles intended to make Lincoln conform to the FHLBB's philosophies
and bend to its control.

When Lincoln bumped into these impediments, it did not understand
why the FHLBB was being so obstructive. Nor did it understand the
hostility which was beginning to be displayed by certain of the regulators.
Lincoln became concerned. It wondered what was going on with the
regulators.

ACC's purchase of Lincoln placed it on turf that the FHLBB controlled and regulated—turf that would quickly become a battlefield. The
visible signs of conflict between the parties had not yet surfaced. But the
seeds of war were starting to germinate. Hostile feelings were emerging.
Soon, fighting would break out in earnest.

Two

Re-regulation Sets Stage for War

When Garn-St. Germain was signed into law on October 15, 1982, President Reagan touted it as tangible evidence of the fulfillment of his preelection promise to the American people to remove restrictive government regulations that had stifled the economy and increased the cost of doing business. He was not alone in his enthusiasm for this legislation. It was also heartily endorsed by Congress and the S&L industry.

One of the industry people who had lobbied hard for the passage of Garn-St. Germain was a public-relations man who represented a large, Southern California association. His name was Edwin Gray. Typical of public-relations types, Gray was outgoing and affable, with a quick handshake and gift-of-gab that enabled him to sell any concept or idea his superiors in the S&L asked him to sell—even though he may not have had a clue as to what the concepts or ideas really meant. Gray purportedly spent a great deal of time in Washington, wining and dining people and espousing the virtues of deregulation.

Not only a PR-man, Gray was also a political hack. He had worked as Reagan's press secretary when Reagan was governor of California. And after Reagan was elected president, Gray was given a role in the Reagan White House.

Gray was then recruited by the U.S. League of Savings Institutions, and his old friends in the Reagan administration, to become the chairman of the Federal Home Loan Bank Board. He accepted the offered chairmanship and was sworn in on May 1, 1983, approximately six months after Garn-St. Germain became law.

The FHLBB was composed of three members and had several primary functions. First, it supervised the twelve Federal Home Loan banks created by the Federal Home Loan Bank Act and issued regulations and orders affecting those banks. Second, it prescribed rules and regulations that covered the organization, incorporation, examination, operation, and regulation of federally chartered savings and loan associations. Third, it directed the FSLIC, which not only insured depositors' accounts but regulated and examined all insured institutions.

Now, one would expect that persons who had such wide authority over an industry, which held nearly $1 trillion in assets, would be well-grounded in the disciplines of banking, economics, and finance. But such is not the case with government appointments; they are purely political appointments—plums handed out to party loyalists. The law governing the members of the FHLBB was silent as to the minimum credentials each member had to possess, except to say that not more than two could be from the same political party.

Ed Gray was not an expert in banking, economics, or finance. In fact, industry observers considered him to be a lightweight in all of the primary disciplines underlying this troubled and increasingly complex industry. But one has to believe that President Reagan, and his inner circle of White House advisors, didn't really expect Ed Gray to do anything substantive in his role as the FHLBB's chairman. The government deregulated the S&Ls and wanted the regulators simply to stand back and let the institutions work, unfettered, at curing their own illnesses.

Ed Gray was appointed to the FHLBB with one primary role—to be an industry and administration shill—to go around the country giving speeches that said the interest-rate-spread crisis of 1979 to 1983 was over and the industry was on the road to recovery. And early in his term, he did. He crisscrossed the country, giving speeches and hobnobbing with industry leaders—heady stuff for a so-so PR-guy.

Gray quickly took advantage of the "perks" his new position offered. He completely remodeled his office at the FHLBB—at a purported cost of nearly $50,000. He took trips throughout the country and to Europe, with the costs being picked up by the U.S. League or one of the twelve Federal Home Loan banks. Gray was not one to skimp on his expenses. He ate in the best restaurants; traveled by limousine; stayed in world-class, luxury hotels; and even sought, and obtained, reimbursement for personal expenses, such as his wife's visits to beauty and massage parlors, sightseeing trips, gifts for friends, and the like. It was widely reported that Gray was even reimbursed for the contents of a wallet that he carelessly lost on one of his many trips.

While previous FHLBB chairmen had also enjoyed the largess of the U.S. League and the district banks, Gray turned it into an art form, reaching new heights of personal enrichment in his travels.

As Gray was engaged in his initial public-speaking campaign, the industry was in the midst of its massive restructuring. The early rebuilding tendency of most S&Ls was to stay in areas that their executives understood. Remember, these people had always run a business where the government set the rates on both sides of the equation—on deposits and mortgages—

so they had never had to make many sophisticated business decisions. Moreover, some would argue that the highly regulated, traditional S&L business had resulted in institutions attracting more than their fair share of intellectually challenged managers who weren't mentally equipped to venture very far outside of their limited comfort zones.

At first, most of the S&Ls simply tried to grow out of their negative-spread problem. They rushed into the market for brokered deposits and raised as much new cash as they could. They invested the cash either by originating new mortgage loans, with higher interest rates, or by purchasing mortgage-backed securities issued by various government-sponsored entities, such as GNMA, the Federal Home Loan Mortgage Corporation (FHLMC), or the Federal National Mortgage Association (FNMA). The basic strategy was to add layers of higher-yielding securities and loans to the portfolio in order to offset the effects of the lower-yielding paper they already held.

The grow-out-of-the-problem strategy sounds logical, and, for a few associations, it actually worked. But for most associations, it couldn't, and didn't, work. And it certainly couldn't work for the industry as a whole. Consider how the strategy works in practice. If an association holds a $1-billion portfolio that yields a negative 1 percent, in order for the entire portfolio to have an overall yield of 2 percent (the historical average spread and the spread needed to generate a profit), the association must generate another $3 billion in loans that generate 3 percent. Easier said than done.

First, it was virtually impossible to originate mortgages with a 3-percent spread, especially during a period when interest rates were continuing to rise. With all the competition in the mortgage market from other S&Ls, mortgage bankers, mortgage brokers, and the government-sponsored entities, pricing was competitive, and an association couldn't obtain rates that would produce a 3-percent spread. Moreover, once a mortgage was originated, escalating rates ate into the spread, and it soon turned negative.

Second, in periods of high rates, the demand for mortgages goes down, not up. Potential borrowers are either unable or unwilling to pay the higher rates. They sit on the sidelines and wait for rates to recede before they buy a new home or refinance an existing one. So, just when the S&Ls needed increased demand to make the growth strategy work, demand was all but nonexistent. Certainly, there wasn't enough demand for the entire industry to originate two or three times the volume of mortgages they held—it would have taken decades to do that.

Third, the regulations required an S&L to maintain its capital at a given percentage of its assets—about 3 percent at the time. As growth occurred, capital had to increase. But capital wasn't increasing; instead, it was disappearing at an alarming rate. And if an S&L went to the capital markets—Wall Street—and said, "Give me more capital so I can continue to invest it in the mortgage business that is causing me to spread buckets of red ink all over my income statement," Wall Street, who viewed S&L executives as a bunch of not-too-bright guys who barely had the good sense to come in out of the rain, would have reacted with a fit of uncontrolled laughter at the sheer folly of it all.

When attempts to grow out of the problem by expanding the volume of fixed-rate loans didn't work, the S&Ls attempted to introduce a new kind of mortgage—the adjustable-rate mortgage (ARM). It was designed to cure one of the primary defects of the fixed-rate mortgage. ARMs featured interest rates which were tied to a given rate index—the rate on a Treasury security, a given bank's prime rate, or some other rate which served as an indicator of the rate the S&L had to pay on its deposits. As the indexed rate moved up or down, so did the rate on the ARMs. The theory was that the adjusting rates on the ARMs would match the increases or decreases in interest that an S&L had to pay its depositors, thereby eliminating the possibility of spread erosion. The movement in rates was not unlimited, however, as ARMs contained limits on the amount that the rate could go up or down in a given year (usually 1 or 2 percent) as well as the maximum amount that the rate could increase over the term of the loan (usually 5 to 6 percent).

While the use of ARMs may potentially have cured one problem—spread erosion—it still wasn't the answer to the problems facing the industry in the early 1980s. First, because high rates and inflation made housing unaffordable for most potential buyers, there was no demand for new loans, no matter whether fixed rate or adjustable rate. There was no way that enough ARMs could be originated to meet the volume demands of all the institutions in the industry. There simply weren't that many potential borrowers available in the market.

Second, borrowers' early reactions to ARMs were not favorable. With the potential of an interest rate going up 5 percent or 6 percent over a relatively short period, the borrower was uncertain as to the eventual cost of the loan. More significantly, while the borrower might have been able to afford the initial loan payment, if the rate increased, the borrower's income might not be sufficient to meet the higher payments caused by the adjusted rate—and it wasn't difficult for a borrower to figure out what would happen then. So, for the most part, borrowers avoided ARMs like the plague, taking them only when no other reasonable alternative was available.

Thirdly, the rate protection offered by ARMs wasn't perfect—not by a long shot. If rates escalated rapidly, as they did in the late 1970s and early 1980s, they could shoot through the annual cap and the life-of-loan cap and subject the mortgage to rate erosion, reducing the spread and even turning it negative—the same problem that is the Achilles' heel of the fixed-rate mortgage.

There was another tactic that emerged as the S&Ls were engaged in these early efforts to restructure their assets. When an S&L was purchased, the accounting used to record the purchase produced an interesting result. The acquired S&L was required to discount its assets to fair market values. That is, the carrying value of low-yielding mortgage loans was reduced to the point where the cash flow from the loans produced a yield equal to the then-current interest rate. For example, a $1-billion portfolio of thirty-year loans yielding 8 percent (the stated rate on the mortgages) discounted to yield 12 percent (the current market rate) would be recorded at approximately $850 million, a discount of $150 million. Then, as payments were received from borrowers, the acquired S&L would record a portion of what was previously a return of principal (the $150-million discount) as interest income. If the loans were paid off early or were sold, any remaining discount was taken immediately to the income statement. With this simple bookkeeping technique, the income statement could be made to look relatively healthy.

The accounting wasn't quite that simple. The $150-million discount had to be offset elsewhere in the balance sheet or the books wouldn't balance. The answer was an account called "goodwill," an intangible asset, referred to by some as a "plug" to get the books to balance. The accounting rules required the acquired S&L to write the goodwill off—as an expense—over an extended period of time, usually fifteen to thirty years. Everything being equal, the income recognized from the discount was offset by the write-off of goodwill. But everything wasn't equal.

Most acquired associations found that either the mortgage loans paid off early or, as interest rates took periodic dips, the discounted portfolio could be sold at a "book" gain. As a consequence, the income from the discount was recognized earlier than the offsetting write-off of goodwill, producing an income statement that looked healthier than the real underlying economics. The whole process was simply an exercise in bookkeeping which tended to postpone recognition of the acquired S&L's real underlying problems.

Nonetheless, acquirers liked the effects produced by this accounting. It buoyed up their reported earnings and gave them time to address the real issues. More importantly, the regulators accepted—in fact, encouraged and endorsed—this accounting. As such, the accounting at least protected an S&L's capital, allowing it to maintain or grow its asset base.

The illusionary benefits that acquired associations gained by using this accounting technique was the source of envy by other S&Ls. They, too, wanted to sell their portfolios and postpone the recognition of losses in the hope of preserving their precious capital. So, the regulators adopted a regulation which permitted S&Ls to sell loans—and they did by the billions—and defer the recording of any loss. The regulation let S&Ls write the deferred loss off over a period of years, creating the illusion that the S&Ls had more capital than they really did. As a result, the FHLBB could claim that fewer S&Ls were terminally ill than was actually the case. Not a bad political solution to an increasingly sticky mess.

In fact, none of this accounting cured a damn thing. An S&L was just as sick after discounting its portfolio or selling loans and deferring losses as it had been before. It was all smoke-and-mirrors designed to buy time to solve the real economic problems. Unable to generate the profits they needed by simply extending their traditional business or by playing accounting games, S&Ls were forced to seek new lines of business—those permitted by Garn-St. Germain. At first, they increased their construction lending to home builders and financed the builders' acquisition and development of land. To the S&Ls, this was a natural extension of their traditional single-family lending. They were simply picking up the financing of homes earlier in the process, before the homes were ready to be occupied by the end-user.

These loans, referred to as ADC loans (acquisition, development, and construction), more often than not covered 100 percent of the builder's land acquisition, development, and construction costs and were made on a non-recourse basis, exposing the S&L to greater risk of loss if the project didn't work out as planned. In consideration of the increased risk, the S&L usually charged a floating-interest rate—usually a point or two over a local bank's prime rate.

When prime rates hit the mid-teens, S&Ls had a problem with loans featuring an interest rate that was based on and floated with prime. Most states had usury laws which were designed to protect citizens from loan sharks. These laws established the maximum interest rate that a lender could legally charge a borrower. With high prime rates, S&Ls were bumping up against the usury limits.

To get around the usury problem, S&Ls started obtaining a participation in the builders' profits—a form of bonus interest (although lenders argued that it wasn't technically interest) that was generally expressed in terms of a percentage of profits (either net or gross profits), a fixed amount per home sold, a percentage of revenues, or whatever other formula the S&L and builder agreed upon. These profit-participation arrangements were referred to as equity kickers, because the participation didn't kick in until profits occurred or a given milestone was achieved by the builder.

Some S&Ls extended the equity kicker concept farther by entering into a joint venture, or partnership, with a builder, taking an actual equity position in the builder's project. Their reasoning was: If we have to suffer losses when the builder hits bad times, we might as well share in the builder's profits during good times. And they felt a joint venture gave them more say in a project than did a lender-borrower arrangement.

These early deals were very profitable to S&Ls that entered into them. As such, they caught the attention of other S&Ls who also wanted to establish the same kinds of arrangements with builders. But housing was still in a down-cycle, and there wasn't enough of this business to satisfy all the S&Ls' demands. So, the S&Ls simply extended this business to commercial properties and other real estate. They made similar loans to, and entered into joint ventures with, developers of office buildings, apartments, shopping centers, industrial parks, hotels, mini-warehouses, and virtually every other kind of real estate, including raw land held for speculation.

This extension, or mutation, of the S&Ls' traditional real-estate-lending business reached its logical conclusion when S&Ls simply decided to bypass the builders, or developers, and did the projects themselves. The reasoning was: If it's profitable, why share the profits with someone else, especially since, as a non-recourse lender, we have to absorb all losses if the deal doesn't work out right.

By mid-1983, S&Ls were pursuing these new loans and real-estate ventures with a vengeance. It was a feeding frenzy as they competed with each other to find and close the next deal. And it came at an opportune time. The real-estate markets were starting to recover, inflation was easing, and interest rates had peaked and were coming down. S&Ls started to record profits. Some were real, but others—the product of the generally accepted accounting principles which were in effect at the time—were somewhat imaginary and later vanished. Nonetheless, S&Ls felt they were on the road to recovering from the spread problem which had haunted them for years. The road was not without its bumps and potholes, however.

Many S&L executives were in over their heads. They barely understood the fundamental economic characteristics underlying the projects they were financing. Fish out of water, they were easy prey for some of the slicker developers who sought their backing. Some S&Ls failed to make the necessary inquiries into and analyses of the deals that were pitched to them. It was not unusual for several institutions to turn down a project—because it didn't make economic sense—only to have one of the more unsophisticated, or overly greedy, associations make the loan or enter into the project as a joint-venture partner. As a result, many projects which should not have been financed were.

Rapid growth strained the capabilities of even the better-managed shops. Data-processing systems were proven to be archaic and needed to be totally redesigned or, at a minimum, upgraded. New people, with new skills, had to be hired. Internal procedures required revamping in order to keep pace with the new kinds of business the associations were conducting.

All these improvements took time to implement. Until the changes were made, the associations suffered from weak controls and deficient records, resulting in errors of both commission and omission that might have been avoided if growth had been less frenetic.

Again, despite their internal-management deficiencies, S&Ls were recording profits—for many, large profits. The developers and builders started to view S&Ls as more than lenders; they were competitors, eating into the sources of profits that the builders and developers had traditionally enjoyed. Many developers said to themselves, "Hell, if an S&L can take over my turf and make such good returns, I ought to buy one of the damn things." Other entrepreneurial types came to the same conclusion. When S&Ls were engaged solely in residential lending, and were hemorrhaging red ink, no one in his right mind wanted to own one. But now, with their new earning power, S&Ls became desirable businesses to own. As previously discussed, this is, in part, what drew ACC to join the throng of people seeking to buy an S&L. There was an all-out stampede to open a new S&L or to buy an existing one, especially in Texas and California.

As new players entered the game of owning an S&L, real-estate lending simply became one of the many businesses that S&Ls pursued as they searched for ways to generate profit. Soon, they were buying equity securities; investing in a host of debt instruments—junk bonds, mortgage-backed products, and hybrids; developing and selling land; building and leasing commercial buildings; making unsecured business loans or loans secured by collateral other than real estate; operating hotels, insurance companies, and other businesses; and so on and so on. As the new operators succeeded in recording profits from these diverse endeavors, other associations copied them, converting an industry of sleepy S&Ls into one of complex, diversified, financial companies.

This was the environment which greeted Ed Gray when he was handed the reins of the FHLBB: rapid growth; frenzied diversification into complex transactions and new lines of business; changing ownership and management; new associations springing up every day; revived profits; and S&Ls beset by internal systems problems and outmoded procedures. And on top of the hectic activity of the revitalized associations, there were still numerous associations that remained in the categories of the walking-wounded and brain-dead, without any hope of survival and awaiting a decent burial.

While the executives in the S&L industry generally viewed the changes that were occurring within their respective associations, and the industry as a whole, with favor, Ed Gray was forming an entirely different opinion. His public remarks in early 1984 indicated that he believed that too many S&Ls were growing too fast and that diversification was leading them into very dangerous waters—waters that threatened the FSLIC insurance fund which he administered. His opinion appeared to be that freewheeling S&L managers, who were seeking to grow their associations at what he thought was an imprudent pace, were investing too much money in dubious ventures that offered more potential risk than rewards to the associations. Gray considered brokered deposits to be the primary culprit. He believed that the existence of brokered deposits made it too easy for associations to raise large sums of cash simply by bidding up the price (the interest rate) they paid for these deposits. Gray believed that if the flow of brokered deposits could be stemmed, growth rates could be reduced to what, in his mind, were more acceptable levels.

So, in mid-January 1984, Ed Gray announced a proposed regulation that would severely limit the amount of deposits that a given broker could place in a given association and still receive insurance coverage on the deposits from the FSLIC. In the eyes of most observers, the effect of the proposed regulation would have been, for all practical purposes, to eliminate brokers as a significant source of deposits and would have made S&Ls, once again, dependent on branch networks for deposit dollars.

The proposed regulation drew fire from all quarters. The Reagan White House was extremely upset with Gray. Donald Regan was reported to be particularly irate. Regan had been the prime mover in eliminating all restrictions on the use of brokered deposits. Since 1982, when the last limitations were lifted, brokered deposits had soared by the billions, allowing Wall Street firms, where Regan had plenty of friends, to reap millions in commissions. Now, Gray was planning to strike a death-blow to one of Regan's sacred cows.

The administration attempted to persuade Gray to back off the issue, but he steadfastly refused to do so. Because of his refusal to go along with the administration—and Regan in particular—Gray was viewed as a traitor. His intransigence made Gray the bitter enemy of many of his former supporters and allies.

Not everyone in official Washington was opposed to Gray's proposed regulation, however. William Isaac, head of the Federal Deposit Insurance Corporation (FDIC), supported it. To observers in the S&L industry, Isaac's support didn't come as a surprise. The FDIC insured commercial banks and, thus, was subject to pressure from the banks' lobbyists. The commercial banks didn't rely as heavily on brokers for their source of funds, so limiting brokered deposits was no big deal.

Limiting the growth of S&Ls was, however, a big deal to the banks. As S&Ls diversified, they ate into the business of the commercial banks and, therefore, became a concern to the banks, which didn't want or need any more competition. Gray's regulation clipped the S&Ls' wings, inhibiting their growth. The lobbyists for the banks were grateful for any regulation that put the upstart S&Ls back in their traditional place as mortgage lenders who presented little or no threat to the banks' prime business. So, the banks probably applauded and encouraged Isaac's support of Gray's proposal.

Before discussing the S&L industry's reactions to Gray's proposal, it may be helpful to provide some perspective on brokered deposits. Brokered deposits were often referred to as hot money. Most brokered deposits were for relatively short terms, generally six months. An association could quickly attract them by offering a favorable interest rate and could lose them just as fast if, when they came up for renewal, other associations offered better rates. Brokers looked at the rates offered by associations across the country and moved their customers' deposits wherever the highest rates were available. Thus, brokered deposits were an unstable source of funds.

In contrast, deposits garnered through branches tended to stay in a given association for long periods of time because branch customers often valued service as much as rates and, therefore, didn't move their accounts as renewal dates came up. But offsetting their stability, branch deposits were generally more expensive to obtain than brokered deposits. With a branch, an association had to pay for space, the cost of tellers and managers, and for relatively expensive equipment. Competition was also intense, for there seemed to be a bank or S&L branch on virtually every street corner in most urban areas.

With brokered deposits, the only equipment needed was a telephone. One or two people could raise literally millions and millions of dollars each day simply by placing a few calls and offering the right rate. The only real cost, aside from higher rates, was the commission paid to the broker. For most S&Ls, the commission was less than the cost of maintaining branches.

Most small, well-established associations didn't vigorously oppose Gray's proposal, and, in fact, some supported it. The supporters were much like the commercial banks. They didn't use brokered deposits, and they feared competition from the new, or growing, associations. So, supporting Gray served their self-interests.

But larger associations, those with spread problems that they needed to outgrow, and start-up shops vigorously opposed Gray's regulation. They also felt Gray had betrayed them. He had gotten the FHLBB job with the active support of the U.S. League, and now he was turning on the industry. They viewed him as a re-regulator who was blocking their efforts to dig out of a deep, deep hole. During the sixty-day comment period, when the FHLBB was supposed to listen to the views of concerned or affected citizens, letters opposing the regulation outnumbered those supporting it by more than a two-to-one margin.

As for Keating and ACC, they were opposed to any attempt to re-regulate the industry. But since Gray announced the proposal on January 15, 1984, and ACC's application to acquire Lincoln wasn't approved until February 22, 1984, the comment period was almost over before ACC was free to speak. After all, it would not have been politic to have opposed Gray vociferously at a time when he could have scotched the deal to buy Lincoln. Thus, ACC's opposition to Gray's re-regulation of deposits was voiced through a trade association ACC belonged to—the National Council of Savings Institutions, a lobby group that, in effect, competed with the U.S. League.

Despite industry protests, Gray went ahead with the regulation against brokered deposits. It was approved by the FHLBB on March 26, 1984, and was to go into effect on October 1, 1984. The protests were immediate. Brokers started a campaign against Gray. Congress held a hearing on the issue. Finally, a lawsuit was filed. The judge in the case ruled against Gray, stating that only Congress, not the FHLBB, had the authority to set the limitations imposed by the regulation against brokered deposits. Even then, Gray wouldn't give up. He asked Congress to give the FHLBB the authority to pass such regulations. His request fell on deaf ears and was not acted upon.

Ed Gray paid a steep political price for his dogged insistence on limiting brokered deposits. He was attacked by both the S&L and broker-age industries, the Reagan administration, Congress, and even by long-time employees of the FHLBB. He was viewed as a guy who didn't understand the industry that he was charged with regulating and, as such, was simply not qualified for the job. Even many of those who had supported his appointment to the FHLBB thought he should resign.

While Ed Gray was fighting his battle against brokered deposits, Keating and ACC's management team were in the midst of restructuring Lincoln. Old management was replaced, and new managers were installed. Data-processing systems were completely redesigned. Branches were revamped. A program was started to raise brokered deposits—not hot-money deposits, but long-term (three- to ten-year terms), nonwithdrawable accounts which would assure Lincoln of a stable core of deposits.

Lincoln also materially altered its investment practices. California-chartered associations, thanks to a piece of legislation known as the Nolan Bill, named after its sponsor, Patrick Nolan, had the broadest investment powers in the nation. The Nolan Bill permitted an S&L to invest its money any way it wished. If it didn't want to do so, a California-chartered association was not required to make any single-family, residential loans.

Lincoln took advantage of these broad powers. It discontinued residential lending, because in the rate environment which existed at the time, and given the competition in the market for the limited number of home loans that were available, residential lending was not, in the minds of ACC's and Lincoln's management, a profitable undertaking. Instead, Lincoln focused its lending activities on making construction and ADC loans to builders and real-estate developers. It also made loans which were secured by commercial real estate and, in certain instances, extended credit on an unsecured basis to some of its corporate customers.

The most dramatic changes in Lincoln's operations started to occur in mid-1984. Lincoln started to form a number of subsidiaries (also referred to in the industry as service corporations). Each subsidiary was formed for a specific business purpose. Some were created to acquire and develop land into master-planned communities or into commercial projects, such as shopping centers or apartment sites. Other subsidiaries were designed to invest in corporate debt or equity securities. Others were formed to purchase, construct, and operate hotels. And still others were designated to conduct insurance businesses. When all these subsidiaries became fully operational, they represented a complex network of business enterprises that made sense to Keating and his associates, because the structure was similar to that of American Financial Corporation, where Keating got his start. But the convoluted organization confounded and confused outsiders who tried to fathom the multiple layers of related and, occasionally, overlapping entities.

In order to form these subsidiaries, Lincoln was required to obtain permission from the California Commissioner of Savings and Loans, Lincoln's primary regulator. In 1984, the Commissioner was Lawrence Taggart, a man who had worked for over a decade for the same San Diego-based S&L that had employed Ed Gray. Lincoln, as the regulations required it to do, submitted a business plan to Taggart for each subsidiary it intended to form. Taggart and his staff reviewed the business plans and applications submitted by Lincoln and met with Lincoln's executives to discuss the plans for the various subsidiaries. After the state's review, most, but not all, of Lincoln's applications were approved, and the subsidiaries started to conduct business.

In November 1989, when a congressional committee asked Taggart about ACC's restructuring of Lincoln and the formation of the subsidiaries by Lincoln, he had this to say:

Prior to American Continental's acquisition of Lincoln in 1984, Lincoln Savings had been a traditional conservative thrift operating in Southern California. . . . For the few years prior to its acquisition, Lincoln was floundering and losing money. In fact, for the year ending 1982 . . . Lincoln lost

$3,153,624, and out of 106 State Chartered Associations that year, ranked 100 as having the least net income.

It was obvious and apparent that some other management strategy and philosophy was going to be necessary to restore Lincoln's financial strength. Apparently, American Continental had recognized this as an opportunity, and submitted an application for change in ownership. . . .

After acquiring Lincoln, relatively progressive plans were submitted for approval to the Department of Savings and Loan in their efforts to strength [*sic*] the financial base of the association and improve profitability. . . .

Taggart's office approved Lincoln's plans and Lincoln aggressively implemented them.

Lincoln embarked on a plan to raise approximately $1 billion in long-term, nonwithdrawable, brokered deposits. The monies raised were to be used to fund newly formed subsidiaries which, in turn, would invest the funds in the manner that the state commissioner had approved.

As the funds were raised, investments were made. A Lincoln subsidiary, using Drexel Burnham Lambert and other investment bankers as advisors, purchased high-yield, corporate bonds (otherwise known as junk bonds). Another subsidiary purchased a hotel in Detroit. Another started to acquire large tracts of land in Arizona and other states and began the planning process to develop the land into master-planned communities. Insurance operations were initiated. And Lincoln bought the equity securities of a number of corporations, including some stocks which were acquired in connection with leveraged buyouts and hostile takeovers.

All of these new activities were ones in which Keating and his executives had extensive previous experience. They were investments that Keating believed he and his people thoroughly understood—both the risks and rewards inherent in the investments. These investments would also become the bases for the skirmishes and battles that ACC and Lincoln would fight with the FHLBB and its allies.

There was one other important step that occurred in this restructuring process—one that Keating later regretted taking. Committed to using Lincoln as its primary subsidiary, ACC converted itself into a pure holding company by transferring most of its productive assets into Lincoln or one of Lincoln's subsidiaries. When the transfers were completed, ACC was completely dependent on Lincoln for its future income—a dependence which made ACC vulnerable to attack by the FHLBB.

As Keating and ACC were proceeding full steam ahead with their transformation of Lincoln into a diversified financial institution, Ed Gray was still smarting from the defeat he had suffered in his attempt to rein in brokered deposits. He continued to believe that the rapid growth spawned by these deposits placed the FSLIC in imminent danger.

Gray's fears concerning brokered deposits appear to have been based on, or were at least reinforced by, an economic and regulatory disaster that had surfaced in a Texas S&L. In March 1984, Gray and the FHLBB were asked to declare Empire Savings and Loan of Mesquite, Texas, insolvent. Empire had invested funds raised through brokered deposits into numerous condominium projects in Dallas. Virtually all of the units funded by Empire's loans—literally hundreds and hundreds of units—were either under construction, unoccupied, or abandoned. The units had been subjected to vandalism, weather damage, and neglect, and all represented certain losses to Empire. Gray purportedly watched a video-tape that panned across a stretch of Dallas where these projects were located, and what he saw apparently shocked, angered, and sickened him. It also proved to him that his fears were not unfounded—as almost everyone else believed them to be—and he renewed his resolve to stop the growth rate in the industry that he was responsible for overseeing.

Two days after Gray watched the Empire tape, the FHLBB passed its regulation limiting the use of brokered deposits. Empire's failure later became an embarrassing problem for Gray and his fellow regulators. Congress wanted to know where the regulators were when Empire was placing all the bad loans on its books. Hearings were scheduled to look into the matter.

These hearings had to be a concern to Ed Gray. He had been crisscrossing the country, socializing with his friends from the U.S. League and living lavishly on funds provided by the League and the district banks. His image in the industry, and with the White House and Congress, was that of a glad-handing lightweight who was ill-equipped to handle the industry's problems. Now the spotlight was being focused on the performance of his agency and on whether it had acted prudently and appropriately in the Empire affair. The logical question was: What had Gray done to prevent a situation like Empire from occurring? The Empire situation could be used to confirm what many were saying about him—that he was disorganized, inattentive to the real needs of the FHLBB, incompetent, and lacking in the executive presence and toughness needed to be effective.

About a month after the FHLBB's seizure of Empire, and approximately a week and a half before the hearings were to start, Gray fired the president of the Federal Home Loan Bank of Dallas. The timing of this action and the action itself—no one had been similarly fired by the FHLBB in many decades—raised questions and concerns within the industry, especially in Texas, and within the FHLBB structure. Many believed that the Dallas president was simply a scapegoat. The theory was that he was fired so that Gray could tell the congressional committee that he had taken strong action in the matter. The person Gray named as the new president of the Dallas bank didn't help to invalidate the scapegoat theory. He was an executive of the League and a cohort of Gray's close friends in the industry, making his selection smack of cronyism on Gray's part.

In the hearings, the regulators offered the committee a host of reasons why they had been precluded from taking earlier actions against Empire. They asserted that Empire's accounting for the loans made Empire appear to be one of the most profitable associations in the country. How could they discipline a highly profitable shop? They blamed Empire's outside audit firm for failing to detect the fraud in Empire's financial statements, saying that they were relying on the auditors to do just that.

In spite of all of the defenses offered by Gray and other regulators in the hearings, the investigating committee concluded that as early as 1982, the regulators had had sufficient data to allow them to determine that Empire was a problem shop. Even outside parties, using public documents, were able to identify that Empire had severe problems. The bottom line to the committee was that the regulators had simply failed to act in an appropriate manner. Gray was chastised and humiliated by the committee.

The public rebuke by the congressional committee, combined with the stinging defeat he had suffered in his attempt to limit brokered deposits, seemed to harden Gray's resolve to do something about the rapid growth and asset diversification in the industry. He fastened on a new approach. If he couldn't limit brokered deposits, he could limit the manner in which the proceeds from such deposits were invested.

Garn-St. Germain and the companion state-sponsored actions promoting deregulation resulted in S&Ls greatly expanding their investments into two areas that particularly troubled Ed Gray—real-estate projects and equity securities. He also pointed to some of the more exotic investments made by some associations—windmill farms, fast-food outlets, airlines, and oil-drilling operations—as other examples of excessive investment risk.

Gray proposed a regulation which would limit the percentage of assets that an association could invest in real estate and equity securities (referred to in the regulation as direct investments). The regulation was originally proposed in mid-1984, but, because of a barrage of criticism and the poor language of the draft regulation, it was withdrawn and redrafted.

The revised regulation was approved by the FHLBB in January 1985 and was to go into effect in March 1985, with a retroactive date back to December 10, 1984. The regulation restricted an S&L from investing more than 10 percent of its assets in direct investments. An S&L could complete any direct investment to which it was committed at December 10, 1984, but could not enter into any new direct investments if that would cause the total of all such investments to exceed 10 percent of its assets.

Industry reaction to both the original and revised regulation was immediate and intense. Virtually all comments received by the FHLBB opposed the direct-investment regulation. One of the most forceful and vocal opponents of the regulation was Lincoln.

Lincoln had committed itself to a strategy of investing a substantial portion of its assets in its subsidiaries, real estate, and corporate equity securities—all of which met the definition of direct investments. Gray's regulation threatened to drive a stake through the heart of Lincoln's basic strategy.

Keating was dismayed and incensed by Gray's actions. He had acquired Lincoln solely because of the investment alternatives that deregulation (Garn-St. Germain and the Nolan Bill) permitted. Were it not for these broad investment powers, he never would have purchased Lincoln nor would he have transferred ACC's productive assets into Lincoln. He viewed Gray's re-regulation as a stab in the back of anyone who had heeded the regulators' urging to invest in the industry.

Keating reacted in customary fashion to the situation. He engaged the best consultants and lawyers he could find to advise him on the regulation. The two most prominent consultants used by Lincoln were Alan Greenspan, a distinguished economist and economic advisor to President Reagan and, now, chairman of the Federal Reserve Board, and Professor George Benston of the University of Rochester.

Both consultants determined that direct investments did not inherently pose undue risk to the FSLIC insurance fund. They testified before Congress in opposition to the regulation and presented the committee with the logic and reasoning supporting their conclusions.

Some of Greenspan's conclusions, as set forth in a letter to the FHLBB dated November 1, 1984, are as follows:

> Accordingly, direct investments constitute an investment option that is necessary to the financial health—and, in many cases, the survival—of savings and loan associations. Any artificial restriction on rational investment opportunities reduces the overall efficiency of the economy, and restrictions that directly impede efficient adjustments to broad and fundamental changes in the economy can only be detrimental to the associations and to the nation as a whole. . . . The risks currently imposed on the industry by fundamental changes in economic conditions and by asset-liability mismatch are severe and immediate, and the use of direct investments to avoid or minimize them would lessen the risks facing both the savings and loan industry and the economy as a whole. . . .
>
> In view of the powerful reasons why direct investments are necessary for the financial health of the savings and loan industry, only overwhelming evidence of imminent and acute risk from direct investments could rationally justify the Proposed Rule. Professor Benston's study, with which I concur,

demonstrates . . . that the Proposed Rule could seriously harm the savings and loan industry.

Gray's reaction to Lincoln's use of these consultants was expressed to a congressional committee in November 1989:

> I will never forget my first candid thoughts when I was told that Mr. Greenspan had been hired by Lincoln. How much money had Lincoln paid for this extraordinary representation service, I wondered to myself. I had known Alan Greenspan when I worked in the White House. I knew he had an awful lot of clout in the Administration and I wondered whether Lincoln had hired him so that the effect would somehow unnerve me enough that I might back off from going through with the direct investment regulation. God knows it was awfully unpopular. I didn't back off, despite opposition from my own administration. OMB [Office of Management and Budget], true to form and as intransigent as ever, would not approve the regulation, under the Paperwork Reduction Act. We summarily overrode OMB.

This testimony reveals that Gray felt it was somehow improper, or unusual, for Keating to have engaged a person of Alan Greenspan's stature to represent Lincoln. He also implies that Greenspan accepted the assignment solely because of the size of the fee paid to him, as reflected in his query, "how much money had Lincoln paid," and as expressed later in his testimony when he said, "he [Keating] hired Alan Greenspan to do his bidding—for money."

These comments to the congressional committee, and the attitudes they exhibit, raise more questions than they answer. Why should Alan Greenspan, a noted economist, not take a natural interest in a regulation that could potentially adversely affect the national economy? Why should Greenspan's prior or continuing service as an advisor to Washington preclude him from accepting such an assignment, especially since he was not on the federal payroll at the time? Did Gray even know what Greenspan was paid, and, if so, did he have any evidence indicating that the fee paid influenced, in any way, the conclusions Greenspan reached? Why does Greenspan's political standing with the administration become a factor in evaluating the objectivity of his findings? Since he believed the regulation threatened Lincoln's viability and future economic existence, why shouldn't Keating engage one of the most respected economists in the country to analyze the issues and assess their impact on Lincoln? Would it have been wiser, from Keating's standpoint, to engage an economist who had no national standing and who didn't understand how Washington worked, or was it wiser, in light of what was at stake for Lincoln, to get the best and most experienced consultant he could find?

In the context of this story, Gray's comments are even more significant, for they make it apparent that he took Keating's opposition, and the
use of prominent consultants, as a personal affront and challenge. Rather
than view their opposition as a reasoned position based on what the
consultants believed were competent and reliable data and observations,
Gray viewed the use of respected people like Greenspan and Benston as a
macho challenge to his courage and manhood. To Gray, it was not a matter
of whether the arguments made by the consultants were valid or not, it was
an issue of whether he would be "unnerved" and tempted to "back off."
Thus, his insistence to go ahead with the regulation, despite the input of
learned experts and opposition from virtually everyone in the industry, the
Congress, and the Reagan administration, does not appear to have been
based on reason and sound economics but, rather, on his emotional need
to avoid being viewed as a weakling who backed down in the face of
pressure.

The overwhelming opposition to the direct-investment regulation
didn't stop with consultants' reports and testimony before congressional
committees. After the FHLBB approved the regulation, a resolution was
circulated in Congress demanding that the implementation of the regulation be postponed. The resolution had over two hundred cosponsors,
including well over half of the members of the House of Representatives'
Committee on Banking, Finance and Urban Affairs, the primary committee that was charged with overseeing the operations of the FHLBB.

Gray summed up his reactions to the pressure he felt from Congress
in his November 1989 testimony as follows:

> . . . [W]e pursued the direct investment regulation early on with vigor, and dug
> in our heels to adopt it in the face of unbelievable pressure from many
> quarters, including incredible pressure from this House (of Representatives)
> itself.
>
> . . . [Y]ou will recall that more than half the members of this House signed
> a resolution, authored by Congressman Annunzio, the sole purpose of which
> was, frankly, to derail and bury the direct investment regulation.

Once again it was a personal issue to Ed Gray. His testimony should
make one wonder how, in a representative form of government, a bureaucrat who has obtained his position via political appointment can thumb his
nose at the majority of the elected members of the House of Representatives and the rest of the president's administration and simply do as he
pleases because of concerns over how people will view his personal
courage.

More significantly, from Lincoln's standpoint, Gray viewed Keating
as the primary person who was challenging his authority and courage. It

was personal. Keating was his enemy—a person who, because he had the temerity to challenge Ed Gray, would be dealt with in due course.

With the direct-investment regulation approved and in place, Lincoln applied for an exemption to the limitations imposed by the regulation. The request was, as one might expect, denied.

The stage was set for the first real battle between Lincoln and the regulators and, because of the acrimony harbored by Ed Gray toward Keating as a consequence of the direct-investment skirmish, it promised to be a heated contest.

Three

The First Shot: 1986 Examination of Lincoln

Most of the participants in the Lincoln Savings War would say that the conflict started on March 12, 1986, when the FHLBB began to conduct a routine examination of Lincoln. Although, even this is in dispute, as Lincoln contends the examination actually commenced on March 4 rather than March 12. Irrespective of which date is the correct starting point for the examination, the fact is this examination was the first real confrontation between the staff of the FHLBB and the management of ACC and Lincoln.

The FHLBB's field troops came out of the Los Angeles and San Francisco offices of the Federal Home Loan Bank of San Francisco (FHLB-SF), one of the twelve district banks in the FHLB system. The San Francisco bank was charged with overseeing all of the institutions in the states of Arizona, California, and Nevada—the Eleventh District. Each district bank is owned by its member institutions, who are required as a condition of membership to purchase stock in the bank. As such, the district banks are private corporations, not government entities.

The primary function of a district bank is to serve as a source of credit for its members. Member institutions, after pledging acceptable collateral, can borrow funds on either a long-term or short-term basis from the bank at advantageous interest rates. Also, institutions can deposit their liquid funds with the bank and receive interest income on those funds.

The district bank also acts as the agent for the FHLBB and the FSLIC in supervising the periodic examinations of the institutions within the district. There is a district director of examinations who is in charge of a staff of field examiners stationed in each of the districts. The director and his staff, under the direction of a principal supervisory agent (PSA), conduct the examinations. The PSA is also the president of the district bank and is the official agent of the FHLBB and the FSLIC.

The purpose of an examination is to determine whether the institution is complying with the applicable regulations and whether it is operating in a safe and sound manner. The examination is conducted primarily in the institution's offices, with review and report writing being done at the offices of the district bank. The member institution is charged for the full cost of the examination, as determined by the district bank, including the cost of any appraisals or other studies the examiners deem necessary.

Prior to 1986, the examiners were on the federal payroll and, as such, were subject to the pay limitations affecting all federal employees. In late-1984, Ed Gray started complaining to Donald Regan and David Stockman, the director of OMB, that he needed additional examiners, and he needed the ability to pay them more than the then-current federal pay standards permitted. At the time, the FHLBB had about seven hundred examiners, who were paid about $14,000 a year to start, with the average salary for an experienced examiner being around $25,000 per year. In 1984, the turnover rate for FHLBB examiners was about 25 percent. The FHLBB contended that salary limitations made it difficult to attract and retain the kind of people it needed to cope with the deregulated environment.

Gray's pleas were ignored. The Reagan administration was committed to balancing the budget, and it wasn't about to increase federal spending by hiring more examiners or by raising the pay of existing ones. And, for the FHLBB to do so, it needed OMB's permission and approval. OMB wouldn't grant its approval.

Gray's actions relative to brokered deposits and direct investments amply demonstrated that he was not one to listen to the concerns of the Reagan administration, nor was he inclined to follow the administration's policies. Gray solved this problem, as he solved most others, by simply executing an end-run around OMB. His FHLBB legal advisors had concluded that the FHLBB could transfer all of its field examiners off the federal payroll and into the employ of the twelve district banks, where, because the banks were nongovernment corporations, the federal hiring and pay standards would not apply. The supervisory personnel who oversaw the work of the field examiners were already on the district banks' payrolls.

Gray described this action to Congress by saying the following: ". . . [I]n mid-1985 the Bank Board, having given up on any prospect of help from Donald Regan, or from OMB, the Bank Board unilaterally, on our own, transferred its examination force out from under OMB and out to the Federal home loan banks." He also added, "We had to do it. We were so outmatched and outgunned by the industry that we were supposed to regulate, that we had to get the examiners out from under OMB and the ridiculous salary controls on them by the administration through the Office of Personnel Management."

This unilateral action by Gray was not without its obvious problems. Each district bank has its own board of directors. Some of the directors are elected by the member institutions and are frequently officers of member institutions. The remainder are appointed by the FHLBB. Virtually all of the directors have ties directly to the industry.

The board of each district bank chooses the bank's president. These selections are viewed by many as being heavily influenced by political considerations, including the input of the U.S. League and its inner circle. Not surprisingly, the various district bank presidents also have strong allegiances to the industry and, often, to particular institutions.

Thus, Gray's move placed the entire examination force into the hands of the industry—the very people the examiners were supposed to regulate. The League, and those associations that had representation on the board of one of the twelve district banks, had to view Gray's unilateral action as a very sweet deal. They now had control of, or at least influence over, the examination process. But what about those associations, like Lincoln, that didn't have representation on the board of a district bank or that were not supporters of the League? They were now subject to an examination that logically fell under the control of their competitors and, perhaps, their enemies.

This problem appeared to be most acute if an association was located in the Eleventh District, as Lincoln was. The Eleventh District was considered to be Ed Gray's power base. The board of the San Francisco bank was seeded with people who were his mentors—the people who had influenced his appointment to the FHLBB chairmanship—and the people he most frequently listened to on a regular basis. Moreover, James Cirona, the president of the bank—the PSA to whom the examiners reported—was active in the League and had previous, long-time ties to the industry.

So, the examiners who showed up on Lincoln's doorstep on March 12 (or March 4, depending on which date is actually the correct one), 1986, were on the payroll of the Eleventh District. Lincoln's management was understandably concerned that these examiners might be directed, controlled, or influenced by Ed Gray, who, by this point, was viewed to be hostile to Lincoln and Keating, and/or by one of Lincoln's competitors, which was almost as bad.

The field examination team was led by Joe Kotrys, whose title was Examiner-in-Charge. Joe was an experienced examiner who had been with the FHLB-SF for a long time. The bulk of his prior experience had therefore been in examining associations that conducted the traditional S&L business of extending mortgage loans to home-buyers. He had not previously been exposed to an association whose organizational structure was as complex as Lincoln's, nor had he had any real experience with transactions whose nature and level of technical sophistication were comparable to those routinely entered into by Lincoln. But Joe appeared to be realistic about his level of knowledge and was aware of his technical limitations. If he didn't understand a transaction, he asked Lincoln's people to explain it to him.

Kotrys' team of examiners was comprised largely of young people who had had little or no previous experience as field examiners. Most were part of the influx of new people who had joined the FHLBB examination staff after it was moved to the Eleventh District's payroll. Unlike Kotrys, if they didn't understand a transaction, they didn't ask Lincoln's personnel for complete explanations. Instead, they filled in missing gaps in the data, or in their understanding of a given deal, with assumptions and speculation. As the examination progressed, the assumptions that these people made, which were often unfounded or erroneous, created tremendous problems for both Kotrys and Lincoln. Moreover, because of the prominence of some of the people with whom Lincoln conducted business, or because of the size and nature of certain of the transactions, the younger examiners tended to get sidetracked on matters that were not germane to the basic thrust of the examination.

The activities of the young, inexperienced examiners seemed, at times, too much for Kotrys to handle. Kotrys, while an experienced examiner, didn't strike the Lincoln people as a strong manager. At one point, a Lincoln executive pointed out to Kotrys that the "kids," as Lincoln came to refer to the younger FHLBB personnel, seemed to be missing the point of some of the transactions they were examining. Kotrys acknowledged the accuracy of this observation by saying that he was letting them "run free," and later he would "bring them back to reality."

The primary person from Lincoln's side who was charged with interfacing with Kotrys and the examiners was Judy Wischer. Judy was the president of ACC and a member of Lincoln's board of directors. At the time of this examination, Judy was in her mid-thirties. An accountant by training, she had joined Keating before he acquired ACC and, therefore, had been with him from the first day he assumed control of ACC. Over the years, she became the second most powerful person within ACC's network of companies.

Judy is an attractive woman who looks younger than her chronological age. Her voice is high-pitched and has a little-girl quality to it, which reinforces the impression of youthfulness that her physical appearance produces. Because she looked and sounded young, people often assumed that she lacked forcefulness and resolve. Those who made this assumption rapidly learned that they were dead wrong. Underneath her pleasant veneer was a tough-minded business executive who could be as hard as nails. Well organized and able to grasp the basic elements of the most complex transaction, Judy Wischer could negotiate with the best of them, and, as was usually the case, she drove a hard bargain. If one of her subordinates stepped out of line or failed to perform satisfactorily, she could fire the person without so much as a moment's hesitation. Within ACC, Charlie Keating may have been the person who negotiated many of the deals, but it was Judy Wischer who managed the people and got the deals closed.

Judy and Kotrys met frequently to discuss the progress of the examination. At first, the examination seemed to be proceeding as Lincoln expected it would. The examiners asked for Lincoln's account trial balances and for listings of its loans, investments, and real estate. They initially focused on the loans by selecting a sample and asking Lincoln's staff to pull the applicable files. They used standard checklists to see whether Lincoln had followed acceptable procedures in processing the loans and had the necessary documents in its files. They also took samples of other transactions and reviewed them. Everything was routine.

A few weeks into the examination, Kotrys got a telephone call from someone in San Francisco asking whether Lincoln had any investments connected to Ivan Boesky. Apparently, San Francisco had been called by someone in Washington who had read a newspaper article reporting that a number of S&Ls had invested in Boesky-sponsored securities which were the subject of lawsuits. The paper said these issues were going into default.

Ivan Boesky was a Wall Street financier and investment manager who was accused (and later convicted) of insider trading—using confidential, nonpublic information to take unfair advantage of the markets. Prior to these accusations, Boesky was considered to be one of the real investment gurus of Wall Street, and many individuals and corporations had placed funds under his management. He had also formed a number of investment vehicles in which investors took either a debt or equity position.

Lincoln did, indeed, have an investment in a Boesky-sponsored partnership. Lincoln was in a senior position, relative to other debtholders and to limited partners, and firmly believed that it was protected from any loss. Lincoln told Kotrys about its investment and gave him all of the files pertaining to it. Kotrys passed the information on to San Francisco who, in turn, sent it to Washington. Later, Kotrys told Judy Wischer, "It was the fastest thing I have ever seen to go to Washington and bounce back," the first indication to Lincoln that someone in Washington might be directly involved in the examination.

In all of Judy's weekly progress meetings with Kotrys, the Boesky investment became a topic of discussion. Kotrys kept asking for more information but admitted he didn't have the expertise to judge the quality or soundness of the investment. He told Judy, "I write up the information and pass it on to someone else to make the determinations." Thus, it became obvious that someone in Washington—and not Kotrys—was the person who had an interest in the Boesky deal.

The Boesky investment was just the start. After it surfaced, it became routine for San Francisco or Washington to raise an issue and for Kotrys and his people to collect data from Lincoln's files just so they could pass it up the line. Lincoln didn't know who was making the decisions and, apparently, neither did Kotrys, because, when asked by Judy who the others were who were involved in the process, he pled ignorance.

The examination team conducting Lincoln's exam was employed by the San Francisco bank and, therefore, was under the control of its board of directors. These directors presumably had a say in whether an examiner was hired, promoted, given a raise, or fired. Lincoln began to question whether the board of directors' control over employment matters provided it with the power to influence the conduct or outcome of specific examinations. If the board had this ability, it was a concern to institutions, like Lincoln, that were not directly represented on the board. The fear was that a person who sat on the district bank's board could take vindictive actions against a competitor; could receive favorable treatment when the director's own institution was examined; or could obtain access to otherwise confidential information.

During one of their weekly meetings, Judy Wischer asked Kotrys whether the Eleventh District's board had any influence over the examiners. Kotrys told her, "I think if I examined a board member's bank and found deficiencies, the board member would simply have me pulled off the examination." Whether Kotrys would actually be removed from examining a board member's institution, simply because he found problems, wasn't the issue. The mere fact that Kotrys made this comment was the issue. It gave validity to the notion that the board could exert influence over the examination process. It also made Lincoln's management increasingly uneasy about what might be going on with the examination that was in process, especially since a lot of information was flowing from the examiners to someone in San Francisco.

There may have been nothing to Lincoln's early concerns. The field examiners did report to people in the district bank. The supervisors in San Francisco could merely have been asking for the data they needed to provide routine advice and counsel to their subordinates. But Lincoln didn't think that was the case.

As the weeks passed, Lincoln's concerns continued to grow. The examiners were beginning to make frequent comments about Lincoln's investments being too risky. They even said this about deals that were closed. For example, in 1984, Lincoln had invested about $130 million in the stock of Gulf Broadcast Company. The investment was considered to be a hostile takeover. That is, Gulf's management was adverse to Lincoln's purchase of large blocks of Gulf's stock. Lincoln believed that Gulf's shares were substantially undervalued and wanted to obtain control of Gulf, so it could force a liquidation of the assets. Because of Lincoln's actions, Gulf's management decided to sell the company's assets. When Lincoln got its share of the liquidation proceeds, it made over $50 million on the entire deal.

Chuck Deardorff, one of Kotrys' supervisors, thought that Lincoln should not have done the Gulf Broadcast deal. When the deal was completed, Deardorff complained that, after Lincoln had told him it would make $51 million, it had made only $50 million. Kotrys didn't understand Deardorff's continued negative attitude concerning the Gulf transaction and, at one point, told Judy, "I think the FHLB-SF should have written Lincoln a letter of congratulations on the Gulf Broadcast deal." Instead, Lincoln continued to hear criticism.

As the examination progressed, this became the constant pattern. The field examiners looked at Lincoln's records and, after talking to Lincoln's people about specific transactions, told Lincoln that everything looked fine. Then, Lincoln heard, usually from Kotrys, that San Francisco or, worse, Washington wanted more data. Lincoln knew the examiners were receiving pressure from somewhere. But Lincoln didn't know from whom the pressure was emanating, and, more importantly, it didn't know why the pressure was being applied.

It then became difficult for Lincoln's people to ascertain what was going on in the examination. Even though Judy met frequently with Kotrys, he became very closemouthed. He told Judy what information he and his team needed but was not forthcoming in discussing the real issues the examiners were concerned about or what their tentative conclusions were. Nonetheless, Lincoln was aware, simply by the nature of the requests for data and from comments that Kotrys let slip, of what some of the more troublesome matters were.

The most critical issue concerned Lincoln's direct investments. At the time of the examination, Lincoln had over $900 million in direct investments, about 40 percent of its assets. The regulation, as finally adopted by the FHLBB, provided that if an association was committed to an investment, either legally or pursuant to a "definitive plan," on December 10, 1984, it could complete the investment, even if it exceeded the 10 percent of assets limitation contained in the regulation. Pre-December 10, 1984, investments were referred to as "grandfathered" investments. An association could not, however, enter into any new direct investment if the new investment, when added to its existing investments, caused the total of all such direct investments to exceed the limitation. Since Lincoln exceeded the limitation, and by a sizable margin, it could complete any grandfathered investments, but it could not enter into any new ones.

The direct-investment regulation allowed an association the option of designating either its investment in its subsidiaries or the assets held by those subsidiaries as its direct investments. Lincoln contended that its direct investments were represented by its investments in its subsidiaries. Lincoln itself owned very little land and no equity securities. The subsidiaries did own land and equity securities (over $900 million of such assets), because that was the purpose for their creation and existence—to hold such assets.

Lincoln further contended that, as the regulation required, each of the subsidiaries was formed under a definitive plan that was in existence prior to December 10, 1984. Lincoln gave to Kotrys the plans filed with Taggart and the California Department of Savings and Loan, as well as numerous other documents, as evidence that a definitive plan did, indeed, exist for each investment. Kotrys and his field examiners reviewed the documents which Lincoln provided and indicated to Judy that they seemed to fulfill the requirements of the regulation. Lincoln thought the issue had been put to rest.

Then, the examiners started asking Lincoln for documents and files supporting the acquisition of land and equity securities by the various subsidiaries. Judy asked Kotrys, "What's going on? Why are you looking at the subsidiaries' investments?" Kotrys told her that they were simply gathering more data and asked for the board of director's approvals of the specific assets purchased by the subsidiaries. Then, Kotrys reaffirmed that his interim report would note that Lincoln believed, and the field examiners concurred, that Lincoln's investments were grandfathered based on the investment in subsidiaries and not on the specific assets owned by the subsidiaries. So, Lincoln was still not sure what was going on.

ACC found out later that Kotrys had received a directive from Washington, albeit thirdhand, stating that the investments in subsidiaries were not grandfathered simply as a consequence of receiving approval from the state. They were grandfathered only to the extent that they were *actually funded* by December 10, 1984, and not by the amount approved and committed to in the business plans.

This was a critical point, since only a fraction of the investments in the subsidiaries had actually been funded by December 10, 1984. If the investments were not grandfathered, the FHLBB could, presumably, force Lincoln to liquidate the nongrandfathered portion. If this happened, all of Lincoln's investment plans would be stopped dead in their tracks, and Lincoln could suffer losses by prematurely liquidating the investments. Kotrys was told not to discuss the issue with Lincoln but simply to gather information and forward it on to San Francisco, who would then send it to Washington.

Washington should not have had any active role in the examination. The regulators in Washington were essentially concerned with policy issues. There wasn't a field examination staff in Washington. Unlike the district banks, Washington didn't have any institutions it was responsible for examining. So, it didn't make sense that any Washington-based regulators would have direct involvement in a field examination. It wasn't their role or their jurisdiction. If they were involved in the examination of Lincoln, it raised the question: Why?

Lincoln's management believed they knew the answer to the question. Lincoln had presented the most visible and aggressive opposition to Ed Gray's direct-investment regulation. They had heard from sources within the industry that Gray had taken Lincoln's opposition personally. Shortly after the conflict over direct investments, Keating and Gray had attended an industry meeting in Hawaii. The two men had never actually met each other, but Gray knew who Keating was. As Keating passed by Gray's table, Gray is reported to have pointed at Keating and said, "I'm going to take that fucker down." Keating had also heard from one of the other FHLBB Board Members, Donald Hovde, that he was on "Ed Gray's shit list." These reports made it clear to Keating that Ed Gray might try to drive him out of the S&L industry. Now Keating believed Gray was using the examination of Lincoln to do just exactly that.

Keating's conclusions were consistent with the information that Lincoln was receiving from the field examiners. The field examiners had concluded that Lincoln's direct investments met the requirements of the regulations—and had told Judy Wischer that that was the case—but they were apparently being overruled by Washington. Keating believed that the person in Washington was Ed Gray, or one of his henchmen. It made sense. Direct investments was the issue over which Lincoln had opposed Gray, and now Gray was using that precise issue to attack, and possibly destroy, Lincoln.

As the examination continued, Keating and his associates began to view the entire process as a vendetta launched by Ed Gray against Lincoln. They began to discover other areas in which the field examiners were being directed and overruled by San Francisco and Washington: evidence to them that the examination was anything but routine, as the examiners had originally told Lincoln.

For example, there was the issue of appraisals of the collateral that Lincoln held for the loans it had made, as well as appraisals of the real estate it owned. In an examination, it is not unusual for the examiners to request that an association get new appraisals to update those that are in the association's files or, if there is not an appraisal in the files, to ask the association to get one. In these instances, the association usually provides the examiners with the names of the appraisers it intends to use, and, after gaining the examiners' approval of the intended appraiser, the association engages the appraiser to do the necessary work. That's not what happened in the Lincoln examination.

The FHLBB appraisal staff in San Francisco obtained a list of properties that Lincoln owned or held as collateral for loans from the field examiners who were in Lincoln's offices. Then, the San Francisco group selected and engaged its own outside appraisers, cutting Lincoln entirely out of the process. In fact, they prohibited Lincoln from even talking to the appraisers.

Without any input from Lincoln, the appraisals became a nightmare for Lincoln. Some of the appraisers were not qualified to appraise the properties assigned to them. Because the field examiners didn't collect all of the necessary data, collateral was omitted from some appraisals. Some of the appraisers were not familiar with the market in which the subject property was located; as a result, many of the appraisal assumptions and market data used by the appraisers were erroneous. Other appraisals contained simple mathematical or computational errors that affected the values in the appraisal. But because the FHLBB had hired the appraisers, the persons who had done the hiring would steadfastly, throughout the course of the examination, refuse to acknowledge or address the deficiencies in the appraisals they had commissioned.

A prime example of the unusual nature of the fieldwork in this examination is the subject of the Wolfswinkle loans. Lincoln had made a series of loans to Conley Wolfswinkle (a prominent Phoenix land developer) and his company, Wolfswinkle Group, Inc. (WGI). The primary loans were used to acquire and develop a project in Tucson known as Rancho Vistoso. There were also some other loans associated with another property in Tucson known as Marana, and a loan on property in Phoenix called Hidden Valley. These loans totaled approximately $100 million, which was less than 75 percent of the appraised value of the properties pledged as collateral. Lincoln was to receive a 50-percent equity participation in the profits produced by the Rancho Vistoso property which Wolfswinkle was financing.

The loans were considered to be acquisition, development, and construction (ADC) loans, a type of loan that, at the time, could have been, depending on the characteristics of the loan, accounted for as either a loan or an investment in real estate. Lincoln accounted for the transactions as loans. Kotrys and the examiners, after consulting with San Francisco, said that the transactions should be accounted for as "joint ventures."

ADC loans were prevalent throughout the industry during the 1980s. These loans are generally secured by land which the borrower intends to develop into residential, commercial, or industrial lots. ADC loans feature provisions which permit the lender to participate in a portion of the profits realized on the sale or refinancing of the subject property. The participation generally is called an equity kicker. With an ADC loan, the loan amount often provides a reserve to cover interest, and the payment of principal is not required until the financed project is completed or sales occur. Many ADC loans are non-recourse, ones where the lender can only look to the collateral in the event of default.

The American Institute of Certified Public Accountants (AICPA), one of the rule-making bodies in the accounting profession, became concerned about the accounting for ADC loans in 1983. The AICPA believed that in some of these transactions the lender had "virtually the same risks and rewards as those of owners or joint venturers." If that is the case, the transaction should, according to the AICPA, be accounted for as an investment in real estate and not as a loan. As such, the lender has to defer the income recognition of some, or all, of the interest and loan fees it collects from the borrower.

A more important issue than income recognition, from Lincoln's standpoint and in the context of the examination that was in progress, was, if the transaction was accounted for as either a joint venture or an investment in real estate, it was considered a direct investment. Thus, depending on the accounting, another $100 million could be added to Lincoln's direct investments. This was significant because the FHLBB was already contending that Lincoln had exceeded the limitations specified in the regulation.

In November 1983, the AICPA issued the first, in a series of three, "Notice to Practitioners" which discussed the accounting for ADC loans. The notice described a number of criteria causing a transaction to be treated as either a loan or an investment in real estate.

Essentially, a transaction, even though it contained an equity kicker, was considered to be a loan if the borrower had equity in the property which was not funded by the lender; if the lender had recourse to other assets of the borrower, either through a pledge of assets or a personal guarantee; if there was a take-out commitment that would pay off the loan; or if there was an existing, noncancelable sales contract or lease for the property. Each of these factors reduced the lender's risk and made the transaction more akin to a loan than to an investment.

Even with the guidance provided in this notice, there was a lack of uniformity in the industry's accounting for ADC transactions. So, two more notices were issued: one in November 1984 and another in February 1986. The focus of these additional notices was largely on whether personal guarantees were effective in reducing the lender's risk to the point where loan accounting was appropriate. The notices discussed a number of criteria which personal guarantees had to meet before they could be relied upon in determining whether a transaction was a loan.

Suffice it to say, ADC arrangements can be complex, and the accounting for them requires the exercise of judgment. In this case, the outside auditors for Lincoln and ACC, Arthur Andersen & Co., had addressed these specific transactions. Based on the personal and corporate guarantees

of Conley Wolfswinkle and WGI, which were backed by financial statements that Arthur Andersen had either reviewed or audited and that
showed a current-value net worth of $190 million for Mr. Wolfswinkle
(which included his investment in WGI) and $170 million for WGI, as well
as other characteristics of the transactions, Andersen concluded that the
transactions were properly recordable as loans.

Now, at the time of the examination, the FHLBB's examiners had
some accounting knowledge, but they were by no means experts in
accounting matters. Certainly their knowledge wasn't close to the knowledge and skill that a firm like Arthur Andersen possessed and knew how
to exercise. Yet, the examiners challenged Andersen's conclusions with
respect to the Wolfswinkle loans, even after Andersen issued a specific,
separate report addressing these very transactions. Something didn't add
up. The separate Andersen report should have put the issue to rest, but it
didn't.

The examiners' actions, such as rejecting Andersen's opinion and
continuing to criticize the Gulf Broadcast deal, didn't make sense. It
seemed to Lincoln that the examiners' role had changed from that of
conducting a routine examination into one of trying to find or create an
issue which San Francisco or Washington could use to take some action
against Lincoln and Keating. The belief that the exam was a vendetta
intensified, and Lincoln became more and more concerned about where
the examination was headed.

It was the controversy between the FHLBB and Lincoln over the
Wolfswinkle loans that drew me into the Lincoln War. When the FHLBB
rejected Arthur Andersen's report on these transactions, both the FHLBB
and Lincoln decided to ask another major accounting firm to review the
transactions and to express its opinion as to the appropriateness of
Lincoln's accounting for the loans.

At the time, I was the managing partner of Arthur Young & Company's
Phoenix office. Arthur Young was one of the so-called "Big Eight"
accounting firms.

I'd been in public accounting for over twenty years. Primarily an
auditor, I also conducted management-consulting assignments and possessed a reasonable working knowledge of the federal tax laws. Some of
my clients were, or had been, start-up businesses that struggled to make
ends meet and employed rudimentary financial and accounting systems.
Others were large, publicly held corporations that featured complex
financial structures, sophisticated data-processing systems, and international business operations.

From 1979 to 1986, an increasing percentage of my professional time
was devoted to savings and loans and related industries, such as home

builders, land developers, mortgage bankers, construction companies, property managers, and real-estate syndicators. Two of the Phoenix office's most significant clients in the S&L industry were Merabank and Pima Savings. I served as the account partner for both of these associations.

Merabank was a Phoenix-based savings and loan association with total assets of approximately $5 billion. Pima was a Tucson-based association with assets of over $2 billion. By industry standards, they were large institutions. They were also well respected, both within the state and nationally.

I had seen, firsthand, the S&L industry convert from one which was comprised of fairly mundane businesses into one consisting of complex, diversified, financial-services enterprises. Merabank and Pima were a microcosm of the industry. They experienced all of the problems affecting the industry as a whole. I worked closely with their management groups and, therefore, I understood most of the factors affecting the S&L industry.

I also saw the effects which spread erosion had on all of my clients. The most dramatic erosion was at a San Diego-based association, Central Savings, with which I became involved in the early 1980s. Central failed, in large part, due to losses resulting from its negative spread. It was also crippled by foreclosure losses which were the direct result of the high interest rates and inflation prevalent at the time. Unlike my other clients, Central ran out of time and was not able to adapt quickly enough to survive.

Merabank and Pima, on the other hand, did react to their spread problems. For example, Merabank (then First Federal Savings and Loan of Arizona) took advantage of the new rules that permitted a mutual association to convert to a stock association. In 1983, it offered its stock to the public and raised approximately $60 million in new, and badly needed, capital. It also issued subordinated debt which qualified as regulatory capital. Merabank, as did Pima, invested its capital by entering into real-estate joint ventures, making commercial and ADC loans, and diversifying in other ways. Both associations, as well as the other institutions I served, took full advantage of the flexibility offered by deregulation, although not to the degree that Lincoln did.

Arthur Young had a number of committees which dealt with specialized industries. Each committee consisted of about a dozen partners who were heavily involved in the subject industry. The purpose of the committees was to identify the emerging problems facing the industry and to develop approaches for solving those problems. The committee members also were a resource to other partners within the firm who needed counsel and advice regarding accounting, auditing, regulatory, or business problems impacting the firm's clients.

I was a member of Arthur Young's real estate and savings and loan industry committees. In this role, I received frequent calls from people within Arthur Young, as well as from outside parties, including the partners of other major accounting firms who wanted to discuss issues involving savings and loan associations.

It was in this context that I was introduced to Lincoln. Judy Wischer had gotten my name from one of Arthur Andersen's partners as the person in Phoenix to call for a second opinion on the Wolfswinkle loans. She called me in June 1986 and asked if Arthur Young & Company would accept the assignment.

After Judy explained the situation which had arisen with the examiners concerning these loans, I recall asking her, "Judy, if Andersen has already addressed these transactions in a separate report, why do the examiners want a second opinion?"

"They don't seem satisfied with Andersen's report," Judy said. "They want another firm to look at the loans. It's a mystery to us why they have rejected Andersen's report."

It was a mystery to me, too. As a consequence of my experiences with other clients, I had dealt with the FHLBB's examiners and its staff in Washington on a fair number of occasions. It was my observation that the FHLBB's field examiners had, at best, a very elementary understanding of accounting. Based on my experiences, they were ill-equipped to deal with a complex ADC issue.

As for the staff in Washington, the full-time, permanent FHLBB employees knew just enough accounting to be dangerous. Recognizing the technical inadequacies of its own staff, the FHLBB borrowed several young people from major accounting firms—people not yet admitted to a partnership but who hoped to be admitted in the future—to augment the full-time staff. While these on-loan people—referred to as interns—were better equipped than the FHLBB's permanent staff, for the most part they were still cutting their teeth on the more complex areas of accounting. I had dealt with these people in connection with acquisitions and securities offerings and, each time, a great deal of time was consumed educating them on the most basic of issues.

So, neither the FHLBB's field examiners nor its Washington staff were accounting experts, and, certainly, they didn't come close to equaling the technical-skill levels of Arthur Andersen's partners. It was almost inconceivable to me that the FHLBB people would view their own conclusions about ADC loans to be superior to Arthur Andersen's written opinions. I believed that they were aware of and understood their own technical limitations better than that.

In fact, it was a mystery to me why ADC accounting would become an examination issue in the first place. Every S&L was required to have its annual financial statements examined by a certified public accountant.

The FHLBB and the various state commissioners reserved the right to approve the accountants that a given association sought to appoint as its auditors. Once appointed, the regulators relied on the CPAs to determine whether an association's accounting for its transaction was appropriate or not. The field examiners did not, in my experience, get involved in the accounting at all; instead, they deferred to the outside auditors. Thus, it was very strange that Lincoln's examiners were even raising these matters, let alone rejecting Andersen's opinions. It was, indeed, a mystery.

More out of curiosity than anything else, I agreed to meet with Judy, her staff, and the Andersen people in order to gather more information before deciding whether to accept the assignment of rendering a second opinion or not.

I had no sooner finished talking to Judy and hung up the telephone, when I received a call from one of my partners in Arthur Young's Los Angeles office. He told me that he had just been talking to the FHLBB's Los Angeles staff, and they had asked him to accept the very same assignment that I had discussed with Judy.

He, too, was baffled by the request. It was almost unprecedented for the FHLBB to call a firm, other than an association's own auditors, to ask about the accounting for a transaction. The examiners were always very secretive about what they were doing and almost never revealed anything to an association's auditors. In fact, they wouldn't even show the auditors their reports on an association; the auditors had to get these reports from an association's board of directors, if they were to get them at all. So, a call directly from the FHLBB to a firm other than an association's own auditors was completely out of the ordinary.

I told him about my conversation with Judy, and we agreed that the best way to handle the situation was for me to proceed with the meeting I had already scheduled. Then, we could decide what, if anything, to do about accepting the assignment—with either Lincoln or the FHLBB as our client.

I took our audit manager who had the most experience in auditing S&Ls and ADC transactions with me to meet with Lincoln. She had been involved in auditing S&Ls for over six years and had looked at literally scores of complicated ADC transactions. If we accepted the assignment, she would be the person responsible for analyzing the details supporting the subject loans.

We spent several hours discussing the transactions with Lincoln's and Andersen's representatives. As the discussion progressed, it became obvious that Andersen believed it had sufficient, competent data to support their opinions, and they were both perplexed and miffed by the FHLBB's actions. They and Lincoln's people agreed to give us full access to all of the audit work papers and to any, and all, of Lincoln's records. Based on these discussions, the assignment appeared to be straightforward, and we accepted it, with Lincoln insisting on being our client, not the FHLBB.

Lincoln was concerned that, if the FHLBB were the client, the examiners would try to influence the outcome of our work, as Lincoln believed the FHLBB had done with the various appraisers it had engaged. We didn't see any problem with Lincoln being the named client, especially since, even if the FHLBB engaged us, Lincoln would have to pay our bill.

My partner in Los Angeles called the FHLBB and told them that we had decided to render the second opinion, and Lincoln was our client. The FHLBB representative said that he was upset that Lincoln had contacted us—he said that they were interfering with the examination—but told us to go ahead with the work, adding "We reserve the right to hire another firm if we don't agree with your opinion." His closing admonition confirmed that this was, indeed, a very peculiar situation.

The audit manager finished her analysis of the ADC loans about two weeks later. She had reviewed all of the loan documents, the other data in Lincoln's loan files, the financial statements of the guarantors, and Andersen's work papers. She found Andersen had ample support for their opinion.

During the second week of July 1986, we issued our report, which concurred with Arthur Andersen's earlier opinion. Our report should have resolved any concerns that the examiners had regarding Lincoln's accounting for these loans. They now had opinions from two major accounting firms concluding that Lincoln's positions were appropriate.

At that point, I believed that my involvement with Lincoln and ACC was over. They appeared to have a good relationship with the Andersen firm and valued its services. This looked like a one-shot assignment.

I was wrong. It wasn't the end; it was just the beginning. Unknowingly, I had become involved in what would become a prolonged, all-out war.

Four

Keating Meets the FHLBB's Field Troops

By the first of May 1986, Lincoln's examination had been going on for eight weeks, the normal elapsed time for most routine examinations. An exit conference signals the completion of the examiners' fieldwork. Lincoln, wanting the examination to end, tried to get an exit conference scheduled with the examiners.

In mid-May 1986, Kotrys told Judy that an exit meeting would be held on May 27, as the examiners would "be pretty much done and gone by May 31st." But this meeting was never held. In fact, Kotrys' superiors denied that it was ever scheduled.

Another meeting was scheduled for June 24. Judy Wischer, Rob Symes, who was then president of Lincoln, and Tim Kruckeberg, who was Judy's assistant and a person who performed special projects for Lincoln, met with Kotrys on June 17 to review the meeting agenda. Kotrys began by telling the Lincoln people that the exit conference scheduled for June 24 was canceled, and he didn't know when it would be rescheduled.

Judy asked, "What happened? Why is the meeting being called off?"

Kotrys said he had been called to San Francisco on Monday, June 15, where he was given additional instructions and a list of items San Francisco wanted reviewed before they would end the exam.

"What are those items?" Judy asked.

Kotrys replied, "There won't be anything more than what is already listed in my June 13 memo [which had previously been given to Judy]. However, some of those will be expanded."

Judy asked Kotrys, "Who was in the meeting in San Francisco?"

Kotrys responded by naming about a half-dozen of his supervisors, after which, Judy asked, "What kind of things did they want to talk about?"

Kotrys explained that the meeting had only been about an hour long, but, prior to that, the others had held their own private meeting. He then said, "I've never been so disgusted as an agent. I've never been to San Francisco before, nor have I ever had an audit that was so totally finished where I was told to go back and re-look at things. I was finished with this audit in May, and I'm still here, and I'll be here at least another two weeks, although you can't quote me on that—it may be longer. I have nothing additional to do. They have asked me to restate some of the things that I have already written up—to look at them in another way, and to readdress some of the questions."

This response immediately got the Lincoln people's attention. Kotrys was an experienced examiner. He had been in the FHLBB system for a considerable number of years. He was clearly competent to recognize when his fieldwork tasks were complete. He said that he knew his work was done in May. That's why he had scheduled an exit conference for May 27. Now, his supervisors, who had never seen any of Lincoln's records or reviewed the details of any of its transactions, were telling him to "re-look" at things. In effect, they were telling him "keep digging until you find something wrong." And, as Kotrys told Judy and the others, the actions of his superiors "disgusted" him.

Judy had known something wasn't right with the examination for several weeks. She had heard Kotrys say that he was "passing things on to others to make the determinations" too many times. Moreover, Kotrys said that he had "never been to San Francisco before." He had spent a long career with the FHLBB, and "never" in all those years had any supervisors asked him to come to San Francisco. But now they had, and they had done so in order to direct him to continue an examination that Kotrys knew was finished—something no supervisor had ever asked him to do before. These occurrences reinforced Lincoln's belief that someone was out to get Lincoln.

After Kotrys said that he didn't have anything else to say about the meeting, he went over the list of items contained in his agenda memo, adding clarification for the benefit of the Lincoln people. When he had completed discussing the list, Judy, following up on the concerns Kotrys' earlier comments had raised, asked a series of questions: "What's really going on with this audit? What are they trying to do? Why was that meeting held?"

Kotrys said, "I really don't know."

He then added, "Until recently I have been a civil servant, and I couldn't be called by supervisory until the examination report was written and sent on to supervisory."

This further alarmed Judy and the others because it was the second time, in the space of just a few minutes, that Kotrys had indicated that someone was trying to guide or influence the examiners in a preconceived direction. If, in the past, Kotrys' supervisors hadn't gotten involved in the process until after he drafted his report and sent it to them, why were they interceding in this examination?

In response to the question regarding what the FHLBB was going to do to Lincoln, Kotrys said, "I'm not aware of any specific actions that will be taken."

He then said, "The reason I feel they are concerned about Lincoln is they are running scared from recent failures of other savings and loans which have resulted in congressional hearings looking into those failures. Those hearings have resulted in criticism of the regulatory personnel involved.

"I've assured San Francisco that Lincoln is different," Kotrys said. "The San Francisco people have noted that Lincoln has investments and operations similar to those of thrifts which have failed. They have specifically talked about San Marino, American Diversified, and Beverly Hills. I told them again that Lincoln is different from those associations, and, in my opinion, the personnel at Lincoln are quite competent, and there aren't any substantial losses in Lincoln's assets.

"I repeated that additional work in the field would not turn up anything new," Kotrys concluded.

Nothing Kotrys told Judy during the course of the examination indicated that the field examiners had any concern about Lincoln's viability. In fact, the examiners had specifically said, on every occasion when Lincoln inquired, there weren't any "substantial losses" disclosed by the examination procedures. So, Lincoln had to ask itself, "Why are they mentioning us in the same breath with failed associations like San Marino, Beverly Hills, and American Diversified?"

Judy then asked, "What's Glen Sanders' [the FHLB-SF's appraiser's] approach to the audit?"

"What do you mean?" Kotrys asked.

Judy replied, "Is he finding problems? Is he in favor of continuing the audit? Where does he stand?"

"Sanders tends to showboat somewhat and talk to you like he's at a podium giving a speech," Kotrys said. "But he told me he has not seen any case of loss in the association. He has found some deficiencies in some of the appraisals, but he doesn't expect to find losses. Although, he is still putting his list together."

Judy asked Kotrys about Sanders' attitude because, earlier in May, she had had conversations with Sanders about the reappraisals that the examiners had ordered. She had asked Sanders how long the reappraisal process would take. Sanders had told her, "It can go on forever." Now that it was clear that San Francisco was trying to extend the examination, Sanders' comment took on added significance. San Francisco could use the reappraisals to stall the whole examination while the other examiners looked for something on Lincoln.

Kotrys then promised there would be no surprises at the exit conference when it was eventually held. He said that he would get with Sanders and would meet with Judy to go over all of their findings. He reiterated that all he was going to do was re-look at the work which had already been done, so he could satisfy San Francisco. With that, the meeting concluded.

Later that day, Bob Dove, Kotrys' immediate supervisor, in a telephone conversation with Bob Kielty, who was ACC's in-house legal counsel, confirmed what Kotrys had said about the meeting which had been scheduled for June 24. Dove stated that officials in San Francisco had canceled the meeting because of "continued questions regarding Lincoln's investments in land, high-yield bonds, and acquisition and development loans."

Later, in a letter defending the appropriateness of San Francisco's actions and condemning Lincoln for being "hostile and uncooperative," B.J. Davis, Dove's boss, refuted the comments made by Kotrys and Dove. He stated that the meeting had merely been "postponed, not canceled."

The issue wasn't whether the meeting had been "postponed" or "canceled." It was: Why? Kotrys' remarks set off renewed speculation that some party, whom Lincoln still hadn't identified, was turning a normal, routine examination into an attempt to harm Lincoln. Perhaps the unknown party was, as Keating strongly suspected, Ed Gray, who was seeking revenge for Lincoln's opposition to the direct-investment rules, or maybe it was a competitor who sat on the San Francisco bank's board? Lincoln's management knew that it had to find out what was really going on before the situation got totally out of hand.

During the week of June 23, Lincoln was informed that another exit conference had been scheduled for July 3, 1986. It was to be held in Irvine, and the examiners would discuss "all of the issues" and "all of our findings" with Lincoln.

Charlie Keating had not, until this point, been involved in the examination. He had been content to let Judy, Bob Kielty, and Lincoln's own management team deal with the regulators. But he had received periodic briefings and was aware of the comments about possible corruption of the examination by the supervisory personnel in Washington and San Francisco. Like Judy, he was apprehensive about what that connoted. Was someone out to do him harm? If so, who and why? To answer these questions, Charlie decided that he had to interject himself personally into the process of dealing with the examiners.

With that decision, the examiners were about to face a very unique individual. Charlie Keating is an intense competitor with a deep-seated need to excel and succeed. Accounts of his youth demonstrate that these attributes were acquired at an early age, when he was confronted with and learned to overcome adversity.

Charlie was seven years old when his father contracted Parkinson's disease and was never able to work again. His father's condition became more severe when he lost a leg as the result of a hunting accident. In spite of his physical problems, Charlie's father maintained a positive attitude and taught his sons to "accept what life gives you and keep on going." Charlie describes it as "a midwestern value system, where your goals are realistic, and you do whatever you have to as situations come along."

As a result of his father's disabilities, the family lived on limited resources. Charlie and his younger brother, Bill, performed all the heavy chores around the house, helped care for their father, and held odd jobs. By the age of fourteen or fifteen, Charlie was working fifty to sixty hours a week in a local dairy, earning money to help meet the family's basic needs. It was fatiguing, backbreaking work, but Charlie never complained.

These early experiences taught Charlie an approach to work which he illustrates by saying, "I've never thought of myself as a workaholic. But I've always enjoyed work. I've always thought you could make it as much fun as playing, if you took the right approach to it."

Charlie's youthful, competitive spirit was honed in the Naval Air Corps, where he flew carrier-based, night-fighter planes. It carried over to his days at the University of Cincinnati, where he was an All-American swimmer and NCAA champion. And it played a strong part in his decision to enter law school and the legal profession.

By attending classes twelve months a year, Charlie graduated from the University of Cincinnati's School of Law in two years. After graduation, he joined a Cincinnati-based law firm. He was compensated through a base salary but earned added income based on business he brought to the firm. He said, "That was a real incentive to start getting clients in. I started doing a lot of business in a hurry." Charlie rapidly discovered that, from the standpoint of personal satisfaction as well as economic reward, he enjoyed attracting new clients, more than actually rendering legal services. The ability to make a sale became one of Charlie Keating's strongest business attributes.

In 1951, Charlie formed his own firm with his brother and a former classmate. Charlie's role, as the rainmaker, was to find clients while the others provided the services. Charlie found business law was where his talents lay. He acted as a consultant to his clients, a role he described by saying, "I would put clients together with the experts they needed and, then, worked along with them. I wouldn't interfere with what the experts were doing, but I would challenge them to make sure they did their job."

He said that his value to his client was: "I was able to understand all aspects of a business deal. I was able to understand the entire picture better than the client or the attorneys or the experts we would bring in. That made me valuable. There were a lot of transactions where, if I hadn't been involved, the client never would have gone forward with the plan. I found

I could inspire them, give them the confidence to try new things." It was through working in this part of his practice that Charlie learned the art of deal-making, a skill which was his real business forte.

In 1959, Charlie began to work with American Financial Corporation. It was here that he first became involved with savings and loan associations. He negotiated the acquisition of numerous businesses, including savings and loans, for American Financial. He learned to identify companies who held undervalued assets and to differentiate between the good and not-so-good acquisition opportunities. After the businesses were acquired, Charlie participated in directing their management. Again, his role was deal maker and consultant.

In 1976, when he got the opportunity to obtain control of American Continental from American Financial, Charlie used his acquired skills to build his own company. Under his direction, ACC reflected Keating's most prominent attributes. The company was an intense competitor in the markets in which it operated; its business, with resultant profits, was deal driven; it employed people with excellent technical skills who were willing to work long, hard hours; marketing, or salesmanship, was a significant element in the business' success; and acquisitions played a role in the company's growth. Later, ACC exported these same attributes to the newly acquired Lincoln.

But it's not these acquired skills that set Charlie Keating apart from the crowd; it's the man himself. When Charlie enters a room, his presence is immediately felt. His physical appearance grabs attention, and then he proceeds to dominate any meeting with his forceful personality.

In excellent physical condition, Charlie is lanky—six feet, five inches—and lean. His piercing blue eyes look out from wire-rimmed glasses and are accented by his reddish-blonde hair. His normal office attire was a custom-made, light-blue dress shirt with French cuffs, fastened by cuff links made of gold or large gemstones. By early morning, his collar was open, his tie loosened, his sleeves rolled up and the cuff links deposited in a pocket or on his desk.

Charlie normally arrived at the office about 4:00 A.M. and, sometimes, earlier. He is a voracious reader and would pour over books, magazines, newspapers, reports prepared by staff or advisors, and other written materials which sparked his interest. By the time his secretaries arrived, their desks would be piled with items to be distributed, notes or letters to type, and instructions to be followed. In the morning hours, free of distractions and interruptions, Charlie could accomplish more than most people can in an entire workday.

Charlie is spontaneous, hyper, and impatient, with a short attention span and an incessant need to be doing two or three things at once. After the staff arrived, he would walk through the office, yelling out in his nasal voice "get me so-and-so on the phone." Before the call could be placed, he would shout to another secretary "get me what's-his-name." In short order, he would have two or three calls going, each on a different phone on different desks, and, simultaneously, he would be carrying on a discussion with another executive or staff person. Even in meetings with outsiders, there were constant interruptions for phone calls, most of which he had asked to be placed on the spur of the moment during the meeting. He kept up this frenetic pace until he left the office, usually around 6:00 P.M. Even then, he often was leaving only to attend church, another meeting, or a business dinner.

Charlie is anything but subtle. He says exactly what pops into his head. He has strong opinions, likes, dislikes, and beliefs. And he voices them—frequently—and often stridently. Most people don't have to guess what he's thinking. He is also prone to use exaggerated phrasing in order to make his point. People who haven't been around him much often take this hyperbole literally and are either shocked or misunderstand him. While this trait is often evident in his speech, it showed up more in notes he wrote to his staff or in comments he scrawled on letters and reports.

The examiners hadn't had to deal with Charlie. They were going to now as they entered Lincoln's conference room on July 3, 1986, for the scheduled exit conference which ACC expected would bring the examination to a close.

There were six examiners and supervisory personnel from the FHLB-SF; four representatives from the California Department of Savings and Loan (CDSL or DSL); and thirteen people from ACC and Lincoln in attendance.

At the onset of the meeting, Kotrys distributed an agenda. As he handed Judy her copy, he said, "This is new, Judy." The agenda was totally different from the one Kotrys had reviewed with her a few weeks earlier. This agenda indicated that the meeting was a "preliminary conference" and not an exit conference. This was news to Lincoln, the field examiners, and the representatives of the CDSL, all of whom were there because they thought the meeting was the final exit conference. None had been informed of the new agenda.

Before Kotrys could begin discussing his agenda items, Charlie interjected and said, "I've got some preliminary questions I want answered. First, whom do you work for?"

"The Federal Home Loan Bank of San Francisco," Kotrys said.

"Does everyone here work for the FHLB-SF?" Charlie asked.

Kotrys replied that except for the CDSL representatives, everyone worked for the FHLB-SF. Charlie then asked, "Under what authority do you work for the bank?"

"What do you mean?" Kotrys asked.

"Well, when we deal with government agencies, someone advises us of the authorities under which its agents operate. Since the FHLB-SF is not a government agency, I'm curious whether you can tell me the code section or something of that nature which gives you the authority to examine Lincoln?"

Kotrys said that he didn't know how to answer the question.

Charlie was trying to find out whether the movement of the field examiners from the federal payroll to the FHLB-SF's payroll had created any confusion as to what their roles were. Kotrys' response indicated that the examiners were, indeed, confused. They weren't sure what authority they now operated under—were they government employees, or were they private examiners who were directed by the board of the FHLB-SF? They didn't seem to know.

So, Charlie said, "Okay, tell me about the handling of the information Lincoln provides to you. Where does it go? Who keeps control of it? Who has authority over it? I'm asking this because the FHLB-SF's chairman and directors are direct competitors of Lincoln."

Kotrys couldn't answer the questions, but Del Fassett, who was the vice-president of examinations for the FHLB-SF's Los Angeles office, described the delegation of authority from the FHLBB to the district banks. He referred Charlie to the regulations. Fassett also described, in response to a follow-up question from Bob Kielty, the reporting relationships of the various examiners.

Then Fassett answered the questions about the materials which Lincoln gave to the examiners by saying: "Everything collected during the examination is kept as part of the agency function. All the material is confidential and is kept in the agency's organization in the sense that the work papers for Lincoln are retained in the office in Los Angeles, with copies going to Mr. Sanchez in San Francisco."

Mr. Sanchez, to whom Fassett referred, was Richard Sanchez, Lincoln's supervisory agent, who had recently been inserted into the process as one of Kotrys' bosses and was also in this meeting. Sanchez was a relatively young man and one of the more recent additions to the FHLBB supervisory staff. He had worked in the financial-services industry but was not an experienced examiner. Certainly, he had far fewer years of experience working with S&Ls than did Joe Kotrys, the man he was supervising.

In meetings like this one, Sanchez generally sits with a sullen, noncommittal expression on his face, content to let others on his team do the talking. When asked questions, he has a tendency to be defensive, as if his authority is being challenged, and gives very curt and abrupt responses.

Fassett continued, "The directors of the FHLB-SF don't have the authority or the right to delve into any examination work that has taken place, and they aren't privy to anything that Lincoln is doing or not doing."

Charlie then said, "If that's true, and they are prohibited from overseeing the work of the Bank's employees, they are exposed to great personal liability, given their fiduciary obligation to oversee the bank's operations."

Charlie's comment was meant to convey that he didn't find it plausible that the directors of the FHLB-SF weren't privy to the data that the examiners had in their possession. Who was going to deny them access? Surely not an employee whose career was totally in their hands?

Glen Sanders, the FHLB-SF's chief appraiser, seeing that Charlie didn't buy Fassett's explanation, then said, "Let me clarify this. I just appeared before the Dingle Commission on the failure of Beverly Hills Savings Association. The FHLB-SF is divided into three sections: supervision, examinations, and banking. There is a 'Chinese wall' between what's done in examinations and supervision and what goes on in banking. Nothing done in the course of the examination passes over that Chinese wall."

Charlie hadn't expected the examiners to admit it if the FHLB-SF's directors did have access to Lincoln's information or could influence the conduct of the exam. Rather, he simply wanted the examiners to know that Lincoln was concerned about the appearance of a conflict of interest. He was making the point because of Judy's earlier conversations with Kotrys where Kotrys specifically indicated that potential conflicts of interest existed.

Charlie then moved to another topic. He distributed copies of a report, dated June 24, 1986, which had been written by the law firm of McKenna, Conner & Cuneo. The chairman of the FHLB-SF was a member of this firm. The introduction to the report stated:

Recent months have given rise to a pattern of increased enforcement activity by the Federal Home Loan Bank Board with respect to FSLIC-insured thrift institutions. The pattern of enforcement once was focused on recently chartered institutions, but now has expanded to include long-existing, "traditional" thrifts as well.

The enforcement strategy seems to be to raise a number of criticisms with respect to such matters as acquisition, development and construction ("ADC") loans, deviation from the institution's "business" plan, underwriting and documentation errors or insufficient oversight by the institution's board of directors. A history of profitability or of compliance with minimum net worth requirements does not appear sufficient to exempt an institution from this pattern of enforcement.

The criticisms, which are characterized as unsafe and unsound practices, are followed up by a request for a meeting between the directors and the institution's supervisory agent who, in many instances, asks the directors, on behalf of the institution, to sign a supervisory agreement restricting, often in sweeping terms, the institution's growth and operations and mandating various remedial steps. Often the request to enter into a supervisory agreement is coupled with a thinly-veiled threat to initiate cease and desist proceedings should the directors refuse to sign the agreement.

Referring to this report, Charlie said, "You will note the report concludes that regardless of operational successes, institutions that are not operating consistent with the wishes of Ed Gray are being coerced into executing supervisory agreements and submitting to formal cease-and-desist orders. This is wrong, and it's completely inconsistent with the FHLBB's statutory mandate. This kind of extra-statutory behavior forces us to approach your examination of Lincoln with concern about your motives."

The situation described in this report was exactly what Lincoln saw happening in its examination. The areas which the report said that examiners would attack, in order to force an institution to enter into a supervisory agreement, were the precise ones that the examiners, after receiving instructions from San Francisco and Washington, were raising at Lincoln. Charlie didn't believe it was by coincidence that this was occurring. It was by deliberate design.

Charlie had thrown down a gauntlet, but none of the examiners chose to pick it up. They remained silent. And an uneasiness settled over the room.

After a brief pause, as some of the tension drained, Kotrys presented the examiners' comments regarding Lincoln's operations and loan-documentation deficiencies. Kotrys said, "Lincoln is not a traditional savings and loan. Interest expense exceeds interest income, and most of Lincoln's income is generated by service-corporation activities." With respect to loan-documentation deficiencies, Kotrys referred to a list that he had provided earlier to Judy. He said that the list contained the deficiencies "identified in our initial review of the loan files."

Kotrys acknowledged that he had received rebuttal materials from Lincoln and said that the examiners were still looking into the information. He then said, "That's where we stand right now." It had become very clear that this meeting was not an exit conference as Lincoln had been told and had anticipated.

At this point, the heat began to build under Charlie's collar, and his frustration with the entire examination process started to show. Judy had reported to him that Kotrys felt the examination was over but that he had been ordered to keep going and to revise his conclusions regarding certain areas that he had examined. It now looked like the examination was still not finished. Charlie, Judy, and the other Lincoln people were increasingly concerned that someone, as yet unknown, was intent on finding, or manufacturing, something which could be used against Lincoln. It was clear to Charlie that the field examiners' findings were being altered or changed by people above them in the regulatory structure. The question again was: Why?

Charlie responded to Kotrys' remarks by saying, "When we took over Lincoln in February 1984, it was headed for the same bloodbath encountered by numerous other institutions. It had a poor loan portfolio, and its records were in bad shape. We couldn't run a normal savings and loan and, at the same time, salvage Lincoln. We don't intend on continuing to operate with a negative spread. We'll fix that situation. It results, in large part, because a significant amount of cash is invested at overnight rates. We will invest the cash in qualified assets, but we need to do that prudently. But you should at least acknowledge that we literally bailed out Lincoln. And these things take time."

Judy then followed up on the comment about all the earnings coming from the service corporations. She said, "The service corporations are heavily capitalized. Had we chosen to make loans to the service corporations, Lincoln would have earned interest income on these investments. But because we decided to make capital contributions, it created $700 million to $800 million in non-earning assets on Lincoln's books. You have to recognize that the level of Lincoln's operating income is determined by this capital structure. The service corporations have made interest-earning investments, but it doesn't show up as interest on Lincoln's books. It's accounted for as other income and doesn't figure into the spread numbers. And Lincoln is profitable."

Kielty then asked, "Given those comments," referring to Charlie's and Judy's responses, "are you still concerned about Lincoln's operations?"

"We are not attempting to characterize things as either good or bad," Sanchez said. "We are just stating that we have observed certain conditions."

"We are here to address Lincoln's situation directly," Charlie said. "There is no question San Francisco and Washington don't like Lincoln's operations. We are keenly aware of their views. We know there are discussions between Washington and San Francisco regarding Lincoln's operations. So it's neither possible nor factual to say Washington doesn't have a bone in its throat over Lincoln.

"There are some very, very decent people in the examination system," Charlie continued. "But as so often happens when a government agency becomes perverted, those peoples' strength and decency are shut out. This situation is dreadfully wrong. I resent the fact this examination has, to date, cost Lincoln at least $5 million in management time, expenses, and lost opportunities.

"In addition to the economic cost, I walk around with a hollow feeling in the pit of my stomach trying to run a profitable business," Charlie said. "The direction of this examination from Washington and San Francisco constitutes rank discrimination and harassment.

"The last time we were asked to discuss Lincoln's operations, we did so proudly," Charlie said. "We've lived up to our promises. But after $5 million and box cars full of information, I don't see any point in discussing Lincoln's operations any further. Given the gross discrimination by the FHLBB, additional explanations will have little relevance on the FHLBB's view of Lincoln."

At this point, Judy made a few comments correcting some of the examiners' comments regarding other aspects of Lincoln's operating results. In part, she was creating a diversion to let Charlie calm his anger about the fact that this was not an exit conference and the examination was not over.

When Judy finished, Charlie, in a slightly less agitated fashion, noted, "Lincoln has out-performed all of the banks and savings and loans in Arizona, of which there are approximately twenty-seven, during the time period from January 1, 1985, to the present. Given this, we resent being told the FHLBB has a neutral view on the examination. This isn't true. And we are not a Beverly Hills."

Charlie then said, "The time for new forays into real estate has passed, and that is a very unfortunate fact for the S&Ls, because real estate constitutes the type of investment in which S&Ls can profitably engage. Lincoln currently has about 39,000 acres in Arizona real estate, of which about 65 percent will be used for single-family development, providing at least 104,000 residential units. Only about 10 percent will be devoted to townhouses and apartments, and another 10 percent will be commercial and industrial. If the FHLBB forces investors like Lincoln out of the development business, the housing industry will critically suffer.

"When we took over ACC in late 1976, it was almost bankrupt. We were able to revive ACC and made good earnings. But we predicted a worsening in the housing market by 1985. So we decided almost five years ago to move out of the housing business. When the California legislature wisely deregulated the investment authority of California-chartered S&Ls, we decided to acquire a California thrift. This authority has been turned into a joke.

"After we acquired Lincoln," Charlie said, "we attempted to put everything we had into the S&L business. We found it impossible to do because of the tax statutes and regulations. Nevertheless, we have done everything we can to achieve this goal, and our decision has turned out to be exactly wrong because the predilection of the FHLBB has changed.

"Now, ACC is stuck with Lincoln and is forced to exist like a cornered rat," Charlie said. "Since Lincoln is all ACC has, we're forced to fight."

In a less cynical tone, Charlie went on to talk about Lincoln's real estate. "Our land portfolio is sufficient to last through the 1990s. With the exception of some tracts acquired to implement existing holdings, and tracts representing quick in-and-out profit situations, we won't be buying more land.

"Look at Estrella. It provides Lincoln with a unique advantage in that it is tied closely to a growing regional airport and is benefited by extraordinary cooperation from the local municipality. Our basis is about $3,500 per acre. It'll appraise at about $5,000 to $6,000 per acre and can be sold for at least $10,000 to $11,000 per acre. Properly liquidated, the ground will produce a profit of between $100 million and $150 million."

The Estrella property was Lincoln's largest and most controversial land-development project. Beginning in 1984, and continuing into 1986, Lincoln, through its subsidiary AMCOR Investments, purchased a number of contiguous parcels of land southwest of Phoenix. These assembled properties aggregated over 17,800 acres and, when combined with some industrial property which was purchased at a nearby airport, were referred to within Lincoln and ACC as the "Estrella Assemblage."

The property was intended to be a large, master-planned community which could ultimately house over 250,000 people; thus, it would become a city in its own right. The plan was to develop the property over a period of twenty to twenty-five years, with new phases of the overall project opening up in approximately five-year intervals. Initial development began on the north end of the assemblage, which was referred to as "Estrella—Phase One," and consisted of a little over three thousand acres. The second phase, which was south of and adjacent to Phase One, experienced some limited development work, but the intention was not to do any extensive work on this phase until Phase One was substantially sold. The southern portion of the project, which was often called "Hidden Valley," was not scheduled for development by AMCOR until after the second phase was completed, sometime near the year 2000. But starting in late 1986, large parcels of Hidden Valley, usually ones consisting of one thousand acres or more, were sold as undeveloped land to home builders and investors.

At the time AMCOR began assembling this property, the southwest section of the greater Phoenix area was the one portion of the valley which had not experienced any real growth. The northeast valley was represented by the prestigious communities of Scottsdale, Paradise Valley, Carefree, Cavecreek, Pinnacle Peak, and Fountain Hills, all of which were growing. The southeast valley consisted of the cities of Tempe, Mesa, and Chandler, as well as the smaller communities of Gilbert and Apache Junction. The northwest included Glendale, Peoria, Sun City, and Deer Valley. Each of these areas had the advantage of being near major roads and highways, which facilitated transportation into Phoenix as well as between these established communities.

There were two primary interstate highways serving the Phoenix area in 1984–1986. Interstate-17 started in mid-Phoenix and ran north to Flagstaff. It connected the northwest and northeast areas with Phoenix, and population expansion followed its path. Interstate-10 ran east and west, from Florida to Southern California, except for one small stretch of unfinished highway which started in downtown Phoenix and ran for several miles southwest of Phoenix. The southeast valley was able to reach the downtown business area using I-10 and the Superstition Freeway, a spur route of I-10; therefore, growth occurred rapidly in this corridor. But that little stretch of unfinished highway was enough to restrict the growth in the southwest, rendering it time-consuming to travel from anywhere in that part of the valley to anyplace else in the metropolitan area. Consequently, over the years, the southwest remained largely agricultural land, with occasional industrial sites being located nearer to Phoenix.

The problem of transportation access to the southwest valley was essentially solved in the early 1980s, when the federal government started construction on this last piece of Interstate-10 (construction was completed in late 1988). The finished interstate made it possible to reach downtown Phoenix faster from the southwest, in part because of the smaller population, than from anywhere else in the valley. With ease of access, this area could now be expected to emulate the rapid growth of the other three quadrants.

ACC and Lincoln quickly recognized the potential existing in the southwest valley. Land prices had not reacted to these possibilities when AMCOR focused on the Estrella area and started to assemble its property. AMCOR was able to buy the entire 17,000-plus acres for an average price of about $3,200 an acre.

For AMCOR's purposes, this assembled property was ideal. It was bounded on the east by a mountain preserve, insuring that a wilderness park area would always be available to those who lived in the Estrella project. Some of the land ran into the foothills and up the slopes of the Estrella Mountains, a small low-lying range which made up the preserve. The rest of the assemblage had been either agricultural land or desert and lent itself to easy development. Most importantly, the property was just a few miles from Interstate-10.

The industrial piece was located around the airport in the small city of

Goodyear and was only a couple miles from the larger property. The airport featured a modern runway which was long and wide enough to accommodate virtually any private or commercial aircraft. AMCOR intended to market the industrial land to manufacturers and distributors in order to create a larger employment base to support the Estrella project. From AMCOR's viewpoint, the property offered a potential user an economical site with convenient ground, rail, or air access to the California market. Arizona's tax structure, wage costs, utility rates, and land prices were all favorable when compared to the cost of doing business in California.

Development started with extensive engineering, soils testing, hydrology studies, and land planning. AMCOR was able to get the project annexed into the city of Goodyear and laid out the zoning for Phase One. After the primary planning was completed, there were several major construction activities carried out almost simultaneously, or at least in rapid succession.

Two artificial lakes were built and stocked with fish. The lakes were surrounded by parks and recreational facilities. The lakes were big enough to accommodate small sailboats and offered buyers the option of lakeside lots and scenic views.

A four-lane divided highway was constructed to join with a state highway leading to an exit on Interstate-10. The highway required that a bridge be built over the Aqua Fria River, which was dry most of the year, and this bridge, totally constructed by AMCOR, was purportedly the largest privately built bridge in the state.

Streets were built throughout the entire Phase One. Electric, gas, water, and sewerage lines were installed with capacities sufficient to accommodate the entire assemblage. Literally thousands of mature trees were planted on the property.

One of Lincoln's objectives in Phase One was to establish the standards for the entire project, whether future development was done directly by AMCOR or by another developer who bought acreage farther south in the assemblage. ACC had learned from its days as a home builder that if a developer offers unique amenities in a project and maintains high, consistent, quality standards, sales will be strong, even in down markets.

The Estrella project highlights the depth of the disagreement in philosophies between the FHLBB and Lincoln. As Charlie indicated to the examiners in this meeting, this was exactly the kind of investment that Lincoln believed was ideal for an S&L. It had great profit potential; it contributed to the housing industry; and it would provide a stream of income over an extended number of years. The FHLBB, on the other hand, believed that direct investments, like Estrella, posed undue risk to the S&L and, ultimately, to the insurance fund.

These large projects were also difficult for the examiners to assess adequately. Appraisals were rarely reliable because they relied on comparable property values, and there was nothing in the market that was truly comparable to a project of this magnitude. In addition, none of the examiners had ever had any experience in evaluating the probable success of such a project, because they had never been exposed to large-scale land-development projects. As a result, they treated Estrella, and other Lincoln investments, with an undue amount of skepticism.

"Comparisons have been made during the examination between Lincoln and Beverly Hills Savings," Charlie said. "That's insulting. When Beverly Hills started its explosive growth, I personally labeled their deposits as hot money."

Charlie said, "Lincoln has used nonwithdrawable certificates of deposit with maturities of three, five, seven, and ten years to extend its liability maturities. We wanted to become impervious to a run because of the constant specter of a FHLBB cease-and-desist proceeding. We have rid Lincoln of the hot money we inherited from former management. You can look at Lincoln's current liabilities, and you won't find even a million dollars of withdrawable jumbo certificates. Lincoln has chosen not to play the 'we are higher than you are' game other thrifts play. We've lost some customers as a result, but we have garnered deposits that don't move.

"If you compare Lincoln's deposits over the last two years," Charlie said, "you'll see we increased by 22 percent, while Beverly Hills' deposits increased over four years at a rate of 680 percent and Butterfield Savings' [another failed thrift] increased by 1700 percent over three years. Lincoln's return on assets in 1985 was 3.98 percent, Beverly Hills' was a negative 3 percent and Butterfield's was negative 4 percent. Lincoln's return on net worth was 33 percent and both of the others' were negative. Lincoln's ratio of net worth to assets is 5.3 percent, compared to negative .3 percent for Beverly Hills and negative 3 percent for Butterfield. Now, I simply don't understand the FHLBB's concern.

"Everyone in the FHLBB system seems to enjoy finding fault with Lincoln's $80 million net income for 1985," Charlie said, "yet it's real money and earnings, compared to Beverly Hills' loss in 1985 of $84 million and Butterfield's 1985 loss of $32 million. I'll be happy to give you similar comparisons against any association taken over by a supervisory agreement. You shouldn't mention any of these associations in the same breath as Lincoln."

Charlie then turned to the topic of Lincoln's investments in high-yield debt securities (popularly referred to as junk bonds). "We are where we said we would be and where we intended to be. The FHLBB cannot eliminate the reality of the capital market's reliance on high-yield bonds. The world is deregulated and that's the way it is.

"ACC was the inventor of the first retail, mortgage-backed bonds. This is documented in SEC filings. We've sold $650 million worth of these bonds and, because of them, ACC was ranked as one of the top ten builders in the United States for seven or eight straight years. As a result of bonds like these, and other financing techniques, the home-building industry is no longer a source of single-family mortgages for thrifts. If the FHLBB intends to rely on single-family mortgages, all institutions are going to have real problems," Charlie said.

"Recently, Ed Gray said associations should not do fixed-rate home loans," Charlie continued. "If thrifts are only to fund adjustable-rate mortgages, the market will prove inadequate to absorb all of the available investment dollars. We have about 10 percent of our assets in high-yield bonds. I've been investing in such companies for years. I personally know many of the people who run the companies that we have invested in. Some high-yield issuers will suffer losses, but we have reserves to protect against such losses. Remember, when we bought Lincoln, we didn't start out with the Rock of Gibraltar."

The regulators from the FHLBB were by now rather somber. They had expected that the meeting would be routine, as they had not planned to discuss any controversial findings. Instead, they had intended to focus on simple file deficiencies and innocuous observations regarding Lincoln's operations. It was a classic battlefield tactic—stall until you can outflank the enemy. This meeting had been billed as an exit conference, but the supervisory people in San Francisco wanted the examiners to do more work. The goal was to give Lincoln a little information and then to announce that the exam would continue for a few more weeks. They had not anticipated that Charlie would confront them so strongly.

Kielty, following up on the foundation that Charlie had constructed, asked the examiners as a group, "Do any of you believe there are specific facts suggesting that Lincoln is comparable to either Beverly Hills Savings or Butterfield?"

Glen Sanders responded, "A few months ago I had a conversation with Judy, and I made a comment that, based on my experience with Beverly Hills, Butterfield and American Diversified [another troubled S&L], there is a general profile that fits these institutions. They exhibited rapid growth, heavy direct investments, ADC-type lending, and brokered deposits."

"Well, at this point in the examination, what significant characteristics link Lincoln's operations to these institutions and why?" Kielty asked.

Sanders started to respond but was interrupted by Sanchez, who said, "The examination process is not complete, and it wouldn't be proper to make any judgments like that until the examination is finished."

Kielty, now showing the agitation that Charlie had previously exhibited, retorted, "Why, after four months of fieldwork, can't he answer that question?"

"I'm telling you no one here is going to make a judgment on Lincoln until the examination is finished," Sanchez responded.

Sanchez was so new to the examination that he couldn't have known all the details of Lincoln's operations. Lincoln believed that he had purposefully been interjected into the process in order to force Kotrys and his examiners to alter their conclusions and find the information that was necessary to support a supervisory action against Lincoln. He didn't have that information yet. He needed to stall; to buy more time to build his case. And he wasn't about to let the examiners go on record with Keating that they hadn't found any real problems in Lincoln's operations. He wanted to close off the discussion before any of his troops responded to Lincoln's probing questions regarding the conclusions they might have reached.

"Okay. When is the examination expected to end?" Judy asked.

"I can't tell you when we will be finished, but I don't think you want anyone making judgments until we have collected all the information," Sanchez replied.

"I'd love to see the people who actually conducted the field examination make these judgments. They've seen the evidence that has been collected. They can answer the question that Bob asked," Charlie said. "But if you're telling me that, after four months, the examination is not complete, the FHLBB will have a lot worse problems than just Lincoln to deal with."

Judy then asked, "If Joe and the people working for him aren't making the decisions about Lincoln, who is?"

Charlie, pointing to Sanchez, said, "He is! He just called off the people who know the facts."

"Look, the examination is not complete. It's that simple," Sanchez said. By this time, he was clearly uncomfortable. He had thought that it would be easy to put Lincoln off and stall the examination. It wasn't turning out to be as easy as he and his bosses had anticipated.

"Again, when will it be done?" Judy pointedly asked.

"I don't know at this point," Sanchez said.

"Judy, why are we having an exit meeting if they're not done?" Charlie asked.

Sanchez said, "The memo indicated this is a 'pre-closing' meeting and the purpose was to go over loan deficiencies and loan underwriting. Until we complete our work in all of the other areas, I don't think it is appropriate to make any judgments about Lincoln's operations."

"Give us a list of these other areas. We have gone over all the loan items already with the field examiners. We don't need to do that again," Charlie said.

"This isn't a closing meeting," Sanchez replied. "When we do have a closing meeting, you will be given all of our findings. But, again, it would not be appropriate for us to make any judgments until we have all the facts."

"If, after four months, you haven't got the facts, you aren't ever going to have them," Judy said, with growing frustration and anger.

"Look, you appear to be a honest guy," Charlie said. "Why don't you just tell us what's really going on?"

"I am," Sanchez replied.

"No way!" Charlie shot back.

"Well, you're entitled to your opinion," Sanchez said. "I'm being honest with you. The examination isn't finished. I can't tell you when it will be done. And we aren't going to make any judgments until everything is complete."

"I would ask Joe to tell me the examination isn't complete, but I don't want to make the decent people in your organization have to lie," Charlie said.

Charlie, now very upset with the way Sanchez was stonewalling, continued, "Do you think you are dealing with a bunch of kids? Do you think this is some kind of game? We have everything we own in Lincoln. I resent the problem the FHLBB is creating for us. You," he was glaring at Sanchez, "don't have the slightest idea what Lincoln's management has done or what the examiners have actually seen. You ought to be ashamed for coming to this meeting with nothing more than the preliminary stuff when you knew we expected to have a closing meeting.

"This examination isn't a game. We are not only dealing with a lot of money, but our lives are involved in this," Charlie said. "You are dealing with honest, hardworking, competent, and intelligent people, and continuing the FHLBB's charade isn't going to be worthwhile. Why don't you go ahead and do something so that at least we can go into court and get the FHLBB monkey off our backs? If we get into a court, we can find out who is personally responsible and liable for the costs we have incurred in this examination. You take that thought back to the FHLBB, the FHLB-SF's directors, and the people in Washington. You people are going to find out that Lincoln is not a tiger without teeth like the rest of those associations the FHLBB has buried!"

Charlie, by this time, was completely frustrated and extremely angry. He knew that he was being stalled, and he knew that the reason for all the stalling was to give the FHLBB time to build an inappropriate and unfair case against Lincoln. And there was nothing he could do that would bring the examination to a close. He was at the mercy of Sanchez and his superiors. Charlie had talked to Lincoln's lawyers about this, and they had told him that, if the FHLBB persisted in trying to build a false case, Lincoln's only recourse might be the courts.

Once again, Judy tried to defuse the situation by attempting to pin Sanchez down on the open items in the examination. The essence of her questions was simple and straightforward: What are the open questions in the examination? What information do you need to answer the questions? How long will it take you to finish?

Sanchez didn't provide the answers to these questions.

Sanchez' unresponsiveness reignited Charlie. He knew that these were the people who were conducting the examination. If they could not, or would not, answer basic questions like Judy had posed, then someone else was definitely pulling the strings on the examination—someone in San Francisco or Washington. His now long-held suspicions and concerns were being confirmed.

Looking directly at Sanchez, Charlie said, "You couldn't make any money if you ran Lincoln, and there isn't a group of people in the entire FHLBB who could make a nickel in Lincoln if they managed it. Yet, you and the FHLBB think you can sit in judgment on Lincoln's management. We're facing a tough business world, but we're coping with it and we're doing very well. But it takes a lot of time and attention, and I'm not going to let the examination distract management from its obligations. I'm going to turn the examination over to our lawyers, and we are going to get back to running our business."

Charlie continued, "If we don't do this, the FHLBB will say, 'See, we told you so!' Ten years from now, you and others in the FHLBB will look back and ask, 'What have we done to officials like Lincoln's management?' But, in the meantime, we aren't going to roll over and play dead.

"Your people threatened to interfere with our transaction to sell Continental Foothills. We were forced to spend over $1 million closing the transaction in June in order to prevent that interference. This is notwithstanding the fact we had been negotiating the sale of the Foothills with three or four buyers over the last year. We finally sold it to a subsidiary of Arizona Public Service Company, but we had previous contracts with other parties. One of your appraisers said he'd stop the sale if he wanted to. As a result, we made $1.75 million in concessions to accelerate the closing. Who in the FHLBB should pay for this sacrifice? We should be able to collect it from the directors of the FHLB-SF and the staff who are running the exam."

Charlie concluded, "I'm not stupid and neither are Lincoln's lawyers. You aren't listening to the field examiners. Now, if you don't want to answer the basic questions or speak about something meaningful, we have better things to do with our time."

Sanchez knew that he had reached the end of the line. It was time to fold his tent. "Maybe we should adjourn," Sanchez replied. Looking at Judy, he said, "We'll be getting in touch with you about a closing meeting in San Francisco. You can bring whomever you like."

"We're not attending any such meeting," Charlie said.

With that, the meeting further disintegrated. It was clear that, while the field examiners believed that the examination was completed and they were prepared to discuss their findings, San Francisco's supervisory personnel were not of a like mind. The report from the law firm McKenna, Conner & Cuneo had alerted Charlie to the fact that San Francisco might have an enforcement strategy in mind.

Unbeknownst to ACC or Lincoln, this meeting was a pivotal event in the eyes of the regulators. In his testimony before the House banking committee in 1989, Alvin Smuzynski, one of the primary regulators with the FHLBB in Washington and a person who played a central role in the entire Lincoln affair, stated the following:

> In July 1986, Michael Patriarca was named Director of Agency Function at the District (San Francisco). Mr. Patriarca had a reputation as an aggressive regulator, which fit with the emphasis on tough supervision which was desired by the FHLBB. In July 1986, the examination of Lincoln appeared to take a new direction, in my opinion. After a meeting with the Lincoln Board, which ended in heated disagreements between the Supervisory personnel and the institution, the management of the examination was revamped. A new Field Manager, and a new Supervisory Agent were named, and a generally more aggressive posture toward Lincoln was adopted. This new emphasis was fully supported by myself and my supervisor, John Price. Relations between the District and Lincoln's management deteriorated, to the point that Lincoln insisted upon transmitting examination information through a law firm in New York. The Office of Enforcement was called in, which negotiated a settlement of this issue.

Charlie is a person who wears his emotions on his sleeves. When he is upset or thinks he doesn't have someone's full attention, he is prone to use dramatic language, hyperbole, and intimidation. When Sanchez got his blood boiling, he did all of that and more. But if he had known how his actions would be interpreted and the effect they would have on the course of the exam, he could have, and would have, held himself in check. Unfortunately for Lincoln and him, he did not.

Later, it became even more apparent that the examination was far from over. The week following this meeting, Lincoln received a whole new list of requests for documents. Examiners also showed up in Phoenix, unannounced and unexpected, to examine the real-estate files. One examiner told Lincoln that the team had been told by San Francisco that "*they hadn't found enough and that they were to return and stay until they had something on Lincoln.*" This was verified when, in his testimony before Congress in 1989, Darrel Dochow, a top FHLBB officer, who would also play a very large role in the Lincoln situation in later years, said:

> . . . I was further informed by a former Bank Board member, Mr. Don Hovde, who served under Chairman Ed Gray at the time, that he was approached and would testify that an examiner, during the 1986 examination, approached him and said that they were being asked by unnamed sources to more stringently examine some of Lincoln's activities, even though that examiner apparently considered those activities thoroughly examined and not to be of supervisory concern.

Lincoln and ACC viewed the continuance of the exam with concern and a certain amount of trepidation. They knew there were some significant issues still on the table. The examination was clearly out of the hands of the field examiners, and all of the shots were being called by either San Francisco or Washington. These people had been consistently critical of Lincoln's operations, including transactions which were undeniably successful and highly profitable. Management was truly concerned that there was an agenda within the FHLBB structure to find fault with Lincoln so that punitive actions could be taken against Lincoln and its management.

Both Smuzynski's and Dochow's comments verify that Lincoln's concerns were justified. The newly hired supervisors in San Francisco were out to prove they were tough regulators who could implement the "tough supervision" policy which Smuzynski cited. They ordered the field personnel to keep looking until they found something which could be used against Lincoln and which would advance their standing and careers within the FHLBB structure. Lincoln was the ideal target because it was highly visible in the eyes of their superiors in Washington. If the field examiners could not find information to be used against Lincoln, the supervisors would create it.

Charlie asked the law firm of Kaye, Scholer, Fierman, Hays & Handler (Kaye Scholer), one of the country's largest and most prestigious firms, for assistance. Charlie had a long-standing relationship with Peter Fishbein, Kaye Scholer's managing partner and a nationally renowned attorney. Kaye Scholer had also provided legal services to ACC for many years, going back to the days when it was headquartered in Cincinnati. So, ACC held the firm in high regard and trusted their advice.

One of the first steps taken was to ask the examiners to channel all the requests for documents through one of Kaye Scholer's attorneys, who would be located in Irvine, or through Mark Sauter, Lincoln's general counsel, in Phoenix. This would enable ACC and Kaye Scholer to monitor the requests and to get a feel for the direction in which the examination was going.

The FHLBB reluctantly went along with the arrangement but warned it would do so only "so long as it imposes no burden on our examination process." It also said: "We will not permit any effort to interrogate our examiners while they are trying to do their jobs. Further, any attempt to obstruct the examination process by inappropriate interrogation in response to requests for specific information will be considered a refusal to produce documents."

These admonitions further raised Lincoln's suspicions about San Francisco, since there had never been any mention of questioning or interrogating the examiners. In fact, Lincoln believed its relationships with the field examiners, excluding the appraisal team, were very good. Thus, San Francisco's words of warning raised questions about what they were trying to hide from Lincoln that could be discovered if questions were asked of the examiners.

During the next weeks, the examiners requested vast numbers of files. Instead of merely testing the files, as was their normal practice, the examiners made complete copies of virtually every file. The volume of copying was so great that Lincoln said it had to commit two high-speed, high-volume copy machines exclusively for the examiners' use. Lincoln reported that the machines were in constant use from early in the morning until the close of the day. The examiners were using dozens of boxes of paper each day. Since a box of paper consists of five thousand sheets, the daily volume was fifty thousand sheets or more. The copying reportedly went on for weeks. Lincoln also noted that the field examiners were not looking at the copies. Instead, the copies were being shipped to the FHLBB offices.

By this time, Judy had stopped being the liaison with the examiners, and that role rested with the attorneys. Throughout the exam, Lincoln kept logs of the examiners' various requests for documents and information. By late summer, when the field examiners' activities were winding down, these logs filled several binders and consisted of hundreds of pages. The volume of requests, many of which were duplicative, was truly amazing by normal standards.

In early August, it appeared San Francisco had formulated its plan of attack. Lincoln believed their intention was to move toward an enforcement action. The examination was still in process, but Lincoln felt that the top people in San Francisco, and their colleagues in Washington, were already drafting such an action. To Lincoln, it seemed a little like a jury reaching its verdict and setting punishment before the trial even begins.

Charlie feared that the FHLBB might be contemplating such actions because the report he had received from McKenna, Conner & Cuneo described this very strategy. It should be noted that the law firm's report had not been prepared specifically for Lincoln, although, under these circumstances, it was certainly relevant to Lincoln. The report had been sent to executives in all of the thrifts with which the firm had a relationship. Because of the report's wide distribution, it leads one to the conclusion that the FHLBB was following the same strategy it was now planning to use on Lincoln with other thrifts and that Lincoln was probably not an isolated case. Charlie was not paranoid; his fears were justified.

The body of the McKenna report offered institutions some insight into the use of supervisory agreements as a regulatory tool (some would say trap rather than tool). This is what the report said:

> Apart from its immediate impact upon operations, the chief significance of a supervisory agreement is that it constitutes a "written agreement" with the FHLBB. Under the Enforcement Provisions, violation of such an agreement is prima facie grounds for a formal C&D order. Absent violation of a written agreement, the Enforcement Provisions provide that a C&D order generally may be issued only upon proof, produced at a formal hearing, that an institution, its officers, directors or employees have violated or are about to violate applicable law or regulations or are engaging or about to engage in an unsafe or unsound practice. Thus, although a supervisory agreement is an alternative to the costly C&D procedure, it can also make obtaining a C&D order relatively simple for the FHLBB should the institution violate the terms of the agreement.

This was the regulatory trap San Francisco was setting for Lincoln. The examiners were charged with getting the bait—even if they had to create it.

Five

FHLBB's Line of Attack

By the first of October 1986, the examination of Lincoln had been going on for seven months and still wasn't finished. The escalating conflict between Lincoln and the FHLBB was beginning to affect ACC's and Lincoln's relationships with others who were caught up in the process. On October 1, 1986, Charlie received a letter from Lincoln's auditors, Arthur Andersen & Co., which included the following paragraph:

> As I discussed with you on September 29, 1986, our Firm believes that the regulatory environment surrounding Lincoln Savings' operations places us in an untenable position over which we have little or no control. We have weighed very carefully the risks we believe we face and have concluded that we can no longer serve as auditors of Lincoln.

In an earlier conversation with Judy Wischer, the Arthur Andersen partner who wrote the letter had elaborated on his firm's concerns. He had told Judy that he did not want to get caught between Charlie Keating and Ed Gray. He is quoted as saying that he "would be the whipping boy and the FHLB would hire other Big Eight firms to keep chipping away at AA's work until they found something."

He had a sound basis for this belief, since Arthur Young had already been called upon to render the second opinion on the ADC loans. Moreover, other purely accounting matters were emerging as issues in the examination. This was an unusual approach by the examiners and was obviously unsettling to Arthur Andersen's partners.

The Form 8-K (an information form) filed by ACC with the SEC regarding Arthur Andersen's resignation included the following statements:

> On October 1, 1986, Arthur Andersen & Co. ("AA"), the Registrant's independent accountant, advised the Registrant that AA was resigning from the Registrant's account effective October 1, 1986. In resigning the account,

AA confirmed to the Registrant that, in connection with the audits since AA's engagement in 1981, including the two most recent fiscal years and subsequent interim periods preceding such resignation, AA and the Registrant have had no disagreements at a decision-making level in any matter of accounting principles or practices, financial statement disclosure or auditing scope or procedure. None of AA's reports on financial statements of the Registrant or its subsidiaries contained an adverse opinion or a disclaimer of opinion or was qualified as to uncertainty, audit scope or accounting principles. AA confirmed to the Registrant that AA's resignation was not the result of any concern by AA with the Registrant's operations, recordkeeping, books and records, management cooperation, or asset/liability management; AA expressed full confidence in the Registrant's financial disclosure. AA advised the Registrant that the resignation was a result of AA's concern over the potential liability in representing certain savings and loan associations in view of the very litigious environment controlled to a large degree by regulators. In particular, AA cited the regulators' criticism over thrift institutions' rate of growth and asset mix (although consistent with applicable statutes and regulations), and AA's concern over the considerable publicity generated by the FHLBB's and its Chairman, Mr. Gray's, disagreements with the policies of the Registrant.

It's rare to see an auditor resign without some disagreement with the company, even if the issue is as simple as disagreeing over fees. Here the only issue appears to have been the environment created by the regulators. Thus, the effects of the regulators' actions touched many aspects of Lincoln's relationships with the parties with whom it did business as well as Lincoln's own internal operations.

On October 1, the same day that Andersen informed Charlie it was resigning as Lincoln's auditors, Judy and Andy Ligget, ACC's chief financial officer, asked to meet with me. They told me about Andersen's resignation and asked if Arthur Young would agree to serve as ACC's and Lincoln's independent auditors. I said that I would have to make some inquiries of Arthur Andersen and of ACC's legal counsel before I could make that decision. They requested me to make the necessary investigation as quickly as possible because their year-end was rapidly approaching, and they needed to know who their auditors would be.

I called the local managing partner of Andersen's Phoenix office, who also happened to have been the account partner for ACC, and asked why Andersen had resigned the account. He confirmed that the reason was the litigious environment surrounding S&Ls in general and the circumstances of Lincoln's prolonged examination in particular. He believed that the conflict between Lincoln and the FHLBB would escalate, and he didn't want to be caught in the middle of the warring factions. He was specifically concerned about the fact that the examiners were focusing on accounting-related issues which called the work of his firm into question.

As to Lincoln and ACC per se, his comments were all very favorable. He told me that the companies were well managed, and, while the transactions Lincoln engaged in did entail an element of risk, he said that the company understood the risks and had the practices in place to manage them. Essentially, he confirmed exactly what Ligget and Wischer had told me earlier.

I called Karen Katzman, one of the Kaye Scholer lawyers who was working at ACC's offices, and received favorable reports on both ACC and Lincoln. I also performed a review of Lincoln's and ACC's prior years' financial statements and reports which had been filed with the SEC. None of these procedures disclosed any reason why Arthur Young should not accept an assignment as ACC's audit firm.

Accordingly, I notified Judy that Arthur Young would serve as their auditors. In so doing, I reentered the war between Lincoln and the FHLBB.

One of the first things I did following acceptance of ACC as a client was to meet with Charlie. I wanted to get his impressions of the status of the examination and his thoughts as to where it was headed. In light of the apparent conflict between his philosophies and those of the FHLBB, I also wanted to understand what his immediate plans for Lincoln were. We set up a meeting to be held in his office.

Charlie's office occupied the north end of the top floor of ACC's building. The office was sizeable, but not as spacious as the offices of many of the other chief executive officers I knew in the city. The office contained a conference table with seating for eight to ten people, which I learned Charlie seldom used, a table-style desk, a comfortable sitting area consisting of sofas and chairs and glass-enclosed cabinets, which contained a few pieces of china and memorabilia. At the north end of the office, there was a large globe of the earth, which was constantly lighted, symbolizing Charlie's international view of business and life.

The walls of Charlie's office, like those in the offices of ACC's other executives, were unadorned by pictures, degrees, diplomas, or other personal mementos. ACC had a policy which required all employees to clean off the surface of their desks at night and prohibited the hanging of personal pictures or diplomas on the office walls. The figurines and other knickknacks in the cabinets had been picked out by Charlie's wife and were there for decorative purposes only. They held no personal significance for Charlie. The only truly personal items in the room were a picture of Charlie and his entire family and a crystal Madonna which sat on the corner of his desk.

We sat in the corner of his office. Charlie was relaxed; his tie had already been loosened; and he stretched his feet out on the coffee table in front of him. After a few minutes of introductory small talk, he turned to the examination. "This FHLBB examination is absolutely killing us. They've been at it for over seven months and aren't done yet. They've copied all our records and are distracting all of our people. We aren't able to concentrate on the things that are important to our business, and we are running up huge costs for lawyers and consultants. It has to end or they'll ruin us."

"Charlie, I understand, from talking to Judy and the Andersen people, that you believe Ed Gray, in a retaliatory move, is causing this exam to be extended. Is that correct?" I asked.

"We think that is what is happening. I'll tell you something funny. I've never met the guy. Yet, I've heard he's turned the exam into a personal vendetta against me. The story is he's upset about our opposition to the direct-investment regulations, and he thinks I was personally responsible for the congressional pressure he received.

"We certainly opposed the direct-investment regulations, and we are still fighting them," Charlie said. "We bought Lincoln because the industry was deregulated. We wanted to do the things a California charter permitted us to do. As soon as we bought Lincoln, we started to move all of our operations into its service corporations. Now all of our business is in Lincoln. We can't turn back. We are totally committed.

"If we had known there were going to be restrictions imposed on what we could do with Lincoln, we'd have never bought it. But what do I do now? Everything I own is tied up in this business. My family is dependent on being able to make Lincoln work the way we planned. We can't allow the FHLBB to destroy those plans or our profitable operations. We have to fight them."

At this point, Charlie told me a little about his family and their dependence on Lincoln and ACC. Charlie and his wife, Mary Elaine, have five married daughters—Kathy, Mary, Beth, Elaine, and Maureen—and one son, Charles III ("C-III"). All of the children live in Phoenix. Four of the sons-in-law worked for ACC/Lincoln—Bob Hubbard, Bob Wurzelbacher, Brad Boland, and Tom Mulhern—as did C-III. The fifth son-in-law, Gary Hall, a three-time Olympic swimmer and an ophthalmologist, served on ACC's board of directors. Moreover, Mary Elaine and Charlie's daughters were often involved in various ACC projects. So, the entire family had a direct interest in the business. They were also ACC's major shareholders.

"The FHLBB has said our operations are risky," Charlie said. "That's not true. I'm not stupid. I'm not going to take undue risk with everything my family owns. We have more at stake in Lincoln than anybody else.

"When we put our plans for Lincoln together, we tried to balance risks. We have created a number of sources of revenue. Each of which is influenced by different factors. The risk is spread out and diversified.

"Our primary activities are centered on real estate," Charlie said. "We develop our own projects, and, therefore, we are not dependent on the performance of outside parties. While a major portion of our real estate is here in Arizona, we also have major developments in Colorado, Texas, Georgia, and Louisiana. We've spread risk by diversifying the markets we are in. We should be able to sell between $150 million and $250 million of real estate a year at an average gross profit of 25 to 35 percent.

"We've also made a lot of loans with real estate as the collateral," Charlie said. "We know these borrowers. We've done a lot of business with them over the years, and we know they are good risks. We also know their projects. They're good projects. If it becomes necessary to foreclose, we can take over the development and make good money off the collateral. In the meantime, these loans produce above-average interest returns. As you know, many of the loans feature equity kickers. If these projects are as successful as we think they will be, we share in the success.

"The second part of our plan is investing in high-yield debt securities," Charlie said. "Again, we are diversified. We have guidelines which limit how much we will invest in any given issuer and in any given industry. We know the management of many of the issuers. We rely on the best investment bankers and investment advisors in the business. We track the prices of our investments every day. We monitor the issuer's performance. If we see problems, we sell the security. We haven't suffered any significant losses, and we don't expect to in the future.

"The examiners have been concerned over an investment we have in a partnership which Ivan Boesky sponsored. All their concerns result from Boesky's insider-trading problems. But they don't understand the investment we hold. We are protected and won't lose a dime. We told the examiners that, but they don't seem to believe us. The field examiners believe us; they've seen the information we've given them. It's the higher-ups in San Francisco and Washington who are the problem.

"The investments provide high returns," Charlie continued. "First, we earn good interest rates. Second, if prices go up and premiums are available over what we bought the bonds for, we sell the bonds and capture these gains. Third, many of the bonds we buy are new issues, and we receive either warrants or stock in addition to the bonds. These equity securities have produced, and will produce, significant gains. When you factor in the capital gains, our overall returns average around 20 percent on the debt securities and sometimes are higher.

"But because of the concerns they have about the Boesky deal, and their lack of investment experience and knowledge, the examiners call these high-risk investments. Yet, they can't find any losses. All they can find are gains—big gains. When your people do the audit," Charlie said, "they'll see what I'm telling you is fact, not opinion.

"The next part of our strategy is investing in equity securities. I understand that you know about the Gulf Broadcast deal," Charlie said. "We made over $50 million on that deal. We knew what we were doing. We knew the company was undervalued. We knew we could either gain control or force a liquidation. We knew what we had to do to eliminate the risk of loss. But even after we've made a large gain and have explained our strategy to the examiners, they still don't understand the deal and call it risky. How can they do that after the deal is done and it was successful? What do we have to do to get through to them?

"This year we entered into some partnerships with Sir James Goldsmith, one of the wealthiest and shrewdest investors in Europe," Charlie said. "One of the partnerships invested in the stock of the Goodyear Tire and Rubber Company. We were in the deal for about three months, and we made about $25 million. The second partnership is General Oriental Securities Limited Partnership (GOSLP)."

Charlie described the GOSLP investment, which was one of the largest deals Lincoln had done. Beginning in late 1985, Lincoln, through its subsidiary AMCOR Funding, invested $75 million to obtain a 20-percent partnership interest. The partnership used its $375 million of capital, plus about $250 million in borrowed funds, to purchase common shares of Crown Zellerbach Corporation (CZ). The partnership believed CZ's assets were undervalued and wanted to force a split-up, or liquidation, of the assets. The partnership's efforts forced a tender offer in which it initially received $90 million in cash and all of the stock of three corporations from Crown Zellerbach.

One of the corporations was sold by the partnership in 1986 for over $225 million. Another held over two million acres of timberland which were located in the southeastern and northwestern United States and were appraised at between $900 million and $1.3 billion. (In 1990, the stock of the timber company was exchanged for stock in the largest gold-mining operation in North America in a deal purportedly valued at $1.3 billion.) Thus, the aggregate assets received by the partnership carried a value of between $1.3 billion and $1.7 billion. The partnership borrowed $250 million against the timberland and paid off the debt it had incurred to buy the CZ shares. By October 1986, Lincoln had gotten back much of the cash that it had invested and still held an investment with an unrealized gain of over $100 million.

Charlie said, "These are the major equity deals we have done—Gulf, Goodyear, and GOSLP. All of them have been tremendously successful. How can the FHLBB criticize these transactions? Doesn't a proven track record count for something in this world? We intend to do at least one equity deal a year. It's good business, and we would be foolish not to take advantage of good opportunities.

"We have also entered the insurance business," Charlie said. "We bought American Founders' Life Insurance Company, a Texas-based life insurance company. We plan on offering our customers the option of investing in annuity contracts and other life-insurance products. Again, our objective is to diversify risk as well as to earn healthy profits.

"The final piece of the strategy is our hotels. In 1984, we bought the Pontchartrain Hotel in Detroit. We syndicated it in 1985 and have retained management of it. We are currently building the Crescent Hotel, a businessman's hotel on the west side of Phoenix, and the Phoenician Resort, a luxury, destination resort in Scottsdale. We think the hotels are an excellent hedge against inflation. If price levels go up, we can adjust room rates on a daily basis. Again, the examiners think these are risky investments for an S&L.

"So our risk is well diversified. We aren't dependent on a single source of income. Our investments are spread out geographically. And we've been profitable. I don't know what more the FHLBB can expect us to do," Charlie said.

"All right, I understand that the examiners are saying they don't like Lincoln's risk profile, and I understand that you think they are dead wrong. What else are they criticizing?" I asked.

"As you know, they think we violate the direct-investment limitations. They're wrong. We hired the best lawyers in the country when we funded the service corporations, and we followed their advice explicitly. We've also had Kaye Scholer look at the issue, and they agree we are not in violation. But I want you to look at our situation, too. I know you have other S&L clients with direct investments, so we'd appreciate your input.

"They've raised some appraisal issues. Our people think there are errors in the appraisals," Charlie said. "We are having people look at the appraisals, and we will rebut those that we think are incorrect.

"The examiners are also raising some accounting issues," Charlie said. "That's the reason Arthur Andersen resigned. They didn't want the examiners chipping away at their work. You'll have to talk to Judy and Kruck [Tim Kruckeberg] about the specifics the examiners are concerned about.

"Then they are raising some questions about our records and files. But these questions are minor compared to the other issues," Charlie said.

"From what you have described, you are justified in being concerned about the examination," I said. "Usually an examination lasts sixty days, ninety days at the extreme. This examination has taken twice that long, and they aren't done. The issues are also atypical. It's normal for the examiners to comment on the records and files. It's also normal for them to ask for appraisals. But it isn't normal for them to delve into accounting issues or to second-guess investment decisions. So, you are right, something doesn't pass the smell test here."

"That's why I have Kaye Scholer's litigation people in here right now," Charlie said. "I hope we can avoid a court battle, because this examination has already cost us millions of dollars. But if we have to go into court, we want to be prepared. In some respects, we would be better off if the exam would end right now and the FHLBB would issue a cease-and-desist order. Then, we could sort out the issues before an impartial judge. We are certain we would win. Then, we could get on with our business while the lawyers argue with the FHLBB.

"We have to do something," Charlie said. "We've turned ACC into a pure holding company and transferred our income-producing activities into Lincoln. ACC now needs dividends from Lincoln to meet its obligations. We figure that Lincoln can pay about $50 million in dividends right now. But we are going to get the FHLBB's approval before we pay any. We've filed for approval to pay $20 million in dividends, but the exam could affect that approval. If we don't get it, ACC has to rely on issuances of preferred stock and debt. The exam affects everything we want to do.

"Because the exam is so critical, I'd like you to get personally involved in it," Charlie said. "I'd like you to talk to our people—Judy, Bob, Kruck, Sauter, and the others—as well as Kaye Scholer's people. I'd like your ideas on all of the issues raised by the examiners. And I'd like you to attend some of the meetings with the examiners. I know the audit is important, but we have to solve the problems with the FHLBB."

I agreed to get involved with the examination and to learn the specifics of the various issues. I turned some of the day-to-day audit requirements over to a principal and another partner and began trying to understand where the examiners were going with their examination.

Charlie's concerns about Lincoln's ability to pay dividends were fully justified. On September 8, 1986, Lincoln sent a letter to the FHLBB informing the FHLBB of its intention to pay a $20-million dividend to ACC. Since its acquisition in 1984, Lincoln had paid only $5 million in dividends, even though it had been very profitable.

On October 8, 1986, the FHLBB opposed the proposed dividend in a letter from C.A. Deardorff which said, in part:

> . . . Because of the unusually large amount of dividend proposed and in light
> of the issues that have arisen in connection with the ongoing examination

process, including the reappraisal and valuation of a substantial amount of the association's assets, we request that the Board of Directors reconsider its decision to pay the proposed $20 million dividend until such time as the examination is completed.

A blind copy of the letter was sent to Al Smuzynski, who reported to Ed Gray, in Washington. The use of blind copies concealed Washington's involvement in the examination and supervision of Lincoln.

The first area that I decided to delve into was the one which was the most critical to Lincoln's future—direct investments. I met several times with Bob Kielty, Mark Sauter, and Karen Katzman to gain information about the examiners' position on this issue.

Bob Kielty is a native of Cincinnati and has known the Keatings since his days as a youth. He served in the Peace Corps and received a degree in law. After gaining experience as a practicing lawyer, he joined ACC and moved with it from Cincinnati to Phoenix.

If Charlie is hyper, Bob is super-hyper. Full of nervous energy, Bob appears incapable of sitting still or remaining silent for any extended period of time. He is an extrovert with a boisterous, outgoing personality. He will not hesitate to shout across a crowded room or restaurant. In the office, he's in constant motion. He walks in and out of his office, paces from one office to the next, shouts out instructions to his secretary, moves from one phone call to another, and stands rather than sits behind his desk.

Bob was responsible for hiring and directing the in-house attorneys. He seldom prepared documents or performed other legal services himself. Rather, he designated a staff attorney to carry out the various legal tasks, confining his role to delegation and review. He also interfaced with the numerous outside law firms that ACC used when special skills and expertise were required.

Perhaps because of their backgrounds as lawyers, Bob and Charlie often viewed litigation as a routine tool or response to a situation. Judy seemed more inclined to seek compromise and negotiation as the best way to resolve disputes. Bob and Charlie, on the other hand, would consider throwing down a gauntlet by filing a lawsuit to neutralize an opponent and then negotiating.

Mark Sauter is a lawyer, with experience in private practice before joining Lincoln. He was a vice-president and general counsel of Lincoln. In his early thirties, Mark was a serious, studious-looking person with a very dry sense of humor. His primary role was to advise Lincoln on all regulatory matters and to assure that transactions and the related records complied with the regulations.

In his role, Mark had frequent contact with the outside counsel who were engaged to assist Lincoln with its regulatory affairs and the various regulators. He therefore played an instrumental role in determining whether Lincoln complied with the direct-investment regulations. He had more detailed knowledge than Kielty about Lincoln's arguments and the FHLBB's counterarguments concerning Lincoln's compliance.

Karen Katzman is a litigator with Kaye Scholer who had started in July to gather information on Lincoln's affairs vis-à-vis the examiners. She led a team who interviewed Lincoln employees, outside auditors and attorneys, appraisers, borrowers, brokers, some regulators, consultants, and others. They reviewed the files related to loans, investments, and real estate. They looked at procedural manuals and Lincoln's written policies. They tried to learn as much about Lincoln as they could in order to be prepared to deal with whatever course of action the FHLBB decided to take with respect to Lincoln.

As we talked about the direct investments, Mark supplied all of the background information on how Lincoln had originally made the investments and what the FHLBB's objections were. Karen described Lincoln's defenses against the FHLBB's arguments. Bob, as was his habit, would make a comment, leave the room, reenter to curse at the stupidity of the examiners, talk about filing suit against the FHLBB, and then would leave again.

In 1986, direct investments were defined as equity securities, real estate, the S&L's service corporations (a type of subsidiary), and the S&L's operating subsidiaries. Under the regulations, a S&L could not make direct investments which, in total, exceeded 10 percent of its assets (or, if greater, twice its regulatory net worth) without prior approval of a principal supervisory agent (who was Jim Cirona, president of the San Francisco bank, in Lincoln's case). The regulations also contained a "savings clause" which exempted, or "grandfathered," direct investments made or planned as of December 10, 1984.

Mark said the examiners were claiming Lincoln's direct investments exceeded the amounts permitted under the regulations by approximately $600 million. He believed that the excess included the following components:

a. Approximately $428 million related to Lincoln's investments in its service corporations.
b. Approximately $55 million related to loans to an entity known as Continental Southern.
c. Approximately $29 million related to Lincoln's investment in a piece of property where the Crescent Hotel was to be built.
d. Approximately $64 million related to loans to the Wolfswinkle Group.

e. The remainder related to some relatively small investments in several equity securities.

Much of the issue hinges on how one reads and interprets the savings clause. Mark and Karen didn't believe that there was a great deal of argument, although there was some, over the factual issues surrounding the various investments. The real issue was that the regulators interpreted the language and meaning of the savings clause differently than Lincoln did.

When the regulations were first proposed in early 1984, the savings clause read as follows:

The requirements of this section shall not prohibit an institution whose aggregate investment on May 10, 1984, in direct investments exceeds the applicable limitation set forth in paragraph (b) of this section from maintaining such investments in which it had already invested as of that date; however, the institution shall not make any additional direct investments until its aggregate investment is less than the applicable limitation. In addition, an institution is not required to reduce any investment because of a subsequent change in its assets or regulatory net worth, but additional investments may not be made until the institution is in compliance with the applicable limitation.

The key words here are "already invested as of that date." They meant funds had to have been expended by May 10, 1984, and the so-called grandfathering applied only to the extent of those expended funds.

The FHLBB received various comment letters directed at the language contained in the proposed clause. They suggested that the clause should be broadened to extend to ongoing transactions and investment projects to which an institution was committed as of the effective cutoff date. The most detailed comment letter came from the National Council of Savings Institutions, dated July 16, 1984, which said the following about the savings clause:

As written, the savings clause for direct investments in place on May 10, 1984, does not appear to take into account the nature of an on-going business venture. While grandfathering all investments actually made by May 10, the proposal does not allow any additional investments over the appropriate limit. We believe that the clause should be rewritten to grandfather fully projects or business ventures begun on the date of adoption. For example, institutions which have real estate development projects can't stop developing parcels undeveloped as of May 10; they have to be able to complete the whole project. Similarly, an investment in a service corporation, or a subsidiary business, which was in existence on May 10, should not be limited to the investment level obtained as of that date, if it was always contemplated that the business would be capitalized or supported at a higher level throughout the life of the investment. Thus, we recommend that the savings clause be rewritten to change the date to the date of enactment and fully grandfather outstanding projects, including commitments at the date of adoption.

Other comment letters echoed the substance of the comment cited above. All encouraged the FHLBB to adopt a broader scope in the language of the savings clause in order to encompass commitments existing at the effective date of the clause.

The FHLBB took these comments into account in writing the final regulations. In its explanation of the final regulations, the Board stated:

Many of these commenters also questioned the extent of the coverage of the savings clause. Suggestions were made that the savings clause should also encompass commitments to invest and the completion of pending projects as well as completed transactions. . . . The Board agrees with these comments and has therefore revised the proposed rule to permit the performance of commitments to make direct investments to which an institution was legally committed on or before December 10, 1984, as well as the completion of projects pursuant to definitive plans in existence on that date.

The pertinent part of the final savings clause, as adopted by the FHLBB, reads as follows:

An institution whose aggregate or specific types of actual or prospective direct investments on December 10, 1984, would not conform to the requirements of this section shall not be prohibited solely for that reason from maintaining such investments, making investments to which it was legally committed on that date, or completing projects pursuant to definitive plans in existence on that date; nor shall an institution be required to divest any investment solely because of a subsequent change in its assets or its regulatory capital.

Thus, the transaction did not have to be completed (or funded) by December 10, 1984, in order to be grandfathered. The investment was grandfathered even if funding occurred after December 10, 1984, as long as a legal commitment or definitive plan existed at that date.

California required an institution to file an application and a business plan for each subsidiary it proposed. The institution had to specify the fixed dollar amount it wanted the state to authorize to be invested in the subsidiary. Lincoln did this. It met frequently with the commissioner, who at the time was Lawrence Taggart, and his staff to explain its plans and gain approval for each subsidiary.

In the case of Lincoln's service corporations, the following had occurred prior to December 10, 1984:

1. Each of the service corporations had been incorporated, and each of the respective bylaws had been approved.
2. Lincoln had submitted to the California Department of Savings and Loan applications for approval of the formation of each of the service corporations.
3. The Department of Savings and Loan had given written approval for each of the service corporations, and the service-corporation agreements had been executed by all of the pertinent parties.
4. The Department of Savings and Loan had authorized a specific planned dollar amount of investment in each service corporation.
5. Lincoln had submitted business plans documenting the activities in which each service corporation was to engage.

Apparently, the examiners did not dispute that each of the above actions had occurred prior to December 10, 1984.

As of December 10, 1984, Lincoln obtained approval from the Department of Savings and Loan to invest approximately $900 million in the service corporations. On that date, the actual funding of the service corporations was $372,841,000, and $531,893,000 of the approved investment amount remained to be funded by Lincoln. With one exception, the examiners were not challenging these investment numbers.

There were discussions at the time of the exam, and in later congressional hearings, concerning the timing of the formation of some of the service corporations as well as the timing of the state's approvals. Many of the actions related to the formation and approval of the service corporations occurred in October and November and as late as December 7, 1984. Lincoln's critics said, in effect, "Lincoln worked hard to squeeze its service corporations in under the wire. They did everything at the last minute before the regulations went into effect." From what I learned, the critics are probably correct. Lincoln did try to get its service corporations grandfathered. One would suspect that many other S&Ls also tried to grandfather projects that they believed were important to their long-term future and success.

The source of much of the criticism lies in Lincoln's subsequent relationship with Commissioner Taggart. On January 1, 1985, Taggart resigned as commissioner and became an officer in TCS Financial, Inc. (TCSF), a company which provided consulting services to savings and loans. On January 4, 1985, Lincoln sent TCSF a check for $50,000 and executed a consulting agreement which contemplated $200,000 of services. On January 18, 1985, Lincoln purchased 578,000 shares of TCSF's common stock—88 percent of the public offering—for $2,890,000. Critics have tried to draw a connection between these transactions and Taggart's prior approvals of Lincoln's various applications. Taggart and Lincoln have steadfastly denied that there was any connection whatsoever between Taggart's role as commissioner and Lincoln's decision to invest in TCSF or to use TCSF's services. Nonetheless, the critics remain skeptical.

The direct-investment issue, as it relates to the service corporations, comes down to the interpretation of the words "project pursuant to definitive plans in existence on that date," as contained in the savings clause. The San Francisco regulators claimed that the phrase is limited to "real-estate projects pursuant to definitive plans." They did not believe that the phrase encompassed definitive plans to invest in a service corporation. Following their interpretation, they contended that Lincoln was grandfathered only to the extent of the "actual" investment at December 10, 1984. Further, because the actual investment exceeded the applicable limitation in the regulation, the investments made after December 10, 1984, constituted violations of the regulations. The logical consequence of the violations is that Lincoln should liquidate assets in the service corporations, and the nongrandfathered investment amounts should be returned by the subsidiaries to Lincoln per se.

Lincoln's argument was, if the FHLBB meant to restrict the word "projects" to only "real-estate projects," the regulation would have been explicitly so worded. It was not. Therefore, a project appropriately includes an investment in a service corporation or operating subsidiary or equity security and is not limited to real estate. Lincoln also pointed out that elsewhere in the regulations, when a term was to be restricted to a single asset type, the language of the regulation was clear and precise as to the limited definition. Moreover, the examiners' interpretation flies in the face of the public-comment letters and the Board's reaction as well as published remarks relative to its agreement with those comment letters.

Funding a subsidiary or service corporation over a period of time makes logical and good business sense. If an S&L receives approval to fund a service corporation at the level of $300 million, it's unlikely that it would be able to make the investment in lump sum. S&Ls simply don't have that much cash on hand. It's equally unlikely that the subsidiary could invest the capital it receives all at once. The more logical and prudent sequence of events would be for the S&L to make its capital contributions as the subsidiary needed the funds—over a given period of time. That was the basis of Lincoln's various business plans and was the same basis on which the state approved those plans. To stop the funding of a service corporation in midstream would be just as economically devastating as stopping a real-estate project before it was completed. The examiners' interpretation, from Lincoln's viewpoint, made no logical or economic sense and was totally inconsistent with the clear language of the savings clause.

Having listened to the arguments, I think that the examiners were trying to correct, after the fact, a problem the FHLBB and Ed Gray had not foreseen when the direct-investment regulations were adopted. The regulations allowed an institution to determine its direct investments on either a consolidated or an unconsolidated basis. On a consolidated basis, the institution basically ignores its investment in service corporations and looks directly at the assets the service corporation holds for purposes of determining aggregate direct investments. On an unconsolidated basis, the investment in the service corporation is the direct investment—it doesn't matter what kind of assets the service corporation holds.

For example, first consider the consolidated basis. Prior to December 10, 1984, an S&L invests $300 million, which is 30 percent of its assets, in a service corporation. The service corporation invests $100 million in U.S. Treasury securities and $200 million in real estate, all prior to December 10. Using the consolidated basis, the S&L looks through the corporate veneer of the service corporation and determines its direct investments are $200 million, the amount invested in real estate. Thus, its direct investments are 20 percent of its assets, and it exceeds the limitation set forth in the regulations. The direct investment of $200 million is grandfathered. But if the S&L liquidates the real-estate investment, it can only reinvest in other real estate or equity securities a maximum of $100 million, an amount equal to 10 percent of its assets and the regulatory limit.

Now, consider an example of the unconsolidated approach. Again, prior to December 10, 1984, the S&L invests $300 million, which is 30 percent of its assets, in a service corporation. The service corporation, in turn, invests the entire $300 million in real estate. The S&L's direct investments are $300 million, the amount of its investment in the unconsolidated service corporation. The entire $300 million is grandfathered and will remain grandfathered so long as the investment in the service corporation is not reduced. If the service corporation liquidates its real-estate investment, it can reinvest all of the proceeds in other real estate, equity securities, or whatever asset it chooses. Additionally, if the service corporation chooses to, it can borrow additional funds from a third party and can invest those funds in real estate or equity securities. Assuming the service corporation borrows another $300 million and invests it all in real estate, increasing its investment in real estate to $600 million, the S&L's direct investments remain at $300 million, the amount of the investment in the service corporation, and it is still grandfathered.

Lincoln and other S&Ls realized that, if they made all of their investments in equity securities, real estate, or other operating subsidiaries through grandfathered service corporations and elected the unconsolidated method, they could maintain the dollar amount of their direct investments virtually forever. They also knew that they could constantly reinvest or leverage the service corporations without violating the direct-investment regulations. Therefore, if they could get the investments in service corporations approved at the maximum possible level before December 10, 1984, they could substantially diminish the effects of the regulations.

I don't believe that the FHLBB understood the differences that could result between the consolidated and unconsolidated approaches when they adopted the regulations. They didn't appreciate the fact that investments in real estate or equity securities are fundamentally different from investments in service corporations or operating subsidiaries. An S&L sells real estate and equity securities in the ordinary course of business. If these assets exceeded the targeted limit at the date the regulations were adopted, the investment level would be reduced as these assets were routinely sold. But S&Ls don't routinely sell their service corporations and operating subsidiaries. If these assets exceeded the targeted level at the date the regulations were enacted, the excess would stay there forever. It would never be reduced.

When examiners began to examine S&Ls like Lincoln, the FHLBB discovered the oversight. The language in their own regulation allowed the effects of the regulation to be diluted. What were they to do? It had to be particularly infuriating that Lincoln, the staunch opponent of the regulation, was one of the S&Ls who had discovered the glitch in the regulations. There was only one thing they could do under the circumstances. They had to say, "The regulations don't mean what they say; they really mean something else." Or, "Now that we understand what they really say, we didn't mean to say what we said." They were forced to say that their own words, which were now cast in stone, were subject to differ.ng interpretations. After all, this was much more palatable than simply saying, "We screwed up."

This may be why the FHLBB was fighting Lincoln on the issue. They had screwed up. Lincoln was the strongest proponent of direct investments and the S&L who had put up the most aggressive battle against the regulation. The FHLBB didn't want to see Lincoln take advantage of this gaping loophole. Remember, it was a personal issue to Ed Gray. So, in effect, the FHLBB was rewriting the regulation to block Lincoln. To put it simply, the FHLBB and Ed Gray didn't want Lincoln to make them look bad.

Trying to get out of the box they had built for themselves, the examiners were also grasping at another phrase—"definitive plan." Lincoln was told that the FHLBB had unpublished opinions which stated that only real estate could be covered by a definitive plan. Lincoln's understandable reaction was that if such opinions had, in fact, been issued, they were inconsistent with the clear language of the published savings clause. The term "definitive plan" was not specifically defined, and therefore limited to real estate, anywhere in the published regulations. Again, this appears to be nothing more than the FHLBB trying to change the published rules-of-the-game after the FHLBB figured out that the regulations weren't producing the result the FHLBB had originally desired. Lincoln contended that for the rules to be changed, the FHLBB had to issue new rules with a new effective date. Meanwhile, transactions, actual or prospective, which met the clear language of the existing regulations, and were therefore grandfathered, remained grandfathered, even if new regulations were adopted.

Bob Kielty said that he had tried to get copies of the opinions which the examiners said they were relying on and was told they were not available. They were unpublished opinions of the FHLBB's general counsel and were restricted to the agency's own use. Bob argued that if the opinions were unpublished, how in the world could they be binding on an association? Lincoln didn't know, and could not have known, that such opinions existed, much less what they stated, at the time it made the investments. He believed that these opinions were nothing more than a false card which the FHLBB was attempting to play.

The examiners were also arguing that, putting aside the issue of whether service corporations could be covered by a definitive plan, Lincoln's actions prior to December 10, 1984, with respect to its service corporations, may not have been sufficient to constitute a definitive plan. Lincoln pointed out that prior to December 10, 1984, every service corporation had been validly incorporated; bylaws had been adopted; business plans had been submitted to the state; the state had approved the dollar amount of capitalization or investment; service-corporation agreements had been executed; and, in almost all cases, very specific assets had been identified for the various service corporations to acquire. The only thing that remained was for the funding of the service corporations to occur. In that regard, at December 10, 1984, Lincoln was in the process of issuing long-term, nonwithdrawable certificates of deposit, the proceeds of which were to be used to fund the investment in the service corporations. The use of such certificates of deposit as the specific funding vehicle was part of Lincoln's overall plan and had been thoroughly discussed with the state. When asked, "What else could a definitive plan possibly have included?" the examiners were at a loss for words.

Finally, with respect to the service corporations, the examiners raised one additional issue. They contended that documents relating to one of the service corporations, Continental Homes Corporation (CHC) (later renamed AMCOR Investments Corporation), were "backdated" to make it appear that the investment had occurred prior to December 10, when, in fact, it had actually occurred later. The examiners said that the computer-generated accounting and related records which show Lincoln had completed the transaction before December 10, 1984, had somehow been prepared and inserted into the computer after December 10. They also said that formal land-transfer documents had not been prepared until early 1985 and that the dates on those documents were inconsistent with the effective date of the transaction.

Because Lincoln thought conducting its land operations in a subsidiary would yield both tax and organizational advantages, CHC had been created as a service corporation in April 1984. Lincoln's plan was to use CHC as a vehicle to acquire land that would be developed into residential lots which CHC would sell to home builders.

In April 1984, Lincoln applied to the state to invest up to $300 million in CHC. The business plan accompanying the application described the general plan for buying and developing residential real estate and identified specific parcels of land that CHC intended to acquire. A table in the plan allocated the $300-million investment to specific, anticipated acquisition and development expenditures.

Starting in September 1984, Lincoln held a series of meetings to determine exactly how to structure the entire investment in CHC, so as to obtain the desired tax advantages. The meetings were attended by a number of officers and directors of Lincoln and CHC. Also in September, Lincoln's regulatory counsel was instructed to analyze the applicability of any state or federal regulations relating to the transaction.

On November 16, 1984, Lincoln filed with the FHLBB its revised "Three-Year Operating Plan," which described the planned investment in CHC and the structure of that investment. The document states: "As early as December 31, 1984, Lincoln will have a total investment in CHC of approximately $220 million, consisting of land and notes receivable from the sale of land."

In November 1984, Judy, then Lincoln's president, instructed Lincoln's chief financial officer to make the appropriate accounting entries reflecting the investment transaction. The transaction is reflected in accounting entries, including computer runs, which predate December 10, 1984. In depositions taken by the FHLBB, Lincoln's data-processing personnel testified that these entries could not have been placed on Lincoln's books unless they had been made prior to December 10, 1984. The computer had a fail-safe mechanism which protected against any otherwise undetectable backdating of data entered into the computer. The mechanism was part of the computer's routine security system and could not be overridden.

The loan agreement, promissory notes, and purchase agreements relating to the CHC transaction were prepared after December 10, 1984. Some of the documents bear the date of November 30, 1984, and some are dated "as of November 30, 1984." Apparently, almost all of these documents had been prepared by outside counsel.

The formal land-transfer documents, the deeds, and deeds of trust bear several different dates: the effective date of the transaction, which was November 30, 1984; the dates on which they were signed and notarized (which were in the spring and summer of 1985); and the subsequent recordation dates, which were stamped by the local government entity.

The documents with the most troublesome dates were the minutes and consents memorializing Lincoln's decision to invest in the service corporation. These bear the date of November 30, 1984, and are signed by Lincoln's directors. In their depositions, directors were unable to testify to the exact date on which the consents were signed. In many cases, the consents were signed by others authorized by the directors to sign on their behalf, most often the individual director's secretary. The majority of the directors were able to recall that the meetings they attended which dealt with CHC and the asset transfer were held in the early fall of 1984. It was these documents which drew most of the FHLBB's attention and caused the entire transaction to be viewed with extreme skepticism.

Lincoln personnel pointed out that, because of the large volume of documents and the need to involve outside attorneys, it was not possible to execute and record the documents contemporaneously with the effective date of the transaction. They also noted that the transaction was between a parent and its own subsidiary, and not with a third party; therefore, there was no compelling reason to complete the documentation by a given date.

Lincoln strongly believed that the record, taken as a whole, amply demonstrated that it had transferred control of the assets on November 30, 1984, and that it had no longer carried the asset on its own books after that date. Lincoln believed that the assertion that it had backdated documents in order to deceive the examiners, or any other person or persons, was ridiculous. Lincoln had enough experience to know many of the documents had to be notarized or recorded by the local government. This would make it clear that they were executed after November 30. Why then would it feel compelled to backdate other documents? In any event, the most telling evidence that the transaction had occurred before November 30, 1984, was the computer-generated records which could not have been altered or backdated.

The whole argument involving the dates of documents has no real significance if Lincoln's contention that the investment was grandfathered because it was pursuant to a definitive plan which was in existence before December 10 is valid. There can be no question that the plan existed and had been approved by the state before December 10. Thus, the real issue is still whether the examiners fairly interpreted and applied the regulation and its savings clause.

Leaving the service corporations, the next investments that the examiners contended were not grandfathered were two real-estate projects—Continental Southern and the Crescent Hotel property.

Continental Southern was a Georgia corporation with three shareholders—Lee H. Henkel, Jr. (who would later be appointed to the FHLBB), James C.V. Nalley III (who would later figure in a controversial series of transactions involving a project known as the Crowder Water Ranch), and Richard C. Wernick. Continental Southern had been formed to purchase a number of parcels of land near Atlanta which were to be assembled into larger parcels that would then be developed into commercial and industrial parks or projects. Continental Southern applied for loans from Lincoln to acquire and develop the subject properties.

This was another case involving acquisition and development loans. As stated earlier, under certain circumstances, a transaction that is legally structured as a loan can be accounted for as, in substance, a real-estate joint venture or an investment in real estate. In the case of Continental Southern, loans were eventually accounted for as a real-estate transaction, even though the legal form of the transactions was that of a loan. The direct-investment regulations treated loans accounted for as joint ventures or real-estate investments as direct investments. The issue with the examiners was whether this transaction was grandfathered or not.

Lincoln contended that by December 10, 1984, it had advanced $2,450,000 to Continental Southern and estimated that Continental Southern would require, and Lincoln would finance, an additional $50 million to acquire the land. Lincoln further contended that by December 10, 1984, it had orally committed to provide the financing.

The terms of Lincoln's commitment apparently were reached in early November 1984 during a meeting with Richard Wernick. Lincoln was represented in the meeting by Charlie Keating, James Conner (an in-house lawyer and at the time assistant secretary for Lincoln), Kathleen Wade (senior vice-president of Lincoln), and Mark Sauter. Wernick showed the Lincoln people a map which displayed the target areas to be acquired. During the meeting, it was agreed that Continental Southern would acquire and combine land parcels from different sellers within the target areas and assemble the parcel into even larger tracts which would have greater development potential. It was agreed that as Continental Southern located the individual parcels, Lincoln would provide acquisition loans to fund the purchases.

On November 14, 1984, Lincoln closed the first of the intended land-acquisition loans to Continental Southern in the amount of $2 million. On that same date, Lincoln extended a line of credit to the officers of Continental Southern, in the amount of $750,000, to be used as earnest money deposits for other proposed land purchases, for Continental Southern's overhead costs, and for proposed contributions to joint ventures. Draws of $450,000 were taken against the line of credit by December 10. By December 31, 1985, Lincoln had provided over twenty loans, totaling $49,197,000, in connection with Continental Southern's acquisition program.

Lincoln contended that the meetings and funding of the initial loans constituted a definitive plan. Therefore, the investment was grandfathered. The examiners contended that Lincoln needed legally binding, contemporaneous documents or written evidence corroborating each and every fact that Lincoln asserted had existed prior to December 10, 1984, before the existence of a definitive plan could be established. Lincoln believed that there could be a definitive plan without legally binding agreements and that there was no requirement in the regulations for a definitive plan to be in writing.

The other contested real-estate project was a parcel of land located on Interstate-17 in northwest Phoenix. Lincoln had acquired the parcel to develop a master-planned, mixed-use project which would consist of an upscale businessman's hotel, restaurants, and office buildings.

On October 31, 1984, Lincoln had purchased a thirty-one acre parcel for $13 million. On August 14, 1984, the board of directors had approved the purchase of twenty-three acres of this property for $9 million, pursuant to the terms of a purchase agreement executed by the parties on that same day. On October 1, 1984, the board had authorized the purchase of six additional acres for $3.8 million, pursuant to the terms of a purchase agreement executed on August 28, 1984. By December 10, 1984, Lincoln had invested approximately $12.7 million developing the property. At that time, Lincoln estimated that in order to complete the project, an additional $17.7 million would be needed to complete the funding of the land acquisition for an office building and $46.2 million would be needed to finish the hotel construction.

Other activities related to this property had also been carried out before December 10, 1984. As early as August, Lincoln had begun negotiations and received proposals for the leasing of restaurant space; entered into negotiations for hotel food services; and commenced discussions with an architectural-design firm for the planning of a proposed health club. In September, detailed descriptions of the hotel design and preliminary site plans had been completed and documented. A market survey for the hotel had been completed, and the architectural firm had begun designing the hotel in accordance with a proposed budget. By October, a preopening budget for the hotel had been completed and an appraisal of the property had been finished. By the middle of November, a master plan for the hotel and office building had been completed. A comprehensive engineering report on the entire site had been done. A zoning application had been filed with the city of Phoenix on November 20 to rezone a portion of the property to allow for construction of a fourteen-story building for the hotel. And advertisements had been placed in a national publication announcing the availability of office space in the project.

Lincoln contended that all of the above activities amply demonstrated that a definitive plan for the entire project existed before December 10, 1984. Therefore, Lincoln believed that the project was grandfathered as provided for by the savings clause in the regulations. The examiners did not agree that the activities and related documentation were sufficient to constitute a definitive plan.

The remaining direct-investment issue centered on the Wolfswinkle loans. Lincoln believed that these transactions were properly classified as loans and therefore were not subject to the direct-investment regulations. The examiners believed that the transactions should be considered as either an investment in real estate or as an investment in a real-estate joint venture. The classification hinged on how an accounting pronouncement was interpreted and applied.

The direct-investment issues were the most controversial and the most important ones being raised in the examination. The issue was subjective and judgmental, as opposed to an issue which could be resolved on the basis of completely objective evidence. This was the main reason why the subject was so frustrating to Lincoln's management and advisors. They truly believed that the examiners were guilty of making arbitrary, unfounded interpretations of the regulations. The examiners' interpretations were not supported by the legislative history or published language of the regulations. Further, Lincoln felt that these interpretations threatened Lincoln's very existence by eliminating its ability to continue to conduct profitable operations in the future. Thus, in the collective minds of Lincoln's management, these were life-and-death issues.

The examiners' references to interpretations of the regulations and unpublished opinions also added more credence to the contention that either San Francisco or Washington was calling the shots in the examination. These are not the kinds of things field examiners would be aware of in the normal course of their duties. These are the types of arguments lawyers engage in, and that argued strongly that the FHLBB's lawyers in Washington were involved in the process.

Moreover, the issue had broader connotations than Lincoln's compliance with the regulations. Its resolution could establish a precedent which other associations could follow in challenging the FHLBB. So, the issue was elevated from a mere disagreement with Lincoln to a more serious and wide-ranging policy issue for the FHLBB.

Washington's involvement was consistent with the comments that Kotrys had made to Judy during the course of the examination. He had said that he agreed with Lincoln's position that the investments were grandfathered. He had also received instructions that he could not discuss with Judy. And he had been told to send the data to San Francisco and Washington, where someone else would make the "determinations." Thus, Washington had to be at the center of this issue.

I understood Lincoln's inclination to take this matter to a court for resolution. It was a disagreement which logically could not be resolved by the parties to the dispute. They each had lawyers who interpreted the regulations and the legislative history differently. Lincoln couldn't appeal to the examiners' superiors in either San Francisco or Washington because they were the very same people who were making the interpretations and decisions for the FHLBB. An impartial party needed to rule as to whose interpretation was appropriate.

The next areas that I researched were the various accounting issues that the examiners were raising. Tim Kruckeberg had been meeting with the examiners in an attempt to understand their concerns and to provide them with information which supported Lincoln's accounting treatments.

Tim was in his twenties. He is a CPA and had worked for Arthur Andersen for a couple years before coming to ACC. For a while, he was Lincoln's controller and later became, essentially, an assistant to Judy, performing special projects, many of which related to the FHLBB examination.

We first talked about the Wolfswinkle ADC loans. The examiners, in spite of receiving separate reports from both Arthur Andersen and Arthur Young, were still maintaining that these loans should be accounted for as investments in real estate. Lincoln's personnel had talked to the field examiners ad nauseam and had gotten nowhere with them. It was apparent that someone other than the field examiners was making these accounting decisions.

We then turned to the capitalization of interest and certain farming expenses. The capitalized-interest issue centered on two projects: the Uplands, a 3,250-acre development near Austin, Texas, and Castle Meadows, a 4,153-acre development in Castle Rock, Colorado. The capitalized farming expenses related to the Crowder Water Ranch, a 13,857-acre parcel in western Arizona.

Starting in 1973, the Financial Accounting Standards Board has had the responsibility for establishing generally accepted accounting principles (GAAP). It does so by periodically issuing "Statements of Accounting Standards" which address specific accounting issues. These standards are to be followed by all preparers of financial statements in the United States.

The standard dealing with the capitalization of interest is standard no. 34, issued in October 1979. The standard states: "The historical cost of acquiring an asset includes the costs necessarily incurred to bring it to the condition and location necessary for its intended use. If an asset requires a period of time in which to carry out the activities necessary to bring it to that condition and location, the interest cost incurred during that period as a result of expenditures for the asset is a part of the historical cost of acquiring the asset." In effect, the standard treats interest cost the same as any other component of an asset, such as bricks or mortar.

The standard further states that:

[I]nterest shall be capitalized for the following types of assets ("qualifying assets"):
a. Assets that are constructed or otherwise produced for an enterprise's own use.
b. Assets intended for sale or lease that are constructed or otherwise produced as discrete projects (e.g., ships or real estate developments).

The first category of qualifying assets includes the hotels which Lincoln was building and was going to use as operating assets. The second category includes the real-estate projects Lincoln was developing either for sale or for lease to others.

The standard says interest "shall be" capitalized. It's not a matter of choice, or election, one makes about whether to capitalize interest or to expense it as it is incurred. Some of Lincoln's critics have said, "Lincoln's net income would have been less if it had expensed rather than capitalized all interest costs." This wasn't an option available to Lincoln—or any other enterprise. Lincoln was appropriately following the standard when it capitalized interest costs.

The standard states:

The capitalization period shall begin when three conditions are present:
a. Expenditures for the asset have been made.

b. Activities that are necessary to get the asset ready for use are in progress.
c. Interest cost is being incurred.

It further says:

Interest capitalization shall continue as long as those three conditions are present. The term "activities" is to be construed broadly. It encompasses more than physical construction; it includes all the steps required to prepare the asset for its intended use. For example, it includes administrative and technical activities during the preconstruction stage, such as the development of plans or the process of obtaining permits from governmental authorities; it includes activities undertaken after construction has begun in order to overcome unforeseen obstacles, such as technical problems, labor disputes, or litigation. If the enterprise suspends all activities related to acquisition of the asset, interest capitalization shall cease until the activities are resumed. However, brief interruptions in activities, interruptions that are externally imposed, or delays that are inherent in the asset acquisition process shall not require the cessation of interest capitalization.

On January 6, 1981, the FHLBB issued a technical memorandum, T 59–3a: "Accounting Guidelines Re Capitalized Interest Costs Related to 'Qualifying Assets' Allowable for Regulated Institutions." In the opening paragraph of the memorandum, the following is stated: "The principles embodied in SFAS No. 34 are acceptable for purposes of regulatory reports to the Federal Home Loan Bank Board." But then, later in the memorandum, it states: "For FHLBB purposes, *institutions may not capitalize interest for any period in excess of six months unless ongoing and substantive physical construction has commenced in a manner which in the judgment of the FHLBB will result in the completion of the asset within a reasonable period of time*" (emphasis added).

The provisions of the FHLBB's technical memorandum were made retroactive to all fiscal years beginning subsequent to December 31, 1979. The arbitrary six-month requirement was not only inconsistent with standard no. 34, it was inconsistent with the opening paragraph of the memorandum itself. It was this six-month limitation that the examiners were relying on in challenging Lincoln's accounting.

To appreciate fully the significance of the six-month rule, consider what a developer, like Lincoln, does with a property. Lincoln buys raw land, arranges for annexation and zoning, plans and constructs the physical infrastructure, and then sells parcels to builders who construct the single-family homes and other subdivision improvements. The "activities" Lincoln engages in "to get the property ready for its intended use," including planning, zoning, and obtaining all governmental approvals, are necessary prerequisites to actual construction. These activities can be the most arduous and time-consuming aspects of the entire development process.

During the planning and zoning process, architectural drawings are prepared; a detailed annexation development contract is negotiated; and a zoning plan is submitted for approval. Master engineering plans for utilities, transportation, and drainage are prepared and submitted for review. Specifications for individual roads and subdivisions are also submitted in a process known as "platting." Depending on the municipality, this entire process can take several years.

Only after the necessary approvals have been obtained does physical construction begin. The initial construction work consists of the marking, grading, and leveling of roads on the property and the construction of drainage systems. Thereafter, the utilities are constructed. These include water and sewer mains, storm sewers, water and sewage treatment plants, gas mains, telephone lines, and electric and cable television lines. Every road and utility requires planning, engineering, and governmental approval. In addition, each phase of the project must comply with all applicable ecological regulations and, therefore, must include erosion control and other environmental protection. Then, all the work must be inspected by the local authorities. All this has to be done before builders can start to construct the subdivisions and homes.

The technical memorandum T 59–3a was issued prior to the enactment of Garn-St. Germain, in an era when S&Ls were not empowered to develop real estate for sale to others. In most communities, it is not possible to secure the necessary plans and permits to build a simple, single-family residence in less than six months. It is virtually impossible to begin substantive, continuous physical construction on a large-acreage, mixed-use real-estate project in less than six months from the time the land is initially acquired. Some construction could occur in the six-month period, but not continuous construction. The arbitrary six-month limitation adopted by the FHLBB is a concrete example of the FHLBB's lack of understanding of the real-estate development process.

The examiners were asserting that Lincoln had improperly capitalized interest on the Uplands property because "the property is not undergoing substantive development as required by the applicable regulation, FHLBB Memorandum T 59–3a." Further, the examiners said that they did not find evidence that "the project was undergoing activities which would result in its completion within a reasonable period of time." They determined that Lincoln should reverse $14.5 million of capitalized interest.

With regard to Castle Meadows, the examiners could not determine whether the project qualified for interest capitalization. The examiners said that it did not appear that "a significant amount of construction work had been performed during the capitalization period." They hadn't requested the reversal of any capitalized interest but did ask for additional information on the project. If such information didn't demonstrate that substantial physical construction had taken place, they said that they would require a reversal of the capitalized interest.

Lincoln had voluminous records showing construction had begun on both projects within the six-month period following Lincoln's acquisition of the properties. Interest capitalization had begun on Castle Meadows in January 1985, and physical construction had started in June 1985. Construction activities were being performed at the Uplands at the time Lincoln acquired the property and continued thereafter.

At Castle Meadows, for example, two major roads, as well as connecting roads, had been built, requiring over 50,000 cubic yards of concrete. Eight wells had been drilled. Approximately 1.5 million cubic yards of dirt had been moved. Over 2.5 miles of telephone cable, 2.5 miles of water and sewer lines, 50 miles of irrigation lines, and 50,000 feet of gas mains had all been laid. Over 40,000 tons of rocks had been put in place to control erosion. And a 3-million-gallon water tank had been built.

Tim said, "If that's not considered substantial construction, something's really wrong."

The Uplands project involved a lengthy and complex public-approval process in Austin. It would literally take years of continuous activity before all of the necessary permits and authorizations would be obtained and the property annexed into Austin. The delays which took place in this process were the "delays that are inherent in the asset acquisition process." Nonetheless, a water supply and treatment facility and a major road had been constructed.

In both cases, Lincoln and its auditors believed that capitalization of interest was required throughout the entire period. If Lincoln reversed the capitalized interest on the Uplands project, as the examiners wanted, Lincoln would literally have to maintain two sets of books—one for financial-statement purposes and another for the FHLBB. The cost basis of the Uplands would be different in each set of books as would the gain or loss on the sale of each piece of property.

The situation was a little different with respect to the Crowder Water Ranch. At the time Lincoln acquired Crowder, the groundwater laws in Arizona were in the process of being revised. Beginning in the year 2001, in order to develop any additional land or obtain a construction permit, a developer will have to assure that the project has at least a one-hundred-year supply of water.

The municipalities and cities in the major urban areas of Arizona are rapidly reaching the point where, based on their traditional sources of water, they will not be in a position to assure a one-hundred-year supply.

The consequence of not being able to grant such assurance will be that the cities will not be able to grow or expand in the future. To overcome this problem, the major cities and municipalities began to seek permanent alternative sources from which they could import water into their boundaries.

One such source is the Central Arizona Project (CAP). The CAP is a huge canal which has been built by the state and the Federal Bureau of Reclamation. The canal starts at the Colorado River and runs into Phoenix and then down to Tucson. Arizona is entitled to extract a given number of acre feet of water out of the Colorado River each year and can transport that water across the state through the CAP. The annual water allotment has been allocated to a number of users, including Indian tribes, cities, and others. Even after such allocations, there may not be a sufficient amount of new water available to the cities to address completely the supply problem. Four major cities purchased large ranches in sparsely populated portions of the state and intend to extract water from these properties and export it into their respective communities. These properties became known as water ranches, and their value lies, not in the agricultural products which can be grown on them, but in the amount of water which can be mined from beneath their surfaces.

Lincoln intended for Crowder to be a water ranch. Lincoln's objective was to maximize the water rights associated with the Crowder land and to sell the rights or the actual water to cities that had not purchased their own water ranch.

The law was unclear as to how much water could be extracted from a given property. One measure was thought to be the historical amount which had been used on the property to grow agricultural products. Another measure might be a maximum amount set by the state legislature, such as 3.5 acre feet per year. Another might be any amount so long as the remaining supply under the water ranch would always last at least one hundred years. At the time Lincoln bought Crowder, the issue of how much could be extracted and exported had not been resolved.

There is at least one other problem in owning a water ranch. Once water is raised to the surface, there has to be a means of transporting it to the intended urban area. If the ranch is remote, the cost of constructing a water-transportation system can far exceed the cost of acquiring the ranch itself. In this regard, Crowder is ideally located. It is very near the CAP. The idea was to pump water from Crowder into the CAP canal and transport it through the already-existing canal. Lincoln expected that it would have to pay a fee to the CAP to use the canal, but the fee should have been much less than the cost of constructing a separate delivery system. Thus, Lincoln believed that Crowder possessed attributes which could not be matched by other potential water ranches.

Lincoln thought that the existing law would permit, at a minimum, the amount of water which had been used for agricultural purposes to be extracted and transported. Therefore, it sought to establish the highest level of agricultural use, or consumption, it could. It brought new acreage into production and planted the ranch with alfalfa and Sudan, high water-usage crops which do not require excessive management. In order to farm the additional acreage, Lincoln had to laser level approximately 1700 acres; construct a dike and channels for flood control; and repair various wells.

Total agriculture costs incurred and capitalized during 1986 were about $2.7 million. More than 40 percent of these costs were associated with providing water. The water used per acre was approximately 9.6 feet. Offsetting a portion of the costs was the revenue generated by the crops which totaled almost $650,000 for 1986. Lincoln expected that these costs and corresponding revenues would persist from year to year, because it was necessary to continue farming the property in order to establish and preserve the water rights.

The accounting literature related to the capitalization of the net farming costs is Financial Accounting standard no. 67, "Accounting for Costs and Initial Rental Operations of Real Estate Projects." The relevant section of this standard states: "Project costs clearly associated with the acquisition, development, and construction of a real estate project shall be capitalized as a cost of that project." The farming costs were, in Lincoln's opinion, clearly associated with the development of Crowder Water Ranch and were necessary if Crowder was to reach the point of its intended use.

The examiners were asserting that the farming costs on the site "do not qualify for capitalization because such expenses are not increasing the value of the property and appear to be incurred to maintain existing water rights as the property is not undergoing development." The entire object of farming additional acres was to enhance the water rights of the property, thereby making the property more valuable. Lincoln's activities had nearly doubled the water use on the property. Without such activities, the value of the water rights would have remained the same or could even have been reduced. Leveling new acres, extending wells, and planting new types of crops were the development activities taking place at Crowder.

In 1986, water ranches were valued at approximately $1,000 per acre foot of water which could annually be exported from the property. Lincoln's management believed, for every acre foot of additional water consumption added and maintained at Crowder, the value of the property would increase by $1,000. If Lincoln could increase the water use at Crowder by three feet for each acre of the ranch, the value of Crowder could increase by over $40 million. It was this magnitude of added value that Lincoln was seeking to achieve by the farming activities.

Once again, these issues required an understanding of the relevant literature and its application. Field examiners do not have that level of understanding. In fact, without knowing the accounting requirements, they didn't have sufficient knowledge even to know whether they were obtaining the data necessary to make the accounting judgments.

The last accounting issue involved a sale of loans. The examiners were contending that Lincoln should reverse approximately $12.5 million in profits recognized on a sale of loans which had taken place in the last quarter of 1985. They did not explain how they came to their conclusion that the accounting for this transaction was incorrect.

In November 1985, Lincoln had entered into a simultaneous purchase and sale of loans with San Jacinto Savings Association of Houston, Texas. Lincoln purchased $123.5 million and sold $123.7 million in loans. Lincoln realized a gain of $12.3 million from the transaction.

In April 1986, disagreements arose, and both associations made demands upon each other for the repurchase of the loans. The transaction was rescinded on September 25, 1986; however, the profit was not reversed because Lincoln viewed the rescission as a separate transaction from the sale.

The rescission was precipitated when San Jacinto attempted to put the loans it had purchased back to Lincoln, notwithstanding Lincoln's satisfactory performance with respect to the loan portfolio it had delivered. Lincoln did not believe that San Jacinto's effort to put the loans back was enforceable. Lincoln did not intend to acknowledge the put or to effect the loan sale rescission unless the entire loan portfolio could be resold with no impairment to Lincoln. At the time the loans were taken back, Lincoln had clear indications that it could resell the loans at no loss. In the fourth quarter of 1986, Lincoln did resell all of the loans, for cash, at prices which approximated, or exceeded, the carrying value of the loans, resulting in no loss.

The original sale had been examined by Arthur Andersen as a part of the 1985 annual audit. Arthur Andersen considered the literature relating to the simultaneous purchase and sale of loans and did not take exception to Lincoln's accounting for the transactions. The events leading to the rescission had been independent from the original sale transaction, and all had occurred in 1986. Lincoln appropriately accounted for these events in the fiscal year in which they occurred. Lincoln believed that the adjustment being proposed by the examiners, which required reversing profits in 1985 and booking them in 1986, was misleading and improper.

It took me most of the month of October 1986 to obtain the information on the direct investment and accounting issues. Discussions with Andersen's people verified that they had, indeed, reviewed these accounting matters as a part of their audits and that they concurred with Lincoln's accounting.

While I was looking into the direct investments and accounting areas, I became aware of two other issues, both of which were being pursued by the Kaye Scholer attorneys. The first issue related to the origin and the dating of certain documents in Lincoln's files. The examiners were making noises about documents being "backdated" and about documents having been "stuffed" into files on an after-the-fact basis. Second, there was growing evidence that the FHLBB was using a number of outside, or nonagency, consultants in the examination.

I talked to a number of people, primarily Sauter, Katzman, Kielty, and Judy, about the issues surrounding Lincoln's files. The issue first surfaced during the discussion of the direct investments. The examiners were asserting that documents had been backdated to make it appear that events had occurred earlier than they actually had.

I learned that Lincoln had been examined in 1984 and that the examiners were critical of Lincoln's files. They said the files lacked required documents; the files were not organized properly; and the files and Lincoln's minutes did not reflect the decisions made by the board of directors and various committees.

In 1985, in anticipation of another examination, Lincoln had engaged the law firm of Jones, Day, Reavis & Pogue, whose attorneys were considered to be experts in regulatory matters, to review its procedures and make recommendations for improvement. The attorneys reviewed Lincoln's files to determine whether the necessary documents had been obtained and maintained. It didn't take long to determine that the files were not complete. This is what the examiners had found in 1984 and what Lincoln's auditors had discovered in their annual audit of Lincoln's 1984 financial statements.

The attorneys said that the basic problem was that the files needed to be better organized and that there needed to be uniformity among the various files. Essentially, a file format had to be created and adopted, and all of the documents for a given transaction had to be placed in a single, comprehensive file.

Lincoln's task was complicated because it kept two complete, duplicative sets of files. One set was kept in Irvine, which contained all the original documents, and the other set, containing copies, was in Phoenix. Thus, procedures were needed to assure that when a document was added or deleted from one set, the same thing happened to the other set, so they would always be identical.

Lincoln was also advised that it needed a comprehensive written "loan summary" for each loan. The summaries had to set forth all of the pertinent factors relating to the purpose of the loan, the attributes and value of the collateral, the history and financial status of the borrower, the terms of the loan and any other factors having a bearing on the decision to make the loan. Similar summaries were recommended to document the decisions made in the investment and real-estate areas. Since the summaries, as envisioned by Lincoln's advisors, didn't exist, it was suggested that they be created.

In order to address the documentation problems, Lincoln formed teams to attack each area. Separate teams were assigned to investments, lending, corporate minutes, and accounting, where Lincoln had to catch up on some routine account reconciliations. Judy, who was at that time serving as president of Lincoln, spearheaded the effort along with Mark Sauter.

To augment Lincoln's staff, Judy arranged for some staff people from Arthur Andersen to be assigned to the project teams. The Arthur Andersen personnel on the teams were what is known as loaned staff. Arthur Andersen made bodies available to Lincoln. The loaned staff reported to Lincoln personnel, who assigned tasks to them, supervised them, and reviewed the work product they produced.

In the investment area, team members first gathered all the available information on each security Lincoln had purchased. This meant going to each person in the investment area and asking them to go through their personal files and retrieve any relevant documents or analyses. If documents had not been retained, the team got new copies from investment bankers or from other sources. Documents included prospectuses, newspaper clippings, press releases, annual reports, investment analyses prepared by investment bankers or consultants, and other relevant data. The intent was to try to duplicate the data which had been available and considered at the time the investment decision was made.

The team also talked to the people who made the investments to learn the primary factors the investment group had considered with respect to each security, including whom they had talked to and when the conversation had occurred.

The team used all this information to assemble an underwriting summary for each security. The summary is a written document which sets forth the rationale for buying the security and generally is written in the present tense rather than the past tense. That is, it has the appearance of having been created prior to the time the investment decision was made. Lincoln's management believed that the summary merely documented what had occurred; therefore, the present tense was appropriate because the summary was merely a surrogate for what would have been written if the decision maker had recorded his considerations at the time. Lincoln did not believe the summaries presented data received after the decisions were made.

The team then took the underwriting summary and the other materials they had gathered and placed them in the file for each security, thereby augmenting what was already in the file. The added materials were supposedly undated, as opposed either to being backdated or to bearing the date on which they were placed in the file. The examiners questioned whether the added data was, in fact, backdated, thus making it appear that the data was in the file earlier than it actually was. But, in discussions I had with Lincoln's personnel, its attorneys, and Arthur Andersen's people, and in written materials that I saw, the evidence is that the added information was simply not dated.

Similarly, in the lending area, missing documents were located and placed in the file. Also, loan summaries, comparable to the underwriting summaries, were prepared. The files were reorganized to conform to a standard file index. These files actually consist of several large, ringed, hard-covered binders for each loan. Again, materials, including the loan summary or loan underwriting, were undated.

The corporate minutes were more difficult for Lincoln to deal with. Transactions were actually entered into by one of Lincoln's subsidiaries. Except for taking in deposits, purchasing U.S. government securities, and lending, Lincoln's business was conducted through the network of subsidiaries.

When it came to reviewing minutes, and resolutions or corporate consents to enter into specific transactions, the team had to look at the activities of well over a dozen corporations. They found minutes and resolutions were often incomplete or nonexistent. The various meetings had actually been held, but the proceedings simply hadn't been recorded.

The team drafted minutes, consents, resolutions, and/or ratifications for each transaction. There were some minutes already in existence. The team was merely filling in the missing documentation.

I wasn't able to determine how the various minutes and related documents drafted by the team were dated. Some may have been dated to appear as if they had been prepared at the time the meeting or actual decision took place. Others may have had an "as of" date. Others may have been dated with the date on which they were drafted by the team and were structured as a ratification of a decision which had taken place at an earlier date. Different people described each of these dating alternatives. Perhaps there was some of each.

There was another problem with these documents. Because there were so many of them which needed to be signed, and they required the signature of each director or committee member, it was difficult to coordinate getting all of the already busy executives to sit down and sign the hundreds of documents needing their personal signatures. So someone, probably Mark Sauter, made the decision to get the executives to agree to let another person sign for them. Then apparently a group of people, most likely secretaries or paralegals, signed the documents, using the names of the executives whose signatures were required.

Several problems arose as a result of this decision to use surrogate signatures. First, there was no concrete evidence that the executives had ever read the documents or that they concurred with the contents or accuracy of the documents. Second, the signatures did not indicate that they were facsimiles. Third, there is disagreement as to whether some or all of the executives gave their consent for another person to sign on their behalf. Finally, there are indications that some of the executives may not have even known these documents were being prepared by the team.

In any event, the documents were signed, by someone, and became a part of each affected corporation's records. The legal department did learn something from this exercise. Procedures were put in place to assure that minutes were prepared for all future meetings and corporate decisions.

The examiners, and in later years other persons who were adverse to Lincoln, asserted that these efforts constituted "file stuffing" and, with respect to the minutes, "forgery," designed intentionally to mislead examiners or others who reviewed or used Lincoln's files. And, in fact, there were a number of depositions taken of Lincoln and Arthur Andersen personnel by the FHLBB's lawyers who looked into these assertions.

I was told that Lincoln's management was very up-front in stating that they wanted to be sure their records were complete. The attorneys knew they were reviewing files so that deficiencies could be identified and corrected before the examiners arrived. Arthur Andersen knew that their staff was being used to prepare Lincoln for the examination. So, Lincoln appeared to be very straightforward about their activities with both their attorneys and auditors. But what about the examiners? Was Lincoln also straight with them?

There are indications that when Judy met with Kotrys in their weekly meetings, she discussed the fact that materials, which were undated, had been added to the files in anticipation of the examination, so that the files would be complete.

Mark Sauter was asked about the subject by a supervisory person from San Francisco in September 1986, and he told this person that "The documentation was in fact not dated or signed, but the information was pulled together solely for the purpose of the examination."

Arthur Andersen people remember talking to the examiners in late 1986 and early 1987, before the examination was completed and a report was issued, and confirmed Sauter's comments.

But perhaps a more basic question is: What would have happened if Lincoln had not gone through this extensive documentation and house-keeping exercise before the examiners arrived? Well, obviously the examiners would have noted more recordkeeping deficiencies than they did.

What would have been the consequences of the existence of more deficiencies? Certainly, the examination report would have been more critical of Lincoln's procedures, practices, and files. But the examiners' remedy or directive would, in all likelihood, have been to tell Lincoln to correct the deficiencies and improve its procedures. In effect, they would have asked Lincoln to do that which it had already done. Again, with respect to the deficiencies they were citing, they were requesting that the files be corrected and procedures be improved. They also admonished Lincoln to be more mindful of the regulations in the future.

There are also some things that the examiners probably would not have done as a result of discovering more exceptions in the files. They would not have increased loss reserves. The absence of a few documents, unless they affect the enforceability of liens, does not affect a loan's value. They would not have issued a cease-and-desist order solely as a consequence of documentation problems. And they would not have closed Lincoln's doors because of recordkeeping problems like the ones that Lincoln addressed in its housekeeping.

In later years, some of ACC's and Lincoln's detractors have argued that if the regulators had been aware of the housekeeping, some of these dire consequences would have occurred. But that's basically nonsense. First, as stated, there are pretty strong indications that the examiners did, in fact, know about these activities before they issued their report and, probably, while they were conducting their fieldwork. Secondly, they didn't have any statutory authority to take such drastic actions based solely on recordkeeping deficiencies.

There have been those who have asserted that because of the signature problems and the dating issues, fraud was involved in the case of the minutes. But a much more plausible explanation than fraud is that someone simply screwed up in trying to save time and in making the project easier to complete. Using hindsight, and with an agenda that's adverse to Lincoln and/or its executives, it's easy to see how a completely innocent act could, however, be painted differently.

The Kaye Scholer attorneys also learned that the examiners had engaged consultants to look into Lincoln's investment practices and policies. Other consultants had been hired to prepare economic studies of Phoenix and Tucson, with emphasis on land values and growth trends. And, of course, there were the outside appraisers. The attorneys were concerned about the number of outside parties who had access to Lincoln's records and transactional data. The examination process was supposed to be confidential. This clearly wasn't the case with this examination. Again, the question was: Why?

After learning about the various issues that the examiners had raised with Lincoln's people, I formed some impressions about the direction of the examination which I passed on to Charlie.

With the direct investments, the examiners might be taking a number of possible paths. First, they could be making a case for Lincoln having to liquidate its excess investments. Second, they could be trying to increase Lincoln's required capital. Finally, they could be trying to show that Lincoln willfully violated regulations.

If Lincoln had to liquidate assets, it would destroy Lincoln's business plans, and Lincoln could incur losses in selling the assets. If the required capital were increased, Lincoln might not meet its capital requirement and the FHLBB could take enforcement actions. If Lincoln violated the regulations, the FHLBB could move to get a cease-and-desist order. None of these consequences was good.

With respect to the accounting issues, the examiners could be heading in only one direction. They were looking to reduce Lincoln's capital. That also argues that they were trying to do the same thing with the direct investments, but one couldn't be sure of that.

The capital requirement for an S&L is an important test. In 1986, the minimum capital requirement for an S&L was equal to 3 percent of its insured deposits. The minimum requirement could be increased by a number of contingency factors. If the S&L's actual capital did not equal or exceed its required capital, the FHLBB could take supervisory or enforcement actions against the S&L.

In this case, the examiners could be trying to increase Lincoln's required capital by an amount equal to 10 percent of the direct investments that the FHLBB claimed were not grandfathered, or an amount of approximately $60 million. The accounting issues decrease actual capital. In both cases, the result is that Lincoln's excess of actual capital over its required capital is reduced.

From what I was able to learn, Lincoln had evidence to support its position on both the direct-investment issue and the accounting matters. But both of these areas involved subjective judgments and interpretations of the regulations or accounting pronouncements. Apparently, the examiners had not been willing to listen to the evidence Lincoln provided them with, and they might continue to reject that evidence.

Moreover, because the issues rested on interpretations of the regulations and accounting literature, it might not be possible to resolve the issues with the examiners. Where did that leave Lincoln? What alternatives were there to resolve a dispute with the examiners? If the decisions were made by the FHLBB people in Washington, Lincoln couldn't appeal to them. So, where did Lincoln lodge any appeals to resolve the matter?

Lincoln filed suit on the direct-investment regulations themselves and got Kaye Scholer involved because it might have to go to a court in order to obtain a fair hearing on the other examination issues. But Lincoln couldn't do anything else until the FHLBB took some action that would serve as the basis for pursuing a legal action.

Keating didn't want to go to court. It was expensive and a further distraction. But he felt that Lincoln was being treated differently from other associations. Keating thought that Ed Gray was behind the examination problems—an attack because Lincoln had resisted Gray's attempts to re-regulate the industry. Keating believed that Gray's goal was to destroy ACC and Lincoln. But to do so, Gray first had to have a case. That's what Keating thought the examiners were doing. They were not doing an examination; they were building a case. They couldn't find any real losses, because there weren't any. So, they were trying other things, stretching all the rules of the game.

At this point, the battle lines were clearly drawn. The FHLBB appeared to be heading down the path toward an aggressive enforcement action. Lincoln was preparing to defend itself against the expected assault. Bitter warfare between the two parties was inevitable.

Six

Tightening the Screws on Lincoln

When Lincoln's request to pay dividends to ACC was opposed by the FHLBB, ACC had to look to other avenues for cash to finance its operations. ACC had been converted into a pure holding company. It still had some income-producing assets, and it had direct subsidiaries other than Lincoln, primarily finance companies which held GNMA certificates collateralizing bonds which had been issued to the public, who provided additional income to ACC. But these sources of income were not sufficient to meet ACC's cash requirements.

ACC had a substantial payroll, as none of the Keating family members was on Lincoln's payroll, even though they spent virtually all of their time working on Lincoln's behalf. Additionally, other executives, such as Judy Wischer and Bob Kielty, were also on ACC's payroll rather than Lincoln's. Charlie never wanted the compensation of his family members or ACC's other top people to be an issue with the FHLBB, so he kept them off of Lincoln's payroll.

In addition, ACC had other expenses which, if they had been paid by Lincoln, would have been the subject of controversy. For example, ACC owned, or leased, three corporate planes. The planes were housed in a large private hangar at Phoenix' Sky Harbor Airport. The company also employed pilots and copilots for the planes and had a staff of maintenance and support personnel.

These aircraft were used almost exclusively for Lincoln's benefit. There were daily flights, often several, between Phoenix and Irvine. There were also frequent trips to Lincoln's properties that were located in other states. And the planes were used to shuttle ACC's and Lincoln's executives and staffs back and forth to meetings throughout the country and occasionally to Europe or other foreign destinations.

Many of ACC's critics have claimed the aircraft were a symbol of corporate extravagance and waste. They say the operation of the planes cannot be cost-justified and, as a result of owning and operating the small fleet, ACC incurred excessive expenses. They further assert that the real reason ACC owned the planes was to satisfy Charlie's ego and penchant for luxury.

ACC, on the other hand, defended the use of the planes as being cost-effective. The private aircraft saved ACC's executives from wasting valuable time waiting for commercial airline flights, which are often delayed or canceled. The planes provided flexibility, freeing ACC's executives from the limitations inherent in commercial air carriers' schedules. ACC's executives could work on the planes, because each aircraft had telephones and the largest plane had a secretarial work station. In fact, on most trips, the flight provided ACC's people with an opportunity to meet and discuss issues, free from the interruptions which invariably occurred during meetings held in the office.

Whatever point of view one chooses to believe, it is precisely the argument that Charlie did not want to have with the regulators. He did not want them to assert that the corporate aircraft were inappropriate for an insured institution to own. So, ACC, not Lincoln, owned and operated the planes. There were other expenses that Charlie believed would be the source of disagreement with the examiners, and these, too, were paid by ACC.

As a consequence of these expenditures, ACC needed operating cash. Additionally, ACC had incurred debt to purchase Lincoln and to purchase some of the assets which it had transferred to Lincoln's subsidiaries. This debt required periodic payments of principal and interest.

ACC planned to meet its cash needs through periodic dividends from Lincoln. When ACC acquired Lincoln, it entered into an agreement with the FHLBB that permitted Lincoln to pay annual dividends equal to 50 percent of its net income for any given fiscal year. Any dividends which were not paid in the year when the income was earned could be deferred and paid in a subsequent year. However, all dividend payments were subject to the FHLBB's prior approval. If the FHLBB determined, by fact or opinion, that Lincoln had failed to meet its net-worth or capital requirement, Lincoln could not pay any dividends. At the end of 1985, Lincoln believed it had met its capital requirement and, therefore, believed that it could pay ACC up to approximately $50 million in dividends.

So, having been told it would have to await the outcome of the examination to pay any dividends, ACC turned to the issuance of debt to meet its cash requirements. Already in 1986, ACC had issued, or had filed registration statements with the Securities and Exchange Commission (SEC) to issue, debt securities.

Its first offering was an issue of senior debentures that was sold, on a best-efforts basis, by the firm of Offerman & Co., Inc., of Minneapolis,

Minnesota. These bonds had a stated interest rate of 12 percent per annum, payable monthly. The underwriting commission was 8 percent, or $2 million, if the entire issue was sold.

A company generally uses an underwriter, or investment banker, to issue its securities because the underwriter has the means to sell and distribute the securities to the public. In a small offering, a single underwriting firm may handle the entire issue. In larger offerings, several investment banking firms join together in a syndicate to sell the securities, with each member of the syndicate agreeing to handle a given portion or allotment of the entire issue. It is this distribution network which a company seeks when it engages an underwriter, although the underwriter will generally perform other functions in connection with an offering as well.

The investment banker generally agrees to underwrite the proposed issue on either a firm or best-efforts basis. In a firm underwriting, the investment banker agrees to purchase any portion of the total offering which it is unable to sell to the public (the issuer and the investment banker have already agreed on the price the securities will be sold for). Accordingly, the issuing company is assured that the entire issue will be sold and also knows the amount of the proceeds it will realize from the offering. In a best-efforts deal, the investment banker merely promises to try to sell the offered securities. If, at the end of an agreed-upon period, some of the securities remain unsold, the investment banker does not purchase the unsold portion. The company merely realizes a smaller amount of proceeds from the offering. There are also deals where a minimum amount must be sold or the whole offering is called off and no securities are issued. This is more common in equity issues.

The investment banker charges for its services, and the company also agrees to pick up all the expense of the offering, such as lawyer's and accountant's fees, printing and mailing costs, and registration fees, known as blue-sky fees, paid to governmental agencies. The commissions and related fees charged by the investment banker can easily exceed 10 percent of the amount of the offering. A company can incur significant costs before the investment banker commits to handling the offering. Factors, such as the price that the securities will be offered at and the investment banker's compensation, can remain in a state of flux right up to the very last minute. So, there is a lot of uncertainty in an offering, even when an underwriter is used.

In the summer of 1986, ACC started to plan the issuance of $100 million of subordinated debentures (bonds), which would be sold by ACC employees, not by an underwriter or investment banker, through the network of Lincoln branches. ACC concluded that by using its own personnel to sell the issue, and not using an underwriter, it could save a substantial amount of money on the distribution costs of the issue. The concept wasn't unique. Other savings and loans had sold debt securities in their branches. For example, pursuant to an offering circular dated December 30, 1985, Atlantic Federal Savings and Loan Association of Fort Lauderdale, Florida, sold a $25-million issue, in minimum denominations of $2,500, through its branches. The difference in Atlantic Federal's case was that the S&L, and not the parent company, was the issuer; but the concept was the same.

In the fall, ACC drafted a registration statement for the proposed offering of subordinated debentures. The registration statement contemplated a shelf offering, where the debentures would be offered periodically in series, with each series conforming to the description of the debentures set forth in the registration statement and the related prospectus. The only attribute which would differ between the various series would be the interest rate that the bonds in each series would bear. The interest rate from series to series fluctuated with the market rate of interest.

The registration statement was filed with the SEC. The SEC typically reads the prospectus and provides the company with comments about the disclosures contained in the document. The company, its attorneys, and other advisors consider the comments and make appropriate changes in the document. The SEC neither approves nor disapproves the securities; that is, it does not judge the merits of the issue. Neither does it make any independent investigation or determination of the accuracy or adequacy of the disclosures. In this case, ACC also presented the prospectus to state agencies, most importantly those in California, to obtain what is known as blue-sky approval, which allows the securities to be sold in that state.

Before the registration statement for the $100-million issue became effective, ACC filed another registration statement for $200 million and withdrew the earlier filing. The registration statement became effective in November 1986. After the effective date, ACC could sell the first series of debentures. Thus, when the intended dividend payment from Lincoln was denied by the FHLBB, ACC was ready to sell these bonds.

ACC leased a small amount of space in each of Lincoln's branches, where a desk, or kiosk, was placed. Only ACC's employees were authorized to sell the debentures, not Lincoln's employees. The sales were to occur only at the designated ACC desk and nowhere else in the branch. The ACC desks were to be physically separated, by distance as well as appearance, from Lincoln's teller windows.

Each prospective debenture purchaser was to be given a prospectus, prospectus supplement, Form 10-Q for ACC (a company's quarterly financial report which is filed with the SEC), and ACC's current annual report. There were also sales brochures. These brochures had been reviewed by outside counsel in order to assure that nothing was contained in them which was inconsistent with the prospectus.

On the front page of each prospectus, the following appeared in bold, capital letters:

THE DEBENTURES BEING OFFERED ARE THE SOLE OBLIGATION OF THE COMPANY AND ARE NOT BEING OFFERED AS SAVINGS ACCOUNTS OR DEPOSITS AND ARE NOT INSURED BY THE FEDERAL SAVINGS AND LOAN INSURANCE CORPORATION.

The title caption on the front page indicated in large, bold, capital letters that the issuer was American Continental Corporation.

On the front page, in bold type, the following sentence appeared: "For a description of certain risks and other factors, see Special Factors." The intended purpose of the Special Factors section was to alert any potential security purchaser to the risks inherent in the issuer and, in turn, the offered security. A prudent investor was expected to read the prospectus, especially the Special Factors section, before buying the offered security. An issuer can only provide the prospectus; it cannot force a potential buyer to read the document.

Because these debentures were subordinated, the prospectus also clearly indicated that these debentures were junior to, and therefore ranked behind, $207 million of senior debt. In the event of a liquidation, including one caused by bankruptcy, the senior claims would be settled before any monies would be available to the subordinated debenture holders.

Each aspect of the drafting of the prospectus and the formulation of the plan of distribution was overseen by ACC's outside counsel, Kaye Scholer. The lawyers reviewed the instructions to be given to the ACC bond sales representatives. They reviewed proposed brochures and advertisements. They had frequent conversations and correspondence with Ray Fidel and David Thompson, the people who were responsible within ACC for overseeing the sales and distribution of the debentures. From all appearances, ACC was doing the things necessary to ensure that the sale of the debentures was entirely proper.

The bond sales force was recruited and supervised by Ray Fidel, with assistance from Rob Symes, Fidel's immediate supervisor. Fidel and Symes were responsible for all of Lincoln's branches. They directly supervised the branch managers and, indirectly, were responsible for all teller operations. They also were responsible for maintaining the level of Lincoln's retail deposits as well as the other financial products Lincoln offered to its customers. As long as deposit levels were maintained, and no complaints were received in Phoenix about branch operations, top management appeared to give Fidel and Symes free rein in running the branches. They were Lincoln's top managers in Irvine.

In 1986, Ray Fidel was in his twenties. At the time, he was responsible for recruiting and supervising the people in Lincoln's branches. Later, he would hold the title of Lincoln's president. Fidel didn't fit the same mold as most of ACC's other people. His hallmark wasn't a legal or accounting background but rather his salesmanship and showman's flair. He showed traits of being undisciplined, often finding excuses to miss meetings, especially those dealing with the FHLBB regulators. Later, when he was on Lincoln's board, he attended few meetings. He pretty much operated autonomously, a condition that Charlie and others seemed to accept as long as the branches ran smoothly and, later, bonds were sold.

Rob Symes was, in 1986, executive vice-president of Lincoln and was later, at differing times, its president and chairman of the board. Extremely intelligent, he holds a Ph.D. in operations research and is a whiz in computers and mathematical models. He was responsible for Lincoln's sophisticated computer systems and for the analysis of interest rates to be paid on deposits as well as for creating models for investment analysis.

To most people, Symes is drab and cerebral. Social skills are not his long suit. He finds it almost impossible to engage in small talk or social conversation. This, of course, affected his ability to manage others and, as such, he was usually teamed with an outgoing person, like Fidel, who would communicate to others for him. He was, however, considered to be very valuable because of his sheer intellect and conceptual skills.

On November 24, 1986, David Thompson, Rob Symes, and Ray Fidel conducted an all-day compliance seminar for the ACC employees who were to sell the debentures. A memo describing this meeting indicates that the salespeople were instructed that they were to make it clear to potential debenture purchasers that the debentures were not insured, not the same as insured accounts, and not issued or recommended by Lincoln.

On November 25, 1986, a similar seminar was conducted for the Lincoln branch managers. They were instructed not to permit any Lincoln employees to engage in any debenture-related activities, such as distributing prospectuses, taking orders, and the like. They were also instructed that if any customers of the branch had questions about the debentures, they were to be directed to the ACC desk and its representative. Lincoln's people were not to answer any debenture-related questions.

Following these meetings, the sale of the debentures started in earnest in the various Lincoln branches. Monthly sales averaged about $7.5 million, with some months' volume exceeding the average by several millions of dollars. It was my observation that the ACC executives based in Phoenix had minimal contact with the actual bond sales representatives. ACC's executives received updates from Fidel and Symes, which were almost always upbeat and favorable, indicating that the sale of the debentures was proceeding without problems. With the program appearing to be running successfully, there was no real reason for the top ACC people to intercede or to become directly involved in supervising the sales force.

As the subordinated-debenture program was being put together, the FHLBB scheduled another exit conference. The meeting was held on November 7, 1986, which was roughly four months after the meeting of July 3 and nearly eight months after the start of the exam. As Keating anticipated, this did not turn out to be a true exit conference. It was merely a status report. It became evident that there were still many unfinished portions of the exam, including appraisals and reports from consultants.

Kotrys did most of the talking for the FHLBB and listed some of the FHLBB's primary concerns, which included the direct-investment and grandfathering issues; the classification of and accounting for the Wolfswinkle loans; appraisal results and loan classifications; reserves for losses; criticism of investment policies and risk diversification; accounting disagreements; and loan documentation deficiencies. And once again, the examiners expressed concern that the majority of Lincoln's operations were conducted through subsidiaries. They pointed out that Lincoln, standing alone as a parent company, did not generate enough income to cover its expenses. Lincoln was profitable only because of the income produced by its subsidiaries.

When Symes, the person who was representing Lincoln in this meeting, asked for details supporting the examiners' comments, he was told that Kotrys or another examiner would supply it in a few days or that the information wasn't presently available but would be shortly. Symes asked Sanchez when Lincoln could expect the FHLBB's report and asked if Lincoln would have a chance to respond to it before it became final. Sanchez said that he thought the report would be issued by the end of the month (November 1986) and that Lincoln would be able to respond to it.

Lincoln again wondered why this meeting had been scheduled. It obviously wasn't a closing meeting or exit conference. It was apparent that the examiners were still gathering information from their consultants and appraisers. Lincoln concluded that this was another stalling tactic designed to give Lincoln the illusion that the examination was nearing a completion point.

A few weeks after the November meeting, at Lincoln's request, I attended a meeting in San Francisco to discuss the accounting matters raised by the examiners. I was accompanied by Kruckeberg and Sauter, among others. The FHLBB was represented by Sanchez, John Ashton, and George Shiffer, a recent addition to San Francisco's supervisory staff who was apparently senior to Sanchez. This was the first time that I had met any of the regulators working on Lincoln's examination.

Before the meeting started, I was able to chat briefly with Ashton. I asked what his background was and whether he had worked in public accounting. He said that he had spent several years in accounting and had some experience with financial institutions. I wasn't able to determine why he had left public accounting, but surmised that, like many young people, he may have reached a point where future promotions were either going to come slowly or be nonexistent. Public accounting firms move people out pretty quickly if the partners determine the person doesn't fit the mold they seek.

I didn't speak to Shiffer before the start of the meeting. He appeared to be older than either Sanchez or Ashton. Before we arrived, the Lincoln people knew that Shiffer was going to attend the meeting and hoped he would be someone they could reason with in order to reach agreement on the outstanding differences between Lincoln and the FHLBB. However, he projected an unfriendly attitude and a demeanor which bordered on arrogance. He quickly appeared to be a person intent on enforcing his will and positions on others. He didn't look like he was willing to listen or that he would change his mind on decisions that he had already made. I understand that, within a year of this meeting, he was asked to leave the district bank because of certain aspects of his conduct. He is also said to have blurted out in a public bar that he "would get Charles Keating."

The meeting dealt with the accounting issues that Tim Kruckeberg and I had discussed earlier in October. It was very clear that Lincoln's and the FHLBB's position on each of the issues differed. After Lincoln's position was explained and information was provided that the regulators didn't seem to have, there was still no change in their opinions. They said that they simply didn't agree with Lincoln and never would. They had made up their minds and weren't about to change. We asked them to explain the reasoning underlying their conclusions, but they weren't willing, or able, to do so. The information they did present seemed to overlook certain facts or represented narrow interpretations of the accounting literature.

As a result of their positions, they were asking Lincoln to reverse over $30 million of previously recorded income. Seeing that we were not going to reach any agreement on the issues, we tried to address some peripheral matters. The examiners had subtracted the proposed reversals from Lincoln's net worth without taking into account the effects of income taxes. Since net worth consists of previously taxed income, not reducing these income reversals for the effects of taxes was like combining apples with oranges. Ashton and Shiffer both agreed that their numbers should reflect the effect of taxes and, therefore, were incorrect. But they said they didn't know what tax rate to use and, therefore, were not going to change their numbers. They said that Lincoln could make any changes after receiving their report. We said that we would supply them with the appropriate tax rate. They said, "Forget it, we're not interested. You deal with the taxes later."

On the interest-capitalization issue, we discussed the FHLBB's technical memorandum which interpreted generally accepted accounting principles (GAAP) as described in the Financial Accounting Standards Board Statement. We pointed out that GAAP had to be followed by all preparers of financial statements. We explained why the six-month limitation in the FHLBB memorandum was too narrow to be useful in the environment of deregulation. Ashton agreed that the interpretation in the memorandum, if followed, could produce a difference between the answer determined under the regulations and that obtained following GAAP. Nonetheless, he said that he would follow the FHLBB interpretation and would not reconsider his position.

On the accounting for the Wolfswinkle loans, we reiterated that both Arthur Andersen and Arthur Young had rendered opinions on the transactions. We told the examiners that Arthur Young's opinion had been sought by both the FHLBB and Lincoln.

I asked Ashton, "Who reached the opinion for the FHLBB?"

"I did," he said.

"Did you consult with anyone, or is this your own personal opinion?" I asked.

"It's my opinion, and I don't need to consult with anyone about it," he said.

"Doesn't it concern you that two, well-respected firms have looked at these transactions?" I asked. "They have considered all the same facts that you have. Independently, they have reached different conclusions than you have reached."

"No, it doesn't concern me at all," he responded. "I'm sure that I'm right, and I think they're wrong."

The meeting ended with both parties in complete disagreement with one another. I wasn't surprised by the attitudes of the FHLBB people. I had heard about what had happened in other meetings and had been told that the FHLBB would not listen to new information and were rigid in their positions. But I had hoped they would be open and reasonable. They weren't. I fully appreciated Lincoln's and Kaye Scholer's concerns. The concerns were valid and completely warranted under the circumstances.

On December 19, 1986, Sanchez sent to Smuzynski, who was in Washington, what he described as "the final draft of the Statement of Supervisory Concern Regarding Lincoln Savings and Loan Association." In the cover letter, he added that "The examination is in its final stages with an asset classification meeting to be scheduled with the association's management within the next few days. Any changes to the draft should be minimal."

In other words, the association might not agree with any of the findings of the examiners, but that wouldn't change the examiners' conclusions. Their minds were closed to anything Lincoln might present to them.

The draft was over two hundred pages long. It contained all the subjective theories and arguments that the regulators had discussed with Lincoln, plus other issues that had never been disclosed to Lincoln. It was clear that San Francisco had succeeded in getting the field examiners to "re-look" at their work. But even then, the examiners were still hard at work trying to find data that would support their theories, since many of the findings in the draft were nothing more than that—theories and theories only.

Also, the report did not state what supervisory actions the FHLBB examiners in San Francisco intended against Lincoln. But it was clear that they planned to take some action—just as the report from McKenna, Conner & Cuneo, which Charlie had cited to the examiners in July, had said they would attempt to do.

About this time, information started appearing in the press regarding Lincoln's affairs. Lincoln had always been concerned that the information it provided to the examiners might not be held in strict confidence. It had heard things from other people in the industry indicating that the examiners were revealing confidential information. But now it was appearing in the press, and Lincoln had to stop the leaks before any damage was done to it or its customers.

On December 31, 1986, Peter Fishbein, of Kaye Scholer, wrote to Stephen Hershkowitz, of the Office of Enforcement in Washington, about leaks of confidential information regarding Lincoln which were appearing in the press. Some of the pertinent parts of the letter are:

> . . . This letter constitutes Lincoln Savings and Loan Association's ("Lincoln") request that the Federal Home Loan Bank Board ("FHLBB" or "Board") conduct an immediate and thorough investigation to determine the identity of the Board officers or employees who are leaking to the press highly confidential information about Lincoln obtained during the course of the pending FHLBB examination. Since this is not the first time that confidential information obtained from Lincoln during the examination has been leaked, it is apparent that a deliberate campaign against Lincoln is taking place. It is

highly damaging to Lincoln and constitutes a patent violation of federal criminal statutes as well as the Board's policies and regulations.

The letter went on to provide specific examples of the articles containing the leaked information. Those examples were:

Enclosed are articles that appeared in the December 24, 1986, Wall Street Journal and the December 28, 1986, Mesa Tribune which are obviously based on leaks that could only have come from the FHLBB of information obtained by the Board during the course of its examination of Lincoln. There is no conceivable explanation as to how the press could have obtained the information in the articles except from Board personnel. Thus, the Wall Street Journal article specifically identifies the information as coming from "Bank Board sources." Further, the articles refer to specific numbers pertaining to Lincoln's financial condition which are not publicly known and come directly from the confidential documents. For example, the Wall Street Journal article states that the Board contends that Lincoln has $615.4 million of direct investments in excess of the Board's 10% limit which are not grandfathered. This figure obviously comes from a December 15, 1986, letter from Supervisory Agent Richard A. Sanchez to Lincoln. That figure was very recently calculated by the Eleventh District personnel involved in Lincoln's examination and could not have come from any other source.

Similarly, the Mesa Tribune article quotes from an internal FHLBB memorandum, the author of which is described in the article as "one of Gray's investigators," listing specific concerns raised by the memorandum. It is apparent from the article that the reporter had a copy of the memorandum which, again, could have been obtained only from FHLBB personnel.

The subject of these leaks came up in the 1989 congressional hearings on Lincoln Savings. The congressman asking the questions was Mr. Annunzio, and the following series of questions and answers took place:

Ms. STEWART [an attorney with the FHLBB's Office of Enforcement]: I know there were at least two inspector general inquiries into leaked Lincoln information. And neither was conclusive about the source of the leaks.

MR. ANNUNZIO: Now, Ms. Stewart, I was interested and that is what lead [*sic*] me to that question in the portion of your testimony that dealt with leaks of confidential information at the Bank Board. You said you wrote a memo to Chairman Gray complaining about leaks, and you were told that the Chairman was mad at you because he was the source of the leaks. Would you please expand on that statement. What was he leaking? Who was he leaking to? In your opinion, did Chairman Gray ever leak confidential information such as examination reports?

Ms. STEWART: The specific disclosure I described was in December 1986, in which information from the still ongoing examination of Lincoln was delivered to a member of the press. It appeared in a Wall Street Journal article on Christmas week of 1986. That was the specific disclosure that I complained of in my memo of early January 1987 to Mr. Gray.

I was told shortly after sending that memo by the then acting general counsel, Harry Quillian, that my memo had caused quite a stir, that Chairman Gray and his chief of staff were very angry about it, because it was indeed Mr. Gray who had authorized the disclosure.

MR. ANNUNZIO: Mr. Smuzynski, were you ever asked to provide any information? And if you were, who did you give the information to?

MR. SMUZYNSKI: I have been asked for a lot of information on Lincoln. And I normally do supply it.

MR. ANNUNZIO: While you were giving information on Lincoln, 2 days after you were given the information, it showed up in the press. Do you recall that?

MR. SMUZYNSKI: Yes, I do.

MR. ANNUNZIO: Who asked about that information?

MR. SMUZYNSKI: Well, the parties here are Mr. Black and the others at the table I believe is what you are referring to. I was requested by Mr. Black to provide information to him on the possibility of a large violation of a direct investment violation. This was in December of 1986.

That information was not in Washington. I called San Francisco district, was provided the information over the phone, and provided it to Mr. Black, who had a legitimate interest in that information.

MR. ANNUNZIO: Mr. Black, can you add to that statement? Mr. Black, did you leak that information? You are under oath. Now, remember, you are under oath.

MR. BLACK [an FHLBB attorney]: Yes, sir, I do not need to be reminded of that. I am under oath. And I never made any unauthorized release of information. What is being asked about is the following circumstances: Mr. Henkel, as his first substantive act as a Board member, made a proposal as an amendment to the direct investment rule. His proposal would have eliminated Lincoln's $600 plus million violation of the direct investment rule.

After the Board meeting, I informed first Board member White and his special assistant, and then Chairman Gray, of what this Henkel proposal would have done. I then went back to my office.

I was later called up to the offices of Chairman Gray. And there was an ongoing television conversation with Ken McClean [*sic*], who was a chief staffer to Senator Proxmire. And I was asked to explain by Mr. McClain what had gone on at this Board meeting. I then ended up going over, at McClain's request, and briefing Mr. McClain in person.

They wanted to know the dollar amount of this violation. I do not remember when I got it from Al. I have no reason to believe that I did not.

There was at that time a statement of supervisory concern. It was in writing, and it had been given to the institution already as to those numbers.

MR. ANNUNZIO: You made a statement that you never leaked any unauthorized information. Did you ever leak any authorized?

MR. BLACK: As part of my job, I released tons of information. And everyone at this table releases tons of information about institutions.

MR. ANNUNZIO: That are authorized?

MR. BLACK: Yes. And they are not leaks, as anyone uses the terms as I know it.

The facts are that someone did leak information to the press. It could be that Black (a person whose role in this war will be discussed in greater detail later in the story) was being cute. He may have been told by Gray to release the information and, therefore, considered it authorized. If this was the case, if Gray told someone to break the law, the implication was that it was okay since he had authorized it. I just don't think the real truth came out here. The articles specifically identified a source within the FHLBB, not some senator's staff person. Anyway, the senator's staff person was no more entitled to specific information from the exam than was some guy on the street. That disclosure was, I believe, contrary to the law, and that's what Rosemary Stewart was saying.

In Bill Black's testimony he mentioned Mr. Henkel. Lee Henkel is one of many fine people who have had their good reputations tarnished merely because they had an association with Lincoln. His story fits into the chronology of events at this time.

Lee Henkel is a lawyer from Georgia, specializing in tax and corporate law. In 1971, he was appointed by the president to be the chief counsel of the Internal Revenue Service and the ranking assistant general counsel of the Treasury Department. He supervised the regulatory function of the IRS. He was repeatedly commended for his service by both the IRS and the Treasury Department. At one point, Henkel was asked to consider assuming the position of commissioner of the Internal Revenue Service but declined.

Henkel met Charlie Keating in 1979, when both of them were working on John Connally's campaign to gain the Republican Party's nomination for the presidency. Both served as fund-raisers—Henkel in the East and Keating in the West. After the campaign, Henkel's law firm was engaged to do some tax work for ACC and the Keating family.

After ACC acquired Lincoln, two limited partnerships in which Henkel held small, limited partnership interests borrowed money from Lincoln. The total loans to these partnerships were approximately $23 million. In addition, Henkel held a minority stock interest in a corporation, Continental Southern, that borrowed around $55 million from Lincoln to acquire land in the Atlanta area. Henkel did not manage the day-to-day affairs of Continental Southern; this was done by another shareholder. The appraised value of Continental Southern's assets exceeded the amount of the loans that it received from Lincoln. Henkel also had a personal line of credit from Lincoln.

In the fall of 1986, Henkel was appointed to the FHLBB by President Reagan and was sworn in on November 11, 1986. There was plenty of talk at the time that Keating was responsible for Henkel's nomination. Henkel testified that those rumors simply weren't true. He had been approached by Senator Mattingly of Georgia, who was his personal friend. Henkel testified that it was Mattingly and his numerous friends in the Republican Party who were responsible for his nomination. Charlie was certainly supportive of Henkel's going onto the Board, and actively campaigned to garner support for Henkel's nomination and confirmation, but to suggest that he was responsible for the appointment just plain overstates Charlie's influence in Washington.

At the time of the appointment, Henkel told Congress that he was mindful of his relationship with Lincoln. He paid off his line of credit. He disposed of any general partnership interests he held. He resigned from the law firm and resigned any officer or director positions he held in any corporations. He later sold his stock in Continental Southern to Lincoln for less than the appraised value of the equity it represented. He also recused himself from any matters involving Lincoln. The evidence shows that he did what any reasonable and prudent person would do to assure that no conflicts of interest existed, in either fact or appearance.

Black essentially accused Henkel of proposing a rule change which would specifically benefit Lincoln, implying that Henkel had undertaken to do so because of his past relationships with Lincoln. Henkel testified that he drafted his proposal in response to letters and documents that he had received from the U.S. League of Savings Institutions. Henkel told Congress:

> I had no idea that responding to a request from an organization representing 3,500 institutions would cause me to be accused of trying to help a past business associate.
>
> Although I learned that Board members Gray and White were inclined to extend the existing regulation, I, nonetheless, made the proposal relating to the direct investment regulation at the December 18 open meeting recognizing that it had no chance of passing.
>
> I had written this proposal the night before. It was after that meeting that Ed Gray talked about, it was late at night when I wrote it.

He then went on to describe, in detail, the elements of his proposal. He explained that he was attempting to clear up the confusion existing over the provisions in the regulations dealing with "a definitive plan to complete a project." In this regard, he said:

> All my proposal said, in effect, was that if a thrift had started a project on land it owned on December 10, 1984, the cutoff date, according to a definitive plan, the thrift could continue and/or complete—those words are right from my proposal—continue and/or complete—I don't see how you can continue or complete something unless you owned it to start with—to continue or complete the project without the Board questioning whether the thrift followed every minute aspect of the plan.

He then described three conditions under which an investment could be grandfathered. The third of these conditions is the one that Black said would benefit only Lincoln. Henkel described it as follows:

> The third type of direct investment had to do with a commitment which must have been in existence on December 10, 1984, to either purchase a real estate project or to invest in other assets such as stock in service corporations.
>
> The Board had previously defined commitment to mean a binding contract under state law.

My proposal was limited in scope and only addressed No. 2, but I later learned that apparently Lincoln's principal dispute with the Board was with respect to three above having to do with a commitment to invest in a service corporation.

Understand at this point in time, I was recused, I had no way of knowing anything about Lincoln's situation, none of the disputes had been reviewed with me at the Board because of my complete recusal.

Immediately stories appeared in the press suggesting that my grandfathering proposal would principally benefit Lincoln.

I did not know until the last several days that this conclusion was Mr. Black's, who reported it to Chairman Gray, who in turn passed this information on to Senator Proxmire and I might add somebody also immediately called the Wall Street Journal because it was in there within the next day or two.

I find it very interesting and sort of disappointing frankly that neither Black nor Chairman Gray had the courtesy—I was only a short walk down the hall— to bring this purported conclusion to my attention, particularly since they knew that I had recused myself as to all Lincoln matters and thus was not aware of Lincoln's apparent dispute with the Board.

There was an investigation of the whole Henkel affair by both the Board's Office of Inspector General and the Department of Justice—all because of Black and Gray. Henkel was completely exonerated. Even though Henkel was exonerated, the investigation had a devastating effect on him. Investigators questioned many of his business associates and friends, and the tone of their questions implied that Henkel had done something wrong. Simply by asking the questions, they damaged his reputation. And stories continued in the press, and rumors continued to surround him. When these investigations showed no wrongdoing, there was scant mention of the exoneration in the press. The smell of scandal sells newspapers—not the fact that all of the previous stories run by the paper were incorrect and falsely accused a person of acts that he did not commit.

On March 31, 1987, fed up with the whole situation, Henkel resigned. About this he said: "I considered that the attacks against me were largely an attempt to remove me from the Board so that others more acceptable and perhaps more susceptible to certain interests could take my place."

Finally, there was no evidence—none—that Charlie Keating had had any contact with Lee Henkel while he was a member of the FHLBB. Henkel appears to have been a victim of not agreeing with Ed Gray's viewpoint on the direct-investment issue. Because the press got the information from an "inside source," they didn't find out whether it was true or not—they just printed it. The use of leaks is a tactic that the FHLBB people would use again and again to inflict severe damage on ACC and Lincoln.

One other series of observations concerning the Henkel situation is in order. Gray was opposed to Henkel because he believed that Henkel's appointment was instigated by Donald Regan, at Charlie Keating's urging. He testified that Keating used political influence—supported by campaign contributions—to obtain the Henkel appointment. In November 1989, he told Congress:

> So, here you had this unbelievable situation in which Charles Keating had finally achieved his wish. He was now in a position to greatly influence the Bank Board, to checkmate and frustrate my re-regulatory initiatives and, yes, to quite possibly see to fruition the elevation of Mr. Henkel to the Chairmanship of the Bank Board. Mr. Keating had gotten this far because of his political influence (translate that as money)—yes, all the way to and through the White House Office of Presidential Personnel and the White House Chief of Staff— and with friends like Senators DeConcini, McCain, Glenn and Cranston, what was to stop him.

Once again, Ed Gray took it personally. Keating was out to "frustrate" his initiatives, confront his policies, and challenge Gray's manhood and standing in the Bank Board. So, it became a personal matter for Gray to oppose Henkel and to block his enemy, Charlie Keating.

Gray then told the committee that Henkel acted improperly and for the benefit of Keating, by saying:

> Mr. Henkel's appointment was to turn out to be one of the most embarrassing selections in the history of federal financial regulation. For, in only a matter of weeks, Mr. Henkel—who also was the choice of Charles Keating, Jr., Senators DeConcini, McCain and Cranston and others—proposed in his first open meeting of the Federal Home Loan Bank Board, a regulation intended to benefit Charles Keating. . . .

Lee Henkel's version of the events surrounding the proposal he made, and the intent of the proposal itself, have already been covered, and Henkel's account differs substantially from the one offered by Ed Gray.

Finally, as previously stated, it is obvious that Gray took Henkel's nomination as a challenge and threat to Gray's own standing on the Bank Board. Gray's attitude is reflected in his testimony to Congress, as follows:

> We at the Bank Board watched Mr. Henkel strut in and out of meetings in his early days on the Board and it seemed clear to him, because he left no doubts about it, that he had been sent over to the Board by Don Regan to straighten

the place out, get things going in the right direction, and to stop second-guessing the judgments of thrift operators (who were, to him, the same as other businessmen). He apparently thought that since he had been appointed to the Republican seat on the Board that he was my likely successor as Chairman of the Bank Board. At least his demeanor conveyed that impression. It sounded plausible with Donald Regan running things.

Gray's testimony leaves the impression that Henkel was the only person appointed to the Bank Board as a consequence of political considerations and political influence, assuming, of course, that political influence had had something to do with Henkel's appointment. What about Gray himself? How did he get on the Bank Board? He was appointed because of his loyalty to Ronald Reagan, and as a consequence of political influence, lobbying, and, probably, campaign contributions by the U.S. League. And once there, didn't he do the League's bidding? Public reports indicate that Gray actually allowed the League to draft some of the regulations that the FHLBB later adopted—something Henkel certainly never let Charlie Keating or anyone else do. And didn't Gray willingly and eagerly accept cash payments from the League for his expenses? Gray's comments are, at the very least, the pot calling the kettle black.

The tactic of destroying anyone who crossed into the FHLBB's gunsights or threatened its leader's authority—people like Henkel—became commonplace in this war. And, as in this case, the attack was often launched by illegally leaking confidential and distorted information to the FHLBB's allies in the press.

On January 27, 1987, another closing meeting was held in San Francisco where, once again, Lincoln was led to believe that the FHLBB would disclose, in detail, all of its examination findings. The FHLBB was represented by eleven people, with Sanchez being the person in charge of the meeting. The state of California sent three people. Lincoln brought twelve people, including three outside attorneys who had helped Lincoln analyze expected issues. At Lincoln's request, I also attended.

With the size of the group, the meeting room was crowded, and people were jammed together. The FHLBB people aligned themselves at one end of the room, while the Lincoln contingent lined up at the opposite end. The state group was seated in the middle—occupants of a demilitarized zone surrounded by warring factions.

In order to reduce confusion and to allow the meeting to move along with a minimum of interruptions, the Lincoln people decided beforehand to have Karen Katzman speak for Lincoln. If others had questions for the regulators, they were to write Karen a note, and she would pose the question at the appropriate time. Alternatively, if Karen needed someone else to answer a question or respond to an issue, she would call on the person for assistance. It was felt that this would eliminate side conversations, or tangential interruptions, which could bog down the meeting and prohibit Lincoln from learning as much as it could from the examiners.

Unfortunately, the regulators appeared to misinterpret Lincoln's intention. Because Karen was an attorney with a litigation background, the regulators became very cautious and defensive, appearing to believe that they were going to be attacked. This reaction undoubtedly inhibited their openness and candor.

The first part of the meeting dealt with the classification of assets and was led by Dennis Fitzgerald, one of the field examiners. Basically, assets could be classified as substandard, doubtful, or loss. If the asset were deemed substandard, Lincoln would have to increase its minimum regulatory capital requirement by an amount equal to 10 percent of the asset value classified as substandard. If the asset were considered doubtful, the minimum capital requirement would have to be increased by an amount equal to 50 percent of the classified amount. If classified as loss, Lincoln would have to record a reserve, and corresponding reduction in income, on its books for the amount the regulators considered a loss.

The matter was further complicated because, in this instance, the regulators classified portions of an asset in more than one category. For example, a $1-million loan could be classified as $100,000 loss, $400,000 doubtful, and the remaining $500,000 substandard. The classification could be based on either collateral weaknesses (appraisal results) or problems with borrower creditworthiness (purely subjective conclusions by the person doing the classification).

Karen Katzman asked the regulators to explain and elaborate on the classification procedures, so Lincoln could better understand the process. Marirose Lescher, an attorney representing the FHLBB in the meeting, responded that the procedures had just recently been revised to conform more closely with those used by commercial banks, implying that the examiners were not very familiar with the new procedures. When asked if Lincoln could have a copy of the revised procedures, Lescher responded, "The procedures are internal to the agency and are not available to persons outside of the agency." There was no further elaboration.

Fitzgerald then went through a list of loans that they were going to classify. Certain classifications were based solely on creditworthiness, while others were based on a combination of appraisal results and creditworthiness. Fitzgerald gave a very brief explanation of the reasons for the classification of each loan. Katzman responded to each loan, pointing out factors the examiners apparently had not considered or discussing what Lincoln believed were fundamental flaws in the appraisals. Basically, each conclusion reached by the examiners was refuted. In each case, Katzman said that Lincoln would provide the additional information to the examiners.

The back-and-forth nature of the discussion between Katzman and Fitzgerald set the tone for the rest of the meeting. The regulators stated their findings and conclusions; then, Katzman offered additional information that she felt the examiners had overlooked or ignored. This process polarized the two groups, as each side felt compelled to defend its position. It became clear that the regulators were not interested in any additional information. They were obligated to hold an exit meeting, and they were just going through the motions. The Lincoln people, therefore, kept their rebuttals short and to the point. There was no effort to enter into meaningful dialogue.

The next topic was direct investments. Fitzgerald stated that the examiners had concluded that approximately $628 million of Lincoln's direct investments were not grandfathered; therefore, the investments exceeded the amount permitted under the regulations. Fitzgerald said that Lincoln's investments in its subsidiaries were not covered by a definitive plan; therefore, they were not grandfathered. Fitzgerald said that the FHLBB had issued opinions to the effect that only real-estate investments were covered under definitive plans.

Bob Kielty said that that was interesting because Lincoln had requested, under the Freedom of Information Act, all opinions issued by the FHLBB on the subject and had been told there were none. Ms. Lescher, with obvious embarrassment and reluctance, then agreed to provide redacted copies of the opinions to Lincoln.

Katzman concluded this portion of the discussion by saying that there were clearly differences in interpreting the law, and the matter would have to be settled at a later time, perhaps through litigation.

We then discussed the subject of income reversals that the examiners were basing on the accounting for certain transactions. Ashton led the discussion, and his comments and the FHLBB's positions were a virtual repeat of those given in the November meeting. Lincoln obviously voiced the same objections that it had raised earlier. Katzman again asked Ashton whether he had consulted with any outside accountants. He said that he had not. Lincoln later learned that San Francisco had not only consulted with an outside accounting firm but that the examiners had also engaged outside lawyers to review numerous documents of Lincoln's. Once again, the FHLBB did not appear to be open and truthful in dealing with Lincoln.

Appraisal losses were then covered by Everett Fenton, an FHLBB staff appraiser, and one of the persons who had told Judy that the examiners would stop the sale of the Foothills property in June 1986. The list of appraisal losses totaled over $135 million, with approximately $80 million of that amount attributable to the Phoenician Resort.

The Phoenician was a hotel which was under construction near the city boundaries of Phoenix and Scottsdale. Located on the south side of Camelback Mountain, it was being built on one of the best and most valuable pieces of land in the entire Phoenix area. The resort would not be completed until October 1988. Even though the resort was in the midst of construction, the examiners had already concluded that it should be written down. Lincoln was absolutely convinced that the appraisal was seriously flawed and that the appraiser used by the FHLBB was not qualified to appraise such a project.

Lincoln's representatives were also concerned about the other appraisals. They contended that appraisers had overlooked items of value and had made mechanical and theoretical mistakes. They were concerned that some of the appraisers were not familiar with the markets in which the properties they had valued were located. And the credentials and qualifications of some of the appraisers were, in Lincoln's opinion, very questionable.

Sanchez then made an incredible statement. He said that Lincoln would have to record the appraisal losses *before* the FHLBB would consider any rebuttals of its appraisal loss conclusions. Lincoln simply couldn't do this. ACC was a publicly held company with an active public market for its stock. Its earnings were directly affected by Lincoln's earnings. If Lincoln recorded the appraisal losses, ACC's earnings would be reduced and the value of its shares could go down. If the rebuttal arguments were successful, the losses would then have to be reversed. This would cause ACC's earnings to fluctuate improperly and could unnecessarily harm its shareholders. Since ACC and Lincoln believed that the FHLBB findings were absolutely incorrect, they could not properly reflect them on their books. The FHLBB's position was arbitrary, punitive, and totally irresponsible. Nonetheless, when they finally issued their report, they demanded that Lincoln record all of their adjustments before any rebuttals would be considered.

Kotrys then discussed Lincoln's net worth. He said that, based on the adjustments proposed by the FHLBB, Lincoln failed to meet its minimum net-worth requirement. Since Lincoln had already pointed out many serious problems with the examiners' conclusions, both sides agreed that any further discussion of this subject would be fruitless.

While there was no further discussion of the net-worth issue, the Lincoln people understood the significance of Kotrys' comments. If an institution fails to meet its net-worth requirement it can be subjected to severe enforcement actions—a cease-and-desist order or worse. The examiners' determination that Lincoln failed this important test was the first clear warning that serious trouble was on the horizon.

There were a number of other subjects discussed, but the discussions were neither informative nor fruitful. Lincoln was convinced that the examiners would not provide any substantive information and that it would be better to wait for their report and deal with the issues at that time. At least then they would have to place all of their cards on the table and abandon their evasive tactics. Sanchez said that if Lincoln would submit the information it had promised, the FHLBB would issue its report within fifteen days thereafter.

This meeting, which lasted a couple of hours, was the final meeting between Lincoln and the regulators before the regulators issued their report. As the weeks passed, the tension built. Lincoln knew the report was going to be critical, and it was anxious to receive it so that defensive measures could be taken to protect against any enforcement actions. On the basis of this last meeting, Lincoln believed that the examiners were way off base, and it wanted the opportunity to set the record straight.

A few days after this meeting, the examination took another ominous turn. The FHLBB began to enlist other federal agencies to assist them in their attack on ACC and Lincoln. On January 30, 1987, Stephen Hershkowitz sent the following letter to Gladwyn Goines of the enforcement division of the SEC:

> This confirms my telephone conversation with Bruce Heiler on January 23 and you on January 28, 1987, concerning American Continental Corporation's ("ACC") offering of securities, periodic filings and purchases of securities.
>
> The Bank Board's 1986 examination of ACC's principal subsidiary Lincoln Savings and Loan Association will be completed next month. It appears that the examiners will question the adequacy of loan loss reserves, the accounting treatment for various loans and direct investments, as well as other regulatory deficiencies. Therefore, we are referring for your review the possibility that ACC is selling securities based upon a false and misleading registration statement and that its periodic filings during the last two years may have been false and misleading. In addition, it appears that certain of ACC's securities purchases may have been based on nonpublic information. We will be happy to share this information with you.

As a consequence of this letter, the SEC started an investigation of ACC. The investigation caused ACC, its accountants, and attorneys to supply, pursuant to subpoena, literally thousands of pages of documents. The investigation did not conclude until 1994.

There are a few things that Hershkowitz' letter didn't say. First, just a few days before the letter was sent, in the January 27, 1987, meeting in San Francisco, Lincoln took strong exception to virtually all of the examination findings. Second, the letter did not indicate that discussions were surfacing within the FHLBB system in which actions, such as conservatorship or receivership, were being bandied about and that, if such actions occurred, they would have a much more profound effect on ACC than any of the exam findings per se.

One has to be curious as to the timing of this letter. The exam was not finished, nor were all of the issues resolved. In fact, the exam wouldn't be done and a report issued for nearly three more months. Why didn't the FHLBB wait until their work was done before involving another agency? Were people within the FHLBB looking for help to buttress their arguments? Were they trying to put more pressure on ACC, so it would accede to any actions the FHLBB was planning to take against Lincoln?

This part of the story gets even more curious. The examiners began to intensify their criticism of the underwriting analyses Lincoln had made prior to purchasing securities. They became concerned that Lincoln had relied almost exclusively on the advice of its principal investment banker, Drexel Burnham Lambert, who they believed was becoming the primary brokerage firm being scrutinized by the SEC during the investigation of Ivan Boesky and insider trading.

The examiners began analyzing specific securities purchased by Lincoln and appeared to conclude that many were the same issues being scrutinized by the SEC and Justice Department. They seemed to be asserting that Lincoln did not do a meaningful underwriting analysis prior to its investment decisions. They asked questions about what had prompted Lincoln to make these investments. In so doing, they compiled a list of debt and equity security transactions of various takeover candidates referenced in published media accounts concerning the Boesky and Drexel Burnham insider-trading investigation.

At this same time, they also started asking questions about a number of sections of the November 12, 1986, registration statement. They felt that the disclosures in the document were inconsistent with their examination findings. None of their speculations about the registration statement and insider-trading concerns was commented on in the Report of Examination, nor, to my knowledge, was any ever proven to have substance.

Whether the speculations of the examiners had substance or not is not the real issue. The FHLBB was not the federal agency charged with reviewing suspected instances of insider trading or the adequacy, or lack thereof, of the disclosures in documents filed with the SEC. The examiners were not securities lawyers, nor were they expert in the security laws and related regulations; therefore, they were not qualified to review a registration statement for compliance with the applicable securities laws or to determine whether laws regarding the use of insider information were abused. That was not their domain. Their charge was to determine whether Lincoln had complied with the regulations they were specifically charged, by law, with administering.

Their excursion into potential insider trading was also based on questionable information as it was predicated mostly on articles in the media and not on reliable data. The SEC and the Department of Justice were the responsible agencies, and they had the proper staff, as well as access to reliable data, in order to carry out their regulatory and legal obligations. In effect, the FHLBB examiners had just enough knowledge and information to be dangerous—and they were. This tangential excursion appears to have been driven by a combination of misplaced priorities and a desire to use any avenue available to get something on ACC.

On February 18, 1987, Sanchez wrote a letter to Lincoln which followed up on the examiners' concerns regarding Boesky, Drexel Burnham Lambert, and insider trading. The letter requested additional data and asked Lincoln to conduct an internal investigation to look into possible insider trading or market manipulation. On March 5, 1987, Lincoln responded to the letter. Lincoln supplied the information which was sought and indicated that it would conduct an internal investigation. Lincoln also stated, in pretty clear terms, that the regulators "do not understand the nature of the securities market and insider trading practices." Nonetheless, Lincoln undertook the costly task of responding to the examiners' misguided speculations and unfounded concerns.

Lincoln believed that it had thoroughly responded to the same issues surrounding Boesky and the examiners' concerns over insider trading in December 1986. Lincoln's management was, therefore, concerned with this follow-up request, especially its tone, which was accusatory. The letter suggested to Lincoln that the examiners were now on a witch hunt and were not pursuing normal procedures. This was all on the heels of numerous articles which had appeared in the press confirming that Ed Gray harbored ill feelings toward Keating and Lincoln.

The Lincoln people became further convinced that Gray's feelings were resulting in a prejudgment of Lincoln and that the exam had devolved into nothing more than an effort to make a case which could be used in some adverse action against the association.

Seven

The Keating Five

Charlie Keating and ACC always maintained good relations with their elected officials at both local and national levels. Local officials, and the policies they adopted, affected the various projects ACC developed. Policies regarding zoning and land-use planning dramatically impacted property values. Local and state tax laws contributed to the cost of doing business and determined the growth rate for a community, which, in turn, influenced the demand for housing. Likewise, federal tax laws directly affected property values, the cost of doing business, and the strength of the economy. Therefore, candidates' positions on tax and economic issues were of continuing interest to ACC.

Keating also maintained contact with elected officials as a result of his long-time efforts to counteract and eliminate child pornography in America. He founded an organization, Citizens for Decent Literature through Law, which waged a national campaign to protect children from pornographic literature and exploitation. These efforts brought him in contact with governmental officials throughout the country. He knew how legislation was formulated, sponsored, and passed into law.

Keating's experiences left him with the strong belief that if a citizen—any citizen—had a problem with a governmental body, that citizen had an absolute right to seek assistance from his or her elected representatives. Our representative form of government is founded on the principle that the people we elect are obligated to serve the needs of their constituents. One of their fundamental purposes is to act as a liaison between individual citizens and the bureaucracy they are charged with overseeing. Charlie believed, and quite properly so, that a person should not hesitate to ask for assistance from any officeholder. The purpose of officeholders is to serve and not to be served.

When the FHLBB sought to re-regulate the thrift industry by enacting the direct-investment regulations, Keating and hundreds of other S&L owners let their elected representatives in Washington know that they opposed such initiatives, and they asked for legislation to stop the FHLBB.

ACC expressed its views through Jim Grogan, a former aide to Senator John Glenn. Grogan is an attorney who worked for ACC and Lincoln and was responsible for tracking legislation and regulations which could have an impact on Lincoln's business and well-being. Grogan maintained contact with members of Congress, senators, and lobbyists in Washington.

Keating and his ACC associates also contributed to various political campaigns or political parties. Politicians have a constant, never-ending need for campaign funds. First, to get elected and, then, to get reelected. Their campaign managers enlist fund-raisers who go out and browbeat their friends and associates into making contributions or buying tickets to fund-raising dinners and other affairs. Each election, their money requirements seem to increase.

Beginning with the advent of deregulation, people associated with S&Ls became significant contributors to campaigns and parties. They were certainly not unique. Virtually every major industry, or interest group, supports candidates. And many, if not most, hedge their bets and support both parties and more than one candidate in the same race. This is simply the reality of our political system.

Charlie and his associates were no different from thousands of people across the nation. They supported candidates they knew and who they believed had a realistic chance to win. They supported both parties and, in a given race, might support more than one candidate.

Why did they do this? It's simple. Like most contributors, they wanted access to the person if he or she was elected. They wanted the person to accept their phone call and to listen to their concerns and ideas. If necessary, they wanted the elected official to represent their interests before the bureaucracy. They wanted the elected official to pay real attention to their needs rather than simply answering ACC's calls for assistance with a form letter.

In the summer of 1986, Charlie and Grogan began to discuss their concerns about the course of the examination with various congressmen and senators. They sought advice about how to deal with the situation and wondered whether they were being treated fairly or whether the regulators, in retaliation for Lincoln's visible opposition to the direct-investment rules, were out to get Lincoln. As the examination wore on into the fall and winter months, Charlie's and Grogan's concerns heightened, and contacts with elected officials were more frequent. The message also changed. By this point, Charlie was convinced that the examiners' actions constituted harassment and that their agenda was to inflict serious damage on ACC and Lincoln.

There were five senators with whom Keating and Grogan had the most contact regarding the examination. Senators DeConcini and McCain from Arizona, Senator Glenn from Ohio, Senator Cranston of California, and

Senator Riegle of Michigan. ACC had a connection to each of their states, and Keating believed that each was ACC's valid representative.

ACC's principal operations and a large portion of its assets were in Arizona. ACC was a significant employer in Arizona and a major source of revenue for the state. Keating and his associates had contributed to both of the Arizona senators' election campaigns. McCain and his family had vacationed at Keating's home in the Bahamas on several occasions. Keating knew both men well and thought he could seek their advice and counsel.

ACC was incorporated in the state of Ohio. Many of the ACC people still had family members in the Cincinnati area. Grogan had worked for John Glenn in Washington and knew most of his staff on a personal basis. He felt comfortable stopping by Glenn's office whenever he was in Washington. People associated with ACC had contributed to Glenn's campaigns.

Lincoln was chartered in California and employed hundreds of people there. Lincoln's depositors were largely California citizens. The examiners were also located in that state as was the district bank. ACC people had also contributed to Cranston's campaigns, and ACC had contributed to voter registration and get-out-the-vote organizations sponsored by the Democrats—Cranston's party.

The Pontchartrain Hotel, which was managed by a Lincoln subsidiary and was owned by a partnership which included people associated with ACC, was located in Detroit. It was one of the city's premier hotels and was considered to be very important to Detroit's convention center, which was undergoing a major expansion program. And again, ACC-related people had supported Riegle's campaign.

In the latter part of February 1987, Jim Grogan called me and asked if I would go with him to Washington to attend a meeting of the FHLBB on February 27. The FHLBB was going to discuss a proposal to extend the scope of the direct-investment regulations, and Grogan wanted me to listen to the discussion, so I could determine how the revisions might impact Lincoln. Grogan's request was not unusual. Many clients asked their auditors to consider the effects of proposed changes in regulations or tax laws. It was something both my partners and I had done for our clients in the past.

We left very early on the morning of the 26th in one of ACC's corporate aircraft. During the flight, Grogan said that he and Charlie had been discussing the progress, or lack thereof, of the FHLBB's examination with several senators and that he planned to see some of them later that day to update them further on recent events. He said that they might like the chance to ask about the audit and to inquire about my personal impressions of Lincoln and the meetings I had attended with the regulators. He didn't have anything firmly scheduled and was going to play things by ear. He used a phone on the plane and tentatively scheduled a meeting with Senator Riegle's office for midmorning.

When we landed, we went straight to Senator Riegle's office. After a few minutes' wait, Senator Riegle came out to greet us. The senator had some papers clutched in his hand and seemed to be harried and pressed for time. This was confirmed when he said to Grogan, "My schedule's really busy today, and I have to be at a meeting in about ten or fifteen minutes, so we'll have to make this brief."

Grogan said, "Senator, I just wanted to bring you up to date on the FHLBB examination. We still haven't received any report, and the exam is still going on. As you know, Charlie is very concerned about the situation. I can tell you more when we have more time. Jack's been the audit partner on Lincoln's account, and his firm has just completed the annual audit. He has also attended some of the meetings with the San Francisco examiners. If you have any questions about Lincoln that you'd like him to answer, he'd be happy to do so."

"I do have some questions," Riegle responded. "I've listened to Charlie and Jim, and maybe you can give me your viewpoint on some of the issues. I'll tell you what my questions are, and maybe you can send me a letter responding to them."

With that, the senator recited a brief list of questions, which I wrote down. I told him that, when I returned to Phoenix, I would think about his questions and send him a response. He thanked me and said that he really had to run to his next appointment. The whole meeting lasted ten minutes or less.

We then met separately with Senators Cranston and Glenn in their respective offices. The questions asked and responses given were almost the same in both meetings.

The senators asked, "Who else have you met with and what was said?"

Grogan answered, "We had a real brief meeting with Senator Riegle who was on his way to a meeting. He left some questions with Jack, and Jack's going to answer them later in a letter to the senator."

The senators asked what Riegle's questions were. After I read Riegle's questions to them, they each said, "Those are the same questions I have. Why don't you send me the same letter that you send to Senator Riegle?"

I said I would do that.

There were further discussions among Grogan, the senators, and their aides. Grogan discussed the lack of progress in ending the examination and told them about Lincoln's frustration with the whole process. He said, "The examiners completed their fieldwork months ago. They promised to send a final report, but no report has been issued. All Lincoln wants at this point is for the exam to be concluded, so Lincoln can get on with its business, free of the disruption caused by dealing with the examiners."

At a point in each meeting, I was asked about my impression of the exam and the examiners. I recall responding, "The process is longer than I have seen at any other S&L. In the meetings I have attended, the examiners have taken rigid positions and weren't receptive to Lincoln's comments or presentations of added information. And on some occasions, the examiners have admitted that their positions are not correct, but they still will not revise their findings. As a result, the relationship between the parties is strained and adversarial."

Each meeting lasted about thirty to forty-five minutes. At no time during the meetings did Grogan ask either senator to take any action on Lincoln's behalf. And at no time did either senator volunteer to do anything for Lincoln. Before we parted company, each senator asked to be kept advised on any further developments in Lincoln's relationship with the examiners.

After we left Senator Glenn's office, the last of the two meetings, Grogan suggested that we meet with Senators DeConcini and McCain. I said, "We have already had a long day, and we'll probably have to cool our heels in their waiting rooms before we can see either of them. Based on the other senators' reactions, they are probably interested in the same questions that Riegle wants answered. Why don't you call them later and tell them about the other meetings and Riegle's questions? If there are other questions which interest them, I can answer them in a phone call, or we can see them in Arizona, or you can tell me what their questions are and I can write to them. But for now, let's call it a day. We've got to get to that FHLBB meeting early tomorrow, and that's enough for this trip."

The next morning Grogan and I attended the FHLBB's open meeting regarding the extension of the direct-investment rules. The meeting was held in a large conference room in the FHLBB's building. There was a long conference table in the front of the room where the Board members and their aides sat facing a gallery crammed with interested spectators and members of the press. Across the table from the Board members was a group of FHLBB staff members who where there to answer questions and to present the proposed rule changes.

There were three FHLBB Board members: Chairman Ed Gray, Larry White, and Lee Henkel. White and Gray sat together at one end of the conference table with aides at their sides. Henkel sat at the other end of the table, separated from the other Board members by several people. It was obvious that White and Gray were allies and Henkel was an outsider.

As the meeting started, Henkel, because of the furor raised by his earlier proposal regarding direct investments, the one Gray and Black asserted would have inappropriately benefited Lincoln, announced he was not going to vote on the issue and, as such, was recusing himself from the discussion. The adverse publicity and resultant investigations spawned by Gray and Black removed Henkel from the game, leaving the field open to Gray and his teammate White.

The proposal that the FHLBB was considering expanded the definition of direct investments to include "land loans and non-residential construction loans with loan-to-value ratios greater than 80 percent." The loan-to-value ratio is the ratio of the loan amount to the market value of the pledged collateral. The proposal also amended the limits on direct investments by limiting them to the greater of 3 percent of total assets or three times tangible net worth for institutions whose capital was greater than 6 percent of insured liabilities or two and one-half times tangible net worth for institutions who meet their net-worth requirement but whose capital is less than 6 percent of insured liabilities. Tangible net worth is essentially actual net worth, as reflected on an institution's books, less goodwill and other intangible assets.

When an S&L was acquired, regulators allowed goodwill to be reflected on its books. Goodwill is an intangible asset which represents the difference between the fair value of the assets acquired and the sum of the fair value of the liabilities assumed and the purchase price paid by the new owner. In effect, goodwill is the amount the buyer is willing to pay to acquire a going concern as opposed to merely buying a collection of assets. Some would say that it is the value of the S&L's franchise. And regulators expressly acknowledged that goodwill was a part of the S&L's capital or net worth.

In the late seventies and early eighties, when hundreds of S&Ls began bleeding red ink as a result of their eroded spreads, the government encouraged healthy S&Ls to buy the walking-wounded and deceased S&Ls. In 1983, the government encouraged non-S&Ls, such as ACC, to become acquirers. Virtually every acquired S&L ended up with a significant amount of goodwill being recorded on its books. When ACC acquired Lincoln, $124.5 million in goodwill was reflected on Lincoln's books.

All of the acquirers purchased an S&L for the same reason—the deregulated nature of the industry. They did the same things that ACC did with Lincoln. They invested in land and equity securities. They made loans secured by land and engaged in nonresidential construction lending. They formed subsidiaries who entered into nontraditional businesses.

With this proposal, the Bank Board delivered a one-two punch to these recent acquirers of S&Ls. It expanded the definition of direct investments, and, effectively, it reduced the aggregate amount of direct investments an institution could hold from 10 percent of assets to 3 percent of assets. This meant that large numbers of S&Ls exceeded the allowable limits. Their existing investments were grandfathered under this new proposal, but, as investments were sold, the institutions would not be permitted to reinvest in other direct investments. Instead, they would have to invest the proceeds into traditional investments—essentially residential mortgages and government securities.

The adoption of the tangible capital standard was a particularly cruel blow. It affected primarily those institutions who had heeded the government's call to infuse new capital into the industry. In approving each acquisition, the government explicitly approved the goodwill resulting from the transaction. Here, with a stroke of Ed Gray's pen, they were eliminating goodwill. This reduced the aggregate capital in the industry for purposes of the direct-investment rules by billions of dollars.

This was not an accident. In this open meeting, White and Gray discussed the effects of adopting a tangible-capital standard. In the discussion, Gray said, essentially, "Goodwill is a worthless asset." When someone mentioned goodwill was the equivalency of a franchise value, Gray basically answered, "With all the losses in the industry, how can there possibly be any value in an S&L's franchise?"

At one point in the discussion, Gray stated, in essence, "The new regulations will stop institutions from undertaking risky ventures like building hotels." Grogan and I believed that this comment was directed specifically at Lincoln.

Grogan and I were struck by several things during this meeting. First, Gray and White didn't understand the industry. They wanted it to return to the business of making home mortgages. But they didn't appreciate that the profit margins in that business were razor-thin and that there wasn't enough volume out there to satisfy all of the associations. Second, they were totally willing to betray those acquirers who had rescued the industry during the years 1980 to 1987.

We left the meeting with the firm belief that Charlie should be worried about Ed Gray. He didn't appear to be a person who could be trusted. And he appeared to act without fully understanding the consequences of his actions.

After we returned to Phoenix, in fact a few weeks later, Grogan called me and said that he had talked to DeConcini's and McCain's office and that they wished to receive the same letter as Riegle. I never talked with either of these senators.

There hadn't been any urgency in Senator Riegle's request for answers to the questions he had asked. March is still a very busy time for CPAs, and it was several weeks before I had the time to answer the senator's questions. On March 13, 1987, I sent letters to Senators Riegle,

Cranston, and Glenn. On March 17, 1987, after some minor changes to the opening paragraph, I sent essentially the same letter to Senators DeConcini and McCain.

The following addresses the basic content of those letters with some added comments directed to the criticisms that I have received for visiting the senators and sending the letters answering their questions.

Riegle's first question was: What is Lincoln Savings' financial condition at December 31, 1986, and its operating results for the year then ended?

I responded that Arthur Young & Company examined the financial statements of Lincoln Savings for the year ended December 31, 1986, and issued an unqualified opinion, dated February 17, 1987, on such financial statements. Lincoln Savings' consolidated statement of financial condition at December 31, 1986, reflected stockholder's equity, as determined in accordance with GAAP, of $193,024,000 (or approximately 6.8 percent of its FSLIC-insured deposits) at that date. Its consolidated statement of operations reflected earnings before income taxes of $81,689,000 and net earnings of $48,958,000 for the year ended December 31, 1986.

The second question was: In determining its earnings and stockholder's equity, did Lincoln make provisions for potential losses?

I wrote that Lincoln's stockholder's equity was after valuation allowances of approximately $28,000,000 at December 31, 1986, and the pretax earnings for the year were net of provisions for losses of $32,500,000.

It is interesting to note that if the loss reserves the examiners were proposing in January 1987 were adjusted to exclude the Crescent and Phoenician hotels, which Lincoln believed were operating assets and not subject to valuation allowances based on appraisals, the requested reserves would have been approximately $50 million. Lincoln contended that appraisals relating to $32 million of the adjusted amount were fundamentally flawed. If Lincoln's contentions were correct, then the adjusted reserves would have been $18 million as compared to Lincoln's recorded valuation allowances of $28 million.

Riegle's next question was: Is the Federal Home Loan Bank Board currently conducting an examination of Lincoln Savings?

I answered that the FHLBB began an examination in March 1986, and as of the date of this letter had not yet concluded the examination. Accordingly, the examination had been ongoing for approximately one year. I also noted that the examination was characterized by duplicative procedures and redundant requests for information.

At times, the examiners have said that their redundant requests for information resulted because Lincoln was uncooperative and had failed to give them the data when they asked for it or because Lincoln had provided them with incomplete data. There may have been instances where this occurred. It's my experience that auditors sometimes ask for data which they assume the entity that they are examining routinely keeps in the ordinary course of business. Their assumption is frequently incorrect. Often, the entity has to assemble and process the requested data because it is not a part of the routine records.

Also, auditors often describe the data in terms that are different from what the entity uses; as a consequence, they are given something different from what they are seeking. Such instances of miscommunication are frequent and are, or should be, expected in any examination. When these things occur, it's almost always the fault of the auditor and not the entity being examined. When auditors complain about these instances, it's usually a rationalization for the auditor's own unfamiliarity with the entity's records and terminology. I think that's, in part, what happened between the examiners and Lincoln.

The next question was: In your experience, is the duration of the FHLBB examination unusual?

I answered that examinations generally are conducted over a period of two to three months by field examiners. Final reports are usually issued within six months from the start of the examination. Hence, the duration of this examination appeared to be clearly outside normal standards.

I am not aware of any examination which lasted over a year without a report having been issued. Is it possible there were other prolonged FHLBB examinations which were comparable to Lincoln's? Certainly, it is possible, because I don't know the statistics of every examination ever conducted by the FHLBB. But that wasn't the question. The question dealt with my experience. Even if there was another exam which lasted a year or more, and I'm still not aware there were any, it would also be outside the norm. I've heard people from the FHLBB say that the Lincoln exam was the longest they are aware of, and no one has ever mentioned one that lasted longer.

Again, the FHLBB says that the duration of the exam was Lincoln's fault. They point to the fact that they had to channel requests for data through one of Kaye Scholer's attorneys as contributing to the delay. But that procedure wasn't put in place until after the exam had been going on for over three months.

The fact is, in January 1987, the FHLBB still hadn't received all of the appraisals that it had ordered, nor were consultant reports finished. They told Lincoln that on January 27, 1987. They, not Lincoln, made the arrangements with the appraisers and consultants. Lincoln was not permitted to talk to these people. So how could Lincoln have caused the delay? The FHLBB's attempts to make Lincoln responsible for the extended duration of the exam simply don't wash. We found out later that the FHLBB used other consultants, accountants, and attorneys they never told

Lincoln about. Their reliance on outside parties was a significant contributor to the extended duration of the examination.

Riegle's next question was: Have the procedures conducted by the examiners appeared to be different or more extensive than you believe is typical?

I said that, while I didn't have first-person knowledge of the examiners' procedures, I had discussed the procedures with Lincoln Savings' management and legal counsel. Based on these discussions, the extent of loan-file reviews, the number of appraisals ordered, the nature of the appraisal process, including the experience of appraisers selected, the redundant procedures and requests for data, and the types of transactions examined were unusual. I also provided the senators with several examples of requests made by the examiners which I thought were atypical.

The next question was: Was the unusual duration of the examination and type and extent of the procedures used caused by the nature of Lincoln Savings' operations?

The response to this question provided background information regarding Lincoln as well as my perceptions of the nature or character of the examination the FHLBB had conducted. As such, it was a fairly lengthy answer. Some of the key elements were:

> While Lincoln Savings is not a typical association in that it is not a significant single family residential lender but rather tends to concentrate on land development and construction lending, it engages in transactions comparable to those entered into by other associations in Arizona and California. The focus of the FHLBB examination appears to have been centered on (a) land development projects, (b) investments in equity and noninvestment grade debt securities, and (c) commercial and construction loans. . . .
>
> In February 1984, when ACC acquired Lincoln Savings, Lincoln was in the position of other traditional thrifts in that its interest spread was insufficient to provide a level of profitability. Since ACC's primary business was land development and homebuilding, it looked to what it knew best to improve Lincoln's profits and reduce risks. . . . Since this strategy was put in place, Lincoln has realized aggregate after-tax earnings of more than $141,000,000.
>
> Because the experience of most of the FHLBB's more senior examiners is with traditional single family lenders, Lincoln Savings is different from their prior experience. Also, the more junior examiners generally lack the business acumen to understand complex real estate development projects or complex investment strategies. Hence, while the examiners' decision to focus on real estate, commercial and construction lending, and equity and debt investments may have been proper, they appear to have had neither sufficient experience nor knowledge to deal with Lincoln's transactions effectively, thereby causing the examination to be more protracted than necessary.

Moreover, because Lincoln does not concentrate on single family residential lending, it does not fit the pattern for member institutions that the present FHLBB leadership has espoused publicly and has reflected in recent regulations. This fact has, based on my observations, led to unusually antagonistic positions and actions by the FHLBB toward Lincoln. This is difficult to understand because Lincoln's strategies have thus far proved successful and have turned an association headed for failure into a strong and viable financial entity. . . .

Thus, the nature of Lincoln's operations should not have resulted in the protracted period of the examination or the unusual procedures employed. But, because the examiners did not have the requisite experience and knowledge to evaluate the types of transactions entered into by Lincoln, the nature of the business did, in fact, cause the examination to be inordinately protracted.

As to the nature of the procedures employed, the experience factor contributed to some of the redundant procedures. Others, I believe, based on observation of FHLBB personnel, were the result of the FHLBB's resistance to Lincoln's nontraditional business profile and the fact that Lincoln does not fit into the mold desired by the FHLBB leadership.

The contents of the response have drawn criticism from a wide variety of sources. The regulators say that I improperly characterized the pre-1984 Lincoln as being in financial trouble; the comments about the experience and knowledge of the examiners are too harsh or inaccurate; Lincoln is inappropriately praised; and Lincoln is the real cause of the protracted period of the exam. Some say that the comments represent "advocacy" of Lincoln and assert that the comments represent an "opinion" by Arthur Young & Company. Others say that the comments are those of a "promotor," in the sense of promoting a company's stock, and also say that the response "praised ACC/Lincoln management and was highly critical of the Federal Home Loan Bank Board," apparently in an inappropriate fashion.

Lincoln had been examined by the FHLBB in 1982, and the Report of Examination had expressed specific concern over Lincoln's eroded interest-rate spread and the level of its earnings. The concern was high enough for the regulators to classify Lincoln as an association that had to be watched carefully, so as to not become a threat to the insurance fund. A letter from the FHLBB to Lincoln in November 1982 stated: "If the Association continues to incur operating deficits at the same monthly rate, its September 30 net worth of $16.4 million, equal to 2.0% of assets, could be depleted in approximately 12 months."

Lincoln had lost $13 million in 1980. In 1981, it had lost more than $4 million (the loss would have been more than $12 million had it not sold a valuable branch). In 1983, Lincoln had earned $3 million, but it had had to sell another branch to do so. Somehow the regulators who argue that Lincoln didn't have profit problems before 1984 have failed to read their own agency's reports.

As to criticism that the comments about the regulators' experience and knowledge are harsh or critical, the facts are what the facts are. During this period of time, the FHLBB was conducting classes in an attempt to improve the knowledge of its examination force. Kotrys admitted to Judy that he didn't understand many of the issues and was just collecting data to be passed up the line. Kotrys was equally candid when he said that his staff were inexperienced and had to be reined in and controlled. It's fact that the FHLBB had to employ outside consultants to deal with many of the issues, like debt securities, because they didn't have the expertise in-house. And don't forget the outside appraisers, real-estate-market studies, and outside accountants and attorneys. Lack of experience and knowledge was a real problem. I believe that one of the real reasons the examiners came in a second time was to get the information for the consultants that they didn't get the first time around.

As to the comments that procedures may have been influenced because Lincoln didn't fit the desired mold, the examiners' comments and actions provided ample evidence to support this observation. Deardorff was critical of the Gulf Broadcast transaction as being too risky after it resulted in a $50 million gain. Even though Lincoln never suffered a loss on the Boesky investment, the examiners continued to cite it as evidence of unreasonable risk. The consultant studies were ordered for only one reason—to support the examiners' preexisting conclusions about Lincoln's risk profile.

As to praising ACC/Lincoln, I believe that the response simply states the economic results reflected in Lincoln's financial statements and comes to what I think is the obvious conclusion that, at the time, Lincoln's strategies were producing favorable results, certainly when compared to how Lincoln had been doing just before ACC acquired it. I don't believe that pointing out the amount of Lincoln's reported profits constitutes either promotion or advocacy.

Finally, as to whether these comments, and the others expressed in the letter, constitute an opinion by Arthur Young & Company, one merely has to read the letter and have a basic understanding of the English language. The questions were asked of me—as an individual—and not of Arthur Young—the firm. The letter is written entirely in the first person. There is no use of the third person or the institutional "we" or "the firm." The letter presents personal observations and comments.

The next question was: Lincoln Savings' representatives have asserted that the FHLBB examiners were unreasonable in their decision making and that at times their conduct bordered on "harassment." Did you observe personally any such conduct by the FHLBB?

The letter provided six examples which supported Lincoln's assertions.

First, there were the requests for separate reports from both Arthur Andersen and Arthur Young and the FHLBB's rejection of both reports, which was made by John Ashton, a relatively inexperienced accountant.

Second, the FHLBB was demanding that reserves be recorded before Lincoln could respond to them. This was despite the fact that the FHLBB had not taken into account the already-recorded reserves on Lincoln's books; despite the data showing that certain appraisals were seriously flawed; and despite the fact that certain properties didn't fall under the appraisal requirements.

Third, the FHLBB had repeatedly said that the examination was completed and a report would be issued, yet the exam was still ongoing.

Fourth, there was the start-and-stop nature of the examination and the expense and distraction it caused Lincoln.

Fifth, there were the redundant and excessive requests for data by the examiners.

Finally, there were the pejorative nature of the examiners' interpretations of regulations and their hostile and inflexible attitudes toward Lincoln's representatives.

Each of these was cited as conduct that could be viewed as harassment.

The last question was: Do you believe the eventual outcome of the examination will be detrimental to Lincoln's well-being?

I responded as follows:

> Based on the draft reports presented to Lincoln, I believe the results will indicate Lincoln fails to meet the minimum net worth requirements as determined by the FHLBB staff. I don't believe the facts and circumstances will, if objectively viewed, support such a conclusion. Thus, the final report will in all likelihood be detrimental and inappropriately so. This is not to say that Lincoln could not, or should not, improve certain of its internal procedures. But based solely on my personal observations to date, the final report can be expected to be unduly harsh.

Before writing this response, I made a series of calculations to adjust the findings in the FHLBB's draft reports for mechanical errors as well as the various assertions Lincoln had made, and was making, regarding the inappropriateness of certain appraisals. The results of these calculations indicated that Lincoln did meet its minimum net-worth requirement. The basic adjustments to the FHLBB's findings provided for the effects of income taxes on the various adjustments and reserves requested by the FHLBB. Even the examiners admitted that the failure to take into account income-tax effects was wrong, yet in their draft reports (and ultimately their final report) they failed to do so.

Another basic adjustment was simply to eliminate double counting between their various classification categories. For example, assume an appraisal indicates that the market value of the collateral for a $10-million loan is only $8 million. The examiners required a reserve of $2 million, the difference between the loan amount and the appraised value of the collateral. If the appraisal was accurate, Lincoln could lose only $2 million on the loan. But in Lincoln's case, the examiners went one step farther. They classified the remaining $8 million as substandard, increasing Lincoln's net-worth requirement by an additional $800,000, an amount equal to 10 percent of the substandard classification. By so doing, they were requiring Lincoln to set aside $2,800,000 for a loss that they themselves didn't believe would exceed $2 million. This double counting was done in several instances.

In the January 27, 1987, meeting with the FHLBB, this result was pointed out to the examiners, and their attitude was, "So what? We see the problem, but we aren't going to do anything about it." The "so what" is that the double counting unfairly affected their determination of Lincoln's net-worth requirement—and the FHLBB knew it did.

My calculations indicated that Lincoln met its net-worth requirement after making the adjustments discussed above. But an even more significant factor was the appraisal losses on the two hotels—the Crescent and Phoenician. The FHLBB was asserting that these properties should be written down by a total of about $85 million. Lincoln provided evidence showing that the underlying appraisals were seriously flawed and, therefore, useless. Of equal importance, the hotels were not investments or loans; therefore, they did not fall under the appraisal regulations. These were operating assets, analogous to a branch office building; as such, their cost was to be charged to earnings via normal annual depreciation charges. Lincoln was adamant that the FHLBB was wrong in indicating appraisal losses on the hotel properties.

So, there were plenty of reasons to conclude that the FHLBB's final report would be unduly and inappropriately harsh. The results indicated in the draft reports were simply erroneous, and the FHLBB knew, or should have known, that was the case. But that did not deter the FHLBB from putting forth these faulty results in both their draft and final reports.

The letters didn't ask the senators to do anything on Lincoln's behalf.

Nor in the meetings with the three senators were they asked to do anything, except to consider Lincoln's situation vis-à-vis the FHLBB and to provide Lincoln and ACC with their counsel and advice.

On March 20, 1987, Lincoln filed a "Petition for the Recusal or Disqualification of Chairman Edwin J. Gray" with the secretary of the Federal Home Loan Bank Board. The petition essentially requested that Gray remove himself from participating in any deliberation or decision by the Board or by the FSLIC involving Lincoln. The petition cited, as the basis for the requested action, numerous examples which had appeared in the press over several years. Lincoln said that the articles documented Gray's "personal bias and enmity toward Lincoln and Charles H Keating, Jr." The petition further stated that Lincoln believed, and it could establish, that Gray had "specifically prejudged such crucial issues as whether Lincoln's investment practices are 'unsafe and unsound' under federal law." Lincoln also asked the Board, if the request for disqualification were denied, to permit "discovery and conduct an evidentiary hearing on an expedited basis for the purpose of exploring the extent of Gray's bias and prejudgment toward Lincoln."

The one area cited in the petition which perhaps upset Gray the most involved press articles accusing Gray of unethical and potentially illegal conduct regarding the payment of his travel and related expenses. The *Washington Post*, in its December 8, 1986, edition, carried an article on the subject, entitled "Bank Board Lived Well off S&Ls: Industry Picked up Tab for Cruises, Gifts, Alcohol, Limosines," which recounted many of the alleged improprieties. A February 23, 1987, article in *Barron's*, entitled "War on the Bank Board," contained the following:

> The fight between Keating and Gray is linked to the furor surrounding the chairman's expenses. Word that the regional Home Loan Banks had been picking up the tab for Gray began filtering out several months ago. And though Gray has refused to grant interviews, those close to him say he believes Keating leaked those reports. Recently released records show that his spending practices raised questions as far back as his first days on the board in 1983, when he submitted a travel voucher to be reimbursed for air fare from San Diego to Washington to begin work. Despite regulations stating that it is the employee's responsibility to get to his duty assignment, the board approved the voucher. After revelations about Gray's expenses surfaced some weeks ago, he repaid nearly $12,000 in bills run up by his wife, including beauty-parlor appointments.

The March 6, 1987, edition of the *American Banker* contained an article, entitled "Bank Board Is Rebuked on Expenses," which said :

Federal Home Loan Bank Board members and their staff never had any legal basis for accepting millions of dollars in travel and lodging expenses from the agency's 12 district banks, according to the General Accounting Office, the watchdog arm of Congress.

"It is our view that neither the board nor its officers and employees have the legal authority to accept payment or reimbursement from banks for the travel-related administrative expenses of board personnel," GAO general counsel Milton J. Socolar wrote in a letter to Rep. Edward P. Boland, D-Mass., chairman of the House Appropriations subcommittee on independent agencies.

Such expenses must be paid by the board, using its own funds . . . subject to any limitation on the board's administrative expenses contained in the annual appropriation act.

The bank Board staff ran up millions of dollars in transportation and lodging bills between 1984 and 1986 while attending district bank meetings, according to expense records. The banks paid or subsidized many of the expenses, both directly and through a shared expense fund.

"Bank Board Chairman Edwin J. Gray alone accounted for $327,697 of the expenses," he said. . . .

Gray's expense-account troubles led not only to an internal ethics investigation by the FHLBB, but the Justice Department was also called in to look into the situation. Keating denies that he ever had anything to do with reporting Gray's expense problems. If the payments came from the district banks, how would Charlie Keating ever have gotten the information? He wasn't exactly on close terms with any of the district banks. But Gray believed Charlie was responsible for his problems, and that's what counts in this saga.

Apparently, for several months in early 1987, a combination of Charlie, Kielty, and Grogan had conversations with various of the five senators, asking them if they could find out from Ed Gray what the status of the examination was and when it was going to conclude. And there may have been some conversations among some of the senators as what to do about these requests. I was unaware that any such conversations had occurred, or would occur, when I met with the senators or when I wrote the letters.

I did watch the Senate Ethics Committee hearings regarding the so-called "Keating Five," but even in those proceedings, absent the testimony of Charlie Keating, the record is very confused as to who said what, to whom, and when. Some of the senators had pretty porous memories, and their recollections, the assertions of the committee's special counsel, and the testimony of the other witnesses were inconsistent and, in my mind, inconclusive as to what actually happened and when it happened.

In any event, the record does indicate that on the evening of April 2, 1987, Gray was asked to stop in DeConcini's office where Senators Cranston, Glenn, and McCain were also present. Apparently, there was some discussion of the examination, the direct-investment issue, Lincoln's suit against the FHLBB challenging the regulations, and other matters. Gray apparently indicated that he was not the appropriate person to talk to about the exam; instead, Gray told the senators they should talk to Jim Cirona, who was president of the San Francisco bank.

In congressional testimony, Gray said that he told the senators, in response to a question about why the exam was taking so long:

I said I didn't know. I said the most that I knew was that in the fall of 1986 I had received a report from the principal supervisory agent in San Francisco which said that the reason the examination was going on longer than normal was because Lincoln was not being cooperative with the examiners. What the situation was since then, I said, I didn't know, but that I had full confidence in the regulators in San Francisco, and I said there had to be a good reason for the length of the examination, or it would have been finished by then.

Gray further testified:

I said, in response, that I was responsible for the regulation of some 3,000 thrift institutions across the country and that I shouldn't be expected to have instant knowledge of any one institution, even if it was Lincoln. Further, I said that in my view it would be unseemly for me to have particularly unusual knowledge about this institution or how it was being regulated, given the repeated statements of their friend [Charlie] that I had a personal vendetta against Lincoln. I said this was, of course, false.

One certainly has to wonder about Gray's truthfulness. We know that Washington, which had absolutely no jurisdiction over Lincoln, had been getting materials regarding Lincoln from San Francisco for months, if not years. Sanchez had sent Smuzynski a report that consisted of over two hundred pages, much of which dealt with the direct-investment issue—the issue that was personal to Ed Gray. Why was so much information being sent to Smuzynski, Black, Stewart, Hershkowitz, and others? Is it credible to believe that the information was never discussed with Gray—that he didn't read Sanchez' report? After all, Lincoln was "the" institution that had challenged him over the direct-investment regulations and was "the" institution that he blamed for the congressional opposition to those regulations.

Gray knew about Lincoln's direct-investment situation, because he and Black had discussed it after Henkel made his proposal. If Lincoln wasn't an issue, how did Black know Henkel's proposal would benefit Lincoln, and why did he bring it to Gray's attention? It was the cause of Henkel's resignation from the FHLBB. Wouldn't Gray have logically followed the Henkel investigation and been prepared to respond to questions about the Henkel/Lincoln connection?

There were scores of press articles referring to disputes between Gray and Keating. The press attributed remarks to Gray that accused Charlie of creating his expense-account problems—a problem which resulted in Gray having to repay thousands of dollars. Just a few days before this meeting, Lincoln had filed the petition for recusal, thoroughly blasting Gray and accusing him of improper conduct.

Then, there is this April 2 meeting. If you knew that Charlie Keating and ACC were in Arizona, and you were asked by a senator from Arizona to attend a meeting, would you have asked some questions about Lincoln before you went to the meeting? If you also knew that the examination was one of the longest in the FHLBB's history, if not the longest, and was very controversial, might not you have fended off questions by pleading ignorance of the subject and shifting the focus to San Francisco, while you bought some time to figure out how to answer the tough questions? Is this what Ed Gray and the regulators did?

Is it credible, given all these circumstances and all the publicity about the dispute between Gray and Keating, that Gray would be as disinterested in Lincoln's affairs as he told these senators? All the information was in the hands of his own staff. Lincoln had to be a hot topic in the hallways of the FHLBB. It simply does not seem possible that Gray did not, indeed, know a great deal about Lincoln—as "unseemly" as it might be.

Pursuant to Gray's suggestion, arrangements were made, apparently between DeConcini, or his office, and Cirona, for the Eleventh District examiners to meet with the senators on April 9, 1987, to discuss the examination. The examiners who attended were Cirona, Michael Patriarca, Richard Sanchez, and William Black. Patriarca was the director of agency functions for the Eleventh District. Black had just become or was about to become, the general counsel for the Eleventh District. Black had been with the FHLBB in Washington in the litigation area prior to going to San Francisco. Since Black's title at the time of the meeting was still apparently deputy director, FSLIC, his real duties at that time were still in Washington, where he reported to Ed Gray.

During the April 9 meeting, Black was apparently the only person who took notes. After the meeting, he converted his notes into a report to Gray which took the form of a transcript of the meeting. In the memorandum, Black acknowledges that his notes were not verbatim, but he indicates they were extensive. He says that he used the notes and his independent recall to write the memorandum. It's unfortunate that there is no true transcript of the meeting or that none of the senators took notes, because, in the absence of any other evidence, Black's memorandum is the only record of the meeting. The various senators have been forced to accept Black's record of what transpired at the meeting.

Black's attendance adds to the speculation about the truthfulness of what Ed Gray told the senators. The San Francisco regulators said that they directed all aspects of the exam and didn't receive any instructions from Gray or Washington. Yet, Black attended the meeting and appeared to be knowledgeable about the exam. Black's answers to some questions were specific as to Lincoln's condition, and he voiced strong opinions on other subjects. If Black and Washington were not deeply involved in the exam, how did he come to have this information and the opinions he expressed? His title indicated he was still in Washington at the time of the meeting. His notes on the meeting were directed to Ed Gray. Why? It simply doesn't add up. If Black was informed about Lincoln, was Gray as much in the dark about the exam as he has said he was? If Black knew about Lincoln, it seems logical that Gray also had to have had specific knowledge.

The Black memorandum has been published in many places and was extensively discussed in various hearings and proceedings. I don't intend to repeat all of it here. But it is useful to consider some of the questions and comments made in the meeting in order to see whether the regulators were playing it straight with the senators.

First, consider how the regulators described their backgrounds to the senators:

PATRIARCA BY CIRONA: Mike has joined us recently from the Comptroller of the Currency, where he was in charge of multi-national banks. Before that he was a lawyer for seven years.

BLACK BY CIRONA: Also with me is Bill Black, our general counsel. Bill was formerly director of litigation for the Bank Board for three years.

SANCHEZ BY CIRONA: He's been with the San Francisco Bank for __ years. Before that he was an auditor for a commercial bank and before that he was in school.

The backgrounds of these three people are telling. Neither Patriarca nor Sanchez, the two people in the group most directly responsible for the Lincoln exam, had had any real prior experience with savings and loans. Their experience had been with banks. While their experience with banks may be analogous to working with S&Ls, it is by no means the same. There are major, critical differences between the two types of financial institutions. The rules they lived under, at that time, were simply not the same. This is one of the problems Lincoln was concerned about throughout the exam. The regulators didn't understand their own regulations and were holding Lincoln to standards which didn't exist in the written regulations, at least not as Lincoln and its counsel read the regulations.

Black's introduction was interesting. It gives the impression that

Black had been in San Francisco for some period of time. There was no indication that he still was in Washington and reported to Gray. What might the senators have concluded, or asked, if they had been told that Black had ties to Washington and Ed Gray? Would they have taken his later comments differently? One can only speculate.

In their opening comments to the regulators, the various senators made it clear that their purpose was not to seek any favors or special treatment for Lincoln. Some excerpts demonstrate this attitude taken by the senators. For example:

McCAIN: I wouldn't want any special favors for them.

McCAIN: I don't want any part of our conversation to be improper. We asked Chairman Gray about that and he said it wasn't improper to discuss Lincoln.

GLENN: To be blunt, you should charge them or get off their backs. If things are bad there, get to them.

RIEGLE: The appearance from a distance is that this thing is out of control and has become a struggle between Keating and Gray, two people I gather who have never even met. The appearance is that it's a fight to a death. This discredits everyone if it becomes the perception. If there are fundamental problems at Lincoln, OK.

GLENN: I'm not trying to get anyone off. If there is wrongdoing I'm on your side. But I don't want any unfairness against a viable entity.

The first real issue discussed was the use of appraisals. The issue was posed to Sanchez, and the following dialogue ensued.

SANCHEZ: An appraisal is an important part of underwriting. It is very important. If you don't do it right you expose yourself to loss. Our 1984 exam showed significant appraisal deficiencies. Mr. Keating promised to correct the problem. Our 1986 exam showed that the problems had not been corrected—that there were huge appraisal problems. There was no meaningful underwriting on most loans. We have independent appraisals. Merrill Lynch appraised the Phoenician. It shows a significant loss. Other loans had similar losses.

DeCONCINI: Why not get an independent appraisal?

SANCHEZ: We did.

DeCONCINI: No, you hired them. Why not get a truly independent one or use arbitration—if you're trying to bend over backwards to be fair. There's no appeal from your reappraisal. Whatever it is you take it.

SANCHEZ: If it meets our appraisal standards.

CIRONA: The Phoenician reappraisal process is not complete. We have received Lincoln's rebuttal and forwarded it to our independent appraisers.

There are some interesting things omitted from Sanchez' answer on the appraisal issues. First, he could have said that Lincoln disagreed with virtually every appraisal and had submitted specific reasons for such disagreement. Second, he could have said that the one appraisal most strongly contested was the one on the Phoenician, including Lincoln's specific concerns regarding the competency of the Merrill Lynch appraiser. Lastly, Cirona could have said that the independent appraiser, to whom Lincoln's rebuttal was forwarded, was Merrill Lynch, the very same appraiser Lincoln objected to so vigorously.

Right after Cirona's comment, the senators left the room for a vote. When they returned, the examiners chose to avoid the sticky issue of appraisals and shifted gears.

SANCHEZ: Lincoln had underwriting problems with all of their investments, equity securities, debt securities, land loans and direct real estate investments. It had no underwriting manual in effect when we began our 1986 exam. When the examiners requested such a manual they were informed that it was being printed. The examiners looked at 52 real estate loans that Lincoln had made since the 1984 exam. There were no credit reports on the borrowers in all 52 of the loan files.

DECONCINI: I have trouble with this discussion. Are you saying that their underwriting practices were illegal or just not the best practice?

CIRONA: Their underwriting practices violate our regulatory guidelines.

BLACK: They are also an unsafe and unsound practice.

DECONCINI: Those are two very different things.

SANCHEZ: You need credit reports for proper underwriting.

RIEGLE: To recap what's been said for Senator Glenn (who had just returned to the room): 52 of the 52 loans they looked at had no credit information. Do we have a history of loans to folks with inadequate credit?

SANCHEZ: $47 million in loans were classified by the examiners due to lack of adequate credit to assure repayment of the loans.

GLENN: How long had these loans been on the books?

SANCHEZ: A fairly long time.

GLENN: How many loans have gone belly-up?

SANCHEZ: We don't know at this point how many of the 52 loans have defaulted. These loans generally have interest reserves.

GLENN: Well, the interest reserves should run out on many of these.

CIRONA: These are longer term investments.

BLACK: I know that Lincoln has refinanced some of these loans.

RIEGLE: Where's the smoking gun? Where are the losses?

Again, the regulators conveniently failed to tell the senators that Lincoln disputed the contention that there was no evidence of credit analysis in the loan files. Lincoln admitted that it was not in the form the examiners wanted but strongly argued that adequate credit checks had been performed. For example, Lincoln made multiple loans to many borrowers. In these instances, the credit information was contained in the file for the initial loan and was not duplicated in all the other loan files. The examiners considered it a deficiency if there wasn't credit information in each and every loan file.

The regulators also didn't answer the questions regarding the existence of losses. Sanchez cleverly mentioned that $47 million in loans had been classified. But he didn't say that Lincoln refuted the classifications and had provided information which indicated the examiners' analyses regarding specific borrowers' credit had overlooked significant facts. The regulators couldn't be specific about losses because they didn't know that any existed. And they sure didn't volunteer that Lincoln's investment returns had, in fact, been very profitable.

Black's comments were especially interesting. He trotted out the regulators' favorite standby, the old "unsafe and unsound" argument. But the senators didn't appear to take the bait. He also said, "I know that Lincoln has refinanced some of these loans."

How did he know that? Neither Sanchez nor Patriarca seemed to pick up on the point, and they were the closest to the examination. Was it a red herring, or was Washington more closely involved in the examination than they had ever admitted? And if there had been refinancings, was there anything improper about Lincoln having done so? Black certainly looked like he was trying to get the senators off the subject of actual losses.

The discussion then turned briefly to Lincoln's historical performance.

RIEGLE: These people saved a failing thrift. ACC is reputed to be highly competent.

BLACK: Lincoln was not a failing thrift when ACC acquired it. It met its net worth requirement. It had returned to profitability before it was acquired. It had one of the lowest ratios of scheduled items in the 11th District, the area under our jurisdiction. Its losses were caused by an interest spread problem from high interest rates. It, as with most other California thrifts, would have become profitable as interest rates fall.

DeCONCINI: I don't know how you can't consider it a success story. It lost $24 million in 1982 and 1983. After it was acquired by ACC it made $49 million in one year.

While Black seemed to know Lincoln's ratio of scheduled items, a rather arcane statistic, he apparently didn't know its operating history or that it was only profitable because it had sold its better branches to cover operating losses. He also apparently hadn't read the correspondence which warned Lincoln that it would deplete its net worth in only twelve months if it couldn't generate profits. It looks like he tried to throw a fastball past the senators, but DeConcini wouldn't fall for the pitch.

McCain then returned to the primary issue of the length of the examination.

McCAIN: I haven't gotten an answer to my question about why the exam took so long.

SANCHEZ: It was an extremely complex exam because of their various investments. The examiners were actually in the institution from March to October—8 months. The asset classification procedure is very time consuming.

McCAIN: What's the longest exam you ever had before?

CIRONA: Some have technically never ended, where we had severe problems with a shop.

McCAIN: Why would Arthur Young say these things about the exam—that it was inordinately long and bordered on harassment.

GLENN: And Arthur Andersen said they withdrew as Lincoln's prior auditor because of your harassment.

RIEGLE: Have you seen the Arthur Young letter?

CIRONA: No.

At this point, Cirona was given a copy of the letter to read. The answers to McCain's question about the length of the exam were not responsive. The regulators could have provided a brief chronology about the examination activities. But to have done so would have revealed things that they probably wanted left unsaid. They wouldn't have wanted to explain why the field examiners left, only to return. They wouldn't have wanted to talk about the outside help they needed from consultants, lawyers, and accountants.

A candid chronology would also have disclosed the massive effort of copying Lincoln's records and would have again raised the whole subject of appraisals. It was probably easier for them to brush the question off and hope that the senators wouldn't return to it later.

While Cirona was apparently reading the letter that I had sent to the senators, Patriarca made some provocative comments.

PATRIARCA: I'm relatively new to the savings and loan industry but I've never seen any bank or S&L that's anything like this. This isn't even close. You can ask any banker and you know about these practices. They violate the law and the regulations and common sense.

GLENN: What violates the law?

PATRIARCA: Their direct investments violate the regulation. Then there's the file stuffing. They took undated documents purporting to show underwriting efforts and put them into the files sometimes more than a year after they made the investment.

GLENN: Have you done anything about these violations of law?

PATRIARCA: We're sending a criminal referral to the Department of Justice. Not maybe; we're sending one. This is an extraordinarily serious matter. It involves a whole range of imprudent actions. I can't tell you strongly enough how serious this is. This is not a profitable institution. Prior year adjustments will reduce that reported $49 million profit. They didn't earn $49 million. Let me give you one example. Lincoln sold a loan with recourse and booked a $12 million profit. The purchaser rescinded the sale, but Lincoln left the $12 million profit on its books. Now, I don't care how many accountants they get to say that's right. It's wrong. The only thing we have as regulators is our credibility. We have to preserve it.

DeConcini: Why would Arthur Young say these things? They have to guard their credibility too. They put the firm's neck out with this letter.

Patriarca: They have a client. The $12 million in earnings was not unwound.

DeConcini: You believe they'd prostitute themselves for a client?

Patriarca: Absolutely. It happens all the time.

At this point, the senators had to leave the meeting for a vote. Look closer at what Patriarca said and didn't say. He started off by saying that he was new to the S&L industry. He then made the sweeping statement that he had never seen any bank or S&L like Lincoln. That's understandable. Being new to S&Ls, he wouldn't have seen many S&Ls of any kind—like Lincoln or otherwise. And banks are not like any S&Ls. They conduct very different businesses and are governed by different rules and regulations, especially after the S&Ls were deregulated by Garn-St. Germain and state laws, like California's Nolan Bill.

That was part of the problem. Regulators like Patriarca didn't understand the distinctions between the banks that they had prior experience with and the institutions they were now regulating. They constantly made comments like "if this was a bank." But S&Ls weren't banks. Big differences existed between the kinds of transactions that S&Ls were permitted to do under the law and what the new regulators thought they could or should be able to do.

He said that Lincoln had violated the direct-investment regulations. He didn't say that Lincoln had a suit pending against the FHLBB regarding these same regulations. Nor did he say that Lincoln vehemently disagreed with the regulators' interpretation and application of the regulations. He made the issue sound cut and dried. It was anything but that.

The file stuffing and criminal referral discussion was an interesting gambit. The San Francisco people had known almost from the start of the examination that Lincoln had placed undated documents and loan and investment summaries in their files. Judy had discussed this with Kotrys. An Arthur Andersen partner had discussed it directly with people in San Francisco. The addition of materials to the various files was no secret or mystery.

Since the regulators knew about what Patriarca called "file stuffing," and accepting his comment that such activities were "an extraordinarily serious matter," why did it take so long to make the criminal referrals? Why didn't the regulators contact the Department of Justice as soon as they discovered what had happened? After all, they had been done with their fieldwork since October 1986—six months prior to this meeting. Surely, they had known about the file-stuffing activities at least since the conclusion of the fieldwork.

A skeptic might be inclined to believe that the idea of criminal referrals was hatched just prior to the meeting with the senators. In fact, in a recently published book on the S&L industry, the author asserts that the regulators decided to make the referrals during a brainstorming session that occurred just a few hours before this meeting. It was a hell of a good way to stop the senators in their tracks. Not even a senator is going to venture into areas where criminal activity is alleged. The comments regarding criminal referrals definitely put a chill on the senators' curiosity.

Apparently, the FHLBB did make the criminal referrals regarding file stuffing. What choice did they have after Patriarca's comments to the senators? The Department of Justice did not elect to pursue the matter. Later, the enforcement arm of the FHLBB conducted a series of depositions which looked into the issue, but, to my knowledge, nothing ever came of this matter.

With respect to the sale of "a loan with recourse," the facts are different from what Patriarca described. This was the sale of the pool of loans totaling well over $100 million to San Jacinto Savings. As you will recall, at the same time, Lincoln purchased a pool of loans with dissimilar characteristics from the other institution. Such reciprocal purchases and sales were rather common in the industry. The agreements provided that loans could be returned if the loan documentation was not as represented.

Arthur Andersen examined the transaction when it occurred in 1985 and concurred with Lincoln that sale treatment was appropriate under the circumstances. A gain of about $12 million was recorded by Lincoln. In 1986, Lincoln found that the documentation on the loans it had purchased was not satisfactory and demanded that acceptable loans be substituted, or it wanted its purchase money returned. This started a dispute between the two S&Ls which resulted in each party returning the loans each had previously purchased.

When Lincoln got the loans back, they were almost immediately sold to another party at slightly more than Lincoln had received in the original transaction. Under the applicable accounting literature, the repurchase in 1986, and the subsequent resale, were events which were independent of the 1985 sale. There was no need to reverse any previously recorded profits. Lincoln's profits at the end of all of these events exceeded the amounts recorded in 1985. Patriarca's recitation of the transaction left a little to be desired and omitted pertinent facts.

Finally, there is the subject of the letter that I sent to the senators. The fact that the senators had to break for a few minutes was convenient for the regulators. It gave them some time to figure out how to deal with the letter. They had several options. First, they could respond to each of the issues in the letter and provide their rebuttals. This could be difficult, because the letter basically recited events which had happened, and believable counterarguments would be hard to present. Second, they could say that they weren't prepared to respond at that time. They needed to study the contents of the letter. But the senators, who wanted answers, probably wouldn't buy that tactic. Third, they could attack the credibility of the writer of the letter. That's the approach they used.

CIRONA: I also wanted to note that the Bank Board has had a lot of problems with Arthur Young, and is thinking of taking disciplinary action against it.

BLACK: Not for actions here. Primarily because of its Texas office, which has never met a direct investment. They think everything is a loan. This has quite an effect on the income you can claim.

Empire of Texas is a perfect example. It did acquisition, development and construction loans that were really direct investments because the borrowers had no equity in the projects. It booked all the points and fees up front as income. It created interest reserves so the loans couldn't go into default. It provided take out financing and then end loans so the loans couldn't go into default for many years. All this led it to report record profits. Even when the losses started, as long as it grew fast enough and could book new income up front it could remain "profitable." It gets to be kind of a pyramid scheme with rapid growth. Lincoln has grown very rapidly.

Many Congressional hearings have been very critical of the Bank Board for not acting more quickly against unsafe and unsound practices. Rep. Dingell our . . . our . . . I grew up in the 16th District. His hearings were very critical about Beverly Hills [Savings], which had a clean accounting opinion, and then, at last count, is over $900 million insolvent.

Then there was Sunrise [Savings], also with a clean opinion and it is expected to cost FSLIC over $500 million. And Congressman Barnard's hearing was very critical there.

CIRONA: Also San Marino.

BLACK: Yes. I can tell you from my experience as former litigation director, where I sued many of these failed shops, that it is routine for the accounting firm to serve as management's expert witness and adopt an extremely adversarial tone.

Black's performance, with supporting roles by Cirona and Patriarca, seemed to work. It's too bad the senators didn't know that the histories of the other institutions that were cited were completely irrelevant to the matter of the Lincoln exam. I wrote the letter to the senators, and I certainly had never had any association with any of the institutions cited, and I don't believe that Arthur Young had either. Black appeared to have but one purpose—to discredit the letter and Lincoln by trying to tie them to completely unrelated situations.

The discussion then returned to more relevant matters. The examiners escaped from having to address the specific issues in the letter.

SANCHEZ: Our exam has found that $— million has to be written off Lincoln's books. That will leave them with a regulatory net worth of $25 million. They will fail to meet their net worth requirement. They have $103 million of goodwill on their books. If this were backed out they would be $78 million insolvent.

PATRIARCA: They would be taken over by the regulators if they were a bank.

DECONCINI: You're saying they're insolvent.

BLACK: They'd be insolvent on a tangible capital basis, which is basically the capital standard for banks.

DECONCINI: They'd be insolvent if they were a bank, but by law you have to use a regulatory capital standard, and under that standard they have $25 million in capital. Is that what you're saying?

Once again the regulators tried to confuse the issue by referring to regulations which apply only to commercial banks—not to savings and loans. The concept of "tangible net worth," and the subtracting of goodwill, simply didn't apply to Lincoln or any other S&L. DeConcini seemed to pick up on this and asked for clarification, at which point the regulators avoided the subject.

PATRIARCA: By regulation we have adopted a regulatory capital standard.

DECONCINI: And you'll take control of them if they fail your net worth standard— you'll take operational control of them.

CIRONA: That's speculative. We'd take steps to reduce their risk exposure.

RIEGLE: What would you require them to sell?

CIRONA: We'd probably have them decrease their growth. Time and again we've found rapid growth associated with loss. Lincoln has grown rapidly.

BLACK: Are you sure you want to talk about this? We haven't made any recommendation to the Bank Board yet. The Bank Board decides what action to take. These are very confidential matters.

DeCONCINI: No, then we don't want to go into it. We were just asking very hypothetically and that's how you were responding.

CIRONA: That's right.

DeCONCINI: Can we do something other than liquidate them?

CIRONA: I hesitate to tell an association what to do. We're not in control of Lincoln, and won't be. We want to work the problem out.

McCAIN: Have they tried to work it out?

CIRONA: We've met with them numerous times. I've never seen such cantankerous behavior. At one point they said our examiners couldn't get any association documents unless they made the request through Lincoln's New York litigation counsel.

RIEGLE: Well, that does disturb me—when you have to go through New York litigation counsel. What could they do? Is it too late?

The regulators backed off the talk of taking Lincoln over because they saw that DeConcini recognized the difference between the regulatory capital requirements of banks and S&Ls. They shifted to a more moderate stance of working with Lincoln to reduce risk. But Black didn't want to go far in this direction, either. Moderation would make it more difficult to recommend strong punitive action against Lincoln. So, he kind of cooled the discussion with the suggestion that all of a sudden everything was very confidential.

Cirona was able to get in a neat point. I'm not aware that any of the regulators present, other than Sanchez, had met with Lincoln in connection with the exam. The implication that all the top regulators had met with Lincoln to "work things out" was a nice touch—it just wasn't accurate. As I recall, ACC's and Lincoln's top people had met Cirona only once or twice and not in regard to the exam. Yet his remark, "I've never seen such cantankerous behavior," would lead one to believe that he had met often with Lincoln.

The bit about the New York litigation counsel was also shifty. Cirona could have said that the Kaye Scholer lawyer was in Irvine, but that wouldn't have had the effect that omitting that small detail had on the

senators, especially Riegle, who bought the idea completely.
We finally get to the question which had brought everyone together.

DeConcini: How long will it take you to finish the exam?

Patriarca: Ten days.

The examination report was issued on April 20, 1987. This was one of the few straight answers given by the examiners during the entire meeting. If the meeting had not been held, and DeConcini hadn't asked the question, there is no telling how long the exam might have continued. Patriarca's answer finally set a deadline for ending the exam.

There were a few questions about what the senators could or could not say to Lincoln about what was discussed in the meeting. It was left that if Lincoln wanted to know anything, Lincoln should call the regulators. The senators were advised not to say anything, except that the exam would be completed in about ten days.

Then there is this last bit of discussion. It is illuminating with respect to the use of outside parties other than appraisers.

Riegle: Is this institution so far gone that it can't be salvaged?

Patriarca: I don't know. They've got enough risky assets on their books that a little bad luck could nail them. You can't remove the risk of what they already have. You can reduce what new risks they would otherwise add on.

Black: They have huge holdings in Tucson and Phoenix. The market there can't absorb them for many years. You said earlier that ACC was extremely good but ACC has gotten out of its former primary activity, homebuilding. I'm not saying they're bad businessmen but they had to get out of one homebuilding market after another. They had to get out of Colorado when they had bad models and soil problems. They also had to get out of their second leading activity, mortgage banking. They're now down to Arizona.

That's not a bad market but no one knows how well it will do over the many years that it would take to absorb such huge holdings in Tucson and Phoenix.

DeConcini: So you don't know what you'd do with the property even if you took them over?

Black: Bill Black doesn't. Bill Black is a lawyer. We hire experts to do this work. Our study of their Arizona holdings was done by top experts. Our study of below investment grade corporate debt securities—what folks usually call junk bonds, but I avoid it because I don't know where you stand on such bonds—was done by top outside experts. I see in this Arthur Young letter that they criticize us for having an accountant with "only" eight years experience. Well, I think . . . I don't see how you can claim eight years as inexperienced. But we didn't simply rely on him. We had . . . wasn't it Kenneth. . . .

SANCHEZ: Yes. Kenneth Laventhol [*sic*].

BLACK: We had Kenneth Laventhol, outside accountants, work on this. These are also some of the reasons the exam took time.

Kenneth Leventhal is an accounting firm known for specializing in the real-estate industry. Many of their clients in 1986 and 1987 were home builders, land and commercial real estate developers, real-estate syndicators, mortgage bankers, and property-management companies. Their practice included auditing, but they were probably stronger in the tax and real-estate consulting practice areas. They were not considered a significant factor in serving as auditors for savings and loans, certainly not the larger, publicly held institutions.

At some point in time, I can't recall whether it was before this meeting or not, the FHLBB asked Lincoln if Kenneth Leventhal could come into Lincoln to conduct some tests for the FHLBB. Charlie and Judy went ballistic. They told me that there was not another professional firm, of any kind, whom they trusted less or had less respect for than Kenneth Leventhal. There was no way that they would allow the Leventhal firm to have access to any of their records or any other information regarding either ACC or Lincoln.

When ACC was active in home building, it developed a program of financing home sales, known as the builder-bond program. Kenneth Leventhal was engaged by ACC to assist in certain aspects of this program. ACC was, according to Judy, protective of the details of the program, because it gave ACC some distinct advantages over ACC's competitors. Within a short time after it started the builder-bond program, ACC learned that some of its competitors in Tucson and Phoenix had banded together and were offering their own builder-bond program. The advisors and accountants for these competitors were members of the Kenneth Leventhal firm. Later, a partner in Kenneth Leventhal left the firm to head up a finance company formed by ACC's competitors. And the National Association of Home Builders, a client of Kenneth Leventhal, also promoted a similar program on a national basis.

Charlie and Judy were convinced that Kenneth Leventhal had taken ACC's valuable idea, which it was supposed to hold in strict confidence, and exploited the idea for its own benefit and to ACC's detriment. Charlie and Judy vowed that they would never have anything to do with the Leventhal firm again. They believed, and apparently with justification, that the firm could not be trusted with any important data or information which was supposed to remain confidential. From Lincoln's prospective, the FHLBB could not possibly have selected a more inappropriate firm with whom to discuss Lincoln's affairs. When Charlie and Judy learned that Kenneth Leventhal played a role in the exam (they learned this much later in time), they were appalled.

Lincoln also repeatedly asked the examiners whether they had consulted with any accounting firm. They were told "no" every time the question was asked.

The issue of the use of outside consultants and accountants is interesting from another standpoint. The law and regulations specifically provide that appraisals can be obtained in connection with the examination of an insured institution. I can find no permitted use of outside consultants, or any other outside parties, in either the law or the regulations. There are, in fact, sections in the regulations which specifically cite that the FHLBB is prohibited from divulging any information on an insured institution.

These sections were clearly designed to protect the member institutions from disclosure of the information that they were required to make available in connection with examinations. In Lincoln's case, the examiners provided public parties, namely, the accountants and consultants, with information that Lincoln had every right to expect would remain within the FHLBB structure. Kenneth Leventhal was among the public parties who received this information. I'm certain that Lincoln would have absolutely refused to make the information available to the examiners if it had known Leventhal would have access to any portion of it.

Aside from disclosing the existence of outside parties, Black's comments confirm that the use of these consultants contributed to the length of the examination. It also is conclusive evidence that the FHLBB didn't have the in-house expertise to deal with an institution of Lincoln's complexity. Which is what I said in my letter to the senators.

Finally, Lincoln would, and did, take strong exception to Black's characterization that the consultants used were "top experts." Lincoln believed that the reports prepared by these people were seriously deficient and therefore invalid.

The meeting with the senators ended with one last parting shot.

PATRIARCA: I think my colleague Mr. Black put it right when he said that it's like these guys put it all on 16 black in roulette. Maybe, they'll win, but I can guarantee you that if an institution continues such behavior it will eventually go bankrupt.

RIEGLE: Well, I guess that's pretty definitive.

The FHLBB would try its best to make Patriarca's prophecy come true.

The meeting could have been very brief if the regulators had said at the onset that "the exam will be done in ten days." That's all the senators really wanted to know. I've gone through this meeting in some detail because it later became a critical issue in the Senate Ethics Committee hearing. I've read Black's report of this meeting dozens of times. Each time, I see nothing wrong in the senators' conduct. There was no attempt to have the regulators do anything improper. There was no pressure placed on the regulators. Some of the questions may have been pointed, but only after the regulators tried to blow smoke at the senators.

The main accomplishment of the meeting was that the report finally got issued, and the 1986 exam appeared to have ended. A new stage in the war was about to begin.

Eight

Dirty Tricks and the Regulators' Report

On April 20, 1987, the FHLBB issued its long-awaited Report of Examination on Lincoln Savings and Loan Association. The examiners' findings were not a surprise to Lincoln or its attorneys. As a consequence of the various meetings that Lincoln's people had attended, and from the correspondence Lincoln had received from the examiners, Lincoln had anticipated most of the issues. None of Lincoln's rebuttals to the preliminary findings had influenced the examiners, and their conclusions remained unchanged from the positions they had articulated earlier.

Two of the major areas of the Report of Examination—direct-investment violations and accounting matters—contained the same findings that the examiners had previously disclosed to Lincoln. The response to the examination report that Lincoln filed with the FHLBB presented the same arguments discussed earlier. On both sets of issues, Lincoln continued to believe that the examiners were misinterpreting the regulations and the applicable accounting literature; therefore, the findings were without merit. Nonetheless, Lincoln supplied, once again, the factual evidence supporting its argument that all of the direct investments were properly grandfathered and that its various accounting treatments were appropriate under the circumstances.

The examiners' treatment of the Wolfswinkle loans, which was the most controversial accounting issue because of the reports by Arthur Andersen and Arthur Young, is typical of the treatment they afforded direct investments and the other accounting matters. They asserted that the transactions should be accounted for as a real-estate joint venture rather than as loans, because they did not believe that the Wolfswinkle personal and corporate guarantees had substance. The Report of Examination stated: "Conley Wolfswinkle's guarantee is not of substance. . . . His financial statements show a negative net worth on an historical basis and a positive but illiquid net worth on a current fair market basis. The fair value of net worth consisted mainly of unrealized appraised equity in properties encumbered by debt. . . ."

The net worth of the Wolfswinkle Group, Inc., on a current-value basis, as set forth in financial statements which were audited by Arthur

Andersen, was $153.2 million on January 31, 1987. The personal net worth of Mr. Wolfswinkle, on a current-value basis, as set forth in financial statements reviewed by Arthur Andersen, was $170 million at January 31, 1987.

The examiners' comment expresses concern about the liquidity of each reported net worth. Both WGI and Mr. Wolfswinkle had a number of established lending relationships with financial institutions that were totally independent of Lincoln. The financial statements disclosed a capacity to service a substantial amount of additional debt, and both parties had a considerable amount of unencumbered collateral value available to support any added debt. Thus, while neither WGI nor Mr. Wolfswinkle was carrying substantial liquid assets, it appeared that if circumstances required greater liquidity, they could become liquid.

The examiners also indicated that when evaluating the substance of a guarantee, historical financial statements should have greater weight than current-value financial statements. The current values were based on appraisals. Lincoln argued that the examiners' position was inconsistent with the FHLBB's own insistence on requiring appraisals as a measure of the value of collateral. In effect, the examiners use appraisals when it suits their purpose but reject appraisals if they detract from the examiners' arguments. Lincoln's exact words were: "To calculate Wolfswinkle's net worth based on historical cost is absurd. It neither serves any logical purpose nor does it accurately measure the ability of the guarantor to perform."

The issue of the personal guarantee, and Wolfswinkle's ability to perform under it, is key to any determination of the proper accounting treatment for the subject loans. This is a determination which had to be made as of the date the transactions were entered into by Lincoln and the borrower. For the examiners to reject the conclusions of the two accounting firms, the FHLBB's assessment of Wolfswinkle's financial status should have been absolutely ironclad and beyond question. If there were any doubt about the strength of the financial capabilities of the borrower, the issue should have been conceded and resolved in Lincoln's favor. Based on comments made in various meetings, the examiners had substantial doubt about the position they had taken regarding the financial strength of Wolfswinkle, and their assessment was anything but ironclad.

The Report of Examination also presented the results of the examiners' appraisal efforts. The examiners were asking Lincoln to record loss reserves for the difference between the book values and the values shown in the appraisals for fifteen different properties or loans. The total amount of the requested reserves was $135 million.

Of the $135 million, $85 million related to the Phoenician Resort and the Crescent Hotel. These indicated losses were based on appraisals conducted by Merrill Lynch Capital Markets (MLCM). In a letter dated January 14, 1987, from Lincoln's outside counsel, Lincoln noted numerous deficiencies in the MLCM appraisals with respect to both hotels. After the issuance of the Report of Examination, the examiners finally acknowledged that the appraisal on the Phoenician was fundamentally flawed and ordered a new appraisal and withdrew the recommendation that a loss be recorded on the property.

With respect to the remaining properties, Lincoln did not contest the appraised losses on four properties which were located in Colorado. Lincoln also accepted the loss recommended for one of the loan transactions. Lincoln contested all the other losses. The response provided detailed information, which had previously been given to the examiners, as to why Lincoln and its consultants believed the examiners' appraisals were deficient. The deficiencies were varied, but the most common were the use of inappropriate comparable values in the appraisals; the use of unreasonably low demand, or absorption, studies; the failure to include water rights or other property interests in the appraised value; the failure to use the highest and best use or to use the proper zoning for the property; and the use of an improper rate when discounting estimated future cash flows from the property.

For financial-statement purposes, Lincoln's recorded allowances for potential losses exceeded the amount of the appraisal losses that it agreed were appropriate. Once the recommended losses associated with the hotels were no longer a factor, the remaining appraisal issues were not of great significance.

As indicated in the January 27 meeting, the examiners classified six loans as either substandard or loss. If an asset is deemed to be substandard, an institution must increase its required regulatory capital by an amount equal to 10 percent of the asset value that is so classified. If an asset is classified as loss, the institution must record a reserve on its books in the amount of the asset value so classified. The examiners classified a portion of three loans as loss. The loss amount was based on appraisals. The remainder of those three loans, as well as the entire outstanding balance of three other loans, an aggregate amount of about $39.6 million, was classified substandard. The substandard classification was based on the examiners' evaluation that these loans exhibited credit "weaknesses."

Lincoln asserted that the examiners were not following their own internal guidelines and the applicable regulations. The examiners classified a loan that they felt had any weakness. The regulations indicated that the weakness had to result in the "distinct possibility" that Lincoln would "sustain some loss if the deficiencies are not corrected."

In the case of the three loans where no appraisal loss was indicated, Lincoln argued that the collateral value was sufficient to provide adequate protection against loss. Moreover, Lincoln asserted that, in some of the cases, the examiners did not properly assess the borrower's ability and resources to repay the loan. Lincoln believed that there was ample evidence showing no losses were probable and, that in these instances, classification as substandard was not appropriate.

In regard to the three loans where appraisal losses were indicated by the examiners, Lincoln felt that the regulations were not being properly applied. Lincoln argued that if the appraisals were correct, and Lincoln was not necessarily conceding they were, then the difference between Lincoln's book value and the appraisal value (the amount the examiners classified as loss) was the most Lincoln could lose on the asset. Once that amount was recognized, the regulations required no further classification. Lincoln felt that the examiners were asking it to take a double hit on the asset by including the portion of the asset not deemed to be loss in the substandard category.

The findings in the Report of Examination relating to direct investments, appraisal losses, asset classifications, and accounting adjustments had an impact on the examiners' calculation of Lincoln's net worth. If the examiners' findings, including their computation of the proposed adjustments, were correct, Lincoln did not meet its regulatory capital requirement at September 30, 1986. This, in turn, provided the FHLBB with grounds for taking potentially severe regulatory action against Lincoln and its management. Absent a demonstrated net-worth deficiency, the FHLBB did not have an adequate foundation for taking any strong action against Lincoln. So, the findings, and their effect on the net-worth calculation, were of paramount importance to both Lincoln and the FHLBB.

The following table shows the examiners' calculation of Lincoln's net worth as adjusted for their findings. Since Lincoln argued that the proposed adjustments were not proper, the table also reflects Lincoln's net worth as Lincoln believed it should have been calculated. The table is presented in thousands of dollars.

	Examiners' Analysis	Corrected Analysis
Appraised losses	$(135,241)	$(23,335)
Capitalized interest and expenses	(16,288)	0
Joint-venture reclassification	(3,608)	0
Loan sale	(12,300)	0
Subtotal	(167,437)	(23,335)
Tax effect	0	11,667
After tax impact	(167,437)	(11,668)
Reported net worth	197,937	196,513
Adjusted net worth	30,500	184,845
Minimum requirement	(73,663)	(73,663)
Direct-investment adjustment	(59,995)	0
Substandard-loan adjustment	(7,919)	0
Excess (deficient) net worth	$(111,077)	$111,182

As the table demonstrates, the effect of the examiners' findings and proposed adjustments has a tremendous impact on the status of Lincoln's regulatory net worth. Note that the examiners did not remove the appraisal loss on the hotels in presenting this table, even though they had conceded that the appraisal was not, at this time, valid. This simply made the results in the table much worse than even the examiners believed they appropriately should have been.

Lincoln believed that virtually all of the examiners' findings were erroneous and that its true regulatory net worth exceeded the required level by over $111 million. The gap between the examiners and Lincoln was over $222 million. This gap quantifies the extent of the disagreements between the two parties. If the examiners were right in their findings, Lincoln was in serious trouble and faced strong regulatory consequences. If Lincoln prevailed in its arguments against the findings, it comfortably met its requirements and should be able to continue its strategies and operations free of regulatory interference.

The fact that every proposed adjustment was essentially the result of subjective opinions of or decisions by the examiners was particularly frustrating to Lincoln's management. When they saw the impact that these judgmental issues had, when reduced to numbers, they understood the power the examiners possessed. Literally, with the stroke of a pen, they had erased Lincoln's net worth. The animosity that, in Lincoln's opinion, the examiners had exhibited throughout the examination now took on new dimensions. Armed with their net-worth calculation, the examiners had set the stage to proceed against Lincoln's and ACC's management in an all-out assault. To survive, Lincoln would have to devote all its energies and resources to proving that the examiners' conclusions were erroneous or inappropriate under the existing regulatory laws.

The other findings in the Report of Examination didn't have an impact on the determination of Lincoln's regulatory net worth. Under normal circumstances, these findings would have been viewed merely as differences in investment philosophies. But, given the net-worth calculation in the Report, the other findings now had to be viewed more seriously. They represented additional ammunition that the FHLBB could use to discredit Lincoln and to claim Lincoln's operations were not safe and sound. These findings were a consequence of the examiners' assertions that Lincoln's investment practices involved unacceptable risks to the FSLIC insurance fund. They focused on several areas—securities investments, real-estate investments, and real-estate lending.

There were two sections of the Report which addressed Lincoln's securities investments. The first section focused on the examiners' perceptions of the risks inherent in the transactions. The second dealt with

Lincoln's underwriting practices and related records.

A number of transactions were cited by the examiners as examples of risk exposure that they considered to be "inordinate." The first two were the Gulf Broadcast Company and Crown Zellerbach, or GOSLP, investments. From the onset, Lincoln's objective in these transactions had been to gain control of two companies where its own analysis indicated substantially undervalued assets could be acquired and ultimately sold to others at a very substantial gain.

In the Gulf case, for example, the examiners said:

> Although the association made a substantial profit on this investment, it was a risky undertaking. Since Gulf paid no dividends, the association could receive a return on its investment only if the stock were undervalued by more than 30%. According to Valuline Investment Service, in an analysis written shortly after the association's purchase, the stock was recommended to ". . . speculative investors," and it was anticipated that the price would fall approximately 30% if the company were not sold. A decline of 30% would have dropped the price to approximately $10 per share from the $15 per share at the time of the analysis, or approximately $2 per share less than Lincoln's purchase price. Thus, the association was speculating on the sale of the company rather than investing based upon anticipated increase in earnings or other sound underwriting criteria.

The examiners' comments demonstrate their naïveté regarding equity transactions. Significant blocks of stock, especially ones which result in gaining control of a company, don't trade based on the market price for a single round lot. These blocks are often private transactions and, depending on the circumstances, are priced at a premium or discount. And while Valuline may be a useful tool to small investors, its analysis is not intended to be used in major block transactions. The examiners' analysis and related comments are simplistic and don't reflect either the complexities or the reality of the transactions they were attempting to critique.

Between 1986 and 1988, Lincoln, through its subsidiaries, participated in at least three other transactions with takeover connotations. All resulted in substantial gains. Lincoln had never engaged in a takeover-related transaction which produced a loss. Hence, Lincoln's track record in such transactions was extremely good and reflected its ability to identify appropriate targets of such transactions.

The examiners also cited Lincoln's investment in the Boesky-sponsored partnership as another example of "high risk" investing. Lincoln responded to the examiners by stating: "That investment (1) contained numerous covenants for Lincoln's protection, (2) was itself well diversified, and (3) was liquidated at a return of 9.2% to Lincoln."

Again, while the examiners perceived that the investment was unduly risky, Lincoln maintained its analysis was sufficient to provide reasonable assurance against the risk of loss. And in fact, even though the partnership had to be prematurely discontinued because of Boesky's personal problems, Lincoln suffered no loss.

The examiners cited a number of concerns that they had regarding Lincoln's underwriting and files related to its high-yield securities portfolio. The most interesting comment was: "The files for these investments did not contain adequate underwriting and financial analysis information. According to Mark Sauter, written analyses were prepared after investment decisions were made and the analyses provided to the examiners on investments in some 23 companies selected for detailed review were not used in the decision-making process."

This was the so-called file stuffing that Patriarca told the senators was the basis of criminal referrals. Sauter and the other Lincoln people maintained all along that they never set out to deceive the examiners. This is proof that their claims were, indeed, true. The examiners, in this report, acknowledged that they were told that the summaries and other materials had been added to the files after the fact. How can that be criminal? Who was misled?

The examiners go on to say that, because of the concerns they cited:

> . . . [T]wo independent consultants were contracted to evaluate the association's corporate securities investments. These consultants, Alan C. Shapiro and Mark I. Weinstein of the University of Southern California, and the valuation consulting firm of Houlihan, Lokey, Howard, and Zukin, Inc., produced conclusions that these securities investments exposed the association to inappropriately high levels of risk.

The examiners said that in their report, "Investment Practices of Lincoln Savings and Loan Association," Shapiro and Weinstein concluded:

> . . . [T]he association managers of Lincoln Savings and Loan Association are engaging in investment practices that expose the FSLIC to a level of risk that is, given the insurance fees charged, inappropriately high. This is accomplished by concentrating the corporate bond portfolio almost exclusively in below-investment-grade issues which have a high degree of credit risk and appear to be highly illiquid. Further, Lincoln fails to properly analyze these securities prior to purchase, fails to properly monitor the securities on an ongoing basis and fails to properly diversify the debt portfolio. In addition, there is evidence that Lincoln is investing in particular securities issued by firms that are engaged in merger contests and "risk arbitrage." These

conclusions are based on a comparison of Lincoln's management policies to both current academic thinking and standard practice in the investment industry.

The Houlihan report, entitled "Risk Analysis of Springfield Savings and Loan" ("Springfield" was used by the authors for internal security purposes), said:

The individual investments comprising the [Lincoln] portfolio are generally highly speculative issues which have probabilities of default, on average, many times greater than most New York Stock Exchange corporations.

The report also concluded, "Lincoln's portfolio is concentrated in a small number of issues and is not well diversified."

As might be expected, Lincoln countered the reports that were commissioned by the examiners with consultant reports of its own. These reports, of course, took exception to the reports submitted by the examiners.

The use of consultants, or so-called experts, is a common tactic of lawyers. The consultant provides support for the lawyer's argument by expressing opinions that, because of the consultant's academic or professional credentials, have an aura of high credibility. In reality, if the issue is one involving judgment or subjective measurement, a consultant can be found to support just about any position the lawyer wishes to take. The consultant's opinion is dependent only on the question asked and the degree to which related data can be skewed or interpreted. Because of the subjective nature of defining risk, as in the case at hand, any of the consultants could have demonstrated that Lincoln's investments were either risky or prudent. There was sufficient data and enough subjective variables to sustain either conclusion. Consequently, none of the consultants' reports was very meaningful.

What is meaningful are the facts which cannot be disputed or distorted. One is that, through the date of the examination, Lincoln's investments were very profitable. Secondly, the examiners were not able to, and therefore did not, cite the existence of any losses in the corporate-securities portfolio. Thus, even though one may have viewed Lincoln's practices as risky, the perceived risks had not resulted in any demonstrable adverse consequences to Lincoln.

There were also a few false cards in the examiners' arguments which should be briefly dealt with, because they raised totally irrelevant issues. One of their comments said that the portfolio had a "potentially high degree of illiquidity." Their focus on the liquidity of the portfolio is not appropriate. This portfolio was acquired to produce long-term investment returns and was not intended to be a cash equivalent. The investments were in a service corporation and had been funded by long-term, nonwithdrawable deposits. As such, there was no risk that the investments might have to be liquidated rapidly in order to meet depositor withdrawals or other unexpected short-term cash needs. If Lincoln's objective had been to assemble a portfolio of liquid securities, it would have purchased short-term, U.S. Treasury obligations. These instruments would have been very safe and very liquid. They would also have yielded far less than the corporate bond portfolio.

The examiners and their consultants also framed the concept of risk in terms which equated Lincoln's investment risks to the insurance premium charged by the FSLIC. This is a totally inappropriate comparison. The FSLIC charged the same premium rate to every S&L in the country. Most insurers base the premiums they charge on the risks they perceive in the party or object they are asked to insure. The FSLIC rate was not risk-based. The FSLIC certainly had the ability to adopt a risk-based premium structure, but it did not. It is not Lincoln's fault that the FSLIC didn't price its insurance coverage properly to compensate the Fund for the varying degrees of risks it was insuring.

With respect to the inherent risks of an S&L holding junk bonds, there were absolutely no restrictions in the regulations pertaining to such investments. If a state-chartered S&L wanted to invest 100 percent of its assets in junk bonds and state law permitted, as California's law did, it could have done so. These securities didn't even fall under the definition of direct investments; therefore, there were no required additions to regulatory net worth if an institution held junk bonds. If the regulators truly believed that these investments were by their nature subjecting institutions to "inappropriately high levels of risk," the place to address the issue was in the regulations and not in the Report of Examination for an individual association like Lincoln.

Lastly, regarding the underwriting deficiencies cited by the examiners, it is again interesting to note that the regulations, at that time, didn't discuss the extent, or even the nature, of the underwriting necessary for corporate securities. A FHLBB memorandum dated August 27, 1984, did address the subject. The memorandum stated: "Associations which choose to invest in such bonds under applicable state laws or under the corporate debt securities authorization . . . should be advised that prudent and especially careful underwriting should be employed. Failure to exercise demonstrable caution is to be cited as an unsafe and unsound practice."

The memorandum didn't establish specific underwriting standards or recordkeeping requirements. Therefore, a deficiency could only represent the personal preferences or judgments of the examiners. In June 1988, another memorandum dealing with commercial loans, including junk bonds, finally provided specific underwriting guidelines.

As in the securities area, the examiners were very critical of Lincoln's underwriting and related files in the real-estate investment and lending areas. For real-estate investments, they cited several appraisal deficiencies, the lack of feasibility studies, the absence of cash-flow projections, and the absence of certain other data in the real-estate investment files. In the lending area, the cited deficiencies included the lack of evidence of a financial analysis of the borrower, the absence of credit reports, loan approval prior to receiving an appraisal, absence of signed and/or completed loan applications, inconsistent loan-settlement statements, and loans with little or no borrower equity. In its response, Lincoln acknowledged that its records could have been better. Lincoln stated it had adopted new procedures to improve the documentation of its underwriting and its files.

The more significant issue was the examiners' finding that:

> The concentration of land in Arizona appears to be excessive, especially when combined with the $228.6 million in land loans originated in Arizona. The examiners believe that this concentration is excessively risky when combined with the lack of feasibility studies or other documentation to support the marketability and the absorption rate for the vast acreage. In addition, recent indicators of absorption rates in Phoenix and Tucson indicate that an overbuilt condition may be developing.

In its response, Lincoln indicated that the examiners' concerns regarding overbuilding in the Phoenix and Tucson markets were essentially unfounded for three basic reasons. First, Lincoln believed that the studies obtained by the examiners were flawed in their methodology, data, and calculations. Second, the examiners' studies used unrealistically long absorption periods. And third, the studies didn't take into account Lincoln's actual absorption rate for its own projects, which was much more favorable than the general market rate.

Part of the problem was that the examiners' studies defined absorption as sales from a builder to an end-user buyer. This definition really didn't apply to Lincoln, because Lincoln no longer was engaged in home building. Lincoln sold to home builders parcels of land that required further development before homes could be constructed. There was lead time between the point when the builder purchased land from Lincoln and the commencement of home sales. This lead time could be as much as two years and wasn't factored into the examiners' studies.

The examiners also didn't allow for land banking, where builders and investors purchase parcels (particularly during periods of favorable interest rates and tax deductions) in order to secure positions in popular communities years ahead of construction. In many cases, the investor's intent is to keep the land off the market for an undetermined number of years in order to realize greater appreciation in its value. This practice results in the absorption of land that Lincoln was marketing but wasn't reflected in the examiners' more narrow definition of absorption.

The examiners' studies also failed to consider that not all of the land in Lincoln's projects was intended for residential use. In the master-planned projects, much of the acreage was intended for commercial, office, and industrial space. This was also true for non-Lincoln master-planned communities in both the Tucson and Phoenix markets. By not considering these other intended uses, the examiners' studies overstated supply and understated demand.

As in the corporate-securities area, the conclusions reached in these various studies, whether commissioned by the examiners or by Lincoln, will always be debatable. Since the studies were necessarily dependent on assumptions and projections, the conclusions can be second-guessed and criticized. In all likelihood, none of the studies was completely wrong, nor was any totally valid.

The real bottom line is that the examiners did not find any projects in Arizona, except for one property known as Garden Lakes, which, at the time of their examination, exhibited losses or a negative difference between book value and estimated market value. Even the appraisals ordered by the examiners, including those related to lending transactions, demonstrated significant potential gains in those Arizona properties which were appraised. With respect to Garden Lakes, Lincoln maintained that the appraisal was erroneous and failed to consider adequately the actual sales prices that were being realized in the project.

The examiners' concerns may have been more valid regarding loans than they were for Lincoln's own projects. Lincoln was able to control its own projects and could alter its plans and spending levels as market conditions changed. Because Lincoln's projects were long-term in nature, they went through several market cycles—ups and downs—before they were completely sold out. Lincoln had the ability to adjust its activities and development efforts as the market changes occurred—developing aggressively during the up periods and conserving during the down cycles.

This flexibility isn't present in lending situations. A borrower typically has to maintain a constant level of activity, whether in an up or in a down market, because there is debt that needs to be serviced. Therefore, the pressure of the debt load can cause a borrower to spend when conservation is a more prudent course of action. If the borrower becomes overextended during a down market, the project can fail. Also, the projects undertaken by Lincoln's borrowers were not as diverse as the master-planned communities Lincoln developed. Therefore, they were much more sensitive to the balance between supply and demand for residential lots, even on a short-term basis. A short-term condition of oversupply can cause serious financial problems for a thinly capitalized builder.

Hence, the examiners' focus on the issue of supply and demand, as it relates to the loans Lincoln extended, wasn't necessarily off base. The only issue is the reliability of the data that they used to determine the market conditions existing at that time.

The letter accompanying the Report of Examination concluded with the following directives to Lincoln:

> In view of the foregoing, we request that the association file revised Quarterly Financial Reports for the periods ending December 31, 1986, and March 31, 1987, to reflect all of the adjustments to earnings and net worth as noted herein, with the exception of the indicated appraised loss on the Phoenician Hotel property.
>
> In view of the serious deficiencies and violations noted above, we recommend that a special meeting of the Board of directors be convened to discuss the Report of Examination, and that the Board prepare a detailed response to this office. That response must address all areas of concern, and provide a detailed description of the steps to be taken by the Board to correct each deficiency and/or regulatory violation addressed in the report, including the Board's plan to bring the association into compliance with Insurance Regulation 563.13(b) respecting its net worth requirement. We also ask that you submit copies of journal entries verifying the requisite accounting adjustments. Your response should acknowledge receipt and review of the enclosed Report of Examination, be signed by each member of the Board of Directors, and be submitted to this office no later than June 5, 1987.

Lincoln responded to the Report of Examination on June 26, 1987. Lincoln did not make the requested accounting entries, as it believed that the examiners' findings and related adjustments were erroneous.

What Lincoln did not know, until many months later, was that the San Francisco examiners also issued another, and much more detailed, report on the examination to the FHLBB in Washington. This report, which Lincoln never had a chance to rebut, included additional findings and was much more critical of Lincoln than was the Report of Examination sent to Lincoln. The Report of Examination was approximately 60 pages in length. The report sent to Washington consisted of 285 pages. Had Lincoln seen this report, it would have taken strong exception to the accuracy of its contents, but it never was given the opportunity.

This second report also disclosed the true agenda of the people in San Francisco. An agenda which other documents show was being actively pursued during the course of the field examination and was the factor which caused the examination to last as long as it did. The intent of San Francisco is stated near the end of the report (on page 279), where the following conclusion is reached:

> Lincoln is unsafe. As it is currently operated, Lincoln is a threat to the FSLIC insurance fund and to other insured institutions. In view of Lincoln's unsafe and unsound condition, we believe it should be placed into receivership or conservatorship or, at a minimum, required to cease and desist those unsafe practices that have led to its currently unsound condition.

This conclusion is evidence that Charlie Keating's fears about the course and conduct of the examination were not misplaced. The examiners' findings and conclusions were based on contested facts, subjective judgments, opinions, and controversial interpretations of the regulations. There were no clear-cut, unambiguous findings of unrecorded losses, nor was there any evidence of wrongdoing on the part of Lincoln's management. If the examiners' findings regarding appraised losses and accounting issues are corrected for the obvious errors, such as failing to take into account the effects of income taxes on the adjustments, Lincoln still met its net-worth requirement, notwithstanding the fact that Lincoln believed that virtually all of the adjustments were dead wrong.

In reading the findings in the examination report, one has to ask: Were they grounds for a receivership or conservatorship, which would mean seizing Lincoln and placing it under government control? Or, as Charlie Keating maintained: Were they the result of a conscious, deliberate scheme to remove him and his associates from the industry because they were not conforming to the FHLBB's philosophical desires?

On May 1, 1987, San Francisco forwarded to Smuzynski its "Recommendation and Statement of Supervisory Concern," the 285-page document. It contained the recommendation that "prompt action should be taken—either by means of a receivership or conservatorship or cease and desist order—to prevent further evasions and misrepresentations by Lincoln's management." The report was written by Sanchez and Deardorff, with Cirona concurring with the report and recommendation.

San Francisco was fully committed to taking forceful action against Lincoln. Yet, at this date, it hadn't received Lincoln's response to the examination report. Sanchez had repeatedly told the Kaye Scholer lawyers and Lincoln's other representatives that, before any final decisions were made by the regulators, Lincoln would have an opportunity to address any findings that it believed were in error. But this "Recommendation and Statement of Supervisory Concern" is clear evidence that San Francisco didn't care what Lincoln thought about the examination findings.

To San Francisco, anything that Lincoln said in its response was going to be considered "evasions and misrepresentations." They had already made up their minds. Nothing Lincoln could say or do was going to alter the regulators' conclusions—even if those conclusions were wrong.

Representatives of the FHLB-San Francisco also tried to gain support for its pending actions against Lincoln from the California DSL. Apparently the DSL was also considering a cease-and-desist order for Lincoln. But they were concerned that their examination findings were "stale." They needed to verify that the alleged conditions still existed. So, DSL wanted to send in a team of examiners to update the findings in the Report of Examination.

When San Francisco met with the DSL, they were apparently told that trying to remove Charlie from his position, which is what San Francisco wanted to do, would be very difficult, and, more importantly, such a removal could cause losses to the FSLIC insurance fund. The DSL was concerned that if Charlie were removed and a receiver appointed, the value of the Arizona land which Lincoln owned would fall. Also, they didn't think that the FSLIC would be as successful in acquiring the zoning changes necessary to complete many of the unfinished projects.

The DSL and the FHLBB were always concerned with what the other agency might do with regard to Lincoln. Neither wanted to be upstaged by the other. In addition, DSL appeared to believe that the FHLBB merely tolerated the state regulators, treating them almost as a nuisance, except when there was dirty work to be done. Then, the FHLBB tried to put the DSL in a position where it was forced to take action, thereby giving credence to the FHLBB's own actions. And if something went wrong, the FHLBB could then blame the DSL. The DSL often counteracted the FHLBB's suggestion that action was required by asking for additional examination procedures. These "stalling" tactics bought DSL extra time before they had to bite the bullet and bow to the "feds'" pressure. This tug-of-war between the two regulatory agencies was a constant process—Lincoln served as the rope which the two pulled in their contests with each other.

The FHLBB was also continuing its "dirty tricks" activities against Lincoln. Sensitive information was constantly being leaked. In July 1987, *Regardie's*, an East-Coast publication, contained an article on Lincoln and Ed Gray entitled "Renegade vs. Regulator." The article included information from the examination which came from the internal 285-page report which Lincoln had never seen. The article actually stated:

What follows is a rare look into the inner workings of federally insured financial institutions. The window is the most sensitive and secret variety of information produced by federal regulators, the bank examiners' reports. These reports are never shared with the public, indeed, only sanitized versions of them are shown to a financial institution's top management. This article was written after a six-month investigation during which "Regardie's" gained access to more than 300 pages of secret reports, memos, correspondence and other documents from the Federal Home Loan Bank Board. . . .

The article was terribly damaging to Lincoln. It identified borrowers, such as Wolfswinkle. The article disclosed the amount of funds that he had borrowed and the appraised value of his real estate. It presented all of the examiners' highly contested conclusions about the Rancho Vistoso project, including their opinion that the project could take forty-five years to complete. That disclosure, in and of itself, could have permanently damaged the project. It also discussed the details of Wolfswinkle's net worth. Thus, the article not only disclosed confidential information about Lincoln, but it discussed information that customers, like Wolfswinkle, would never have made public. Why would people ever do business with Lincoln in the future if their personal affairs were going to be made public by the FHLBB?

The article also threatened Lincoln's deposit base. The article was a clear message that the regulators were after Lincoln. Why should a person deposit money in an institution that might be closed by the government? If people don't have confidence in an institution, they'll take their business elsewhere.

There was no question—none—that someone within the FHLBB had illegally released the examination information with the premeditated, deliberate objective of destroying ACC and Lincoln. There can be no other reason. This is not the kind of information that is inadvertently released. As the article said, it is the "most sensitive" information the FHLBB ever has in its hands.

Whoever gave the information to *Regardie's* did so intentionally and knew its contents would be widely repeated and that Lincoln would have an extremely difficult time controlling the devastating effects of the *Regardie's* article. The "leaker" also had to know that Lincoln believed that most of the examination findings were inaccurate, incorrect, or inappropriate. If the information were released later, after Lincoln's response had been delivered and considered by the FHLBB, there was always the chance that the examination findings might be revised in

Lincoln's favor. Thus, the person leaking the information needed to get it out while it was worded as strongly as it would ever be.

If anybody at Lincoln had any doubt that the examination was simply a ruse to carry out a vicious, illegal attack on the association, the release of the information to *Regardie's* erased that doubt. The publication had information that even Lincoln didn't have, and wouldn't have until it was produced in connection with a lawsuit Lincoln filed. Lincoln's and ACC's management, and their lawyers, knew that they could never trust San Francisco again and that the examination could be resolved only if Lincoln could drag the FHLBB into court. What was really appalling to Charlie was the fact that the FHLBB was constantly saying that Lincoln was in violation of regulations when, at the same time, the FHLBB itself seemed routinely to disregard the regulations and the law.

No one has ever been identified as the leaker. The FHLBB and the FBI paid lip service to investigating the leaks, but their hearts didn't appear to be in it. After all, the only one they thought was affected was Lincoln—and who the hell in government cared what happened to Lincoln. They were planning on trying to seize the association anyway; therefore, no harm, no foul.

Lincoln's and ACC's people always believed that the person leaking the information was Bill Black. Lincoln believed that he was transferred from Washington to San Francisco for two reasons. First, in San Francisco, he could take a more proactive role in directing the war against Lincoln. He would no longer have to function as a rear-echelon advisor to the commander-in-chief; instead, he could take battlefield command and join the other field generals—Cirona and Patriarca. Second, the transfer off the federal payroll and onto San Francisco's private payroll undoubtedly resulted in a handsome increase in Black's compensation—perhaps a reward for eliminating Henkel and performing other useful deeds for Ed Gray?

Lincoln may have been right about Black being the source of the early leaks. But there was another possible suspect for this much more egregious offense. A person who may have had motive and one who consistently exhibited intense dislike for anyone associated with Lincoln and ACC: Kevin O'Connell.

O'Connell joined the FHLBB staff in Washington in late April 1987, at which time he was assigned to Lincoln. Prior to that, he had been on the staff of the FHLB of Chicago, which he joined in 1984. Before that, he had reportedly spent six years as a loan officer and executive assistant to the president of a Chicago-area savings and loan. But in this story, his most significant attribute is that he is the son of William O'Connell, who was president of the U.S. League. There is the possible motive to "get" Lincoln. William O'Connell and Ed Gray were very close, as reported by the *Wall Street Journal*, July 16, 1986, in an article entitled "Friendly Terms— Thrift's Trade Group and Its Regulators Get Along Just Fine." Some pertinent excerpts from the article are:

> Edwin Gray, the Chairman of the Federal Home Loan Bank Board, lived nicely during the recent Montreal conferences of the U.S. League of Savings Institutions. He had chauffeurs and good meals, and even a typewriter was provided in his $233-a-night hotel room.
>
> One reason Mr. Gray was able to live so high on the hog was that the League, the trade group for the thrift institutions that Mr. Gray and his board regulate, picked up the tab for $735 of his expenses.
>
> From pampering the bank-board chairman at an expensive hotel in Canada to hardball lobbying tactics, the U.S. League gets its job done in Washington. "There is a symbiotic relationship. I'm trying to avoid using the word incestuous" says Steven Goldstein, a former official of the bank board. "It is a very close rapport between the regulated and the regulator."
>
> Not only does it (the U.S. League) have easy access to the board's top officials, but also it receives confidential agency briefings and internal drafts of regulations. And it has virtual veto power over many proposals by the independent agency. "God knows how many times we've taken actions or changed regulations for the League" says one bank-board official who asks not to be named.
>
> Three bank-board officials flew into Chicago's O'Hare Airport and were escorted to the O'Hare Hilton Hotel. The League told the officials the changes it wanted in the proposed rules—involving the limits on the kinds and amounts of direct investments that thrifts are allowed to make. By the end of the day, according to participants, the bank-board officials were essentially helping the League staff to draft the group's official comment letter. Such meetings are questionable under federal rules. The League's changes were later adopted.
>
> Sometimes agency officials initiate the contact. When Chairman Gray was preparing to make a new legislative proposal this spring, he called William O'Connell, the League's president, in England the night before Mr. Gray was scheduled to testify at a congressional hearing. According to Mr. O'Connell— and Mr. Gray confirms the conversation—the chief regulator read a couple of paragraphs from his prepared text. "How does that sound to you?" Mr. Gray asked. The trade association leader said it sounded fine to him, and Mr. Gray delivered the testimony the next morning on Capitol Hill.
>
> And then there are the "countless" informal meetings between Messrs.

Gray and O'Connell, as the latter puts it. Mr. O'Connell had Mr. Gray over to his Watergate apartment last winter for an afternoon of viewing pro-football playoff games, has lent him his golf clubs and takes him to lunch and dinner a few times each month. Messrs. Gray and O'Connell call each other good friends. . . .

The closeness between the bank board and the League is grist for the black humor among agency employees. At last year's Christmas party, one staffer who is a ventriloquist performed a routine with a dummy. The staff member played Bill O'Connell doing the talking for Ed Gray.

William O'Connell's cozy relationship drew him and the League into the controversy surrounding Gray's travel-expense problems. The investigation was critical of the close ties between a regulator and the very institutions he was supposed to regulate and, therefore, caused O'Connell's own behavior to be questioned. Since Gray blamed Keating for spilling the beans on his shoddy practices, one can reasonably assume that O'Connell shared Gray's belief and, thus, viewed Charlie with a considerable degree of animus.

The O'Connell and Keating conflict didn't end with Gray's expense-reimbursement problems. As you will recall, Lee Henkel was appointed to the FHLBB in late 1986. In the summer of 1986, another person with ties to Charlie Keating was also being considered as a potential nominee to the FHLBB. Professor George Benston was a candidate for the FHLBB. During the debates over the direct-investment rules, Dr. Benston was the coauthor of an academic study which rejected the need for limits on direct investments in the S&L industry—a viewpoint shared by the majority of those who commented on the proposed rules, including many members of the U.S. League. The cost of Benston's study was underwritten by Lincoln.

On July 2, 1986, O'Connell wrote to Senator Jake Garn, chairman of the Committee on Banking, Housing and Urban Affairs, commenting on Benston's potential nomination. The pertinent parts of the letter are:

. . . Though the U.S. League acknowledges the President's prerogative to send to your Committee his choice for that independent regulatory agency (the FHLBB), Professor Benston has actively participated in a recent campaign to undermine the FHLBB and the FSLIC fund which it administers.

On behalf of our FSLIC-insured member institutions, I ask you to notify the President that you consider the nomination of Professor Benston to be inappropriate for this important regulatory post.

I also enclose an article from the February 18 issue of the American Banker revealing the sponsorship of Dr. Benston's campaign against the direct investment regulation by American Continental Corp., a conglomerate which is the parent of Lincoln Savings, a California-chartered FSLIC-insured Thrift. In addition I enclose an article from Business Week explaining why direct investments through the S&L subsidiary is part of the corporate takeover strategy of Mr. Charles Keating, Chairman of American Continental Corp.

Your distinguished Committee will be considering an important legislative proposal to recapitalize the FSLIC fund in the very near future. The continued application of the 1985 direct investment rules to FSLIC-insured institutions is an important component in the FHLBB's program to prevent additional caseload demands on the resources of the FSLIC. Appointing an outspoken opponent of those rules to the bank board at this time would seriously undermine any FSLIC recapitalization plan adopted by your Committee and the Congress and the future viability of the separate FSLIC fund.

Therefore, I make this extraordinary request that you alert the White House to the inappropriateness of Dr. Benston's name as a nominee for this important regulatory position.

When Lincoln learned of the letter to Senator Garn not long after it was sent, Charlie recognized it for what it really was. Gray couldn't scuttle Benston's nomination, because everyone knew where he stood on the direct-investment issue. So, he needed a credible source to speak for him. Who better than his near and dear friend, who could cloak the opposition to Benston with the mantle of his industry organization? If propositioned in this manner, O'Connell probably would help Gray out because he knew the League couldn't control Benston. From O'Connell's perspective, it was better to get rid of Benston and try to find another nominee who would serve as the League's stooge just as Gray apparently had. Thus, it appears O'Connell served as Gray's mouthpiece.

Lincoln and Keating reacted to this charade. On July 16, 1986, Peter Fishbein, representing Lincoln, wrote O'Connell a scathing letter, with copies to Senator Garn and all of the directors of the U.S. League. The significant sections of the letter are:

Your letter makes grave charges against a reputable, highly respected professional without any basis and falsely represents for whom you purport to speak. You have misused your position as President of the U.S. League to mislead the Congress and unjustifiably disparage an individual who possesses the highest qualifications to fill the position to which he has been nominated. Moreover your letter contains reckless and uncalled for defamatory comments against Lincoln.

Despite your declaration that you are speaking "on behalf of [the U.S.

League's] FHLBB-insured member institutions," we understand that your comments were made without the knowledge and approval of the U.S. League's Board of Directors; there can be no doubt that your comments do not reflect the strong views maintained by many of the savings and loan associations which you purport to represent.

At the heart of your letter is the preposterous assertion that because Professor Benston commented on and objected to the direct investment rule during the period of time that it was being considered for promulgation, he is a subversive who "has actively participated in a recent campaign to undermine the FHLBB and the FSLIC fund which it administers." You have, of course, conveniently failed to inform Senator Garn that the note and comment period for the direct investment rule saw a landslide of opposition to that rule—opposition voiced by virtually everyone who had any connection with the savings and loan industry, including Senators, Congressmen, savings and loan associations, state regulators, trade associations and prominent economists. . . .

. . . In these circumstances, it is difficult to tell whether you are acting as a spokesman for the Chairman [Ed Gray] or purporting to speak for the League's members. Whatever the motivation, it is disingenuous, to say the least, to attempt to give Senator Garn the erroneous impression that the views you are expressing are shared by either the League's Board of Directors or its member associations.

Your conduct is nothing short of a blatant misuse of your position as President of the U.S. League, as well as a defamation of Lincoln for which you personally or the League must bear responsibility.

The letter also cited numerous statistics regarding the number and nature of the responses which had been submitted regarding the direct-investment rule.

If William O'Connell wasn't an enemy of Lincoln before this incident, he must have been after receiving Fishbein's letter and having to face his directors. He got caught trying to front for Gray. Added to the allegations of the impropriety of the relationship between O'Connell and Gray, this had to hurt him. And therein lies a motive for Kevin O'Connell, his son, to pay Lincoln back. This motivation, coupled with the intense dislike exhibited by Kevin toward anyone affiliated with ACC and Lincoln, makes him a prime candidate as the person who gave the FHLBB materials to *Regardie's* and so damaged Lincoln.

At the end of June or in early July 1987, Lincoln delivered its response to the Report of Examination to San Francisco. The response actually served two purposes. First, it was a last attempt to convince the regulators that their findings and conclusions were incomplete or erroneous. Lincoln hoped that the Report would be revised to reflect what Lincoln believed were the true facts and circumstances of the association and its operations. Secondly, if the Report were not revised and the regulators sought to take some action against Lincoln, the response provided a foundation for Lincoln's legal defense in the appropriate court venue.

Smuzynski and Kevin O'Connell were chomping at the bit to get on with action against Lincoln. To them, Lincoln's response was nothing more than a hurdle that they had to leap before they could get on with the actions they intended to take. They simply wanted to dispense with the response as quickly as they could, without devoting any real attention to its contents and the validity of the facts and arguments contained therein.

The FHLBB's lawyers, on the other hand, understood that if they had to go to court and hadn't at least given a little consideration to the Lincoln response, they would be in trouble. Therefore, they were obliged at least to give a cursory look at the response. And this would necessarily slow down any actions Smuzynski and his cohorts wanted to take against Lincoln.

It is critical to note at this juncture that Smuzynski had for some considerable period of time completely embraced the concept that Lincoln was a rogue association that ought to be placed into receivership—taken over—by the FHLBB. The commitment to this course of action had been formed while he was working with and reporting to Ed Gray and, indirectly, Bill Black. He was as much a part of the decision to move vigorously and decisively against Lincoln as anyone in San Francisco, if not more so. When O'Connell joined Smuzynski, he too, for whatever reasons, was also committed to a takeover of Lincoln.

For the next two years, these two people, Smuzynski and O'Connell— who were completely unknown to anyone at ACC or Lincoln at this time, as their names had never surfaced or been mentioned—played a central role in shaping all of the FHLBB's actions against ACC and Lincoln. They were the silent, anonymous architects of many of the regulatory actions and directives used against ACC and Lincoln. They, along with people like Cirona and Patriarca in San Francisco, carried on the war after Ed Gray left the job as chairman of the FHLBB. Because for each of them, the destruction of Lincoln and Keating had also become a personal goal. They had taken a written stand on the severe regulatory actions that San Francisco wanted to take against Lincoln. To get ahead in the new environment of the FHLBB, one had to be a tough regulator. None of them wanted to soften the position against Lincoln and be viewed as a person who vacillates and is a weak regulator. They were, for all intents and purposes, committed to taking Lincoln and Keating down—the promise Ed Gray had made in Hawaii.

On July 23, 1987, a briefing memorandum under William Robertson's signature (he was then the top staff person at the FHLBB) was sent to the Bank Board. The memorandum was actually drafted by O'Connell and Smuzynski. The conclusion in the memorandum regarding Lincoln was as follows:

> Given the litigious nature of the association, ORPOS [Office of Regulatory Policy, Oversight and Supervision—the FHLBB constantly reorganized itself and changed the name of its departments; this used to be basically the Office of Examinations] believes that no Cease and Desist Order will be honored. Further, there will be some time before any such C&D will take effect, as we fully expect the association to seek a temporary Restraining Order against any Temporary C&D, and to go through the entirety of the administrative process. We therefore believe the only way to stop the association from speculating with the FSLIC funds is through receivership, a receivership based on unsafe and unsound practices and dissipation of assets. . . .

The memorandum also asked that ORPOS be designated as the organization within the FHLBB structure to coordinate all enforcement actions and other matters related to Lincoln. The person within ORPOS who would logically draw this assignment was Al Smuzynski. He wrote a memo which would, if the Board went along with the proposal, let him run the whole show.

Now, I'm not a lawyer, but let me give you a layman's view of the practical difference between what would happen if the FHLBB got a C&D and what would happen if it put Lincoln in receivership.

With a C&D, the FHLBB would serve the order on Lincoln. Immediately, Lincoln's attorneys would go to a federal court and seek a restraining order—an injunction—against the enforcement of the C&D order pending the outcome of administrative proceedings. Then, a formal proceeding would commence before an administrative law judge, who is basically a hearing officer retained by the FHLBB, to consider the merits of the charges supporting the C&D order.

The FHLBB would argue that Lincoln was unsafe and unsound; therefore, the C&D was warranted. Lincoln would counter saying that, as a matter of law, the FHLBB's charges were unfounded and insupportable and that the C&D should be voided. If Lincoln prevailed, the C&D would be lifted, and Lincoln would go on about its business. If the FHLBB prevailed, Lincoln would appeal the decision to a federal court, which was not under the administrative auspices of the FHLBB, and reargue its case.

This process could go on until there was no higher court to appeal to or until Lincoln prevailed. Depending on the calendars of the various courts, the process could take a considerable period of time. If the FHLBB ultimately prevailed, ACC would still own Lincoln, but Lincoln would be precluded by the C&D from engaging in the practices specified in the order. Also, the order could seek to remove certain named people from engaging in the management or affairs of Lincoln. Because Lincoln would retain its assets through this whole process, it could finance the entire appeal process using its own resources.

With a receivership, the FHLBB would show up one day at all of Lincoln's facilities with a small army of federal agents and rent-a-cops and simply seize all of Lincoln's assets. It would throw out any of Lincoln's employees it chose to and would ban them from Lincoln's premises. It would then take over the management of all of Lincoln's affairs.

ACC would turn to a court—using its resources, not Lincoln's, to finance the defensive efforts—to try to get an injunction, which probably wouldn't be granted. ACC would then have to file an action contending that the taking of Lincoln by the FHLBB was not legal. While this action was being heard, the FHLBB would be selling all of the assets it didn't approve of, probably at a loss, thereby confirming that the assets were, in fact, very risky. If ACC were to prevail in its lawsuit and the receivership was voided, the Lincoln that was returned to ACC would bear no resemblance to the Lincoln that was seized.

In effect, the receivership is a final, irreversible event. Whatever equity ACC and its shareholders had in Lincoln would be erased—forever. And even the Report of Examination, with all of its flaws, indicated that Lincoln's net worth, and ACC's equity, was $30.5 million ($110 million, if you toss out the Phoenician appraisal loss). Thus, the FHLBB was seriously considering depriving ACC's shareholders, by their own calculations, of as much as $110 million.

What ORPOS was contemplating was a fatal blow to ACC and Lincoln. It was basically saying, "We don't want these guys to avail themselves of the protection of the due process the judicial system offers, because they might win. Therefore, let's just grab the sucker." Not bad if you can do it, except, of course, if you're on the receiving end of this little gambit; then it looks curiously like the practices used by banana-republic dictators.

Now, to put an association into receivership, the FHLBB was, at this point in time, required to show it was insolvent. Was that a problem? No. The possibility that an association placed into receivership will ever be shown not to be insolvent doesn't exist. The first thing that the FHLBB does is to get its appraisers and managers to trash the assets; thus, if there was any doubt, it is eliminated by manufactured red ink. This creates a slight problem—the trashed assets have to be sold at a loss. But what the hell, it's not the FHLBB's money. They just stick it to the taxpayers and blame prior management. They have become real pros at this game. If the regulators are determined to seize an association's assets, no association can stand up to them.

On August 4, 1987, the Kenneth Leventhal firm, which was described in some notes made during a meeting among the examiners as "our hired gun," wrote a letter to Pillsbury, Madison & Sutro, a law firm retained by San Francisco, suggesting an approach they would take to identify accounting-related issues which could be used to attack Lincoln's reported financial results. Basically, they proposed to look at any area requiring the exercise of judgment.

This is a pretty common approach for accountants who are asked to be expert witnesses. Wherever judgment is exercised, any skilled accountant can argue for alternative treatments and can usually force the underlying data to lend support to the alternative positions. This doesn't mean the original accounting is incorrect; rather, it means that you can always cast some degree of doubt on the accounting. It is a given in the accounting profession that whenever the element of judgment is involved, two equally skilled and knowledgeable people can come to different and supportable conclusions. What the expert witness tries to do is raise as many alternative treatments as possible in order to cast doubt on the reliability of a company's financial statements. The expert will almost always cast its position as conservative and the other party's as aggressive.

In August, the examiners started questioning the sale of the Phoenician and Crescent hotels. When the Phoenician was initially planned, it was not of the scope and magnitude that it later had. One of Charlie's primary plans was to syndicate the hotel as an investment for higher-income taxpayers. He believed that the Phoenician would be a good hedge against inflation. Unlike an office building, where long-term lease arrangements expose the owner to inflation risks, a hotel can adjust its room rates on a daily basis, thereby allowing the hotel to keep up with increases in inflation.

In the early years, Charlie thought that the Phoenician would throw off tax deductions resulting from depreciation and interest to the investors. These deductions could be used to offset otherwise taxable income which for people in the upper tax bracket was taxed at a rate of 52 percent. Later, as its operations stabilized, the hotel was expected to appreciate, and it could be sold at a gain. At the time, capital gains, which this gain would be, were taxed at a maximum rate of 25 percent. Therefore, the investors reduced income which was taxed at a high rate and, later, recognized a gain which was taxed at a low rate.

But in 1986, after Lincoln had already acquired the land for the hotel, Congress changed the tax law. The ability for the average investor to deduct the losses produced by depreciation and interest deductions was effectively eliminated, as was the lower capital-gains tax rate. This killed any plans to syndicate the Phoenician.

The Phoenix and Scottsdale area already had several nationally renowned, destination resort hotels—the Arizona Biltmore, Camelback Inn, and the Wigwam. These were older properties, with long lists of clientele who returned to the respective resorts each year for conventions, conferences, or vacations. Each resort featured golf courses, tennis and swimming facilities, meeting rooms, ballrooms, and excellent food and beverage services. But because of their age, these resorts needed modernization and refurbishing; thus, they were vulnerable to new competition, especially if the competitor offered up-to-date facilities, attractive amenities, and comparable guest services.

Charlie saw an opportunity for a new world-class resort to capture much of the highly profitable business that the older hotels had enjoyed for many years. The plans for the Phoenician were changed. The ballroom was enlarged so it could accommodate major corporate conventions. More meeting rooms, in a variety of sizes, were added to serve as break-out rooms for large groups or to handle small meetings. The quality of construction and furnishings was upgraded to surpass the features offered by the older establishments. Pools and other water features, the tennis courts, golf course, and health spa were all upgraded.

These revisions increased the budget for the Phoenician. But in Charlie's opinion, and those of his other executives and their advisors, these changes were needed if the Phoenician was to capture the business from up-scale, corporate conventions and affluent vacationers and winter visitors. For these potential guests, higher room rates and increased prices for other services were not significant barriers to their booking space in the resort, as long as the quality of the guest services was consistently high.

Even with the increased construction cost, Lincoln believed that the numbers for the project worked. Because of the expanded meeting space, food and beverage revenues were expected to be much higher than for other facilities with a comparable number of guest rooms. The resort also expected to capture a great deal of local business for meetings, charity gatherings, weddings, and other celebrations. Additionally, with completely new rooms and furnishings, it was expected that the resort could charge the highest room rates in the market without adversely affecting its occupancy levels. All these added revenues made the cash-flow numbers work. Moreover, the plans called for adding up to another 250 guest rooms a few years after the resort initially opened and once it attained a stable level of operations. These additional rooms would have a construction cost much lower than the initial rooms, thereby reducing the overall average cost per room.

Knowing the project was now much larger, Charlie sought an equity partner. He believed that such a partner would come from Europe or Japan, where U.S. tax laws would not play a significant role in the investment decision. He looked in both geographic areas for a large, stable partner.

Through a person who was affiliated with the Swiss financial institution, Credit Suisse, Charlie was introduced to executives of the Kuwait Investment Office (KIO), the investment arm of the government of Kuwait. Charlie presented the Phoenician and Crescent hotels to the KIO, and they expressed interest in the properties. The KIO was an experienced and sophisticated investor with real-estate investments throughout the world that purportedly totaled more than $200 billion.

Over the course of a few months, the KIO visited the properties, reviewed the cost records on the hotels (the Crescent was already completed and in operation), examined construction plans and budgets, reviewed construction contracts, studied projected operating budgets, had consultants look at the projects, and performed numerous other analyses and due-diligence procedures. After this intense investigation, the KIO decided to invest in the hotels.

The KIO had a very specific investment structure in mind. In order to meet their requirements, Lincoln had to reorganize all of the corporate entities that owned the hotel properties. The KIO did not want majority ownership, nor did they want any responsibility for managing the properties. They made it clear that their interest was in the long-term real-estate value of the properties. So, part of the structure was to create a management company, to be operated by Lincoln, which would manage the properties for a fee.

The KIO had some other deal points which were very important. The contract specifically stated that the KIO's identity was to remain confidential and was not to be disclosed by Lincoln. Because of tensions in the Middle East, the KIO wanted anonymity. Also, the KIO was very particular about whom it did business with and whom it would accept as an investment partner. Thus, the contract contained a provision stating that if either partner received an offer to sell its interest in the hotels, the other partner had a right of first refusal to sell its interest or buy the other partner's interest on the same terms and conditions as the outside offer. This provided both partners with the ability to avoid inadvertently becoming a partner with an unacceptable party.

The KIO paid $173.7 million, all in cash, for a 45-percent interest in the corporation that owned the two hotels. The price was based on agreed-upon values of $275.7 million for the Phoenician and $77 million for the Crescent. The price also included a development fee of $12.7 million, and

$2.2 million for the hotel-management company.

The examiners asked Lincoln for all the documents related to the sale of the hotels. Lincoln only sent them a portion of the documents they requested. The reason why the examiners in San Francisco didn't receive all of the documents related to the sale was very simple. The KIO wanted its identity to remain confidential. The FHLBB was a sieve. Any data it received on Lincoln was immediately leaked. So, Lincoln held any documents which identified the KIO. For months after the deal closed, the FHLBB pressured Lincoln to give them all of the documents. Lincoln, after receiving assurances that the documents would remain confidential, finally relented and gave the FHLBB the documents. Not long thereafter, the KIO was identified in the press as the purchaser of the interest in the hotels.

The FHLBB fretted for months that the deal wasn't a sale. First, they said that the KIO wasn't sophisticated and didn't know what it was buying. Then they said that the KIO didn't understand the values of the hotels, because they hadn't seen the existing appraisals (the KIO had seen the appraisals but in general completely discounted their value and usefulness.) Then, they worried over the right of first refusal. Finally, while they conceded that a sale had taken place, they argued about how much profit could be recognized. Later, they argued that a new appraisal was more indicative of value than the price paid by the KIO, and they wanted Lincoln to write down its interest.

Lincoln started to see evidence that the regulators had moved beyond routine supervisory activities and were gearing up for litigation. They made another attempt to visit Lincoln, under the guise of completing the examination, with a team of people, including several from Kenneth Leventhal, in order to gather the evidence they needed for the lawyers. This way they would have a head start on Lincoln and, thus, would force Lincoln into a catch-up game if a suit were filed.

On August 31, 1987, Sanchez sent a letter to Lincoln regarding the planned on-site visit. The letter read as follows:

This is to confirm Charles A. Deardorff's telephone conversation with Mr. Robert Kielty on August 28, 1987, in connection with Lincoln Savings and Loan Association's (Lincoln) June 30, 1987, response to the Report of Examination as of March 13, 1986. Our staff has been reviewing your response to the examination findings. This review, however, is inconclusive. As indicated to Mr. Kielty, we believe the outstanding issues can best be resolved through an on-site visit. Please be assured that this review process will be conducted expeditiously in order to minimize any disruptions to your staff. We request your cooperation in providing the following additional information.

First, we have compiled a list of documents and other information to be supplied by the association. This list is attached as Exhibit I and is keyed to your response. Second, we request that the association make certain files available for the examiners who will conduct an on-site review of these and any other pertinent documents beginning September 14, 1987. Included in the scope of this on-site visit will be a review of Arthur Young's audit workpapers for Lincoln's 1986 audit. The list of files/documents to be made available is attached as Exhibit II. Third, Mr. Steven Rushmore, a hotel appraiser whom we have retained, plans to visit Phoenix September 14 through 16, 1987, to inspect the Phoenician Hotel project and meet with project officials.

As also discussed with Mr. Kielty, our examiners will be accompanied by several accountants from Kenneth Leventhal & Company, whom we have retained as consultants. While reviewing the audit workpapers, they would like to have an opportunity to speak to the Arthur Young accountants who worked with John Ashton and Monica Gawet of this office during their visit in April.

Exhibit I was a list of thirty-seven different areas where Lincoln was asked to supply analyses or files. Exhibit II was a list, usually for "all files," covering an additional twelve major categories. All of the documents requested had previously been made available to the examiners. This was simply a disingenuous attempt to provide the FHLBB's lawyers and expert witnesses with the information they needed to perfect their planned legal action against Lincoln. Information which, under normal circumstances and due process, they would have had to subpoena after the legal action was filed.

On September 11, 1987, Kielty sent a letter to Patriarca stating two things. First, Lincoln would have Kaye Scholer prepare responses to each of the items listed on Exhibit I to Sanchez' letter. Second, there would be no on-site visit or any additional information provided until the examination was resolved. On September 23, 1987, Lincoln supplied answers to all of the thirty-seven items in Exhibit I.

The request for the on-site visit triggered a new phase in the 1986 examination. Kielty knew something strange was afoot in San Francisco. They were planning an action of some kind. If Lincoln didn't take some initiative to bring the exam to a final conclusion, whatever was happening in San Francisco could get out of hand. So, Lincoln began its own strategy to end the exam. A process which would take over seven months to complete.

Meanwhile, San Francisco continued its efforts to get a C&D or stronger action filed against Lincoln. These efforts would draw San Francisco into a bitter conflict with some of the FHLBB regulators in Washington.

Nine

San Francisco Rejects Peace Overture

By October 1987, the prolonged examination process had exacted a tremendous toll from ACC and Lincoln. At the time, estimates of the monetary costs incurred by Lincoln for attorneys, consultants, appraisers, and accountants, as well as by the time and expenses of internal personnel, reached as high as $50 million. And Lincoln not only had to pay the costs of its own defensive actions related to the examination, it was also billed for the FHLBB's examination costs. This economic drain started in 1985 when Lincoln started preparing for the examination and continued, unabated, for the two years that followed. In October, there was no sign these costs would stop anytime soon. In fact, if the FHLBB decided to take supervisory action against Lincoln, resulting in extended legal battles, the expenses for Lincoln's defense could accelerate and get much worse.

Effectively, Lincoln was paying an even higher cost as a direct consequence of the examination. The examination was a constant intrusion—consuming the time of Lincoln's and ACC's management and diverting their attention from the crucial business decisions that needed to be made each and every day. They found themselves pulling and reviewing old files in order to retrace information they had considered and decisions they had made months or years ago. The incessant questions from the examiners and Kaye Scholer's attorneys had to be researched and answered. Lincoln's people had to deal with consultants and appraisers, not for the purpose of advancing the company's business, but merely to satisfy the examiners or to support Lincoln's response. There were countless meetings relating to the examination process which Lincoln's people were forced to attend.

This diversion from the real tasks at hand fatigued and frustrated Lincoln's top executives. Key projects became stalled because the people didn't have time to make the decisions necessary to keep things moving at a steady pace. Opportunities, of which Lincoln normally would have taken advantage, escaped them. Morale, which had always been extremely high in ACC and Lincoln, sagged.

Charlie recognized that something had to give—and soon—or Lincoln would not recover from the debilitating effects the exam was producing. In early October 1987, he scheduled an all-day meeting to discuss strategies for ending the exam. His mission was to devise a battle plan to allow Lincoln to seize the initiative in resolving its dispute with the FHLBB. He believed that the FHLBB was content to drag out the process; in the meantime, Lincoln was being condemned to a slow and painful death, taking ACC with it to the grave.

During the first hour of the meeting, people simply vented their frustrations. Each person recounted his or her exasperation in dealing with the regulators. They talked about endless requests for information; the feelings of hostility and distrust they felt emanating from the San Francisco people; the destructive nature of the leaks; the erroneous findings in the Report of Examination; and the tremendous cost of the entire process. They needed this cathartic relief before they could address the alternatives available to end the ordeal.

Emotion out of their systems, the group speculated about what the FHLBB's most probable course of action would be. The lawyers in the meeting believed that the FHLBB would try to issue a cease and desist order. In fact, they were surprised that a C&D action had not already been filed. They concluded that the FHLBB didn't have a strong enough case. The request for a new on-site visit appeared to be an attempt to clean up the examination findings, so the regulators could rebut Lincoln's response and shore up their case for a C&D.

The lawyers didn't believe that stronger actions could be taken until the FHLBB first tried the C&D route. They thought that other alternatives could be used only if the C&D were violated or if Lincoln were, in fact, insolvent. Since the Report of Examination didn't indicate insolvency, the C&D was, in the lawyers' minds, the most logical step for the FHLBB to pursue.

The attorneys with litigation backgrounds actually welcomed a C&D order. Kaye Scholer's litigation attorneys, led by Karen Katzman, had been preparing for such an eventuality since mid-1986. The attorneys believed that they would be successful in obtaining a restraining order against the enforcement of any C&D. Once a restraining order was issued, an administrative hearing would be held. Since administrative hearings are under the auspices of the FHLBB, and the hearing officer or administrative law judge who conducts the hearing is retained by the FHLBB, the attorneys didn't hold out much hope for success in that venue. They more or less likened an administrative hearing to being invited to a fight where the judge gives Lincoln a butter knife with which to defend itself while, at the same time, issuing the FHLBB an assault rifle. It didn't figure to be a fair fight.

After the administrative process, where the FHLBB would probably prevail, Lincoln could move the action to a federal district court. Here the attorneys expected a fair hearing. They were confident that in this arena, Lincoln could defeat the FHLBB's C&D. During the process of preparing Lincoln's response to the Report of Examination, the lawyers became convinced that the preponderance of admissible evidence supported Lincoln's position; by the same token, they didn't think that the evidence would enable the FHLBB to sustain its arguments.

The problem with waiting to defend against a C&D order was that, even if Lincoln won, as the attorneys thought it would, the legal process would be expensive. The entire effort could take several years. The cash outlay for attorney fees, expert witnesses, consultants, and related costs could be in the tens of millions of dollars. More significantly, the distractions management faced would not only continue, they'd get worse. Lincoln might win the battle, but it could also lose the war. No one in the room believed that ACC and Lincoln could endure several more years of conflict without suffering irreversible damage. While it was comforting to know that the lawyers were confident they could win in court, there had to be a better way to resolve the matter.

With these considerations in mind, the discussion turned to the possibilities of negotiating a settlement with the FHLBB. There were certain issues Lincoln could concede. There were others that Lincoln would not accept under any set of circumstances. And there were issues where compromise was possible. If Lincoln structured a package which allowed the FHLBB to believe that the examination had resulted in changing Lincoln's practices and operations, without giving away the store, a deal could be made.

Lincoln was willing to accept some of the appraisal losses. It could reclassify a portion of the general reserves that it had already recorded on its books to specific reserves—the reserve category the FHLBB was seeking—without having to revise its previously issued financial statements. It could also agree to create better manuals, revise files, improve underwriting procedures, and prepare a comprehensive operating plan. These were things management knew could, and should, be improved, whether the FHLBB insisted on the improvements or not.

Lincoln was not willing to agree to any of the so-called income reversals related to accounting issues. Lincoln believed that its accounting was correct and that the FHLBB was simply wrong on these issues. There were also certain appraisals, especially those on the hotels and Garden Lakes, which Lincoln would never agree were proper. Nor was Lincoln willing to concede the issue of excess direct investments, although a compromise regarding the net-worth requirement related to direct investments was possible. Lincoln would not agree to the reclassification of the

Wolfswinkle loans. These were all deal breakers from Lincoln's perspective.

Finally, Lincoln would not enter into any agreement viewed as either a supervisory directive or supervisory agreement. If a settlement were made, it would be precisely that—a settlement—there would be no admission of any inappropriate activities or of any unsafe, unsound, or risky operations or practices by Lincoln.

Lincoln believed that its actual net worth, excluding the effects of the FHLBB's findings, exceeded its required net worth by $120 million. Therefore, if it would facilitate a settlement, Lincoln could agree to an increase in its minimum net-worth requirement. It shouldn't matter to the FHLBB whether actual net worth was reduced (an action which would cause Lincoln to revise its financial statements) or the minimum requirement was increased (an action which would have no effect on Lincoln's financial statements). Either way, the difference between the actual and required net worth would be reduced. The concern of the FHLBB should simply be that there was excess net worth, not which component of the equation was adjusted. If Lincoln could get the FHLBB to appreciate this point fully, settlement was possible.

There was one other factor in the deal-breaker category. Lincoln wanted out from under the supervisory jurisdiction of San Francisco. Everyone knew that this would be politically difficult for the FHLBB to swallow. But the animosity between Lincoln and San Francisco was so strong that no one thought Lincoln could receive fair treatment from San Francisco's examiners and, especially, its supervisory people. At this stage, Lincoln didn't know exactly how it would be able to escape the Eleventh District, but there had to be a way.

Having established these concepts, the group sketched out the parameters for a Memorandum of Understanding (MOU) which, when drafted, would be submitted to the FHLBB as a settlement vehicle. The group rapidly agreed on the basic elements of the MOU. Karen Katzman, along with Peter Fishbein, was asked to draft and circulate an appropriate document to the meeting's participants for review and suggestions.

Charlie was pleased with the strategy of an MOU, as were the other top executives of ACC and Lincoln. The concept spawned real hope that the examination could be resolved short of total, all-out warfare; then, everyone could return their attention to running the business. It was the first time in many months that a light appeared to be at the end of the tunnel.

During this same period in time, I introduced Charlie to Bill Hinz, a friend of mine who was a seasoned S&L executive. Bill had started his career in 1962 with First Federal Savings and Loan Association of Phoenix (later Merabank). In 1982, Bill became president and chief operating officer of

Home Federal Savings and Loan Association of Tucson. While Bill was its president, Home Federal converted from a mutual association to a stock company through an initial public offering of its common stock. Following the conversion, the association experienced rapid and profitable growth. In 1986, Home Federal was acquired by Great American First of San Diego, and Bill was assigned the task of managing the real-estate operations of the combined entity. In order to realize certain benefits which carried over from his Home Federal employment contract, Bill retired from Great American in October 1987. After his retirement, I suggested to both Bill and Charlie that the two should meet and explore the possibility of Bill joining Lincoln.

Prior to Lincoln's acquisition, Andy Niebling was the only ACC executive who had had extensive S&L experience. Andy had worked for several financial institutions, including one owned by American Financial Corp. in Cincinnati, which is where Charlie and he had become acquainted in the seventies. Andy was responsible for Lincoln's basic S&L functions, its high-yield bond investments, and the operations of ACC's mortgage finance subsidiaries. Andy left ACC in mid-1987 to pursue a mortgage banking business that he was starting up.

After Andy Niebling left Lincoln, no one in Lincoln's upper management had an extensive background in the operation of a traditional savings and loan. With the pressure that the regulators were applying to force Lincoln to move away from its nontraditional operations and to reenter the single-family residential mortgage market, Lincoln needed someone with the requisite experience to guide it through any transition it decided to undertake.

Charlie and Bill met a number times over the span of several weeks to discuss their individual objectives. Agreement was reached, and Bill entered into a three-year employment contract to be chairman of Lincoln. Aside from providing for normal compensation and severance benefits, the contract provided that Bill would receive a substantial commission if he found a buyer for Lincoln and successfully negotiated a purchase/sale contract. This was in keeping with Charlie's view that, given the attitudes of the regulators, one option that ACC should consider was selling Lincoln.

While the MOU was being drafted and Hinz was coming on board, the FHLBB continued to pursue a C&D or other supervisory action against Lincoln, as did the CDSL.

The CDSL sent Lincoln a letter containing certain "directives" which it ordered Lincoln to follow. The letter contained the words "unsafe and unsound." Kielty asked the CDSL to remove this language from the letter. As an alternative, Kielty apparently said that Lincoln would send the

CDSL a letter agreeing to about 75 to 80 percent of the directives, but would delete any reference to "unsafe and unsound" practices.

Commissioner Crawford also spent a day in Phoenix reviewing, by helicopter, several real-estate projects and speaking with Lincoln's real-estate sales people and feasibility consultants. Afterward, he met with Kielty and others on Lincoln's staff to discuss the "directives" letter. No agreement was reached on the subject.

At the time, William Crawford appeared to be in his mid-sixties. He was a gruff, crusty, highly opinionated guy who gave one the impression that he knew all there was to know about everything. After just a few minutes of conversation, Crawford's remarks clearly indicated that he didn't have the foggiest notion of what was involved in developing a master-planned community. It was apparent that his knowledge was limited to small, single-family subdivisions and that anything on a larger scale was beyond his experience and comprehension.

For example, at one point, the value of the Estrella project and the demand for housing in that area of Phoenix were discussed. Crawford told Judy that he didn't need to see the project in order to appraise its value. All he required was for Judy to send him "the zip codes in Estrella." He would compare the zip codes to the latest census, use the census to determine the population in the area, use his population number to calculate demand, and then use his calculated demand figure to determine the value of Estrella. It was simple, he said: The key to value is population by zip code.

Someone pointed out to him that as a new, planned community, there weren't any people in Estrella's zip code. Crawford smiled and said, "See that's my point. If there's no one in the zip code, there's no demand. Without demand, the project's not worth much."

So much for sophisticated market research. All Lincoln needed to achieve success was a postal directory, so it could build all of its large developments in the most densely populated areas of the country. By Crawford's reasoning, the ideal place for a 17,000-acre development was midtown Manhattan.

Crawford's attitude was reflected in the CDSL's directives (contained in an October 21, 1987, letter) to Lincoln. One of the directives said: "Refrain from making any investment in any future construction loan or participation interest therein, in excess of $500,000 to one borrower or project for the development of land. . . ." This was basically saying, "Get out of the construction lending business and confine your activities to single-family residential lending." In many sections of Phoenix, a $500,000 loan limit would restrict a project to not more than two residential units for a given builder.

Some of the other remarks that Crawford made were equally simplistic. Others demonstrated that, since he didn't understand real-estate development, he didn't trust it. This easily enabled him to buy into the FHLBB's belief that real estate was inherently risky. This may have been why San Francisco tried to use the CDSL so much. They knew that they had a sympathetic ear. I suspect they also figured out that, because Crawford was opinionated, unsophisticated, and possessed a short-fused temper, he was easy to manipulate. From his remarks, Crawford appeared to view himself as a crusader who was out to rescue the industry from the policies of his predecessor, Lawrence Taggart. Thus, reining Lincoln in was right up his alley.

During October 1987, there were several meetings involving the people from San Francisco, including representatives from both Pillsbury, Madison & Sutro and Kenneth Leventhal, and the Washington-based regulators. Smuzynski, O'Connell, and the San Francisco folks seemed to agree on the issues raised in the examination and on filing a C&D order against Lincoln.

There were signs, however, that the lawyers in the enforcement division in Washington were convinced that San Francisco's plans for a C&D were inappropriate. In her 1989 congressional hearing testimony, Rosemary Stewart recited, in response to a claim in the same hearing by Patriarca that Washington's enforcement program was "abysmal," a series of instances where San Francisco had not performed well in enforcement situations. As a consequence, she concluded:

Each of the above examples, which were selected by Mr. Patriarca as the best examples of what he considers to be an "abysmal" enforcement program, in fact demonstrates that the San Francisco District failed to exercise effective supervision over a protracted period of time, that effective supervision would have identified problem areas much sooner than they were identified, that the resulting delays rendered effective enforcement action more difficult (and in some cases meaningless), and that consequently, the District's credibility is extremely low. As such, anything the District sends to Washington Headquarters for action is necessarily carefully reviewed.

Thus, while some of the Washington people endorsed what San Francisco wanted to do, others were apparently inclined to move more cautiously.

On November 3, 1987, Kielty sent Darrel Dochow, the FHLBB's top staff person in Washington, a copy of Lincoln's draft of a Memorandum of Understanding. When the MOU arrived in Washington, it started a chain-reaction series of events. The FHLBB now had something other than a C&D order to consider. It raised the possibility, as Lincoln hoped it would, that some other action could be used to settle the exam. Apparently,

Dochow raised this possibility with Patriarca.

Patriarca sent Dochow a letter via electronic mail (e-mail) on November 3, 1987, commenting on the status of the Lincoln situation. Some of the more pertinent comments in the e-mail message are:

> We consider a C&D the least stringent vehicle appropriate to the circumstances. I assume our thinking on this important issue was conveyed to you. If you prefer that we justify our position in writing or wish to discuss it personally with me, please give me a call. . . .
>
> Overall, I'd have to say that the handling of this case has been really quite distressing to those of us who have been trying to deal with a serious problem for a long time. I'm sincere in my desire to put the hard feelings that have resulted behind us and get on with the problem addressed.

This was a clue to Patriarca's growing impatience. He was anxious to get the C&D order filed but must have run into roadblocks in Washington. He also was becoming aware that control of the Lincoln case was slipping out of San Francisco's hands and was being taken over by Dochow. This was a real problem in the political world he inhabited. His power base rested on being in absolute control over everything that happened in his district. If Washington took control, it would be viewed throughout the FHLBB structure as a vote of "no confidence" in San Francisco and, more importantly to Patriarca, in him.

On November 13, 1987, the Pillsbury firm sent a draft of a proposed C&D order to Steve Hershkowitz. The cover letter to the C&D rejected the MOU approach and asked Lincoln to consent to the C&D order. Thus, in spite of Dochow's growing concerns about the effectiveness of their approach, San Francisco was sticking to its position. Ominously, the cover letter accompanying this document was captioned "Pre-Litigation—Lincoln Savings and Loan Association," another strong indication of the FHLBB's mind-set toward Lincoln.

On December 9, 1987, Kevin O'Connell and Carol Larson, an accounting fellow who was on loan to the FHLBB from one of the major firms, met in New York with people representing Lincoln to talk about the sale of the Phoenician to the KIO.

Larson appeared to believe that the transaction should not be accounted for as a sale because of a right of first refusal in the sale contract. At about the same time she was expressing this concern, Dochow received a letter from Arthur Young & Company explaining the circumstances of the right of first refusal and asserting that the existence of such a provision did not preclude sale accounting.

The Phoenician was a major part of San Francisco's case. If the sale was valid and the accounting was appropriate, the $80-million reserve that San Francisco wanted Lincoln to record, which was being held in abeyance pending a new appraisal, would no longer be an issue. Therefore, the regulators were trying to find some way to discredit Lincoln's treatment of the transaction.

During the meeting, O'Connell and Larson were told that the buyers did have access to the association's appraisal. They were told this because they seemed to feel that Lincoln may have withheld the appraisal from the KIO. Once they knew that the KIO had the appraisal, they wondered why the KIO decided to buy into the hotels at a much higher cost than what the appraisal showed. They were told that enhancements to the Phoenician, which were indicated by the increased cost to complete the hotel, were a contributing factor to the buyer's analysis that the price paid represented a good long-term investment. Lincoln's people also said that the buyer's price confirmed that appraisals were not as useful as the FHLBB believed they were. Sophisticated buyers used their own judgment in deciding on what price to pay rather than relying on the theories which appraisers employed.

O'Connell and Larson also seemed disturbed that the sale had been tailored to meet the KIO's requirements. Lincoln's people told them that Lincoln would have preferred a different structure than the one used—a partnership rather than a corporation—but that the buyers had insisted on the form used. From Lincoln's perspective, the form of the transaction had no real effect, except on the timing of certain tax considerations. The form of the transaction simply wasn't a big deal. But the FHLBB people thought it was. At one point, they even suggested that Lincoln shouldn't have met the buyer's demands. To use their words, they felt that "Lincoln should have told the buyer to buzz off and sell the hotels to someone else."

The naïveté represented by these people was nothing short of incredible, especially when one considers that they were among the most important decision makers in the FHLBB regulatory group in Washington. To think that they actually believed that any sale of an asset for $173 million, in cash, doesn't require the transaction to be tailored to the negotiated needs of both buyer and seller is mind-boggling.

They implied that all one has to do to sell a multi-million-dollar property is to put an advertisement in the classified section of the local newspaper and then wait for the offers to pour in. The idea that anyone would tell a serious, cash buyer to "buzz off" because you have to agree to some tax concessions (which only affect timing in this case and not the absolute amount of taxes ultimately to be paid) defies logic. There is not now, nor was there then, a glut of purchasers in the market who could pay $173 million in cash for any asset. If a reasonable deal can be structured, no sane person says "buzz off." Market value results from negotiations between two motivated and able parties where neither has an advantage over the other. It does not result from an appraisal, nor does it result from setting a price and asserting that that's the only price which is market. Market is the result of negotiation—give and take.

The idea that the KIO overpaid, which O'Connell and Larson seemed to believe, is preposterous. The KIO had over $200 billion in assets compared to Lincoln's approximately $4 billion. If there was a David and Goliath at the bargaining table, Lincoln sure wasn't Goliath. Moreover, there was no motive that compelled the KIO to purchase, except their own judgment of value. They were free to walk away at any time. Charlie, on the other hand, had the likes of O'Connell and Smuzynski nipping at his heels, threatening all kinds of nasty actions if he didn't sell the hotel or prove its value. In these circumstances, logic dictates that if any money was left on the bargaining table, it was Lincoln's, not the KIO's.

This meeting in New York was the first time that any Lincoln people could recall meeting O'Connell. Their reactions were not favorable. They used the term zealot to describe him. He was further described as intense, distrustful, sarcastic, and impolite. Unfortunately, at the time, no one fully understood or appreciated his role in regard to the FHLBB supervision of Lincoln.

After this meeting, the Phoenician issue seemed to be put to rest. To put the Phoenician issue once again in perspective from the regulators' viewpoint, it was central to their entire case against Lincoln. Lincoln had total assets of about $4 billion. The examiners had spent eight months pouring over all of Lincoln's assets, looking for unrealized losses. After looking at virtually every asset, they had determined that there were $135 million in unrealized losses—$85 million of which was related to the hotels. If you remove that $85 million, you are left with $50 million. Lincoln had solid evidence that appraisals relating to $32 million were flawed and, thus, there were no losses. That leaves $18 million of unrealized losses. Lincoln had reserves of $28 million on its books—$10 million more than it needed.

It's pretty hard to make a case about undue risk and unsafe and unsound practices when, after considering all of Lincoln's assets, there are no unreserved losses. This was San Francisco's and O'Connell's problem. The lawyers for the FHLBB in Washington also knew that this was the problem in trying to take any strong regulatory action against Lincoln.

On December 18, 1987, after only a few weeks at Lincoln, Bill Hinz met with Deardorff, Sanchez, and some of their assistants in San Francisco. Patriarca also joined the meeting for a little while. Bill had several objectives that he wished to accomplish in this meeting. First, he wanted to introduce himself to the regulators who were involved with Lincoln.

Second, he wanted to see how entrenched they were in their attitudes toward Lincoln. Third, he wanted to learn what enforcement action, if any, they were planning to take. Fourth, he wanted to discuss the concept of using the MOU to resolve the differences between Lincoln and the FHLBB. Finally, he wanted to gain time to formulate a plan for profitably restructuring Lincoln's operations toward a more traditional profile of a savings and loan association.

Early in the meeting, Bill introduced the subject of the Memorandum of Understanding as a means of resolving the examination. He explained that Charlie felt Lincoln's Memorandum of Understanding could be used, with some give and take, to work out the issues. He explained that there were several areas of common ground between Lincoln and the regulators in the approach. For example, the bond portfolio would not increase, Lincoln wouldn't acquire additional land, and the proceeds from the sale of real estate would be invested in more traditional assets.

Bill's comments and the concept of a Memorandum of Understanding had little effect on Patriarca, who continued to assert that there was a wide gap between the Federal Home Loan Bank of San Francisco and Lincoln in terms of "an appropriate operating philosophy and strategy for the association." Patriarca was concerned that there hadn't been any "meeting of the minds" on any of the examination issues, and he was disappointed by Lincoln's lengthy denial of the examination findings. Patriarca told Hinz that the Federal Home Loan Bank Board had undertaken an independent review of Lincoln's response to the Report of Examination and found that the examiners' conclusions were warranted. He then told Bill that San Francisco and ORPOS had every intention of proceeding with a cease-and-desist order, with the possibility of negotiating a supervisory agreement, if the supervisory agent found Lincoln's future operating strategy "acceptable."

This was the first time that the FHLBB had actually disclosed to anyone associated with Lincoln that a cease-and-desist order was, in fact, the direction in which they were heading. Lincoln had long suspected that San Francisco was intent on taking strong enforcement action against Lincoln; now these speculations had been confirmed. And interestingly, Patriarca couched the FHLBB's concerns "in terms of an appropriate operating philosophy and strategy for the association." As Charlie had contended from the beginning of the examination, Lincoln's problems with the regulators were not the result of losses or imprudent investments; instead, they were the result of philosophical differences between the FHLBB and Lincoln's management.

The hard-line approach by the regulators continued throughout the meeting. At one point, Sanchez indicated that the regulators would ask Lincoln to increase its capital to in excess of 6 percent of total assets (the requirement at the time was 3 percent). This is known as establishing an individual capital requirement, a power the regulations granted to a principal supervisory agent to protect the insurance fund from excessive risk. This was another tactic that Charlie feared the regulators might resort to in attacking Lincoln. By establishing an individual capital requirement, the PSA could set aside the regulations and impose whatever capital requirement the FHLBB deemed appropriate. If used abusively, as Charlie believed would happen in this instance, the FHLBB could make it virtually impossible for an association to meet its capital requirement, thus setting the association up for an enforcement action.

There was then a discussion of the direct-investment issue. Sanchez said that Lincoln was in violation of the direct-investment limitation by approximately $600 million. Sanchez then explained that the proposed enforcement document would require Lincoln to submit a plan for the disposal of the excess direct investments that would bring Lincoln's investments down to a level equal to two and a half times its tangible capital. Sanchez also said that no time frame for such disposition would be specified; instead, Lincoln would be required to submit a proposal acceptable to the supervisory agent.

Bill replied that he was unable to commit to any resolution of the direct-investment issue, because Lincoln's senior management did not agree that any violation existed. But he said that he would discuss the issue with Charlie and Lincoln's board of directors. Bill did say that Lincoln's board would be highly concerned about any imposed target level or any retaliatory action should Lincoln fail to meet the target level.

Again, for the first time, the examiners gave Lincoln confirmation that they were going to try to force Lincoln to dispose of certain of its investments based on their belief that Lincoln violated the direct-investment limitations. It was clear that the regulators were holding firm on their position that Lincoln's investments in its service corporations were not grandfathered; in addition, they were continuing to reject the nonconsolidated method for determining Lincoln's direct investments. These were fundamental areas of disagreement which Lincoln would never accept unless a court ruled in favor of the regulators' positions.

Also, the regulators' proposal to make Lincoln submit a plan for reducing its investments to the regulators for approval and monitoring was something that Charlie would never agree to, and Bill knew it. Such a proposal would allow the FHLBB to retaliate against Lincoln for even the slightest deviation from the plan. This was a position that Charlie would not allow Lincoln to be placed in, because he knew it would be tantamount to putting a gun at Lincoln's head.

Bill tried to explain what the regulators' proposal meant in practical terms. He said that it would take Lincoln, at a minimum, three to five years to work through its current real-estate holdings, even if Lincoln agreed not to acquire any new real-estate assets. He also told the regulators that Lincoln intended to continue to invest in equity securities. At which point Sanchez said that if Lincoln was to do so, it would have to file an application for a waiver to invest in equity securities and that Lincoln would still have to decrease its overall level of equity-risk investments. He made it clear, however, that any purchases of equity securities without such a waiver would be further violations of the equity-risk investment regulation.

Once again, the regulators demonstrated a lack of flexibility. They were insisting that Lincoln dispose of its equity investments and that it refrain from purchasing any other such investments without the prior approval of the FHLBB—an approval which would never be granted, given the FHLBB's philosophies. Bill tried to explain that if these very profitable investments were removed from Lincoln's operations and if Lincoln were limited to investing in assets which produced lower profit margins, Lincoln would have to grow its asset base significantly. That was simple logic. If an institution is forced to dispose of $600 million of assets producing a net yield of 10 percent and must reinvest in assets yielding a net of 2 percent, the institution must purchase $3 billion of the lesser-yielding assets in order to achieve the same net income. As Bill pointed out, this would necessitate a growth waiver.

Sanchez indicated that a growth waiver probably would not be granted, but Lincoln could submit an application, and it would be reviewed by several people and be decided on "at the highest level." That's not surprising—Charlie believed that all aspects of this examination were being decided by people "at the highest level." Charlie believed that that was what was wrong with the exam. These people "at the highest level" converted a routine examination into an attempt to rewrite or reinterpret the regulations in order to curtail the otherwise permissible activities of a nontraditional association like Lincoln.

The meeting closed with a discussion of a letter of intention that the regulators wanted Bill to submit to them. The letter was to describe the changes that Bill was going to make in Lincoln's operations. Deardorff stated that it would be an important guide in determining the FHLBB enforcement document. Bill requested that any enforcement document not be referred to as a cease-and-desist order or supervisory agreement. He said that such a document could be harmful to Lincoln. The regulators gave little hope that they would be agreeable but said that they'd think about it.

The regulators also said that they would be starting another exam around March 1, 1988. This time, they would have people from Kenneth Leventhal and consultants on their team.

Bill's report to the other management personnel of Lincoln and ACC was not encouraging. The regulators' proposal that Lincoln dispose of its assets was unworkable and unacceptable. Lincoln knew that the only way to realize the maximum benefit from its investments was to proceed in an orderly fashion with the development plans that it already had in place. They understood that this was not a three-to-five-year process. Some of the assets—like Estrella, Castle Meadows, and the Uplands—would take up to twenty years to complete. If these assets were sold "as is," Lincoln would not realize any developer's profit. Moreover, because of the size of these projects, there were not many development companies that had the ability to stand in Lincoln's shoes. What San Francisco was proposing was not workable and was an unsafe and unsound course of action.

Bill was convinced that San Francisco was absolutely committed to a supervisory action. All that could be gained by submitting a letter of intention was that Lincoln could buy some time to try to get Washington to accept a negotiated settlement. He also felt that Lincoln should start looking for potential buyers as soon as possible. The die was cast in San Francisco. As long as San Francisco was the supervisory district, Lincoln would not be able to continue to operate as it had in the past. The only options were to sell or change.

Lincoln put three strategies into play. First, in order to stall any actions against Lincoln, Bill would prepare something for San Francisco. Second, Bill would begin to look for potential buyers. Third, and most important, Lincoln would use some of its contacts in Washington to set up a meeting with Dochow to try to get an MOU negotiated. With a little luck, San Francisco could be cut out of the decision-making process, and, perhaps, Lincoln could find more reasonable people to listen to and consider its case.

Based on Bill's report, Lincoln was convinced that San Francisco was not going to agree to a negotiated settlement with Lincoln; instead, it was going to go ahead with its plans for a C&D order. This course of action also appears to have been completely embraced by both O'Connell and Smuzynski, who were assembling support in Washington for the enforcement document. This was in spite of the fact that a C&D proceeding would not accomplish their objectives.

They had to know that a C&D order would be opposed and that the ensuing legal conflict could take years, and a lot of dollars in legal expenses, to resolve. In the meantime, if their concerns about Lincoln being a threat to the FSLIC were valid, the threat would continue unabated as the C&D wound its way through the court system. Thus, the strategy of a C&D order doesn't seem to have been very well thought out by any of its proponents. Aside from making San Francisco look like tough regulators, the C&D route would fail to achieve any of the FHLBB's purposes. This result was clearly evident to some of the cooler heads in the FHLBB, who started to take more seriously the idea of reaching a workable compromise with Lincoln.

Lincoln's management faced a dilemma as they contemplated how to transform Lincoln. Lincoln's real-estate and equity-security activities created over $150 million a year in gross profits. Since the average spread on mortgage-backed securities or residential mortgages was around 200 basis points (or 2 percent, as one percentage point is equal to 100 basis points), a billion-dollar investment in GNMAs would yield net interest income of about $20 million, on average. To cover the earnings generated from Lincoln's nontraditional activities, the association would have to purchase and hold $8 billion or more in GNMAs or single-family mortgages. Since Lincoln's total assets at the end of 1987 were about $5 billion, that would mean Lincoln would have to grow at an annual rate of as much as 50 percent—almost double the permitted growth rate. There was no way that San Francisco would allow Lincoln to grow at that rate.

Even if such growth were permissible, it was laden with risk. In order to generate the deposits necessary to finance the GNMA purchases, Lincoln would have to increase the deposit interest rate which, in turn, would decrease the spread, which would increase the investment volume Lincoln would need. The result was a vicious circle. And if rates rose during the period that the strategy was in play, Lincoln would create a new problem rather than solve an existing one. Lincoln would convert itself into an institution with a negative interest-rate spread, plunging asset values, and lots of red ink. Betting that rates would remain constant or fall was a big gamble.

Now, the feds and the CDSL would have some easy answers to this dilemma. First, they'd say, "Don't buy GNMAs. Originate your own single-family mortgages, just like traditional associations have always done." Easier said than done. The economics and market for originating mortgages changed dramatically in the 1980s.

When a lender originates a mortgage loan, it charges the borrower a fee, called origination points, equal to 1 percent to over 2 percent, depending on the market. Prior to December 1986, the S&L could take these points into income. In December 1986, the Financial Accounting Standards Board issued standard no. 91, "Accounting for Nonrefundable Fees and Costs Associated with Originating or Acquiring Loans and Initial Direct Costs of Leases." The standard stated: "Loan origination fees shall be deferred and recognized over the life of the loan as an adjustment of yield (interest income)." The standard also provided for the deferral of the incremental direct costs of originating loans. The effect of this standard was to reduce the income that loan originators were able to reflect in their financial statements.

Also, the single-family loan market, by 1987, was dominated by a few government-sponsored enterprises (GSEs), namely, GNMA, FNMA, and FHLMC. These organizations, through their ability to issue mortgage-backed securities, have effectively erased the position once held by S&Ls in financing housing in the United States. These organizations pay no taxes, can issue securities without having to file with the SEC, and operate independently of the federal government, even though the government guarantees some or all of their obligations.

The GSEs basically set the rates for mortgages in the United States. They purchase mortgages originated by S&Ls, mortgage bankers, brokers, and home builders. They put the mortgages into batches or pools. The pools secure certificates, whose principal and interest are guaranteed, in whole or in part, by the government. Then, the pools are sold to investors.

Because of the ability to sell loans to the GSEs, mortgage originators no longer have to have the wherewithal to hold the mortgages for collection. They can establish a line of credit—a warehouse line—with a financial institution which allows them to fund a pool of mortgages. Once the pool is originated, the loans are sold to one of the GSEs, and the proceeds of sale are used to pay off the warehouse line. Then, the process starts all over again. The originator makes its income off of the origination points. This cycle has allowed hundreds, if not thousands, of entities to become mortgage originators—a role which once was almost exclusively filled by S&Ls. The new people in the market are not burdened with a branch network; therefore, they can run very low overhead operations.

In the early- and mid-1980s, S&Ls could not cross state boundary lines, so many of them created mortgage-banking subsidiaries that could conduct multistate operations. Some of these operations became very large, capturing significant market shares. The parent S&Ls served almost as warehouse lenders, buying the subsidiary's loan production and selling it in the secondary market. By 1987, when Lincoln was considering its dilemma, the markets in which Lincoln operated, primarily Arizona and California, were virtually saturated with mortgage originators. The only way that Lincoln could have gained a sizeable piece of the market would have been to offer prospective borrowers a lower cost—either lower points or a lesser interest rate—than others in the market. This would have reduced the already thin margins that originators were realizing.

If Lincoln opted to enter the mortgage-origination business, the entry cost would be steep. Lincoln would have to lease space; hire loan processors, loan servicing, and secondary market specialists; and acquire sophisticated computer hardware and software systems. Since most of the skilled mortgage-origination people were already employed, Lincoln would have to pay above-market wages to attract the best producers. The investment was high to enter a business characterized by intense competition, low profit margins, and inherent risks.

As to interest-rate risk, the feds could be expected to offer some dubious advice. They'd say, "Avoid the interest-rate risk by offering only adjustable rate mortgages (ARMs)." Again, easier said than done. The public has never been very enthusiastic about ARMs. In the 1980s, in an attempt to get the public to accept ARMs, many lenders offered teaser rates. These were lower rates that were charged for the first year or so and were designed to "tease" the borrower into accepting an ARM loan. The effect was to reduce the lender's yield in the years when the teaser rate was charged; consequently, the spread was negatively impacted. Teaser rates also made it difficult to sell the ARMs at a profit.

With respect to fixed-rate loans, the feds would say, "Hedge the risk with financial futures contracts." Many associations tried hedging, including Lincoln. Very few of them ever achieved the results they were looking for in their hedging programs. Most of these programs resulted in increased costs over the long run, not lower costs. The fact is that it wasn't really possible to eliminate interest-rate risk.

Therefore, the return to a traditional operation was no panacea. While there were successful associations that conducted traditional operations, most, but certainly not all, were smaller, relatively new organizations not saddled with a portfolio of loans with low fixed rates that had been originated in the 1970s. The market was such that some niche shops could succeed, but it was no longer a market that could support all of the nation's S&Ls. Those days had ended when Congress deregulated deposit rates. The almost guaranteed spread that S&Ls had enjoyed in the years before the rampant inflation of the late 1970s had disappeared.

The effects of deposit deregulation and escalating interest rates are clearly evident in the industry statistics. Eroded spreads caused many S&Ls to experience operating losses in the late 1970s and early 1980s, when all of them conducted traditional businesses. A study prepared for Lincoln by Lexecon, Inc., showed the percentage of S&Ls who had GAAP net worths below 3 percent, including those with negative net worths, for each year from 1977 through 1985. These statistics were derived from data obtained from the FHLBB and were as follows:

1977	-	5.5 percent	(223 out of 4,055).
1978	-	5.0 percent	(204 out of 4,048).
1979	-	5.2 percent	(208 out of 4,038).
1980	-	7.9 percent	(315 out of 3,993).
1981	-	19.9 percent	(744 out of 3,743).
1982	-	34.6 percent	(1,137 out of 3,287).
1983	-	38.3 percent	(1,205 out of 3,146).
1984	-	42.8 percent	(1,343 out of 3,135).
1985	-	40.7 percent	(1,294 out of 3,180).

These statistics show that an increasing percentage of the industry, with a growing amount of assets, were in the trouble zone before nontraditional operations were widespread.

By the end of 1985, there were 461 insolvent thrifts (GAAP net worth below zero) with total assets of $112.7 billion. Also, between 1980 and the end of 1985, nearly 600 institutions failed and went out of existence. The peak year was 1982, before Garn-St. Germain was effective, when over 250 institutions failed and ceased to exist.

So, contrary to the popular myth, the deregulation created by the Garn-St. Germain legislation didn't cause the problem—it may have contributed to making it worse, but it didn't cause it. The industry had plenty of sick institutions who had contracted a fatal disease while conducting the touted risk-free, traditional operations that the FHLBB was insistent on pushing Lincoln to adopt.

Lincoln saw the problems in trying to convert to a traditional S&L operation and realized that it would be difficult, if not impossible, to turn profitably into a single-family lender like San Francisco wanted. A better alternative was to sell the association. Bill Hinz knew a large home builder in Tucson who was interested in buying an S&L, probably in concert with another equity partner. This party, who wanted Bill to run Lincoln if they bought it, was introduced to ACC by Bill. In early 1988, they started their due-diligence investigation.

In the meantime, as Bill Hinz was beginning to insert himself into managing Lincoln, he ran into problems. Bill thought that being the CEO of Lincoln meant that he was responsible for all of its operations, including those conducted in the subsidiary service corporations. Charlie, Judy, and Kielty, as well as others in the ACC organization, meant only the branch operations, and not the service corporations, when they referred to Lincoln. If Hinz was responsible for the entire consolidated Lincoln group, that meant Judy and Kielty essentially reported to Hinz, since ACC itself had limited operations. And Judy and Kielty thought that Hinz reported to them.

This lack of understanding, as one might imagine, caused immediate and serious conflicts and confrontations among the people involved. Bill Hinz quickly found himself isolated—a stranger looking from the outside into an organization that was rejecting him. He was unable to accomplish the tasks he set out to do. He ran into deep resistance at every turn in the road and became very frustrated with the whole situation.

Bill also had another problem. On the one hand, he was responsible for seeing that ACC got the best price possible for Lincoln. On the other, with the potential buyer wanting him to run Lincoln if it were purchased, he wanted that party to pay the lowest price necessary to make a good deal. He couldn't serve both masters. In late February 1988, as a result of this conflict of interest, combined with the resistance he was getting from Judy, Kielty, and others, Bill and Charlie decided to sever Hinz' employment. In early March 1988, even though the Tucson people opted not to purchase Lincoln, Hinz' ties to Lincoln and ACC ended completely.

With Bill Hinz' departure, any plans to move Lincoln to a more traditional operation also ended. That left the negotiation of an acceptable MOU as Lincoln's only option to end the war with the FHLBB peacefully. In late January 1988, Lincoln started to devote all of its energies to pursuing the MOU.

Ten

Negotiating a Peaceful Solution

In late January 1988, Lincoln called on Margery Waxman, of the Sidley & Austin law firm in Washington, to set up a meeting between Lincoln and the FHLBB staff to discuss the proposed MOU and to determine whether a negotiated settlement was possible. If the meeting did not reveal any sign that the FHLBB was willing to negotiate, Lincoln would make the necessary preparations to litigate a potential C&D order.

Margery Waxman, like many Washington-based attorneys, had previously worked for the federal government. Her value to her clients was therefore not necessarily her legal skills but rather her contacts—contacts who allowed her to cut through the layers of bureaucracy to reach governmental decision makers. This is the norm in Washington. The law firms in the city are heavily seeded with lawyers who have spent several years working for one of the federal agencies before entering private practice. Once in private practice, they can enjoy extremely high earnings from trading on the contacts they made while employed by the government. Many function as lobbyists and influence peddlers, while others serve as liaisons between their citizen-clients and the self-anointed royalty of the three branches of government, including the legions of bureaucrats who have almost permanent tenure in the halls of government.

The nameless, faceless bureaucrats wield much of the real power in Washington. They remain in their positions, while elected or appointed officials come and go every two, four, or six years. To identify, let alone gain access to, these people, one needs a guide and sponsor. That's where the Washington lawyer becomes important.

Lawyers, like Margery Waxman, know whom to call, and they know, when they do call, the person on the other end of the line will listen. This system works because the person in government knows that someday he will want to cash in on his own contacts; then, people like Waxman can gain them entry into the right law firm or think tank.

One of Margery Waxman's key contacts was Darrel Dochow, who became the top person in the FHLBB's Office of Regulatory Policy,

Oversight and Supervision (ORPOS) after M. Danny Wall replaced Gray as chairman of the FHLBB in the summer of 1987. Waxman believed that Dochow had the power to overrule San Francisco and would be amenable to considering a negotiated settlement. It had been that reasoning that had caused Kielty to send a draft of the MOU to Dochow some months earlier.

Waxman was able to reach Dochow while he was on vacation in Hawaii, and they set up a meeting for either February 4 or 5, 1988.

In preparation for the meeting, on February 2, 1988, Bill Hinz, Jim Grogan, and I flew to New York, where, in Kaye Scholer's offices, we met Charlie, Peter Fishbein, Tim Kruckeberg, Bob Kielty, Mark Sauter, and some of the other Kaye Scholer attorneys. We discussed the various enforcement options available to the FHLBB, including how each could affect Lincoln and how each could be countered through litigation. However, the consensus of the group was to try to avoid litigation. No one believed that Lincoln or the FHLBB would derive any benefits from a prolonged legal battle. Thus, the focus turned to the scheduled meeting with Dochow and the MOU.

The first concern was: Who would be representing the FHLBB? If the meeting included people from San Francisco, it was unlikely that the MOU concept would be given a fair hearing. Everyone was convinced that San Francisco had decided how they wanted to proceed, and no one believed that they were about to change their position. Charlie called Waxman and asked her to find out who would be attending the meeting.

Waxman was not able to talk with Dochow, but she did speak to O'Connell. O'Connell told her that at least Patriarca and Sanchez would attend. This wasn't good news. It was decided that Waxman should talk to Dochow and tell him that if anyone from San Francisco attended, the meeting wouldn't be fruitful. In fact, Lincoln might cancel the meeting and take its chances in court.

The next day, the entire group flew to Washington and reconvened in Sidley & Austin's offices. For the rest of the day, the MOU was drafted and redrafted. In each version, something was added or deleted or the lawyers played with the language of the document. Each lawyer wanted to change and revise the document to leave his or her mark on the MOU. In the meantime, a small army of secretaries was run ragged making the various changes. In the end, the MOU was the same as the one that the lawyers had started out with at the beginning of the meeting.

One thing was accomplished that day. The meeting with Dochow was fixed for the next morning, February 4. The Lincoln group decided that if Charlie took anyone else with him, Dochow would feel compelled to do the same. If there were too many people in attendance, the meeting would get sidetracked and the purpose would never be accomplished. With just two people, Charlie could focus Dochow's attention on the central issue—

the MOU and the importance to both sides of avoiding a legal struggle. Thus, the only people in the meeting would be Charlie and Dochow.

While the Lincoln group was meeting, Dochow conducted a series of his own meetings to determine who should meet with Lincoln. There was a meeting on February 3, involving Patriarca, Sanchez, Black, Dochow, O'Connell, and Smuzynski. In a letter to Alan Litman, of the Pillsbury firm, dated February 16, 1988, Black described the events which took place in the meeting. Some of the key discussion items, as reported by Black, were:

... Waxman described the meeting as a final attempt to resolve the situation. She requested that our representatives tell Lincoln what we wanted done and Lincoln would either say yes or no at that meeting to what we wanted done. If no, then they would litigate. Darrel also informed us that Lincoln had taken the position that it would not agree to anything with the Eleventh District and that a requirement for them agreeing to anything was that the Supervisory Authority of the Eleventh District over Lincoln be removed.

Darrel indicated that he was inclined to agree to the removal of the Eleventh District's jurisdiction over Lincoln, or at least agree that no examiners from the Eleventh District be used in the upcoming March 1988 examination of the institution, and rather that some kind of a Blue Ribbon Group composed of examiners from multiple districts be brought in to conduct the next examination. Mike Patriarca indicated our belief that these things were totally unjustified and would cause a devastating precedent to the system; that the concept that a institution could pick its supervisors and could veto its supervisors was a terrible precedent for the system.

Mike and I stressed that ORPOS [primarily O'Connell and Smuzynski] had reviewed the work of the Eleventh District, that it had found that we were correct in our conclusions that the institution proposed a severe regulatory problem, and that they and the Office of Enforcement had agreed that a stringent Cease and Desist Order was necessary and that all parties had agreed on the form, the central form of the Cease and Desist Order that was needed to bring this severe supervisory problem under control.

We also discussed the Cease and Desist Order that the Office of Enforcement and the Eleventh District had agreed was necessary. Rosemary Stewart said that if Lincoln was willing to sign the Cease and Desist Order we had proposed the Bank Board should definitely enter into it because she didn't think we could get that much relief in a litigated proceeding.

... Darrel claimed that it was necessary to go forward on the basis of removing the Eleventh District's jurisdiction because this was the only way of securing a prompt restriction on Lincoln's unsafe and unsound practices. He argued that unless Lincoln was willing to consent to relief it would take many months to get such relief through a contested Cease and Desist Order and that if the price for securing Lincoln's consent was removal of our jurisdiction that was what would need to be done. . . .

Dochow's comments in this meeting show that he was definitely leaning toward removing San Francisco's control over Lincoln. He said that the reason he concluded that it might be best to remove San Francisco centered around the various leaks which had occurred. All of the San Francisco people, with support from both O'Connell and Smuzynski, denied that they had anything to do with the leaks.

It was also clear that the lawyers in Washington concurred with Dochow's inclination to remove San Francisco. The comments attributed to Rosemary Stewart demonstrate that there was little support in Washington for the idea of pursuing a C&D order requiring litigation. Yet, that was the course of action San Francisco was taking.

This was the first time that San Francisco had been advised that their continued supervision of Lincoln was seriously in doubt. As Patriarca indicated, he thought that the removal of San Francisco would be "a devastating precedent." It also threatened the standing of people like Patriarca and Black in the FHLBB structure. So, the concept of San Francisco's removal was not merely an organizational problem. It was a personal problem for some of the regulators, who saw such an action as a vote of "no confidence" in their regulatory judgment by their superiors. This personalization of the issue increased Patriarca's resistance to the idea of any MOU which threatened San Francisco, in general, or him, in particular.

The other subject which received considerable attention was Dochow's decision to exclude Black from the planned meeting with Keating and Lincoln. The San Francisco people, to a person, thought this decision was the same as allowing Lincoln to pick and choose which regulators it would deal with and which ones it would not. The Eleventh District's position was that this was not proper and that the regulators should select whomever they wanted to serve as their representatives. Again, the argument was that this decision established a bad precedent. But the subtext was that Black viewed such an action as a personal affront, and his ego was injured.

Because of the personal and organizational implications of a negotiated settlement, the Eleventh District rejected the concept of an MOU. The San Francisco regulators really wanted a conservatorship, feeling that a C&D order was being lenient with Lincoln. They thought that using a new examination as a basis for stronger enforcement was wrong, because Lincoln would not be subjected to the stronger restrictions the C&D would impose during the course of the new examination. They also thought that the idea of a negotiated settlement sent the wrong signal to other institutions, because it implied that the institutions had a say in how the rules of the FHLBB would be enforced.

The San Francisco group also thought they were receiving shabby treatment. They believed that they, not Washington, should retain control of any regulatory decision involving Lincoln. They also thought that the issue of who controlled the enforcement of Lincoln had already been decided and that Dochow and the other Washington folks had agreed control rested with the Eleventh District. Thus, their argument was that Dochow was changing his position without sufficient justification.

Later that day, the regulators held another meeting. This time the attendees were Dochow, O'Connell, Smuzynski, Stewart, Cirona, Patriarca, Sanchez, Black, and FHLBB Board member Larry White. White was the only one of the three Bank Board members who was a carry over from Ed Gray's term on the FHLBB. He, like Gray, had supported re-regulation and was in favor of stronger enforcement actions. He had also been around when the Henkel and Benston appointments were being considered, so he definitely knew about the long-standing controversy between the FHLBB and Keating.

Again, Black's letter described this meeting. Some of the content of his letter is as follows:

> Darrel began with a factual description of Lincoln that did not correspond with either the fact findings of our examination or the fact findings of the ORPOS review of that examination. He then indicated that he believed that we could get Lincoln to agree to the terms of the Cease and Desist Order if we were willing to call the Cease and Desist Order something other than a Cease and Desist Order. We indicated our disagreement with that and noted that Mr. Hinz had already rejected the proposed Cease and Desist Order's terms and that Lincoln was continuing to insist on a Memorandum of Understanding approach, the terms of which were totally unacceptable to all the parties involved.
>
> We stressed again that once the Bank Board indicated that it could be extorted with threats of a law suit [related to the leaks], it was a never-ending process and set a terrible precedent far broader than Lincoln and explained again the terrible precedent that removing our jurisdiction would have in our district and all the other districts. We also noted that Lincoln had had an entire series of meetings with board members and with ORPOS that we had been excluded from, that Lincoln apparently used these meetings to make claims of personal misconduct on behalf of various Eleventh District employees and that the Bank Board had, and ORPOS had, taken actions that impeded the examination without even checking with the Eleventh District to determine whether Lincoln's claims were correct. We stressed that this was not a good way to run a railroad, and that it was improper as a matter of fundamental

fairness to the individuals in the Eleventh District who were subject to these claims but had no opportunity to know the charges or to respond to them.

Board Member White asked why the meeting had to take place the next day, Thursday [February 4, 1988]. He stressed that both policy issues [the removal of the Eleventh District and the exclusion of Black from the meeting] brought to him were very important and deserved greater consideration and should be based on more knowledge of the facts. We agreed that there was no reason why the meeting had to go forward at that juncture and that it was critical that Lincoln's factual allegations be investigated so that the Board act on the basis of facts and not simply claims. Darrel and Rosemary Stewart strongly favored going ahead with the meeting the next day. They suggested that the meeting go forward but not discuss the issue of the removal of the Eleventh District's jurisdiction. Larry White indicated that would not deal with the issue of excluding Bill Black from the meeting, which he considered an important issue, and while he was only one Board Member, he certainly voted that no meeting occur. Darrel indicated that he should not have brought it to the Board's attention, and should have proceeded, but Board Member White interjected that it was too late that Darrel had already brought it to the Board's attention, it was at the Board, if he hadn't wanted it at the Board's level, he should have never brought it to him.

To some extent Dochow wasn't very smart meeting with White, although he was probably maneuvered into it by San Francisco. White was the one Board member most likely to oppose giving consideration to what Lincoln had to say.

But Dochow made up for the lapse in judgment and apparently talked to both Board members Wall and Martin. A memo written by Monica Gawet, dated February 8, 1988, said: "Kevin verified that a meeting was held on Friday between D. Dochow and Charles Keating. The meeting was held at Chairman Wall's request, and he recommended that a 'peaceful solution' be agreed upon."

Thus, in spite of the two meetings which San Francisco attended, the meeting with Keating was back on track, and no one from San Francisco would be in attendance. There are a couple of other things which should be noted about these two meetings.

First, San Francisco was always quick to point out that ORPOS agreed with the examination findings. In this context, ORPOS is really Smuzynski and O'Connell, both of whom had been in on the examination for a considerable period of time. They were always part of San Francisco's team, although Lincoln didn't know that was the case. It is therefore disingenuous to refer to their review as independent, because they were involved in the decision making on this examination almost as much as anyone in San Francisco. Also, their knowledge appears to have been largely limited to what they gained from reading reports and discussing matters with other FHLBB personnel. They didn't visit Lincoln's facilities, review detail examination work papers, or spend much time with the field examiners. Therefore, much of the information they received had been run through a filter before it reached them.

Secondly, the San Francisco people were experiencing some of what Lincoln had gone through in their hands. They resented Dochow's interpretations and his representations of what he considered to be fact. They were upset that they had been accused of acting improperly without receiving a fair hearing. These were precisely the kinds of things that Lincoln had been objecting to for nearly two years. Black and the others felt the same frustration and anger that Charlie felt and had to endure.

On Thursday, February 4, 1988, Charlie and Dochow met. The meeting lasted about five hours, from around 8:30 A.M. to 1:30 P.M. A wide range of subjects were discussed in this meeting, but the essence of Charlie's message to Dochow was that he was willing to compromise in order to resolve the issues emanating from San Francisco's examination of Lincoln. Charlie said that ACC would contribute an additional $10 million to Lincoln's capital and that Lincoln would try to sell $50 million in subordinated debt that would qualify as added regulatory capital. Charlie also agreed to improve Lincoln's underwriting practices and said that Lincoln would curtail certain of its investment activities.

The heart of Charlie's proposal was the MOU, in which the concessions which Charlie expressed orally to Dochow were committed to in writing. In return for Lincoln's concessions, Charlie wanted a new examination by a district other than San Francisco and, after that exam was completed, he wanted Lincoln transferred to the new district. As for the 1986 examination findings, Lincoln would agree to some of the appraisal losses but not to most of them. Lincoln would not agree to any of the other adjustments proposed by San Francisco. Charlie also told Dochow that he believed that the issues related to direct investments should be resolved by a court, as the parties were simply too far apart on the issues.

Throughout the meeting, Charlie emphasized the inherent quality of Lincoln's assets. He stressed the fact that San Francisco's examiners simply did not understand the assets, nor did they understand Lincoln's operations, particularly the land-development activities and Lincoln's debt and equity security investments. In effect, he told Dochow, "If you give us the room to operate, we will make strong profits in Lincoln." But he also told Dochow, "If Lincoln is to be run by regulators, it won't work. If I have to lose a fortune, I'd rather do it quickly, rather than being crippled by the regulators, where Lincoln dies a slow death."

Midway through this meeting, I received a telephone call asking me to go to the FHLBB offices to meet with Carol Larson regarding some accounting questions.

When I arrived at Carol Larson's office, Kevin O'Connell was also present. The two issues they wanted to discuss were Crowder Water Ranch and the Uplands project.

With respect to Crowder, I explained my understanding of the status of Arizona's ground-water law and the necessity for Lincoln to farm the property in order to establish and maintain the water rights related to the Crowder land. We talked about the intended use of the property and the fact that its value was the water rights, not the land per se. We discussed Lincoln's expense-capitalization theory under FASB standard no. 67 and why the theory could be supported under the circumstances. Larson was noncommittal and indicated that she wanted to think about Lincoln's theories before coming to her own conclusions.

Even though he wasn't an accountant, O'Connell interrupted several times to express his opinion that Lincoln was wrong and that the expenses shouldn't be capitalized. It was clear to me that he didn't understand the accounting issues and he didn't want to.

When we turned to the Uplands, Larson asked about Lincoln's capitalization of the costs of a management agreement related to the property. The management agreement was with two people, Barnes and Connally, who were developing the property before Lincoln took total control and ownership. I explained to Larson that Lincoln had, indeed, capitalized these costs, but that both Arthur Andersen and Arthur Young had thought that the use of the management agreement as the basis for capitalization was not correct. The firms believed that the capitalized management fees should be reversed and that, instead, interest should be capitalized. I told her that calculations done by each firm demonstrated that the difference between capitalizing management fees versus interest was not material. She said that she understood the distinction between the two costs and that it explained what Lincoln was doing. She didn't say, one way or the other, whether she agreed with Lincoln.

At this point, O'Connell butted in again. He had a copy of a consent agreement which Charlie had entered into with the SEC in the 1970s. The consent agreement was to settle, without any admission of wrongdoing by Charlie, a dispute which arose while Charlie was with American Financial

Corporation. O'Connell asserted that the deal with Barnes and Connally was a violation of the consent agreement, involved self-dealing with friends, and was a violation of law. As he made these accusations, he got very agitated, his voice became strident, his speech rapid, and he waved the copy of the consent agreement around in the air like it was a battle pennant. When he paused for a breath, I asked if I could read the consent agreement.

I read the agreement and couldn't see any connection between the facts recited in it and the Uplands situation. I told O'Connell, "Look, I'm an accountant, not a lawyer. But I don't see any connection between this agreement and the subject we are discussing. I don't have the facts of Lincoln's acquisition of the Uplands committed to memory, and it wasn't my firm that audited the acquisition, but, from what I do recall, you appear to be off base on this. I can discuss the accounting issues, as we have been doing. If you want to know more about the acquisition of the property and the precise relationship between Barnes and Connally and Keating, you'll have to talk to Lincoln's lawyers."

Before O'Connell could react, the phone rang in Larson's office, and O'Connell and I were asked to go to Dochow's office. This was the first time I had met Dochow. Darrel is a round-faced, somewhat rotund man, with sandy-colored hair and a bland personality. His demeanor is calm; his speech slow and precise; his voice is so quiet you have to strain to hear him; his language reflects the regulator's jargon; and he exhibits no visible emotions.

Dochow asked if we had agreed on the accounting issues we were discussing. I told him we had not.

"Has Lincoln recorded the various reserves contemplated in the draft MOU Mr. Keating has given me?" Dochow asked.

I responded, "Lincoln has general reserves recorded on its books which are greater than the specific reserves that it says it will record as part of the MOU. If the MOU is entered into, Lincoln has indicated that it will reclassify the required amount of general reserves to specific reserves." I indicated that the MOU didn't contemplate setting up all the specific reserves requested by the examiners, because Lincoln did not agree with certain of the examination findings.

"Are the auditors satisfied that Lincoln's reserves are appropriate?" Dochow asked.

"The audit of Lincoln's 1987 financial statements is still in progress," I said. "As part of any audit, the audit team performs tests of the client's allowances for losses. That is being done in the Lincoln audit."

"If the audit tests show a need for additional reserves, will Lincoln record them?" Dochow then asked.

"If the tests disclose that the reserves are materially misstated, we will propose adjustments to the company. It's the company's decision to record the adjustments or not," I said. "If the company doesn't record the adjustments that we believe are necessary for a fair presentation of its financial condition and results of operations, we address that in our report."

At this point, Charlie said, "Lincoln will record any material adjustments proposed by the auditors."

That ended Dochow's questions of me, and, with that, the meeting ended. Charlie said that he would send Dochow a revised copy of the MOU and that they should meet again the next day to discuss the draft. Dochow agreed.

As Charlie and I were going back to Sidley & Austin's offices, I asked him what he thought of Dochow. Charlie said that he couldn't really read Dochow, because he didn't show any reactions, but he did say that Dochow was the first regulator he'd dealt with who seemed willing to listen and to try to work out the problems. Charlie felt that the meeting had been successful and that eventually Dochow would accept the MOU concept.

When we reached Sidley & Austin's offices, Charlie recounted his meeting with Dochow. He indicated the things that he thought had to be changed in the draft MOU as a result of the discussion. The rest of the afternoon was devoted to making these changes.

At several intervals, Charlie and Waxman left the conference room where we were and called Dochow to clarify a point. Late in the day, a revised draft was sent to Dochow. There was some fine-tuning done after the draft was sent, and Waxman called Dochow at his home to discuss some issues.

On February 5, 1988, Charlie and Margery Waxman met with Dochow and Rosemary Stewart to go over the draft MOU. The draft was reviewed on an item-by-item basis, with the two regulators pointing out those areas that they believed still needed to be changed. Waxman noted their comments, and the regulators were told that a revised draft would be sent to them. On February 12, 1988, Charlie sent a revised draft, with the changes underlined, to Danny Wall and Dochow.

On February 16, there was a telephone conference involving Jordan Luke, who was the FHLBB's general counsel, Hershkowitz, Stewart, O'Connell, William Robertson, who was on the enforcement staff, George Barclay, who was with the FHLB-Dallas, Karl Hoyle, who was the FHLBB's public affairs director, and Dochow, all of whom were in Washington, and Bill Black and some Pillsbury lawyers in San Francisco. Minutes of that conference call, which were included as an exhibit to the transcript of congressional hearings, reflect the comments made by the various participants.

Barclay, Dochow, Luke, Hoyle, and Rosemary Stewart made up a group known as the Enforcement Review Committee (ERC). This committee was formed by the Bank Board in December 1987. Its purpose was to draft enforcement policies and to advise the Board, as well as the district banks, on specific enforcement cases or proposals which presented policy questions or controversial issues. The committee was also delegated the authority to initiate formal examination and investigation proceedings and to approve consent cease-and-desist orders as well as other enforcement actions.

As the meeting began, Jordan Luke addressed the presence of the Pillsbury people by saying, "I object. These are internal discussions. Also, I previously made my objection to using fee counsel on Agency matters. We need to discuss this."

There was a brief break while the Washington group debated whether it was appropriate to proceed with the Pillsbury people present. Evidently, Luke appreciated the fact that the use of Pillsbury, of necessity, involved disclosure of information that the regulations required the FHLBB to hold in strict confidence. A fact which didn't seem to bother San Francisco.

When the meeting resumed, Luke said, "I am not at all comfortable with Federal Home Loan Bank's using fee counsel in performing Agency functions. Notwithstanding that, the strong feeling here is that because your fee counsel has been relied upon so heavily in this matter, it would not be fair to exclude them. I'll recede from that concern for this matter, but I continue to hold my opinion strongly."

It is worth noting that the use of fee counsel could be one reason why San Francisco was pushing the C&D concept so hard. They were relying on Pillsbury for direction. If a C&D order were pursued, everyone conceded that litigation, which could drag on for years, would result. As litigators, Pillsbury would probably represent the FHLBB and could realize substantial fees. On the other hand, if the situation resolved itself peacefully, Pillsbury's role could be over. No big fees. It is therefore conceivable that the fee counsel's advice may not have been driven by the counsel part of its title but, rather, by the fee part of the title.

Dochow opened by saying:

The intention of this meeting is to make sure that both Mr. Barclay and Mr. Luke get a good sense of what is going on and provide them full access to all information to determine the appropriate supervisory response for Lincoln. The issue is what to take up to the Bank Board on how Lincoln should be dealt with. The Committee can either make a new recommendation or pass through the existing recommendation. Hope to have that at the end of the meeting today. On the issue of change of district banks, we should use this week to gather information. We still do not have a final document from Keating. The result is that we are still waiting for a final recommendation.

Dochow then gave a brief history of Lincoln and its relationship with the examiners and the FHLBB. Dochow concluded his recital with:

San Francisco wanted a C&D. Mike [Patriarca] was willing to settle for agreement. In the midst of this, Mike suggested a redraft of the C&D that ORPOS and San Francisco had agreed upon, to make it stand alone and individual paragraphs not related so closely. That never happened. ORPOS was going to have a sit-down discussion with Keating and Margery Waxman, local counsel hired to deal with regulatory issues. Lincoln used New York counsel on issues for litigation. We were told they have drafted portions of that litigation that alleges everything. They had previously agreed not to file this if they could get a separate hearing. Lincoln made a commitment to representatives of the Bank Board that they would not file if things moved forward and they got an objective review.

Then, after some clarifying comments by Luke, Dochow said,

Then Mr. Keating came in within a week or two. He met with the Chairman, myself and three or four other people. Basically, at that time Mr. Keating wanted us to look at what's happened. It was decided ORPOS should take a fresh look at what is happening. That is the best we can do—try to make a determination. We met with FHLBSF and had accountants meet with us. ORPOS confirmed 90 percent of the asset classifications and the institution's high risk, direct investment violations, loan documentation deficiencies, and other factual patterns previously asserted by the examiners. [Remember, the ORPOS review was conducted entirely by O'Connell and Smuzynski.]

Dochow then discussed the meetings with San Francisco concerning delaying his meeting with Keating. He followed that by describing his February 4 meeting with Charlie.

Following Dochow's description of the meeting with Charlie, Barclay asked, "What could happen if Lincoln was presented with a document that was acceptable to Lincoln, except it didn't contain a transfer?" Dochow responded:

I don't know. On the issue of transfer, I'm not sure they will get a recommendation of this office. It would be a major policy change. The thrust of the document is, at this stage, as drafted . . . it has a cover letter from Keating saying he has reviewed the document and supports it. The document starts off with . . . lending policies, investment securities policies. Keating expects to receive advice and recommendations of an appropriate Supervisory Agent. They will consider abiding by the business plan. . . . Three years in time, one year detailed. Any changes will be made with adequate notice to the Agent; Lincoln reviews the recommendation but will not be bound over prior approval. Document says they will take writedowns.

"What say does the PSA [Principal Supervisory Agent] have?" Barclay then asked.

Dochow answered:

They're not willing to agree to any requirement for PSA approval of their underwriting policies. In the area of writedowns, the document lists assets for which they will take writedowns. It omits two that were income reversals, Uplands and Crowder Ranch; they say those are proper accounting entries. For not taking these writedowns, he will increase the contingency factor of the net worth requirement. Keating says, I will make sure my net worth stays at a level that takes into account direct investment.

Dochow went on to say:

In addition, changes need to be made in two provisions that deal with the capital question—one says that the PSA will not impose high minimum capital requirements. My intention there was that that was unacceptable. Keating proposed a compromise whereby during the time the examination is underway, or six months (whichever is shorter) no action would be taken . . . another one says the document can't be renegotiated, modified, altered, or other action taken. Basically, it takes the form that we are frozen and we are freezing supervisory action until the examination is done.

Dochow briefly talked about some other aspects of the proposed document, and then he asked this rhetorical question: "If goal [*sic*] in life is to stop failure and reduce risk, what is the best approach?"

Answering his own question, he said:

In my mind, the answer is to take whatever action to get corrective measures. The issue of transferring to a different district mucks it up. Lincoln suggested that ORPOS should have a role. I don't like it. The Bank has an obligation to lend and supervise. If there is litigation—would we win on all issues? Prevail? Yes. Do I think a court would find the basic condition of the institution intolerable? No. I could argue that, if we go to litigation, we run a higher risk that the institution would go unabated for a year or more. If we sign a document today, if they don't live by it, I'd recommend a conservatorship. I think this is a classic institution that can be saved even with existing management. San Francisco in August recommended conservatorship. I think that was premature, but the recommendation is on target if they continued doing the same things. If we find in the next examination, they have continued to do these things, then it is absolutely clear that management cannot be trusted.

Barclay asked, "Jordan, what is the next step? My question is, what do we do next? Do we present a C&D?"

"If it's a consent C&D, we have the authority to pass on it," Luke answered. "Or if asked, we can give a recommendation and advice."

This prompted Dochow to say, "I hoped to get a final decision to the Board Friday. Obviously that is not possible. I intended to bring this to the Enforcement Review Committee because we have a classic case where precedent could be set, where the district bank feels very strongly, where I will recommend a decision. I don't know what I will say on the transfer issue. This is a case for the Committee. It can make a recommendation."

There was then a great deal of discussion regarding Lincoln's claims of leaked information and of misconduct by the San Francisco people. This prompted several attempts by Black to get the ERC to let the Eleventh District present its full case to the entire committee. This internal controversy dominated the rest of the meeting. The ERC agreed to hear whatever San Francisco wanted to present in a meeting scheduled to be held in Washington the next week.

This conference-call meeting was the beginning of a shift in the internal politics of the FHLBB. Initially, it looked like it would benefit Lincoln. In reality, it ultimately worked to Lincoln's detriment. The MOU forced the ERC to consider the removal of the supervision of Lincoln from the Eleventh District. The internal debate changed the focus of the ERC from how best to regulate Lincoln to a policy issue of whether Washington could replace a district bank's supervision of a given institution.

To counteract the threat to its prestige within the FHLB structure, San Francisco was forced to defend its assessment of Lincoln by painting the worst picture possible of Lincoln as a rogue institution. The Eleventh District also appealed, through the internal grapevine, to the other district banks asking them to understand that if San Francisco's authority could be stripped by Washington, so could theirs. The debate was watched closely throughout the entire system, and people, like Dochow, were about to put their reputations on the line.

If San Francisco's authority were removed, Lincoln would become Dochow's responsibility. If there were any sign in a new examination that San Francisco's findings were correct and Lincoln was out of line, Dochow would have no choice but to react hard and fast with the conservatorship that he had promised in this conference call. If the MOU were entered into, this would effectively reduce the future enforcement options to either no action or a conservatorship. Flexibility would be removed from both Lincoln and Dochow.

The argument also placed Smuzynski and O'Connell in an awkward position. They had been supportive of San Francisco for two years. In fact, they had encouraged the examiners to take the strong actions that they were proposing. They had also conducted the so-called independent ORPOS review, concurring with the Eleventh District's findings and conclusions. So, they were as committed as anyone to, at the very least, a C&D order or, preferably, a conservatorship or receivership. But now they worked for Dochow, who was definitely leaning toward an MOU which would remove San Francisco. This forced them to go along with their boss and against their friends in San Francisco, putting them in the posture of betrayers of the Eleventh District.

The focus on the internal politics also obscured the real issues Lincoln was concerned about, which were: (1) Were the examination findings representative of Lincoln's true status and the risks it represented; (2) were the examiners wrong in their risk assessment because they failed to understand the transactions they were examining; (3) was the examination biased because of differences in philosophy between the examiners and Lincoln; and (4) would regulatory action which caused Lincoln to alter its operations cause more problems than it cured? These were some of the questions, among others, that the ERC should have been asking rather than the ones centered on the internal FHLBB issues.

The central question that the ERC should have asked about any enforcement action was: What are the probable economic consequences of the actions we are demanding of the institution? There should have been a requirement to prepare a detailed financial projection of the effects of any proposed regulatory action. There was none. As a result, the FHLBB didn't have the slightest idea what effects their actions would produce. It's the central reason they were never able to know the depth of the hole they dug whenever they forced institutions into failure and receivership. They never asked the most important questions about their own actions. This was certainly true in this instance.

Lincoln had analyzed the consequences of trying to convert to more traditional operations. The conclusions were: It would take a long time; it would require considerable growth and capital investment; and such actions were themselves laden with risk and might not be successful. The only regulator who seemed to focus on the question was, surprisingly, Crawford of the CDSL. He admitted that Lincoln could manage its assets better than any regulators and that the regulators could lose a lot of money if they took over Lincoln. So, at least he'd thought of the question.

On February 22, 1988, the ERC met to hear the Eleventh District's presentation regarding Lincoln and San Francisco's recommendation for an enforcement action. The Eleventh District prepared and submitted a thirty-three-page document which was signed by Cirona and dated February 22. The document set forth San Francisco's view of Lincoln and the course of action that they recommended. Needless to say, the document was extremely negative. Some of the sections of the document and the comments made by San Francisco are as described in the following paragraphs.

Section (B)(1) was entitled "Lincoln's reported profitability has declined sharply." The section presented a table purporting to show Lincoln's net income for the years 1985 through 1987. I'm not sure where San Francisco got their numbers, but they aren't the same as Lincoln's actual reported net income. The actual figures and those shown in the report are as follows (in millions):

YEAR	ACTUAL	AS IN REPORT
1985	$79,850	$79,526
1986	$48,958	$48,042
1987	$41,020	$28,547

Using the erroneous numbers, especially for 1987, the report stated that Lincoln's net income had declined sharply and that 1987's return on average assets was "less than one-fourth of the rate for 1985." The report also omitted the fact that Lincoln's expenses during 1986 and 1987 included nearly $50 million related to Lincoln's efforts to defend itself from the 1986 examination findings.

Section (B)(2), entitled "Lincoln's reported net income is misleading," made these assertions:

ORPOS estimates that Lincoln booked $400 million in "self-funded" income from real estate investments and ADC loans, namely interest reserves, fees and capitalized interest.

Lincoln's other recorded profits come primarily through gains on sale of assets. The gains are attributable to:

   a. Sale of pre-acquisition loans on Lincoln's books (marked to market at the time of acquisition).

   b. Gains on sale of takeover stocks.

   c. Income from transactions with its parent, ACC, totaling in excess of $7.0 million.

The examination identified improper income recognition of over $31 million.

After the examination, Lincoln recorded a $10.3 million profit from the "sale" of a 45% interest in the Phoenician and Crescent hotels, despite the fact that the Phoenician Hotel is nowhere complete and the costs to complete have risen dramatically.

Each of these claims was misleading in that the assertion implied that Lincoln's reported earnings were somehow improper. Aside from the alleged improper income recognition identified in the exam, the only thing which could be said about the sources of income cited was that the FHLB-SF didn't like them. There was nothing misleading about the reported income—it was derived from permissible activities. And as to the $31 million in improper income recognition, by the time this report was written, the FHLB-SF accountants had already reversed themselves on some of the items included in this number.

Section (B)(3) was entitled "Lincoln's reported losses are under-stated." This title itself was misleading, as a previous section clearly indicated that Lincoln reported net income in each year, not losses. Having said that, the assertions made in this section were:

After the examination, Lincoln was directed to book $53.7 million in specific loss reserves. Lincoln recorded only $36 million in appraised losses. . . .

If Lincoln had recorded the specific loss reserves it was ordered to book in 1987 it would have reported a loss for the year.

If Lincoln had recorded the over $31 million income reversals it was directed to establish by the SA it would have reported negative income for 1987.

Notwithstanding the adjustments recommended by the examiners, Lincoln has ignored numerous unrecognized losses, particularly the mark to market losses on its debt portfolio—$35 million as of 12/31/87. Lincoln's substantial trading in its junk bond portfolio evidences a trading portfolio that is required to be recorded at the lower of cost or market. If Lincoln had recorded this loss in its junk bond portfolio it would have reported negative income for 1987.

San Francisco really pulled out all stops in this section. They failed to state that none of their adjustments had been tax-effected; their own accountants could no longer support some of the income reversals; Lincoln had recorded the specific reserves they requested; Lincoln had general reserves on its books which the examiners chose to ignore; and neither the FHLBB regulations nor GAAP required the mark-to-market treatment they suggested.

These arguments by the Eleventh District were also a stretch because all of the examination adjustments related to transactions which had occurred in either 1985 or 1986, yet this report suggested that the adjustments should be booked in 1987, the year the FHLB-SF understated

Lincoln's net income. The so-called mark-to-market issue related solely to 1987, a period falling after the examination; thus, the examiners could not have examined any securities transactions in 1987. Therefore, the assertion that Lincoln should have recorded losses on securities held at December 31, 1987, in the amount of $35 million lacked foundation and was groundless.

Section (B)(4) was entitled "Lincoln's financial statements should not be relied upon." The specific comments were:

> The FHLBSF made a referral to the SEC regarding ACC's financial statements and Lincoln's possible involvement in insider trading.
>
> The SEC is actively investigating ACC's financial reporting practices. The SEC is also about to subpoena the FHLBSF's records regarding Lincoln in connection with its investigation arising from the Boesky insider trading matter.
>
> OE's investigation also developed evidence that Lincoln's backdating of documents was designed to achieve possibly improper tax benefits. An IRS investigation is ongoing as a result of a referral regarding this activity.

The Eleventh District, with the aid of a few of their friends in Washington, did make referrals to the SEC, the IRS, and the Department of Justice. All of these agencies investigated San Francisco's charges, at a cost of millions of dollars to ACC and Lincoln, and none of the investigations led to any actions against ACC or Lincoln. The referrals were largely a product of the Eleventh District's naïveté and intent to inflict maximum damage on ACC, Lincoln, and Keating for having the temerity to reject the erroneous examination conclusions. It also should be ample proof that if a group of bureaucrats wants to make life miserable for a corporation or individual, the referral trick is effective.

Section (B)(5) was entitled "Lincoln's future prospects for increased risk, losses and probable failure." The key comments were:

> ORPOS staff states that Lincoln will report substantial losses by 1990 and will fail no later than 1991 simply on the basis of existing, unrecognized losses.
>
> As the table indicates, Lincoln's reported profitability has been steadily declining. Lincoln has and must continue in higher risk activities to cover its negative interest margin. . . .

There were other comments in this section, most of which indicated that if interest rates increased, Lincoln would experience difficulties and the FSLIC's risk would increase. The key comment, however, was the one about ORPOS' dire prediction. The prediction was that Lincoln would fail because of "existing, unrecognized losses." This was, to say the least, a surprising conclusion for ORPOS to reach, since the examination report did not cite any such losses. One has to wonder where ORPOS discovered all the alleged losses if, after eight months of serious searching, the field examiners could not find any.

This prediction, which was largely the product of Smuzynski and O'Connell, was widely quoted in the internal FHLBB organization. In the months ahead, those responsible for the prediction used all their power to see that the prediction came true.

The next major section was a litany of San Francisco's allegations that Lincoln had broken numerous promises to the Eleventh District; Lincoln's management lacked credibility; and Lincoln had a disregard for regulatory compliance. The diatribe filled about five pages of the report and was replete with untruths and half-truths. Having thoroughly castigated Lincoln's behavior, the next section, consisting of four and a half pages, explained how "the examination and supervisory process has been conducted in a scrupulously fair fashion."

Then, there was a section entitled "Lincoln's alleged basis for removing FHLBSF does not withstand scrutiny." Again, the truth was bent and trampled on as San Francisco rewrote history. Nothing in any of these sections was anything other than self-serving statements by the Eleventh District, and the ERC probably saw that was the case.

There were two specific comments in these sections related to leaked information. The Eleventh-District report stated:

> Commissioner Crawford states that Mr. Binstein [author of the Regardie's articles] indicated to him that the source for his information concerning the conservatorship recommendation is in Washington D.C.
>
> The alleged recent leak to Mr. Binstein is of a document that the FHLBSF never had access to, only the Bank Board has such access.

These comments add credence to a theory that O'Connell, maybe with help from Smuzynski, was a logical candidate as the source of the leaks which so damaged Lincoln and ACC. This theory was further buttressed by the fact that the leaks continued well after the involvement of San Francisco was reduced. To this extent, Lincoln's belief that Black was responsible for all the leaks was misplaced. Black may have been at the center of the leaks in 1986, but the two people in Washington were more likely culprits for the later leaks. Since Smuzynski was also around in 1986, in theory, he cannot be ruled out as the source of some of the early leaks as well.

The next section of the Eleventh District's report argued that "The appropriate remedy is conservatorship." The basic arguments made for this position were:

ORPOS agrees that Lincoln is in unsafe and unsound condition and that there has been a dissipation of assets and earnings arising from violations of regulations.

ORPOS agrees that Lincoln's reported income does not accurately reflect its financial condition.

ORPOS estimates that even on information already gathered, Lincoln will be reporting losses by 1990 and will be a FSLIC case by 1991, and that if a conservatorship is delayed it will represent a much greater cost to FSLIC. In the proposed MOU Lincoln proposes to grow by more than $3 billion in the near term.

ORPOS states it will recommend a conservatorship if there is a material breach by Lincoln of the proposed MOU. Since breach of the MOU does not itself constitute grounds for a conservatorship, one must conclude that ORPOS is of the view that grounds now exist for conservatorship.

The Eleventh District's approach in arguing the appropriateness of a conservatorship was simply to present O'Connell, Smuzynski, and, to a lesser extent, Dochow with their own words. The fact that Smuzynski and O'Connell had jumped on San Francisco's bandwagon, and had at times actually driven the wagon, now became a real hurdle to overcome. Dochow, their boss, and Rosemary Stewart, also senior to them, weren't buying the conservatorship argument. In this argument, San Francisco was cleverly saying to Dochow, Stewart, and the rest of the ERC, "Hey, don't take our word that this is the best option—listen to your own staff. It's really their recommendation." Smuzynski and O'Connell were faced with the difficult political choice of continuing to support San Francisco or supporting their new boss by backtracking and saying there weren't sufficient grounds "at this point" for a conservatorship.

The Eleventh District then argued that if a conservatorship were not sought, the "only other reasonable alternative would be a temporary Cease and Desist Order." To support this option, they made a comparison of each element of the proposed MOU and their proposed C&D order. Of course, the comparison showed that the C&D was superior to the MOU for every point analyzed. They were not willing to concede that even a single attribute of the MOU had merit when compared to their C&D.

The analysis was followed by two pages summarizing San Francisco's conclusion that "ORPOS's proposed MOU should be rejected." The conclusion was based, in part, on the assertion that the MOU would not be effective in resolving the problems that the Eleventh District felt Lincoln presented to the FSLIC. The second basis for the conclusion was that the MOU established precedents that San Francisco did not feel were appropriate for the FHLBB to adopt.

The ERC convened on February 22, 1988, to hear the Eleventh District's presentation. San Francisco was given the opportunity to express its views regarding Lincoln to the ERC members.

A Pillsbury lawyer, Bruce Ericson, made notes of the meeting, which he distributed to four other lawyers in his firm. These notes, dated February 23, 1988, demonstrate the gulf which had developed between San Francisco and the Washington-based regulators. Throughout the meeting, as San Francisco, often aided by O'Connell, made a point, someone from Washington delivered a counterpoint.

First, consider the ever-popular subject of file stuffing.

"The examination uncovered evidence that Lincoln engaged in file stuffing," O'Connell said.

Hershkowitz responded, "Lincoln has admitted the file stuffing."

The file-stuffing reference by O'Connell was made in support of Sanchez' comment that "Lincoln's underwriting is inadequate." This brief exchange is evidence that Hershkowitz, and the others within the FHLBB, knew that Lincoln had not attempted to do anything improper by adding information to its files. Yet, the file-stuffing charge was used as the basis for referrals to the Department of Justice and was used constantly by San Francisco and its supporters, like O'Connell, in attempts to discredit Lincoln and to imply wrongdoing on the part of Lincoln's management.

There were then a series of comments by Sanchez and O'Connell which continued to assert that Lincoln's underwriting was not acceptable and that its portfolio of securities presented risk. And at one point, Sanchez indicated that the portfolio should be marked to market prices by stating: "Lincoln has a portfolio of $600 million in junk bonds, which have not been marked to market. If one subtracts out the unrecognized losses on this portfolio, Lincoln's net worth is approximately $6 million."

The Washington people responded to Sanchez's comments with the following remarks:

"Lincoln has retained underwriting experts that say Lincoln's underwriting is appropriate," Hershkowitz said. "Lincoln has other experts who say that Lincoln is safe. This case could be a battle of experts. Lincoln's portfolio is concentrated. They are traders but have a history of making money. Pillsbury was looking for securities losses but did not find them last summer, not even unrecognized mark to market losses. I don't know what has changed since."

"I would not agree that Lincoln has churned its portfolio and I do not think that trading activity means that a portfolio need be marked to market," Dochow added.

"The SEC staff has been urging mark to market accounting for 15 years, but the SEC has not yet required this," Hershkowitz said.

Barclay added, "We do not have a regulation that requires a mark to market accounting."

"It would be hard to bring an enforcement case against Lincoln," Hershkowitz said. "It would be hard to find an accounting expert who would say that Lincoln was wrong."

The whole issue of mark to market was an attempt by San Francisco to show somehow that the underwriting and investment practices that they had so severely castigated had resulted in losses. Their problem was that they couldn't point to any actual losses. So, they were seeking to assert that Lincoln's portfolio contained unrealized losses which should be reflected as actual losses through a mark-to-market technique. But, as the ERC members were stating, the use of mark-to-market accounting was not required by the regulations or by GAAP. This was simply another attempt by San Francisco to play a false card, and the ERC called them on it.

The San Francisco regulators then tried another approach to assert that Lincoln's earnings lacked quality and were misleading. Sanchez said, "Lincoln claims it has strong earnings, but ORPOS concluded that Lincoln has nearly $400 million in self-funded income. This means that Lincoln must successfully sell its real estate if it is to realize profits."

Jordan Luke asked, "Are you saying Lincoln's income figures are inflated or simply that Lincoln's assets are concentrated?"

"According to Tom Bloom [a FHLBB accountant who had recommended that the FHLBB use Kenneth Leventhal as its "hired gun" and later joined that firm], Lincoln has capitalized $160 million of real estate interest on properties held for sale," O'Connell responded. "This represents very liberal or very aggressive accounting but is not necessarily improper."

Lincoln's capitalization of interest was in compliance with the applicable professional accounting standards. It was neither liberal, aggressive, nor improper. O'Connell was, in a backhanded fashion, condemning Lincoln by using the words liberal and aggressive.

Luke asked, "What I want to know is whether Lincoln's accounting practices are not standard practices?"

O'Connell answered, "Lincoln's practices are aggressive but defensible."

The above discussion was a continuation of the attempts by San Francisco to cast Lincoln's operating results as being unusual in the industry. In fact, most of the so-called nontraditional associations relied on ADC, commercial, and construction loans as primary sources of earnings. Many of these loans featured interest reserves which provided funds for the payment of interest during the period when the asset was being developed or constructed; as such, income was self-funded. Lincoln was not at all unique. San Francisco was criticizing Lincoln for practices that were commonplace in the industry.

Having failed to convince the ERC that Lincoln presented unusual risks or that its earnings were suspect, San Francisco turned to more subjective areas of criticism. They addressed Lincoln's management. There was nothing new in the discussion. It was basically a rehash of ACC's action after its acquisition of Lincoln and San Francisco's belief that promises had been broken.

San Francisco also claimed that ORPOS was holding them back from conducting a new examination. To this, Dochow replied that the reason they weren't doing an exam was that they would need a court order to do so.

They then turned to what was labeled in Ericson's notes as the "attack on the Eleventh District." The discussion centered on Lincoln's assertions regarding the leaks of information. San Francisco insisted that it was being falsely accused of being the source of the leaks and insisted, instead, that the leaks had to have been made by someone in Washington. There was also discussion of Lincoln's claims regarding Gray's involvement in the examination as well as the assertion that Lincoln was being harassed.

Again, San Francisco denied that Gray had been involved in the examination, and it denied any harassment of Lincoln. Of course, it's possible—maybe highly probable—that Gray had simply used Black and Smuzynski as the conduits through which he influenced the examination. If so, the San Francisco people were able to deny that they had received any instructions directly from Gray.

There was also some discussion that shed light on the role of outside parties in the examination of Lincoln. The more pertinent comments were as follows:

Black said, "There is nothing unusual about hiring an accountant. It is standard practice to hire needed experts as part of an investigation."

"I agree with Black," Ericson said, "but he did not participate in the hiring of the accountant. I did, so let me speak. I told the San Francisco Bank that they needed experts. I suggested that we hire an accountant. I discussed this with Tom Bloom, the FHLBB's chief accountant, as well as Anne Sobol and Steve Hershkowitz. They all recommended Kenneth Leventhal. I know a hint when I hear one. Therefore, I recommended that we retain Leventhal and we did."

"That's true," Hershkowitz confirmed. "We had been using Leventhal in another case and they are good."

Ericson then added,

I can also speak to junk bonds. Early in the examination, the San Francisco Bank realized it did not have the expertise. We consulted with them and agreed that good junk bond experts should be hired. Once they were hired, I directed that the experts be given Lincoln's complete files. This is vital in any work with experts. You have to give them everything or they are vulnerable on cross-examination. They wanted complete files. The examiners did not enjoy doing all the photocopying but it was necessary.

It looks like Pillsbury was the party who directed the examination. The discussion on the junk bonds confirms Lincoln's suspicions about the inordinate copying that was going on during the exam. This was not a routine exam. It was conducted like litigation discovery from the very start. The Eleventh District's claims to the five senators that the exam was not unusual, therefore, were untrue.

The meeting then focused on San Francisco's recommendation to the ERC.

Patriarca stated San Francisco's position by saying: "We recognize that this is an unusual case, and that Lincoln is not book insolvent. However, a cease and desist proceeding would be time-consuming. Therefore, our first choice is a conservatorship. The MOU is extraordinarily unlikely to be effective or reduce the risk."

What Patriarca was essentially admitting was that San Francisco had no legitimate regulatory or legal basis for the recommended conservatorship action. They were recommending it simply because it was easier on them—less "time-consuming." This is how these people thought. They would, without a moment's hesitation, wipe out ACC's $100-million investment in Lincoln just to save themselves some time and effort.

"The other issue is transfer," Patriarca continued. "Lincoln's allegations are all baseless. This is a smokescreen. This is also Peter Fishbein's pattern of operations. He claims personal animus in every one of these cases. This is an effort to buy time in hopes that growth and good luck with speculative investments will bail out Lincoln. Lincoln is doubling down with our money."

It should be noted that Peter Fishbein was not representing any other S&Ls in cases similar to Lincoln's. Therefore, Patriarca's statement that Fishbein claimed animus "in every one of these cases" was without merit. One should also note the attitude of the regulators, as represented by Patriarca's phrase, "Lincoln is doubling down with our money." The regulators did not have one thin dime invested in Lincoln. Yet, they acted like they, not ACC, were the true owners of Lincoln.

Patriarca then continued his comments on the subject of a transfer of districts:

A regulation covers transfers from districts. There must be a merger plus a change in headquarters. It would be crazy to let Lincoln acquire another institution. We recently turned down, on CRA grounds, Lincoln's application to acquire one branch. How can we justify a merger? If we do this, it will be window dressing and just an attempt to pacify Lincoln. If you are going to do any such thing, and you should not, please do not do a merger. It will be a bad signal to the industry that problem shops can engage in forum shopping.

The remainder of the meeting consisted of San Francisco asserting that the concept of an MOU would not work, while Washington defended the MOU as a reasonable means of resolving the 1986 examination. When the meeting adjourned, San Francisco had failed to convince the ERC of the merits of its recommendations. If anything, San Francisco's presentation reinforced the growing feeling in the minds of many of the Washington-based regulators that the Eleventh District's personnel exhibited an inordinate, unjustifiable, and unhealthy degree of animosity toward Lincoln and its management.

The ERC next met on February 29, 1988, at which time the committee decided to invite Lincoln in to make a presentation. They also decided to limit attendance to the five ERC members, a few staff, and one representative from the FHLB-SF. That meeting was scheduled for March 14, 1988.

In anticipation of this next ERC meeting, San Francisco submitted another twenty-page document, dated March 3 and signed by Patriarca, which was entitled "Further Thoughts on the Appropriate Supervisory Response to Lincoln's Current Condition." This document basically made a case for a C&D order, assuming that a conservatorship, which was still what the Eleventh District wanted, was not recommended by the ERC. Much like the earlier document of February 22, 1988, this letter compared the relative strengths of a C&D versus an MOU on a point-by-point basis.

One added element was that this document highlighted the information needed really to make a decision. The scope of the additional information that San Francisco needed was such that it essentially represented an admission by the Eleventh District that the 1986 exam findings were now too dated to support the actions that San Francisco wanted to take. To update their findings, they needed to conduct a new examination.

The most relevant parts of the document were its last two sections. One entitled "Examination and Supervision" blasted ORPOS and showed the width of the gap which had grown between the two groups of regulators. The last section presented San Francisco's conclusion. Some of the contents of these sections of the document were as follows:

We know that Lincoln is a problem shop. We know its management has no credibility. We know that Lincoln is growing rapidly. ORPOS predicts that Lincoln will be a FSLIC case no later than 1991. Yet the FHLBB has done nothing to remedy the situation, and the examination and supervision activity has all but ceased. Why? Because ORPOS has ordered such activity to cease.

The FHLB-SF recommended a conservatorship last May; nothing has happened. The FHLB-SF ordered a field visit to obtain information requested by FHLBB-retained experts; ORPOS canceled the visit. Small wonder that Lincoln's cooperation is at an all-time low. ORPOS has done essentially nothing to obtain information or require any cooperation from Lincoln; instead, it retreats from each new baseless threat of litigation.

Lincoln bluffs and bullies because those tactics work. The people in Washington who fear litigation should ask themselves if Lincoln really wants its persistent illegal conduct, backdating, file-stuffing and attempts to buy regulators spread on the public record.

Lincoln has said it will buy another savings and loan sight unseen, with no underwriting, if that will facilitate a transfer to a new district. This would be some "remedy" for a shop whose forte is slipshod underwriting and speculative investments.

This document left no doubt about San Francisco's position regarding Lincoln and the actions that it thought were most appropriate. It was also a direct slap at Dochow and Stewart. While it may have given Patriarca, or the lawyer who probably actually wrote it, the pleasure of letting off some steam, it wasn't a very good move politically. Dochow and Stewart were two of the five members of the ERC, and the attack on them could not have done anything but convince them that San Francisco was no longer objective when it came to Lincoln.

The meeting on March 14, 1988, was held, but Lincoln did not attend. Lincoln had been told that San Francisco would have a presence at the meeting and asked that another meeting, which excluded San Francisco, be scheduled. Another meeting was scheduled for March 25, 1988.

The minutes of the March 14, 1988, meeting indicate a number of topics were covered. The most significant discussion was the recommendation of the Office of Enforcement which was presented by Rosemary Stewart. The minutes reflect the following:

She stated that OE was in favor of Lincoln's transfer out of the 11th District in order to address the seriously adversarial relationship that has developed with the FHLBank and to compensate, in an indirect manner, for the leaks of FHLBB information that have injured Lincoln's operations and opportunities. She said that the transfer would not necessarily set a bad precedent because of the unique situation Lincoln presents in that it *has* been the subject of unprecedented leaks of confidential Bank Board information. She stated while she was not criticizing the FHLBank of San Francisco for any particular action, it has been aggressive in its supervision of Lincoln, and many of the contacts with Lincoln have been confrontational—on both sides. She stated her belief that litigating a cease-and-desist proceeding would not produce the same Cease and Desist Order the FHLBank of San Francisco requested. R. Stewart then described OE's experience with attempting to prepare the C&D case that San Francisco recommended last year, for which supporting evidence was lacking in several key areas. She recommended instead a more modest cease and desist order, or a supervisory agreement, coupled with the transfer. She emphasized that the acquiring District Bank should be consulted regarding the contents of the Cease and Desist Order or Supervisory Agreement. She concluded by saying that if Lincoln remains in the 11th District, it is inevitable that the FHLBank will declare the association insolvent and recommend an immediate conservatorship/receivership, but that if it is transferred to another district, there is a chance that the institution will survive.

D. Dochow agreed with R. Stewart that a transfer would not set a bad precedent in light of the unique situation Lincoln presents and agreed that the 11th District's supervision of Lincoln has had a "harsh edge."

About a week prior to March 25, 1988, Charlie told me about the scheduled meeting with the ERC. He said that Margery Waxman had told him that Dochow wanted someone from Arthur Young to attend, so the ERC could ask questions about Lincoln's most recent financial statement and the audit related to those financial statements.

There was a brief meeting among the FHLBB people before anyone representing Lincoln entered the meeting room. Minutes indicate this discussion dealt with the desire of Commissioner Crawford to meet with the ERC and with San Francisco's request for another meeting after the ERC had met with Lincoln.

The people representing Lincoln at the meeting were Charlie, Waxman, Kielty, Grogan, and me. The FHLBB people were Luke, Dochow, Barclay, Stewart, Hoyle, and Hershkowitz. In addition, O'Connell, Sanchez, and Beth Mizuno, a FHLBB lawyer, were present to observe and take notes.

In a memo to Deardorff, dated June 5, 1988, Sanchez summarized his recollections of this meeting. The memo does, I believe, contain some inaccuracies but, in general terms, describes what occurred.

Jordan Luke more or less acted as the chair for the meeting. He explained that the purpose of the meeting was to allow an opportunity for Lincoln to update the ERC on its current financial condition as well as on its relationship with the FHLBB and FHLB-SF. Waxman indicated that I could answer questions about the current financial statements; Grogan could address the relationship with the regulators; and Charlie would discuss questions about Lincoln's future plans.

Jim Grogan started by describing Lincoln as a strong institution with very competent management that found itself in an unfortunate set of circumstances. He said, "Lincoln has very specific information that has come from the highest levels of the FHLBB that Lincoln had been 'targeted' by the FHLBB."

He added, "Lincoln feels the examination was oppressive and it was conducted in an illegal manner because of the leaks of confidential materials and information to the press. We have been told by former Board Members that they are willing to testify in support of Lincoln's claims of unfair treatment. The report of Examination is unequivocally and purposefully wrong and incorrect."

Barclay interjected and asked if Grogan would describe the specific issues or give examples which supported his assertions. Before Grogan could do so, Waxman said it might be more useful if the committee looked at the current financial status of Lincoln, so that any further remarks that Grogan made would be in a better context. Luke agreed and asked me to describe how Arthur Young had become the auditors for Lincoln.

I described all of the circumstances surrounding Arthur Young's initial involvement with Lincoln, including my understanding of the reasons underlying Arthur Andersen's resignation as Lincoln's auditors.

I then was asked to talk about the 1986 audit. I indicated that the 1986 audit had required approximately twenty-five thousand man-hours and had resulted in an unqualified opinion on the financial statements.

Luke asked whether loss reserves were reviewed in conjunction with the audit. I responded that they were considered and that the audit team concluded that the recorded reserves were fairly presented in relation to the consolidated financial statements taken as a whole.

"What contact have you had with the examiners during the audit?" Luke asked.

I said, "I have attended several meetings with the examiners in order to determine what disclosures regarding the exam might have to be made in the footnotes to Lincoln's financial statements." I went on to say:

We were concerned about the length of the exam and the fact that when the firm had to express its opinion on the financial statements, there was no final exam report. The examiners had expressed some preliminary conclusions, but Lincoln's position is that the examiners' preliminary conclusions were based on incomplete and erroneous data.

I attended a meeting in San Francisco, in January 1987, where Lincoln was requested to book specific reserves and submit a Board resolution before it could take exception to the requested reserves. To me, that was unusual and unreasonable, because Lincoln told the examiners about specific errors in appraisals which were the basis for the requested reserves. As a public company, ACC cannot book reserves if they have a reasonable basis to believe that the requested reserves are not correct. Therefore, Lincoln's only option was to record the reserves for regulatory accounting purposes only until the differences can be resolved. The examiners were told that this was the situation and it would have been more reasonable for them to work out the differences before issuing demands.

The other disturbing event in 1987 is that someone in the FHLBB structure has given a copy of the preliminary exam findings to the SEC, causing the SEC to launch an investigation of ACC. It is my understanding that the contact with the SEC is not the normal formal communications between the two agencies but, rather, someone in the structure is acting on their own without Board authorization. The SEC investigation has resulted in Arthur Young having to produce over 17,000 pages of documents at a substantial cost. If contact between the two agencies is appropriate, it seems logical that the FHLBB should have waited until all the facts are in and the examination is resolved. But in this case, the logical course of conduct was not followed.

I have heard the 11th District is also making remarks regarding Arthur Young's offices in Texas and implying that the circumstances in Texas are comparable to Lincoln's situation. I find it inconceivable that people in San Francisco can be fully knowledgeable about any situation in Texas when there is so much disagreement over whether they understand the facts regarding Lincoln. I feel that it is more appropriate for the 11th District to confine its concerns to Lincoln and let the Dallas Bank worry about Texas.

At that point I was asked about the 1987 audit and Lincoln's financial results for 1987. I said, "I would be happy to discuss the subject, but ACC is a public company and it has not yet released its earnings for 1987. I am concerned that any numbers remain strictly confidential. Therefore, before discussing any specific numbers, the Committee has to assure me that I won't see the numbers in the press following this meeting."

George Barclay said that because of the history of leaks related to Lincoln, the committee couldn't give that assurance. Therefore, he didn't want any specific numbers discussed.

I responded that Lincoln's reported net income for 1987 was not as high as its 1986 reported net income but that it was in the same approximate range.

I was then asked about the recorded reserves for 1987. I indicated that the 1987 reserves were higher than 1986 and that the increase was attributable to different assets from what the 1986 reserves related to. I said that I believed the 1987 provision for losses was in the range of $10 million to $15 million and the reserves at that the end of the year were about $33 million.

Luke wanted to know if Lincoln's assets presented a high degree of risk to the association.

I said,

Lincoln is not like more traditional institutions. The traditional thrift becomes involved with real estate primarily as a consequence of foreclosure; therefore, it may not have the resources to adequately deal with the real estate it acquires, as the acquisition of the asset is not planned. Other associations engage in real estate through joint ventures formed with developers. In these instances, while the asset acquisition is planned, the association is dependent on the outside developer for the project's success. Thus, the association isn't really in control of the decisions and performance affecting the asset.

In Lincoln's case, not only are the real estate acquisitions planned, but Lincoln employs internal people to develop the asset. Lincoln has over a hundred people involved in its real estate operations, including engineers, field superintendents, planners, zoning specialists, project managers, real estate accountants and attorneys, tax and insurance clerks, and salespeople. Thus, while there are risks, as there are with any asset, Lincoln has assembled the resources it believes are necessary to manage the risk. In my judgment, because Lincoln is in control of its real estate assets, it is in a better position than those associations who are relying on third parties or partners.

With respect to investments in debt and equity securities, Lincoln also has an internal staff who are responsible for acquiring and managing these assets. Lincoln does rely on advice from investment bankers in deciding whether to buy or sell securities, but the actual decision is an internal one. Again, Lincoln has tried to employ the resources to manage the risks inherent in the assets it holds. Thus far Lincoln's experience appears to be better than industry averages.

If one considers the percentages of assets which are in real estate, debt securities, equity securities, loans, mortgage-backed securities, and other assets, Lincoln is diversified. My discussions with Lincoln's management indicate that they are aware of the various asset risks and they have obtained the resources that they believe are appropriate to manage the risks. That doesn't assure continued success but it does mitigate against loss.

Jim Grogan then continued with his discussion about the relationship with the FHLBB system. He indicated that it was difficult to go through everything. He said that Lincoln had eyewitnesses who would testify that they had seen Ed Gray point to Charlie Keating at a U.S. League meeting in Hawaii and say he was going to "take that fucker down." Grogan said that this event was not imagined by Lincoln and that the association believed it was a clear indication that the 1986 exam had been "orchestrated."

He then turned to the numerous leaks. First, he discussed the article in *Regardie's*, which referred to a nearly three-hundred-page FHLBB report that Lincoln had never seen. He called Michael Binstein (the author of the article) a "mouthpiece" for Ed Gray. He said that Binstein had called Lincoln and threatened that additional leaked material would soon be published. Grogan said that Lincoln did business with some of the finest people in the world and that the committee could not appreciate how seriously the leaks had affected Lincoln's business. Grogan said that Binstein knew about the ERC meeting with San Francisco and the memo from San Francisco recommending conservatorship, subjects that Lincoln could not have known about because Lincoln wasn't represented in the meeting.

With respect to other leaks, Grogan commented on the well-documented history of the other leaks. He said that the *National Thrift News*, which published some of them, was very "solicitous of Ed Gray." That Binstein also had a memo related to Lincoln's possible transfer to Seattle. That the identity of the KIO had been confidential until information was provided to the regulators. He concluded by saying that the damages to Lincoln were real and that Lincoln had its attorneys prepared to litigate the matter and was now ready to file the action. He offered to discuss the suit in more detail with Jordan Luke.

Luke asked Grogan whether Lincoln felt it was dealing with the residual effects of Ed Gray. Grogan said "no." The leaks and misconduct were continuous and still very active. Luke said that he thought the proposed transfer to the Twelfth District had been disclosed by Lincoln. Grogan replied that the reporter had the actual transfer memo and that it was also obvious that San Francisco didn't want to see the 1986 matter resolved without an enforcement action. Also, Binstein had documents from both the summer of 1987 as well as 1988 dealing with the conservatorship recommendation. The misconduct had not stopped when Gray left office.

Barclay inquired if Lincoln were absolutely convinced that someone within the Bank Board system was responsible for the leaks. Grogan said "absolutely" and added that he thought he knew who was responsible for at least some of the leaks.

At this point, Charlie went over his background and how his experiences had led to ACC acquiring Lincoln. He said that he "would go to his grave with a Bible in one hand" that he had known Lincoln was in trouble when it was purchased. He had believed that with growth, the problems could be dealt with and overcome. He said that the deregulation of direct investments had been a godsend and was the only reason he had bought the S&L. It allowed diversification and growth.

There was some discussion about the former management of Lincoln. Charlie said that once ACC's people had to deal with the former management on a day-by-day basis, they realized what a "disaster" they were. There was no real choice but to remove them.

O'Connell pointed out, quite aggressively, that Lincoln's actual operations were inconsistent with the growth and diversification set forth in the original business plan. Charlie said that he could not recall what was in the plan or that a plan was a requirement. O'Connell again referred back to the original plan and wanted explanations for why Lincoln hadn't abided by the projections in the plan. Barclay interjected by asking Charlie if he thought the plan could have anything to do with the relationship with San Francisco. Charlie responded by saying that following the acquisition there were frequent communications with the CDSL about Lincoln's direction. Charlie said that there were also meetings with San Francisco, and he didn't recall any concerns being expressed.

Barclay asked about the criticism of Lincoln moving into real estate and away from home lending. Charlie said that ACC simply took Lincoln into the business that ACC knew best. He described the Estrella project in some detail and said, "It is the best thing we have ever done." He indicated that the project still had well over $100 million in potential gains in it.

There were then some questions regarding Charlie's political contacts. He explained that most of them were the result of his anti-pornography activities and weren't really related to ACC or Lincoln.

The committee asked what Lincoln was willing to do to resolve the issues. Charlie said that he believed everything Lincoln did was permitted by the regulations and that issues could be resolved if two things happened. First, Lincoln had to be in a district it could communicate with. Second, Lincoln could either transfer assets to the holding company or must be permitted to complete them. There was some discussion as to how transfers to ACC might occur.

Luke then inquired again about the risk associated with the real estate, the nonearning gap, and the interest-reserve issue. Charlie said that Lincoln had always made money, but, if he had to get out of the assets he held, he would do so, provided the market would permit it without incurring losses.

Charlie said that there was no way that Lincoln would sign a supervisory agreement or agree to a C&D. He said that he would rather fight in court.

There was discussion about the differences between a n MOU and a C&D. Both Charlie and Grogan reiterated that Lincoln would not agree, under any circumstances, to a C&D or to any document that was in any way called a supervisory agreement.

Finally, there were brief discussions about the issues of file stuffing, backdating, and attempts to hire regulators or have them fired. Each area was considered to be a series of misunderstandings which had been blown out of proportion. The meeting adjourned after the discussion of these minor items.

On March 30, 1988, the ERC met with Commissioner Crawford and his deputy, William Davis. The purpose of the meeting was to get the CDSL's view of the appropriate supervisory action against Lincoln as well as to learn the status of the exam the CDSL was conducting. One passage from the minutes of the meeting sums up the nature of Crawford's input to the process:

> In response to G. Barclay's questions, W. Crawford acknowledged that his views are based on accepting the FHLBank of San Francisco conclusions and not on independent exam findings by the State of California. He stated that Lincoln could be highly profitable or a serious loss depending on circumstances.

As these minutes indicate, Crawford didn't have a factual basis for his concerns about Lincoln other than what he had been told by the Eleventh District. This was a consistent pattern. The Eleventh District fed the CDSL information supporting their conclusions and then asked, "What do you think?" Because the CDSL lacked resources and information, it bought in to San Francisco's conclusions. The Eleventh District would then run to Washington and say, "the CDSL concludes that. . . ." Hence, the CDSL was little more than the Eleventh District's puppet when it came to Lincoln. The fact that Crawford disliked Keating also made matters easier for San Francisco.

The ERC again met on April 14, 1988. The purpose of the meeting was to formulate recommendations for the Bank Board to consider. The minutes show that the committee agreed to present several different options to the Board. They were:

> 1. The informal agreement—Lincoln agrees not to sue on the leaks, no promise of a transfer but an assurance that it will occur if the exam findings are adequately dealt with;
> 2. The cease and desist order—Lincoln agrees not to sue on the leaks, the terms of the Order are determined by ORPOS and the acquiring District, transfer is guaranteed immediately;
> 3. Lincoln is allowed to choose between Options #1 and #2; and
> 4. No transfer, supervision by FHLBank of San Francisco.

The minutes of this meeting show that the ERC had a primary concern not shared by the Eleventh District. The ERC did not want Lincoln to sue over the leaks. This committee knew there had been leaks; Lincoln could prove that in court; Lincoln had been damaged; and the FHLBB, and probably some individuals, would, in fact, be found liable for these damages if the issue were ever tried. They also knew that a successful civil suit by Lincoln would, inevitably, lead to criminal charges as well. This was a strong motive to reach agreement with Lincoln before any suits were filed; indeed, it overrode all other considerations. Their use of options was merely an attempt to find a politically acceptable solution should it ever be questioned.

The ERC met once again on April 25, 1988, to refine its recommendation to the Bank Board. The minutes show that option no. 3, giving Lincoln a choice, was removed. Also option no. 1, the Agreement/MOU, was amended to provide for an on-site FHLBB monitor to oversee Lincoln's activities while the new exam was being conducted.

The ERC recommendations were scheduled to be presented formally to the Bank Board on May 8, 1988. At that time, the Bank Board would make the decision as to how to resolve the 1986 exam, which had now gone on for over two years.

Eleven

Cease-Fire Agreement

The Bank Board convened on May 5, 1988, in a special closed meeting to consider the ERC recommendation regarding Lincoln. There were numerous people from the Washington staff of the FHLBB in attendance.

Jordan Luke opened the meeting by providing a brief description of the ERC's process in considering the Lincoln situation. He then presented the three options that the ERC was recommending to the Bank Board. He described them as follows:

Under the first option, there is an attempt to maintain a somewhat fluid position for a period of time to permit further examination, and then to attempt to reach some resolution of the matter at the end of that time. More specifically, as it says, Lincoln would execute a Supervisory Agreement that would address regulatory matters and generally freeze its current level of investments. A new exam would begin under the direction of the Washington Supervisory Office. There would be no participation by the Federal Home Loan Bank of San Francisco. An examiner would be assigned to perform on-site monitoring of all significant business decisions during this period of time. If the exam findings warrant, and if problems disclosed by the examiner are then addressed appropriately, that is in a form and substantively satisfactory to the Washington Supervisory Office, Lincoln could apply to transfer to another Federal Home Loan Bank District. Lincoln would agree not to sue the Federal Home Loan Bank, its employees or agents in return.

The second option would take stronger action at the front end. . . . Lincoln would be permitted to transfer Federal Home Loan Bank Districts immediately. That agreement, however, would be conditioned upon its executing a final cease and desist order that is acceptable, both to the Office of Enforcement and to the receiving Federal Home Loan Bank. Such orders are immediately enforceable in U.S. District Court. That Order would address all regulatory violations and underwriting concerns and it would require a phasing down of Lincoln's high risk assets and other direct investments. A new exam would be initiated as soon as possible by Lincoln's new Federal

Home Loan Bank District. Again, Lincoln would agree not to sue the Bank Board, its employees or agents.

The third option would have Lincoln advised that the Bank Board will not entertain its request to transfer Federal Home Loan Bank Districts, and the examination and supervision functions would be handled by the Federal Home Loan Bank of San Francisco, which would then pursue those Supervisory options that it thinks are appropriate.

Having presented the various options that the Bank Board was asked to consider, Luke then offered his opinions on the positions that the two parties to the dispute had taken. He said:

> . . . Lincoln, on the one hand, represented by Mr. Keating, came in and spoke to us for several hours. And while I can't represent what position he may be willing to negotiate to, I do think it's fair to say that he was quite unequivocal in telling us that he will not sign a cease and desist order, nor will he sign a supervisory agreement. In his view, it is necessary that he have the flexibility to try to bring his institution into line with a risk profile that is acceptable to the Bank Board and its supervisors. And as he put it, it's simply going to be necessary for me to have the freedom to do that, for you to trust me for a period of time.
>
> On the other side of the ledger, the San Francisco Bank, as I understand it, has stated its position quite clearly that it thinks the risk profile of the institution at this point is sufficiently unacceptable; that they think it should be placed into a conservatorship—the institution should be placed into a conservatorship without further adieu [*sic*]. . . .
>
> San Francisco has indicated that if they are unable to prevail in their conservatorship recommendation, that the second to best option is a cease and desist order acceptable to them and through all of this, they have been quite clear with us, without knowing whether their position is changed recently, that they think it would be an absolutely unacceptable concession to the institution to permit it to move out of that District.

Luke then turned to Darrel Dochow and asked him to provide the Board with additional background data. The most pertinent remarks that Dochow made concerned his perceptions of Charlie's role in the management of Lincoln and the examination process. Some of his comments were:

> . . . In the applications for the change of control and the acquisition, Lincoln essentially parroted that they would continue on the same line of business, they essentially parroted that there wouldn't be substantial management changes, and the like. It is not clear that the application was really focused on much by Mr. Charlie Keating, the major stockholder, but rather was prepared by his staff, who were familiar with what they represented then and have essentially tried to say, when they got into the institution, they saw that it

couldn't make money in that line of business. I personally, believe that Mr. Keating simply bought the institution purposely to engage in the types of business lines that it's currently engaging in and that the application at the time filed was not focused on by him, it was just focused on "we need the institution. . . ."

. . . They have reaped their income consistently and have been quite profitable from these endeavors, primarily what I refer to as "doing deals." Mr. Keating has said that his whole life he has generated income from "making one deal work after another deal," that being the real estate business. He does have a philosophy that the traditional S&L cannot succeed unless it already has a market share and a lending network that allows them to compete, and that Lincoln Savings did not have that. . . .

. . . The result, however, on the profit statement has been quite remarkable. They're consistently reported as one of the highest earning institutions in the nation, and the profits have been regular; they have not been sporadic. . . .

The issue also in my mind is one that Mr. Keating, until recently, appears to have not been actively involved in dealing with the regulatory affairs of the institution. Instead he has been at the holding company. He's not a director nor an officer of Lincoln Savings. He has been dealing with the development activities and the like, doing a lot of things to get major improvements done, major zoning changes done, to properties that benefit Lincoln and American Continental, the holding company.

Since this event with the examination and the animosity with the San Francisco Bank heated up and got to the stage of lawsuits being filed, Mr. Keating has now taken a very active role, in my opinion, into the affairs of Lincoln directly. He is basically representing that he, personally, now has made a commitment to have Lincoln be a good regulatory citizen. . . .

He further points to the fact that he thinks Lincoln has been irreparably harmed through a series of information that has hit the press, information that I believe he truly believes has come from Federal Home Loan Bank System sources. And the consequence of that is, and I think in Mr. Keating's mind, he feels the institution, where he has substantial funds invested, has been harmed, has not been given an opportunity to correct itself, and has not been given an opportunity to be run in a fashion that it must be run to survive. His opinion, stated more bluntly, has been if the regulations get enforced to the degree that you can't do business—in other words, if the regulators themselves come in and run my institution, we will fail. And I won't let that happen without a fight.

When Dochow finished giving the above background comments, he offered his opinion on the solution for resolving the stalemate between Lincoln and San Francisco.

. . . I'm comfortable myself that something could be negotiated with Lincoln that would freeze them as to where they are and would, in an orderly fashion, reduce their exposures in high-risk areas while at the same time increasing their capital position.

My fear is that we're at the threshold where regulatory involvement can be justified now; I believe involvement that takes a traditional form of going in and doing every transaction, overseeing everything, with prior approval. When it deals with land loans, and the Arizona economy, and big developments, it will, in fact, cause predictions to come true that Lincoln will suffer additional losses. But, rather, I think a preferable approach is to let Lincoln have a little bit of room to demonstrate that this new involvement of Charlie Keating is, in fact, a legitimate involvement. . . .

Dochow was acknowledging that if the Board opted for a traditional regulatory approach which placed the decision making related to Lincoln's assets in the hands of the regulators, losses would result and Lincoln would fail. Dochow had good reason to come to this belief, because that is precisely what had occurred in every other situation where the regulators attempted to make management decisions for an institution—the institution had experienced a slow, agonizing death as a direct consequence of the regulators' business ineptitude and poor decisions. George Barclay echoed Dochow's observation by saying:

I believe also that Keating probably is the only one who can preserve a significant amount of the value for Lincoln. I believe that he is a—and he proved to us, he is a very strong sales oriented individual and I believe, although he says he has no political connections, that only he can get some of the zoning changes that are necessary to enhance the value of the properties, otherwise there would be substantial losses for the association.

The comments by both Dochow and Barclay are acknowledgments that Keating and his management team were the most qualified people to preserve the value of Lincoln's assets. They knew that government bureaucrats or FHLBB-appointed managers would take actions which would produce losses. So, even though no formal analysis had been done by the FHLBB staff regarding the effects of a conservatorship, these two people had seen a sufficient number of closed institutions to know that losses inevitably result. The only way that the losses, if any, to the FSLIC could be minimized was to let Charlie Keating complete the development of Lincoln's major assets.

The discussion then turned to more details about the various options, with much of the concern focused on the possible removal of the Eleventh

District's authority, rather than to Lincoln's status per se. However, at one point, Rosemary Stewart was asked about her views regarding the various options. Her first comments were directed to the actions which San Francisco intended to take against Lincoln. She said:

> ... [O]ne of the contributions that OE made to the Enforcement Review Committee was to summarize the work that we had done for the last year in attempting to work with the San Francisco Bank and build a cease and desist case. There are a few regulatory violations, for which we're confident that a clear reg violation would get us an order. But most of this case is not regulations, most of this has to be an unsafe and unsound practice charge. . . . [T]he evidence . . . does not demonstrate losses, does not demonstrate abnormal risk, or loss, or damage, even anticipated to Lincoln in a manner that we're confident we could prove. And that's what the case law says you need for unsafe and unsound practices, unlike regulatory violations. . . .

She was effectively saying what Charlie had contended all along. If Lincoln was unsafe, unsound, or excessively risky, where was the evidence? The examiners had not uncovered any losses. As Dochow noted, Lincoln was profitable—and consistently so. Thus, while there may have been conditions which the examiners believed represented regulatory violations, they didn't rise to the level required to support the strong action which San Francisco was recommending. In effect, Stewart was admitting that San Francisco had no legitimate basis for the actions they were proposing to take. Her observations should have prompted the questions: Absent a valid basis for their actions, why is San Francisco so intent on taking such drastic measures against Lincoln; what underlies their decision; and what drives them to such levels of intensity? But these questions were not asked.

Stewart went on to give her views about the investigations into the allegations of file stuffing and backdating by saying, "I find them not particularly startling, not particularly indicative of criminal activity . . . there are defenses, there are explanations that are plausible. . . ."

She explained the basis for her recommendations to the Board by saying:

> I believe very strongly that Lincoln has been victimized by deliberate leaks of information. My own recommendation is, in large part, based upon that belief. How the Bank Board deals with that kind of situation, when we do not have a person that we can prove is responsible for those leaks, becomes

difficult. But I think what the Committee has done is recognize that this is a
very unique situation, one that should be dealt with in a very unique fashion
and therefore need not set a precedent for other unhappy institutions who
might not be happy with their supervisors.

Stewart's comments reflect that her inclination was to believe Lincoln's
assertions rather than those of the Eleventh District. While she believed
that a C&D could be obtained to protect against certain regulatory
violations, which were minor to the overall situation, she didn't believe
that the FHLBB could prove Lincoln was unsafe or unsound. On the other
hand, her remarks indicate that she did believe that Lincoln could prove
that the leaks resulted in damages to Lincoln. Therefore, she supported the
concept of an MOU to avoid litigation and to compensate Lincoln for the
damages it had suffered.

Steve Hershkowitz was then asked to share his views with the Bank
Board. Some of his more pertinent remarks were:

> . . . [T]his is not a traditional regulatory case. The institution is not doing
> anything illegal; in fact, it is engaging in those types of transactions that have
> been contemplated by Congress and contemplated by this Board as the
> general direction that the industry might go in order to increase its profits
> outside traditional business. . . .
> . . . [T]his institution has management with a personal stake in the transac-
> tions and have been successful in turning real profits, not paper profits, in
> these kinds of transactions. However, the situation is such that San Francisco
> and the institution itself believes that the institution will fail if they continue
> in the current supervisory structure.
> . . . [I]f the institution remains in its current supervisory situation, it will,
> inevitably, fail. An institution that engages in high-risk transactions requires
> extra supervisory surveillance, and it needs a regulator that will permit
> management to make management decisions. San Francisco has demon-
> strated in the past with this institution that it believes that its current assets and
> risk profile is such that it will not permit them to do that.

Hershkowitz' comments are disturbing. He acknowledged that Lincoln was engaged in permissible activities—ones which the FHLBB and
Congress had encouraged in the past. He acknowledged that Lincoln was
profitable and that Keating had a real stake in the business. And he
understood that leaving Lincoln in the hands of the Eleventh District
would result in Lincoln's eventual failure. These comments are a condemnation of the regulatory process that Lincoln had complained about for two
years. The regulators truly understood that Lincoln was not doing anything
improper, yet they were still debating Lincoln's fate. The debate would
never have occurred had the Eleventh District acted responsibly and
without bias.

Then, Karl Hoyle was asked if he had any comments that he wanted to share with the Board. He said:

> One thing I'd like to add and that is, I think Mr. Keating has made it clear, when we talked with him, that he would like out at this juncture, if that's what we would like. He says the only way to do that is to put the thing in shape and get out, because he has a good deal of his family's and his own personal funds involved in the institution. That's one of the reasons he's adamantly opposed to a cease and desist; one of the reasons I think he would be a good regulatory citizen for that period of time, should we go with 1 or some other option of that. He feels that he's tired of the fight. He'd like to clean up the institution and, at that juncture, he would get out. And he can't do that if there's a cease and desist or somebody telling him how to make the business decisions every day, because he'll lose what he views as a considerable sum of his and his family's investment.

At this point all of the ERC members had expressed their respective opinions on the various options. All, except Jordan Luke, supported some form of a negotiated settlement. Luke supported a C&D order. His concern with a negotiated settlement was twofold. First, he said, "I am still not comfortable with something less than an immediately enforceable cease and desist order." Secondly, he said, "I'm concerned that Option 1 has the potential to strike a public impression that we're not stepping up to the matter and dealing with it in a definitive fashion."

None of the ERC members, including Luke, expressed comments indicating that they actually believed that Lincoln had suffered losses or that Lincoln's practices could be shown to be unsafe or unsound. They did share San Francisco's concern that Lincoln's assets were nontraditional and that, as such, they presented risk. They each indicated that they wanted to see a mechanism in place which would restrict Lincoln from expanding its risk profile and would allow the regulators to monitor Lincoln's future operations closely. The majority believed that the appropriate mechanism was a properly negotiated agreement similar to the proposed MOU.

The ERC was also convinced that San Francisco's and Lincoln's differences were so great that a change in supervisors was not inappropriate. Certainly, because of internal, political considerations, there was concern over changing districts, but none seemed to believe that Lincoln would survive if it stayed under San Francisco's control. The change in districts was the area that the various Bank Board members were most concerned about.

Board member White, the only carry-over from Ed Gray's era, spoke to his concerns about a change in supervision by saying:

> ... I think, first of all, that the issue of forum shopping is terrifically important. Yes, other insured institutions have left one District and gone to

another, but this, for better or worse, has been raised to quite a prominent and public level and there is no getting around the fact that were we to agree to let them shift Districts, it would be seen by one and all as blatant forum shopping. And I just don't like that, don't like that, at all.

Having said this, White went on to recite all of San Francisco's concerns, primarily those expressed in the letters which Cirona and Patriarca had sent the ERC. He clearly indicated that he favored the Eleventh District's view of Lincoln and rejected Lincoln's arguments against San Francisco's examination findings. After his recitation, White indicated his position by saying:

And, so, despite the recommendations of the ERC, I believe that option 3 is the appropriate option. I believe we have an insured-institution, whose processes and procedures are seriously deficient; who is, as everyone agrees, in a high-risk profile situation. I believe the forum shopping is just a terrifically worrisome problem. And given the history and everything else I know, despite my concerns about the leaking and my concerns about the hostile situation between San Francisco and Lincoln, I believe that Option 3, turning jurisdiction back to San Francisco and—I do not—I'm not convinced at this point that a conservatorship is appropriate, but I do believe a very tough C&D order is appropriate.

With that, White indicated that he was in favor of the one option that not a single ERC member supported. All of the ERC members fully understood that if the decision were simply to return Lincoln to San Francisco—that is, maintain the status quo—litigation and continued acrimony would be certain results. But in order to avoid internal controversy and to preserve the FHLBB's public image—political considerations—White was more than willing to condemn a $5-billion institution to a certain death. With leadership like White's, it's no wonder that the industry was a mess and so many institutions had been seized.

After White's comments, the other Board members and the ERC representatives returned to a discussion of why option one—the MOU—made the most sense. This led to a motion by Board member Martin that the FHLBB adopt option one. White immediately made this comment:

First, from a public perception, we end up looking weak; and, again, the forum shopping to me is a very, very serious problem. And with respect to substance, I believe the problems that have been revealed already in this institution are so serious that I believe more direct action is taken.

This set off another long series of attempts to address White's concerns over "forum shopping." The conclusion was that if Lincoln complied with everything in the proposed MOU, and then purchased an institution in another district and applied for a transfer, Lincoln would not be receiving any special treatment. Rather, Lincoln would simply be doing what any association was permitted to do under the regulations. This satisfied Board members Wall and Martin but did not alter White's beliefs.

The FHLBB then voted two to one to adopt option one. With that, the meeting adjourned. The Board had decided to pursue the MOU, coupled with a supervisory agreement, to resolve the 1986 exam issues. The Board's real objective was to start a new exam of Lincoln as soon as possible in order to ascertain the true status of Lincoln and to determine what further supervisory action, if any, should be taken. Several of the speakers indicated that the new exam was to be by "disinterested parties or examiners," so none of the biases which may have been inherent in the 1986 exam would cloud the findings of the new examination.

When Dochow supported option one during this meeting, he made one comment which committed his future actions regarding Lincoln. He said,

I believe the consequences of not abiding by what's in the agreement should be a conservatorship, not a cease and desist. At this stage, this agency has gone a long ways, over a considerable time period, to try to be as fair as possible and as reasonable as possible, given all of the circumstances that tend to cloud the basic issues, to not abide by—If Option 1 is chosen, to not abide by what's agreed on, essentially, in my mind, removes any probability of additional chances.

Dochow was running the risk that internally, within the FHLBB system, he would be viewed as soft on Lincoln. To counteract the possibility of such internal charges, he made the above comment, taking the position that, if the exam revealed any real problems, he was prepared to go directly to a conservatorship, bypassing all other remedies. This position was never disclosed to Lincoln. Had it been, Lincoln's attitudes toward the MOU and a new exam may have been different from what they were.

To a very large extent, the Lincoln situation was converted into an internal struggle within the FHLBB structure. It was San Francisco against the regulators in Washington. Lincoln had simply become the bone that these two big dogs were fighting over.

On the same day as the Bank Board meeting, May 5, 1988, the ERC met briefly to discuss how to implement the Board's decision. The minutes of the ERC meeting indicate that they agreed to draft a traditional supervisory agreement and another agreement which (1) incorporated Lincoln's consent to the supervisory agreement, (2) included a mutual agreement not to bring suit, (3) provided for an examination by a "blue ribbon" national team to commence as soon as possible and to conclude within six months, and (4) assured Lincoln's transfer to another district, providing it met all normal requirements.

These points demonstrate what the FHLBB's two primary concerns were when it agreed to a negotiated settlement. First, they didn't want Lincoln to sue the FHLBB over the illegal leaks of confidential information. Second, they wanted a new, unbiased examination of Lincoln. These were the prime factors which motivated the members who voted for the MOU approach.

Darrel Dochow called Charlie Keating and informed him, in general terms, of the Bank Board's decision. The negotiations between the FHLBB were to be handled by Rosemary Stewart, with Dochow in close consultation with her.

Dochow also called San Francisco and told them about the Board's decision. San Francisco, in turn, called the CDSL and told them that the Eleventh District would not be examining Lincoln in the future. The CDSL and the Eleventh District had been just about ready to start a new joint examination. In fact, the CDSL had already started, anticipating that the Eleventh District examiners would join them any day. The CDSL wanted to use the exam as the foundation for strong action against Lincoln, probably a tough C&D. The removal of the Eleventh District pulled the rug out from under Commissioner Crawford's feet. He didn't have the resources, either in numbers or experience, to deal with Lincoln by himself. He had been repeatedly goaded by San Francisco into taking a stronger and stronger stance against Lincoln, for which he was receiving political heat. Now, San Francisco was gone—leaving him up the proverbial creek without a paddle. He had no choice but to postpone the examination that he was conducting.

When Dochow's call came in to Charlie, it started a series of meetings to decide who should negotiate with the FHLBB. Up to that point, the lead person had been Margery Waxman. But there was concern about whether she was the right person to conduct the final negotiations. Waxman's real asset was her access to people like Dochow. This created the possibility of a conflict of interests. If things reached a stalemate, the negotiator had to feel free to stand up and walk away from the table. Some of ACC's people weren't sure that Waxman had such freedom. If she walked, the negotiations might collapse, leaving Dochow in a difficult position. There was a feeling that Waxman might not get tough with Dochow, for fear of destroying a valuable contact; thus, she might agree to things that Lincoln wouldn't necessarily have to agree to, just so she could maintain her own relationship and standing with the FHLBB staff.

Therefore, it was decided that Peter Fishbein ought to conduct the negotiations for Lincoln. Peter is an extremely skilled negotiator and was completely familiar with all of the issues. Also, he was not carrying the baggage that Waxman was. So, Peter immediately started meeting with Rosemary Stewart to hammer out a settlement acceptable to Lincoln. The negotiating sessions went on for about two weeks, with new versions of documents being faxed to Phoenix almost every day. As each new version came in, there were discussions about which elements were acceptable and which were unacceptable. The process involved considerable give and take by both Lincoln and the FHLBB.

On May 20, 1988, three documents were executed between Lincoln and the FHLBB. These were: a Memorandum of Understanding, an Agreement, and a letter signed by Rosemary Stewart. The key elements of each of these documents are described in the following paragraphs, starting with the MOU.

The MOU started with four "Whereas" clauses which essentially read as follows:

1. The Federal Home Loan Bank of San Francisco conducted an examination of Lincoln in 1986 and 1987 which resulted in a report of examination dated April 20, 1987 ("1986 examination");
2. Lincoln believes that the 1986 examination does not present a fair portrayal of the association's financial condition or operations as set out in Lincoln's written response to the 1986 examination;
3. Lincoln has indicated a desire to acquire a savings and loan association in another FHLB bank district and move its headquarters to that district; and
4. FSLIC, the FHLBB, and Lincoln are desirous of amicably resolving all the issues outstanding as a result of the 1986 examination and the negotiations concerning it between Lincoln and ORPOS leading to this Memorandum of Understanding (except for the issues involving Lincoln's equity-risk investments, which are addressed in paragraphs 8 and 9 of a separate Agreement between the parties of even date).

The MOU then sets forth the following understandings reached by the parties:

1. FSLIC agrees to initiate and complete a new examination of Lincoln and submit a report of examination within seven (7) months from the execution of this Memorandum of Understanding, under the direction of ORPOS ("the new examination"). This examination will be performed by an examination team with no examiners from the FHLBank-S.F. It will be a regular, periodic FHLBB examination conducted in the ordinary course. It is the intention of the parties that the new examination will not rehash the findings in, or

transactions, procedures or events covered by, the 1986 examination and the
negotiations concerning it between Lincoln and ORPOS leading to this
Memorandum of Understanding; but rather will focus on the current situation
at Lincoln and changes since the 1986 examination. Lincoln agrees to fully
cooperate with and facilitate the new examination.

2. In consideration for Lincoln's agreements set out in this Memorandum
of Understanding, FSLIC and the FHLBB agree not to initiate any administrative or enforcement proceedings against Lincoln or its parents, affiliates,
officers, directors, employees or agents relating to any findings in, or
transactions, procedures or events covered by, the 1986 Examination and the
negotiations concerning it between Lincoln and ORPOS leading to this
Memorandum of Understanding. Lincoln agrees not to initiate any litigation
against the FSLIC, the FHLBB or their members, employees or agents for
actions taken through the date of this Memorandum of Understanding within
the scope of their employment or official capacity.

3. FSLIC, the FHLBB and Lincoln agree to resolve all the issues described
in or stated by the 1986 Examination and the negotiations concerning it
between Lincoln and ORPOS leading to this Memorandum of Understanding
(except for the issues involving Lincoln's equity risk investments which are
addressed in paragraphs 8 and 9 of a separate Agreement between the parties
of even date) by executing that Agreement to, inter alia, increase Lincoln's
capital, decrease the risk profile of Lincoln's assets, and enhance its underwriting procedures.

4. In the spirit of regulatory cooperation during the new examination and
in an effort to provide the FSLIC a better understanding of Lincoln's current
operations, ORPOS agrees to designate a senior examiner who will remain at
Lincoln during the examination to facilitate such cooperation and understanding. Lincoln agrees to notify the Executive Director of ORPOS or his designee
of any highly material and controversial transaction or event, prior to its
consummation. Such notification shall be in writing unless the matter
involves confidential or inside information. The failure to object to such
transaction or event shall not under any circumstances be construed as
approval of it by the FSLIC or the FHLBB. Lincoln also agrees to inform the
designated senior examiner of any other significantly material transaction
either before or within five business days after its consummation.

5. The parties will make every effort in good faith to promptly resolve any
issues raised in the new examination, and will work together to discuss such
issues at the earliest practicable time and develop procedures to resolve them
reasonably and expeditiously. When the new examination is resolved, Lincoln will submit an application to the FHLBB to move its headquarters to a
district in which it proposes to acquire a savings and loan association. Based
on the nature of the new examination findings and Lincoln's resolution of any
material issues arising from the new examination in a manner and in a form

satisfactory to ORPOS, the FHLBB and the FSLIC agree that Lincoln will be allowed to transfer its headquarters upon having made an appropriate application and having met normal requirements related to such a transfer. The FSLIC and the FHLBB agree to act expeditiously on such an application. Upon such approval, all supervisory and examination authority over Lincoln will be transferred to the FHLBank for the new District.

6. From the date of the execution of this Memorandum of Understanding ORPOS will have exclusive supervisory and examination authority over Lincoln and will act as Lincoln's principal supervisory agent. ORPOS will continue in this capacity at least for a reasonable time after the new examination is completed so that any issues raised by the examination can be resolved and Lincoln's application to be transferred to a new district can be acted upon.

The MOU was signed by Darrel Dochow, for the FSLIC and FHLBB, and by Jim Grogan, for Lincoln.

The Agreement, of the same date, began with a series of "Whereas" clauses which were essentially the same as those contained in the MOU. The specific provisions of the Agreement, which for the sake of brevity will be summarized without changing their meaning, are as follows:

1. Lincoln will comply with the regulatory capital rules unless a waiver is granted pursuant to an application.
2. By October 1, 1988, Lincoln will sell to ACC $10 million of preferred stock that qualifies as a contribution to its regulatory capital.
3. By June 30, 1989, Lincoln will make reasonable and diligent efforts to sell a minimum of $50 million and a maximum of $150 million in securities that qualify as contributions to its regulatory capital. The FHLBB agrees to process Lincoln's application for approval of the securities expeditiously.
4. Of existing reserves at December 31, 1987, Lincoln has designated as specific for regulatory purposes $18,269,000 related to assets questioned in the 1986 examination.
5. (a) Lincoln will submit manuals describing its underwriting and operating procedures, within 60 days, and will take into account any advice by ORPOS about the contents of the manuals. The manuals will cover the underwriting for real estate, equity, debt, government and mortgage-backed securities and loans. The manuals will establish lending limits for geographic or economic areas, borrowers, and projects. Transactions with affiliated persons will be addressed.
5. (b) Lincoln will provide notification of any modifications to or deviations from the manuals.
5. (c) Lincoln will comply with the manuals.
6. Lincoln will prepare and submit, within 60 days, a business plan

covering the remainder of 1988 and calendar year 1989. Lincoln will provide notification of material modifications or deviations from the plan and will consider the advice and recommendations of ORPOS.

7. During the "interim period" (the earlier of the completion of the new examination or seven months) Lincoln won't apply for a growth waiver. However, Lincoln can submit applications for approval of the acquisition of another savings and loan association or the opening or acquiring of additional branch offices.

8. During the interim period, Lincoln will not increase the dollar amount of its aggregate equity-risk investments, as of the date of the Agreement, except that the increase in real estate resulting from the capitalization of costs and the incurrence of expenses which are reasonable and necessary to develop, improve and/or market existing real estate projects will not be counted against the limitation. Ten percent of the amount of Lincoln's equity-risk investments in excess of $550 million will be added to Lincoln's minimum capital requirement. This amount is in lieu of the amount that would otherwise be required by the regulations.

9. Paragraph 8 will not prejudice the positions of either Lincoln or the FHLBB as to whether Lincoln's equity-risk investments are grandfathered. Lincoln will file an application for a waiver to allow it to maintain equity-risk investments in an amount equal to one-third of its total consolidated GAAP assets, and the FHLBB will act on the application in conjunction with the resolution of the new examination.

10. During the interim period Lincoln will not pay any dividends unless it notifies the Agent a least two weeks prior to the proposed payment and the Agent does not object.

11. Lincoln agrees to cooperate with and facilitate the new examination.

12. This Agreement has been arrived at through voluntary negotiations and accommodations between the parties. The enforcement of this Agreement will be undertaken by the FSLIC and the FHLBB only for material violations. . . .

These two documents represented a negotiated, contractual settlement of all issues raised in the 1986 examination, including "transactions, procedures and events covered by" the 1986 examination, whether or not they were specifically mentioned in the Report of Examination. The new examination was to address "the current situation at Lincoln and changes since the 1986 Examination." In reaching these agreements, each party agreed to certain undertakings which constituted consideration for the contracts they had entered into by signing the two documents. The FHLBB almost immediately, and repeatedly, breached these contracts.

In entering into the contracts, there were many issues raised in the 1986 examination that Lincoln did not agree with and, as a consequence, did not reflect on its books. For example, it did not agree to any of the so-called income reversals resulting from accounting issues, nor did it agree to certain of the appraisal losses requested by the examiners, nor did it agree to the ADC accounting for the Wolfswinkle loans, among other things.

Later, when the FHLBB was questioned about these documents, some people within the FHLBB system, notably, Dochow, O'Connell, and Wall, said they believed that Lincoln had recorded all of the various adjustments to income that the examiners had requested in the 1986 Report of Examination. In fact, some, particularly O'Connell, said, even to a congressional committee, that Charlie and/or I told the FHLBB that Lincoln had recorded all of these requested adjustments. Those assertions are utter nonsense. If Lincoln had been willing to record, and had recorded, all of the adjustments, then the two documents which were so heatedly negotiated would have been largely unnecessary. The FHLBB had been told that Lincoln had recorded only those few appraisal losses that it agreed with—and no more. That's why it was necessary to negotiate a settlement in order to resolve the other unrecorded differences between the parties.

Purely in the context of the struggle between San Francisco and Lincoln, the MOU and Agreement represented a victory for Lincoln and a defeat for the Eleventh District. As a result of not having to record the income reversals and appraisal losses, Lincoln's actual net worth exceeded its required net worth by over $60 million. Lincoln was not required to dispose of any assets, and its subsidiaries were free to continue their nontraditional operations. Neither was Lincoln subjected to any onerous restrictions on its other activities. In effect, all of the actions that the Eleventh District had contemplated taking against Lincoln were negated. San Francisco, on the other hand, suffered a tremendous political loss within the FHLBB system. The removal of its supervision over Lincoln was clearly viewed as a vote of "no confidence" and a criticism of its performance in the Lincoln examination. The decision was a viewed as a direct slap to the faces of Patriarca and Black.

In addition to the two primary documents, Rosemary Stewart, as the director of the Office of Enforcement, wrote Lincoln a brief two-paragraph letter. The first paragraph was simply an opening introduction with a reference to the MOU and the Agreement of the same date. The second paragraph read as follows:

Based on the findings made in the 1986 Examination and the information presently known to FHLB-S.F. and ORPOS, FSLIC and the FHLBB have no present intention to refer any matter to, or to request any other governmental agency to take any action, involving Lincoln or its parents, affiliates, officers, directors, employees or agents.

At the time it was received, this was considered a significant letter. But because Lincoln did not know that the FHLBB had already made referrals, both formal and informal, to about every agency they could, this letter was basically meaningless. The damage that referrals could cause had already been inflicted.

Nonetheless, Charlie and the other people in ACC's and Lincoln's management groups, who had struggled with the 1986 examination for over two years, viewed the signing of these documents as a great victory. The initial belief was that the battle was over and that Lincoln had survived. Lincoln soon learned, however, that this was not the end of the war; it was merely a temporary lull in the hostilities.

Twelve

FHLBB Violates Peace Accord

Public accounting is, like all professions, demanding. Audit partners who handle clients face a constant stream of tight deadlines which must be met as well as numerous business and technical accounting problems that clients seek to have answered. Managing partners are confronted with a myriad of financial, personnel, marketing, and logistical problems that an active practice continuously produces. Beginning in 1980, I performed both an extensive client-handling role and the managing-partner duties for the Phoenix office. By 1986, the stress induced by these dual roles was taking its toll on my health. I found myself with peptic ulcers, high blood sugar, periodic episodes of shortness of breath, dizziness, and chest pains. These symptoms resulted in several trips to hospital emergency rooms and numerous diagnostic tests by physicians and cardiologists.

In mid-1987, I asked my superiors in Arthur Young to reduce my client-handling responsibilities or to appoint another person to assume the office-managing-partner role. I did not believe that I could continue to perform both functions and still maintain any semblance of reasonable health. As events unfolded, my client-handling duties did not decrease; instead, they increased significantly. In addition, I retained the managing-partner position until April 1, 1988. Consequently, neither my health nor my concern about my physical well-being improved during this period of time.

When ACC's audit was completed, I started to think about the changes that had to be made in my role as a partner in Arthur Young if my health were to improve. In that connection, I also considered leaving Arthur Young in order to escape the stress endemic to public accounting.

On April 8, 1988, as I was visiting ACC's offices on routine matters, Charlie asked me to meet with him in his office. He said that the audit was now over, and he wanted to talk to me about joining the ACC management team. He said that he needed someone to deal with the restructuring or sale of Lincoln and to assist him in deciding the future course of ACC's operations. He didn't believe that any of ACC's present executives could plan the transformation of Lincoln, but he thought, because of my experience with the industry, that I could. Moreover, he wanted to devote more of his time to the major equity deals which had been so profitable in the past, and he didn't believe that he could do that and handle the resolution of Lincoln's problems at the same time.

As we discussed what my role might be, it became clear that I would function as an internal consultant. I would not be responsible for managing a group of people; rather, I would formulate conceptual solutions to Lincoln's structural problems as well as plans to effect those solutions. We both believed that this role would substantially eliminate the stress conditions that I had been operating under for the past eight years.

After due deliberation, I told him, on April 11, that I would accept his offer. The next day I informed Arthur Young that I would be leaving the partnership to join ACC. My superiors in Arthur Young decided that April 30, 1988, was an acceptable separation date. Thus, on May 1, 1988, I became a senior vice-president in ACC.

Some have questioned the timing of my departure from Arthur Young, implying that, because it was so close to the date the audit was completed, something was improper. Actually, the only time I could have exited the firm without creating a potential conflict of interest was during the April-May period. At any other time of the year, I would have been in the midst of an audit for one or more significant clients; therefore, either a conflict would exist, or my departure would require a duplication of effort because another partner would have to redo portions of my work in order to sign off on the audits.

Others have questioned whether it is proper for an audit partner to leave a firm to join a client that he or she has served. The fact is that most partners who leave public accounting firms before normal retirement age do so in order to join clients. It is a natural transition. Both parties know each other. The partner, as an incoming executive, is productive from the first day forward, because he or she is already familiar with the company's personnel or operations. Moreover, the partner knows what to expect in the new environment. Therefore, both parties benefit. For this reason, many companies recruit executives from the professional firms that serve them.

The timing of my entry into ACC was fortuitous because the MOU was signed just a few weeks after my arrival. The MOU resolved the outstanding conflict with the regulators and placed Lincoln in a position to move ahead with its operations.

Shortly after I started at ACC, I met with Charlie and told him that I thought Lincoln had to be fundamentally changed or restructured. With the re-regulation of the industry, I believed that even if the 1986 exam were peacefully resolved, Lincoln could not maintain its present asset mix and have a lasting peace with the FHLBB. As I saw it, either Lincoln had to acquire another significant S&L, resulting in a new, combined institution where real estate and corporate securities became a lesser percentage of total assets, or ACC had to sell Lincoln.

I thought that a gradual transition of Lincoln's business would require a large capital investment. Even then, Lincoln faced the likelihood that the economy would adversely affect the transition, and losses could result, particularly if interest rates increased. I believed that if the problem were to be solved without undue economic risk, a major transaction which instantly changed Lincoln's characteristics was the answer.

I told Charlie that it was not possible to sell Lincoln at a fair price in the environment existing in mid-1988. The FHLBB had already announced its intention to dispose of a number of Texas-based thrifts in what was known as the Southwest Plan. Under the FHLBB's plan, prospective buyers expected to receive all kinds of goodies from the government, including the ability to acquire institutions that had their bad assets stripped away; yield-maintenance agreements which guaranteed a specific return on assets; tax incentives; forbearances that waived certain regulatory requirements; and other valuable inducements that no private seller could match.

Under these circumstances, a potential buyer had the choice of negotiating with a private seller, like ACC, who understood value and would drive a tough bargain, or they could deal with the government negotiators, perhaps the most inept negotiating group ever assembled. With ACC, they would actually have to buy Lincoln. With the government, they would be given an institution.

In addition, Lincoln's own characteristics made it a hard sell. Its branch network was in California, and its management offices were in Arizona. Its real-estate assets were scattered in a number of other states. Any buyer, other than an existing S&L, who bought Lincoln "as-is" faced the same philosophical problems with the regulators over Lincoln's risk profile that ACC had been struggling with for years. Another S&L could average Lincoln's assets in with its own, thereby diluting the effects of the direct investments that Lincoln held. But the new tangible capital requirements made it difficult for an existing S&L to swing such a large acquisition. So, a sale appeared to be the least likely of the two primary options available to ACC.

With respect to the purchase of another S&L, I knew that Pima Savings and Loan Association of Tucson was for sale. Pima was owned by Heron International, a large, privately held company headquartered in the United Kingdom. Heron, like ACC, was disenchanted with the re-regulation that had occurred since it acquired Pima. Heron was also facing business difficulties at home. Therefore, Heron had engaged an investment-banking firm to sell Pima. I had the package which Pima gave to prospective purchasers, and I was personally familiar with Pima's operations. My first reaction was that Lincoln and Pima were an ideal fit for each other.

Pima had branch operations in both Phoenix and Tucson as well as a large mortgage-banking business in California. Geographically, Pima complemented Lincoln, and the mortgage-banking business addressed the concerns of both the FHLBB and the CDSL with respect to the Community Reinvestment Act. I thought it would be possible to reduce operating costs substantially by eliminating duplicative operations in such areas as accounting, data processing, branch administration, and other overlapping functions. Pima, at the time, had about $3 billion in assets, so it was big enough, but not too big, for Lincoln to consider. I suggested to Charlie that we should at least explore such an acquisition. He agreed.

I set up a meeting for Charlie to meet the two top people in Heron. We met in late May in Phoenix. Charlie gave them a brief tour of ACC's facilities, and then we went to the Crescent Hotel for dinner. Over dinner, we agreed that Lincoln would be given the opportunity to structure a deal to buy Pima. We agreed to perform some preliminary due-diligence work, and, if things looked favorable, we would enter into a letter of intent. If we agreed on general terms, we could complete our due diligence and, pending a continued favorable assessment, could negotiate a contract. Both parties agreed that we should be able to accomplish everything by early August, and that became our objective.

On the Monday following the signing of the MOU, a group met in the conference room adjacent to Charlie's office to begin preparing for the upcoming examination. Charlie asked me to coordinate the preparation of the business plan and to organize a presentation to orient the examiners to Lincoln's various operations. Tim Kruckeberg and I were also asked to coordinate all responses to requests for information that Lincoln would receive from the FHLBB examiners. Our role was to see that these requests were channeled to the people who had the most knowledge about, or who had control over the data related to, the specific areas of interest to the examiners. The intent was to keep track of the examiners' requests and to make sure that the information was provided as quickly as possible. We were to meet periodically with the lead examiner to determine whether any issues had surfaced which the examiners were concerned about. We wanted to resolve these issues before a report cast in concrete was drafted. Jim Grogan was to coordinate responses to requests received from the CDSL examiners.

Grogan, Kruckeberg, and David Thompson, who replaced Mark Sauter as Lincoln's in-house regulatory counsel, were to coordinate the updating of the various manuals cited in the MOU and the agreement.

Randy Conte, who was in charge of the loan-servicing area, and Anne Oakley, one of the in-house attorneys, were responsible for seeing to it that all of the Lincoln's files were in order. They were to work with the accountants in the various business areas and with Joe Kotrys, who had joined Lincoln in Irvine and was responsible for the main file room, to make sure that the files were well organized.

The business plan and the various manuals were all completed and submitted to the examiners within the time frame contemplated by the MOU and the agreement.

With respect to the files, Lincoln asked both Arthur Young and Kaye Scholer to perform separate reviews of the files and to report any deficiencies they noted to Lincoln's board. Lincoln's file requirements, at the time, were more stringent than what the regulations required. These reviews disclosed deficiencies that related to the higher standards which Lincoln had established, but compliance with the regulations, per se, was reported to be good. The deficiencies noted were addressed by the people who were responsible for the files. There was no attempt to create new files or to backdate any documents.

These preparatory efforts went on through June and into early July. As a result, when the examiners arrived, Lincoln believed that it had complied with the requirements of the MOU and the agreement.

Also in May, ACC filed another registration statement to sell additional subordinated debentures. In connection with the filing, the California Department of Corporations asked ACC for additional information regarding its cash flow and debt-service capabilities. The Department of Corporations was provided with various cash-flow analyses and other data which answered their basic questions. ACC was seeking to register an additional $300 million of debentures. On May 26, 1988, the state granted qualification to ACC to sell $100 million of the requested amount.

While the Department of Corporations was reviewing the proposed sale of the subdebt, the CDSL was also looking into the matter. The CDSL first tried to get the Department of Corporations to deny ACC's application. On May 18, 1988, seven people from the CDSL, including Commissioner Crawford, met with representatives of the Department of Corporations and argued against ACC's application, expressing doubts that ACC could service the debt. When the application to sell additional debt was approved, the CDSL tried a different approach. On June 20, 1988, it wrote to ACC and Lincoln and said that, effective with the completion of the sale of the original $200 million or August 1, 1988, whichever came first, it was denying ACC's right to lease space in the Lincoln branches.

In order to continue the debenture sales, ACC had to locate and lease space outside of Lincoln's premises. So, for the next two months, Ray

Fidel and the others involved in the bond sales located space, usually near a Lincoln branch, negotiated leases, moved the bond sales offices, reprinted sales materials, changed the advertising, and did a host of other things to move the debenture sales away from all of Lincoln's branch offices. By August, there were no more ACC bond representatives in any of Lincoln's branches.

While ACC and Lincoln were getting ready for the upcoming examination, the FHLBB was making its own plans. Dochow circulated a request for experienced examiners to all of the FHLB bank districts, except San Francisco and Dallas, which was neck-deep in its own troubles. As a result of his requests, Dochow assembled a team of about twenty experienced examiners with, on paper, solid credentials to handle the examination of Lincoln.

The examiner-in-charge was Steve Scott from Seattle. Steve held the title of supervisory agent, a position similar to that held by Sanchez from San Francisco. He was an experienced examiner of both S&Ls and commercial banks. Steve is articulate, intelligent, tactful, well-groomed, and several cuts above the examiners Lincoln had seen in the past. His demeanor is thoughtful and professional.

Steve's three team leaders were: Charles ("Chuck") Gozdanovich, from Pittsburgh, who was in charge of lending and real estate; Steve Rohrs, from New York, who was in charge of operations; and, Jim Clark, from Indianapolis, who was responsible for investment securities.

Gozdanovich and Rohrs appeared to have comparable temperaments. They are quiet and subdued but are thoughtful, inquisitive, and bright. Their experience appeared to be considerable and relevant to their assigned areas in the examination. Their questions and observations demonstrated competency and an understanding of the operations and transactions they were reviewing. Their attitudes didn't indicate a bias either for or against Lincoln or ACC.

Clark was also an experienced examiner, but he didn't project the same confidence and competency as the others. His assigned area was a difficult one, from both a technical and an intellectual standpoint, and he seemed to be in way over his head. His questions and comments indicated only a minimal understanding of corporate finance and debt and equity securities. Perhaps as a defensive mechanism to overcome his lack of knowledge in the area of corporate securities, he displayed an aggressive personality and was close-minded and abrupt. He appeared to be the weakest of the three team leaders.

The CDSL also put together a team of about ten examiners. The examiner-in-charge was Gene Stelzer. Stelzer was fairly typical of the more senior CDSL examiners, although he had been with the CDSL for only about four years. Where the FHLBB team leaders showed some class and professionalism, Stelzer was at best a journeyman. He was inarticulate, abrasive, and mechanical and was way out of his depth intellectually and in terms of experience. He acted like he had a large chip on his shoulder and appeared to want to show the hotshots from Lincoln and the FHLBB that he had power and clout.

The more junior members of the CDSL team were a real mixed bag. Many were of foreign origin and English was actually their second language. As a result, while they appeared to be quite intelligent, language barriers made it difficult to communicate with and to understand them. They also lacked the training and supervision necessary to grasp some of the more technical areas of Lincoln's operations.

On June 20, 1988, a meeting was held to give the team leaders of both the CDSL and FHLBB examination teams an overview of Lincoln's operations. The FHLBB people attending the meeting were Dochow, Scott, Rohrs, Clark, and Gozdanovich. The CDSL people were Tommy Mar, who was one of the CDSL's senior examiners, Stelzer, Gerald Castillo, who was the CDSL's sharpest field examiner, and Harvey Shames, who was the CDSL assistant chief examiner and the person immediately senior to Mar.

Immediately prior to the meeting with Lincoln, the federal and state examiners held a brief meeting, so Darrel Dochow could lay out the FHLBB's game plan for the CDSL. Apparently, Dochow started by saying that the examination would look only at Lincoln's current financial status. Dochow purportedly said that the exam would cover only three basic areas: loans/real estate, securities, and operations. The CDSL had been pushing for an examination of ACC as well as Lincoln, but, at this time, Dochow purportedly indicated that the FHLBB was not contemplating a holding-company examination. He is also said to have emphasized that the exam was to be a "fresh look" at Lincoln and that the team was not to dwell on the findings of the 1986 examination. This may not have jibed with the CDSL's intentions, as they were still intent on nailing down the open issues from 1986.

The meeting with Lincoln opened with the various examiners introducing themselves to the Lincoln people. We had assembled about fifty people who were introduced to the examiners as their respective areas of operations were discussed. Our presentation was by business area—that is, lending, investments, real-estate management, real-estate development, hotel operations, branch operations, insurance operations, information processing, legal, and financial reporting. The principal business person in each area introduced the other managers, accountants, and attorneys who worked in the area.

At the conclusion of the presentations, I discussed one key concern with the examiners. The 1986 exam had been conducted in Irvine. I told the examiners that there were duplicate sets of records in Phoenix, and all of Lincoln's key people were in Phoenix. While it was their decision, I encouraged them to conduct their examination where they would have access to the people—in Phoenix—not Irvine. I pointed out that one of the problems in 1986 had been that the examiners could not, or would not, discuss their concerns with Lincoln's decision makers; thus, no one had agreed on a common set of facts. I felt that this problem could be substantially eliminated if the examiners were able to talk to the people who bought the securities or developed the real estate, rather than just relying on the paperwork to tell the whole story. I concluded that if they really needed to see the original documents, we could bring those from Irvine to Phoenix.

Dochow said that it made sense to him to conduct the examination in Phoenix and that that's what the FHLBB team would do. The CDSL was a different matter. Tommy Mar said that the state didn't have the budget to pay for any out-of-state travel; thus, the CDSL had to conduct its exam in Irvine. Frankly, this argument didn't make a hell of a lot of sense. None of the CDSL examiners lived in Irvine, so they had to pay for lodging, meals, and travel costs. The only added cost was the difference between the airfare to Phoenix and the auto-mileage cost between Los Angeles and Irvine.

The other issue Mar raised concerned Lincoln's records. He said that there was no way that the commissioner would allow any original records to be transferred to Phoenix, even on a temporary basis. The CDSL's position was that Lincoln was legally headquartered in California, and that's where all of its original records had to be maintained.

The Lincoln people left the meeting feeling that the federal examiners sounded realistic and sincere and as if they intended to live up to the commitments made in the MOU. We also concluded that the CDSL was going to be as impossible as ever to deal with, and, before the whole process was completed, they would be a problem, for both Lincoln and the FHLBB.

While Dochow was apparently committed to complying with the MOU and, therefore, confining the examination to the events which had occurred after the 1986 exam, that view was not shared by the CDSL, O'Connell, or Smuzynski, all of whom still had old axes to grind. Congressional testimony indicates that about this time Commissioner Crawford raised several issues with the FHLBB people which were carryovers from 1986. The most significant was the CDSL's concern over a tax-sharing agreement between ACC and Lincoln. The CDSL had looked at this agreement and didn't understand it, so Crawford requested that the FHLBB examiners review it. This innocuous request launched one of the major controversies of the 1988 examination.

Crawford, Smuzynski, and O'Connell were kindred spirits. They each had a bone in their craw over the 1986 exam; none really let facts cloud or alter his opinions; and each thought that he was manipulating the others. They would cause poor Steve Scott untold problems and headaches as the exam unfolded.

The very first issue to arise after the examiners arrived in Phoenix concerned the potential acquisition of Pima Savings from Heron International. Lynn Fisher, from Kaye Scholer, Ron Stoll, an in-house attorney, and I had been meeting with Heron's people and their lawyers structuring a deal. By late July, we had a definitive structure worked out. Lincoln would acquire Pima for a total price of $125 million, with $50 million to $75 million represented by cash and the remainder of the purchase price by subordinated notes which qualified as regulatory capital. Heron would purchase from Pima more than $300 million in real estate or delinquent loans, paying 20 percent in cash and giving interest-bearing notes, secured by first liens and Heron's corporate guarantee, for the remainder of the purchase price. In addition, Heron would purchase, on the same terms and conditions, any loans which became delinquent within a specified period (as I recall, 180 days) after Lincoln's acquisition of Pima.

We determined that Lincoln could eliminate close to $30 million in duplicative operating costs after an acquisition. The purchases which Heron agreed to make increased Pima's spread and pretax income by eliminating over $300 million in nonearning assets. The combination of these factors enhanced Pima's projected earnings by over $60 million a year. The result was a very good economic deal for Lincoln which required no government assistance.

I had talked to Dochow in June about the possible purchase of Pima, and he had said that he didn't want to consider such an acquisition until after the examination was over. I discussed Dochow's reaction with Charlie, and we both agreed that the deal could not be put on hold for that long. Heron wanted to sell. If Lincoln was to be a buyer, we had to get something down on paper while the opportunity was at hand. Moreover, the MOU contemplated an acquisition by Lincoln and specifically provided that one could be approved within the "interim period," the time covered by the examination. Now, we had negotiated a preliminary agreement which laid out all of the elements of the deal.

On July 13, Charlie called Dochow and again discussed Pima. He was told not to sign anything until Dochow found out more about Pima and determined how long it would take to process an application. Dochow repeated that he preferred to wait until the examination was over to consider the issue.

A few weeks later, when the Pima deal was solid, I sat down with Steve Scott and went over the proposed transaction in detail. I discussed with him the earnings projections and how such an acquisition would change Lincoln's operations and asset profile. I gave him copies of the draft documents. I told him that Heron had contributed over $70 million to Pima's capital over the past few years, even though it didn't have a capital-maintenance agreement requiring it to do so. I told him that it was my impression that Heron would not continue to shore up Pima's capital indefinitely; as a result, Pima could become a "troubled" association. Following the discussion, Steve expressed the opinion that the deal made sense to him and said he would talk to Dochow.

After additional correspondence, Dochow wrote to Charlie saying that he was not in favor of the proposed acquisition until after the examination was finished. He said that Lincoln could file an application, but he didn't think it would be acted on favorably by the FHLBB. Both Charlie and I understood his message. He would advise the Board to turn down the deal. Given Dochow's position within the FHLBB structure, the Board would accept his advice. We were screwed. We decided to tell Heron that the FHLBB probably wouldn't approve the transaction and the deal had to be called off.

I believed then, and I believe now, that this acquisition would have assured the continuance of both Lincoln and Pima. It was a sound transaction that produced enough economic benefits for the combined entity to prosper and survive. The combined association would have had an excellent asset mix, strong branch operations, low overhead and administrative costs, and a strong, positive spread. Dochow was simply unwilling to analyze the advantages that this deal offered. He'd made up his mind that the exam had to come first; he therefore didn't give the proposed transaction any meaningful attention.

While the Pima issue was going on, the examiners pursued Crawford's questions about the tax-sharing agreement between ACC and Lincoln. The field people gathered information and forwarded it to Smuzynski and O'Connell in Washington.

ACC and its subsidiary companies filed consolidated income-tax returns. In a consolidated return, the members of the consolidated group are basically treated as if they are a single entity. The operating losses of one member are offset against the taxable income of the other members to produce a single operating loss or taxable income against which a single tax is assessed. The parent company is responsible for paying the tax or receiving any refunds due from or to the entire consolidated group. In 1984, following its acquisition by ACC, Lincoln's income and deductions entered into the determination of ACC's consolidated taxable income.

Income and deductions for tax purposes can be substantially different from the revenues and expenses which are reflected in a company's financial statements. Income and deductions are a product of the Internal Revenue Code, while revenue and expenses are determined in accordance with generally accepted accounting principles (GAAP). Because of differences between the Code and GAAP, some items of income are reflected sooner in a company's financial statements than they are in its tax return. For example, the entire gain on the sale of a piece of real estate may be recorded for financial-statement purposes in the year the sale occurs, but, if the company elects the installment method, the same gain may be spread over a series of years for tax purposes. Similarly, a company may elect to deduct certain expenses in its tax return in the year the expense is incurred, but GAAP may require that the expense must be capitalized and reflected in the financial statements through annual amortization charges or at the time the related asset is sold.

Because of the differences between tax and financial-statement accounting, companies, such as ACC, must go through an extensive process of identifying and tracking these differences. When the consolidated group is made up of many companies, as was the case with ACC, the process is further complicated because this reconciliation routine must be done for each company in the group. As a result, most companies only go through this laborious exercise once each year, usually in the months following the end of the fiscal year.

In order to allocate the overall tax burden to the component members of the consolidated group, many companies adopt tax-sharing agreements. The purpose of such an agreement is to see that each company within the group pays its appropriate share of the taxes and that a member with an operating loss receives the equivalency of a refund if other members use the loss to reduce overall taxes. The form and content of these agreements vary from company to company. Some base the allocation on the tax liability, or expense, determined for financial-statement purposes, while others base the allocation on the actual income and deductions reflected in the tax return. It's really up to the individual company and its subsidiaries as to what basis is used and how they allocate their tax burden.

In 1985, the management of ACC reviewed the financial statements of several holding companies that owned savings and loan subsidiaries. They noticed that the footnotes to some of these financial statements discussed the existence of tax-sharing arrangements between the holding

company and the subsidiary savings and loan. When it filed its consolidated return for 1984, ACC became aware that Lincoln had absorbed a
substantial part of ACC's operating loss carryforward (ACC had a big
operating loss carryforward because, when it was a home builder, it had
elected to use the installment method for reporting real-estate sales). By
using ACC's losses, Lincoln was able to offset its income and eliminate
any taxes it would otherwise have had to pay.

In early January 1986, Charlie and Judy Wischer called Sidney Mar,
who was Lincoln's supervisory agent at the time, to discuss what they had
to file with the FHLBB, if anything, in order to adopt a tax-sharing
agreement between ACC and Lincoln. Mar mentioned that several other
institutions in the district had agreements and told Charlie and Judy what
he thought they had to file.

On January 23, 1986, Lincoln sent Mar a letter requesting the
FHLBB's approval of a Tax Preparation and Allocation Agreement. The
section of the letter, and the attached agreement, which established how
the arrangement would work was stated as follows:

> Lincoln will pay to AMCC [ACC] the amount of tax which Lincoln and its
> subsidiaries would owe, calculated as if the tax liability of Lincoln and its
> subsidiaries were determined on a stand-alone basis. Such liability will be
> measured by the total provision for such taxes as computed for financial
> reporting purposes in accordance with Generally Accepted Accounting
> Principles, consistently applied.

On March 7, 1986, Sidney Mar responded to Lincoln's request. Mar's
letter cited several factors that he believed would result in a transfer of
assets from the S&L to the parent without any offsetting benefit to the
S&L. One of those was if "the association transferred its deferred tax
account to the parent along with an equivalent amount of cash or earning
assets."

The letter then listed three conditions that an agreement had to meet
before Mar would approve it. The most pertinent was included as a part of
the first condition and said: "No transfer of Lincoln Savings' deferred tax
liability to American Continental."

The proposed agreement called for Lincoln to pay taxes to ACC as
"measured by the total provision for such taxes as computed for financial
reporting purposes in accordance with Generally Accepted Accounting
Principles." The provision for income taxes, as reflected on a company's
financial statements, is comprised of two elements—a current provision
and a provision for deferred taxes. The current provision is the estimated
actual amount of taxes that the company will pay for the year based on the
tax return it files. The provision for deferred income taxes represents the
tax effects of all of the differences between the tax code and GAAP. In

effect, it represents taxes which will actually be paid in the future or refunds which will be received or reductions in taxable income which will occur in the future. The total provision is the combination of these two elements, and it represents the tax which would have been paid if the revenues and expenses appearing in the financial statements had been the income and deductions reflected in the company's tax return for that year. Thus, deferred taxes can be viewed as a means of reconciling the two different methods of accounting—GAAP and the tax code.

As stated, deferred taxes are an estimate of the taxes which will be paid in the future. Depending on the nature of the item giving rise to the deferred amount, those taxes may not be paid for many, many years. For example, if the deferred taxes result from the company's election to use the installment method for reporting the gain on the sale of real estate, such as a house, the deferred taxes will be paid as the company collects payments from the buyer. In this example, the taxes could be spread over the thirty-year period the mortgage is collected. Each year, a little piece of the deferred taxes is actually paid.

This was Mar's concern. He didn't want Lincoln to make a cash payment to ACC if ACC didn't actually have to remit the cash to the government until several years in the future. He viewed such a situation to be the equivalency of Lincoln advancing interest-free funds to ACC. If the agreement based the calculation of taxes, and their payment, on the method of accounting used in the financial statements—the provision for taxes— this result could occur. It should also be noted that if the agreement were based on the provision for taxes determined under GAAP, it was also possible, although not probable under the circumstances, that Lincoln could receive payments from ACC in advance of ACC receiving refunds from the government.

Before and after ACC and Lincoln received Mar's letter, there were a series of telephone calls between Mar and Sonja Rodriguez, who also worked for the FHLBB in San Francisco, and Scott Siebels, an in-house tax lawyer, Mark Sauter, and other Lincoln personnel. During these conversations, the ACC/Lincoln people say that they answered questions about the origination of ACC's net operating tax loss, the length of time before the loss would expire, the amount of the loss, and the benefits to Lincoln if payments to ACC preceded the payments ACC actually made to the IRS. All of the items raised in Mar's letter were discussed, with ACC/Lincoln providing additional information and trying to understand all of Mar's concerns. During the conversations, ACC/Lincoln people say that Mar continued to press for certain changes in the agreement, but in other areas he appeared to be satisfied that no changes were required. The intent of both parties appeared to be to end up with an agreement which could be applied on a consistent basis and could be easily administered.

On March 14, 1986, a new agreement was forwarded to Mar and

Rodriguez. Some of the key provisions and language of that agreement follow.

The preamble to the agreement stated:

[S]uch allocation shall under no circumstances require payment by Lincoln of a tax liability greater than the tax provision computed quarterly *on a separate company basis* and stated in financial statements of Lincoln audited by Arthur Andersen & Company.

Article II stated:

If AMCC [ACC] and Lincoln file a return on a consolidated basis, Lincoln will pay to AMCC an amount of federal income tax, minimum tax or other additional tax (previously enacted or enacted in the future), measured by the total provision for such taxes which is computed for financial reporting purposes, as audited by Arthur Andersen & Co. for Lincoln and its affiliates on a stand alone basis. . . . Where the Lincoln Group is otherwise required to make a payment to AMCC hereunder, and AMCC is in a net loss or non-taxable position due to its own tax status apart from the Lincoln Group, the parties hereto intend that the Lincoln payment computed according to this Agreement shall nonetheless be paid.

This revised agreement still based the determination of the amounts that Lincoln would pay or receive on the total provision for income taxes (which included both the taxes currently payable as well as deferred income taxes) appearing in Lincoln's financial statements. This meant that GAAP concepts would be used and payments would not be based on the amounts appearing in the consolidated tax return. The agreement also required Lincoln to make payments to ACC, even when ACC would not be making any payments to the IRS because of its own tax losses. These elements were essentially unchanged from the original application sent to Sidney Mar.

On April 2, 1986, Sidney Mar responded to Lincoln's revised agreement. The pertinent part of his letter read as follows:

Based on our review of the revised Agreement and representations made by Mr. Sauter, et al., it is our understanding that the Agreement as presently structured will provide for fair and equitable allocation of the tax liability between American Continental Corporation and Lincoln Savings and that under no circumstances will Lincoln Savings' tax liability be greater than its tax liability as calculated on a separate entity basis. Accordingly, we hereby approve the proposed Tax Preparation and Allocation Agreement as revised and signed by each respective party on March 14, 1986.

Whether Sidney Mar intended to waive his concerns regarding the payment of Lincoln's deferred taxes to ACC or not, he approved such payments in this letter. Under the approved agreement, Lincoln would pay the total provision for income taxes shown on its annual financial statements to ACC, even if ACC owed no payments to the government.

On September 2, 1988, Dochow wrote to the Lincoln board, and to Charlie, that there would be a meeting on September 6 to discuss the tax-sharing arrangement, various proposals Lincoln had pending with the FHLBB, and the status of the examination.

Throughout the examination, either Charlie or I, and often both of us, met with Steve Scott. The purpose of these sessions was to ascertain if the examiners had any concerns about Lincoln which needed to be resolved. As of September 2, Scott had not disclosed any significant problems to us. So, when Dochow asked for this meeting, Charlie and I met with Scott and asked what the issue was regarding the tax-sharing agreement. Scott said that he didn't know. It was something that the people in Washington were looking into, and they hadn't told him anything. He seemed as much in the dark about the subject as we were.

There was another subject that we briefly discussed with Scott. During 1988, a large short position developed in ACC's common stock. A short position results from people selling shares they don't own—selling short. The shares sold by a short-seller are borrowed from others. The short-seller is anticipating that the market price of the shares will decline, and he or she can purchase shares to replace the borrowed shares at a lower price. The difference between the price at the time the shares were sold short and the price they are purchased for at a later date determines the gain or loss to the short-seller. If the price, in fact, declines, the short-seller realizes a gain. Conversely, if the share price rises, the short-seller suffers a loss.

In ACC's case, the short position was very substantial when measured against the total number of shares that were outstanding and available for sale in the market. Charlie's concern was that the adverse press which ACC and Lincoln had received as a consequence of the leaks of information by the FHLBB was feeding into the hands of the short-sellers. He was worried that any future leaks could make the short position worse. And he suspected that there could be a connection between the short-sellers and the leaker—that is, they might somehow be working together. He simply wanted Scott to be aware of the situation.

The meeting which Dochow wanted scheduled was held in ACC's main conference room on September 6, 1988. Dochow opened the meeting by saying that the MOU required the FHLBB to bring any issues to Lincoln's attention, so they could be resolved. In this context, he wanted to discuss two subjects which were of concern to the FHLBB.

The first subject was the tax-sharing agreement. Dochow reviewed the written communications between Lincoln and the Eleventh District in 1986 leading to the approval of the agreement. He noted that Lincoln had paid about $93 million to ACC pursuant to the agreement and indicated that the calculations underlying the payments had been properly made. However, he said that Lincoln had made payments of its deferred tax liability in a manner which was inconsistent with the approval granted by the Eleventh District and violative of the regulations, because the payments amounted to an extension of credit to ACC.

Lincoln questioned the propriety of Dochow's inquiries into the tax-sharing agreement, because they were inconsistent with the spirit and terms of the MOU and the related agreement signed on May 20, 1988. These documents made it very clear that Lincoln and the FSLIC and FHLBB, by entering into the agreements, had resolved "all the issues outstanding as a result of the 1986 examination and the negotiations concerning it between Lincoln and ORPOS." Further the MOU stated: "In consideration for Lincoln's agreements set out in this Memorandum of Understanding, FSLIC and the FHLBB agree not to initiate any administrative or enforcement proceedings against Lincoln or its parents, affiliates, officers, directors, employees or agents relating *to any findings in, or transactions, procedures or events covered by*, the 1986 Examination and the negotiations concerning it between Lincoln and ORPOS . . ." (emphasis added). This language was repeated in the agreement of the same date. These are binding contracts. They closed the transactions and events occurring prior to October 16, 1986, the close of fieldwork on the 1986 examination, and arguably prior to April 20, 1987, the date of the Report of Examination.

The tax-sharing agreement had been approved by FHLB-SF on April 2, 1986, after having been entered into by Lincoln and ACC, subject to the FHLB-SF approval, on March 14, 1986. Shortly thereafter, while the examiners were still doing their fieldwork, the first payments under the tax-sharing agreement were made by Lincoln to ACC.

As such, the tax-sharing agreement and related tax payments were "transactions, procedures or events covered by" the 1986 examination. They were, or should have been, closed issues. By contract, the FSLIC and the FHLBB had agreed that they would not ever be the subjects of any administrative or enforcement actions. For this promise, consideration had been given by Lincoln and ACC. For example, they had agreed not to sue the FHLBB, and ACC had agreed to contribute additional capital to Lincoln. Yet, Dochow was bringing up the issue in the new exam.

In his comments, Dochow expressed concern that Lincoln had made payments to ACC which, in turn, were not made to the IRS because Lincoln's payments were for deferred taxes as opposed to taxes currently due. He also raised the question of whether the payments were in accordance with "the spirit" of what Sidney Mar thought he had approved. He didn't indicate that anyone from the examination team had actually talked to Mar; instead, he appeared to base his concern primarily, if not solely, on his reading and interpretation of the two letters which Mar had sent to Lincoln. Therefore, he probably did not know whether or not Mar's discussions with Lincoln's personnel, which had occurred during the period between the two letters, had changed the concerns regarding the payment of deferred taxes which Mar had expressed in his first letter to Lincoln. But Dochow did know that Mar hadn't reiterated any concern about deferred taxes in the approval letter of April 2, 1986.

Dochow also suggested that the payments might be an "unauthorized advance," or extension of credit, from Lincoln to ACC. The payments would have been unauthorized only if one chooses to disregard Mar's approval of the tax-sharing agreement. The agreement contemplated the payment to ACC of Lincoln's deferred tax liability. Dochow admitted that the payment calculations and the payments themselves were in accordance with the agreement. Thus, if one accepts Mar's approval at its face value, the payments were, in fact, authorized by Lincoln's supervisory agent.

Finally, Dochow indicated that the payments were in conflict with the FHLBB's policy and, as interpreted by the FHLBB's general counsel, violated regulations. Again, such payments would be a violation if they had not received prior approval, which is what the regulations required. The only way that one can conclude that Lincoln's payments to ACC had not received prior approval is to disregard Mar's April 2, 1986, letter or not to read it literally.

As to the FHLBB's current policy, that was a matter which Mar, not Lincoln, had to be concerned about when he granted approval to the agreement. The regulation, by its wording, delegated the authority to approve transactions to supervisory agents. The delegated authority was very broad and virtually any payment of any kind and for any purpose could be made by an insured institution, provided there was "prior written approval."

After the discussion of this issue, Dochow requested that Lincoln calculate the amount of the total payments which were based on the deferred tax liability and the amount based on the current tax liability; provide the analysis as well as a written response to his concerns by September 19; and refrain from making any additional payments until the issue could be resolved. Charlie said that no additional payments would be made until after the matter was resolved.

The second issue was the Employee Stock Ownership Plan (ESOP). In 1978, ACC had established an Employee Stock Incentive Plan (ESIP). In 1984, the ESIP was amended to change the plan to an Employee Stock Ownership Plan, allowing the ESOP to borrow funds to purchase shares of ACC's common stock. At the time that the plan was amended, leveraged ESOPs were fairly innovative forms of providing employee benefits.

The plan covered nearly all of the employees of ACC and Lincoln who met prescribed age and service requirements (only the employees of a few small subsidiaries were initially excluded from the plan; later, employees of the Crescent and Phoenician hotels would also be excluded). The ESOP is similar to other benefit plans in that the employer is permitted to deduct for income-tax purposes the amount of its contributions to the plan. Employees also benefit. First, the ESOP gives them an ownership stake in their employer. Second, increases in the value of the stock held by the ESOP and the dividends it receives are tax-deferred. The employee is taxed only when he or she receives distributions from the plan.

A leveraged ESOP, such as ACC's and Lincoln's, borrows money to purchase employer stock. The loans are secured by the acquired stock and are repaid from the funds provided by the employer's annual contributions. Lending institutions also gain an advantage because they can treat 50 percent of the interest they receive from the ESOP as tax free. This allows the ESOP to obtain attractive interest rates on its borrowings.

Even with the tax advantages, lenders will not make loans to an ESOP without adequate collateral. Generally, a bank cannot extend a loan for more than 50 percent of the value of the securities which are pledged to secure the loan. Also, because employer contributions are purely voluntary, lenders are reluctant to lend even 50 percent of the value of the underlying stock. Thus, employers generally have to guarantee the ESOP loans, effectively committing to annual contributions equal to the debt-service requirements of the loan, and these guarantees often have to be backed by collateral pledged by the employer.

When an ESOP purchases employer stock using borrowed funds, the shares purchased are held in a "suspense account" and are not allocated to employees. As employer contributions are made, a portion of the loan is repaid and shares are released from suspense and are allocated to individual employee accounts. The advantage to the employees of leveraged plans is that they have no personal obligation to repay the loans, yet they will benefit if the acquired stock increases in value. Generally, leveraged ESOPs are able to achieve a lower average purchase price, and therefore greater employee benefits, than can traditional nonleveraged plans.

In 1985, the ESOP borrowed $23 million from outside lenders and used the proceeds to purchase ACC common stock. Of the total loans, $20 million was represented by three loans resulting from the issuance of so-called FRESOP notes (Floating Rate Employee Stock Ownership Plan notes). The proceeds from one series of the FRESOP notes, in the amount of $5 million, were used to purchase shares from officers, directors, and employees of ACC. The proceeds from the other two series, totaling $15 million, were used to purchase shares from outside individuals and institutions, including Drexel Burnham Lambert. The FRESOP notes were guaranteed by ACC and Lincoln, with ACC guaranteeing 25 percent and Lincoln the remaining 75 percent. ACC's eligible employees represented less than 25 percent of the total eligible employees; thus, Lincoln guaranteed somewhat less than its proportionate share of the obligations.

ACC represented that the reason shares were purchased from insiders was that there simply were not enough shares available on the open market at favorable prices. This was because ACC's officers and directors owned a substantial percentage of the total outstanding shares of ACC. The officers and directors received an average price for their shares which was below that realized by nonaffiliated parties, in some instances more than 25 percent less.

Dochow's concern was that Lincoln pledged assets to the ESOP which, in turn, used those assets as collateral for notes issued to purchase shares from certain of ACC's management personnel. He wanted an analysis showing whether ACC's management had received personal benefits, to the detriment of Lincoln, from these transactions and whether the transactions were "prohibited affiliate transactions."

Both Bob Kielty and Judy Wischer explained the background of the ESOP and the legal research which had been done before its adoption. They pointed out that only Lincoln's employees benefited from the stock purchased with the portion of the loan to the ESOP that was guaranteed by Lincoln. Also, none of the shares acquired by Lincoln's portion of the ESOP was from affiliates or affiliated persons. They also said that they would send Dochow the analysis he had requested.

With respect to pending proposals, Dochow said that none would be approved until either the FHLBB received more information or the examination was completed and all issues were resolved.

Charlie was disturbed and upset by Dochow's comments regarding the tax-sharing agreement and the ESOP. First, the issues were not being raised by the field examiners—they didn't know anything about the subjects. They had emanated from Washington, and this was reminiscent of the 1986 examination. Moreover, the person or persons in Washington who had provided Dochow with the information on these subjects hadn't given him all the facts. With respect to the few facts that Dochow did seem to have, they were being severely misinterpreted. It appeared as if someone had filled in the gaps in the information with speculations that were simply wrong. Again, this was what had happened in the 1986 exam—the field examiners' superiors had made decisions on the basis of incomplete and misinterpreted information.

Second, the issues involved transactions which had occurred in 1986 and 1985. As such, the MOU foreclosed the examiners from raising these issues. Dochow had to know that was the case, because he had been instrumental in negotiating the MOU. Why then was he breaching the agreement?

Third, Dochow's attitude was dictatorial. He was instructing ACC and Lincoln to do things. In so doing, there was the implied threat that if ACC and Lincoln didn't comply with his instructions, some adverse actions would be taken against Lincoln by the FHLBB. Again, a similar tactic had been used by San Francisco.

The fact that the same things that had plagued the 1986 examination were now resurfacing bothered Charlie. He had believed that Dochow was fair and thorough. But here Dochow was acting before he had all the information he needed to make a reasoned decision. And he was listening to people other than the field examiners—the only FHLBB people who had access to factual data concerning Lincoln. This raised several questions. Who were the people Dochow was listening to? Where did they get their information? What biases did they have with respect to Lincoln? Would Dochow continue to act as he had in this meeting and, if so, would this examination turn into a repeat of 1986? All of these were disturbing questions, and, at this point, Lincoln didn't have answers to any of them.

What Dochow didn't say in this meeting was that a new phase of the examination was being started—an examination of ACC.

Thirteen

Lincoln's Largest Transaction Produces Fallout

Just prior to the September meeting with Dochow, Lincoln entered into one of its most controversial transactions. It involved the exchange of assets that Lincoln had acquired in earlier deals with Sir James Goldsmith for shares in Goldsmith's primary acquisition company.

One of Goldsmith's companies owned the stock of a number of publishing and broadcasting concerns that were located in France as well as the stock of Grand Union, the operator of a chain of supermarkets located in the northeastern portion of the United States. Goldsmith sold this company to the French government, which primarily wanted to own and operate the media companies. After the French government bought the company, Goldsmith was told that the French didn't want Grand Union because it didn't fit in the government's plans. The French asked Goldsmith to find a buyer for Grand Union. Believing that the French government didn't appreciate the full value of Grand Union, Goldsmith organized a group, known as Grand Union Acquisition Corporation (GUAC), to purchase the Grand Union stock. In early 1988, Lincoln, through a subsidiary, bought 25 percent of GUAC's common stock for $12.5 million and also purchased $37.5 million of GUAC's preferred stock. Shortly after Lincoln made its investment, GUAC acquired Grand Union at what Goldsmith believed was an extremely favorable price.

Not long after GUAC acquired Grand Union, a number of parties expressed interest in purchasing the chain of stores. By the early summer of 1988, three groups were considering acquiring the stores, and each group was represented to be a bona fide potential purchaser. The prices discussed by these groups would have produced a gain to Lincoln of $50 million or higher if a sale were actually consummated.

Charlie wanted to capture some of the unrealized gain in GUAC in the second quarter of 1988. To do so, he sold a "profits-participation interest" in the GUAC common shares which Lincoln owned to CenTrust Savings Bank of Miami. CenTrust paid $30 million in exchange for the right to receive 62.5 percent of any gain that Lincoln realized on the ultimate sale or disposition of the GUAC common stock. If such a sale occurred within one year, CenTrust was limited to receiving maximum proceeds of $36 million. After one year, CenTrust would receive the full 62.5 percent of any gain.

This was only a profits interest. First, Lincoln would recover its $12.5 million investment. Then, if there were any profit, it would be split between CenTrust and Lincoln in accordance with the percentages specified in the profits-participation agreement.

Lincoln believed that the entire $30 million it received from CenTrust should be recorded as a gain. Its auditors at the time, Arthur Young, believed that a portion of Lincoln's original $12.5-million investment in the GUAC stock needed to be allocated to the profits interest that had been sold. After a great deal of discussion, Lincoln allocated a little over $5 million of its basis in the GUAC stock to the profits interest and recognized a profit of around $25 million in the second quarter of 1988.

In 1985, when Lincoln had originally entered into the partnership with Sir James Goldsmith to acquire the assets of Crown Zellerbach, Lincoln had anticipated that the GOSLP partnership—the acquirer of the CZ assets—would sell all the assets within two to three years. But in mid-1988, Goldsmith indicated that the operations of the timberlands, which were still in the partnership, were becoming increasingly more profitable and that the partnership might continue to operate these assets rather than sell them. In addition, natural-gas reserves and other minerals had been discovered on the timberlands, making them even more valuable than was originally believed.

Lincoln's investment in the GOSLP partnership was accounted for under the cost method of accounting. Under this method, Lincoln could recognize income from the partnership only as it received cash distributions. If the partnership paid no distributions, Lincoln recognized no profits. Goldsmith's new plans called for reinvesting earnings in the timber operations, as opposed to making cash distributions to the partners. With this change in the partnership's plans, Charlie started to explore the possibility of selling Lincoln's partnership interest to Goldsmith. The first discussion regarding this possibility took place in August 1988 but was inconclusive, because the price Goldsmith wanted to pay and the value Charlie wanted to receive were initially far apart. But Charlie continued to explore the concept with Goldsmith.

In late August, a transaction was proposed wherein Lincoln would exchange its interest in GOSLP, its interest in GUAC (Grand Union), and some cash for 20 percent of the outstanding common stock of Goldsmith's principal acquisition company, General Oriental Investments Limited (GOIL). By owning 20 percent of GOIL, it was believed that Lincoln could account for its investment using the equity method, which allowed Lincoln to recognize its proportionate share of GOIL's reported net income as it was earned, rather than when it was dividended to Lincoln. Additionally, ACC believed that it was entitled to record a gain on the exchange of its assets for the GOIL stock.

A deal was agreed to in principle in late August. A formal contract was entered into on September 2, 1988, with closing to occur prior to October 5, 1988. The terms of the deal were as follows:

1. Lincoln would convey to GOIL: (a) its common stock in GUAC, which was initially valued by the parties at $75 million, to be reduced to $50 million if GUAC was not reorganized or sold by December 31, 1988, in such a manner that GOIL would receive cash and other acceptable securities of at least $75 million, (b) the preferred stock of GUAC valued at $37.5 million, (c) cash in the amount of $8.75 million, to be increased by $25 million if the GUAC reorganization described in (a) did not occur by December 31, and (d) the GOSLP partnership interest.
2. Lincoln would receive 28,630,000 shares of GOIL common stock valued in the agreement at $9.50 a share or an aggregate value of $271,985,000.

Lincoln's side of the deal was complicated by two factors. First, Lincoln no longer owned the entire GOSLP partnership interest. As the result of a series of transactions in 1987 and early 1988, half of the interest which Lincoln originally owned, and which it had now agreed to convey to GOIL, was owned by a subsidiary of Saudi European Bank, a Paris-based bank in which Lincoln held a 10-percent interest. So, Lincoln needed to repurchase this interest. Second, Lincoln had sold the profit interest in the GUAC common stock to CenTrust. In order to deliver the GUAC shares, free and clear of any encumbrances, Lincoln had to settle the profits-participation agreement.

Saudi European Bank's investment in the GOSLP partnership interest was approximately $65.375 million, including a note of $50 million plus accrued interest of about $6.375 million which was owed to Lincoln. After a series of negotiations, Lincoln reacquired this interest by paying Saudi European Bank $12.24 million in cash and assuming the note plus accrued interest, a total purchase price of $68.615 million.

I understand that Saudi European was willing to sell its portion of the GOSLP interest once it learned that Goldsmith intended to operate, rather than sell, the GOSLP assets. Saudi European, like Lincoln, needed to hold earning assets. When Saudi European bought the GOSLP interest, it, too, thought the partnership would sell the timber property in a relatively short period of time. Such a sale was expected to result in a gain. Now, it didn't want to tie up over $65 million in an asset that might not produce any reportable income for several years. By selling the interest to Lincoln, Saudi European could recoup its investment and earn a reasonable profit. So, it was willing to sell.

The CenTrust profits-participation interest was a simpler deal. Since the GUAC shares were valued at $75 million, CenTrust was entitled, according to the terms of the profits-participation agreement, to the maximum, first-year payment of $36 million. This would not be true if the GUAC reorganization were not completed by December 31, 1988, and the value of the GUAC shares reduced to $50 million. But Charlie didn't want to disclose any details of the GOIL transaction to CenTrust and, therefore, was willing to base CenTrust's payment on the $75-million value. Since CenTrust was receiving the maximum amount under the agreement, it didn't have to know who the buyer was or what Lincoln had received in the deal. CenTrust agreed to accept $3.6 million in cash and the remainder in the form of a non-interest-bearing note due December 31, 1988.

A brief description of GOIL is probably in order. Prior to the transaction with Lincoln, Goldsmith owned about 80 percent of GOIL's outstanding shares. The remaining shares were held by the public and were listed on the Vancouver and London stock exchanges. Trading in the shares was light. Primarily for tax purposes, GOIL was incorporated in the Cayman Islands. At March 31, 1988, GOIL held the following assets:

— cash in the amount of $185 million;
— investments in the common stock of companies, such as Ford Motor, Goodrich, Alcoa, Phelps Dodge, and other U.S.-based corporations in the aggregate amount of $239 million;
— other current assets in the amount of $57 million;
— property and equipment of $19.5 million;
— a 25-percent interest in GUAC's common stock at a cost of $12.5 million and $9 million of GUAC preferred stock;
— a 58-percent interest in GOSLP recorded at $114 million on GOIL's books;
— Treasury securities of $45 million.

GOIL's financial statements reflected current liabilities of $76 million; long-term liabilities and deferred credits of $201 million; and shareholder funds of approximately $404 million. GOIL's earnings for its fiscal years ending March 31, 1987 and 1988, were $105 million and $210 million, respectively. GOIL paid dividends of $108 million in 1987 and $56 million in 1988. Lincoln estimated that the unrealized appreciation in GOIL's net assets was at least $700 million.

After the exchange with Lincoln, GOIL would own approximately 78 percent of GOSLP and 50 percent of GUAC's common stock.

Charlie saw four primary reasons to enter into the exchange for GOIL's shares. First, he wanted to participate in any future deals that Goldsmith put together. He was concerned that the FHLBB would not permit any further cash investments in these deals. By owning 20 percent of GOIL, Lincoln would automatically participate in future Goldsmith transactions without having to make any additional cash investments. Second, the ownership in GOIL could provide Lincoln with greater access to investors in the European financial community. Third, Lincoln believed that it could record GOIL's earnings on the equity method, resulting in an earning asset, whereas the assets being exchanged were essentially nonearning because of the use of the cost method of accounting. Finally, he believed that GOIL's asset holdings were very valuable and that the assets would continue to increase in value.

Accounting for exchanges of nonmonetary assets, which is what the GOIL exchange was, is governed by opinion no. 29 of the Accounting Principles Board (APB 29). The Accounting Principles Board was the forerunner to the Financial Accounting Standards Board. Under certain circumstances, APB 29 permits a company to account for exchanges at the fair value of the assets exchanged rather than at the historical cost of the assets surrendered. Lincoln believed that it met the criteria of APB 29 and that it should record the shares of GOIL it received at their fair value. The fair value of the shares was believed to be about $9.50 per share—the amount specified in the exchange agreement—but Lincoln knew that this value would have to be confirmed by an appraisal. This fair-value accounting would have resulted in a current gain to Lincoln of about $59 million and an additional deferred gain, which was contingent on the GUAC reorganization, of $25 million.

Arthur Young did not agree with the accounting Lincoln proposed. Arthur Young looked at GOIL's ownership interest in GUAC and GOSLP, before and after the exchange, and asserted that Lincoln's ownership percentage in these assets had not changed significantly as a result of the exchange. Because of Lincoln's continuing, indirect interest in the assets that Lincoln surrendered in the GOIL exchange, Arthur Young believed that an earnings process did not occur in the GOIL exchange; thus, the profit Lincoln was entitled to recognize on the exchange was, at best, "minimal."

This difference in opinions set off a series of rather heated debates between Lincoln and Arthur Young. There were several meetings in Phoenix that involved a number of Arthur Young's partners, including technical specialists from their national and regional offices, and ACC's and Lincoln's people. The discussions in these meetings centered around the concepts contained in APB 29.

The application of APB 29 requires the exercise of judgment. Two equally skilled and competent accountants can read the principles set forth in APB 29 and can come to different conclusions regarding a given transaction. It is almost never a clear-cut, black-and-white issue when transactions involve the exchange of nonmonetary assets.

Consequently, even though the discussions covered all the various aspects of the GOIL transaction, neither Arthur Young nor Lincoln altered its position as a result of these meetings. Lincoln continued to believe that a large gain should be recognized on the exchange transaction. The Arthur Young partners continued to believe that little or no gain should be recorded.

Believing that Arthur Young's assessment of the accounting for the transaction was wrong, Lincoln consulted with other accountants. Three other Big Eight firms were asked to look at the GOIL transaction and to provide their opinions about the proper accounting for the exchange. As a consequence of future events, none of the three firms ever provided Lincoln with a final conclusion. Lincoln also consulted with a distinguished accounting professor from the University of Chicago, who did reach a final conclusion, and his conclusion was in agreement with Lincoln's position.

In early October 1988, various Lincoln and ACC representatives, along with the professor and other consultants who supported Lincoln's position, met with Arthur Young's chairman and several other top partners. Again, the discussion centered around the proper application of APB 29. Consultants to Lincoln presented their conclusion that the assets that Lincoln received were fundamentally different from the assets that Lincoln surrendered in the exchange. The consultant's conclusion indicated that the legal rights inherent in the assets, as well as the economic characteristics of the assets, were completely different. Lincoln argued that because the assets surrendered in the exchange were inherently different from the assets received, the earnings process had been completed, and gain was recognizable. Arthur Young did not alter its opinion as a result of the arguments Lincoln presented in this meeting.

The relationship between ACC and Arthur Young had been strained for several months prior to the GOIL transaction. Some of the factors leading to the deteriorating relationship were the infrequency of communications between Arthur Young's partners and Charlie and Judy; the ongoing SEC investigation; the new FHLBB exam; and the disagreement over the GOIL transaction. On October 13, 1988, Arthur Young and ACC mutually agreed to sever their relationship as auditor and client. The Form 8-K filed with the SEC on October 28, 1988, reporting the termination of Arthur Young as auditors, cited two disagreements which had occurred between the firm and ACC: (1) the sale of the GUAC profit interest and the issue of the allocation of ACC's cost basis to the interest sold and (2) the accounting for the GOIL transaction. The 8-K also mentioned several reportable events, which were essentially questions that Arthur Young had raised but which had not been answered or resolved because of the termination.

Immediately following the severing of its relationship with Arthur Young, ACC started to seek new auditors. I believed that the firm of Coopers & Lybrand (C&L) was the most qualified, primarily because their clients in Phoenix included a major commercial bank and a large international operator of hotels. Thus, they had relevant experience within their local office with some of the lines of business in which ACC and Lincoln were engaged. We contacted C&L's local managing partner and asked the firm to do whatever investigation they needed to do in order to serve as ACC's auditors. They began to collect data and talked to Arthur Young as part of their decision-making process.

While C&L was doing its due-diligence procedures, ACC received, via an outside attorney who served ACC, an unsolicited proposal from Touche Ross offering to serve as ACC's auditors. Touche Ross had heard about Arthur Young's departure from this attorney. Touche asked him to open the door to ACC for them. At the attorney's request, I met with the local managing partner of Touche Ross for lunch. He asked me if ACC would consider appointing his firm as auditors. I told him that, because of the time constraints we were under, we had decided to ask only one firm to consider accepting appointment as ACC's auditors; therefore, we really couldn't consider his firm. He said that he understood my position and asked if I would be offended if he discussed the subject directly with Charlie. I told him that he was free to do so, but I thought he was wasting his time. That same night, he met with Charlie at the Phoenician. Charlie told him almost the same things that I had told him earlier in the day.

The next day Charlie started to receive telephone calls from major Touche Ross clients in Phoenix and other cities. All of these clients touted the virtues of the Touche firm and encouraged Charlie to engage them. Charlie then received a call from Touche's national managing partner in New York, one of several he would receive from Touche's top partner, asking Charlie to reconsider and give his firm a chance. Charlie was impressed with Touche's persistence and desire to serve as ACC's auditors.

Touche partners continued to pressure Charlie to appoint their firm as ACC's auditors. In the end, over my objections, Charlie offered Touche the engagement as ACC's and Lincoln's auditors. They accepted, contingent only on meeting with Arthur Young to confirm the circumstances surrounding Arthur Young's separation as ACC's auditors. After a brief meeting with Arthur Young, Touche delivered an engagement letter accepting appointment as ACC's auditors.

Between the time Touche indicated its conditional acceptance and the meeting with Arthur Young, Touche expressed a preliminary opinion on GOIL. Subject to auditing the facts as described to them by ACC's people, Touche believed that ACC's proposed accounting was appropriate and gain should be recognized. However, they wanted to obtain the SEC's opinion on the transaction. My own thoughts at the time were that, because of the SEC's two-year investigation of Lincoln and ACC, there wasn't a snowball's chance in hell that, when given the option of gain versus no gain, the SEC would approve any accounting that resulted in gain recognition. Nonetheless, a meeting was set up with the SEC to discuss the accounting for GOIL.

Prior to the meeting with the SEC, Touche prepared a description of the GOIL transaction, removing the names of the parties to the transaction and changing the actual numbers. The description was sent, on a no-names basis, to a senior technical staff person at the FASB for his opinion. This person essentially concurred with the treatment that ACC was proposing.

In November, several partners from Touche, along with Peter Fishbein and Andy Ligget, met with the staff of the SEC. Both Andy and Touche had prepared documents regarding the GOIL deal. These documents were given to the SEC staff and, in an oral presentation, the transaction was described in detail, as were all of the accounting considerations. Touche indicated that they and other accounting professionals concurred with ACC's proposed accounting for the GOIL transaction.

At the conclusion of the oral presentation, the lead Touche partner asked if the SEC staff had any comments or questions. The partner expected that there would be a lengthy discussion and that then the SEC would deliberate about the matter. Instead, the SEC's chief accountant curtly said, "No gain recognition." End of discussion. End of issue. Touche Ross folded up their tent on GOIL, and ACC recognized no gain.

There was also one other important topic discussed with Touche at the time they were appointed auditors. In their unsolicited proposal, they had substantially underestimated the scope of the ACC/Lincoln audits. They were informed that it would take between twenty-five thousand and thirty-six thousand man-hours to complete these audits. The audits had to be done and all reports issued by March 31, 1989. This translated into a requirement that they commit a minimum of twenty-five full-time people to the audits. And to finish on schedule, these people would probably have to work six-day weeks and, at least, ten-hour days.

Fourteen

FHLBB Launches Vicious Attack

By early September, the Lincoln portion of the FHLBB's examination was winding down. Tim Kruckeberg and I met with both Steve Rohrs and Chuck Gozdanovich. They were essentially finished with the fieldwork in their respective areas—operations and real estate/lending—and wanted to give us an indication of their findings.

Rohrs' comments were critical of certain minor aspects of the board of directors' minutes and those of various committees. He also believed that there should be outside directors on Lincoln's board. Further, he felt that Lincoln's employees were too highly compensated, primarily because compensation rates exceeded industry averages and averages for the Eleventh District. Finally, Rohrs said that certain procedures and manuals could be improved and that Lincoln needed an internal-audit function. Rohrs' comments did not disclose any issue that was of a serious nature. Lincoln could easily address all of Rohrs' concerns either by effecting changes or by demonstrating why changes were not practicable or possible.

When we met with Chuck Gozdanovich, Steve Scott and some of Chuck's assistants also sat in on the meeting. The basic topic was the classification of Lincoln's, and its subsidiaries', real-estate assets and loans. Using new classification rules which were adopted in January 1988, the examiners had classified certain assets as special mention, substandard, doubtful, or loss.

The new classification system provided that a portion of an asset could be unclassified or could be classified under a different category from the remainder of the asset. For example, a portion of an asset might be considered doubtful, and the remainder might be classified loss.

Unlike the old rules, which required an increase in an S&L's regulatory capital requirement for any asset classified as doubtful or substandard, the new rules were focused on an institution's GAAP capital. An institution was required to establish specific reserves only for those assets that were classified as loss. However, the examiners could, after reviewing the assets classified as substandard and doubtful, recommend that the institution increase its general reserves. The rules indicated that the establishment of any reserves, including those for loss assets, should be in accordance with GAAP. Further, general reserves were not deducted from regulatory capital.

One effect of the new rule was to remove mandatory or automatic classifications based on appraisals. The examiner was to consider other factors in assessing the risk of nonpayment and asset recovery. Appraisals were still considered by the examiners to be a useful tool, but they weren't necessarily the total or final determining factor in asset classifications.

These new rules were adopted as a result of the Competitive Equality Banking Act of 1987 (CEBA). The intent of CEBA was to eliminate some of the inconsistencies between banks and thrifts. Because the new system was relatively new, the examiners involved in Lincoln's 1988 examination were still not fully experienced with the new methods.

We started the meeting by asking Gozdanovich and Scott to explain their methodology and classification criteria. We needed to understand "what" they were doing before we could determine whether we agreed with the results they reported to us. Chuck indicated that the examiners had reviewed over 60 percent of Lincoln's real-estate assets and loans. The examiners viewed the classification system to be a series of gradations. If they believed that there were problems with an asset, or a borrower, but not, in their opinion, a demonstrable loss or threat of loss, they tended not to classify the asset or to classify it as either special mention or substandard.

We went over the lesser classifications first. They had classified some assets in both the special mention and substandard categories. We did not fully understand the specific criteria they used to distinguish which category an asset fell into, so we didn't contest the classifications, except to indicate that we felt most of the assets should not be classified or, at worst, should be placed in the lowest category. The discussion was not argumentative. Both sides were trying to understand the concepts involved, and Steve Scott and Chuck were not yet comfortable enough with the new classifications to articulate clearly all of their reasoning. So, it was a little confusing to all of us.

The only significant loan which was classified as doubtful was one to the Pontchartrain Hotel. The classification was based on operating losses that the hotel was experiencing and an uncertainty as to when the hotel would return to profitability. We argued that the value of the hotel appeared to be sufficient to prevent the risk of loss from becoming significant. We said that we probably wouldn't argue with a substandard classification but thought that, based on the criteria they had discussed, doubtful was too severe. Chuck and Scott said that they would think about it, but they were inclined to stay with the doubtful classification.

There were some assets for which they felt loss reserves were appropriate. For the most part, these were assets that Lincoln had already covered with either specific or general reserves. We quibbled about some of the assets, but the differences between their findings and Lincoln's own reserves were not great, so there were no real arguments.

After the main meeting broke up and Chuck's assistants returned to the main room with the other examiners, we talked more informally with Scott and Chuck. Chuck indicated that, before the examination started, some of the younger examiners had read about Lincoln in the press. They believed that Lincoln was a "problem shop," and part of the reason they had volunteered for the assignment was because they thought the exam could be a "big deal" with "high visibility within the FHLBB system." They saw it as an opportunity to elevate their careers by being in on a controversial examination.

Scott and Chuck, on the other hand, had taken Dochow at his word and had approached the Lincoln exam with open minds. They found that, while the assets were certainly not traditional, Lincoln was, by and large, managing them well. Chuck indicated that, because the exam had not uncovered any big problems, some of the younger examiners appeared disappointed. He indicated that some of them had tried to create issues where he felt none existed. Chuck also appeared concerned that, because of the actions of his assistants, someone might try to second-guess his decisions and conclusions.

When the examination team was selected, Dochow had picked those people from within the FHLBB system who he felt were the most qualified to be on this blue-ribbon team. Chuck Gozdanovich was deemed to be the most qualified to lead the loan and real-estate reviews. The people assigned to his team were, presumably, less qualified. Therefore, it is logical that Chuck's judgment on specific issues should prevail over those of his assistants.

The exam did not disclose the big losses that some of Chuck's assistants had anticipated it would; thus, the Lincoln exam evolved into just another routine examination. From congressional testimony, it appears that when Chuck's assistants returned to their own offices, they explained to their superiors that the reason the exam was routine was that Chuck hadn't listened to their concerns and had whitewashed the problems that really existed. It was because of the whitewash that their insightful findings hadn't been reflected in the exam results. Had Chuck listened to them, Lincoln would have been exposed as a troubled shop. These stories found their way to Dochow, via O'Connell and Smuzynski, and, apparently, there was some second-guessing of Chuck's work. This is somewhat reminiscent of the treatment that Kotrys had received in 1986.

Tim and I concluded that the reports from Steve Rohrs and Chuck were consistent with what Steve Scott had been telling us each week. No big issues, except for the tax-sharing agreement and ESOP, had surfaced in the exam. It looked like the exam could be completed without the controversy of the 1986 exam. We were premature with this conclusion.

About the same time that Chuck and Steve Rohrs were finishing their portions of the exam, the holding-company examination of ACC by the FHLBB was just beginning. This exam was to be conducted by Alex Barabolak, an examiner from Chicago who specialized in holding companies; a senior assistant, Jack Meek, also from Chicago; and two junior examiners.

Alex was a somber, bearded fellow who had a brusque, blunt manner about him. Meek was a sarcastic, pushy, impatient guy who eventually drove all of the ACC people with whom he dealt up a wall. The tone of the examination changed, and not for the better, shortly after this Chicago team arrived in Phoenix.

Simultaneously, from the West Coast, the CDSL launched an unguided missile, in the form of Richard Newsome, against Lincoln and ACC. The combination of the Barabolak team and Newsome turned into a nightmare for Steve Scott and Lincoln.

Newsome was a real piece of work. He was devoid of all social graces. His suit was wrinkled and stained, and it looked like he'd slept in it for weeks. His tie was at half-mast and covered with a variety of stains. His shirt displayed the remnants of several meals, and the armpits were ringed with the permanent stain of sweat. Lincoln came to learn that Newsome's thought processes, attitudes, and discipline were as disheveled and repugnant as his appearance.

As the Barabolak/Newsome combination moved into their respective examination areas, the nature of the requests for information changed. Barabolak and Jack Meek wanted detailed information on the stock the ESOP had purchased, including the price paid for each group of shares purchased; the identity of the seller; and the bid and asked prices, as well as the high and low price for the day each trade occurred. They asked for similar information on all of the treasury-stock purchases that ACC had made, going back to 1984. They also wanted the identity, and extent of ownership, of every person who had purchased an interest in the Pontchartrain Hotel Limited Partnership. And they wanted detailed compensation data for the period 1984 through 1988 for all of ACC's officers and directors. All of this was in addition to their requests for copies of ACC's annual reports, Form 10-K annual reports, Form 10-Q quarterly reports, annual proxy statements, and the minutes of board of directors' meetings for the years 1984 through 1988.

When Charlie learned about the nature and scope of their requests, he became livid. He asked Grogan and me to accompany him to the examiners' room. When we arrived, Charlie asked Barabolak, pretty bluntly and in no uncertain terms, what his authority was for seeking such information. Barabolak said that he was merely following the instructions he had received from Dochow to examine the holding company and that he needed the requested information to understand the background of certain transactions. Charlie responded, "No way." He told Barabolak that the MOU clearly stated that the examination was to focus on Lincoln's current status. There was no mention of ACC being examined. Furthermore, the periods covered by Barabolak's request were periods covered by the 1986 examination, and the MOU had settled all issues related to the earlier years. Charlie said that he was going to instruct ACC's personnel not to furnish the information and that he—Charlie—was going to talk to Dochow to find out what was going on.

The next day, Charlie heard from Dochow, who cited the statutory authority for the holding-company exam and asserted that it was part of the routine examination process. He said that ACC, per se, was not covered by the MOU, because the MOU dealt with Lincoln only. Charlie retorted that that wasn't the way he read the MOU. Charlie said he would cooperate, so that the exam could be completed, but he didn't like the direction in which the whole thing was headed.

When the 1988 examination first started, Dochow had told the CDSL that the FHLBB would not be conducting a holding-company examination. The decision now to exam ACC probably was the result of several factors. First, because of the MOU, O'Connell and Smuzynski, who were directing the examination, were foreclosed from going after transactions that had occurred in earlier years. By asserting that ACC was not covered by the MOU, they were able to reopen some of these issues by attacking them from the ACC side of the transaction, thereby sidestepping the MOU. Second, the Lincoln portion of the exam was almost complete, and the examiners had not uncovered anything damaging to ACC or Lincoln. If actions were to be taken against Lincoln, the bases for such actions had to be created via the ACC examination. Third, it was almost impossible to attack Charlie or his family through Lincoln. Charlie wasn't an officer of Lincoln, and none of the family members was on Lincoln's payroll. It was only through ACC that O'Connell and Smuzynski could gain access to any payments made to the Keating family. So, the ACC examination became a renewed effort to find data which could be used to harm Keating and ACC. The Lincoln examination had been a failure in that respect.

Newsome was probing into areas that both the federal and CDSL examiners had already covered. As we understood it, and as Newsome himself testified to Congress, he was supposed to be in Phoenix to address certain holding-company issues for the CDSL. But he started looking at the loan to the Hotel Pontchartrain Limited Partnership—a loan that both the state and federal examiners had already reviewed several times. The federal examiners, as Gozdanovich told us, classified the loan as doubtful.

The Pontchartrain consisted of a 420-room tower, with meeting facilities, food and beverage services; motor court with parking; additional parking in another building; and excess land which could be used for hotel expansion, an office building, or other commercial purposes. The hotel is located near the riverfront in downtown Detroit's financial district and is adjacent to Cobo Hall, Detroit's major convention center and exhibition facility. A Lincoln subsidiary acquired the hotel in December 1984 for approximately $19.5 million.

In 1985, the hotel was sold to a limited partnership, in which Lincoln's and ACC's officers and directors held interests aggregating about 35 percent, for $38.4 million. The price was dependent on Lincoln's subsidiary completing substantial renovations to the hotel, including refurbishing all of the guest rooms. The sale was ultimately financed by a loan to the limited partnership from a third-party bank, which was secured by notes from the limited partners, and a note from another Lincoln subsidiary in the amount of $30 million. Lincoln realized a total gain on the sale of approximately $9 million.

During the renovation, which was not completed until February 1986, the hotel incurred operating losses. As the renovation work was in progress, the city of Detroit started a major expansion of Cobo Hall, which, when completed, would make Cobo one of the largest convention centers in the country. Since Cobo is just next door to the hotel, the noise of the construction work, which was often continuous all day and night, disrupted the normal operations of the hotel. To make matters worse, construction also started on a large office building directly across the street from the hotel. Thus, the hotel was surrounded by twenty-four-hour, around-the-clock construction noise, traffic from trucks and heavy equipment, and blocked sidewalks.

The hotel's occupancy was adversely affected by these conditions, which continued into early 1989, and losses continued to be incurred. By December 1986, a Lincoln subsidiary had advanced slightly more than $10 million to the hotel, so that the hotel could meet its cash needs. In late December 1986, these advances were refinanced through the proceeds from a line of credit in the amount of $20 million from another Lincoln subsidiary.

In January 1986, the $30-million note to Lincoln's subsidiary, which financed the sale, was paid off from the proceeds of a $35-million first-mortgage loan to the partnership from a subsidiary of San Jacinto Savings Association of Houston, Texas. In early 1988, because of the constraints which the hotel was operating under and the losses it was experiencing, this loan was modified to reduce the cash required to meet interest on the debt. The expectations were that when Cobo Hall was finished, the hotel would return to profitable operations.

The only mention of the Pontchartrain Hotel in the 1986 Report of Examination concerned the issue of transactions with an affiliated person. The examination finding was as follows:

On December 31, 1984, CHGM (Crescent Hotel Group of Michigan) acquired the Pontchartrain Hotel, a 422-room hotel located in downtown Detroit, Michigan, for $19.5 million. On March 30, 1985, CHGM sold the hotel for $36.7 million to the Hotel Pontchartrain Limited Partnership (HPLP). Charles H. Keating III, a director of Lincoln Savings, and his immediate family owned 16 percent of HPLP. Mr. Keating is an affiliated person . . . as is his family. . . . Therefore, the transaction was subject to supervisory approval. . . . However, supervisory approval was not obtained by the association.

Mr. Sauter stated that the association made a mistake in calculating Mr. Keating's and his immediate family's interest in HPLP and that by the time they recognized the error, it was too late to apply for supervisory approval.

In an attempt to cure or address the problem cited by the examiners, C-III resigned from Lincoln's board. Lincoln viewed this as a closed issue, particularly in light of the MOU.

Newsome believed that the line-of-credit loan should have been classified as a loss in its entirety. He immediately started to claim that the FHLBB examiners were engaged in a whitewash and were ignoring the real problems at Lincoln. With this belief, he and Gene Stelzer changed the focus of Newsome's assignment, and Newsome launched a true witch hunt. He forgot about the holding company and began challenging other loans and initiated an investigation into political contributions that Lincoln and ACC had made.

Steve Scott appeared to be losing control of the examination to Barabolak, Newsome, and the people in Washington. We heard further reports about Washington questioning Chuck's work. Steve mentioned that accountants in Washington were beginning to look into various issues at the direction of O'Connell and Smuzynski. We were concerned about this because, up to this point, Steve had been able to control the examination;

as such, it hadn't turned into a repeat of 1986. Now, we were convinced that the relative peace which had prevailed during the exam would not continue.

The peace was broken and full-scale war broke out when Newsome fired his first shot at ACC and Lincoln. He had typed on his personal computer a letter addressed to Ray Fidel and Judy Wischer regarding the $20-million line of credit to the Hotel Pontchartrain Limited Partnership. This letter, dated September 28, said: "Due to the size of the loan, affiliated party involvement, and the appearance of the loan as a probable total loss to Lincoln, we are requesting that you review the attached tentative analysis of the loan by examiners and respond in writing to the issues raised in these comments." Lincoln was asked to respond within seven days to Newsome, with copies to Stelzer and Scott.

The letter and attached analysis were totally Newsome's doing. They had not been reviewed or approved by anyone else within the CDSL. In fact, both Scott's first name and Stelzer's last name were misspelled in the letter. The analysis also contained numerous typographical errors and misspellings. The analysis was strongly worded, and some of the key excerpts from it are as follows:

> . . . [T]he net realizable value analysis of the association is based on erroneous and questionable assumptions utilizing favorable factors but ignoring negative factors. . . .
>
> The association is basing its analysis on the questionable assumption that the Hotel will be fully available to repay this debt. The unsecured position of the association will not provide any protection to the association in case of any new voluntary or involuntary liens on the Hotel, or foreclosure by the 1st lienholder. Unless a sale can be quickly consummated which will shift the burden of carrying costs to a third party, further borrowings from some source appear inevitable which will be adverse to the prospects of repayment of the subject unsecured note.
>
> Based on the foregoing major points the net realizable value of the unsecured $20 million line of credit appears to be approximately 0 at this time. . . .

On October 5, Judy and Ray responded to Newsome. The cover letter to their response stated: "The Association and the Holding Company do not believe that the unsecured $20 million loan is a potential loss to the Association for the reasons and facts stated [in an attachment]. To alleviate your concern, the Holding Company is willing to purchase the note for $5 million in cash and the balance payable in a five year note. Please advise whether the State will consider such an application for sale." The attachment then responded to the valuation and operating concerns that Newsome raised in his letter.

On October 8, Newsome fired another salvo at Fidel and Wischer. The subject was still the $20-million line of credit to the Hotel Pontchartrain Limited Partnership. The key excerpts from this letter are:

A partnership involving an association subsidiary as general partner and a number of affiliated parties including officers and directors as limited partners acquired the Hotel from the association in 1985. This was in violation of federal affiliated party regulations brought to the attention of management during the March 1986 examination. Subsequently, anticipated project earnings did not materialize and to cover large operating losses the association booked the subject unsecured loan in violation of additional federal regulations. In essence the limited partners apparently usurped corporate opportunity for upside profit potential in the transaction, while transferring the risk of operating expenses through the general partner to the association.

The association thus assumed the majority of the risk exposure in a then nonperforming project while the limited partners benefited directly and indirectly from loan proceeds which serviced project debt and covered operating losses. The five year term of the unsecured note in favor of the borrower (that at the time had a deficit net worth and no plausible ability to repay the loan) with 10 percent interest and principal due at maturity is concessionary. . . .

When booked the subject loan was clearly dependent for repayment on speculative assumptions requiring major appreciation in the project and abatement of operating losses for repayment. The partnership maintained control over upside profit potential and tax benefits while the association bore the increasing risk of an overencumbered, extremely speculative Hotel venture in Detroit with extreme risks and concessionary financing in relation to risk, rate, and terms.

Based on the scenario laid out in the excerpts shown above, Newsome then went on to accuse the association and its officers and directors of:

1. Willful violation of FSLIC insurance regulations.
2. Breach of fiduciary duty by affiliated parties, association officers, and directors who countenanced, participated in, and/or benefited from the association's loan proceeds.
3. Willful diversion of association assets, benefiting affiliated parties

and in violation of regulations, into a high-risk transaction.
4. Material omission in related party disclosures in Form 10-Ks and in
    an offering circular filed with the FHLB on May 27, 1988.

He then requested that the association respond to his charges within
seven days. Again, none of this had been reviewed or discussed with his
superiors at the CDSL before it was delivered to Fidel and Wischer. He did
send a copy to Gene Stelzer, who was his peer, not his superior in the CDSL
structure.

On October 13, Ray and Judy responded. The principal comments in
their response were:

It is important that you understand that the Pontchartrain Hotel was purchased
by Crescent Hotels [a Lincoln subsidiary] for syndication. . . . The partnership raised $10 million cash from limited partners. The partnership agreement
and syndication documents did not provide for the general partner to have
future capital contributions from the limited partners beyond the initial $10
million capital contribution. The syndication terms were identical to syndica-
tions being sold by major Wall Street brokerage firms. . . .

. . . HPLP is not an "affiliated person" of Lincoln and the loan is not
prohibited. . . .

The partners of the limited partnership did not and have not benefited from
this purchase. The partners paid $10 million cash to CH and subordinated all
of their claims and rights to those of the managing partner and the CH
management agreement. The partners have not received tax benefits *as
contemplated in the offering circular* due to the retroactive change in the tax
law for alternative minimum tax and passive loss limitations. In addition,
should the partners lose their $10 million capital investment, they will incur
a tax gain based on the amount of the hotel's operating losses. . . .

You have assumed that the cash flow loan is uncollectible and that the
improvement in the second and third quarter operating results will not
continue. We believe that those trends will continue. Please see Robert
Jenkins', MAI, memo addressing the future operations. Your tone and
accusations are unwarranted. The purchase and syndication of the Pontchartrain
occurred in December 1984 and early 1985, respectively. The State and
FHLB examiners have conducted two audits since the acquisition. It is only
with hindsight and disregard of the $9.5 million profit recognition, that you
raise the issue that an affiliate of the Association should not fund the cash flow
loan. The Association's service corporation is the *general partner* and it has
responsibilities as a general partner. Had the Association's service corpora-

tion kept the hotel and operated it, the service corporation would have $10 million more at risk than it currently does.

The letter refuted Newsome's claims that the disclosures in the Form 10-Ks and the offering circular were not complete. The letter also asked, again, whether ACC could purchase the loan. The state had not responded to the request because neither Newsome nor Stelzer passed the request on to the people who could make such a decision.

There were two more letters on this subject. One was from Newsome to Bob Kielty on October 18, which basically reiterated his contentions that the disclosures relative to the Pontchartrain contained in ACC's and Lincoln's public filings were incomplete. This letter was answered by Lynn Fisher, of Kaye Scholer, on November 4, 1988. Some of the more pertinent portions of Lynn's response letter were:

As a securities lawyer, I was both concerned and perplexed by your letter. I was perplexed because your letter deals exclusively with related party disclosures in AMCC federal securities law filings—an issue which I understand to be far removed from the authority of your department, and totally irrelevant to any question concerning the safety and soundness of Lincoln Savings. I was concerned because you assert serious allegations with respect to matters which are outside of the California Department of Savings and Loan's (the "Department") jurisdiction and area of expertise. Those allegations—that certain items constitute material omissions—would, at best, be considered unwarranted by one knowledgeable in the securities laws.

Then, in eight pages of detail, Lynn discussed why the disclosures in ACC's proxy statements, Form-10Ks, and prospectuses contained all of the information regarding the Pontchartrain Hotel and related loans, guarantees, and lines of credit which were material and which were required in the context of the applicable document. She concluded by saying:

In short, we are both confused and troubled by your October 18, 1988, letter. AMCC has diligently disclosed *all material* information required for each particular SEC filing under the particular SEC rules, regulations and case law relevant to such filing. We do not understand how these SEC filings create an issue under California savings and loan law and regulations. If the issue is the safety and soundness of Lincoln—the only apparently relevant issue—none of these SEC disclosure documents are pertinent. . . .

The examination was rapidly turning into an exchange of increasingly hostile letters between Lincoln and Newsome and Lincoln and Dochow. In response to Dochow's request for information regarding the tax-sharing agreement, Judy wrote to him on September 27. Judy's letter provided a chronology of the events surrounding the agreement. The relevant correspondence between Lincoln and Sidney Mar was attached to Judy's letter. Judy's letter concluded by stating, essentially, that ACC and Lincoln had complied with an approved agreement and that Mar had been fully aware of how the agreement would work when he granted his approval.

Dochow answered Judy's letter with one of his own, dated October 14, 1988. The pertinent sections of this letter are as follows:

> Ms. Wischer's response on behalf of ACC supporting the tax sharing agreement is not considered persuasive. Our concern is not a rehashing of a settled issue but a germane issue that directly relates to the safety and soundness of the ongoing operations of Lincoln Savings. . . .
>
> In reviewing the file on this issue, we have concerns about possible factual misrepresentations. In particular, we note that the April 2, 1986, correspondence from Supervisory Agent Sidney Mar was based on representations from the association's corporate counsel Mark Sauter that the FHLBank of San Francisco's concerns had been addressed by deleting "the provisions cited as being objectionable and adds the language requested." This comment is not supported by the review of Mr. Mar's March 7, 1986, correspondence which clearly states that deferred taxes were not to be paid to ACC. Mr. Sauter's comment that all issues had been corrected per the FHLBank's instructions could be construed as misrepresenting the changes that were actually made in the agreement in response to Mr. Mar's March 7, 1986, letter.
>
> Given the above facts, I have no choice but to formally revoke the April 2, 1986, supervisory approval given the tax sharing agreement. In addition, since we have not received the Board's commitment to abide by the supervisory directive of September 6, we need formal assurance that no further tax payments will be paid to ACC without the prior written consent of this office. Therefore, we ask the board to formally execute the attached consent order that prohibits any future payments, and requires details of its tax liabilities from 1985 to the present.
>
> In addition to officially revoking the April 2, 1986, approval and requiring formal assurance that no further payments will be made, I am also considering requiring ACC to refund all payments of deferred taxes, with interest, to Lincoln Savings. . . .

In the second paragraph cited above, Dochow refers to "possible factual misrepresentations" and states that Sauter's comments "could be construed as misrepresenting." He conveniently fails to mention the telephone calls involving Mar, Sonja Rodriguez, and Lincoln which had occurred between the March 7 letter and the approval of the final tax-sharing agreement. He also ignores the basic fact that Mar had had the actual agreement, which was attached to Sauter's letter, before he issued the approval letter. Sauter and Scott Siebels have said that the comment regarding Mar's concerns being addressed referred to comments that Mar made in the telephone calls when he moderated the comments made in his earlier letter. Dochow chose only to focus on Mar's two letters and Sauter's cover letter. By doing so, he could speculate that Mar might have been misled. Such a conclusion is not plausible. One only has to consider that Mar had had the agreement and could have, and should have, read it before he approved it to make Dochow's speculations unbelievable and inappropriate under the circumstances.

Nonetheless, in the very next paragraph, Dochow converts his speculations into "the above facts" that give him "no choice but to formally revoke the April 2, 1986, supervisory approval given the tax sharing agreement." This is a tactic Lincoln had become all too familiar with in dealing with the regulators. They ignored facts which detracted from the actions they wanted to take. They filled in missing gaps in their logic with speculation. They converted speculation into fact. Using their newly created facts, they issued directives to Lincoln. Directives resting on a foundation of thin air.

In this instance, the directive took the form of a consent cease-and-desist order. Lincoln had steadfastly refused to sign any consent orders throughout its long battle with the Eleventh District. Dochow knew Lincoln's position toward signing such documents. So, he used another common FHLBB tactic. He threatened that he might order ACC to repay the monies representing the deferred taxes that Lincoln had sent up to ACC, with interest, if he wasn't satisfied with ACC's and Lincoln's responses to his demands. It was simple extortion.

In mid-October, Newsome and Stelzer started raising questions about how the CDSL could get the FHLBB, among others, to take stronger actions against ACC. As usual, their observations and ideas were not favorable to Lincoln. Apparently, they discussed their observations with O'Connell. It was becoming obvious that Newsome had formed an alliance, unknown to his superiors, with O'Connell, who supported and may have encouraged Newsome's initiatives against ACC.

In this connection, Newsome started to explore new areas of inquiry. One was a subject which Jack Meek, the FHLBB examiner, had also been delving into. The issue was treasury-stock purchases by ACC and whether ACC had complied with the SEC's rules governing such transactions.

Once again, the examiners, both state and federal, had strayed far afield from their areas of expertise and their regulatory mandate. They were delving into issues which, under federal securities laws, are highly technical. The examiners were not equipped to understand the transactions or the related reporting and disclosure requirements. The regulators' mandate and authority were limited to transactions between Lincoln and ACC and did not extend to any of ACC's transactions not directly related to Lincoln. The regulations did not give them carte-blanche authority to peruse ACC's records to find things which titillated their personal interest and curiosity. Their access to ACC's records was restricted to a specific, limited purpose. The limitations were in place to guard against precisely the things that were happening here—examiners reviewing areas outside their technical training, span of knowledge, and experience.

The consequences of untrained people jumping to conclusions on subjects about which they are uninformed can be disastrous to a company—and, in this case, it became disastrous. Unable to find anything to cripple ACC or Lincoln in Lincoln's records, they were searching in ACC's records for ammunition they could use against these companies. In their zeal, they stepped way out of their regulatory boundaries. And these were not the only instances, there were more to come.

By the middle of October, the focus of Alex Barabolak's examination seemed to be on the following subjects: treasury- and ESOP-stock purchases from the Keating family and other insiders; possible stock-market price manipulation; possible inappropriate insider trading; remunerations paid to the Keating family; the financial condition and cash flows of ACC; the tax-sharing agreement; debt issuances; Hotel Pontchartrain purchase, sale, and loans; transactions with Southmark and its subsidiaries, including San Jacinto Savings; and alleged misrepresentations in SEC-required public disclosures and filings. Of all the issues which Barabolak was addressing, the only ones which arguably fell within the scope of the FHLBB's regulatory authority were the tax-sharing agreement, the collectibility of loans to the Pontchartrain and Southmark, and perhaps the current financial condition of ACC. All of the other areas were not consistent with the FHLBB's regulatory mandate. The focus of the examination made it crystal clear that Barabolak and Newsome were feeding off of each other. The only thing that was difficult to discern was which one was the leader and which was the follower in this tandem effort.

Newsome launched another one of his missiles on October 21. He sent a memorandum dealing with a $30-million subordinated line of credit which been advanced to R.A. Homes, Inc. The loan was current at the time.

R.A. Homes (RA) was a home builder who had operations in Tucson, Phoenix, and Las Vegas. The principals in the company were Harold Cole, Harold Ober, and Ron Ober, Harold's son. Cole ran the operations in Tucson. Ron Ober was in Phoenix. Harold Ober handled Las Vegas. In June 1987, Lincoln lent RA $30 million in the form of an unsecured, subordinated loan with a stated interest rate of 13 percent, and with principal due in various amounts starting in 1992. The proceeds of the loan were used to pay off other loans from Lincoln, to buy property in Las Vegas, Phoenix, and Tucson, and to refinance other debts.

By 1988, the company, in the opinion of some people within Lincoln, had lost its focus. The Tucson market was difficult, and RA didn't seem to be taking aggressive steps to compete in a soft market. In Phoenix, Ron Ober, who was a former aide to Senator DeConcini, became involved in trying to assemble a water ranch. Like Lincoln, Ober thought that the ground-water laws in Arizona created a great opportunity for anyone who had a supply of exportable water. Rather than concentrating on home building, Ron Ober was lobbying the state legislature, negotiating options on land to be assembled into a water ranch, and commissioning hydrology studies. That left Las Vegas, where the company was doing very well. In fact, most of RA's revenues and cash flow were being generated by its Las Vegas operations.

On October 21, 1988, Newsome wrote another of his characteristically bombastic memos regarding the RA loan. The pertinent portions of this memo were:

Lack of company cash flow from operations combined with the highly leveraged position of the company and the subordinated and unsecured position of the association's note in relation to other creditors, who are largely secured by liens on the borrower's real estate holdings, has placed the subject $30 million loan in serious jeopardy. Recovery of the loan appears dependent on assumptions of future profitability that appear speculative and unsubstantiated in relation to past results, particularly given the market conditions in the Phoenix and Tucson areas where the company seemingly must be successful.

The fundamental weaknesses of the association's deeply subordinated position and the uncertainties surrounding repayment of the subject unsecured note are very clear and based on the information presented in this summary there is a need for a large loss reserve to offset the negligible realizable value of the subject in relation to book value.

Newsome arrived at his conclusions in spite of the facts that the loan was current and the FHLBB examiners had examined the same data that he had and had concluded that the loan was not even doubtful. Moreover, the company was solvent, and there was strong evidence that the property which RA held was worth more than the recorded, historical-cost, book values. RA had also been profitable in each of its last three fiscal years.

While Newsome and Barabolak were conducting their attacks, another group of people, whom Steve Scott couldn't control either, were hard at work. These were the FHLBB's accountants, primarily Carol Larson. They were asking questions about Lincoln's policy for the capitalization of interest on real-estate projects, the sale of the equity kicker on the Wolfswinkle loan, and the sale of the Crescent and Phoenician hotels.

From what we could ascertain, Larson was satisfied that Lincoln's policies and practices in accounting for capitalized interest were in accordance with the applicable professional literature. We did hear that she thought Lincoln's policies were aggressive, but apparently she did not conclude that Lincoln was doing anything wrong. We also heard that because she felt that the practices were aggressive, someone might attempt to assert that the policies were somehow either unsafe or unsound.

The two most frightening words that a savings and loan executive can hear are unsafe and unsound. Using these words, the FHLBB's mid-level managers write new regulations on the spot. If they like an association, they can be lenient, even waive compliance with regulations. But, if an association gets on their bad side, they can impose any requirement their fertile imaginations can conjure up, simply by invoking the words safety and soundness.

We also understood that the FHLBB's accountants had concluded that Lincoln's accounting for the Wolfswinkle equity kicker complied with the professional literature. Although, here again, a side issue appeared to be looming. The examiners expressed some concern that prior approval hadn't been obtained for the transaction, leaving open the possibility that someone might assert that it was a prohibited transaction. This concerned us because we had learned that if the FHLBB couldn't skin a cat one way, they would invent another way to get the job done.

The issues regarding the hotels also appeared to be resolved. The expressed concerns of the FHLBB seemed to focus on whether the cost to complete the Phoenician could be determined at the time of the sale. We knew that the FHLBB had never understood the cost estimates on the Phoenician, so we were worried that they might do something out of ignorance. But since, by this time, the Phoenician was completed, and all the costs were known, the issued appeared to be moot.

Even though these accounting issues did not appear to be a problem, Lincoln was nevertheless concerned about the FHLBB's inquiries into them. Lincoln had learned from the 1986 examination that the regulators liked to use accounting matters in their attack because the issues were always judgmental and subjective. Thus, the FHLBB could base its actions on dubious interpretations of the accounting literature. These were therefore difficult issues to defend against.

On November 7, a status meeting on the examination was held. The FHLBB was represented by Scott, Barabolak, and Smuzynski. Since Dochow had promised Charlie earlier in 1988 that O'Connell wouldn't have anything to do with Lincoln, O'Connell was always behind the scenes and never attended any of the formal meetings with Lincoln. The CDSL sent several representatives. And about fifteen people represented ACC and Lincoln, including all of Lincoln's board members except Fidel.

With all these people, the board room was filled to capacity. As is customary in these formal meetings, the regulators aligned themselves on one side of the table, and ACC and Lincoln lined up on the opposing side. Many of Lincoln's folks had to bring in extra chairs, and they were seated around the perimeter of the room. Charlie, Judy, and Kielty sat directly across from Scott, Smuzynski, and Barabolak. The meeting started without any tension in the air—that didn't last long.

We were not expecting this meeting to be confrontational. At this point, the only issues that we believed were potential problems were the tax-sharing agreement and, possibly, the ESOP. Steve Scott had not advised us, at any time, that any other issues existed.

Smuzynski chaired the meeting for the FHLBB and started off by stating that he was the person in Washington who acted as Lincoln's supervisory agent.

Charlie immediately jumped on this declaration and said something to the effect, "I thought Dochow was our supervisory agent. Why isn't he here at this meeting? Steve Scott's supposed to be in charge here in Phoenix, and Dochow's supposed to be in charge in Washington. That's what we agreed to when the exam started. I don't understand this business about you being our supervisory agent. This is the first time anyone here has even met you."

Smuzynski responded by saying that Dochow had delegated the supervisory-agent authority to him when the examination first started. He said that he had kept Dochow apprised of the examination's progress. He then went on to say that the examination of Lincoln consisted of three primary areas—operations, securities and real estate, including lending—and the fieldwork in each of these areas was completed. He said that the examiners would cover everything in this meeting, except for asset classifications, which would be handled later in an exit conference. He then stated that the examination of ACC was separate from the Lincoln examination and suggested that, because it was the more controversial, the ACC exam would be discussed first.

Barabolak started the discussion by saying that the holding-company examination findings related to the relationship between Lincoln and ACC. He repeated that, while the findings tended to overlap, the examination of ACC was a separate exam from Lincoln's.

At this point Charlie asked, "Is Steve Scott the examiner-in-charge of the holding-company exam, too?"

"No," Scott replied.

"I thought you were," Charlie said to Scott. "Dochow said that you were in charge of everything in Phoenix. You're the guy we're to talk to, and you're supposed to tell us what all the issues are as they come up. That was the deal, and that's what the MOU says is supposed to happen. Now you tell me that Dochow is not in charge in Washington and you're not in charge here. No wonder everything is a mess. You guys aren't doing what we agreed to."

Unabashed, Barabolak started through his list of concerns. His first comments were, in essence, that the treasury-stock program, including purchases made by the ESOP, was very troublesome. He said that there was no program to make sure that the purchases were at arm's length; there was no evidence that the lowest price was obtained; the cash used to make the treasury-stock purchases had, from a cash-flow standpoint, weakened the company; and the examiners questioned whether the treasury-stock purchases were being used to support and keep up the market price of ACC's stock. In short, he implied that the treasury-stock and ESOP-stock purchases smacked of market manipulation and unfairly benefited insiders.

These initial comments showed that Barabolak hadn't read the material ACC had given him regarding these programs or, if he had read it, that he didn't understand it. Barabolak wasn't a securities lawyer, and we knew that, based on the questions he and Meek had asked during the exam, he was completely unfamiliar with the SEC's rules governing such transactions. When he originally raised these questions, we were worried that he was getting into an area which was beyond the limits of his experience, knowledge, and training. His opening comments confirmed that our concerns were valid.

Here, he was making serious allegations—allegations that were insupportable. ACC had, in fact, complied with the SEC's rules and guidelines to assure that the kinds of things that Barabolak was alleging did not occur. The purchases of stock by the treasury and ESOP were closely reviewed by ACC's attorneys. All of the forms that the SEC required with respect to such purchases had been filed. ACC had never had even an inquiry from the SEC regarding the transactions. Now, a FHLBB examiner, who had ventured into an area well outside the scope of his regulatory authority, was lodging serious and totally unfounded charges against ACC.

Barabolak then went on to say that the examiners were concerned about the cash flow of ACC. He said that their concern was centered on the financial strength of ACC as Lincoln's parent. Without dividends or tax-sharing payments from Lincoln, ACC's cash needs had to be handled by increasing debt, and ACC was already highly leveraged. He stated that high salaries and other expenses of ACC, such as those related to corporate aircraft, depleted the strength of the holding company by further draining its cash. He continued with this type of a general discussion of ACC's cash position for several minutes.

He then talked about several transactions with foreign entities. Just after the sale of the hotels to the KIO, ACC and Lincoln had entered into a consulting arrangement with Credit Suisse, the Swiss financial institution that had introduced the KIO to Lincoln. The arrangement called for Credit Suisse to assist ACC and Lincoln in finding other foreign investors who might have an interest in the real estate which the companies owned. ACC and Lincoln had paid Credit Suisse a substantial retainer under this consulting arrangement. Barabolak said his concern was that the examiners could find "no visible results" from the arrangement.

Barabolak also commented on ACC's investment practices, particularly trading in stock-index futures and currencies. These practices didn't appear to the examiners to be prudent. Barabolak indicated that losses in the futures trading represented additional outlays of cash which, in his opinion, weakened ACC.

ACC had been engaging in trading in foreign currencies and other commodities for over a year. This activity was conducted primarily by Shelly Weiner and Charlie. ACC maintained a "war room," which was located adjacent to the board room where this meeting with the examiners took place, in which the trading activities were conducted. The war room was equipped with electronic monitors and quotron machines that were used to track price movements in various markets. And on one wall, a series of clocks displayed the time in various cities around the world where active trading markets were located.

ACC had a contract with an organization based in Dusseldorf, Germany, that had designed and operated elaborate computer-based models to track various markets and predict future market trends. This organization provided advice to Weiner on whether and when to buy or sell a given currency or futures contract. Weiner and Charlie considered these recommendations and decided whether or not to act on them. Charlie and Weiner were also in constant communication with commodity specialists in a number of the major brokerage companies.

Prior to going live with these kinds of transactions, Weiner conducted several months of simulated transactions to test whether the information received from Dusseldorf, combined with the data received from the various market specialists, was effective. The simulations were successful, and, in early 1988, ACC began trading in increasing volumes. For the first quarter of 1988, ACC realized substantial gains from this activity.

In May 1988, the volume of transactions increased, and, at any given time, ACC had hundreds of long and short contracts outstanding, often in several different currencies or commodities.

In mid-May, ACC experienced a series of very favorable trading days as the market moved strongly in the direction which ACC had predicted it would. This came at a time when there were hundreds of open contracts, and ACC's daily gains were substantial. As the trend continued, ACC's cumulative unrealized gain reached over $25 million. Charlie and Weiner debated whether to close out the contracts, and realize the gain, or to stay in the market for another day or so in order to capture even greater gains. They decided to stay in the market.

Almost immediately, the market turned abruptly against ACC. In the next week, unable to extricate themselves from a market that was dropping rapidly, Weiner and Charlie watched as the unrealized gains were erased and losses were incurred. When they finally got out of the market, the cumulative loss was about $25 million—a total turnaround of almost $50 million.

ACC continued to take positions in the markets, often sizeable ones, but it never hit the point where a cumulative gain was produced by the activity. In fact, losses continued, on a more modest scale, during the remainder of the year. These were the losses Barabolak was criticizing.

Finally, Barabolak questioned a transaction that had occurred between ACC and Lincoln as being one that denied Lincoln "its corporate opportunity" to realize maximum profits. In conjunction with the purchase of some bonds, Lincoln had acquired shares in Memorex. These shares were one of the equity holdings that San Francisco had criticized. ACC purchased the shares from Lincoln in a transaction which yielded Lincoln a significant gain. Later, ACC sold the shares at an additional gain. Applying hindsight, Barabolak questioned whether Lincoln had been treated fairly, since it didn't get to recognize 100 percent of the total gain ultimately realized. He said that he felt that the gain which ACC realized was a de facto dividend. Presumably, if ACC had realized a loss as a result of holding the shares, the examiners would not have objected to the transaction.

Charlie, who by now had loosened his tie and shirt cuffs, signs he was heating up, immediately brought up the MOU again. He said that the areas which Barabolak was talking about weren't within the scope of the examination contemplated by the MOU. Moreover, he was still upset that Steve Scott wasn't in charge of the holding-company exam. The MOU was, in Charlie's mind, very clear, as were his recollections of his discussions with Dochow. There was supposed be one person in charge. That person was Steve Scott.

Charlie also said that the MOU required the examiners to tell Lincoln about any problems at the time they arose. He said, "You're springing this on us all at once. You were supposed to tell us about this earlier, so we could develop the facts to show you that you are wrong in the things you're criticizing us for."

He went on to say that the examiners needed to know the history of Lincoln in order to understand the operations of ACC. He said that ACC had contributed most of its assets to Lincoln. The decision to put all real-estate activities in Lincoln stripped ACC of its operating assets. ACC then became dependent on Lincoln. After the first year of operations, people had encouraged ACC to take dividends out of Lincoln, but ACC hadn't. Since then, the FHLBB hadn't permitted dividends, even though Lincoln's earnings and net worth would have supported such dividends.

Charlie then said that the direct pipeline from the FHLBB to the press made it difficult to access traditional sources of financing. He said that the adverse publicity from the illegal leaks had hurt ACC's banking relationships and soured investment bankers on ACC. But, in spite of that, ACC had met its cash needs, and it had never defaulted on any of its obligations.

He closed by fixing Barabolak with a piercing glare and asking, "Why didn't you tell us these problems before now?"

Barabolak, squirming a bit, answered, "We gave every bit of this to Mr. Kruckeberg and Mr. Atchison."

That was untrue. I had had little contact with either Barabolak or Meek, and that contact had been limited to seeing whether their information requests were being filled. I had never talked to them about their findings or concerns. Tim reported similar contacts and said that they had never expressed any conclusions to him. Barabolak took the position that because we knew what information they were asking for, we therefore had been informed of their concerns. That didn't sit well. Moreover, like Charlie, we thought Steve Scott was in charge and that he'd be the person who would communicate any problems to us.

Charlie just looked at Barabolak with disgust and said, "That's not the way it's supposed to be and you guys know it."

Smuzynski, trying to regain control, interjected to add support to Barabolak's comments. He said that they were very concerned, now that ACC wouldn't be getting tax payments from Lincoln, that ACC was dependent on subordinated debt for its cash. They were concerned that ACC wouldn't be able to service its current debt and that it could be difficult to sell additional debt in the future.

"Hey, we've been a hostage to the exam process for three years," Charlie said. "How do think we can cope with this?"

Barabolak reentered the fray by commenting that the only operations in ACC were investment activities and that those were producing losses. The losses drained cash and were a strain on ACC. This increased ACC's dependence on debt, which Barabolak saw as the only other source of cash available to ACC.

Barabolak's comments regarding investment results hit an exposed nerve, as the trading losses were a particularly strong disappointment to

Charlie, and Charlie was seething. Kielty saw this and stepped into the discussion. He said that, as a holding company, ACC expected it would receive dividends from Lincoln. Lincoln had refrained from paying dividends pending discussions with San Francisco on the issue, but the discussions had never occurred. Kielty also cited the effects of detrimental publicity. He said that Lincoln and ACC had just settled a libel suit with a magazine that had the FHLBB's three-hundred-page report on Lincoln. Lincoln only got to see the report because it was produced in the discovery related to the suit.

Charlie said that the FHLBB had created the situation that ACC and Lincoln were in, and now they were continuing their attempts to hurt the companies. He said, "Just give us the freedom to operate."

Barabolak said that they were just about done with their "minimum scope" examination. They were still waiting for information. When they received the requested data, they would be done and would leave.

Charlie returned to Barabolak's earlier comments. He said that ACC had removed people from Lincoln's payroll and had added them to ACC's because of prior criticism. Now, the examiners were criticizing ACC.

Barabolak dodged Charlie's comment by attacking other areas. He said that ACC was "pyramiding" debt. ACC was selling new debt to pay off existing obligations, and the debt load was getting heavier and heavier as the process continued. Barabolak reiterated that the debt problem was exacerbated by ACC's poor operating performance, particularly the futures trading. And he again said that the futures trading was a losing proposition.

"That's not correct," Charlie replied. He said that the futures activities had been successful, but they were not at the present. He said that things would turn around and that the investment activities would again be profitable.

Kielty asked Barabolak, "How can a holding company survive when 85 percent of its assets are in an S&L and the S&L can't pay dividends?"

"That's not my area," Barabolak responded. "To make the decision on dividends involves assessing the overall viability of the S&L. My job is to determine whether the holding company is a source of strength to the institution. It's not."

Kielty said that wasn't true. The holding company had absorbed expenses of Lincoln and taken on salaries Lincoln had previously paid. In turn, it hadn't received dividends.

By this point, the frustration levels in Charlie, Kielty, and others were beginning to peak. The FHLBB had encouraged people to acquire S&Ls in 1983 and, following that lead, ACC had done so. ACC had then put its assets into Lincoln, expecting it would receive dividends if Lincoln earned profits. The FHLBB had then changed all the capital rules and, through the examination process, tried to reduce Lincoln's actual capital by proposing various adjustments. The combination of the rule changes and exam-spawned actions made it impossible for Lincoln to pay dividends. ACC was caught in a squeeze that Charlie believed the FHLBB had intentionally engineered. Now, he was being criticized by the very same people who had created the situation. It was only a matter of time before he would boil over.

Charlie, in frustration, said, "People have shorted ACC's stock in cahoots with the FHLBB."

Smuzynski immediately said, "Give us the names of the FHLBB personnel involved in this activity."

"That's not what I said," Charlie replied.

Judy then commented that there was a very clear history of short sales occurring at the same time as the release of information from the FHLBB.

Barabolak, in an attempt to deflect the heat off the FHLBB, changed the subject by saying that the examiners thought that when ACC made treasury- and ESOP-stock purchases, it always paid the highest price. He added that this was detrimental to the company and benefited insiders. He said that the examiners believed that the purchases were intended to keep the price of ACC's stock up.

Charlie curtly said, "Not true."

"We're limited by SEC regulations to when we can buy," Judy added. "If you plot out the prices, we won't be at the high end of the trend." She also recited all of the SEC rules which ACC had complied with in connection with the transactions.

"But you don't have any policies regarding treasury-stock purchases at the holding company," Barabolak said.

Charlie replied that you don't need policies at the holding-company level to the same extent that you do in the S&L because the holding company is not regulated.

Barabolak got in one closing shot on this subject by saying, "Right. But you do need to follow good, general practices."

Smuzynski seemed to be enjoying the by-play between Barabolak and ACC's and Lincoln's people. As Charlie said earlier, this was the first time we had met Smuzynski. He was a slightly built, bespectacled guy with a small, dark mustache. He exhibited a slight smirk and subdued arrogance, leaving the impression that he liked to see people like Charlie squirm. He seemed to be the kind of guy who would not attack you head on but wouldn't hesitate to slip a knife in your back. And he looked like he relished the sense of power that his position afforded him.

The conversation turned to the tax-sharing payments. The examiners asserted that ACC owed Lincoln as much as $93 million for the taxes Lincoln had paid to ACC. They said they were inclined to order ACC to refund the tax-sharing payments to Lincoln. They expressed concern that, because of ACC's cash position, ACC wouldn't be able to return the tax-sharing monies to Lincoln.

Judy responded that ACC didn't have a current obligation to repay Lincoln. Because of the consolidated return, Lincoln benefited from ACC's loss carryovers. She said, "So don't say that we'll have to pay it and can't." She added, "If Dochow wants to stop the tax-sharing agreement, that's okay. But it isn't fair to either ACC or Lincoln to stop it in midstream."

Charlie added that the examiners' comments were "grossly unfair." Dochow had agreed to meet with Lincoln's technical tax people before any decision was made. Until after that meeting, the examiners should hold their comments.

Smuzynski said that he had talked to Kyle Klein, the FHLBB's tax accountant, and she was not aware of any meeting, but it would be held anyway.

Grogan then said that he was aware that ORA [Office of Regulatory Activity, the new name for ORPOS] was reviewing its approach to holding-company examinations. He wanted to know if it was the FHLBB's standard that holding companies had to show earnings on a stand-alone basis.

"No, that's not our policy," Smuzynski answered. "But there should be a Chinese Wall between the holding company and the S&L to protect the S&L. Here, we have a lot of activity going on that the Holding Company Act was designed to prevent."

Smuzynski had cleverly skirted the real problem with the holding-company examination of ACC. Many holding companies had capital-maintenance agreements that required them to infuse capital into their S&L subsidiary whenever the S&L's capital dropped below its required level. The existence of such an agreement provided the FHLBB with a legitimate basis to examine the holding company's level of earnings and financial wherewithal. ACC had no such capital-maintenance agreement. Thus, the FHLBB's examination of ACC should have been restricted to only those transactions which had occurred between ACC and Lincoln. Absent a capital-maintenance agreement, the FHLBB had no legitimate basis for delving into any other affairs of ACC. So the scope of the examination which Barabolak was conducting was totally inappropriate. Smuzynski knew that this was the case.

Charlie responded that Smuzynski's and Barabolak's remarks weren't true. He said, in essence, "We've reduced our debt and are incurring new debt wisely. We have about $85 million in cash that's basically free and clear and always accessible within twenty-four hours. We're extremely liquid. We've got a tremendously difficult environment to operate in, with a berserk industry in general and our situation in particular, which is an unusual one. Generating cash flow without the S&L is difficult but not impossible. It's unfortunate we're back into the old-style exam."

Steve Scott jumped in and said, "Wait a minute, we're doing it right. We're conveying our findings to you."

"Yes, Steve," Charlie answered, "but you're not doing it. People with biases are doing the holding-company exam."

Smuzynski then said, "The MOU only relates to Lincoln and the Lincoln examination. After we got into the tax-sharing-agreement problem, we initiated the holding-company exam. It is separate from the Lincoln examination. We're concerned about the cash flow and the position of the subdebt holders. What happens if you can't sell more subdebt?"

Again, Smuzynski was off base. The cash flow of ACC and the status of ACC's debt holders were of no legitimate concern to the FHLBB—there were other agencies that had that responsibility. If ACC had been subject to a capital-maintenance agreement, these areas might have been fair game for the FHLBB examiners. Absent such an agreement, these issues should have been out of bounds to Barabolak and Smuzynski.

"What do you suggest we do?" Charlie asked.

Smuzynski and Barabolak answered simultaneously, "I don't know."

"Stop purchasing treasury stock," Barabolak then said.

"Then the shorts kill us," Charlie replied.

ACC had two concerns over the short position in its stock. First, the short position eroded the value of the ESOP's assets by driving down the price of ACC's shares. Since the ACC stock was the ESOP's only asset, the value of the ESOP to ACC's and Lincoln's employees was being reduced. Second, Charlie and others had pledged ACC stock to secure various loans. Lenders who accept stock as collateral generally require a borrower to maintain the collateral at a level where its market value is at least twice the amount of the loan. If stock prices decline, the borrower has to pledge more shares. If the borrower doesn't have additional shares to pledge, the lender calls the loan. If the borrower can't answer the call, the lender liquidates the collateral by selling it into the open market. Thus, the squeeze caused by the short-sellers affected both the company and its shareholders.

Scott asked, "How does the SEC view the purchase of treasury shares?"

"That's no problem," Charlie said.

Kielty elaborated by saying, "We disclose the treasury-stock transactions every year in the proxy and everywhere else. As for the MOU, it only talks about Lincoln because that's what the 1986 exam started out as, but it went way beyond just Lincoln. Crawford also said that the DSL would abide by the feds' findings. California hasn't done that either. The MOU does address all issues that occurred prior to the start of this examination. You can't create a strawman by saying 'This is ACC' or 'This is Lincoln'; that's not what the MOU permits."

Charlie said, "The problem before and the problem now is that the examiners have preestablished conclusions."

"We don't have any such conclusions," Smuzynski said. "We are just concerned about ACC's cash flow."

The examiners continued to belabor the points that they had made about salaries, stock purchases, and debt. Finally, Charlie said, "ACC can liquidate many of its assets. We can't sell Lincoln now, because the government gives thrifts away. You should let ACC take back assets in an orderly manner. We can retire the debt, but we need time."

Judy then added, "We've known for two years that we need to get out of Lincoln and put our operations in ACC. We almost put Grand Union into ACC. With Memorex, we should have done a repurchase in ACC, but we knew we'd get criticized by the regulators. We wanted to sell AFL [American Founders Life Insurance Company, a Lincoln subsidiary acquired in 1986] to ACC, but we couldn't figure out how to get that accepted by regulators. You're double-teaming us. If an investment made at the ACC level makes money, you ask why it wasn't made in Lincoln."

"The FHLBB wanted us to issue subdebt out of Lincoln," Charlie said. "Now, they won't let us. The rules keep changing."

Shelly Weiner, who was also in charge of ACC's treasury-stock transactions, then said, "We've heard your concerns regarding the treasury-stock purchases. We have given you information on that and your allegations are not true. We demonstrated that our purchase prices were appropriate with the graphs we gave you."

Charlie looked at Weiner and asked, "Wait a minute. We've already rebutted this?"

Barabolak rapidly responded, "Yes, but we're still analyzing it. Until we're done, our finding stands."

Barabolak's comment reveals the mind-set of the FHLBB. They looked at incomplete data and came to erroneous conclusions. When they were given the data that they really needed, they couldn't understand it, so they put it aside and didn't read it. Then, not having considered what they should have, they stubbornly stuck to their erroneous observations and conclusions. This was a consistent pattern of behavior by most of the FHLBB and CDSL examiners throughout both the 1986 and 1988 examinations.

"Most treasury-stock purchases in 1987 were from insiders or resigning insiders," Newsome tossed in, with agitated impatience.

Charlie replied, "There was no preference given to insiders."

"Andy's [Niebling] stock included warrants," added Judy, referring to the purchase of Niebling's stock when he left ACC. "So, his shares were purchased under market value. Management needs to have the discretion to determine whether to buy out a resigning officer."

Newsome kind of scoffed and said, "It looks funny to have only one purchase in a nine-month period and for that to be a purchase from an insider."

Charlie said, "That's foolish. Andy's not a family member. He was a great S&L guy who just got disgusted."

Barabolak came back with, "You just tell us not to worry. We can't do that."

"We answer your questions in detail," Judy said. "Then we get requests for more documentation. It seems to us that you just don't believe us.

"The holding company is under the MOU and that calls for a different approach and spirit than you've been using. Steve knows that," Judy said. "And you have to understand that some deals are judgment calls by management."

"Alex is in charge of the holding-company exam notwithstanding Charlie's interpretation of his conversation with Dochow," Scott said.

Kielty protested, "You can't separate the two examinations. For Alex to be unaware of the MOU makes his job impossible. We can't have that."

After a few more minutes of debating the appropriateness of the holding-company examination, Steve Scott started to cover the Lincoln-examination findings. His comments on operations were not controversial and dealt primarily with procedural issues. The Lincoln people agreed that the items which Scott pointed out could, and would, be corrected. The group then took a needed break.

During the break, Charlie expressed his displeasure with the attitudes of Smuzynski and Barabolak. He felt that they had an agenda that was adverse to ACC and that they weren't laying all of their cards on the table. He was very disappointed that Steve Scott had lost control of the examination, and Charlie predicted that the exam would turn out to be very detrimental. He said that he would just try to listen to the rest of the examiners' findings without interrupting but admitted that that was going to be tough because they were trying to destroy everything he had worked so hard to build.

After the break, one of the first comments Scott made was that there was the potential that the FHLBB would impose a minimum-capital requirement on Lincoln. Scott said that the level of Lincoln's investments in corporate bonds, real estate, equities, and ADC loans aggregated over $2 billion, or 40 percent of assets, and this was atypical for an S&L. Thus, the FHLBB might increase the amount of capital that Lincoln had to maintain. None of the Lincoln people said anything at this point, but all understood what Scott was saying.

The regulations allowed the FHLBB to set an institution's required capital at any level that the Bank Board or its designee, in this case Dochow, chose. This gave the FHLBB tremendous power over an institution because with the stroke of a pen the required capital level could be raised. If the institution didn't meet the new capital level, the FHLBB could move to take it over. Thus, Scott's comment was viewed as a thinly veiled, extortionate threat.

The fact is that Lincoln had already added $80 million to its required capital as a consequence of the nature of the assets it held. These added amounts were required by the regulations or by the terms of the MOU. So, Lincoln already exceeded the capital requirements that applied to virtually every other S&L in the country. To increase Lincoln's capital requirement by some additional arbitrary amount would simply be a punitive action by the FHLBB.

Scott then said that, while he wasn't going into details, the asset classifications were: substandard—$228 million; doubtful—$34 million; and loss—$30 million. The category of most interest to Lincoln was the loss category. The $30-million number was below the level of Lincoln's recorded reserves, so there was a slight sigh of relief.

Jim Upchurch, who managed Lincoln's corporate bond portfolio, broke in and commented that Lincoln had given Jim Clark's group feedback on the investment classifications. Upchurch felt that Lincoln's comments had either been ignored or rejected in their entirety. He said that the draft he had of Clark's report was dated two days before Lincoln gave Clark its comments on the classifications. Lincoln asserted that this was further evidence that the examiners reached conclusions before considering all the relevant facts. Smuzynski assured Upchurch that there would be a face-to-face meeting regarding the final classifications.

Scott then talked about the interest-rate situation facing Lincoln. He said that the examiners were not worried about Lincoln's ability to manage its own scenario but, if general interest rates increased, Lincoln would be vulnerable. He pointed out that Lincoln's net-interest margin was almost nonexistent, even after a lot of interest had been capitalized. Lincoln needed nonoperating income to cover its expenses. He said that Lincoln's continued reliance on sales of real estate and investment gains resulted in higher risks than the FHLBB would like.

"What's the alternative?" Charlie asked.

"I don't have one," Scott replied.

That answer finally got to Charlie. "Well, I know the alternatives," he said. "These assets have a lot of profit in them. We can realize those profits if you'll just let us operate the assets. Or you can throw us out. If the FSLIC takes over these assets, they'll lose $2 billion to $2.5 billion because they don't know how to manage these assets! The federal government has never made any money on any of the assets it's confiscated from other S&Ls— not a dime! It's lost money on every one of them. No exceptions! With every association that the government's taken over, they've made the situation worse. And that's exactly what'll happen if you take over Lincoln!"

Charlie's comments would come back to haunt him. Later, people took these remarks out of context and said that Charlie Keating knew that Lincoln's assets were overvalued and that they would cost taxpayers at least $2 billion. In fact, the regulators would use this number as a target when they later trashed Lincoln's assets. They wanted to be sure that they lost at least that much, so they could bury Charlie with his own words. But that's not what Charlie said. He was very clear. The assets had unrealized profits—not losses—in them. The only way that money could be lost was if the government tried to manage the assets. Charlie knew that the government would foul up the assets beyond all recognition and, because of their ineptitude, lose billions of dollars. The government's track record provided ample proof to Charlie that he was dead right.

With a deadpan expression, Smuzynski very solemnly said, "We're desperately trying to avoid a FSLIC takeover."

This sent a chill through the room. Everyone thought: Like hell, a takeover is exactly what you're trying to make happen.

Scott then talked about the investment securities but didn't want to go into details. He did say that the examiners didn't approve of Lincoln's investment strategies. He cited, as an example, that Lincoln bought more REVCO bonds after the price had dropped in order to "average down" the cost of Lincoln's position. He also said that the examiners didn't approve of Lincoln's use of margin accounts and its profit taking. He said that Lincoln's philosophy was to "outperform the market." But he said that Jim Clark had concluded that Lincoln couldn't do that, because Lincoln's practices and personnel weren't up to the task.

This comment caught Upchurch's attention. "Are those Clark's conclusions or his group's?" he asked. "How familiar is he with the practices a junk-bond-portfolio management group should have?"

"Jim is in charge of his group, and those conclusions are the culmination of the group's process," Scott explained.

Smuzynski added, "He's got fifteen years as an examiner in Indianapolis. He hasn't dealt with junk-bond portfolios but has lots of experience with commercial loans—the same thing. And Lincoln isn't outperforming the market, except for the Goldsmith deals."

"We've only had one default in two years," Upchurch replied. He was about to strangle Smuzynski. But he calmly pointed out that there was a tremendous difference between commercial loans and junk bonds. He told

Smuzynski that he was very mistaken and naïve if he actually thought they were the same.

Scott continued before Upchurch could react further. He said that the GOIL transaction was very large and that the examiners were waiting for the outside auditor's position on the transaction before taking their own position. But they might object to the booking of any gain.

"Why take a different position from that of our auditors?" Judy asked.

"Because of safety and soundness," Scott said. "We don't know what the real economic value is."

"Odd for you to say that," Judy rather sarcastically commented. She knew that the examiners had failed to appreciate the true economic value of many of Lincoln's assets.

"We want to see the whole process—appraisals, the contract, and the auditors' opinion. We're just not convinced yet," Smuzynski said. "The departure of Arthur Young doesn't raise our comfort level."

The CDSL then asked about the tax-sharing agreement and wanted to know when it would be resolved. There was a brief, but heated, discussion about what role, if any, the CDSL had in the process. After a few questions about what would need to happen to bring the exam to a close, the meeting adjourned.

After the regulators left ACC's offices, Charlie's reaction represented that of the majority of ACC's people who attended the meeting. "We've got to take immediate steps to sell Lincoln," Charlie said. "Those bastards are out to destroy us. They are going to make the exam come out to show we don't have the capital to meet the requirements. They'll invent reasons, even if none exists. We just can't live this way any longer. You can't trust any of them. There's not a honest one in the whole damn bunch."

The most disturbing aspect of the meeting was Dochow's absence. Dochow had promised Charlie that he would be in charge of the entire examination. But his role had been reduced to one of sending letters to ACC and Lincoln—letters that did not appear to rest on facts.

It was also obvious that Steve Scott had no control over the ACC examination. Barabolak had taken over, and he was getting his instructions from Smuzynski and, we believed, O'Connell.

Charlie believed that the only things Dochow heard about ACC and Lincoln were those that had been run through a filter established by a combination of Barabolak, O'Connell, and Smuzynski—people who appeared, for whatever reasons, to be hostile toward ACC and Lincoln. More importantly, these people disregarded any factual evidence that didn't support their preconceived notions and ideas. Thus, this exam was becoming even more biased and unfair than the 1986 exam.

Charlie's final concern centered on Dochow's total disregard for the contractual provisions of the MOU. Virtually every issue that the examiners had raised went back to 1986 or earlier; thus, they should have been resolved by the MOU. The failure to abide by the terms of the MOU was not just a breach of faith—it was a breach of contract. Once again, Charlie believed that the regulators were people who would lie, alter facts, or just make things up in order to achieve their purposes. In this case, the purpose appeared to be the destruction of both ACC and Lincoln.

On November 21 and 22, the FHLBB examiners met again with Lincoln to go over the asset classifications they had made. At the beginning of the meeting, the FHLBB examiners passed out a list of the classifications for loans and real estate. The list showed about $570 million of assets classified as special mention and substandard. The only asset classified as doubtful was the Pontchartrain loan in the amount of $18.6 million. There were about eight assets where a portion was classified as loss. The total dollar amount classified as loss was approximately $8.9 million.

Chuck Gozdanovich went over each classified asset, providing a brief summary of the reasons why the examiners had classified it as they had. The only real disagreement from the Lincoln side of the table centered on some of the substandard classifications. Lincoln's lending folks thought that some of these should have been special mention at the very worst. The examiners also promised to provide to Lincoln, the next morning, detailed write-ups on each asset, so that Lincoln could respond, in writing, to the proposed classification.

After Gozdanovich's presentation, Steve Scott suggested that Lincoln should consider increasing its general reserves because of the dollar amount of assets classified as substandard. Lincoln rejected this recommendation. Lincoln representatives did say that, if its auditors recommended increases in reserves, Lincoln would then record the amount the auditors suggested. It was Lincoln's belief that the issue of general reserves was best left with the auditors and not with the FHLBB, because the reserves could affect the GAAP financial statements.

Jim Clark then began his presentation of the classifications related to securities. Clark spoke in a very aggressive, authoritarian tone. In general appearance, Clark somewhat resembled Smuzynski. He was slightly built and sported a mustache. His nervousness was manifested by a variety of tics and unusual facial expressions. He didn't appear to be very confident of his ability to explain the rationale behind the classifications he was presenting.

Clark started by saying that $228 million of securities were classified as substandard; $34 million were doubtful; and $28 million were loss. As he went through his list, Lincoln's investment people disagreed with many of the classifications. They believed that the examiners' approach was oversimplified and failed to take into account significant attributes of many of the specific securities. For example, Clark indicated that any security that was subordinated was automatically classified as substandard. Upchurch and others said that a consideration like that was ridiculous, since there were many high-quality, subordinated debt issues in the market, including those in Lincoln's portfolio. When pressed for the technical or specific economic reasons for which a given security had been classified, Clark was unable to give a clear explanation of the specific factors that influenced the examiners.

Clark then suggested that Lincoln's portfolio was a "trading portfolio," as opposed to an "investment portfolio." The import being that a trading portfolio should be recorded at market, while investment portfolios are carried at cost. In addition, Clark felt that Lincoln's return was inadequate based on the risks assumed. He said that Lincoln was engaged in trying to "outguess" the market by buying low and selling high. He stated that the examiners felt that Lincoln didn't do a very good job at guessing right. He also suggested that general reserves should be recorded because of the volume of substandard assets.

Lincoln rejected Clark's observations and recommendations. Upchurch pointed to the fact that Lincoln's historical losses had been minimal. He also noted that only one security Lincoln had ever held had defaulted. Moreover, he challenged Clark to identify a single security in the portfolio that exhibited any sign that the issuer might default. He also indicated that where issuers had evidenced signs of financial weakness, Lincoln had been successful in disposing of the security at little or no loss or had been able to restructure the debt in order to avoid loss. Upchurch basically implied that Clark and the examiners who assisted him were inexperienced and simply didn't understand any of the securities they had reviewed. He again pointed out that, contrary to Smuzynski's belief, corporate-debt securities were substantially different from the commercial loans which Clark was accustomed to dealing with in Indianapolis.

The entire discussion of the corporate-debt securities investments, and the examiners' observations about them, was extremely frustrating. The examiners' approach to reviewing these investments was simplistic. They did not understand the technical aspects of the securities; they were unfamiliar with standard analytical techniques; they were not knowledgeable about the price histories of the bonds or the operating results and business plans of the issuers; and they were unwilling to listen to the information presented to them by Upchurch and his associates. Moreover, while they characterized Lincoln's practices as risky and "unsuccessful," the facts were that Lincoln had not experienced losses from defaults and that its overall returns from these investments were higher than market averages and higher than what alternative investments would yield. Because of their inexperience, the examiners were, in Lincoln's opinion, drawing totally inappropriate conclusions based on an incomplete and misguided analysis of Lincoln's actual performance and the true condition of the investments.

The next day, when the meeting continued, Smuzynski indicated that there was a change in the classification of one of the loans that had been discussed the previous day. He indicated that the Pontchartrain loan would be classified as loss rather than doubtful.

I immediately asked, "What could possibly have occurred in the last twelve hours to cause a reclassification? Did the hotel burn down?"

Smuzynski very cryptically stated that he had received information from the FHLBank-Dallas that the appraised value of the hotel was only $26 million and that that, combined with the affiliated-transaction aspects of the loan, had caused him to reclassify the loan.

"Were you the person who made this decision?" I asked.

"Yes," he responded.

I then asked who had done the appraisal. He identified the appraiser as the same firm who had appraised the hotel for the city of Detroit less than two years earlier at $46 million. We said that something had to be terribly wrong with the appraisal. In the intervening year and a half, the financial performance of the hotel had improved, the Cobo Hall convention center had been completed, a major office building across the street from the hotel had been constructed, and the first-mortgage loan had been modified to reduce debt-service costs. If anything, the appraised value should have been higher, not lower. We said that we wanted to see the appraisal on which he was basing the change in classification.

He immediately became defensive and said that because the appraisal had been ordered for a different examination, he didn't believe we could have a copy of it. We responded that if Lincoln's asset classification was based on the appraisal, we were entitled to see it, especially since the appraised value on its face was inappropriate. He wouldn't commit to giving it to us.

It should be noted that Lincoln obtained an appraisal in March 1989 from Pannell Kerr Forster, a specialist in hotels, who valued the Pontchartrain at $53 million. That appraisal value indicated that Lincoln would not incur a significant loss on the hotel loan. The $53-million value was also more consistent with the facts and circumstances surrounding the hotel.

Lincoln believed that the FHLBB had obtained a lowball appraisal by influencing the appraiser. It was common knowledge in 1988 that appraisers in Texas were being sued by the FHLBB over appraisals which turned out to be higher than the liquidation prices that the FHLBB obtained on assets it had seized from Texas thrifts. Appraisers had become frightened that if they prepared appraisals for the FHLBB which later were higher than the selling price of the appraised asset, they too would be sued. All of a sudden appraisals came in with low values—so low that there was no way the asset could be sold for a lesser price. That's what Lincoln figured had to have happened in this case.

After Smuzynski made the classification change, the meeting didn't last much longer. The attitude of ACC's and Lincoln's people was that the FHLBB would continue to screw around with the examiners' findings until they got the answer they were seeking. We figured that we should wait for their report and deal with the issues then. We knew that Smuzynski was going to ignore anything we said in the meeting, so why tell him what our arguments were going to be? If we argued now, the FHLBB would simply adopt a new rationale for their actions. We decided to save our breath.

On November 30, we also had a closing meeting with the CDSL. We didn't view this as a significant event. The CDSL was more a constant irritant than anything else. We knew, based on Newsome's allegations and the remarks the CDSL made in the closing meeting, that they would issue directives or a limited C&D. We believed that the scope of whatever action they took would be restricted to a couple of transactions or assets. We could live with that because we could deal with their restrictions when we had to sell or otherwise dispose of the asset they were concerned about.

The FHLBB was a different matter. We knew that we were back in a full-fledged war with them. We felt that they would attempt to place severe operating constraints on Lincoln. There was even a remote chance that they would try to seize Lincoln. Charlie was right; we had to try to find a qualified buyer for Lincoln. And as we waited for the examination report, that's what we started to do.

Fifteen

FHLBB Moves in for the Kill

In mid-August, a group of California-based businessmen approached ACC and inquired if there was any interest in selling Lincoln. This group consisted of: Spencer Scott, a former S&L executive who said he had been displaced in a management shake-up; Ernest Leff, an attorney who had represented several S&Ls and who had had previous run-ins with the FHLBB; and Herman Rappaport, a consultant.

Charlie indicated that he was always open to a deal and asked what the group proposed. They presented a skeletal outline of a deal which made good economic sense from their standpoint and absolutely none from ACC's. Charlie asked them how they proposed to finance any deal they negotiated. They indicated that they had some capital of their own and that they expected to raise any additional funds that were needed from "Wall Street." Their pitch was common and meant they didn't have the money and didn't know where or how they were going to get it.

Charlie tossed out a proposal that was as badly skewed toward ACC as theirs had been tilted against ACC. Spencer Scott then altered his original proposition slightly and wanted to know if they could obtain some detailed financial data on Lincoln, so they could craft a tighter deal. Charlie, in good humor, said that it had to be tightened about 180 degrees more toward ACC before any discussion became serious. Nevertheless, they were provided with details on Lincoln from its annual reports and from the draft-offering circular for subordinated debt that Lincoln had unsuccessfully tried to get the FHLBB's permission to sell. Charlie suggested that they take the data with them and, after they had read and digested it, and redefined their proposal, we could discuss a possible deal again.

A few weeks later, Kielty, Grogan, and I flew to Los Angeles and met them in Leff's office. They'd added another person to the group, not as an investor, but as an advisor. He was Doug McEachren, a partner in Touche Ross who had recently spent a stint at the FHLBB as an accounting fellow—kind of an intern or on-loan specialist. McEachren was going to assist them with their due-diligence investigation and, with his contacts at the FHLBB, was "going to get any deal rapidly approved."

They started by saying that Lincoln's nontraditional assets made it a difficult association to value and that these assets also made it a tough association to manage. Their initial judgment was that the assets had to be sold and that Lincoln had to concentrate on residential lending. Therefore the assets didn't have the value that ACC believed they had. Also, the fact that Lincoln's administrative personnel were in Phoenix, not California, was a problem. A buyer had to incur the expense of relocating Lincoln's headquarters. All this was preparatory to their saying that their offer wasn't what Charlie might want, but it was fair given Lincoln's circumstances. They then proposed a convoluted transaction which was short on cash and had a total price tag that was less than Lincoln's book value.

I told them that the price we expected was something considerably in excess of Lincoln's book value, and a substantial portion of the price had to be in cash. I added that ACC was willing to buy the assets they didn't want but, if ACC did so, payment would be in the form of a note, and the interest rate on the note would be less than the rate on any debt instruments that they gave as part of their purchase price. I indicated that those were nonnegotiable conditions of any deal.

It was obvious that they weren't prepared to come close to the terms I had laid out. I suggested that they give the deal some more thought and perhaps we could revisit the subject at another time. As we left, we all thought we had seen the last of them.

After the November 7 meeting with the examiners, Charlie decided to contact the Spencer Scott Group to see if a deal could be worked out. This time, we structured a transaction which was presented to them. The deal called for the following:

1. ACC would exchange its Lincoln common stock for $288 million of preferred stock featuring a 10-percent cumulative annual dividend rate.
2. The Spencer Scott Group would contribute a minimum of $35 million to Lincoln's capital and would hold all of Lincoln's voting common stock.
3. ACC would purchase the GOIL stock for $215 million (book value), with the purchase price being represented by a note bearing interest at an annual rate of 9 percent.
4. ACC would buy the 55-percent interest in the Phoenician and Crescent hotels for $193 million (book value), with the purchase price being represented by a note bearing interest at an annual rate of 9 percent.

5. ACC would buy the lots adjacent to the Phoenician for $20 million
    (book value), with the purchase price being represented by a note
    bearing interest at an annual rate of 9 percent.

At first the Spencer Scott Group balked at this proposal but then said
that, depending on what their due diligence disclosed, they might consider
it. They wanted to use the Los Angeles office of Touche Ross to do the due-
diligence investigation.

Within a few days, Judy started meeting regularly with Spencer Scott
and Herman Rappaport, providing them with whatever information they
felt they needed. A Touche Ross team started a week or so later and began
to review loan and investment files. They also, in conjunction with their
people in the Phoenix office, started constructing all sorts of models to
project Lincoln's future earnings under a variety of scenarios.

Meanwhile, we encouraged "the boys," as Judy dubbed the Scott
Group, to get busy lining up the cash they needed. We knew that this was
the hardest part of the deal for them to do. We figured they didn't have the
money and that they would have to sell any investor or lender on the deal
which ACC had proposed.

While this was going on, we also contacted a company in New York
with which Charlie and Judy had done some real-estate deals in 1988. The
company was the Trump Group, a holding company controlled by Julius
and Eddie Trump—not Donald—two brothers who had come to the United
States from South Africa. The Trump Group owned a variety of businesses: a chain of bowling establishments; a large retailer in the Northwest; two very large chains of automotive parts stores; real-estate developments in the Southeast; and other lesser businesses. Charlie had been
introduced to Julius by someone at Drexel, who had financed some of the
Trump Group's other acquisitions.

The Trump Group was presented a deal that was substantially the
same as the one given to the boys. They sent a couple of experienced
financial analysts from their California office to Phoenix, and these folks
spent a week gathering data which they took home to analyze. These
people were considerably more sophisticated than the Scott Group and
assimilated data at a much faster rate.

We heard back from the Trump Group a few weeks after they visited
ACC's offices. They said that the numbers were okay, but they thought the
deal was too big for them. They had recently done some other acquisitions
and felt their management team was stretched too thin to acquire Lincoln.
They left the door open by saying that they might, under the right
circumstances, be willing to participate in a deal with another party.

In late October, a Touche Ross partner introduced me to one of his
clients who had expressed interest in acquiring a savings and loan. The

man, Jim Fail, had assembled a group of insurance companies that were located in several states, including Arizona. Fail had been reading about the FHLBB's Southwest Plan and was considering submitting an application to buy one of the failed Texas thrifts which were being sold under this Plan. We talked a little about Lincoln and the deal which Lincoln had presented to the Spencer Scott Group. Fail agreed to meet with Charlie to discuss the subject further.

A few days later, I arranged for Charlie and Fail to meet. Fail was very candid. He said that he wanted to acquire an S&L. He had decided to submit an application to the FHLBB to participate in the Southwest Plan and was going to bid on one of the Texas shops. He said that everything he had learned about the Southwest Plan convinced him that he could acquire a thrift for virtually nothing. He thought that he could get substantial tax benefits which would recoup any investment he had to make; the government would guarantee a return on assets; and, if an asset which he acquired subsequently went bad, the government would cover the loss. As he saw it, the Southwest Plan allowed him to get in for nothing; guaranteed that as long as he watched operating expenses, he'd make money; and protected him against loss. He had all upside and no downside in the Southwest Plan deal.

Charlie couldn't argue with his logic. Why should a guy buy an S&L when the government not only would give him one, but would guarantee he'd make a profit?

Fail did buy a Texas thrift, and it did return profits. About two or three years later, after it became apparent that people who had acquired thrifts under the Southwest Plan had been given very sweet deals, Congress, with its customary hindsight, raked the regulators over the coals for having given the taxpayers' store away. The regulators reacted by trying to renege on the contracts they'd entered into with the Southwest Plan buyers, including Fail.

Jim Fail learned many of the lessons that the feds had been teaching Charlie for years. They don't honor contracts. They go back on their word. They will immediately accuse you of wrongdoing rather than admit they are inept. If you don't go along with them, they'll destroy you by using their regulatory powers, along with those of other agencies, and then by killing you in the press.

Anyway, by mid-December, the only active deal still under consideration was the one with the Spencer Scott Group. Charlie also contacted people in Europe to see if they were interested in Lincoln or any of its real-estate assets. These people said that they had an interest in investing in ACC, but only if ACC got rid of Lincoln. They didn't want to have anything to do with the regulatory authorities and their arbitrary rules. There also was some interest in specific real-estate assets. So, several packages of information on the various assets were assembled and sent to different parties in Europe.

While the attempts to structure a deal to sell Lincoln were going on, there were still contacts between Lincoln and the regulators. And, internally, the regulators were busy drafting their examination reports and planning their supervisory actions against Lincoln.

Lincoln applied for a growth waiver, which Dochow turned down. The FHLBB contended that Lincoln had already exceeded its allowable growth.

Lincoln had purchased the residual equity interest in a Collateralized Mortgage Obligation (CMO). The dollar value of the interest purchased was not significant, and the transaction was not unusual. GAAP accounting rules required the transaction to be grossed up when it was recorded on Lincoln's books. Lincoln recorded the gross amount of the GNMAs and the CMO bonds on its balance sheet. The effect was to increase both sides of the balance sheet by over $500 million. The regulators assumed that Lincoln had incurred $500 million in new liabilities and had then gone out and purchased the GNMAs. They didn't understand, in spite of repeated explanations, that the whole thing was just a bookkeeping entry and that Lincoln had not, in fact, increased its risks or its liabilities in the manner that they had assumed.

Charlie, David Thompson, and Kielty had a telephone conversation concerning Lincoln's growth rate with some FHLBB personnel, including Dochow and O'Connell. During the conversation, O'Connell made a number of pointed assertions against Lincoln.

On December 5, Thompson wrote to Dochow addressing these assertions. His letter contained the following points:

Mr. O'Connell indicated a concern that the increase in Lincoln's high-yield portfolio might have violated the direct investment regulation. We responded that high-yield debt instruments are not direct investments. He suggested that perhaps Lincoln had advanced funds to AMCOR Funding Corporation [the Lincoln subsidiary that held the securities] in violation of the direct investment regulation and that AMCOR had used such advances to purchase high-yields. We responded that, as Lincoln's thrift financial reports make clear, Lincoln's level of direct investment in AMCOR had not increased at all and that Lincoln's level of direct investment had remained static.

Lincoln remains deeply concerned that erroneous and partial information about Lincoln continues to rise to the top levels of the FHLBB. This misinformation is then used as the basis for making accusations against Lincoln that have no basis in fact. While we willingly respond quickly to correct such misimpressions, Lincoln fears that such misinformation is severely affecting Lincoln's relationship with the FHLBB. . . .

Aside from the erroneous accusations which O'Connell made during the telephone call, his presence in the conversation was very alarming. Dochow had assured Charlie, on several occasions, that O'Connell was not involved in any matters related to Lincoln. And the FHLBB had been careful to keep O'Connell behind the scenes. His participation in this conversation showed Lincoln that O'Connell was, in fact, deeply involved in the examination of Lincoln. To the Lincoln people, his presence explained why the examination had gone so badly and where the predetermined findings had come from.

O'Connell, Smuzynski, and Carol Larson had also taken an interest in what firm Lincoln would select to replace Arthur Young as auditors. Lincoln learned that the FHLBB was thinking about interviewing any firm which Lincoln was considering, and the FHLBB was even suggesting that they, not Lincoln, should select the audit firm.

They were apparently concerned that Lincoln was going to "shop" the different firms by seeking their views on the GOIL transaction. They believed that a firm would be selected only if it agreed with Lincoln's accounting for the transaction. In fact, Lincoln made it crystal clear to both Coopers & Lybrand and Touche Ross that the firm was not to express an opinion on the GOIL transaction until *after* it accepted the engagement as auditors.

Nonetheless, in actions which, to my knowledge, were unprecedented, the FHLBB interviewed both Arthur Young, inquiring into the circumstances of their termination, and Touche Ross. They also had conversations with several lower-level SEC staff members regarding GOIL and the accounting firms which Lincoln was thinking of selecting as auditors.

On December 12, O'Connell and Larson met with Jerry Mayer and Fred Martin, the Touche Ross partners on ACC's account. The questions and comments that they directed to the Touche people indicated that they were trying to find evidence of opinion shopping. But Touche told them that Lincoln had offered the engagement to Touche prior to any meaningful discussion of the GOIL transaction. Touche told the FHLBB that they first indicated the accounting treatment they would support two days after they had accepted the engagement.

We also began to suspect that the FHLBB wanted Touche to agree to support all of the FHLBB's accounting opinions as a condition of their being Lincoln's auditors. This would permit the FHLBB to, in effect, adopt a form of regulatory accounting which would apply only to Lincoln. All other institutions could select the full range of alternatives available in GAAP. Lincoln would be restricted to only those alternatives that were acceptable to the FHLBB. We viewed this as another example of making up regulations as you go and ignoring the regulations as they are actually written.

On December 20, 1988, in the early morning hours, after a full day of negotiations, ACC agreed to sell Lincoln to the Spencer Scott Group along the lines of the deal previously described. The Scott Group said that they had retained Drexel Burnham Lambert, who was going to help them raise $50 million, and, on that basis, the deal called for them to contribute $50 million to Lincoln's capital. If the money wasn't raised by February 1989, the deal was off. The Scott Group also had to obtain the approval of both the CDSL and the FHLBB. They said gaining approval "was no problem." Charlie experienced a sense of relief, because with the sale of Lincoln he could recapitalize ACC and get on with business, free of the regulators' intrusions.

The euphoria of the pending Lincoln sale didn't last long. On the same day, December 20, the FHLBB issued its report on the ACC and Lincoln examinations. The report was accompanied by a series of directives which greatly inhibited Lincoln's ability to do business. The pertinent portions of the letter accompanying the examination reports are as follows:

> ... [T]he examinations reflect that Lincoln is significantly undercapitalized and failing to meet its minimum capital requirements. Assets classified loss and income reversals in excess of $100 million are specified in these examinations and leave Lincoln's capital at an unacceptably low level. Lincoln's capital inadequacy is compounded by the highly concentrated and risky assets remaining on its books. Assets classified substandard and doubtful represent over 500 percent of adjusted capital. Earnings over the past four years have been uneven and solely dependent on nonoperating gains. All of the income reported during the past four years has been self generated either through capitalized interest on large development projects, or sales of assets financed by the association. The examination has identified $33 million of such income that should be reversed.

The letter included a table which set forth the examiners' calculation of Lincoln's regulatory capital deficiency. The table, in thousands of dollars, is as follows:

Association's reported capital:	$255,083
Adjustments:	
Classified losses	59,635
Reversal of income	43,700
Recalculation of capitalized interest (estimated)	15,000
Reversal of tax credit	6,518
Adjusted capital as of September 30, 1988	130,230
Association's reported capital requirement:	179,531
Adjustment:	
Contingency factor for direct investments	65,000
Adjusted capital requirement	244,531
Capital deficiency:	$114,301

The letter then went on with the following additional comments:

Given the association's clear need for increased capital, the board of directors should demand payment of the appropriate deferred tax liability from ACC for the losses and income adjustments noted above. The historical record of the association was to pay up some 40 percent of pretax income to ACC. Given the approximately $118.3 million in losses and income reversals noted above, ACC should now pay Lincoln $48 million in deferred tax payments. Adding in the $6.5 million in tax credits already presented on your financial statements for your third quarter loss, that results in a total payment of $54.5 million from ACC to Lincoln. The board is to immediately demand such a payment from ACC. In addition, the association should take appropriate steps for the attachment of ACC assets in the event that ACC is unwilling to make the required payments.

We find insufficient merit in Lincoln's and ACC's arguments regarding the tax sharing agreement. We have yet to understand the rationale for the association giving up liquid assets to ACC that could earn interest income for Lincoln. The agreement makes no economic sense for Lincoln. All of the benefits go to ACC, and the fact that counsel for ACC transmitted the tax sharing agreement to the Supervisory Agent in San Francisco makes us even more doubtful that the Agreement was structured to be in the best interests of Lincoln. Further, we find it hard to believe that after specifically stating that no deferred taxes were to be paid up to ACC, the Supervisory Agent would go back on his prior directive and violate Bank Board policy by approving an agreement he understood would result in the paying up of deferred taxes to ACC. We have not sent the correspondence relating to the tax sharing matter to the Federal Home Loan Bank of San Francisco, but we believe we already have sufficient information to criticize the agreement and the manner with which the agreement was prepared and presented.

The ploys used in these two paragraphs are interesting. If the FHLBB people in Washington had talked to San Francisco, they would have learned, as the Eleventh District people told Congress, that for whatever reasons Mar did, in fact, approve the tax-sharing agreement. By not talking to San Francisco, the Washington folks could ignore what had actually happened and imply that ACC had done something wrong. They also never acknowledge that the payments could have gone from ACC to Lincoln, which is what would have happened in 1988 if Dochow hadn't suspended the agreement. Lincoln's outside advisors had determined that as a result of the taxability of certain transactions, such as the GOIL exchange, and the expiration of loss carry-overs, payments would have equaled out over the period of another year or two.

The idea that ACC should pay Lincoln the tax effects of the examiners' adjustments is also an interesting trick. It ignores a few things: (1) the taxable consequences of all of Lincoln's other transactions, (2) the fact that Lincoln didn't agree with the examiners' adjustments, and (3) the fact that their estimates are not deductible for tax purposes. This looks like the work of O'Connell and Smuzynski, as many of the other FHLBB people would have known better than to try this approach.

The letter then addressed another of the regulators' favorite subjects—the Pontchartrain loan. Their comment was:

> In regards to the Pontchartrain, this office is dismayed by the willful violations of law and regulations regarding affiliated transactions, conflict of interest and dissipation of assets involved in the transactions surrounding this property. The comment by Ms. Wischer and Mr. Fidel that Charles Keating Jr. is not a controlling person, and hence not an affiliated person, is simply not credible to this office considering Mr. Keating's obvious influence over the management and policies of Lincoln. Further, let us remind the board that Charles Keating III was a member of Lincoln's board in 1986 when the original loans from San Jacinto and the Crescent Hotel Group of Michigan were made, making all of the members of his immediate family affiliated persons.
>
> This office considers the loan to the Hotel Pontchartrain Limited Partnership (HPLP) to be an illegal loan and a gross failure by the board of directors in the performance of their fiduciary duties. . . .

The letter made equally harsh comments about the ESOP, the purchase of stock by the ESOP from Drexel, the Rancho Vistoso transaction, and the purchases of Memorex and Playtex stock. In each case, the letter not only made comments, it asked questions. The questions indicated that the harsh comments were made even though the FHLBB examiners weren't in possession of many relevant facts. The letter ordered Lincoln to address these questions by hiring an independent counsel to look into the following areas: tax-sharing agreement, Pontchartrain loan, ESOP, Rancho Vistoso, and transactions involving Memorex and Playtex stock. The letter ordered Directors Wischer, Kielty, and Ligget to exclude themselves from any discussions surrounding the selection of independent counsel.

The letter then addressed some of the rationale for the "directives" that were attached to the letter. Some of the specific comments were:

> Overall, an underlying concern of both this letter and the Reports of Examination is that Lincoln is being operated for the sole purpose of benefiting ACC, through tax payments, usurpation of corporate opportunity, improper loans, contributions or pledges of assets. . . .
>
> The supervisory directive that prohibits any further purchases of corporate equity or high yield bond securities is intended to prohibit the association from "doubling down" on its troubled assets. . . . [T]he association is only increasing its exposure to high risk, and often non earning assets, for the purpose of trying to "spend its way out" of a troubled investment. Since the source of funds for such activities is FSLIC insured deposits, this office cannot allow such a strategy to continue.

These observations, from Lincoln's perspective, are based on erroneous interpretations of information and improper assumptions made by the examiners. Most of the observations came from Jim Clark's team. The examiners simply didn't understand what they read or what they were told. These botched-up understandings then got communicated to the Washington people, who didn't understand any of it either and who also lost some important details in the translation made by the examiners. The result was that people with little or no practical business experience and acumen were dictating directives to Lincoln.

The directives were intended effectively to freeze Lincoln's operations. Unless approved, in writing, by Dochow or his designee, Lincoln was directed to:

> 1. Engage in no asset growth as measured on an average monthly basis in excess of that level of assets already on the books of the association on the date of this letter [December 20, 1988].
> 2. Purchase no additional equity securities of any type.
> 3. Purchase no non-investment grade corporate debt securities.
> 4. Make no further commercial loans in excess of $500,000, nor guarantee

such loans to other parties, nor pledge assets in support of such loans to other parties, nor purchase any participation of such loans in excess of $500,000; nor restructure, extend or otherwise modify any such loans currently on the association's books.

5. Purchase no commodities, foreign currencies, or mortgage residuals, nor take any short position in any such investment vehicles.

6. Make no further purchases of land, or loans on unimproved land, nor purchase any participation interest in such a loan.

7. Make no purchases nor sell any options, warrants nor any commitment to purchase or sell any of the investment vehicles noted in the paragraphs one through eight [sic] above.

8. Pay no bonuses to officers or directors, nor increase the salary or benefits to any person with a current annual salary in excess of $50,000 when aggregated with all other renumeration [sic] from other Lincoln affiliates, nor to enter into any severance or termination agreement with any such person, nor enter into a consulting contract with any departing employee nor with any relatives of current or departing employees.

9. Hire no employee at an annual salary exceeding $50,000 a year.

10. Engage in no further affiliated transactions.

11. Purchase no non-interest bearing asset in excess of $50,000.

12. Excepting assets qualifying as liquid assets and Federal Agency issues, Lincoln is to execute no transaction in excess of $10 million without prior approval of the Supervisory Agent. . . .

These directives were the equivalency of a cease-and-desist order. In the case of a C&D order, the FHLBB would have had to comply with the due-process protection contained in the federal law and the FHLBB regulations. Here, Dochow attempted to circumvent the law by unilaterally demanding that ACC and Lincoln accede to his directives and bypass the administrative remedies that were available to them.

Lincoln and ACC were caught in a vise, and Dochow knew it. If they ignored the directives, the FHLBB would drag its heels on the application to buy Lincoln filed by the Spencer Scott Group or would deny it. If ACC and Lincoln agreed to the directives, they would lose all control over their respective business affairs and, in effect, Dochow or his designee would make all of Lincoln's business decisions. Moreover, the directives essentially cut off most of the activities which had been the source of Lincoln's profits. The assessment of ACC's management was that they had been placed in a lose-lose situation. They would encounter a major problem no matter which direction they turned.

Not wanting to be upstaged by the feds, the very next day the CDSL joined the game. On December 21, 1988, the CDSL issued a cease-and-desist order. The C&D, in part, prohibited Lincoln from:

Making loans, representing either new or additional extensions of credit, to Pontchartrain, R.A. Homes, Inc. and Southmark Corporation, or any of their subsidiaries, directors, officers, or other affiliates.

The C&D went on to direct Lincoln to "divest its interest in any and all loans to and investments in Pontchartrain, R.A. Homes, Inc. and Southmark Corporation within six months of the date of this Order. Within 30 days of the date of this Order, Lincoln shall file a comprehensive plan for disposal of all such loans and investments. . . ." The C&D was a direct outgrowth of Newsome's allegations and so-called findings.

The state C&D was not a big concern to Lincoln, because its scope was much more limited than the FHLBB directives. Nevertheless, the state's order required Lincoln to gain the approval of the CDSL if Lincoln wanted to resolve problems with the assets that were subject to the C&D order. This was a concern because the CDSL people were very slow in making decisions, and, in Lincoln's opinion, they lacked business judgment. This would make it difficult to work out deals which the CDSL needed to sign-off on in a reasonable period of time. A buyer of these assets would have to have unusual patience waiting for the slow wheels of the state's bureaucratic decision-making apparatus to turn.

When the FHLBB report came in, it was distributed to various people, including Kaye Scholer, so a response could be written within the time allotted. One of the first people to read the report was Joe Sanicola, an accountant who handled Lincoln's regulatory financial-statement filings. Joe immediately concluded that the FHLBB had incorrectly computed certain of the adjustments to Lincoln's capital; therefore, the $65-million adjustment to Lincoln's required net worth was wrong. Joe contacted Andy Ligget with his findings. Andy talked to Kaye Scholer about what Joe had found, and the attorneys advised Andy to engage Touche Ross to verify Joe's conclusions and prepare a letter to the FHLBB pointing out the errors.

Touche Ross reviewed the work which Joe had done and performed other limited procedures related to the components of the net-worth calculation and the adjustments proposed by the FHLBB. Touche concluded that Joe was, in fact, correct and that the FHLBB had made significant errors. The scope of Touche's procedures dealt only with the mechanical or computational errors made by the FHLBB. They did not address whether the foundational facts used by, or substantive conclusions reached by, the FHLBB were correct.

On December 28, 1988, Touche Ross sent a letter to Dochow regarding the computational errors. Some of the key points made in the letter are:

To summarize our findings concerning the calculation errors, and without giving effect to those further accounting issues we address below, the errors made in the letter [Dochow's cover letter dated December 20, 1988] total approximately $88 million, as follows (000's omitted in all further cases):

Contingency factor already included in the Association's reported capital requirement	$58,129
Classified losses already included in the Association's specific reserves	18,017
Incorrect reversal of income for Crescent/Phoenician hotels	7,058
Difference in calculation of capitalized interest applying average cost of funds	4,739
	$87,943

The Touche letter explained the procedures that Touche's staff had applied in arriving at the corrections indicated above. The letter also addressed some of the accounting adjustments proposed by the examiners which Touche believed might not be correct and said that those matters would be addressed in their audit. These matters related to GOIL, the Wolfswinkle equity kicker, gains on the sale of real estate, the Phoenician gain, and the tax-sharing agreement. Touche indicated these accounting matters could result in additional corrections amounting to approximately $47 million.

On December 30, 1988, Dochow sent a letter to ACC transmitting the separate examination report on ACC. Before ACC could incur any additional debt, it had to have its annual debt budget approved by the FHLBB. Dochow's letter contained a paragraph concerning ACC's debt budget which read as follows:

Based on the Report of Examination of ACC, we are concerned with ACC's continued ability to support its level of debt. Therefore, we are disapproving the proposed debt budget filed on November 16, 1988, pursuant to the debt budget authority granted by. . . . However, this office will entertain individual debt applications by ACC, and will take into consideration your response as it pertains to ACC's ability to service its debt and provide support to Lincoln.

This was intended to preclude ACC from incurring any additional debt, including the sale of subordinated debentures. Through its various actions, the FHLBB reneged on its approval of the tax-sharing agreement, thereby cutting off payments from Lincoln to ACC; denied the payment of dividends by Lincoln; ordered the repayment of tax payments previously received by ACC; ordered ACC to repay other amounts to Lincoln; and, now, denied ACC the right to borrow money.

The FHLBB knew, from its examiners, what ACC's cash position was and knew that ACC could not make all of the payments that the FHLBB was demanding. ACC's debt budget clearly showed that, absent dividends from Lincoln, ACC needed new borrowings to service its debt. This action was intended to place ACC in a cash squeeze from which it could not escape. These were deliberate actions by the FHLBB to empty ACC's cash coffers and to debilitate its strength to defend itself against the FHLBB's actions.

When Lincoln read the December 20 letter from Dochow and found the capital requirement to be wrong, people wondered how the FHLBB could have botched the calculation so badly. This calculation, which permitted the FHLBB to assert that Lincoln had failed its capital requirement, was the foundation on which all of the draconian directives rested. These directives threatened Lincoln's very existence by denying it the ability to pursue its primary lines of business. Thus, one would think that this calculation would have been made very carefully.

Lincoln learned that the reason the FHLBB's calculation was wrong was that it was an estimate. The examiners had made a detailed computation for June 30, 1988, but not for September 30, 1988. When O'Connell and Smuzynski put the supervisory letter together, they simply estimated the September requirement based on assumptions they had made. In so doing, they didn't properly calculate the contingency factor for land loans. Neither of these guys appeared to be overly concerned about real facts. If they didn't have facts, they just invented something which supported what they wanted to do.

Steve Scott could have enlightened them. At that time, S&Ls earned a credit against their capital requirement for certain interest-bearing assets whose maturity matched favorably with the maturity of the institution's liabilities. When Scott reviewed Lincoln's June 30, 1988, required capital calculation, he pointed out a way for Lincoln to increase this credit. Lincoln had funded its service corporations with a combination of loans and equity capital. The loans to the service corporations were not secured and, therefore, didn't qualify for the matching-maturity credit. Scott told Lincoln to secure these loans, and then they would qualify for credit.

Following Scott's advice, Lincoln secured the loans with land which the service corporations had owned for several years. If a loan was secured by land and the loan was made after 1987, the land loan became a direct investment. In such a case, while the S&L earned a matching-maturity credit, it also had to increase its capital by 10 percent for the direct-investment portion of the loan. The land securing these loans was already counted as a direct investment; thus, when the service corporations pledged the land to secure Lincoln's loans, there was no additional direct-investment capital requirement associated with these land loans.

When the FHLBB did its estimate, they saw that Lincoln's land loans had increased. Not knowing the real facts, they assumed that a factor had to be added to the capital requirement for the loans. Had they simply asked Steve Scott about Lincoln's capital requirement before they made the estimate, they would have learned the facts. The FHLBB never owned up to this mistake.

Lincoln's response to the Report of Examination was delivered on January 17, 1989. The response was divided into five sections. Section one addressed the overall management of Lincoln. Section two addressed the subject of Lincoln's capital requirements and the errors which the examiners had made in the calculation of Lincoln's capital. Section three addressed the substantive errors that Lincoln believed existed in the examiners' findings and calculated the effects of these errors on Lincoln's capital requirement and actual capital. Section four took exception to the examiners' classification of Lincoln's assets. And section five challenged the examiners' conclusions about the transactions between Lincoln and its affiliates.

The first part of section one presented a series of graphs and charts which traced Lincoln's historical return on its productive assets and then compared these returns against what Lincoln would have realized had it confined its operations to single-family, residential lending. The chart showing historical returns demonstrated that Lincoln's overall quarterly rates of return had been consistently above 11.5 percent and had ranged to over 20 percent for the twenty-two quarters that ACC had owned Lincoln. During that same period of time, Lincoln's cost of funds had remained fairly constant at around 10 percent. Because of the consistency in Lincoln's returns, the response argued: "While the quarterly rates of return on productive assets reflect some fluctuation, as would be expected, they clearly do not reflect the kind of boom and bust pattern that one would expect if the association was engaging in highly risky, speculative activities."

When the rates of return were compared to the earnings rate that Lincoln would have realized from single-family, adjustable-rate mortgages (SFR ARMs), Lincoln's actual rate of return had exceeded the comparable rate every quarter since its acquisition. The margin of excess had generally been over 3 percent, and occasionally more than 7.5 percent, as the return on residential mortgages had started at around 12.5 percent in 1984 and gradually drifted down to about 10 percent. The rates for SFR ARMs, which Lincoln used in this comparison, were obtained from a major Wall Street investment-banking firm and were not rates that Lincoln generated itself. This was done in order to avoid any claim that Lincoln had used a biased rate.

The second portion of this first section argued that there were many unrealized gains in Lincoln's total portfolio of assets. The text of this section stated:

> Given the non-traditional, high-yielding composition of Lincoln's assets, it is very misleading to make a judgment concerning the safety and soundness of the Association (i.e., whether there is sufficient value in the Association to protect the FSLIC fund) by reviewing its portfolio with the sole object to write down or criticize assets which have declined in value, while at the same time totally disregarding assets which have appreciated in value, such as Estrella. Moreover, since the value of Lincoln's assets tends to fluctuate over a wider range than the assets of a traditional savings and loan association, this type of one-sided analysis provides a more distorted view of the Association's health than would a comparable analysis of a traditional association's assets. In looking at an institution like Lincoln, which has substantial non-traditional investments, it is not surprising that some investments have declined in value, just as it's not surprising that some investments have increased in value. However, for such a non-traditional institution, it is especially misleading in evaluating safety and soundness of the institution to write down certain assets and not write up others.

The response cited that Lincoln's actual regulatory capital had exceeded the required amount of capital by only $3 million in 1982, but by 1988, excluding the effects of the examiners' findings, with which Lincoln disagreed, it exceeded the required amount by $125 million.

This section of the response also addressed the examiners' comments regarding Lincoln's investment strategies by saying:

> The examiners' misunderstanding of Lincoln's investment strategy is typified by the Lincoln Examination report's discussion of the Association's investments, where they question whether Lincoln can "beat the market." That is not the issue at all. The pertinent issue is whether, given alternative investment opportunities (within and across the various asset portfolios), the Association has made prudent investments such that its overall return more than compensates for risks taken and is better than other available investment opportunities, such as SFR ARMs.

The response went on to argue: "Lincoln's diversified investments have reduced, not increased, the risk to the FSLIC. The Association's performance has added income—and capital—in excess of what would have been earned had it solely originated SFR ARMs. Moreover, the Association's existing assets have appreciated and provide real value in the asset portfolio which further benefits the Association and protects the FSLIC."

The second section of the response, which addressed the computational errors that the examiners had made in determining Lincoln's capital and capital requirement, duplicated or repeated some of the work done by Touche Ross. It also identified computational errors which Touche did not deal with in its letter. When these amounts were added to the amounts already reported by Touche Ross, the total errors in the determination of Lincoln's capital status amounted to $106 million.

The additional computational errors reflect the ripple effect of the adjustments proposed by the examiners. For example, when the examiners proposed to reduce retroactively the amount of interest which Lincoln had capitalized, this also reduced the carrying value of Lincoln's real-estate assets. The gains on the sales of these assets had to be recalculated because the cost of sales was now less. The examiners failed to appreciate that their adjustments were not isolated transactions but, rather, were changes which rippled throughout Lincoln's books, creating offsetting counterreactions to the income effect of the adjustments. One of the reasons that the examiners didn't focus on the ripple effects was that some of the adjustments had been made by O'Connell, not by the field examiners. O'Connell used estimates, not actual numbers. He also wasn't an accountant; therefore, he didn't understand the full consequences of the adjustments which he had proposed.

The response also made the following point:

> . . . Lincoln's capital [after the correction of the computational errors] is only $8.654 million less than its required capital. Moreover, this alleged "deficiency" exists only because (1) Lincoln's proposed adjusted required capital contains a contingency factor increment of over $56 million reflecting equity risk investments which were grandfathered under the direct investment regulations and which contingency factor is included only because resolution of the grandfathering issue was deferred pursuant to the Memorandum of Understanding, and (2) Lincoln's other contingency factor items, in the amount of approximately $27 million, represent a perceived risk profile of its investments.

This last argument was a very important one. The examiners' main criticism of Lincoln was that its nontraditional assets represented an increased risk to the FSLIC insurance fund. The regulations contained provisions which applied to associations that held such assets and, thus, in the FHLBB's opinion represented a higher risk to the insurance fund. The regulations required such associations to maintain a higher minimum capital requirement by increasing their contingency factors. Lincoln had complied with these regulations and had increased the minimum capital that it was required to maintain by over $83 million. The examiners failed to focus on the fact that Lincoln had already met the statutory requirements associated with its particular risk profile. They may have been blinded by their own calculation errors. In any event, with Lincoln meeting the contingency-factor requirements, the directives were punitive overkill by the FHLBB.

The next section of the response dealt with Lincoln's substantive arguments against the so-called income reversals proposed by the examiners.

The first income reversal that Lincoln opposed concerned the sale of a parcel of land in Hidden Valley to National Realty Limited Partnership (NRLP). The examiners proposed to reverse an $18-million gain on this sale because they believed that Lincoln may have advanced the partnership the down payment it used to effect the sale. The response set forth the following facts related to this sale:

> NRLP purchased certain real estate and paid 25 percent down. At approximately the same time, Lincoln entered into unrelated transactions with entities having the same principals as NRLP. The issue is whether NRLP used funds from Lincoln to make the downpayment. Here, the publicly filed financial statements of NRLP clearly indicate that the partnership had sufficient liquid resources to fund the downpayment. Moreover, as indicated in NRLP's 1987 Form 10-K and its June 30, 1988, Form 10-Q, the funds used for the downpayment to purchase the Lincoln real estate were derived from a line of credit originated by Heller Financial, Inc.

The response continued with these additional facts:

> Furthermore, the loans originated by Lincoln were not made to NRLP, the purchaser, but were made to affiliates of Southmark Corporation which are legally separate and distinct from NRLP. Moreover, these loans were made for the specific purpose of providing mortgage financing for specifically identified apartment complexes which were completely unrelated to Lincoln. Accordingly, the Association has not provided, either directly or indirectly, any portion of the downpayment funds that were used by NRLP for its purchase of land from the Association.

The issue of real-estate sales, and the source of the down payments related thereto, is complex. At this time, a brief discussion of the accounting for real-estate transactions is necessary to understand the issue that was being contested in this specific instance—the NRLP sale.

First, a company has to determine whether the transaction under consideration is a sale or exchange transaction. An exchange, and not a sale, may have occurred if the company (1) engages in sales *and* purchases of real estate with the same entity at or about the same time or (2) the company receives consideration in the transaction which is not measured in units of currency (i.e., nonmonetary assets). These exchange transactions are covered by the concepts set forth in APB no. 29. At times, Lincoln's auditors viewed some of Lincoln's real-estate transactions, ones which Lincoln's accounting personnel had accounted for as sales, to be exchanges. In those instances, the auditors determined that, while the accounting concept that Lincoln applied was not necessarily appropriate, the reported gain on the transaction, whether accounted for as a sale or as an exchange, was materially the same. In this case, the NRLP transaction did not exhibit the characteristics of an exchange; therefore, Lincoln and its auditors considered it to be a sale transaction.

Sales of real estate are covered by the accounting principles discussed in SFAS no. 66. This standard describes numerous characteristics that a transaction must exhibit if a company is to record its full gain on the sale on the transaction date. Certain of these characteristics concern the initial investment, or down payment, that the buyer must make with respect to the real estate being purchased. The standard specifies certain minimum down payments, expressed as a percentage of the selling price, which the buyer must make. For example, in the case of land which is not expected to be developed within the first two years following the purchase/sale date, the specified down-payment percentage is 25 percent.

SFAS no. 66 also, in paragraph 9, specifies that: "The buyer's initial investment shall include only: (a) cash paid as a downpayment, (b) the buyer's notes supported by irrevocable letters of credit from an independent lending institution, (c) payments by the buyer to third parties to reduce existing indebtedness on the property, and (d) other amounts paid by the buyer that are part of the sales value." In this particular instance, NRLP made a cash down payment that was equal to 25 percent of the sales value, which is consistent with paragraph 9 (a).

But there are some restrictions on what can be included in the down payment. These are discussed in paragraph 10 where the SFAS states:

The initial investment shall not include:

(a) Payments by the buyer to third parties for improvements to the property,

(b) A permanent loan commitment by an independent third party to replace a loan made by the seller,

(c) Any funds that have been or will be loaned, refunded, or directly or indirectly provided to the buyer by the seller or loans guaranteed or collateralized by the seller for the buyer.

In accounting for a sale, then, a company must determine whether it directly or indirectly provided the buyer with the down payment to purchase its real estate. This is a factual determination the company must make.

This determination is especially difficult in the case of a financial institution, such as an S&L. The S&L may engage in normal, routine lending transactions or other transactions in the normal course of its business with a person(s), or entity, and its affiliates, who happens to purchase a parcel of real estate from the S&L. In such a case, most accountants would say that the facts and circumstances of each transaction must be considered to see if there was the intent by the parties for the proceeds from any of these transactions to be used solely to provide the buyer with the down payment for the real-estate transaction. This requires the establishment of facts evidencing intent; so the accountant must necessarily exercise judgment.

In making this judgment, there are a number of questions regarding the other transactions between the S&L and the buyer which the accountant should ordinarily ask and have answered.

Was the loan, or purchase of assets, a customary transaction for the S&L?

If the transaction was an asset purchase, did the S&L receive an asset of equal value to the monies expended?

If it was a lending transaction, was the collateral of equal or greater value than the funds advanced?

Was the use of proceeds from the loan for a specific purpose unrelated to the real estate purchased from the S&L?

Was the use of proceeds, as specified in the loan application, consistent with the borrower's corporate purposes, business or investment practices, and financial condition?

Were the terms of the other transaction consistent with the terms of similar transactions with customers who had not purchased land from the S&L?

Did the S&L have a specific business purpose, which was consistent with its existing lines of business, for any assets it acquired from the buyer?

The above questions are not intended to be exhaustive of the questions which the accountant might ask, rather they are merely some representative questions which assist the accountant in determining the proper accounting for the sale transaction.

There are some accountants who maintain that the SFAS should be read literally. They argue that if a seller has engaged in any other transaction with the buyer in close proximity to the subject sale transaction, any proceeds that the buyer received as a consequence of the other transaction(s) should be subtracted from the down payment. In my

experience, it is unusual for an accountant to make such a literal interpretation of SFAS no. 66, except when he or she is acting in an adversarial
position to a company, such as an expert witness who is trying to assert that
the company's accounting is incorrect. In such instances, the adversarial
accountant tries to attack the judgment process and, essentially, ignores
any facts which argue that the real-estate sale transaction and the other
transaction under consideration are independent events. Only by joining
together what are otherwise independent transactions can the adversarial
accountant question the adequacy of the down payment.

That's basically what Lincoln was arguing that the FHLBB had done
in this case. Lincoln contended that the examiners had not asked any of the
relevant questions and were, therefore, ignoring many of the determinative
facts in this transaction. In fact, it's unclear whether the examiners did any
meaningful inquiry into the facts. The comment in the Report of Examination was worded as follows: "Our preliminary review indicates that no
income should have been booked, given the fact that there is substantial
doubt whether any real downpayment was made on the sale." Thus, the
FHLBB's position was not predicated on fact but on "substantial doubt."
In any event, Lincoln believed that the facts demonstrated conclusively
that Lincoln had not directly or indirectly provided NRLP with the down
payment it used to purchase real estate from Lincoln.

The FHLBB report ordered Lincoln to reverse the gain on the
Phoenician Hotel because the examiners believed that the costs to complete the Phoenician were not known or the estimates of completion costs
were uncertain. Lincoln's response argued that the entire gain on the sale
of the Phoenician and the Crescent was properly recognizable by September 30, 1988. The Phoenician was completed and open for business on
October 1, 1988. All of the costs were known by the end of September. It
is clear that by September 30, 1988, all of the gain on the sale of the hotels
was recognizable.

The examiners denied the recognition of income on the sale of the
Wolfswinkle equity kicker. Initially, they attempted to assert that Lincoln's
accounting for the transaction was incorrect. But their own FHLBB
accountants agreed that Lincoln's accounting was, in fact, correct. Then,
they took the stance that the gain could not be recognized because Lincoln
had not gotten prior written approval to sell the equity kicker to ACC.
Based on Lincoln's failure to obtain advance approval, they ordered
Lincoln to reverse the gain and to use the proceeds from the sale of the
equity kicker to reduce the loan balance. Lincoln argued that the accounting was proper and, under GAAP and RAP, the gain was properly
recognizable; Lincoln received all of the economic benefits from the sale
of the equity kicker; and the treatment proposed by the FHLBB was
inconsistent with the regulations.

The FHLBB's position with respect to the Wolfswinkle equity kicker is a clear demonstration of the arbitrary and punitive nature of their decisions. They ordered Lincoln to reduce its capital by $15 million merely because Lincoln didn't ask them for permission to do the transaction. They didn't challenge the fact that the transaction benefited Lincoln or that Lincoln properly recorded the income. Instead, they said, in effect, "You didn't ask us first, and now we are going to penalize you." No wonder there was an S&L crisis in the country. With this kind of attitude, a crisis was inevitable.

The examiners asserted that Lincoln's capitalized interest was overstated by an *estimated* $15 million, and Lincoln was ordered to reverse this amount. The FHLBB's accountants had looked at this issue and concluded that Lincoln's accounting for capitalized interest was "aggressive but not wrong." Since the regulators couldn't order an income reversal on the basis of Lincoln's accounting, they used the argument that Lincoln's interest-capitalization method was somehow unsafe and unsound.

The examiners' report reflects this fractured reasoning. The section of the report dealing with this issue is replete with errors—factual, logical, and typographical. The pertinent segments of the FHLBB report were:

> The association has been capitalizing interest expense oin [*sic*] their real estate investments at the average weighted yield of their brokered deposits. We raised questions about this, since the more normal industry practice is to use the association's total cost of funds rate. In discussions with the Office of Regulatory Activities, Lincoln explained that their logic of using the brokered cost of funds rate was that they would not have begun the brokered deposit program if it were not needed to fund real estate development activities. . . .

The FHLBB had almost listened to and understood Lincoln's explanation—almost. What Lincoln had actually said was that it had entered into the brokered deposits to fund the planned investment in its service corporations which had been approved by the California commissioner in 1984. The planned activity of certain of the service corporations was real-estate development. Since the brokered deposits were incurred specifically for these service corporations, the brokered deposits became specific borrowings, both with respect to the funding of the service corporations and with respect to the real estate they developed. So, the FHLBB was correct that the brokered deposits were intended to fund the real estate, but only because the real-estate development was conducted in the service corporations.

The fact that the FHLBB failed to understand the total purpose of the brokered deposits explains, in part, the next segment of their report, which read as follows:

We are not in a position to judge what the original intent of the brokered deposit program was, but we are in a position to note that whatever the original intent, it is clear that brokered deposits are being used for more than just to fund real estate investments. We note that the association had approximately $9 million of real estate investments as of June 30, 1988, as compared to $1.8 billion in brokered deposits. Whether there was a clearer picture between the two before 1988 was noat [sic] reviewed, the need to identify brokered deposits as spcifically [sic] matched to the real estate investments does not conform to the reality of the association's financial condition.

Where the FHLBB got the idea that Lincoln's real-estate investments were only $9 million is not clear. If that had actually been the case, the entire dispute with the FHLBB would never have existed. Lincoln also never understood what the examiners were trying to say in the last sentence of this paragraph. The only thing that was clear was that the examiners were very confused. However, that didn't stop them from going on to their conclusion, which was stated as follows:

In addition to the fact that there is no clear matching of the association's brokered deposits and its real estate investments that use of a higher than necessary capitalization rate is an unsafe and unsound practice. If an association knows that they can immediately recover the costs of bidding up savings costs through capitalization of interest, there is no economic incentive to try to limit the amount of interest it must offer. Further, the higher the rate of capitalization, the higher the book value of the real estate investment, which only increases the amount of assets not earnings from cash income on the association's books, and increases the amount which must be recovered from future sales. It is therefore directed that the association stop capitalizing interest income at the averaged brokered deposit rate, and to instead use the association's overall cost of funds rate as the capitalization figure. . . .

Because of the grammar errors and faulty logic, it's difficult to understand this paragraph. The FHLBB had, for four years, consistently misunderstood the reason why Lincoln had entered into the brokered-deposit program. It was really quite simple. Lincoln wanted to attract long-term deposits to fund long-term projects. Lincoln also wanted a known, fixed cost for these funds. It did not want to be in a position where the interest costs associated with its longer-term projects fluctuated with short-term interest-rate movements. The brokered deposits met these requirements because they were fixed-rate, long-term, nonwithdrawable deposits. That was the "economic incentive" for obtaining these deposits.

While the use of a high capitalization rate does increase the carrying value of an asset, it is merely a bookkeeping event and not an economic event. The incurrence of an interest cost is what influences the aggregate price that a real-estate developer must charge. Total selling prices must be sufficiently high to recover all interest costs incurred, whether such costs are capitalized or expensed, if a developer is going to realize an economic gain. Lincoln had been incurring interest costs on its brokered deposits since 1985 and would continue to do so until about 1995, when the deposits could be withdrawn. Whether these costs were capitalized or not didn't change the fact that they were, and would be, incurred. So, the argument that the capitalization rate was somehow unsafe and unsound is total nonsense.

The reality of the situation is that O'Connell and others in Washington had several pet peeves regarding Lincoln—the equity kicker, the capitalization of interest, and the Phoenician gain—and they were going to use whatever justification they could to cause Lincoln to reverse these items. When they couldn't get the FHLBB's accountants to support their arguments, they turned to unsafe and unsound as the basis for their actions. The fact that their argument lacked fundamental logic didn't deter them. The frightening part is that their superiors, who presumably reviewed this examination report before it was sent to Lincoln, bought into this half-baked unsafe-and-unsound attack.

Lincoln rejected all of the proposed income reversals. The FHLBB-ordered reversals amounted to $43.7 million. Lincoln believed that the proposed reversals were without merit and should be retracted in their entirety. Even if Lincoln's arguments were not accepted, the reversals were incorrect by $12.7 million, solely because of computational errors.

The next major section of Lincoln's response addressed the subjects of asset classifications and specific and general loss reserves. The examiners classified $59 million of assets as loss, $35 million as doubtful, and $706 million as substandard. They ordered Lincoln to establish specific reserves for the assets classified as loss and suggested general reserves be set up to cover "possible" losses which might result from the assets classified as doubtful and substandard.

In setting up general loss reserves, the examiners suggested that Lincoln review various industry statistics for losses incurred by *other* associations and, then, calculate the relationship of the losses suffered by these associations to the level and types of assets that they held. In following this process, Lincoln was to determine the percentage of each type of asset that it held (i.e., loans, junk bonds, real estate, etc.) that might, based on the industry data, eventually become losses. The examiners had to suggest the use of industry data to make the calculation because Lincoln, itself, had experienced virtually no losses. Had the examiners suggested that Lincoln use its own historical data on losses, no reserves would have been required, since the calculated loss percentage would have been nil.

Lincoln's response first cited the GAAP requirements for recording loss contingencies, which is how accountants technically describe reserves for losses. The GAAP requirements are appropriate to refer to because the Competitive Equality Banking Act (CEBA) required the regulators to follow GAAP, as did the FHLBB's own policy, which stated: "Allowances provided on classified assets should be established consistent with Generally Accepted Accounting Principles."

Financial Accounting Standards Board Statement no. 5 (SFAS 5), paragraph 8, sets forth the requirements which must be met prior to recognizing a loss contingency by a charge against income:

> 8. An estimated loss from a loss contingency (as defined in paragraph 1) shall be accrued by a charge to income if both of the following conditions are met:
> a. Information available prior to issuance of the financial statements indicates that it is probable that an asset had been impaired or a liability had been incurred at the date of the financial statements. It is implicit in this condition that it must be probable that one or more future events will occur confirming the fact of the loss.
> b. The amount of the loss can be reasonably estimated.

As is explicit in SFAS 5, if a loss is not "probable" or if the amount cannot be "reasonably estimated," no allowance is necessary, required, or permitted.

Contingencies which are "remote" or even "reasonably possible" do not satisfy the condition that loss contingencies must be *probable*. SFAS 5 further underscores this point: "General or unspecified business risks do not meet the conditions for accrual in paragraph 8, and *no accrual for loss shall be made*" (emphasis added).

After discussing the applicable accounting requirements for establishing loss contingencies, Lincoln's response argued:

> The examiners' proposed general allowance for "any potential loss exposure" clearly does not meet the first condition of paragraph 8 that loss contingencies must be "probable." In fact, the examiners are proposing an allowance based on nothing more than a general unspecified risk, for which no accrual for loss is *permitted* under GAAP, let alone required.
> The examiners' bases for the classification of individual assets as Doubtful or Substandard are equally, if not more, infirm than the examiners' conclusion that an allowance is necessary for "potential loss exposure." For example, the examiners propose to classify assets as Substandard because of an alleged "sensitivity" to "unforeseen market shocks and surprises," the "possibility of future market deterioration," and "various negatives" affecting the asset. . . .

[S]uch conclusions do not even satisfy the requirements for classifying an asset Substandard. They clearly cannot serve as the basis of a provision for loss in face of GAAP's clear requirements—adopted by CEBA for FHLBB classification purposes—that losses must be *probable* and reasonably estimable.

GAAP also requires a loss contingency to be "estimable." Yet the examiners propose a provision to the general reserve based on "any potential loss," even while conceding that: "it is essentially impossible to predict with any degree of certainty what the eventual loss (if any) will be in regards to the Substandard/Doubtful items. . . ."

Recognizing the impossibility of even "predicting"—let alone reasonably estimating—their hypothetical "potential loss," the examiners suggested that a provision to the reserves be based on: ". . . an allocation factor based on historical precedent and current and future economic conditions."

The response went on to describe why various percentage-of-asset computations of general reserves were not appropriate given the nature of Lincoln's assets and the requirements of GAAP. The response argued that the only reasonable approach was to review Lincoln's total portfolio of assets on an asset-by-asset basis to determine whether "probable" losses existed. This was the approach that Lincoln used internally for financial-statement purposes. Annually, the reserves which Lincoln established were reviewed by its auditors, who either concurred with the reserves which Lincoln established or proposed increases or decreases in Lincoln's reserves as a result of their testing procedures.

Lincoln also addressed the assets that the examiners proposed to classify as loss. To start with, the examiners' findings had to be reduced by $3.915 million for assets which Lincoln had either sold or written off before June 30, 1988. The examiners' numbers had to be reduced by an additional $17.951 million for assets for which Lincoln had already recorded specific reserves. Of the remaining reserves ordered by the examiners, Lincoln agreed with $7.572 million and disagreed with $31.421 million.

Lincoln's arguments were that, for some assets, the examiners had used a method of determining loss which was inconsistent with the regulations. For others, Lincoln asserted that the examiners had had insufficient evidence to support any conclusion that loss was either probable or estimable. For example, Lincoln had appraisal data and other analyses related to the HPLP loan which indicated that the loss, if any, would be minimal on the loan. Also, certain of these assets had been the subject of the 1986 exam, and their condition, if anything, had improved, not declined, since that examination. Lincoln argued that the MOU foreclosed further consideration of these assets.

Lincoln also challenged some of the substandard and doubtful classifications. Lincoln believed that $353 million of the $706 million classified substandard should have been classified no worse than special mention. Lincoln asserted that an additional $232 million should not have been classified at all—not even special mention. Lincoln's primary contention was that the examiners had ignored the regulatory requirement which stated that a substandard asset must "exhibit a well-defined weakness based upon objective evidence."

Supporting Lincoln's contention was the asserted fact that Lincoln's files contained appraisals which indicated that the appraised value of the asset was in excess of its book value. The regulation provides that an asset should not be classified if the value of the collateral shows there is no likelihood of loss, even if the borrower fails to pay. That same logic applies to a real-estate investment where the appraised value of the property exceeds its book value. The examiners' classifications were largely based on their perception that there might be future market conditions which might adversely affect the asset. This was in spite of the fact that the examiners acknowledged that the current realizable value of the asset was in excess of its book value.

The substandard and doubtful classifications didn't have a direct effect on Lincoln's regulatory capital. But if the examiners' classifications were incorrect or inconsistent with the regulations, they colored the assessment of the risk which Lincoln presented to the FSLIC fund. It was this colored perception which had led Dochow and others, who had not seen the details of Lincoln's assets, to act as harshly as they had with their restrictive directives, their intention to consider a conservatorship, and their suggestion that Lincoln was undercapitalized relative to its risk profile. So, while these classifications didn't have a direct impact on Lincoln's capital requirement, the classification errors which Lincoln identified had a profound impact on how the senior FHLBB people viewed Lincoln. For that reason, Lincoln felt that it had to contest vigorously all of the classifications with which it disagreed.

The last section of Lincoln's response dealt with affiliated transactions and the examiners' assertion that ACC had dealt unfairly with Lincoln. The first issue addressed was the tax-sharing agreement. The response started by saying:

> It cannot be disputed that the FHLB-SF had full authority to approve the Agreement. . . . It cannot be disputed that the Agreement was submitted to FHLB-SF for approval, that it was apparent to any knowledgeable person that the Agreement on its face allowed deferred tax payments, and that FHLB-SF approved the Agreement after extensive consideration, negotiations, and revisions, including discussions of the specific points that the Examination Report now says were inappropriate. ACC and Lincoln relied on this approval for over two years and tax payments in excess of $94 million accordingly were made under the operating provisions of the Agreement. Moreover, under the

plan presented to the FHLBB [Lincoln had submitted a new agreement and a plan to the FHLBB before the response was written], by the end of 1989 any difference between what Lincoln paid to ACC under the Agreement and what Lincoln would have paid under the type of agreement now contemplated by the FHLBB would be eliminated, leaving the two companies in an equivalent position. Under these circumstances, retroactive nullification of the Agreement is an abuse of regulatory authority.

The response discussed in detail the discussions that Lincoln had had with Sidney Mar and Sonja Rodriguez regarding the agreement. The response said that in these conversations the FHLB-SF "advised Lincoln's personnel over the telephone of the *precise language* that would satisfy their concerns." It went on to say that only after these extensive conversations was the final Agreement submitted to Mar for approval. Having said this, the response stated:

> Thus, it is apparent from the history of the negotiations and from the plain language of the Agreement that was sent to, and approved by, the FHLB-SF, that anyone familiar with it must have known that the Agreement allowed deferred tax payments. In fact, the FHLB-SF focused on that precise issue. It is simply not credible to suggest otherwise, or to suggest improprieties in the "preparation and presentation" of the Agreement.

The response then addressed the actions which Dochow had taken to revoke the approval of the Agreement by stating, among other things:

> The PSA's claim that ACC should refund Lincoln's deferred taxes paid because of an unpublished General Counsel's opinion barring the payment of deferred taxes is especially unfair and contrary to law. The companies were unaware of this private ruling at the time they entered into the Agreement. Indeed, the FHLB-SF, too, apparently was unaware of this opinion—otherwise it would have disclosed the ruling to the companies. Moreover, to the extent that the FHLBB expected the General Counsel's opinion to be of general applicability, it was required under the Freedom of Information Act to publish that opinion in the Federal Register, which it did not. . . . To penalize the companies on the basis of this opinion would work a harsh and inequitable result not permitted by case law [the response cited the applicable case law].

The next subject which Lincoln addressed was the issue of the ESOP. The response made the following point, among others, regarding the ESOP:

> . . . The Examination Report's criticisms that Lincoln failed to receive regulatory approval for the ESOP—based on FHLBB General Counsel

opinions issued *after* the ESOP was created—are unwarranted and unfair. In foregoing regulatory approval, Lincoln relied, in good faith, on the opinion of respected counsel, which stated in a formal written opinion that such approval was unnecessary. . . . That firm reviewed the transaction on behalf of Lincoln and concluded, in a formal written opinion, that no regulatory approval was required for the pledge of Lincoln's assets, and the transaction did not violate the FHA [Federal Housing Act], the regulations of the FHLBB or the regulations of the FSLIC.

This was the second instance, the tax-sharing agreement being the first, where the examiners used unpublished, or later-issued, general counsel opinions to buttress their actions against Lincoln and ACC. There is absolutely no way that Lincoln or ACC could have known about these opinions. In that respect, these opinions are, or should have been, irrelevant.

It is clear that the examiners—Barabolak, Meek, and Newsome—were not experienced with or knowledgeable about ESOPs. These plans are not very widespread, especially leveraged plans, and it takes an expert in employee-benefit plans to understand the operations of an ESOP. Moreover, the examiners did not understand the sequence of the stock purchases made by the plan, even though they were provided with all of the relevant data, nor did they seem to care to understand the nature of the purchases. They focused solely on the fact that insiders had sold stock to the plan and were blind to whether those sales were beneficial to the plan and detrimental to the selling insiders. The examiners' myopic conclusion was that insiders had received cash from the stock sales to the ESOP, and somehow, to them, that seemed wrong.

The next issue addressed in the response was the matter of the Playtex and Memorex transactions. In both cases, Lincoln had received shares of stock in connection with its purchase of high-yield bonds. Lincoln sold these shares, in the case of Playtex, to ACC and, in the case of Memorex, to E.C. Garcia, a Lincoln borrower who also purchased assets from and sold various assets to Lincoln. Garcia later sold the shares, after the stock-market crash in 1987, to ACC. Months after ACC acquired the shares of both companies, it sold them at gains. The examiners contended that ACC had deprived Lincoln of its "corporate opportunity" to realize the gains which ACC had recognized. They ordered Lincoln to seek recovery of these gains from ACC. Lincoln's general response to the examiners' contentions was:

It is significant that the only basis for the Examination Report's conclusion that these transactions are unfair to Lincoln is the fact that ACC was able to sell the stocks for a higher price approximately nine months after purchase. It must be apparent that, unless there is evidence of unfairness at the time of the transaction, the fact that the price of the stock subsequently rose means nothing. Obviously, no one can know how a stock will trade after a particular sale. Indeed, there are numerous instances where ACC has obtained an asset from Lincoln and suffered a loss due to a subsequent decline in the value of that asset. For instance, ACC lost $1.85 million in connection with its purchase of Warnaco stock from Lincoln (sold by Lincoln for a $2.96 million gross profit), and ACC lost $2.078 million from its purchase of Edgecomb stock from Lincoln (sold by Lincoln for a $2.16 million gross profit). It is just as ludicrous to say that Lincoln took advantage of ACC in these situations as it is to say that ACC took advantage of Lincoln in the Playtex and Memorex transactions.

The response spent several pages on each transaction, providing details of the events surrounding each stock. The details chronicled the movements in each stock's price before and after the sale by Lincoln to ACC. All of this information had been supplied to the examiners, who refused to accept the fact that stocks do increase and decrease in price. Again, the examiners' view of the world was myopic and relied totally on hindsight.

The response then turned to the examiners' overall, broad accusation that ACC had operated Lincoln for its own benefit by siphoning funds out of Lincoln. The first point made was that the response had already demonstrated that the tax-sharing agreement, the ESOP, and the Playtex and Memorex stock transactions were not unfair. Lincoln believed that the information it presented and, indeed, the real facts surrounding each transaction proved the examiners' conclusion was without merit.

The examiners cited ACC's debt structure as a risk to Lincoln and indicated concern that ACC could not service its existing debt. The response took strong exception to these comments by the examiners. The position that Lincoln took on the issue of ACC's debt included the following:

ACC's financial performance has been skewed by the FHLBB's objection to Lincoln's payment of dividends. In approving ACC's application to become a savings and loan holding company, the FHLBB imposed the condition that without prior written approval from the FHLBB, dividends paid by Lincoln in any fiscal year would be limited to 50 percent of net income for that fiscal year, except that any dividends permitted under this limitation could be deferred and paid in a subsequent year (subject to the provision that no dividends [shall be paid] which in fact or in the opinion of the FHLBB would cause Lincoln to fail to meet its capital requirements). Earnings since acquisition total $206.1 million, with one-half totaling $103.1 million.

Despite the fact that Lincoln's capital position from February 1984 (when ACC acquired Lincoln) to date has always been in excess of required capital [accepting that Lincoln is correct regarding the examiners' findings] . . . Lincoln has only paid ACC a one-time dividend of $5 million. In the past, the

FHLBB has objected to the payment of even minimal dividends, despite ACC's right to such dividends. Lincoln and ACC have deferred to the FHLBB's wishes and these dividends have not been paid.

Under these circumstances, it is not surprising that the holding company, viewed in isolation from its principal subsidiary, has a high debt service. It does not take sophisticated financial analysis to conclude that if the holding company retains all of the liabilities, but is allowed none of the subsidiaries' income, its financial picture will be less than rosy. The simplest way to resolve that situation is to allow the subsidiary to make regular dividend payments to the parent. However, as discussed above, the FHLBB has consistently objected to Lincoln's payment of any dividends.

The situation described in the above section of the response is a good summary of why Charlie Keating was so frustrated with the circumstances that had surrounded him ever since ACC purchased Lincoln. He had caused ACC to purchase Lincoln because of the opportunities deregulation offered. He believed that he could direct Lincoln into profitable operations and lines of business. He was so convinced that Lincoln would be very profitable that he caused ACC to transfer all of its own operations into Lincoln. He even retained in ACC those expenses which he knew the FHLBB would object to—the aircraft operations, the salaries of his family members who worked in the business, and other expenses. He expected that, based on the approval which the FHLBB granted when ACC bought Lincoln, ACC would receive substantial annual cash dividends. These dividends would cover ACC's expenses, including its debt-service requirements. But his expectations were not met.

First, the FHLBB changed the required-capital rules, increasing the amount of capital which Lincoln had to maintain before it could pay any dividends. As shown in the response, Lincoln's added capital requirement, due to the contingency components related to the nature of the assets Lincoln held, was $87 million above the otherwise required amount. Second, the FHLBB examiners tried their damnedest to reduce Lincoln's capital through all kinds of appraisal losses and income reversals. Finally, even when Lincoln proved its capital was adequate, the FHLBB denied the payment of dividends.

Charlie felt that he was caught in an impossible situation. He was making the profits that he expected he would. That part of the strategy was working. But no matter how profitable he made Lincoln, he became convinced, by late 1988, that the FHLBB would do everything within its considerable power to retain every dime of earnings in Lincoln and permit no dividends to ACC. In his mind, this wasn't the deal he had made with the FHLBB in 1984.

The FHLBB consistently accused ACC and Lincoln of not having kept their word on ACC's plans for Lincoln. Charlie saw an opposite set of circumstances. He felt that the FHLBB never kept its word: it backed out of agreements; it didn't follow its own regulations; it leaked damaging information to the press; and it was conducting a vindictive, politically driven attack against him. Those were the reasons that made Charlie decide to sell Lincoln. And the irony of it all was that the FHLBB was now saying that it was ACC's own fault that its ability to service its debt was not as rosy as it might have been.

The response then talked about the examiners' accusations that ACC's purchases of treasury stock and the ESOP stock purchases constituted "market manipulation" and "insider trading." These serious charges started with Newsome and Barabolak and found their way into the Report of Examination. This was in spite of the fact that Lincoln and ACC provided the examiners with detailed information on every stock purchase, gave them the various filings the SEC required on insider purchases or sales, and even arranged for the examiners to talk with ACC's corporate-securities counsel. The pertinent portion of the response relating to these issues is:

> The material submitted by Lincoln [to the examiners and as attachments to the response] demonstrate that ACC consistently follows applicable SEC rules and regulations in timing its stock repurchases and ensures that its purchases of ACC stock have neither the effect or appearance of influencing the market. Insiders are not permitted to sell their holdings unless the company has been out of the market for a substantial period of time, thereby ensuring that company purchases will not affect insider prices. ACC consults outside counsel before purchasing insider stock and ensures that there are no material announcements forthcoming. These controls are designed to avoid both any impropriety or any appearance of impropriety.

The response then described, in detail, every major treasury-stock purchase made during 1985, 1986, 1987, and 1988. The details showed that ACC's purchases occurred only after ACC had been out of the market for a period of time. And in each case, the price paid was always below the high for the day and was usually the low for the day, and often for the month.

The treasury-stock purchases were based on ACC's board of directors' belief that ACC's stock was undervalued. The response stated: "ACC's Board believes that just a few investments have a value in excess of ACC's book value in the $150 million to $300 million range. Since ACC has currently outstanding approximately 16 million shares, these investments alone have an unrealized value resulting in an excess of $6.00 to $12.00 (after tax-effecting the excess) over the stock's per share current book value."

ACC believed that its stock purchases were timed to benefit all shareholders and to ensure an orderly market. In this regard, the response said the following:

> ACC has scrupulously followed Rule 10b-18's "safe harbor" provisions in repurchasing stock, which prevents the company from in any way leading the market in stock purchases. Pursuant to the rule, ACC never makes a bid for its stock within the first half hour the market is open, within the final half hour before the market closes, or at a price higher than the published bid or last sale price. Moreover, even in privately negotiated transactions, particularly with respect to insiders, the company always purchases on the bid, rather than the asked, side of the market.

Once again, as was the case with the stock purchased by the ESOP, it was Lincoln's contention that the examiners didn't understand the rules governing treasury-stock purchases, nor did they seem to care what those rules were. Neither did they analyze the details of the various purchases to satisfy themselves that the prices which ACC paid were consistent with the applicable rules. The examiners appeared to be driven by one overriding consideration—insiders had received money and, to them, lots of money for the stock they sold to ACC. This was all they needed to conclude that ACC's practices were wrong or, in their terminology, unsafe and unsound. The fact that ACC had complied with every law and regulation that it was required to follow was irrelevant.

The response then turned to the accusation that the transactions involving Lincoln and the Hotel Pontchartrain were improper. The relevant portions of the response were:

> ... The Examination Report, in a clear violation of the Memorandum of Understanding, rehashes an issue clearly raised and closed in the 1986 examination. Even worse, the Examination Report raises a new aspect of the affiliation issue by alleging that the HPLP is an affiliated person because of the role of Charles H Keating, Jr.—a fact which has been in existence since 1985, was fully known to the 1986 examiners, and was not mentioned in the 1986 examination. Moreover, the examiners' assertion that the HPLP is some kind of a "sweetheart deal," for the benefit of Lincoln's officers, directors, and borrowers and to the detriment of Lincoln itself, is entirely without foundation.
>
> Further, the Examination Report is in error in stating that the HPLP obtained an additional $20 million loan from Lincoln in December 1986 "in spite of the adverse comment noted in the March 1986 examination." In fact, the 1986 examination report was not received by Lincoln until April 1987—four months after the loan was made. To be sure, the loan is a separate transaction, which the examiners are entitled to review and, if warranted,

classify. However, the legal question of whether or not the HPLP is an affiliated person of Lincoln, as defined by the regulations, is not new; that issue was clearly covered by the 1986 examination and examination report—after a review of the list of limited partners and a conclusion that only Charles H. Keating III created an affiliated person violation—and therefore cannot be "rehashed" in the 1988 examination.

The FHLBB had to know all of the above before the examination report was even drafted. Their lawyers knew that Charlie wasn't an affiliated person under the regulations. They knew that the HPLP loan was made before the 1986 examination report was issued. They had to know that the serious allegations in the examination report were inappropriate and not defensible. Yet, they went ahead and accused and criticized Lincoln, using the harshest language, as if this was all some game they were playing. It probably never occurred to them that their game was damaging the reputations and fortunes of their targets, or, maybe, they just didn't care.

It was important to the examiners to find that HPLP was an affiliated person. That was the only way that any of the HPLP transactions could be placed under the rubric of unsafe and unsound. The FHLBB couldn't get there based on the economics of the whole deal, although they certainly tried to do so. The response addressed the idea that the HPLP transactions were only for the benefit of the limited partners—a cornerstone of the examiners' economic argument—as follows:

> The Examination Report fails to recognize the various fees and benefits that were anticipated to inure to the benefit of Lincoln and its subsidiaries. These fees total in excess of $2.5 million. In addition, the general partner, a subsidiary of Lincoln, was to receive 3.5 percent of gross receipts, 4 percent of net operating income, and 15 percent of net proceeds from any sale or refinancing. While it is true that the fees and income in the initial period did not achieve projections, such may be achievable in the future because of developments and improved position of the hotel. Furthermore, the prior projections of this income, fees and other benefits to Lincoln and its subsidiaries were based on reasonable expectations when made, and cannot be dismissed with 20/20 hindsight. Indeed, the examiners refer to the *projected* benefits to the limited partners as if already realized, but dismiss—for no reason—the equal or greater projected benefits due Lincoln and its subsidiaries.

The real question which the examiners failed to ask was: What would have been Lincoln's economic position had it not sold the hotel to HPLP? First, Lincoln would have absorbed the costs of renovation and all of the operating losses. Second, it may or may not have secured the $35-million first-mortgage loan from San Jacinto. Third, it most certainly would not have received the $10 million in cash that the limited partners paid it when it sold the hotel to HPLP. The bottom line is, had Lincoln not sold the hotel to HPLP, Lincoln could have had an additional $35 million of cash invested in the hotel and it wouldn't have received the $10 million it did receive—a $45 million swing. Given that, it's difficult to argue that Lincoln was mistreated in this entire situation. And that's exactly what Newsome was told when he first came to the cockamamie conclusion that Lincoln had been taken advantage of by HPLP.

The baseline position in the response was that Lincoln had clearly met its capital requirement—a requirement which already reflected its risk profile by virtue of the $87-million added contingency component. The computational errors made by the examiners were $106 million; additional substantive errors related to the income reversal were $31 million; the classification losses that Lincoln disagreed with were $31.5 million; and a minor correction to the contingency factor was $3.5 million, for a total of $172 million. The examination report indicated that Lincoln had failed its capital requirement by $114 million. With the corrections that Lincoln believed were appropriate, for all the reasons stated in its response, Lincoln had exceeded its capital requirement by $58 million.

If Lincoln was correct, and it certainly was on the vast majority of the issues, the directives were inappropriate, because Lincoln complied with the regulatory capital requirements. Moreover, the picture painted by the Examination Report was, if Lincoln's arguments were valid, a total distortion of Lincoln's true condition. The rub was that Lincoln's response went to the same people who wrote the Examination Report—not to an impartial third party who would sort out the facts and determine whether Lincoln or the examiners were correct in their views.

The Examination Report and Lincoln's response clearly demonstrate that after nearly three years of almost continuous examination, *the FHLBB had not discovered a single asset, with the arguable exception of the HPLP loan, which exhibited a loss for which Lincoln had not recorded reserves*. The FHLBB's entire attack against Lincoln and ACC was based on judgmental issues which had to be cloaked as unsafe and unsound practices in order to be asserted. The fact that an institution could be subjected to the treatment Lincoln received, when no losses in its operations or assets were disclosed, shows there was something terribly wrong with the regulatory system.

The Lincoln response was not the end of the examination-related matters which Lincoln had to contend with during this period of early 1989. Beginning in December, after the receipt of the Examination Report,

Lincoln started sending Dochow letters concerning the transactions that it was engaged in which were presumably covered by the directives. Lincoln had been advised by Kaye Scholer that the directives were probably neither binding nor enforceable. Nevertheless, with the sale of Lincoln pending and the fact that it required regulatory approval, Lincoln didn't want to upset Dochow.

So, Lincoln sent him letters almost every day outlining the various transactions. Lincoln indicated the date when each transaction was scheduled to close and said, in each cover letter, that if Lincoln hadn't heard from Dochow by the time each deal was to close, his silence would be considered acceptance of the transaction. This wasn't exactly what the directives called for, but Lincoln wasn't going to place itself in a position where closings were dependent on an affirmative response from Dochow. Lincoln's executives had seen enough bureaucrats to know that time was never of the essence in their eyes. They could procrastinate or intentionally stall until a deal fell through, and Lincoln was not about to let that happen.

On January 24, 1989, Lincoln, under the signature of Virginia Novak, an in-house attorney, sent Dochow a letter regarding a transaction with James C.V. Nalley III (Nalley) involving the Crowder Water Ranch. In 1986, Nalley had purchased an interest in the Crowder Water Ranch, paying $5 million in cash with the rest of the purchase price in the form of a $15-million interest-bearing note.

In January 1989, Nalley purportedly claimed that Charlie had told him at the time he purchased the interest in the water ranch that Lincoln was actively negotiating with a number of very interested cities who needed water and that a sale of Crowder would occur in a very short period of time. Based on this representation, Nalley believed that he would be in the Crowder deal for only a short period of time and that his money wouldn't be tied up for an extended period. Purportedly, he also learned that Lincoln had loaned monies to R.A. Homes, which was assembling a competing water ranch. So, in January 1989, Nalley apparently came to the conclusion that the pendency of the sale of Crowder had been misrepresented and that Lincoln was engaged in transactions which threatened to diminish the value of his investment. He purportedly threatened to file suit against Lincoln for the damages he believed he had suffered as a result of the misrepresentations and Lincoln's actions.

In order to avoid the threatened litigation, Lincoln began negotiating a settlement with Nalley. The settlement arrived at contained the following terms:

1. Lincoln would make a cash payment to Nalley in the amount of $7.5 million.
2. Lincoln would take Nalley's interest in Crowder, assuming Nalley's note.

3. Lincoln would receive a comprehensive release from Nalley for any and all claims against Lincoln.
4. Nalley would simultaneously repay all other debt to Lincoln, including accrued interest on that debt, amounting to approximately $3.2 million.

The settlement transaction was scheduled to close on January 25, 1989.

Any transaction involving the Crowder Water Ranch was complicated because of the uncertainty of Crowder's value. The estimated value of Crowder, as represented by appraisals and legal opinions, covered a wide range. The value was a function of how one viewed Arizona's ground-water laws combined with one's assessment of the quantity and availability of suitable water. Opinions on these variables were diverse and often contradictory. So, valuing Crowder was no simple matter.

As the settlement with Nalley was being negotiated, Lincoln wanted to know what the accounting for the transaction should be. We talked with the Touche partner assigned to the Lincoln account. We described the transaction to him. He said that the entire amount of the settlement should be added to the cost basis of Crowder, subject to the appraised or net realizable value of Crowder being sufficient to support the added amount. Concerned, because of the wide range of possible values, that there was a possibility that Touche might find the value of Crowder insufficient to support the entire settlement amount, we asked, if there were a necessity to recognize some loss, whether the loss would be reflected in 1988 or 1989. He answered that the transaction occurred in 1989, and any loss should be recorded in 1989, not 1988.

We confirmed the accounting with Touche several times. Each time, we got the same answer we had previously received. We showed so much concern about the accounting because we knew that the FHLBB would question whatever accounting treatment Lincoln afforded the transaction, and we wanted to be sure that Touche was comfortable with its position on the matter.

Dochow responded to Lincoln's letter regarding the Nalley settlement on February 6, 1989, nearly two weeks after Lincoln had written to him and after the settlement transaction had closed. His reaction was not favorable. His letter contained the following:

As a follow up to our letter of January 30, 1989, which expressed our concern about the lack of time this office has been given to review certain transactions, we wish to specifically note our distress over the January 25, 1989, transaction regarding the Crowder Water Ranch, as summarized in your January 24, 1989, correspondence. This office can not believe that such a material transaction involving the taking back of a $15 million note and paying out

$7.5 million in a cash settlement occurred on such a short notice. We consider the association's action to send us a notification the day before the transaction to be an act of bad faith. . . .

In regards to the Nalley settlement, you are to expense the entire settlement. Further, our files indicate that the association booked a profit of approximately $7.5 million on the 1986 sale, and there was some $2.5 million of accrued interest on the note as of June 30, 1988. The profit and the accrued interest is also to be reversed. In effect, the association is to record the property at its original book value before the sale, for the sale has been effectively reversed. . . .

In effect, Dochow was ordering Lincoln to record a $17.5-million loss as a result of the Nalley settlement. The FHLBB's view of the accounting for the transaction was clearly quite different from what Touche Ross thought was reasonable and appropriate. But given the past positions taken by the regulators, no one was very surprised by Dochow's letter. Lincoln had expected that the FHLBB's position would be the most extreme one possible.

On January 30, 1989, a letter bearing Dochow's signature was sent to Fred Martin of Touche. The letter was in response to Touche's letter of December 28, 1988, which addressed the errors made by the FHLBB's examiners when they computed Lincoln's capital requirement.

The first topic covered in Dochow's letter was the sale of the Crescent and Phoenician hotels. The letter said, in part:

. . . Your letter only addresses that portion that appears to have been allocated to the *Phoenician*, according to our files. Indeed, the total gain on the sale was $12.9 million, with $2.2 million deferred, as of June 30, 1987. The Report of Examination directed that $10.7 million be reversed, but we believe that the entire deferred gain may have been booked as income by September 30, 1988. Since the examination was as of July 11, 1988, the association was given the benefit of a doubt, and only the $10.7 million was used in the examination report. However, since we are now discussing the association's basis as of September 30, 1988, please be advised that the correct figure to be reversed is $12.9 million.

The FHLBB developed a theory that, in determining gain on the Crescent/Phoenician transaction, the proper calculation was to add the costs of the Crescent to the budgeted costs of the Phoenician to arrive at total cost. The amount of profit which could be recognized was then equal to the ratio of costs incurred to date to total expected costs. In effect, every dollar of cost incurred produced an equal amount of profit. This theory ignored any allocation of the total sales price which the KIO and Lincoln agreed to assign to the Crescent and the Phoenician during their negotiations. The FHLBB's theory appealed to O'Connell and others for essentially two reasons: (1) it was simplistic, and (2) it produced the result that O'Connell wanted—an income reversal. The only thing wrong was that the theory didn't reflect reality.

When the KIO bought the hotels, the Crescent was completed and open for business. The value added by the construction process was complete, and the KIO was willing to compensate Lincoln for having created that value. The Phoenician, on the other hand, was only about halfway done. The KIO was to contribute, in cash, the funds necessary to complete its percentage of the hotel. It was willing to compensate Lincoln for some of the value which had been added in the early stages of construction, but it wasn't going to pay Lincoln a profit on the value added by the KIO's own money—to do so would have made no sense at all. Thus, the profit was not the same on every dollar expended on the hotels. There was essentially *no* profit earned on the costs incurred *after* the KIO's investment. From the point when the KIO made its investment forward, Lincoln and the KIO were partners, and neither profited from the other. The FHLBB failed to understand this simple, but fundamental, economic point in the deal. They were so intent on developing a theory that gave them what they wanted that they couldn't see the forest because of all the trees.

But aside from the fact that their accounting theory failed to mirror economic reality, the issue of how the gain was apportioned between the amount which was recognized and the amount which was deferred was a moot point by September 30, 1988, the date of the FHLBB's net-worth calculation. By that date, the Phoenician was completed and *all* of the costs had been incurred. Even under their simplistic and misguided approach, all of the profit would have been recognizable by September 30, 1988. By analogy, this whole issue is akin to deciding how you slice a pie. Do you cut some pieces bigger than others or do you make them all the same size? The question of how big to make the slices becomes irrelevant if you eat the whole pie. That's what happened here. By September 30, 1988, Lincoln had eaten the whole pie, and the size of the slices (i.e., when it recognized each dollar of profit) no longer mattered.

In this letter to Touche, the persons who wrote the letter for Dochow to sign were either demonstrating mean-spiritedness, arrogance, an innate lack of common sense, or all three. The idea that any profit on this transaction should be reversed at September 30, 1988, defies logic, accounting theory, and common sense.

The next point addressed in the letter to Touche dealt with capitalized interest. The letter stated, in part:

> We have no need for further information on the capitalized interest issue at this time, as the amount in the supervisory letter was an estimate. However, please provide us with the specific amount of the difference in income after you have completed the necessary recalculations on all affected assets. As

noted in the examination report, one of the purposes of requiring capitalization at the average cost of funds is to reduce the basis of each asset, which in turn will reduce the sales price necessary to recover the investment in each asset. An aggregate adjustment based on the association's monthly reports is not acceptable. Further, our examiners limited their review to 1988 calculations. Other regulatory authorities may decide to revisit the association's calculations for prior years. Please note that if other regulatory bodies require a recalculation of the association's capitalized interest for prior years, such recalculations are also to be recorded in the Thrift Financial Reports provided this office.

The very first sentence in this comment notes that the FHLBB's order to Lincoln to reverse $15 million of capitalized interest was based on nothing more than a WAG (wild ass guess). It's uncertain who made the WAG, but indications are that this was O'Connell's doing.

The arrogance of the FHLBB is unmistakable in this paragraph. After admitting that their proposed adjustment to Lincoln's net worth was a pure WAG, they tell Touche that Lincoln must calculate the effects of the difference between the two capitalization rates on an asset-by-asset basis. As they put it: "An aggregate adjustment based on the association's monthly reports is not acceptable." It was acceptable for the FHLBB to order a $15-million reduction in Lincoln's net worth and to issue punitive directives based on a WAG, but Lincoln's use of an estimate was "not acceptable." The fact is, at the time of the examination, the FHLBB had all of Lincoln's records and had plenty of manpower to do a precise asset-by-asset calculation themselves, but they did not. Instead, they guessed. What was perfectly acceptable as a practice by the FHLBB is ordered as "not acceptable" for Lincoln.

The comment on capitalized interest again demonstrates the FHLBB's fundamental lack of business judgment and knowledge. They assert that their use of a lower capitalization rate was, "to reduce the basis of each asset, which in turn will reduce the sales price necessary to recover the investment in each asset." As stated earlier, a business has to establish its selling prices at a level that is high enough to recover *all* of its costs and expenses, whether capitalized or not, or it will suffer losses.

The FHLBB's perverted logic perhaps explains why the federal government has lost billions of dollars disposing of the assets it has confiscated from S&Ls. Its basic routine has been to order lowball appraisals, so it can justify writing down assets, thereby proving that the government acted properly when it seized the insolvent S&L. Once the assets have been written down to ridiculously low levels, the government then targets selling prices to recover the new appraised value which it has established. It considers itself successful if it comes close to obtaining those absurdly low values—and most often it hasn't. In fact, there have been numerous public reports in the media that the government has turned down some deals because the offered price *exceeded* their unrealistically low appraisals. The government—as evidenced by this letter to Touche—has no idea of how to run a business or competitively price an asset.

Finally, the FHLBB argued that Lincoln's capitalization rate was unsafe and unsound. If there was even a grain of truth in the assertion, the FHLBB examiners would have found losses—where the book values of the assets on which Lincoln capitalized interest exceeded their net realizable values—and would have proposed loss reserves. But the examiners, who were purportedly the FHLBB's best and brightest, did not propose reserves on a single real-estate project—not one. If the capitalization rate didn't lead to one thin dime of losses, how can it be unsafe and unsound? The answer is simple. The FHLBB's order to change the capitalization rate was arbitrary, not founded on either fact or rational theory, and was purely a punitive measure by unfair and biased regulators.

The letter to Touche then discussed Lincoln's capital requirement, with the following comments:

> The information in both your letter and the association's response regarding the association's capital requirements is inadequate. Although the figure of $244 million in our supervisory letter of December 20, 1988, was an estimate, it was an estimate based on the examination findings of a $210 million capital requirement as of June 30, 1988, plus changes in the association's balance sheet during the quarter ended September 30. Although we understand that the association now claims a maturity matching credit as of September 30, 1988, with an estimated benefit of $30 million according to the examination report, the manner in which the association qualified for that credit was by adding another $640 million in land loans in the three months ended September 30. The contingency factor on such loans virtually eliminated the benefit of the maturity matching credit. Therefore, our estimate gave little net effect to the maturity matching credit. In order to reconcile our differing calculations, we need the specifics of the association's capital requirement calculations. . . .

Once again the FHLBB admits that the real problem was that they have used an estimate rather than taking the care and time to make a bona-fide calculation of Lincoln's requirement based on fact and not assumptions. Had anybody taken the time to discuss the maturity-matching credit and land-loan issue with Steve Scott, he could have told them that he was the FHLBB person who had advised Lincoln on the matter. Lincoln followed Scott's precise instructions and had his prior approval for the way it treated the loans and the related credit. Because the FHLBB people in

Washington made the estimate, and didn't have real knowledge of Lincoln's transactions, they made erroneous assumptions. Even though they had no facts in their possession and never made an actual net-worth-requirement calculation for Lincoln, just an estimate, this didn't stop them from saying that Touche Ross' letter and Lincoln's response, both of which were predicated upon fact, not assumption, were "inadequate." They were arrogant enough to contend that their estimate was superior to calculations that were factual.

Peter Fishbein talked to the FHLBB people in early January about relaxing the directives they had imposed on Lincoln. The basic arguments were that the directives were not specifically permissible under the regulations and, by their very nature and the manner in which they were imposed, deprived Lincoln of the protection offered by due process. Further, Lincoln contended that the directives, if followed to the letter, made it virtually impossible to conduct an orderly and profitable business. The regulators agreed to look into the matter.

On February 3, 1989, Dochow sent Lincoln a letter with an "Interim Agreement" attached. The cover letter stated:

> You will note that the provisions of the interim Agreement differ substantially from those proposed by your outside counsel, Peter Fishbein. The Agreement reflects our heightened concerns with the financial condition of Lincoln Savings, its relationship with American Continental Corporation, and the safety and soundness of its operations.
>
> I would like to give you my preliminary opinion that the proposed sale of Lincoln is a marginal transaction, at best. I am concerned with the management capacity of the proposed acquirers, the viability of the institution, and the method of financing the capital infusion. As a result of those concerns, I consider it highly unlikely that the transaction can be processed expeditiously, as we originally contemplated. I urge you to give serious consideration to finding another acquirer.

The attached Interim Agreement was, in effect, a consent C&D. One of the opening "Whereas" clauses indicated the basis on which it was being presented to Lincoln by stating: ". . . Lincoln and ACC are willing to consent to such restrictions . . . in consideration for forbearance by FSLIC and FHLBB not to litigate an administrative cease and desist order against them for the matters set out below for as long as Lincoln is in compliance with the provisions of this agreement." The Interim Agreement then detailed all of the conditions with which Lincoln had to comply. These conditions were even more onerous than the previous directives which Dochow had ordered. The Agreement closed by stating: "Lincoln and

ACC waive the issuance of a Notice of Charges and the right to an administrative hearing prior to the execution of this Interim Agreement and agree not to challenge the validity of the agreement itself in any later action to enforce it."

Dochow had taken leave of his senses if he actually thought anyone at either ACC or Lincoln would agree to sign this Agreement. Lincoln had filed a detailed response to the Examination Report which rebutted, with factual evidence, virtually every one of the examiners' findings and conclusions. Lincoln believed that it had shown, beyond the shadow of a doubt, that it had met its capital requirements. It believed that it had presented irrefutable factual evidence that the transactions between Lincoln and ACC were not unfair, under any definition, to Lincoln. It also was convinced that it had demonstrated that the examiners had improperly classified its assets and, in so doing, had inappropriately portrayed the risk profile of Lincoln. It was now obvious that Dochow was not going to give any currency to Lincoln's response and that he was sticking with his examiners, even if they were dead wrong.

Lincoln wasn't going to sign a consent C&D. It would be stupid to do so. The only hope that Lincoln had, at this point, was that the FHLBB would take actions that forced the issues into the courts, where Lincoln could prove the exam was fatally flawed. In a court, Lincoln could demonstrate that the FHLBB had repeatedly abused its regulatory authority and had breached the MOU. In this sense, Lincoln and ACC welcomed the prospects of confronting the FHLBB in court. The downside was that Dochow appeared to be using the whole process to scuttle the sale of Lincoln to the Spencer Scott Group. This meant that Charlie had to try to find another qualified buyer who was willing to purchase Lincoln under threatening circumstances. That would not be easy.

On February 9, 1989, for reasons which are still unknown to me, Charlie issued a press release on the pending sale of Lincoln to the Spencer Scott Group. Maybe he wanted to put pressure on either Dochow or the short-sellers of ACC's stock. Or maybe he was just frustrated by the letters he had been getting from Dochow. I don't know. In any event, the press release was headed, "Closing of Lincoln Savings Sale Is Imminent." The first paragraph contained: ". . . [T]he sale of Lincoln Savings and Loan to an investment group headed by Spencer Scott of California is proceeding smoothly and is expected to be completed sooner than originally anticipated."

There was no way the sale's closing was "imminent." Dochow was telling Lincoln he didn't think chances of approval were favorable. The Spencer Scott Group had been asked repeatedly whether they had raised the necessary money. Their answers were not encouraging. They continued to say that Drexel was going to do the deal, but people within Drexel were not making any commitments; in fact, they were saying that it was unlikely they would do a deal with the boys. Spencer Scott also said that Merrill Lynch had shown a strong interest, but Lincoln couldn't get any confirmation from Merrill Lynch. They'd also said that the Bank of Bahrain was interested. None of this sounded like they were even close to raising the money. All we heard from the boys was "not to worry, we'll get the money." But my perception was that everyone was worried that the boys didn't have the remotest idea of how to come up with the required money.

Charlie did have a conversation with Don Hovde, a former FHLBB Board member, who had talked with someone—believed to be Smuzynski—who had essentially told him the deal was on track. Apparently Hovde had been told there were only two remaining problems. First, the application was incomplete, and some additional data was still necessary. Second, there were some concerns about the financing.

Charlie also had several conversations with Dochow between the time that he received the February 3 letter and the date of the press release. It is possible that in one of these conversations Dochow told Charlie something that led Charlie to believe that the sale to the Spencer Scott Group was moving along and that Dochow's earlier concerns had been reduced or eliminated.

Peter Fishbein was out of the country when the press release was issued. But Karen Katzman and Lynn Fisher reacted quickly. They basically demanded that an amended press release be issued which clarified that there were still many things that had to happen before a sale could be concluded. That was done on February 10, 1989. Still, the original press release caused quite a flap with the SEC and the FHLBB. The amended release calmed things down but did not completely erase the bad taste that the original release had left at the SEC and elsewhere.

On February 13, 1989, both Lincoln and ACC were notified that the FHLBB would be starting new exams beginning the next day, the 14th. The expressed purpose of the exams was to look into the compliance with the directives. But, since the real purpose was to prepare for a conservatorship, the letter cleverly said that the exam was "not limited to" the matters specifically stated in the notification letter.

This time around, Lincoln and ACC were not inclined to be very cooperative. It was clear that the examiners were going to find it easier to pull hen's teeth than to get the information they wanted on a timely basis. They were the lowest priority on everyone's list of things to do.

The SEC discovered a gold mine in the persons of Stelzer, Newsome, O'Connell, and Larson, among others at the CDSL and the FHLBB.

Normally, if the SEC wanted to obtain information and documents concerning ACC, it would have to issue a subpoena to ACC. But a coalition developed between mid-level bureaucrats at the SEC and mid-level folks at both the CDSL and the FHLBB. They talked to each other, met, and exchanged information and theories.

Their discussions ultimately focused on a series of sales of land in Lincoln's Hidden Valley project, which was a part of Estrella. Lincoln had entered into other transactions, either purchases of assets or lending transactions, with the buyers of the Hidden Valley land which occurred in close proximity to the sale of the land. In each case, after making a series of assumptions, these people concluded that Lincoln had provided the buyer with all of the funds that the buyer used to purchase the land in Hidden Valley. In virtually every instance, they concluded that there was no evidence that the buyer used its own money for either the down payment or interest payments on the loans.

These assumptions led them to the overall conclusion that the sales were fraudulent and, as such, were improperly recorded on Lincoln's books. They also believed that the heart of the scheme was to allow the transfer of 40 percent of the improperly recorded earnings to ACC in the form of the tax-sharing payments. These people had some of the facts straight regarding these sales, but not most of them. There were just enough, however, to plant suspicions in their minds—suspicions which resulted in their theory being built upon and embellished over the months and years to come.

The examiners had developed many other theories which caused transactions to be regarded as improper or fraudulent—tax sharing, the Wolfswinkle equity kicker, capitalized interest, the HPLP loan, and the KIO sale, to name a few. In all of those cases, Lincoln and ACC had a chance to rebut the allegations. But this would not be the case with their Hidden Valley theory. The theory was never presented to Lincoln for rebuttal. The theory was hatched and nurtured without ACC or Lincoln ever being able to offer explanations for the assumptions these people made.

The Hidden Valley theory marks the start of the fall of Charlie Keating. This collection of bits of data, assumptions, suspicions, and speculation was latched onto by a gaggle of lawyers and prosecutors who were in search of a case to be made against Keating.

The examiners returned to Lincoln and ACC on the 14th of February as Dochow had promised. They immediately flooded Lincoln's people with voluminous requests for information. They were told that they would receive it whenever someone had a chance to deal with them and that that might not be for some time. They were told that they could cool their heels and sooner or later—probably later—they would be given the data they had requested. This prompted an immediate letter to Lincoln which said that Lincoln had better cooperate or the examiners would be forced to use estimates rather than actual data. Lincoln's attitude was: Hell, that's what you'll do anyway, just look at the last exam. Dochow's threats had lost much of their sting because there had been so many of them that Lincoln was building up an immunity to his saber rattling and almost welcomed an all-out confrontation that would wind up in court. Then, finally, Dochow and the FHLBB might have to observe some rules and follow due process.

One thing did happen with the examiners. On February 16, Steve Scott and some of the examiners sat down with Lincoln's regulatory accountants and Touche Ross and went over Lincoln's capital computations. Steve Scott concluded, as did the other examiners who were with him, that Lincoln's calculation was correct. At this point, the FHLBB had been told by Lincoln, Touche Ross, and Steve Scott that the numbers in the examination report were bogus, but Smuzynski and O'Connell were still waiting for more "verification." It also didn't really matter if Lincoln was, in fact, correct. The FHLBB had made up its collective mind that it was going to establish a conservatorship, and Dochow could simply rule that some other element of Lincoln's calculation was not permissible. By the time Lincoln could protest Dochow's ruling, it would be too late, as Lincoln would have been taken over.

By the middle of February, it was painfully obvious to ACC and Lincoln that litigation, or worse, evolving out of the 1988 examination was only a matter of time. It was therefore deemed prudent to establish a written record of what had occurred—a record which could be used in future litigation. This was ACC's and Lincoln's last-gasp attempt to force some reason into Dochow and his cohorts. To this end, Peter Fishbein wrote a letter to Dochow to summarize Lincoln's view of the events that had occurred.

Fishbein's letter addressed each piece of significant correspondence that Lincoln or ACC had received from the FHLBB beginning with the December 20 letter and the supervisory directives. In each instance, Fishbein pointed out the inappropriateness of the FHLBB's actions and the fact that the FHLBB had ignored all of the factual data which Lincoln or ACC had offered in rebuttal of the FHLBB's various assertions and actions.

The following excerpt is representative of the content of the Fishbein letter to Dochow:

> The only purported statutory or regulatory basis for imposing the severe operating restrictions set forth in the Interim Agreement is Lincoln's alleged capital inadequacy. That inadequacy does not exist, as already explained.

Moreover, the Interim Agreement requires Lincoln to reverse retroactively its tax sharing agreement with ACC and to "reflect the losses, income reversals and classifications" cited in the Examination Report without any reference to Lincoln's detailed substantive answer to these points as set forth in the Response. This is a clear violation of the MOU.

Most disturbing, the Interim Agreement requires Lincoln to accede to many FHLBB positions which it strongly believes are in error without any of the procedural due process set forth in the FHLBB's regulations. Notwithstanding that Lincoln does not view the Supervisory Directives as binding, Lincoln recognizes that the FHLBB has statutory and regulatory authority (in addition to its authority to address a failure to meet regulatory capital requirement) under which it could attempt to restrict the operations of an insured institution. No such authority was cited, however, anywhere in the Supervisory Directives, the Interim Agreement, or the February 3, 1989, letter. Moreover, if the FHLBB had attempted to act pursuant to such other laws and regulations, Lincoln would have access to certain procedural protection that would have permitted it to present its case before any restrictions could be imposed. Your demand that Lincoln execute the Interim Agreement ignores the existence of those procedural protections and the Interim Agreement itself, at paragraph 13, includes an express waiver by Lincoln of any right to challenge the validity of the Agreement in any subsequent enforcement action. Execution of the Interim Agreement, therefore, would deprive Lincoln of its entitlement to be heard with respect to the proposed restrictions and your erroneous underlying factual claim.

The opportunity to be heard is of particular importance to Lincoln, given its grave concerns about the fairness of the examination process and your continued failure to comply with the terms of the MOU. Lincoln is especially troubled not only by your failure to reply to the Response but also by the continued involvement in the examination process of Kevin O'Connell of your office, whose clear conflict of interest was the basis of Lincoln's previous requests that he be removed and your assurances that he would be removed.

Fishbein's letter to Dochow demonstrates the depth of the gulf which existed between the FHLBB and ACC/Lincoln. The FHLBB was proposing, in effect, a consent cease-and-desist order, at a minimum, and was threatening worse. Lincoln and ACC, on the other hand, firmly believed that they had met all regulatory requirements and that the FHLBB had breached its contractual obligations under the MOU and had abused its regulatory authority. Lincoln, via Fishbein's letter, offered to sit down and resolve the differences between the parties, as, indeed, the MOU required them to do. But the FHLBB simply dug in its heels and began to pursue stronger measures with even greater resolve.

The situation between the two parties was now more strained than it had ever been in the past. The FHLBB was killing Lincoln with the pens which were in the hands of the examiners. Each of their orders to Lincoln to reduce its capital and each directive was another wound that Lincoln had to bear. Something had to give, or Lincoln would not survive the FHLBB's unrelenting attacks.

Charlie believed that the only real solution was for ACC to sell Lincoln—and fast—before the FHLBB did something really stupid, causing everyone untold grief. The sale of Lincoln remained the number one priority.

Sixteen

ACC Raises White Flag

By mid-February, it was evident that the sale to the Spencer Scott Group was dead. They had not raised the necessary funds to close the deal, and, despite their optimism and reassurances that "the money will be there," there wasn't one chance in a million that they would succeed. They had until the end of February to close the transaction. If a closing didn't occur by then, the deal was off and the contract became null and void.

The indications from Dochow and others in Washington were not encouraging either. The start of another examination was a bad sign. Honest, concerned regulators would have given serious consideration to Lincoln's response. The response was not a shrill protestation that was long on rhetoric and short on fact. It presented easily verifiable factual information.

If Dochow had been conscientious and objective, he should have compared what his troops had documented to what Lincoln was asserting. He should have tried to determine whether something had been overlooked by the people in the field and their supervisors in Washington. And he should have become personally involved. As it was, Dochow, himself, had never seen any of the assets that were being criticized, nor had he asked to look at any detailed records, documents, or correspondence supporting the questioned transactions. Instead, he was satisfied to rely on what others told him, and he appeared to ignore any input from Lincoln.

Given the collapse of the Spencer Scott sale and Dochow's attitude, we were convinced that another buyer had to be found for Lincoln—and fast. We believed that the feds would make a stronger move against Lincoln as soon as the examiners had gathered enough data to weave a credible tale to justify their planned actions. The new examination team members, aside from Steve Scott, were cynical and sarcastic. They didn't request information; they demanded it. They were looking for very specific information that would support their view of Lincoln, and they were not open-minded. It was merely a question of how long it would take them to fabricate their case. Then, the axe would swing on ACC and

Lincoln. A buyer had to be found before the axe came down.

One possibility that we explored was for the ESOP to buy Lincoln. Lincoln would then be wholly owned by its employees. There were three elements to an ESOP transaction. First, ACC would convert most of the Lincoln common stock which it held into perpetual, preferred stock. Second, the ESOP would exchange the ACC stock which it held for all of the remaining Lincoln common stock held by ACC. Third, the ESOP would borrow additional funds to acquire newly issued Lincoln common stock. These three steps would eliminate ACC as Lincoln's parent by removing all voting rights and common-stock ownership from ACC. The leveraging of the ESOP would provide Lincoln with additional capital. ACC and Keating would be removed and Lincoln's capital enhanced.

The initial reactions of Lincoln's and ACC's lawyers to this transaction were favorable. The ESOP's trustees were not opposed to such a transaction. But we hit a snag when the lawyers who specifically handled the ESOP were consulted. They were not negative to the transaction but said approvals were needed from several governmental agencies other than the FHLBB and CDSL. Filings would have to be made with both the U.S. Department of Labor and the IRS. These filings would be extensive, in terms of the paperwork, and an appraisal of the value of Lincoln's common stock by an acceptable, qualified, independent investment banker would be necessary.

This was bad news. Appraising the value of Lincoln would be difficult, if not impossible, given Lincoln's status with the regulators. The process could take months before Lincoln would know whether these agencies would approve an ESOP transaction. Lincoln didn't have the luxury of being able to wait for the process to run its course. Dochow and his group would probably act before a long approval process could be completed.

There was an interim step which could be taken. A group of employees could buy Lincoln. Later, when there were no time pressures, the ESOP could seek the requisite approvals and, if successful, acquire ownership from the initial employee-purchasers. If the ESOP transaction could not be structured, the employee-purchasers could transform Lincoln into a more traditional operation and, once the transformation was completed, could sell the association to other investors who could operate Lincoln for the longer term.

Charlie asked me if I would be willing to put a group together to buy Lincoln from ACC. I was candid with him. Operating Lincoln was not something I wanted to do. But I told Charlie I would study the situation. If the numbers worked, I would put together a workable solution.

First, I obtained all of the projections that Touche Ross had helped the Spencer Scott Group prepare. I had seen most of these projections before but frankly hadn't paid much attention to them. As I dug into the assumptions upon which the projections were based, I found that I agreed with some of them, but many others were unrealistic. Thus, I found it necessary to analyze all of Lincoln's operations, as well as the assets it held, in order to develop more reliable assumptions on which to base the projections.

After completing a thorough analysis of each major area of Lincoln's operations, I addressed the appropriateness of my starting point. Touche Ross had been performing its audit procedures for about three months. I wanted to know whether they had identified any losses which my own review had not disclosed. Along with Andy Ligget, I had a conversation with their lead partner. I told him that I noticed that in all of the projections which they had prepared for Spencer Scott, Touche had started with Lincoln's book net worth. I asked whether Touche's audit had disclosed any problems which made it inappropriate for me to use the book number. In other words, I asked: Has Touche found any areas where Lincoln will be asked to post adjustments which will reduce its net worth below the amount currently recorded on its books?

The partner said that there were still many areas the auditors needed to address, but, based on what they had seen to date, it would be appropriate to use the book figures. He was hedging by saying, in effect, "We don't know of any adjustments right now, but we might have some later." Since Touche should have been well along in its audit, this was encouraging. If he had identified a number of potential adjustments, I would have been concerned about having missed something, but he hadn't. Therefore, I felt comfortable that I had a good starting point.

The terms of the purchase also had to be determined. The logical place to start was with the Spencer Scott deal. That transaction had been agreed to by two independent, unrelated parties. The only problems that Dochow had raised about the transaction were concerns about the management capabilities of the Scott Group and their ability to finance the transaction. Any new group would change the proposed management of Lincoln, and I thought that it was possible to infuse the same amount of cash into Lincoln which had been contemplated by Spencer Scott and his people. If any of the terms of the Scott deal were altered, the FHLBB would assert that the deal was less than arm's length. On the other hand, if the terms of the Scott deal were used, as is, that concern should be eliminated. So, I decided to go with the Spencer Scott deal as it was originally structured. The only changes would be those that the FHLBB might insist upon before they would grant approval.

The Scott transaction increased Lincoln's revenues and cash flow. ACC was taking out the hotels and GOIL in exchange for interest-bearing notes. The annual interest revenue produced by these notes was about $40 million. Lincoln would have to pay dividends on the preferred stock that it issued in the amount of about $32 million a year, assuming the cash infused into Lincoln was also represented by preferred stock.

The accounting for the purchase would result in substantial goodwill. The discounting of both Lincoln's assets and liabilities produced goodwill in the $350-million range. When added to the goodwill already on Lincoln's books, total goodwill exceeded $450 million. This was only a problem with respect to certain of the regulations which were based on tangible net worth and required the subtraction of goodwill from book net worth. Following the purchase accounting, Lincoln's tangible net worth would be a substantial negative number. But the situation was no different from that which existed in any purchase of a savings and loan association, including FSLIC-assisted deals which had taken place in Texas and elsewhere. The FSLIC and the FHLBB could waive the tangible-net-worth requirement, as they had for other purchasers.

The numbers indicated that for the first three years, Lincoln would have substantial earnings, averaging over $50 million a year, and would meet its dividend requirements. If interest rates dropped, earnings would be even greater. For example, for each percentage point that general interest rates dropped, Lincoln's net income would increase by more than $25 million. The annual cash flow was also equal to, or greater than, the earnings numbers. The FHLBB said that Lincoln's earnings were "paper profits," but these projections indicated that the criticism would not apply to the proposed operations of the new Lincoln. The numbers indicated that the deal, as structured, was economically feasible.

The next step was to identify those people who should be part of a buying group. The Keating family, Judy, and Bob Kielty were automatically eliminated, as they wanted to stay with ACC. Moreover, the FHLBB would never approve a deal if any of these people remained, even remotely, connected to Lincoln. Therefore, I focused on three people: Ron Stoll, David Thompson, and Randy Conte.

Ron Stoll is an experienced and extremely competent real-estate lawyer. He was familiar with all of Lincoln's major lending and real-estate assets, as he had drafted many of the purchase or sale contracts and loan documents. He also has good business judgment and, to my knowledge, was in good standing with the regulators. He had good managerial potential, as he is logical, unemotional, unflappable under pressure, and can clearly communicate the objectives that he wants his subordinates to achieve. He could oversee the lending and real-estate operations of the new Lincoln.

David Thompson is an attorney who, after Mark Sauter's departure, had handled Lincoln's regulatory reporting requirements. We needed someone who could deal with regulatory issues, especially if we had to restructure or modify any loans. David could also oversee some of the administrative functions of Lincoln, such as employment and payroll matters.

Randy Conte had been in charge of Lincoln's loan servicing and was familiar with all of the borrowers' current financial conditions and their payment patterns. He was also knowledgeable about the files and records related to the investment portfolio. He was already effectively managing a fair number of people and demonstrated a capacity to take on expanded responsibilities. As an added plus, Randy had a good relationship with the field examiners from both the CDSL and the FHLBB.

I approached each of these people and explained what I was planning and asked them to become a part of an effort to buy Lincoln. Each spent some time delving into the projections and underlying assumptions before committing to the join the effort. Each decided to participate.

David Thompson and Ron Stoll immediately started to put together the application which had to be filed with the FHLBB. They also started to draft the various transactional documents to issue stock, to convey the assets to and from ACC, and to effect the other elements of the purchase. We knew that we didn't have a lot a time and had to move rapidly, as the clock was winding down.

The next big issue that we addressed was raising the necessary capital for the new Lincoln. The logical party to contact was the Trump Group. They had done extensive due-diligence work on Lincoln and had decided not to try to buy the association because of the strain it would place on their management team. If we could convince them that we could effectively manage Lincoln, they might be willing to be the equity partner in the deal. Also, Charlie had talked to them about ACC potentially buying one of their subsidiaries as part of Charlie's plan to recapitalize ACC. The Trump Group had a subsidiary whose primary asset was cash that had been raised by the issuance of long-term debt. If ACC acquired the subsidiary, it could use the cash to service its shorter-term debt, buying time to increase its own internal cash flow.

On March 4, 1989, a group of us flew to New York to meet with Eddie and Julius Trump. Charlie and others were going to discuss ACC's possible acquisition of the Trump Group's subsidiary. Ron Stoll, David Thompson, Randy Conte, and I were going to attempt to get the Trump Group to commit to financing the Lincoln acquisition. During the trip to New York, Charlie agreed that ACC would commit, as part of the deal, to purchase an additional $15 million of Lincoln's preferred stock. This left $35 million to raise from the Trumps.

Charlie also wanted us to consider adding another member to our buying group. He suggested John Rousselot, a former congressman from California who had headed up an S&L lobbying organization after he left

Congress. Charlie felt that we should make Rousselot the chairman of the new Lincoln's board. He believed that Rousselot had good connections in Washington and that his presence would offset the fact that the rest of the group had all worked for ACC or Lincoln.

When we arrived at the Trump Group's offices, we decided that the first topic should be the financing of the Lincoln acquisition. If we couldn't buy Lincoln, it didn't make sense for ACC to buy the subsidiary the Trumps wanted to sell because ACC might not survive the FHLBB's assault on Lincoln. Because of the difference in time zones, it was already late in the day when we started to talk. We first briefed Eddie and Julius Trump on Lincoln's status vis-à-vis the regulators. We went over the entire history of the conflict and didn't pull any punches. The picture we painted of Lincoln's regulatory situation was a bleak one. But we also presented our views on how Lincoln could be restructured. We told them that with a couple of years to achieve the transformation, Lincoln could become a very marketable association. We went over our projections and the proposed transaction to buy the association from ACC.

During the presentation, we were subjected to a constant barrage of questions from the two Trump brothers. Because of the due-diligence work their staff had done a few months earlier, they were familiar with many of Lincoln's attributes. So, their questions were very direct and pointed.

We started this combination presentation and question-and-answer session about four o'clock in the afternoon and concluded after ten o'clock in the evening. After Eddie and Julius Trump appeared to have exhausted all of their questions, it was decided that Julius and the Trumps' attorneys would go with the members of the buying group to another room where we could hash out the details of the Trump Group's investment, if any. In the meantime, Charlie and the ACC people would remain with Eddie, so they could start talking about the subsidiary that the Trump Group wanted to sell to ACC.

The first issue to settle with Julius was the amount of the investment. We started by asking for a minimum of $50 million, and, as I recall, he countered with about $15 million. After some discussion, we agreed on $35 million, the minimum we needed to make the deal work. The issue then became the form of the investment.

Julius suggested a debt instrument. We told him that we needed an equity security if the investment was to qualify as regulatory capital. He then asked us to give them common stock. We told him that we would, but it meant that the Trump Group would have to file a change-of-control application with the FHLBB and to go through the process of being vetted by Dochow and his troops. Julius didn't want any part of that process, so we ended up with a preferred-stock investment.

We then addressed the characteristics of the preferred stock. Julius wanted to be in a preference position, with respect to both dividends and liquidation. That was acceptable. It meant that all of ACC's preferred stock would be junior to that which the Trumps would receive. We then talked about the dividend rate. We said that it should be the same as all of the other classes of preferred. That wasn't acceptable to Julius. He wanted a premium rate. As a compromise, we agreed that the annual dividend rate would be the same as the rate on all other issues but that the Trumps' shares would receive a participating dividend upon any sale of the common stock. If we sold the common shares of Lincoln, they would receive 25 percent of the gain. We also agreed that we would not declare any dividends on the common shares. Any gain which we, as the common shareholders, received from our investment in and management of Lincoln, except for reasonable salaries, would come solely from the eventual sale of Lincoln. That way, even though the Trump shares were nonvoting, preference shares, they shared in any gain that we realized.

Finally, we needed two things from the Trump Group. First, we needed a firm, irrevocable, commitment letter. Second, we needed a letter from their bank stating that the Trump Group had $35 million of uncommitted, unencumbered funds on deposit, combined with a commitment that these funds would remain on deposit and available as long as the investment commitment was in effect. Julius agreed to this. Reluctantly, we added that we needed both letters by the next day. As we explained to Julius, we didn't want to file anything with Dochow which left open any questions regarding the firmness of the financing. This was what had been used, in part, to blow the Spencer Scott deal out of the water, and we didn't want it to be the case with our transaction. He agreed that he could provide those letters by the next day.

By the following afternoon, we had everything we needed. We had a verification letter from the bank stating that the funds were on deposit and were available. We had the commitment letter from the Trump Group which was effective for two weeks. After that, we had to secure extensions on a day-by-day basis. We also completed the descriptions of the preferred stock and gave the Trumps a letter committing to issue the described security.

That evening, March 5, we flew to Washington, and the buying group, now known as Lincoln Savings Acquisition Corporation (LSAC), met John Rousselot and Jim Grogan for dinner. This was the first time that any of the four of us had met Rousselot. John fulfilled my image of a politician. He is a loud, boisterous, out-going, hail-fellow-well-met guy, with an aggressive, let's-get-to-the-point style. But when we began to explain the transaction, his eyes glazed over, and his attention started to wander. All he wanted to know was: How much money do I need to put in the deal, what do you want me to say to the regulators, and when do we close?

John's question—How much money do I need to put in the deal?—was an interesting one. The Spencer Scott Group had planned to buy the common stock for $100,000. The rest of the invested funds, from whatever source, were going to be for preferred shares. We stuck with the same deal. As it stood, the five of us, including Rousselot, would contribute a total of $100,000.

One might conclude that $100,000 wasn't much of a commitment on our part. We were willing to put in all the work necessary to manage Lincoln effectively. We were also willing to accept less compensation than we had been receiving for that effort. But given the attitudes of the FHLBB people, and their disregard for ACC's investment in Lincoln, we were not willing to risk the capital that we had earned during our careers.

On the morning of March 6, 1989, the five of us along with Charlie, Grogan, and C-III met with the FHLBB staff. The FHLBB was represented by Dochow, Smuzynski, Hershkowitz, O'Connell, and Julie Williams, a lawyer with the FHLBB's corporate-finance group. Charlie started by telling Dochow that the five of us had stepped into the Spencer Scott Group's shoes and were presenting an application to buy Lincoln in a transaction that was structured almost the same as the Scott transaction. He told Dochow that the financing was in place and that both ACC and LSAC were ready to close—all we needed was FHLBB approval.

At that point, David Thompson took over and summarized the proposed transaction. He gave Dochow the commitment letters covering the $35 million from the Trump Group and the $15 million from ACC. He said that all of the definitive agreements and documents were either drafted or were being drafted and that they would be submitted as amendments to the application. He also provided a copy of the LSAC business plan and accompanying projections. We had also received a letter from Fred Martin, a Touche partner, expressing Touche's opinion that the transaction, as structured, was a purchase and that purchase accounting applied.

The components of the new Lincoln's capital structure were $288 million of new preferred stock to be issued for the Lincoln common stock which ACC held; $15 million of new preferred to be issued to ACC for cash; $10 million in existing preferred which ACC held and would leave in Lincoln; $35 million in senior preferred to be issued to the Trump Group for cash; and the $100,000 in cash that we would contribute for the new common stock. This resulted in total capital of $348 million.

ACC would purchase GOIL, the hotels, and the Phoenician lots for a total of $428 million in notes. The FHLBB would therefore have to waive the loans-to-one-borrower limitation with respect to the notes that ACC was to issue. The business plan accompanying the application called for decreasing Lincoln's total assets, particularly real estate and junk bonds.

As a result of the transaction, we wanted the FHLBB to agree not to impose an individual capital requirement on Lincoln and to remove its directives. Further, we were willing to be supervised by the Eleventh District or whomever Dochow chose to be the regulator.

At that point, the five of us who represented LSAC, the acquirer, briefly described our backgrounds. We indicated that if the deal were approved, we would sever all ties with ACC, including disposing of any stock or stock options that we held in ACC. We stated that if any of us were deemed unacceptable as purchasers, we wanted to know as soon as possible, so we wouldn't waste anybody's time. We added that we would appoint four outside directors to Lincoln's board, and Dochow could approve or veto each of these directors.

Dochow stressed that the Bank Board would not act without a complete record and application. We assured him that we were prepared to stay in Washington until all of his concerns were adequately addressed. We gave him a telephone number where we could be reached and said that we expected to hear from him the next day regarding any further questions which he had. Charlie closed by stating that time was of the essence and that ACC would also do whatever was necessary to obtain rapid approval.

Notes made by Dochow indicate that, after we left, there was further conversation between Dochow and Julie Williams. In this conversation, Dochow indicated that he would insist that we had to hire a new CEO who had no prior ties to either ACC or Lincoln. He also expressed continued concern about the tax-sharing payments which Lincoln had made to ACC and wondered how the situation could be resolved. He also wanted the ESOP to be unwound but wasn't specific as to how that could happen. And he wanted a more explicit letter from Touche on the purchase accounting. These were all things that he indicated he was going to communicate to us.

The tax-sharing issue was a real quagmire. Lincoln maintained that its deferred tax liability was, at most, $30 million at December 31, 1988. The FHLBB continued to insist that it was $94 million. The difference was largely a consequence of the GOIL exchange transaction.

Every tax accountant and tax lawyer whom ACC had talked to about GOIL concluded that the transaction was taxable and that the share price which had to be used in quantifying the gain was, absent a clear-cut, bona-fide appraisal to the contrary, the $9.50 which was specified in the transaction documents. In fact, these tax specialists didn't think that the GOIL transaction came close to the Internal Revenue Code definitions of a like-kind exchange which permitted gain to be deferred for tax-reporting purposes.

As to the value of the GOIL shares, the IRS always tries to get the highest share price possible to maximize the taxable gain. After all, the IRS' mission in life is to collect as much tax as it can. The IRS wasn't interested in minimizing Lincoln's tax liability. The FHLBB, on the other hand, believed that ACC was causing Lincoln to overstate its taxable income by considering the GOIL transaction to be taxable and by calculating the gain based on $9.50 per share, which the FHLBB thought was too high, just so ACC wouldn't have to return any deferred taxes to Lincoln.

ACC and Lincoln were caught between the competing objectives of two government agencies. In this case, if Lincoln failed to report the proper gain, the IRS could hit Lincoln for substantial penalties and interest. Lincoln was between the proverbial rock and a hard spot. Moreover, ACC didn't have $30 million in cash that it could pay to Lincoln—let alone $94 million.

There had been a continuous series of phone calls and correspondence between ACC and the FHLBB staff regarding the tax-sharing agreement. Even within the FHLB system, the FHLBB staff was still trying to find out what had actually happened with the tax-sharing agreement and its approval. Now that it was so controversial, no one was owning up to his involvement.

Representatives of ACC and Lincoln met several times with Kyle Klein, Smuzynski, and O'Connell to discuss the tax situation. Lincoln was in the process of being audited by the IRS. The IRS had examined Lincoln's 1984 and 1985 tax years and proposed various adjustments that increased Lincoln's taxable income for those years by about $72 million, resulting in additional taxes of around $27 million. Lincoln looked at the effect those adjustments had on its tax years 1986 through 1988 and calculated that its taxes in those years would increase by $18 million. Lincoln also determined that its tax liability for 1988, which included the gain on the GOIL transaction, was approximately $64 million. The combination of the IRS adjustments and the 1988 tax liability equaled $109 million, or about $14 million more than the deferred taxes which Lincoln had previously paid to ACC. Based on these calculations, Lincoln owed ACC, not the other way around, as the FHLBB was asserting.

In these meetings, Klein didn't really dispute the manner in which Lincoln calculated its tax liability or the amount thereof. But Klein did, essentially, suggest different ways for Lincoln and ACC to file their federal-income-tax returns and told ACC and Lincoln how they should deal with the adjustments proposed by the IRS in order to minimize the 1988 tax liability and, thus, not reverse the deferred taxes which were the heart of the FHLBB's case against ACC. This was clearly outside of the FHLBB's regulatory mandate and authority. ACC and Lincoln had to decide how best to use the deductions available to them, so as to minimize taxes, interest, and penalties over the long run. The FHLBB had neither the necessary data nor the expertise to make these decisions.

Al Smuzynski didn't seem to understand the issues or the nature of deferred taxes. He seemed to believe that if Lincoln used the taxable income from GOIL and the IRS adjustments to increase its 1988 tax liability, it would be unable to derive benefits from any future losses. He was, as usual, wrong.

First, deferred taxes result from temporary differences between book and tax accounting. These temporary differences reverse over time. Lincoln had to pay the deferred taxes. The only issue was: when—not if. From LSAC's perspective, those taxes were going to be due before the end of 1989, under any set of circumstances. Lincoln's calculations showed that the entire amount was a current liability at the end of 1988, and those calculations were not unreasonable. It should be noted that because the liability was now current, Lincoln had no longer paid a deferred tax liability to ACC.

Second, Lincoln was not going to be out any money if, as part of the LSAC transaction, it recorded a capital loss on the sale of GOIL to ACC, as Smuzynski also thought it would. If Lincoln recorded a capital loss on the sale of GOIL to ACC, then it had to generate a like amount of capital gains over the next five years, or some of the loss would lapse. That was an average of $10 million in capital gains per year, which was far below Lincoln's historical average. LSAC's plan was to liquidate real estate and securities; thus, it should generate capital gains for tax purposes.

O'Connell was insistent that Lincoln's deferred tax liability was still $94 million—no matter what any tax accountants said. His insistence seemed to be based, in part, on his strident assertion that Lincoln needed to record the adjustments proposed by the examiners. The catch was that most of the adjustments weren't deductible in 1988. Kyle Klein acknowledged that, under any set of circumstances, Lincoln's 1988 tax liability reduced the $94 million by a minimum of $35 million. O'Connell's insistence on the $94 million number indicated that he did not understand Lincoln's tax situation or the nature of book/tax differences in accounting. He did understand, however, that his case against Lincoln and ACC depended on the $94 million, and, right or wrong, he was sticking with it.

On March 10, the LSAC group met again with Dochow to go over his concerns regarding the application we had filed. During the meeting, Dochow presented us with ultimatums rather than suggestions. He acted as if he personally owned Lincoln and was negotiating the sale to us. He gave us a list of twelve conditions that we had to address before he would make a positive recommendation to the Bank Board.

John Rousselot specifically asked him, "If we meet all these conditions, will you make a positive recommendation to the Board?"

Dochow responded, "Yes, I will."

The first condition was: "A president/CEO of Lincoln would have to come from outside of Lincoln/ACC, with a proven track record and be subject to PSA approval."

I contacted a friend and former client of mine about serving as Lincoln's president. He had spent about eight years with one of the largest commercial banks in the Midwest before joining one of the largest thrifts in the West. He was, at the time, executive vice-president of a $6-billion institution. During his career, he had been in charge of virtually every function in the association. He had also served, at the request of the Eleventh District, as acting president of a $3-billion association under the FHLBB's Management Consignment Program (MCP). He clearly had the track record that Dochow was seeking. He agreed to serve as Lincoln's president, but he asked me to keep his identity confidential until LSAC's application was approved. I informed Dochow of this person's background and credentials but withheld his identity pending approval.

Another condition was: "No offset of the preferred stock held by ACC, against the note payable by ACC to Lincoln." This was one that ACC—not LSAC—had to agree to. Charlie was concerned, and understandably so, that after LSAC put $50 million into Lincoln, the FHLBB could seize it anyway. If that happened, he wanted ACC to be protected. The documents were drafted to provide that if, for any reason, Lincoln defaulted on the preferred stock, ACC could offset the face amount of the preferred against the notes that it owed to Lincoln, thereby reducing ACC's debt to Lincoln. Absent such a provision, if Lincoln were seized by the FHLBB, ACC would receive nothing for its investment in Lincoln. That could bankrupt ACC. So, initially, Charlie balked at this condition. Later, under the intense pressure of ACC's worsening cash position, he agreed to this condition.

I think Dochow believed this would be a deal breaker. In light of the increasing political attention that Lincoln was receiving in Congress, I believe that Dochow's real desire was to crush ACC and Charlie Keating to demonstrate that he was a tough regulator. He knew that, absent the offset provision, the deal was terrible from ACC's standpoint. I think Dochow expected that Charlie would reject this and that he would then be able to proceed with his planned conservatorship action.

While that last condition was tough for Charlie to swallow, the next one was hard on LSAC. It was: "No forbearances that restrict supervisory ability to classify assets, or otherwise accurately reflect the condition of Lincoln." The FHLBB didn't know the meaning of the word accurately. I was surprised that Dochow could even spell the word. We had sought this forbearance to give us time to dispose of those assets that the examiners either didn't or couldn't understand. We had also seen—up close and personal—Smuzynski overrule the examiners and classify the HPLP loan as loss. Without the forbearance, we were at the mercy of the FHLBB's arbitrary, subjective classification system. But since our personal economic risk was limited, we reluctantly agreed to the condition.

Another condition demonstrated one of the ways that the FHLBB bypassed the due-process sections of the regulations and the law. It said: "Execution of a prenuptial agreement, with a yet to be determined trigger." In effect, Dochow was asking us to agree ahead of time that if Lincoln's capital dropped below some specified level—the trigger point—we would consent to a C&D or some other specified supervisory action. We didn't like this, because, under the circumstances, we viewed it as extortion. But we weren't playing with a strong hand, so we agreed, subject to knowing what the trigger was and reserving the right to decide whether it was reasonable.

The conditions also required that: "The transaction must meet the accounting and economic tests for a sale, so that purchase accounting is applicable." We didn't think this was a problem. We had a letter from Touche Ross, as did the Spencer Scott Group, saying that the deal should be accounted for as a sale. Unfortunately, this was before Touche Ross had had a couple of friendly chats with the FHLBB staffers. We then learned that what should have been cut and dried didn't quite turn out that way.

The last troublesome condition was: "ACC must repay to Lincoln the deferred taxes, or collateralize the amount, or we will reduce Lincoln's capital by that amount (approximately $52 million)." Again, this one fell into ACC's bailiwick. ACC wasn't opposed to settling up the deferred taxes. The issue was: What is the correct number?

ACC contended that Lincoln owed it $14 million. ACC's position was supported by a number of "expert" tax lawyers and tax accountants. The FHLBB had the opinions of a "tax fellow" and some nontax lawyers, some less-than-expert accountants, and people who were neither accountants nor tax lawyers. LSAC left this for ACC to work out. To us it was a nonissue. We believed that based on everything we had seen and read, the deferred tax liability had reversed to a current liability.

We had addressed all of the other conditions during our first meeting with Dochow. Consequently, as far as LSAC was concerned, none of them was an issue.

On March 10, 1989, O'Connell and Larson met with several partners from Touche Ross. The purpose of the meeting was, I believe, twofold. First, they wanted to know what Touche's position was on various issues. Second, they wanted to bully Touche, so Touche would lean more in the direction of their theories.

During the meeting, Larson asked Touche how the new preferred stock that Lincoln was going to issue would be valued. Touche told her that Lincoln would hire an investment banker to value the stock. This answer prompted questions as to whether the investment banker had already been engaged, and, if so, Larson wanted to know the identity of the investment-banking firm. Touche informed her that an investment banker hadn't yet been hired. Touche said later that they believed her comments indicated that the FHLBB might want to have a say in selecting and "instructing" any investment bankers that Lincoln hired.

The reason an investment banker had not been hired was simple. Touche had never mentioned—not even hinted at—the need to hire an investment banker to anyone at ACC, Lincoln, or LSAC. They had consistently maintained that the stated value of the preferred was market because it had been established through arm's-length negotiations between their client, Spencer Scott, and their other client, ACC. The investment-banker idea emerged only after Larson hammered them a little bit.

A few days after this meeting, when Touche told ACC and LSAC that they had told the FHLBB an investment banker had to value the preferred, someone asked them if they were aware that a complete valuation of the preferred could cost well over $1 million. They were also politely asked to identify which investment-banking firm would undertake such an assignment, given the outstanding examination report, their unfinished audit, and the FHLBB's attitude toward Lincoln. They admitted that they hadn't thought of these considerations when they volunteered that an investment banker would be hired.

It's also interesting that Larson had expressed an interest in "instructing" the investment banker. Did she really want an independent appraisal of the preferred stock, or did she want to tell the appraiser what the value of the stock should be before the appraiser started work?

During the meeting with Larson and O'Connell, the status of Touche's audit work was also discussed. At this time, ACC and Lincoln believed that Touche was on schedule to finish the audit by March 31, 1989, as they had not given any indication to ACC or Lincoln that they were encountering problems. But in this meeting, Touche told the FHLBB that it was having trouble finishing its audit.

Touche told the FHLBB people that if the sale of Lincoln went through, they were approximately 60 to 70 percent done with their work. If the sale didn't go through, they were only 30 to 40 percent finished. They said that the difference between the two estimates was due to the fact that, if the sale went through, some difficult issues from an accounting standpoint became moot and they could finish their work quicker.

Aside from asking questions about the LSAC proposal and other accounting issues, there was another reason why the FHLBB had wanted this meeting with the Touche partners. Touche had defended Lincoln's accounting for transactions that the examination report had criticized and had written a letter disclosing the errors which the examiners had made in calculating Lincoln's capital requirement. This meeting could have been simply an attempt to intimidate Touche, so they would not come to Lincoln's defense in the future.

Both Larson and O'Connell had to know that, if Touche issued reports favoring Lincoln, the FHLBB would not be in a good position to defend its actions in court. So, Touche had to be intimidated and silenced. The pressure was subtle, but the FHLBB was letting Touche know that life could become difficult if they continued to defend Lincoln's accounting. On the other hand, if Touche went along with the FHLBB, the FHLBB would not hassle them.

The Touche conversation alerted us to the fact that the FHLBB staff would probably push for an alternative value to the preferred stock. The standard approach to valuing such a security is to discount the stream of cash that the security is expected to produce by an appropriate discount rate. The selection of the discount rate is largely a function of judgment. We started to look at various discount rates by reviewing the dividend rate on preferred stocks which had been issued in connection with leveraged buy-out transactions. These rates ranged from below 9 percent, the stated rate on our preferred, to over 16 percent.

It was difficult to sort out all these rates because the various securities had different features, such as liquidation preferences or cumulative versus noncumulative payments. The preferred that the new Lincoln would issue to ACC gave ACC the right to convert the preferred into debt after fifteen years. Based on the attributes of the preferred which ACC would receive, we determined that a discount rate of 13 percent was not unreasonable and provided a surrogate value pending a valuation by an investment banker. This rate produced a value for the preferred of about $214 million. We held this calculation in reserve, just in case Touche and the FHLBB insisted on using an investment-banking approach.

On the 13th of March, we had another lengthy session with the FHLBB staff. Few of the FHLBB staff had any real-world business experience, certainly none had ever been a decision maker in any significant transactions. They covered their lack of practical experience by relying on regulations combined with untried, and often impractical, theories, which may have sounded good to them but made no sense in terms of actually operating a business. They made calculations and used statistics, which were only valid in theory, to buttress their arguments. They wanted LSAC to give them a business plan addressing every conceivable contingency, whether probable or not. When our answers to their queries didn't coincide with their views, we were treated to healthy doses of disbelief coupled with acute cynicism.

On the evening of March 17, LSAC was delivered another body blow by the FHLBB. At around five o'clock, Smuzynski faxed us a list of *twenty-one* conditions that we had to meet before the FHLBB would approve the transaction.

Jim Grogan immediately called Smuzynski and asked, "What's going on? We already dealt with the other list you gave us, and we understood that list contained all of your concerns."

Smuzynski said, "These are all of our conditions. If they are addressed, we will make a recommendation to the Bank Board that they accept the transaction. There aren't any more issues other than those on the list. If you can take care of them over the weekend, we may be able to go to the Bank Board early next week." He also gave Grogan his home number in case we needed to talk to him over the weekend.

I was in favor of packing up and calling it quits. I didn't believe Smuzynski. I felt that once we addressed these points, they'd just hit us with another list. Jim Grogan argued that if the deal were not approved, it would be all over for both ACC and Lincoln. He asked us to stay and resolve the issues. He also got Charlie on the phone. Charlie was upset but saw no alternative except to try to meet the FHLBB's demands. I said, "Maybe the FHLBB has it in for some of us, and that's why they keep jerking our chain." Jim said that he would call Smuzynski and ask if that was the problem.

Jim called Smuzynski and said, "Al, there is concern that the FHLBB has a problem with some of the purchasers. If that's the case, tell us. It's not too late to change some of the players, but we have to know if that's an issue."

Smuzynski replied, "That's not an issue. We are not concerned about the buyers. If we had that concern, we'd have told you that at the very start."

"You're sure?" Jim asked.

"Yes. It's not an issue," Smuzynski replied.

We worked through the weekend to address the list of conditions. On some of the items, Charlie had to decide whether ACC could live with the requested changes in the transaction, because they affected the terms of the preferred stock or the notes which ACC was giving Lincoln. Other items had to be discussed with Eddie and Julius Trump, because we didn't want to be in a position where they were not kept fully informed. This process required us literally to work nonstop, around-the-clock, throughout the entire weekend.

We met with the FHLBB people on Monday morning, March 20, to go over our response to their conditions. We had prepared a letter which addressed each item they had raised. The letter opened as follows:

On Friday, March 17, 1989, LSLA Acquisition Corp. (LSAC) received a list of twenty-one (21) conditions which the Office of Regulatory Activities (ORA) recommends for expeditious approval of LSAC's acquisition of Lincoln Savings and Loan Association (Lincoln). As stated below, several of the conditions have already been resolved and are acceptable to all parties. It was believed that others had been resolved in a manner different from that set forth in the list; others are entirely new notwithstanding the representations of ORA personnel earlier in the week that all relevant issues had been raised.

The letter then addressed all of the conditions. We agreed to meet the requirements that the FHLBB was demanding, even though they had the effect of substantially altering the deal.

Given the FHLBB's knowledge of the circumstances surrounding ACC and Lincoln, some of these twenty-one conditions were the regulatory equivalency of extortion. What made these conditions all the more ludicrous was the fact that the FHLBB had, just a few months earlier, given away billions in their Southwest Plan deals. Those acquirers were given a grab bag full of goodies, including forbearances, income guarantees, and huge tax breaks. If the LSAC transaction had been presented as one of the Southwest Plan deals, it would have driven the Bank Board members to the heights of ecstasy. Instead, Lincoln was being treated differently from everyone else.

On March 22, 1989, Lincoln received a letter, signed by Dochow, regarding Lincoln's response to the examination report and Peter Fishbein's February 24, 1989, letter. The letter opened as follows:

Your correspondence not only fails to eliminate our supervisory concerns about the condition of your institution, but rather has increased our level of concern due to the Board of Directors' continuing defiance of our binding supervisory directives and failure to report the association's true financial condition.

Then, after castigating Lincoln for not recording the reserves and income reversals contained in the examination report and asserting that Lincoln had misrepresented some of the findings in its response, the letter stated:

. . . [Y]our response repeated the arguments that the examiners and this office have previously found unpersuasive. *All of the classifications cited in the examination report . . . are hereby affirmed. Further, all of the income reversals noted in the examination are affirmed.* In addition, all of the income reversals and specific reserves that we have required . . . in subsequent correspondence is [sic] also to be set up effective December 31, 1988. . . .

Your letter did not respond to either the ESOP item previously mentioned or the potential classification of the MDC loans and the Phoenician hotel assets. Therefore, we again direct that the $11.25 million ESOP loan is to be immediately expensed. Further, your loans to MDC and its subsidiaries, which our information indicates totals $62.4 million as of January 31, 1989, is hereby classified substandard. The Phoenician Hotel is also classified substandard, which, when combined with the current classification of the Crescent Hotel as substandard, means that the association's total investment in Crescent Holdings, Inc., is classified substandard. . . . [T]he association's net $81.5 million in loans to Southmark and its affiliates is also classified substandard. . . .

Further . . . we believe that the association should set up general reserves equal to ten percent of the carrying value against these assets. We have serious doubt as to the ability of MDC and Southmark to be able to service their debt, and the performance of the hotels indicates that the projected operating losses for 1989 will come about.

This was asking Lincoln to record millions of dollars in general reserves, based on asset classifications that Lincoln did not believe were appropriate under the regulations. The requested reserves were based on doubt, not on any clearly articulated or verifiable weaknesses in the assets. Moreover, the field examiners had looked at these very assets and had not deemed any classifications to be necessary.

But the FHLBB wasn't finished. They then proposed the following:

The association's response as to the criticisms of its investment activities does not allay our concerns. The default rate on your below investment grade securities portfolio is steadily rising, and information that the association purchased additional debt of MDC Holdings and Southmark in September indicates that the potential for future defaults is high. Overall, the record of the association's performance in common stock and below investment grade corporate bond investing is not encouraging. Your performance undercuts the arguments that the association should not have to set up reserves for mark to market losses due to management's belief that their judgment is superior to "the market," as the evidence points to a management philosophy of selling investments with profits, and holding investments with losses. Therefore, this office affirms the examiners' recommendations and directs the association to set up general reserves of $86.2 million as of December 31, 1988, for the mark-to-market losses on your corporate bond portfolio.

Having requested unprecedented general reserves and mark-to-market adjustments, the letter then comments on Lincoln's capital requirement as follows:

Examiners in the association are recalculating Lincoln's capital requirement for September 30, 1988, and December 31, 1988. We will advise you of the results by separate letter as part of the February 14, 1989, examination report.

Our preliminary findings indicate that just as the July 11, 1988, examination determined that the association seriously understated its capital requirement of June 30, 1988, the association is again undercalculating its capital requirement for both September 30, 1988, and December 31, 1988. However, even accepting your calculation of Lincoln's capital requirement, *Lincoln's net worth, after restatement for asset classifications and accounting adjustments, is substantially below its capital requirement. . . .*

The letter ended with yet another of the FHLBB's inventive directives to Lincoln. It read as follows:

. . . [G]iven our concerns about the ESOP, Playtex and Memorex transactions, the association is hereby directed to stop doing business with Drexel Burnham Lambert until further notice. We do not take this action lightly, but given Drexel's refusal to give our examiners the information we requested about the stock they sold to the ESOP, as well as the facts surrounding the Playtex and Memorex transactions, we feel we have no choice but to stop any future dealings with the company.

This letter was drafted many weeks before it was sent to Lincoln. The letter was dated March 22, 1989, yet in one paragraph Lincoln is directed to send work-out plans on all the assets that the examiners criticized to Dochow by *March 20, 1989.*

The FHLBB drafted these things and then held them until they could produce the maximum adverse effect on Lincoln. In this case, the FHLBB was using this letter to influence the LSAC transaction as well as providing a record for their planned conservatorship action. The letter is couched in terms of "serious concerns," but, make no mistake about it, this letter was not a regulatory device intended to achieve resolution of problems existing at Lincoln. This letter was a tool, or game piece, intended to exert pressure on Charlie Keating and to warn him that if he didn't accede to Dochow's demands, the FHLBB, through arbitrary directives, would bury him along with Lincoln.

The demands made in this letter did not conform to either the letter or the intent of the FHLBB's own regulations. The regulations required the FHLBB to conform with CEBA. CEBA, in turn, said that the FHLBB's classification system and other decisions must conform with GAAP. O'Connell, Dochow, Larson, and Smuzynski all knew that these requirements existed. Yet, in this letter, they chose to ignore GAAP and CEBA.

The letter affirmed the income reversals. Arthur Young and the FHLBB's own accountants had agreed that the accounting for the Wolfswinkle equity kicker was proper. The FHLBB's accountants had also indicated that Lincoln's capitalization of interest was in accordance

with GAAP, as had Arthur Andersen, Arthur Young, and Touche. Both
Arthur Young and Touche believed that the accounting for the sale of the
hotels was in accordance with GAAP. Touche told both Larson and
O'Connell that the sale of land to National Realty looked proper under
GAAP. Yet, in all these cases, the FHLBB chose to take contrary positions.

Had this been virtually any other association, these so-called income
reversals would not have been an issue. They were an issue here because
there were no actual losses that the FHLBB could identify in order to
justify actions against Lincoln. The examination disclosed only one
asset—the HPLP loan—that the examiners questioned where Lincoln had
not already recorded reserves. And in the case of HPLP, the requested
reserve had resulted when Smuzynski overruled his own field examiners.
It was also inconsistent with the most current appraisal on the asset. So, the
FHLBB ignored both GAAP and CEBA and manufactured reasons,
usually under the unsafe-and-unsound pretense, for considering these
transactions to be improper.

The FHLBB didn't stop with the income reversals contained in the
examination report. In this letter, they truly outdid themselves. The
demanded 10-percent general reserve on MDC, Southmark, and the hotels
was clearly inconsistent with CEBA, the classification regulations, and
GAAP. The regulations called for specific reserves on assets classified as
loss. There was no similar provision requiring an association to create
reserves for assets which were classified as substandard or doubtful. The
regulations also stated: "The Board may not require an association to
establish reserves against, or write down the value of, any asset in an
amount in excess of the amount which would result from an evaluation of
such asset which is consistent with generally accepted accounting principles. . . ."

Lincoln's response cited the requirements of SFAS 5, which deals
with such reserves. The criteria which the examiners used to classify assets
as substandard or doubtful do not meet the threshold for accruing loss
provisions under SFAS 5. This demand was, therefore, inconsistent with
both GAAP and the regulations.

It should also be noted that the general reserves which the letter
demanded had absolutely no effect on Lincoln's capital requirement. The
regulations permitted an association to disregard general reserves—add
them back—in determining regulatory capital. Therefore, the demand was
simply an attempt to reduce the earnings which Lincoln reported to its
shareholders and had no bearing on any action that the regulators could or
could not take against Lincoln. It was a mean-spirited, punitive measure
being imposed by O'Connell or Dochow, and nothing more.

The demand which required Lincoln to mark its corporate-bond
portfolio to market is even more egregious. Again, the FHLBB *could not*,

under its own regulations, require reserves which were inconsistent with GAAP. Under GAAP, mark to market was only appropriate for a trading portfolio. In this letter, the FHLBB didn't even attempt to establish that Lincoln's portfolio met the definition of a trading portfolio. None of Lincoln's outside auditors—including Touche—had ever made a determination that Lincoln had a trading portfolio. The regulations allowed examiners to make such a determination, but the regulations also contained guidelines that the examiners had to follow. In this instance, those guidelines were not considered, nor, had they been considered, did Lincoln's transactions meet the tests for a trading portfolio. The demand was not supportable under the FHLBB's very own rules.

Prior to the date of this letter, mark to market had not been forced, as Dochow was demanding in this letter, on any other association in the country. There was no precedent for this demand. There were no associations—none—who had trading portfolios that were marked to market. The accounting and regulatory bodies had not established any rules or standards which supported this action because, at this point, mark to market was still only an interesting theory—not an accounting principle that was generally accepted. O'Connell knew that this was the case. Both Dochow and Jordan Luke admitted that mark to market didn't apply, and they had told O'Connell that over a year earlier.

As a final comment on the bond portfolio, the letter asserted that the default rate on Lincoln's securities was "steadily rising." Yet, nowhere in this letter, or in its examination report, did the FHLBB offer any evidence to support this contention. The reason such evidence wasn't presented is simple. It didn't exist. The examiners had not discovered any serious defaults because there weren't any to discover. Reserves had already been established for the few troublesome investments that Lincoln held.

The mark-to-market requirement demanded in this letter had nothing to do with the regulations or GAAP. The fact is that the examiners had botched the calculation of Lincoln's capital requirement. They hadn't calculated the contingency factor for Lincoln's direct investments correctly—a $60-million error. Touche verified that the examiners were wrong, as did Steve Scott. Next, the FHLBB had argued that Lincoln's maturity-matching credit was wrong. But that didn't work either because Lincoln had done precisely what Steve Scott, who had conferred with both O'Connell and Smuzynski, told Lincoln to do in applying for this credit. The FHLBB needed the $60 million because, without it, they could not assert and sustain that Lincoln had failed its capital requirement.

They were doing a lot of things which were predicated on Lincoln's failure to meet the capital requirement—the supervisory directives, the hammering of ACC and LSAC on the sale of Lincoln transaction, and the planned conservatorship. If Lincoln sustained its position that it did, indeed, meet its capital requirement, Dochow, O'Connell, and Smuzynski would have more than egg on their faces. So, they dreamed up mark to market and the 10-percent general reserve to cover their errors.

They also did one very subtle thing to assure that Lincoln wouldn't immediately jump all over this letter and its distorted contents. All other correspondence on this examination had been addressed to either Kaye Scholer or Bob Kielty. This letter was mailed to Phoenix to the attention of David Thompson, as Lincoln's corporate secretary. The FHLBB knew where Thompson was. They had met with him that very day—in Washington, D.C. They knew that it would be days, if not longer, before Thompson would get this letter. And they knew that he was occupied with the LSAC application. If Lincoln didn't respond to their new directives by March 31, 1989, the date they had specified, they could use it to tear into Lincoln one more time.

Aside from the substantive contents of the letter, consider, for a moment, its tone and the use of language in the letter. The letter uses phrases such as "defiance," "deliberately filed false and misleading financial reports," "misaccounted," "deliberately violated," "misrepresents," "arbitrary attempt," "we do not accept," "unpersuasive," "serious doubts," "you are directed," and "hereby directed to stop." This language is typical of the phrases used in virtually all of the correspondence that Lincoln or ACC received from the FHLBB. The language is, by its very nature, inflammatory and pejorative. It is the kind of language that an angry parent might use with a petulant child.

At this time, Charlie Keating was over sixty-five years old, and, for over forty of those years, he had been engaged in operating businesses. He had seen just about every kind of deal there was to see—as a negotiator, buyer, seller, investor, operator, manager, and advisor. He had learned that businesses and business people must be flexible if they are to succeed. There are buyers' markets and sellers' markets. There are risks and opportunities. Sometimes you have to be a buyer, other times a seller, and, occasionally, you have to hunker down and hold tight. Decisions must be made in anticipation of, or in reaction to, the changes in the markets in which the business operates. Not all of these decisions will work out the way the decision maker expects. All businesses have some transactions or investments that don't meet expectations. Successful businesses find ways to minimize the occasional losses, and they capitalize on the unexpected windfalls. But none can succeed if it is forced into a straightjacket that totally eliminates the flexibility to act when market conditions dictate that action should be taken. Charlie understood this; the regulators did not.

The directives that the FHLBB sought to impose in its supervisory letters, and in the various conditions it was placing on LSAC's transaction, reduced and threatened to eliminate the flexibility which was necessary for Lincoln to succeed. The directives and conditions were, in part, based on the regulators' perceptions of risk.

All business transactions involve some element of risk. For example, investing in U.S. Treasury securities, which some might contend are risk free, involves risk. If interest rates rise rapidly, or for a prolonged period, the market value of Treasury securities decreases. If the business requires liquidity and, therefore, must sell its Treasury securities when rates are high, it can incur losses—sometimes sizable losses. The key to any business is understanding the risks inherent in the business and managing those risks in a manner that minimizes loss and captures gains.

The regulators had little or no experience in assessing and managing the risks inherent in the assets they were examining. The lead examiner in charge of examining Lincoln's corporate-bond portfolio had never, in his entire career, examined such securities. He had certainly never had to make the decision of whether to buy, sell, or hold such securities on a real-time basis. Yet, he believed that he was qualified, as did his superiors, to judge the performance of people whose only job was to manage a complex corporate-bond portfolio on a day-to-day basis. These portfolio managers had daily discussions with issuers, investment bankers, market analysts, fund managers, and experts in particular industries. Every day, they tracked prices and market movements in every security that Lincoln held. There was no way that the examiners had the feel for the risks in Lincoln's portfolio that Lincoln's corporate-bond people had.

The order to stop doing business with Drexel shows the regulators' lack of market knowledge. At that point in time, Drexel was still "the" market-maker in the high-yield market. The examiners were peeved because Drexel, who was not subject to their regulations, apparently wouldn't give them some information they had requested. Their solution was to order Lincoln to stop doing business with the most significant entity in the market. This is equivalent to chopping off your hand because you have a hangnail. Later, when the government forced Drexel out of business, the entire market for high-yields went into a tailspin. The FHLBB wanted Lincoln to experience its own, private, market collapse with this directive. It was an asinine solution to a minor problem. But it was typical of the FHLBB's tendency to overreact with draconian directives that made no business sense whatsoever.

The same was true with real estate. In this area, the lead examiner acknowledged that Lincoln's projects were too complex for either him or the examiners who worked for him to understand completely. He visited some of the projects and reviewed all of the files that Lincoln maintained on these projects. Yet, his superiors, who didn't have any more real-estate experience than he had, did not hesitate to criticize these projects and offer their opinions, in the form of directives, about how the projects should be handled.

The point is that the regulators may have been experienced with and knowledgeable about the FHLBB's rules and regulations, but they weren't business people. They thought they understood the business risks Lincoln faced—but they didn't. They were focusing on what had happened historically; they were concerned with arcane theories, doubts, and suspicions which were bred out of a lack of real-world experience; they focused on artificial determinants of value, such as appraisals; and they mistrusted anything that Lincoln or ACC told them. Their solution was to try to freeze Lincoln in place and then to have Lincoln liquidate every asset they didn't understand. That may have made sense to them as regulators, but it was not a good business decision.

Charlie saw the directives for what they really were, just as I understood what would happen if LSAC were subjected to all the conditions the regulators wanted to impose. Lincoln would be placed in a quasi-liquidation mode. Lincoln's customers, borrowers, and competitors would rapidly pick up on the fact that Lincoln was no longer a buyer; it was only a seller—and a distressed seller at that. Once the market recognizes that a company is a forced seller of assets, prices start to drop. The sharks and bottom-feeders move in, and prices drop even farther. Once the liquidation-driven free-fall begins, it's almost impossible to stop. Losses mount at an escalating rate, and the business quickly becomes a candidate for bankruptcy. This was the road map that the regulators were laying out for Lincoln. Either ACC would serve as the liquidator, because of the directives, or the FHLBB would do it directly through a conservatorship. If Lincoln wasn't sold to LSAC, the FHLBB was going to liquidate it. It didn't take a genius to figure out that a liquidation would be disastrous.

After a great deal of discussion and debate, Touche Ross finally issued a letter expressing its conclusions regarding the accounting for LSAC's acquisition of Lincoln. It was a letter that did not completely satisfy anyone, because the language used in the letter implied that Touche was hedging its conclusion.

Touche felt obligated to discuss the transaction that was being discussed between ACC and the Trump Group. This transaction was not finalized. Yet, in drafting their letter, Touche speculated that the price ACC would pay to the Trump Group might reimburse the Trump Group for its investment in LSAC. This disclosure simply raised needless questions in the minds of the already distrustful and somewhat hostile FHLBB staff.

In order to obtain Touche's conclusion, and to make the numbers work under the accounting methods they would accept, there were several changes made in the terms of the transaction. First, at the insistence of one of Touche's geniuses, LSAC's price for the common stock was increased from $100,000 to $1 million. Second, The preferred stock ACC would receive was now redeemable at ACC's option in five equal annual installments commencing in thirteen years (after ACC had paid all of its notes to Lincoln), provided the redemption payments would not cause Lincoln's regulatory capital to fall below 2 percent in excess of its required capital.

Touche's five-page letter was addressed to Dochow and was dated March 23. This letter was intended to put the entire accounting issue to rest. However, the opening paragraph contained one sentence that essentially hedged Touche's conclusion and, thus, left the issue open. The sentence said: "This letter is being provided on the basis that the FHLBB staff will not object to the appropriateness of our conclusion." No one, except Touche, was sure what this meant. If the FHLBB staff disagreed with them, would Touche change its conclusion? Were they saying, we think this is the right answer, but we'll go along with whatever the FHLBB wants us to do?

The FHLBB took it to mean that Touche wasn't sure and that maybe the SEC should be called in to resolve the issue. Of course, the FHLBB had already greased the skids with the SEC and knew they could get an "arbitrary and capricious" decision that would favor their views. When LSAC read the draft of Touche's letter, we asked them to remove the weasel words and extraneous discussion of ACC's negotiations with the Trumps, but they would not.

The conclusion they stated in their letter was:

> Touche Ross has therefore concluded that LSAC should account for the acquisition of Lincoln by LSAC as a purchase business combination, with the purchase price being determined by the fair value of tangible and intangible net assets acquired.

This accounting committed LSAC to engaging an investment banker to establish the fair value of the net assets. Touche commented on this by saying:

> As is the case in many business combinations, an independent investment banker's or appraiser's fair valuation of the identifiable net assets purchased will not be immediately available. LSAC in consultation with the investment bankers or appraisers will be required to use its best estimate of the result to be obtained from the valuation, for purposes of initial postacquisition financial reporting. Under SFAS 38 (para. 4.b.), the time allowed to complete the purchase price allocation usually would not exceed one year.

This was another element that made the FHLBB unhappy, as they wanted to know what Lincoln's capital was going to be right from the onset.

Touche also sent Dochow a letter on March 24, 1989, informing him that they would not complete their audit of Lincoln's financial statements by the due date of March 31, 1989. They requested an extension by stating, "Due to the late engagement of Touche Ross & Co. by Lincoln Savings and Loan Association ("The Association"), we request an extension of time to file the Association's report of audit for the year ended December 31, 1988. With your approval, we will file the required audit report within 30 days of the originally required filing date."

This request was, at the very least, disingenuous. First, had Touche committed the resources to the audit that they had repeatedly been advised to commit, the date of their engagement would not have been a factor. They knew, or should have known, what the time requirements would be when they accepted the engagement. They also knew that both ACC and Lincoln had filings due on March 31, 1989. They had accepted the engagements on November 1, 1988. That gave them five months to do their work. And they had aggressively sought the appointment as auditors with their unsolicited proposal and relentless sales tactics. There was no valid excuse for not being finished.

Second, just a week or so earlier, they had told Larson that if Lincoln were sold, they were 60 percent done, and, if Lincoln were not sold, they were 30 to 40 percent finished. If those statements to Larson were true, they could not possibly have believed that they would complete the audit in another thirty days. It just doesn't compute. Simple math says that under the best of circumstances, which would be if Lincoln were sold, they needed, based on their progress to date, another two or three months.

It should be noted that both ACC and Lincoln had completely drafted their financial statements for the year ended December 31, 1988. They were waiting for Touche's opinion letter and for any adjustments Touche felt were necessary to the draft financial statements. The companies were ready to make timely filings.

Finally, the fact that the audit was not finished was very harmful to ACC, Lincoln, and LSAC in these negotiations with the FHLBB and in the actions that the FHLBB would take later. The auditors, of necessity, had to address the income reversals and classification losses that the FHLBB had directed Lincoln to record. If the auditors concluded these directed adjustments were not consistent with GAAP, they would have been indefensible by the FHLBB under the CEBA provisions. Also, Lincoln's financial statements disclosed, before any adjustments Touche may have proposed, GAAP capital which exceeded $200 million. If the auditors affirmed this net worth via their report, any attempt by Dochow and his troops to establish a lower number would have been thwarted. Absent the auditors' report, the FHLBB had free reign to assert all kinds of theories regarding Lincoln's GAAP capital—and they did.

The importance of the absence of audited financial statements for the year ended December 31, 1988, cannot be overemphasized. These financial statements would have been Lincoln's and ACC's best defense against the FHLBB's onslaught. They would have completely negated all of the efforts of O'Connell, Smuzynski, and Larson. They would have established that Lincoln was, indeed, solvent—and by over $200 million. Without audited financial statements, Charlie Keating's efforts to preserve his investment in the companies were severely crippled.

O'Connell and Smuzynski talked to Patriarca and gave him an update on Lincoln. In the conversation, they told Patriarca that the LSAC deal was still alive. Patriarca indicated to them that San Francisco was opposed to the sale; instead, San Francisco wanted Lincoln placed in receivership.

After the Washington-based regulators talked to the people in San Francisco, we started to hear concerns about the source of LSAC's financing. Apparently, as a result of Touche Ross' letter on purchase accounting, Smuzynski and Larson began to believe that somehow Lincoln was financing LSAC's purchase.

As suspected, the Touche letter raised more questions than it answered. Lincoln was not financing the infusion of capital. ACC may have been squeezed by the Trump Group in their subsequent negotiations with the Trumps, but that had absolutely no bearing on the deal from either Lincoln's or LSAC's perspective. The issues raised in Touche Ross' letter may have affected the way that ACC should account for its transactions, but they were irrelevant to the LSAC transaction. Instead of helping the transaction, this letter harmed the chances of obtaining the FHLBB's approval.

As a brief aside, Touche didn't understand Charlie's plans for recapitalizing and refinancing ACC either. The purchase of the Trump subsidiary was merely a first step. Charlie had strong indications, if not assurances, that, after the sale of Lincoln, several foreign investors would infuse cash into ACC. Accordingly, if ACC had to overpay the Trumps, it wasn't a big deal. The capital which would follow would, through added earning power, more than make up the shortfall.

On March 28, 1989, Patriarca sent Dochow a nine-page letter, with copies to each of the FHLBB Board members, which forced Dochow into a corner and effectively killed the LSAC transaction. ACC, Lincoln, and Keating had escaped from Patriarca in 1988 through the MOU, and he was not about to let it happen a second time. His letter made unfounded accusations; was clearly biased against Keating and LSAC; and was written even though he did not have any direct knowledge of most of the facts. His letter was based solely on conversations with O'Connell and Smuzynski and on the selected documents they had sent him. The letter was, however, so strong in its attack on ACC and LSAC that Dochow either had to refute Patriarca's accusations or had to go along with him. It appears that Dochow was unwilling to stand up to Patriarca, and he feared criticism if he continued to support the LSAC deal.

Patriarca's letter is ample evidence of the deep animus that he had toward ACC and Lincoln. The Eleventh District had not been actively involved with Lincoln for months. The latest direct knowledge that San Francisco had about Lincoln had been obtained in the 1986 examination and was now outdated by almost two years. The opinions he expressed in this letter were, therefore, nothing more than the old biases and hard feelings that he had harbored since the ERC stripped the Eleventh District of its supervision of Lincoln—a move Patriarca had to view as a personal defeat. Accordingly, this letter appears to be, pure and simple, a vengeful act on his part—an attempt to repay ACC and Lincoln for the embarrassment he had suffered.

The letter attacked the members of LSAC who had formerly been employees of ACC or Lincoln. The comments lacked any factual foundation and were merely groundless character assassinations. The purpose in raising the issue was to force Dochow into eliminating each of us from the buying group. Patriarca argued that we were somehow part of the past problems between the FHLBB and Lincoln. He also questioned whether we would, in fact, sever our ties to ACC and Keating, as we had pledged to do in our application to buy Lincoln. His incessant demands in this regard forced Dochow's hand.

At this point, Dochow committed to seek the removal of the four primary parties in LSAC, leaving only John Rousselot. With our removal, the deal was dead.

While Patriarca ranted and raved for nine pages against the sale of Lincoln to LSAC and was in favor of a receivership, not once did he ever consider the economic consequences of a receivership. Nor did anyone else at the FHLBB. They had plenty of experience in closing other institutions, and every closure had cost the FSLIC and the taxpayers dearly. Patriarca was more concerned with eliminating ACC and Keating than he was with arriving at the most economical decision based on facts and not appearances. Even Dochow recognized that Patriarca was out of line and was completely and irrationally biased, but there wasn't much he could do because Patriarca's venomous letter had already gone to all of the Bank Board members and had irreparably poisoned them against the LSAC deal.

At this point, believing we had addressed all of Dochow's twenty-one conditions, I returned to Phoenix to secure the needed directors and to begin making detailed plans for the transition of Lincoln. Stoll and Thompson stayed in Washington with Grogan to draft the transaction documents with outside counsel. On March 29, the group that was working on the documents called Dochow to get the results of the FHLBB's outside counsel's review of the documents, so any needed changes could be incorporated into the new drafts.

The conversation proceeded for about fifteen minutes and focused on the documents that were being drafted. Then, Dochow asked where ACC's $15 million was coming from. He was told that Charlie was going to leverage some of ACC's real estate to raise the funds. Dochow wanted to know whether the real estate could be leveraged even more to pay off the deferred taxes. He was told that wasn't possible. Grogan then told him that ACC's cash was very tight and would be until Charlie could refinance ACC. Dochow was told that Charlie was concentrating on keeping ACC out of bankruptcy, and his efforts were completely dependent on the sale of Lincoln.

Then, Dochow started to give an overview of the things he still found unacceptable about the transaction. Grogan interrupted and said that he thought all of the conditions had been met and that the transaction should therefore be totally acceptable. Dochow said that there were still a couple of open items: (1) the accounting treatment of the capital, (2) the redrafting of the documents, and (3) the problem with the insiders in management.

This drew a quick response from Grogan. He said that we had been given repeated assurances that the four of us were acceptable to the regulators. Dochow replied that one of the conditions gave him the ultimate approval of the management and directors. He said that the four insiders were not acceptable to him. Grogan said that this was a major change in the deal and, in all fairness, Dochow should have spoken up much sooner if he had had a problem, especially since he had been asked that very question directly on several occasions. Dochow tried to say that he had changed his mind when he reviewed the documents and found they favored ACC. He said that was evidence that LSAC didn't have Lincoln's interest at heart. He was told that those documents were part of the Spencer Scott deal and that we assumed he had reviewed them and found them acceptable. He then backed off trying to justify his action. He was asked to provide his specific objections to each person as soon as possible, which he agreed to do, so we would know whether the deal was still alive.

There was no question in our minds that the FHLBB's staff people were playing a game of conditioning LSAC to death. This was their clear and deliberate strategy from day one. The question is: Did Dochow know they were playing this game, or was Dochow being maneuvered by O'Connell and Smuzynski just like we were?

On April 3, 1989, as promised, the FHLBB sent Lincoln a letter regarding its capital calculations at September 30 and December 31, 1988. The letter indicated that Lincoln's required capital was understated because of the maturity-matching credit, as follows:

The maturity matching credit calculation incorrectly included $555.2 million in unsecured loans to subsidiaries as repricing assets. This came about due to the association attempting to classify these loans as secured when in fact the period used to calculate the maturity matching credit was March 31, 1988, when the loans were clearly unsecured.

This was the item that Lincoln had consulted with Steve Scott about. The regulations and the form used to calculate the credit did not indicate clearly that loans to 100-percent-owned service corporations had to be secured, because the parent, in fact, controlled the service corporation which, in turn, allowed the parent to control the assets used as collateral for the intercompany loans. Securing the loans merely involved executing security agreements and recording liens—purely an exercise in paperwork. Steve Scott, after consulting with O'Connell and Smuzynski, had told Lincoln that "technically" the loans should be secured. But because the security for the loans had been owned by the subsidiaries for several years, and had never been encumbered with liens to third parties, the paperwork was only a formality. Scott said that Lincoln was "entitled" to claim the credit in September. In February, when Scott reviewed Lincoln's calculations, he confirmed that this was what he had advised Lincoln to do.

What the FHLBB was doing in this letter was splitting very fine hairs. The letter doesn't acknowledge that the examination report had, in fact, double counted the contingency factor for direct investments, but this letter omits it from the calculation. So, the FHLBB had, in fact, been incorrect in their December 20, 1988, letter to Lincoln. To cover their error, they were now using a meaningless technical point to justify increasing Lincoln's capital requirement by over $50 million, in spite of the fact that Lincoln had followed their instructions to a tee. To add insult to injury, they called this an "error."

The December calculation also eliminated the maturity-matching credit for the same reason.

With respect to Lincoln's actual net worth, the letter cited the reserves and income reversals, which Lincoln had not booked, as "errors" and also required the reversal of the tax credit Lincoln recorded. The effects of these items reduced Lincoln's actual net worth from *$255 million* to *$126 million*, at September 30, 1988. The same adjustments were cited for the December calculation, and Lincoln was required to write off the $11-million ESOP loan. This reduced Lincoln's actual capital from *$250 million* to *$113 million* at December 31, 1988. Note that in both periods, if Lincoln recorded all of the adjustments cited by the FHLBB, it still had actual capital of *over $100 million*. Lincoln was not insolvent, even if all of the contested adjustments proposed by the regulators were taken into account.

We finally learned that Dochow continued to view the LSAC proposal unfavorably and would ask the Board to reject it. The negative recommendation was based largely on the subjective opinions of Dochow and his staff—opinions they are certainly entitled to have and to express—there's no quarrel with that. However, one has to question the business judgment underlying some of their opinions.

For example, Dochow expressed concern that ACC committed to purchase $15 million in new preferred stock in Lincoln but, at the same time, could not or would not reimburse Lincoln for the $94.8 million which the FHLBB asserted was an improper advance to ACC through the tax-sharing agreement. He was upset that LSAC had entered into an agreement with ACC which allowed this issue to remain open, rather than demanding payment.

Dochow knew from the field examiners that ACC did not have the liquidity to repay the deferred taxes—and by December 31, 1988, the amount was not $94.8 million. He also knew that if ACC could not sell Lincoln, it would probably file for bankruptcy. How then did Dochow ever expect to collect the monies that he believed ACC owed to Lincoln? It sure wasn't going to happen by throwing Lincoln into receivership and ACC into bankruptcy.

As another example, Dochow asserted that Lincoln's long-term viability was questionable because of its level of regulatory capital, which, on the basis of the FHLBB's questionable accounting and economic theories, he kept insisting was less than $100 million. He felt that our proposal to infuse $50 million in new capital would not solve the net-worth problem that he perceived existed.

The LSAC transaction may have led Dochow to believe that Lincoln's long-term viability was questionable, but what does a receivership result in? A receivership assures that Lincoln has no future at all, let alone a long-term one. A receivership guarantees only one thing—it's time for the taxpayers to cover the losses produced by every receivership the FHLBB has ever instituted. Why should Lincoln be an exception? Amazingly Dochow never, to our knowledge, addressed anywhere the consequences—in terms of dollars—that would result if this transaction were not approved and receivership became the FHLBB's only option.

Obviously, with Dochow's attitude and expressed intention to make an unfavorable recommendation to the Bank Board, it was the end of the LSAC transaction. John Rousselot tried to form another group, but it was too late. They couldn't raise the money fast enough, and, in any event, their application would have been conditioned to death, just as LSAC's had been. The Trump Group wasn't interested in Lincoln's preferred stock if they didn't know the people who would be managing Lincoln, so John was back at square one, with no time left. If there was any chance for success,

Dochow quickly dashed it by demanding that any deal had to result in Lincoln getting $200 million in new capital. That was ludicrous. There was no way on earth that anyone would commit $200 million in cash to new capital and also pay ACC for its equity. Impossible.

With their decision to turn down LSAC's proposal, Dochow and his staff cost the American taxpayers at least—at least—$50 million. The capital that was to be contributed to Lincoln was real. In a receivership, the government could not, and later would not, get anything close to $50 million for Lincoln's branches. Moreover, our business plan contemplated an orderly liquidation of Lincoln's real estate and junk bonds—a liquidation that would produce no significant losses. The government's receivers could expect to, and did, dispose of these same assets at tremendous losses. Dochow's and the other regulators' desire to crush Charlie Keating, which was the primary motive that led them to turn down this transaction, was one of the most costly bureaucratic blunders in history.

With the death of the LSAC transaction, there were no more viable proposals pending for the sale of Lincoln. The options available to both ACC and the FHLBB were limited and unfavorable, from the perspective of both parties. ACC had tried to surrender to the FHLBB's unrelenting assaults against it by selling Lincoln and getting out of the industry. But the FHLBB wouldn't accept ACC's white flag of surrender; it wanted to see ACC and Keating completely destroyed. Time had run out.

Seventeen

FHLBB Rejects ACC's Surrender

To Charlie, the LSAC proposal made sense. Lincoln would get $50 million in new capital, which it could use to develop and sell assets which he felt were valuable. Absent Lincoln, ACC could, itself, obtain new capital, which would allow it to hold and develop GOIL and the hotels and to continue its investment business. More importantly, if Lincoln were sold, no one would suffer any losses. Not the government. Not ACC's debtholders. And not ACC's shareholders. A sale of Lincoln was the only way, given the FHLBB's attitudes, that everyone could emerge from this protracted war relatively unscathed.

But Dochow and his minions had scuttled any hopes of selling Lincoln. Without a sale, the regulators would inevitably move to seize Lincoln. If this happened, ACC would be deprived of its most valuable asset; as such, it could not possibly meet its obligations. Thus, Charlie needed to prevent the FHLBB from taking these destructive actions.

As a last-gasp effort, Charlie tried to get some of his political contacts in Washington to talk to the FHLBB's Board members to inform them of the consequences that would occur if Lincoln were not sold. If these people did talk to the FHLBB, they obviously didn't have any impact on the Bank Board. The FHLBB remained poised to seize Lincoln. At this point, it became apparent to Charlie that he would have to turn to lawyers and put ACC and Lincoln into the best possible defensive posture.

Earlier, ACC had made contact with some attorneys in Texas who were specialists in bankruptcy. ACC wanted to learn what strategies were available if the FHLBB tried to seize Lincoln. At the time, the discussion with the attorneys was an academic exercise. ACC wanted to know whether they had represented a thrift holding company faced with a FHLBB takeover and, if so, to see if defenses were available. The attorneys had represented savings and loans. Before they could discuss specific options, they needed to know more about ACC's and Lincoln's own peculiar circumstances. They did indicate, however, that, should the need arise, they would be willing to represent ACC and Lincoln.

By late March, the need for the attorneys' services had, in Charlie's mind, arisen. A team from two different firms, the Texas firm and a firm that specialized in regulatory law, arrived in Phoenix and set up shop in the offices adjacent to ACC's legal department. They started pouring over the correspondence from the FHLBB, ACC's corporate structure, and ACC's and Lincoln's financial records. They needed to understand the nature of the beast they were dealing with before a defensive plan could be formulated.

A payment of principal and interest on ACC's subordinated debentures was due at the end of March. The attorneys advised ACC not to make the payment in order to preserve cash. All of the various attorneys who had represented ACC and Lincoln, and who were familiar with the FHLBB's examination reports and other correspondence, had concluded that the positions taken by, and the findings of, the FHLBB were not supportable either as a matter of fact or as a matter of law. Therefore, Charlie believed that if ACC and Lincoln presented their case to an impartial and unbiased judicial forum, any action of the FHLBB could be overturned. If the bankruptcy laws could provide protection long enough to get a fair hearing, ACC might still be able to meet all of its obligations. On the basis of that belief, and not wanting to default, ACC made the payment as scheduled.

Beginning in early April, as the lawyers were planning ACC's defense, the entire Keating family, including all five of the daughters and their spouses, C-III, Mary Elaine, and Charlie, started holding all-day meetings in ACC's boardroom. They convened early in the morning; had lunch brought in; and met until late in the afternoon, at which time most of them left ACC's offices. Occasionally, one of the bankruptcy attorneys joined the family meeting. Otherwise, it was family members only.

While the rest of us were not privy to these meetings, we could see into the boardroom. The family appeared somber and disheartened. It was clear that they were trying to assess the damage that a filing of bankruptcy by ACC or the failure of Lincoln or both would render to the family's fortune and its future.

The Keating family's wealth was entirely dependent on ACC. Its stock ownership in ACC represented the bulk of the asset value that the family held—a value that, before ACC had ever even heard of Lincoln, had exceeded $50 million. Family members did own real estate, including luxurious homes, vacation homes, and investment properties, as well as non-real-estate assets, such as automobiles, jewelry, and artwork. However, many of these assets had been financed by the proceeds from mortgage loans or loans secured by shares of ACC common stock. The loans secured by stock could be called by the lender if the market value of the shares declined. If ACC filed for bankruptcy protection, the stock values would plunge and the loans would, in all probability, be called. This could force the family to liquidate assets to meet the lenders' demands. As such, the family's wealth could rapidly be wiped out.

These meetings were the end of a three-year emotional roller-coaster ride for Charlie. He was physically and emotionally drained. He was faced with explaining to his family the inexplicable. How could one accept, let alone explain, the fact that you might lose everything that had taken a lifetime to acquire to a bunch of regulators who were acting on insupportable and indefensible theories—theories which were driven by dubious motives—and theories which you could not challenge because you didn't have an objective body to which you could appeal?

The toll these meetings exacted from Charlie was clearly visible. He didn't display his characteristic optimism, the bounce was out of his stride, he appeared tired and haggard, and he was almost disinterested in the routine business ACC was still conducting. The decision of whether ACC had to seek bankruptcy protection, and the consequences that the decision might produce, were all-consuming.

The family meetings, which went on for days, also affected the others in ACC. It was agonizing to watch the sullen faces of the Keating clan as they contemplated what might happen. A malaise set in, and ACC's operations ground to a standstill.

The actions of the attorneys on the first floor were cloaked in secrecy. The only ACC people who were privy to their deliberations and strategy decisions were Charlie, Judy, and Bob Kielty. The Keating family members were probably updated by Charlie, so, to that extent, they were also aware of the plans that the attorneys were formulating. This secrecy added to the eerie atmosphere which had settled in ACC's offices. Everyone knew some action was going to be taken. But, other than those few who met with the attorneys, no one knew what that action would be or when it would occur.

One thing was clear. The attorneys felt that it was necessary for ACC to put its defensive plan in motion before the FHLBB had time to act against Lincoln. Even though all of ACC's legal counsel were confident that ACC and Lincoln would prevail against the FHLBB in a court proceeding, they also realized that Lincoln's assets had to be protected, so that the FHLBB could not dismantle them before Lincoln had its day in court. If the FHLBB came in and started to liquidate assets, then even if ACC prevailed and regained its ownership of Lincoln, the damage already done by the regulators to the portfolio would be enormous. If they had control of Lincoln, for even a few weeks, they could destroy the integrity of the real-estate projects; alienate customers and borrowers; sell assets at losses; drive away key employees; ruin the branch network; and much,

much more. The list of damages that the inexperienced, naïve, and economically ignorant regulators could inflict was endless.

No association had ever survived a FHLBB conservatorship without suffering fatal damage. While the concept of a conservatorship is to conserve, or stabilize, an association, in reality it didn't work out that way. Associations did not emerge, intact, from conservatorship as revived entities ready to resume their corporate lives.

Some, usually small associations, were peddled to larger institutions. Most were passed through to a receivership, where they were carved into pieces. One piece, usually dubbed the "good bank," consisting of the branch network and its deposits, along with the "good assets"—cash, U.S. government securities, SFR loans, mortgage-backed securities, and some other assets—was usually sold to another institution. The remaining piece, called the "bad bank" and consisting of the "bad assets"—construction and commercial loans, land loans, real estate, corporate debt and equity securities, and other nontraditional assets—was transferred to the Resolution Trust Corporation (RTC) or its predecessor, the Federal Asset Disposition Association (FADA). These assets were then disposed of individually or in pools—usually at incredible losses. Thus, the concept of a true conservatorship was only a figment of the regulators' imaginations.

The only real purpose that a conservatorship served was to allow the FHLBB to fudge its books by postponing recognition of the inevitable losses it would incur. This way, the White House and the Congress could hide losses and lie to the public about the true cost of the FHLBB's actions and policies.

ACC and its lawyers knew that, once Lincoln was placed in conservatorship, the actual conservatorship wouldn't last very long. The feds would immediately write down assets to their fire-sale, liquidation value, thereby creating huge losses which would allow them to declare Lincoln insolvent. Once Lincoln was pronounced insolvent, the feds would end the conservatorship and place Lincoln into receivership, with either the FDIC or the FSLIC as the receiver. In receivership, the assets would be segregated into good and bad assets. The RTC would be responsible for the bad assets and would begin getting rid of them. So, if ACC wanted to recover Lincoln's assets in an undamaged state, it had to keep them out of the hands of the feds. Once the RTC got their hands on the assets, it was all over, as the value of the assets would be permanently impaired.

The strategy which evolved was to have ACC file for protection under Chapter 11 of the federal bankruptcy laws and also to have all of the first-tier subsidiaries of Lincoln make similar filings. Lincoln conducted all of its business, except for accepting deposits and certain lending, through these subsidiaries. They held all of the real estate, corporate securities, and the hotels—assets that the feds would probably place in the bad category. If these corporations were under the protection of the Federal Bankruptcy Court, the RTC or other federal agencies could not gain access to the assets without first going through the Court. This might give ACC, and the management of the subsidiaries, the opportunity to challenge, in front of an impartial court, the feds' actions. It would also let ACC challenge the legality of the FHLBB's seizure before the assets could be damaged. Then, if the FHLBB's actions were overruled and Lincoln were returned to ACC's ownership, the asset values would still be relatively intact.

While this strategy had a basic logic, no one expected that ACC would ever regain Lincoln per se. It might be able to get the subsidiaries but not the insured institution. This is because a federal takeover would permanently alter Lincoln. There would be a run on the deposits; customers' confidence would be irreparably shattered; certain assets, such as government securities, would, in all likelihood, be sold, and probably at a loss; and the chasm between Lincoln and the regulators would be so wide that it could never be closed again. Therefore, the more practical expectation was that ACC would regain control of the subsidiaries and would be compensated for any damages caused by the inappropriate seizure of Lincoln. At least that was the result the strategy might produce if it succeeded.

Late in the afternoon of Thursday, April 13, 1989, ACC and Lincoln's first-tier subsidiaries filed for Chapter 11 protection. The filings, while not completely unexpected, still came as a surprise. A press release had already been prepared and was released to the media. All work stopped at ACC and Lincoln as people tried to figure out what the filings meant and what would happen next.

Charlie appeared relieved that a decision had been made and that the agonizing was over. He still hoped that the FHLBB would see the light and allow Lincoln to be sold. But if not, a least there was a plan in place to deal with the situation—a plan which still offered the promise that all was not lost for ACC and the Keating family.

Dochow heard about the bankruptcy filings that same Thursday at about 9:00 P.M., Washington time. He stayed in his office for several more hours, working with lawyers, trying to get ready to meet with the Bank Board the next morning to deal with Lincoln.

The Bank Board met at 8:00 A.M. on Friday, April 14, 1989, in a closed meeting to consider the appointment of the FSLIC as conservator of Lincoln. It took them less than an hour to hear the presentation from Dochow's staff and to vote to place Lincoln—an association with $5 billion in assets and more than $100 million of net worth—into conservatorship.

This conservatorship action had been planned for some time. This meeting was a mere formality, as the FHLBB had troops standing by in Phoenix to move against Lincoln. They had court papers prepared to get a temporary restraining order permitting them to gain access to Lincoln. They also had assembled a management team to run Lincoln after they took over.

They believed that their selected managers and advisory board were an outstanding team. One has to suspect that the most outstanding trait of these people was that they had worked for the FHLBB before and the FHLBB knew that they were loyal and would not rock the boat. All but one had been either in the Management Consignment Program or in conservatorship situations before. It should be noted that the other associations they had managed or advised had all experienced slow, agonizing, and expensive deaths at the hands of the FHLBB's expert managers and advisors. So, one could conclude they had proven track records at liquidating shops at big losses, and that may have been a prerequisite to work on this FHLBB team—you had to know how to dispose of assets at huge losses.

The bases for the conservatorship action were dissipation of assets and unsafe and unsound conditions. The alleged instances where assets had been dissipated were: Hidden Valley land sales and related tax-sharing payments; the Pontchartrain loan; the ESOP loan; and the transactions involving Playtex and Memorex stock.

The only information that the FHLBB had regarding the Hidden Valley land sales was a series of schedules that O'Connell had received from Gene Stelzer of CDSL, some information O'Connell had gotten from the SEC, and inferences. The examiners had not yet researched these transactions. The documentation was not completed until months later, when Leventhal supported O'Connell's inferences. Not that Leventhal had much choice—the entire seizure of Lincoln was dependent on supporting O'Connell's conclusions. If Leventhal didn't support him, the FHLBB would lose in court when ACC challenged the conservatorship. So, the hired gun had its back against the wall.

The Pontchartrain loan would never carry the day for the FHLBB. Lincoln could easily demonstrate that had it not sold the hotel to the HPLP, its cash outflow would have been at least $10 million greater—the amount of the limited partners' cash investment. The operating losses would have been exactly the same whether the hotel had been sold or not. It's pretty hard to show any dissipation of assets or injury to Lincoln when it's $10 million ahead because of HPLP.

The ESOP loan wasn't a good case for the FHLBB. As Lincoln's response showed, the value of the ACC stock which Lincoln's portion of the ESOP held was $22 million compared to an $11 million loan. Now, it's true that the value of ACC's stock later went into a free-fall, but that was largely because of the FHLBB's persistent attacks on Lincoln and ACC. The question is: Did ACC or the FHLBB cause the value of the ESOP assets to fall? ACC could contend that, were it not for the FHLBB's inappropriate actions, the ESOP would have had asset values which greatly exceeded any loans; therefore, there was no dissipation of assets.

The Playtex and Memorex transactions were equally arguable. In the case of Playtex, the FHLBB's records show that ACC bought the stock from Lincoln in a transaction which resulted in a substantial gain to Lincoln; months later, ACC sold the stock at a gain; months later, Lincoln repurchased the stock; and several months later, Lincoln realized another substantial gain on the sale of the stock. The FHLBB staff could not possibly demonstrate that each increase in price was not attributable to events which occurred after each purchase or sale. The only way that there could be a dissipation of assets is if the FHLBB could show that ACC bought the stock at a bargain price or had inside information about some future event which would cause it to go up in value. The FHLBB could not demonstrate either of those conditions. Thus, it could not prove any dissipation. So, it argued that ACC's purchase was a prohibited, affiliated transaction. It could not, however, show any direct injury to Lincoln.

In the case of Memorex, Lincoln sold the stock, at a gain, to a third party. The day after the 1987 stock-market crash, the third party sold the stock to ACC at a price which was double the price for which Lincoln had sold the stock over three months earlier. Months later, ACC sold the stock for a gain. The FHLBB argument, using hindsight, was that ACC should have let Lincoln repurchase the stock in October 1987, so that Lincoln could realize the subsequent gain. This, of course, assumes that ACC had a crystal ball or insider information showing that the stock would, in fact, go up in value at the time it was repurchased. It also assumes there were no events after the repurchase date which caused the stock to increase in value. The fact is that the FHLBB could not demonstrate the existence of any of the conditions it needed to in order to prove a dissipation of assets or injury to Lincoln. Also, imagine what the FHLBB's reaction would have been had Lincoln repurchased the stock in October 1987 and it had gone down in value. The words "unsafe and unsound" would have been immediately attached to the transaction.

All of these transactions were also considered to be unsafe and unsound and were the subject of income reversals. If Lincoln wasn't injured, they were hardly unsafe or unsound. The bottom line is that the entire conservatorship action was absolutely dependent on making a case that the Hidden Valley transactions were improper.

The Hidden Valley transactions were the only ones in the FHLBB's kit bag that had not been rebutted by Lincoln. The FHLBB's lawyers had Lincoln's response to everything else and knew, on the basis of the response, that none of the examiners' findings would carry the day if challenged in court. They needed something that Lincoln had not rebutted. This way, they could fabricate some facts and embellish others in any manner they wished. By the time Lincoln or ACC had a chance to respond to the unfounded charges used to support a conservatorship, it would be too late—the deed would be done. Thus, the FHLBB's staff used Hidden Valley as the cornerstone of its recommendation to the Board.

The unusual nature of the Lincoln case is demonstrated by what the regulators could not assert. They could not cite any major appraisal-based losses on real estate or loans—except the HPLP loan and some minor real-estate losses that were fully reserved—because there were no major losses. They could not cite securities that were in default and for which reserves had not been established by Lincoln—there were none. In virtually all of the other conservatorship actions taken, or to be taken, by the FHLBB, the grounds were based on losses in the portfolio which threatened the solvency of the S&L. That was not the case here.

Lincoln may be the only S&L the federal government has ever seized on the basis of accounting disagreements and assertions of "affiliated transactions," such as the tax-sharing payments, the ESOP, Playtex, and Memorex. All of these issues are judgmental and did not involve actual losses to Lincoln.

The tax-sharing issue is moot if one considers the results of the IRS exam and the taxable transactions in 1988. ACC's tax advisors believed that the timing differences which gave rise to the deferred taxes had turned around in 1988 as a result of transactions in 1988 combined with the IRS' findings. Thus, all of the cumulative payments made by Lincoln to ACC represented payments for current tax liabilities, as opposed to payments of deferred tax liabilities. If no deferred taxes were improperly upstreamed to ACC, the FHLBB's entire theory falls apart.

The simple fact is that the FHLBB's position was not supportable based on the evidence existing at the time they considered and voted on this action. Were the FHLBB Board members told about ACC's position with respect to the tax status of Lincoln? Were they told that the assertions regarding the Hidden Valley sales had not been verified by the field examiners or ever discussed with Lincoln's management or Lincoln's auditors? If not, the FHLBB Board members were given a woefully incomplete and misleading picture by their staff. One has to believe that was the case.

ACC filed bankruptcy when it did because it had heard from an outside attorney that the conservatorship action would happen that week. The FHLBB's pattern was to seize an association at the close of business on a Friday afternoon. So, the afternoon of the 14th was the most logical time for it to happen. ACC was undoubtedly right in this assessment. The

FHLBB was ready to move that very day.

The bankruptcy filings just made things a little stickier. The regulators wouldn't be able to get their hands on the assets in any of the subsidiaries. They knew that closing Lincoln would cause a run on the deposits, but they didn't know how bad the run would actually be. To be safe, they'd have to borrow more cash to meet depositors' demands. Without the potential collateral in the subs, they had to obtain guarantees, so the San Francisco Bank and the Federal Reserve would provide the necessary cash.

The Bank Board meeting adjourned at about 9:00 A.M. Washington time, or 6:00 A.M., Phoenix time. This gave the FHLBB people in Washington plenty of time to communicate with their troops and get the invasion of Lincoln completely coordinated. They had to have people at each of Lincoln's twenty-nine branches when they opened in California, as well as people to take over the Phoenix and Irvine offices. All told, they needed a small army. The FHLBB was skilled in this kind of an operation. After all, they had been shutting down associations all across the country.

They hit Lincoln in Phoenix that same Friday morning. They rushed in with over fifty people. Hired security guards, better known as rent-a-cops, were stationed at every door leading into Lincoln's offices. Lincoln's parking garage was sealed off, and nobody could enter or leave the buildings or the garage. A sign declaring the conservatorship was posted on each door.

Once the buildings were secured, the feds entered the buildings and took over all of the interior offices. They secured all of the file rooms, sealed desks and filing cabinets, and evicted people from their offices and herded them into hallways. The feds acted like one would expect the palace guard of a banana-republic dictatorship to act. They were rude, vulgar, disrespectful of people and property, and threatening. Anyone who questioned their actions was threatened with legal action as they waived their court order and credentials under the noses of Lincoln's employees.

The branches and Irvine were also hit by the FHLBB. The depositors in some branches panicked, and the outflow of funds began. The withdrawals for the first two days were $77 million, and the total for the first week was over $180 million. Again, the feds were reported to have acted like a conquering army. They were uniformly threatening and abusive to Lincoln's personnel.

The situation was the worst in Phoenix. In anticipation of the bankruptcy filing, many of ACC's records, which had been stored in the Lincoln buildings, had been moved into ACC's building or had been placed in storage. But not all of ACC's records had been removed from the buildings. Also, several of ACC's operations, such as accounting, data processing, mailroom, switchboard, and real-estate management were housed in the same buildings where Lincoln was located.

When the feds locked up and secured Lincoln's buildings, they locked in ACC's personnel, as well as many of ACC's records. Bob Kielty and Charlie tried to explain this problem to the head fed who was in charge of the takeover operation—a big, burly, bearded, vulgar, lawyer type. His reaction was: "Tough. Nothing leaves these buildings unless we say so. You'll have to prove that anything that goes out of here doesn't belong to Lincoln."

Kielty tried patiently to explain that ACC could not operate without access to functions like data processing and the mailroom, and the feds had to permit access to ACC's legitimate operations and records. He was essentially told to "get lost." Well, this infuriated both Charlie and Kielty, both of whom had, up to this point, been reasonably restrained considering what was happening. The feds' lack of civility and outward hostility then led to a battle between lawyers, with each threatening to haul the other before a judge.

Literally moments after the confrontation between the fed and Charlie and Kielty, one of ACC's secretaries, who had been in Lincoln's offices on a routine business matter, tried to exit the Lincoln building with a couple of files. The files contained ACC's records, and she was unaware of the heated words that had just been exchanged. As she walked toward the door leading out of the building, this very large, and now irate, federal lawyer stepped in front of her, blocking her path. He said, "Give me those files you're carrying!"

"These are my personal records. I'm just going back to my desk in the other building," the secretary said, as she moved to step around him.

He moved to block her way again and literally screamed, "Lady, give me those goddamn files or I'm going to knock you on your fucking ass!"

The young woman dropped the files and, in near panic, ran from the building in tears. When she reached ACC's building, she told the other secretaries what had happened. Word of her encounter rapidly reached Charlie and Bob. They were already angry, and this incident really set them off. They demanded that ACC's attorneys stop the feds' Gestapo-like behavior. But frankly, under the circumstances, there wasn't anything the attorneys could do. The feds occupied the buildings; there were guards at every door; and the feds had court orders in their hands. The attorneys decided to let things cool down before trying to reach a workable peace.

The feds who were inside Lincoln's buildings were not idle. With the help of the FHLBB examiners, they had compiled a hit-list of key Lincoln employees—those most familiar with the records and past transactions. They began to usher these key people, one by one, into private offices and started to interrogate—that is the proper word—them.

They had several objectives in interrogating these people. First, they wanted to let them know, in no uncertain terms, who was in charge and who was now issuing them their paychecks. Second, they wanted to determine whether they wanted to keep the person as an employee. Third, they wanted information about Lincoln's records and customers. Fourth, they wanted any dirt that the person could give them on ACC or Keating.

For most, these interrogations were intimidating and frightening. These were people who had families to feed and bills to pay. The message they were receiving was loud and clear, "Either you play ball with us or you're fired." These interrogations continued for days. Some of the Lincoln people saw what the feds' game plan was. They had a job at Lincoln as long as they were useful and needed. But as soon as the feds had sucked all the information out of them, they were history.

Most of the people in ACC's offices had little time to dwell on what was happening across the parking lot to Lincoln. As soon as the office opened, the phones were jammed with calls from subordinated debenture holders who wanted to know what had happened to their investment. The calls were routed to secretaries, who took the caller's name and telephone number and told the person that someone would call them back. We had assembled about fifteen people who were assigned the responsibility for returning these calls. The attorneys had prepared a brief memo which outlined the potential consequences of ACC's Chapter 11 filing and the seizure of Lincoln. The bottom line was, barring a sale of Lincoln, ACC had lost most of its asset value and, in all likelihood, the debenture holders would get very little, if anything, back. In effect, they had lost their entire investment.

The debenture holders were a diverse group. Many were elderly, and their investment in the debentures represented a substantial portion, or all, of their retirement funds. They had made the investment for the interest return that the bonds paid, and they counted on that interest to meet their daily needs. Others were infirm, and the invested funds were needed to meet medical costs. Some had invested for their children's education. A fair number were professionals—doctors, dentists, lawyers—or small businesses which had invested pension funds. The rest just wanted a place to put excess cash and to earn a return on it.

California is a melting pot, with people of many origins. Many of the callers were not fluent in English. Some spoke only Spanish, others Chinese or Japanese. Thus, it was difficult to understand and communicate with some of the callers.

As we returned these calls, we heard many sad stories of what the loss of the funds meant to the caller. Others were almost casual about the situation, saying that they understood that they had probably suffered a loss, but just wanted to check anyway. If there was any trend at all, and that was certainly difficult to discern, the persons who had invested the larger dollar amounts—usually the business people and professionals—were the least upset with what had happened. They seemed to understand that they had taken a risk and it just hadn't worked out. I remember talking to one man who had invested well over $100,000. He said, "This isn't my year. First, my limited partnership investments all went south and now this. I guess I'd better stick to CDs or Treasuries. This could get expensive." Others were much less sanguine and were extremely distraught over the effects of their loss.

In total, we returned around five thousand calls over a three-day period. Virtually, every caller said that they had purchased the debentures to get the higher interest rates which the bonds paid and that they knew it meant they were taking a higher risk. I don't recall anybody saying that a single caller complained of having been misled or said they had misunderstood the investment risks of the bonds.

Also, they all wanted to know if anything could be done to avoid the loss. Charlie suggested that we should tell them to call Danny Wall in Washington and ask the FHLBB to let Lincoln be sold. He even had Wall's telephone number listed on the information sheet provided by the attorneys. This was at best a symbolic gesture. The moment the FHLBB took over Lincoln that Friday morning, ACC's $100- to $200-million investment was permanently wiped out.

One of the first efforts by the FHLBB's managers was to try to figure out how deep the hole was that they had dug for themselves now that they had to liquidate Lincoln. They began pouring over lists of loans and real estate and formulating all kinds of reserves for these assets. Their approach was to write down virtually every asset. Part of their objective was to throw Lincoln into insolvency as quickly as possible, so they could move out of conservatorship and into receivership.

They started by recording all of the 1988 examination directives. They then made very broad, arbitrary estimates, such as write off 50 percent of all loans, reduce the investments in service corporations by 75 percent, and so on. At this point, there was apparently no attempt to identify these estimated losses with specific, individual assets, even though the people who were now occupying Lincoln's offices could have gone through that exercise.

The Lincoln loss estimate was of great importance to politicians in Washington. The House Banking Committee's chairman, Henry Gonzalez, D-Texas, by April 24, according to the *American Banker*, was asking for Danny Wall's resignation over the handling of Lincoln. The paper estimated that the loss on Lincoln would be $2.5 billion—a number which seems to have been cast in stone, as it is the figure which is most commonly reported. The $2.5 billion number was also needed to elevate Lincoln to the *worst* S&L failure on record. If Lincoln were not forced into this elevated position, it would lose its political sizzle. Congress wanted Lincoln to remain at the top of the loss list, so that Lincoln and Keating could be cast in the role of the symbolic villains of the nationwide S&L debacle.

Under pressure from Gonzalez, Wall held a press interview in which he indicated that criminal referrals had been made in the Lincoln case. He also alleged that ACC had destroyed documents that were critical to Lincoln. And he stated that the recent exam had revealed that assets were being "shifted" between Lincoln and ACC. Of course, most of what Wall said in the press conference was untrue—his comments consisted of the false data and stories that the FHLBB staff had given him.

Wall also wrote Gonzalez a lengthy letter defending the FHLBB's actions relative to Lincoln. He attempted to lay blame for the depth of the losses expected from Lincoln's failure to his predecessor by saying: "When the three member Bank Board was reconstituted in August 1987, it inherited the extremely complex and controversial matter of Lincoln Savings." This would be Wall's constant theme—the prior examinations and FHLBB actions were inadequate, and only after the 1988 exam was completed was the Board in a position to act.

ACC learned from former employees that things were apparently not going well for the new "outstanding" and "expert" management team of Lincoln. All indications were that they were overwhelmed by Lincoln's assets and operations. None had any real experience with the types of assets that Lincoln held or with an operation as large as Lincoln. People said that a Keystone Cop atmosphere had developed within Lincoln.

Data-processing people were resigning and leaving Lincoln in droves. No one was monitoring or managing the junk-bond portfolio. Securities and liabilities weren't being hedged against currency and interest-rate movements. No one was paying attention to the cost of funds, and, as a result, Lincoln's cost of money was much higher than it should have been. No one was in charge of loan underwriting, and funds were being dispersed without a complete understanding of the loan. Real-estate projects were in shambles.

The entire Lincoln operation was in a complete state of disarray. The really good and talented people who were on Lincoln's staff at the time of the seizure thought the FDIC folks were incompetent and poor managers, so they left Lincoln's employ. Those who remained were the people requiring the most supervision. They were put in charge of departments.

An organization which had functioned smoothly on a day-to-day basis suddenly became dysfunctional. The people who remained with Lincoln indicated that the situation didn't improve over time; instead, it progressively got worse. The federal managers were in way over their heads.

The FHLBB had said that ACC's management of Lincoln was unsafe and unsound. Well, their management of the institution gave a whole new meaning to those words. They lost money hand over fist because of basic incompetency.

Real estate projects were left unattended, and development ground to a halt. Many of the loans which Lincoln made were non-recourse. The association could only look to the property for satisfaction of the debt. When people who owed Lincoln money under carry-back notes saw the deterioration in the projects, and the absence of active promotion and development by Lincoln, they defaulted on the notes. There was no reason why they should commit funds to a parcel of land located in a project which was, in effect, being abandoned by Lincoln. The attraction which had compelled them to buy in the first place was that Lincoln was creating value in these projects—value which extended to the land they had purchased. Without the active development and promotion of the land owned by Lincoln, no value was created, and, in fact, because of the lack of activity, values were diminished. They simply decided not to throw good money after bad and gave the land back to Lincoln.

When borrowers asked for loan modifications that would extend terms or reduce scheduled payments, the new management refused to listen.

Between 1989 and early 1990, the government took over Security, Southwest, Universal, Sun State, Western, Merabank, Sentinel, and Pima—virtually all of Arizona's savings and loan associations. These associations held combined assets of over $20 billion and, if Lincoln was added in, over $25 billion. The closure of these institutions destroyed real-estate values, which were already sagging, by throwing billions of dollars of real estate onto the market at distressed prices and by eliminating all sources of credit for builders and developers. As a result, borrowers needed a sympathetic lender who would work with them through a tough cycle. The government managers weren't sympathetic. Their attitude was: Pay up or we'll foreclose. And foreclose is what they did. Consequently, the quality of Lincoln's loan portfolio plunged.

With respect to Lincoln's real-estate assets, the new managers ordered appraisals which were based on the assumption that the property was to be sold within six months, as is, to a single buyer in an all-cash transaction. Appraisers understood that if the appraised value exceeded the ultimate sales price, the government would not view them favorably. So, the appraisals were at rock-bottom, fire-sale levels. And, then, the government let it be known that they would accept deals at 85 percent of the appraised amount. This was welcome news to the bottom-fishers who knew they could clean up by dealing with the government. But they were in for a surprise. Even if they met the government's price, they had to wait for a bid process, or the government's decision regarding their offer took six months or more.

The government managers also adopted very creative sales tactics. They erected a sign on the property saying that it was for sale and then sat back and waited for offers. If no offers appeared, they put the property up for auction, where it went to the highest bidder. Of course, with these practices, they lost money by the millions for each association and, overall, by the billions.

One of the first things that the new managers did was to sell off the interest-bearing securities. They didn't consider whether market conditions were right for a sale—they just sold. They lost money—lots of it. Nor did they have any income stream left to meet ongoing expenses, so operating losses mounted. To cover cash requirements, they borrowed at rates well above market rates. Losses skyrocketed.

In short, these managers did everything possible to create losses. They didn't care. They were able to say that all the money lost as a result of their abject incompetency was the fault of the prior owners, claiming that the losses had existed at the time of the seizure. Well, that's nonsense. The fact is there was no management—the government left Lincoln to run on autopilot and blamed Keating for the resulting losses.

The completion of Lincoln's audit was still an open issue. At the time of the seizure, Touche was far from being done with its work. The issue became: Should the audit be completed? ACC would have loved to see Touche complete the audit, because it would have shown that Lincoln was solvent, and substantially so, when the feds grabbed it. But for the same reason, the FHLBB could not possibly have wanted Touche to finish its work. If the audit were completed, it would have weakened, if not totally destroyed, the FHLBB's contentions regarding the dissipation of assets and insolvency.

Touche Ross was not engaged to complete the audit. After the takeover, there were never any reliable financial statements for Lincoln Savings and Loan. The FHLBB, under the direction of Dochow and San Francisco, forced all kinds of adjustments on Lincoln's books in order to justify the actions they had taken. And the FDIC destroyed the integrity and usefulness of the books with reserves based on dubious appraisals and wild-ass guesses.

ACC also learned that Lincoln was directed to reverse the profits on fifteen land-sale transactions that Kenneth Leventhal reviewed. Not surprisingly, they were the same transactions on which the FHLBB had based the conservatorship. They were also contained in the FHLBB's final examination report on Lincoln—a report that ACC never had a chance to rebut, because it wasn't written until July 1989, even though it was only for the period up to April 14, 1989. The adjustments amounted to $135 million and related to transactions going back to 1986.

ACC heard that Lincoln's accounting personnel were clearly troubled by what they had been directed to do. They apparently resisted recording the adjustments. It was crucial to the FHLBB that Lincoln accept and record the entries related to the land-sale transactions. The FHLBB had based its conservatorship action, and later its receivership, on the income reversals produced by these transactions. If Lincoln's accounting personnel didn't record the entries, the FHLBB, which had by now been sued by ACC, was in real trouble. The FHLBB needed to sustain the assertion that there had been a dissipation of assets and that Lincoln was insolvent at the time the conservatorship was voted on. The subsequent reserves that the FDIC had recorded would not suffice, because they were predicated on Lincoln being liquidated. ACC learned that the issue was resolved when the government "ordered" Lincoln's staff to record the requested entries.

The fact that Lincoln's accounting staff, who no longer had any ties whatsoever to ACC, had to be ordered to record the entries suggests that they certainly were not convinced that it was proper to do so. But it was vital to the government's defense and other legal actions that these entries not be rejected by the government's own managers. This order apparently settled the issue.

The seizure of Lincoln had became a controversial issue. When the FHLBB announced that the aggregate losses from Lincoln's failure could exceed $2.5 billion, making it the costliest S&L failure, Congress jumped all over Danny Wall and the FHLBB. Several congressmen and senators questioned why, if the losses were as bad as reported, the FHLBB hadn't acted sooner. The press cited the 1986 exam results, which had previously been leaked by the FHLBB itself, and wondered why Wall hadn't taken action on the basis of that report. Under intense pressure, on July 6, 1989, Wall released the ERC report dealing with the decision to enter into the MOU. The press release stated:

> While this report was formerly treated as confidential material, it is being made public at this time because of current litigation growing out of recent conservatorship action by regulators involving the thrift, certain criticisms directed at the Bank Board's action and the attendant high level of public interest in these matters.

The information should still have been confidential, but Wall and the FHLBB were under heat, and, as had become the standard modus operandi for the regulators, they ignored all of their own rules and regulations when it suited their own vested interests.

On August 2, 1989, Lincoln was placed into receivership by the FHLBB. A new federal mutual association was created, and Lincoln's assets were transferred to it. The new association was granted a government guarantee to cover up to $2.2 billion in new brokered deposits to fund its operations. The FSLIC was appointed receiver. This action wiped out all of ACC's equity interest in Lincoln. The Bank Board meeting to vote on the action lasted exactly ten minutes, and at 6:25 P.M., Washington time, August 2, 1989, Lincoln Savings and Loan Association ceased to exist. The government had effectively confiscated over $100 million from ACC's shareholders.

ACC and Lincoln had been under almost constant attack by the FHLBB and its agents from March 1986 through April 1989. During the entire period, the FHLBB wasn't able to find a single dollar of uncontested losses which were not covered by reserves already recorded on Lincoln's books. They weren't able to point to a single investment that had resulted in a significant loss, in spite of their continuous assertions that Lincoln's practices were risky. They couldn't claim that a single real-estate project was a loser.

Unable to assert real losses, the FHLBB resorted to rewriting the rules, relying on unpublished internal opinions, and attacks against Lincoln's accounting. These attacks were made by persons with limited training and experience as accountants. The claims often weren't supported by people within the FHLBB structure.

The theft of ACC's equity in Lincoln was accomplished by sleight of hand, illegal leaks, and insupportable arguments about the safety and soundness of Lincoln's operations. This is a case of regulatory abuse. Never before had the government taken over an S&L with so little justification.

Eighteen

Congress Covers Its Tracks

Congress' interest in the Lincoln affair surfaced well before the conservatorship action on April 14, 1989. Congress, most acutely the Committee on Banking, Finance and Urban Affairs of the House of Representatives and the Banking, Housing and Urban Affairs Committee of the Senate, was faced with a major political crisis. The savings and loan industry was crashing down on them. The industry's problems first reached crisis proportions in 1987, when Congress passed a bill providing about $10.8 billion to recapitalize the FSLIC. That was a lot of money, and it was supposed to take care of all of the industry's problems. The appropriated funds were to be recovered later by increased insurance charges to be assessed against the industry. In effect, the funds were loaned to the FSLIC.

Within months of the passage of the bill, the FHLBB changed its estimate of the cost to the industry to about $16 billion but still maintained that taxpayer monies would not be needed on a permanent basis. A few months later, the cost was increased to over $32 billion, and it was becoming obvious that tax dollars would be needed to bail out the industry.

By mid-1989, the number grew to $50 billion. Congress knew, as did the FHLBB, that the number could continue to grow to $500 billion or more. But no one wanted to be the first to tell the American public the real cost of the fiasco that the S&L industry had become. At least not until there was someone, other than Congress, who could be blamed for the debacle.

Congress' role in the industry's collapse started with the passage of the Depository Institutions Deregulation and Monetary Control Act in 1980. The Act was designed to allow insured institutions, particularly S&Ls, to compete with money-market funds by lifting the caps on the rates they could pay depositors and by permitting them to offer different types of deposit accounts. But Congress went one step better. It raised the FSLIC deposit insurance, which was backed by the full faith and credit of the U.S. government, from $40,000 to $100,000 per account. This let the S&Ls compete with major brokerage firms for the jumbo accounts which moved from institution to institution in search of the highest rate. It also laid the foundation for rapid growth for the S&L industry, because a given institution could now raise all the cash it could ever want just by hiking its rate a few basis points over the competition. But it was simply a foundation. For real growth to result, the S&Ls had to have a place to invest the available cash at rates which were high enough to cover the cost of the deposits.

Congress added another step to the industry's ladder to growth with the 1981 tax bill. Prior to the passage of this bill, a vibrant market in tax shelters had emerged. An investment was considered a tax shelter if it featured tax-deductible expenses at the front end and potential capital gains at the back end. The front-end expenses were deducted against income derived from other sources, such as compensation or income from a professional practice, which was otherwise taxable at ordinary tax rates—52 percent for high-income taxpayers. The gain at the back end was taxed at capital-gains rates—25 percent at the time.

The object was to sell an investment for more than the investor had paid or committed to pay—the original cost plus all carrying costs, including interest. Under circumstances where the investor just broke even, the after-tax gain was still equal to 27 percent—the difference between deductions at ordinary rates and the capital gain at 25 percent. Not bad for a break-even deal. If the investment featured either deductible depreciation or amortization, the returns were even better, as these were noncash deductions which, because of the tax-rate differences, produced after-tax cash returns to the investor.

Prior to 1981, the variety of tax-sheltered investments was mind-boggling—limited only by the imagination of their creators. There were farming shelters, such as cattle feeding or certain growing crops. There were oil and gas wells. Others featured master recordings, motion pictures, commodities straddles, book publishing, chinchilla or mink ranches, and you name it. But the "king" was real estate.

By 1981, the IRS considered many of these tax-sheltered investments to be abusive; that is, they had no economic substance. They were merely manufactured deductions, and there was no hope that the investment would ever show a real economic profit. These shelters were a drain on tax revenues. There was no strong, organized lobby that, bearing campaign contributions, touted the virtues of these shelters to Congress. So, they became targets of congressmen who were seeking ways to trim the growing federal deficit.

The 1981 tax bill eliminated most of the shelters and included huge penalties if a shelter were deemed abusive. It also added more luster to the favored status that real estate enjoyed. Depreciable lives were shortened, and accelerated depreciation methods, which increased noncash deductions in the early years, were permitted. Even if the investment were financed by non-recourse loans, the bill allowed the greater depreciation deductions. If the investor were a limited partner, the investor could deduct depreciation to the extent of the investor's ownership percentage in the partnership. As a result, limited partners usually received 99 percent of the deductions, while the general partner received only 1 percent. The bill provided for tax credits for restoration of existing buildings and for fixtures and furnishings. Real estate was no longer king of the tax shelters; it was God.

After passage of the 1981 bill, there was a tremendous rush into real-estate investments, particularly limited partnerships. Office buildings and shopping centers were popular because, once they were rented up, the income stream was stable and predictable. Some investors favored apartments and hotels because, when compared to leases associated with office buildings or shopping centers, rents adjusted more frequently, offering a hedge against inflation. Even though it didn't generate depreciation deductions, raw land was attractive, especially in growth areas, such as Arizona and Texas. The inflation rate on land in these areas had outstripped interest rates, and, since the interest was deductible against ordinary income and the gain was taxed at a lower rate, the raw-land investment penciled out.

The tax status of real estate created a constant demand for product. Many properties rolled over from one partnership to another. Once the partnership burned out—a condition that results when deductions no longer exceed rental income and, thus, the investment throws off ordinary income—the property was sold.

Real-estate syndicators had a stable of investors and partnerships. When Partnership A's property burned out, it was sold to Partnership B, at a gain. Partnership B then sold its burned-out property to Partnership C, who, in turn, sold its burned-out property, again at a gain, to Partnership D, a newly formed partnership. This process could go on indefinitely, creating an almost never-ending demand for real estate at constantly increasing prices, or so the real-estate industry thought.

With the passage of Garn-St. Germain in 1983, the S&L industry entered the real-estate boom, courtesy of Congress. Garn-St. Germain allowed S&Ls to invest directly in real estate and to expand their lending to raw land and commercial real estate—no matter where it was located. And S&Ls could make loans equal to 100 percent of the value of the real estate which served as collateral.

Almost immediately, S&Ls became the primary source of real-estate financing in the United States. Many, like Lincoln, also became active investors and developers of real estate, especially raw land, either directly or through partnerships and joint ventures. Fueled by brokered deposits, which were easy to raise, the balance sheets of S&Ls ballooned with loans secured by commercial real estate and land as well as direct investments. And, because real-estate prices continued on an unabated, upward spiral, these were good investments at the time.

Then Congress slammed the door—hard. It passed the 1986 tax bill. You've heard the phrase, "God is dead." Well, it may not have been a religious reference, it may have been directed at real estate. The 1981 tax bill made real estate the God of tax shelters. The 1986 bill killed it. The 1986 bill, among other things, lengthened depreciable lives; eliminated tax credits; reduced the tax rate on ordinary income; eliminated the capital gains tax rate; limited the deduction of passive losses, which effectively meant that deductions from real-estate investments were limited to the amount of income produced from such investments and that excess deductions could not be used to offset income from other sources; and established an alternative minimum tax. Congress could not have done more damage to real-estate values if it tried—and in the 1986 tax bill it tried.

For the vast majority of investors, the 1986 tax bill removed the incentive to invest in real estate. It probably wasn't until 1988, after investors had had a whole year to see how badly they had been hurt, that all of the effects of this legislation were felt. By then, with demand suffocated, real-estate values plunged. The depth of the drop varied from market to market, but the least affected lost about 25 percent in value, and the worst lost up to 50 percent, almost all attributable to the 1986 tax bill. This terrible result must have been what Congress intended, because they haven't done anything since to remedy the situation. Some would contend that this tax bill was the principal cause of, or at the very least a significant contributing factor to, the recession which followed. Maybe Congress didn't realize the damage they caused—remember these are the same geniuses who have given us a $4-trillion federal deficit.

The effect on the S&Ls was swift and painful. They had made billions of dollars of loans which were secured by real estate, much of them at 100 percent of value. When the tax bill killed real-estate prices, the collateral values dropped in virtually all markets by a magnitude of from 25 percent up to as much as 50 percent. Many borrowers, no longer receiving tax benefits and finding no buyers for their property, simply handed the keys over to the S&Ls and walked. Others demanded modifications to loans to stretch out payment periods, to reduce interest rates, or both. Delinquencies skyrocketed, and, as they moved toward foreclosure, loans became nonperforming.

At this point, the friendly regulators stepped in to give Congress a hand in finishing off the industry. They ordered new appraisals, which, because of plunging values, were, of course, lower. They used the appraisals to force write-downs, reserves, and asset classifications, all of which reduced the capital of the S&Ls. If this were not bad enough, the regulators also made the capital rules more stringent. This created a vise in which S&L operators were squeezed until they expired. And who was charged with overseeing the regulators? You got it—Congress, specifically the same committees who gave us Garn-St. Germain.

Because many real-estate investors and developers had loans with more than one institution, the closure of an S&L had a domino effect. When an investor defaulted at one, the investor defaulted at several others at the same time. With the death of each association, real-estate prices sagged lower, pulling the others in the market down. Because of reduced capital and increased requirements, and faced with a deteriorating market, S&Ls were forced to stop lending, as were commercial banks with real-estate loan portfolios. Credit dried up. People were unable to refinance properties and, with sagging sales, ran out of working capital. As the downward spiral continued, record numbers of builders, developers, property managers, and investors, seeking protection from their creditors, headed for the bankruptcy courts.

In the twelve-month period from February 1989 to March 1990, every major association in Arizona, except one, was seized by the feds. The one exception was closed in 1991. Investors lost billions. These people were small business owners, developers, doctors, lawyers, and other high-income people. Many were driven into bankruptcy.

Some may argue that the 1986 tax bill, by removing tax incentives which artificially inflated real-estate prices, merely eliminated the speculators from the real-estate market. Others may contend that the crash in real-estate values was caused by overbuilding, resulting in a supply of office and shopping-center space that exceeded real demand. There is truth to both of these arguments. There were speculative investors who were primarily motivated by the available tax benefits, and some markets were overbuilt. But this does not change the fact that these projects were, in large part, financed by the savings and loan industry. When the tax law changed, all real estate, whether it was owned by a speculator or not, suffered. In the overbuilt areas, even had there been no tax-law changes, there may well have been drops in value. But at the very least, the provisions of the 1986 tax bill exacerbated the problems in these markets.

Whether one views the 1986 tax bill as the causative factor of, or merely a contributing factor to, the decline in property values, there is no question that the result was a plunge in loan-to-value ratios on existing loans secured by real estate. This was true not only for S&Ls but for commercial banks, insurance companies, and pension funds as well. Moreover, the values of real-estate investments held by these entities, as well as publicly held and private limited partnerships, also crashed.

Congress was, at best, insensitive to the effects of this tax legislation on the economy in general and real estate in particular. The committees charged with overseeing the financial-services industries should have known that the tax bill would render havoc to the already fragile S&Ls. It was certainly no secret that after Garn-St. Germain, S&Ls loaded their balance sheets with large loans secured by real estate and with direct investments in real estate. How then could Congress not know the extent of the damage that reducing real-estate values, by the amount of the tax incentives inherent in them, would cause to these institutions? Was Congress careless, incompetent, ignorant, or all of these?

Congress was not finished with the S&L industry. Under increased pressure from the public, Congress passed the Financial Institutions Reform, Recovery, and Enforcement Act of 1989 (FIRREA), and it was signed by President Bush on August 9, 1989.

FIRREA basically did away with both the FHLBB and the FSLIC. The Office of Thrift Supervision (OTS), directed by Danny Wall, was created to regulate the remaining savings and loans. The Resolution Trust Corporation (RTC) was created to manage and sell the assets of all of the S&Ls that had been, or would be, declared insolvent. Two new deposit-insurance funds were established: the Bank Insurance Fund (BIF) and the Savings Association Insurance Fund (SAIF). Both of these funds were to be administered by the FDIC and were to be funded by premiums, which FIRREA increased. The banks paid premiums to BIF, and the S&Ls paid to SAIF. The FHLB district banks remained intact, but all of the examination and supervisory personnel were put back on the government payroll of OTS, removing the appearance of the conflict of interest which ACC had complained about when these people were on the district banks' payrolls.

FIRREA provided $50 billion in federal monies to resolve the problem of liquidating the failed S&Ls, an amount which would prove woefully inadequate.

A risk-based capital structure for S&Ls was initiated, which based capital requirements on the nature of the assets the institutions held and, overall, increased capital requirements. It effectively disallowed any more direct investments and directed the S&Ls to concentrate on SFR mortgage lending. Under certain circumstances, brokered deposits were severely limited. Loan-to-single-borrower limits were reduced. The overall effect was to unwind Garn-St. Germain and return S&Ls to a very restricted traditional role in the lending arena.

The overall enforcement scheme was radically changed for "insured depository institutions." The reach of the enforcement provisions was extended to include a variety of individuals and entities not previously covered by earlier laws. Enforcement provisions now applied to holding companies, nonbank subsidiaries of holding companies, service corporations, and their subsidiaries. Individuals, referred to as "institution-affiliated parties," who became subject to the provisions included directors, officers, employees, controlling shareholders, persons who filed change-in-control notices, consultants, joint venturers, or others who participated in the conduct of the affairs of an insured depository institution. Under certain circumstances, independent contractors, such as accountants, lawyers, and appraisers also came within the reach of these provisions.

Cease-and-desist authority was expanded, allowing the agencies to require an institution or institution-affiliated party to (1) make restitution or provide reimbursement, indemnification, or guarantee against loss if the institution or party was unjustly enriched by a violation or practice, (2) restrict growth, (3) dispose of any loan or asset, (4) rescind agreements or contracts, (5) employ qualified officers or employees, subject to agency approval, and (6) take any such other appropriate action determined by the agency. FIRREA also defined a "violation" to include, "any action (alone or with another or others) for or toward causing, bringing about, participating in, counseling, or aiding or abetting a violation." Also, FIRREA provided that if certain conditions exist, any institution-affiliated party may be removed from office or prohibited from participating in the conduct of the affairs of an insured depository institution.

FIRREA expanded and increased the civil money penalties which may be imposed on an institution or an institution-affiliated party. Under prior law, these penalties were generally limited to $1,000 per day, but under FIRREA the penalties were increased to $5,000 per day for the least serious violations and up to as much as *$1 million per day* for the most serious cases. Other civil money penalties were added for the failure to make reports of condition (financial reports) to the agency or for submitting or publishing false or misleading reports or information.

Sweeping changes were made in the penalties applicable to banking-related criminal offenses. These offenses include bribery, misapplication and embezzlement, making false entries in bank books, making false statements to a federally insured financial institution to obtain loans or extensions of credit, bank fraud, and, if the violations affect financial institutions, mail fraud and wire fraud. Prior to FIRREA, the maximum term of imprisonment was generally five years for these offenses. Under FIRREA, the maximum sentence is *twenty years per violation*. Maximum fines were also increased from between $5,000 and $10,000 per violation to *$1 million per violation*.

The statute of limitations on these offenses was increased from five years from the date the offense was committed to *ten years*. If the statute of limitations applicable to an offense had not run as of the effective date of FIRREA, this extension also applied to an offense committed prior to the effective date of FIRREA. And it applied to any offense committed after August 9, 1989. So, if an offense were committed on September 1, 1984, the old statute would have run until September 1, 1989; but under FIRREA, the statute would now be extended another five years to September 1, 1994.

FIRREA gave the Justice Department the ability to file civil lawsuits to recover damages for violations of federal criminal banking statutes. It also provided for huge penalties in these actions. The Justice Department was also given the authority to issue administrative subpoenas to conduct investigations before filing these civil suits.

Finally, the RICO [Racketeer Influenced and Corrupt Organizations Act] was amended to add bank fraud. RICO provides for *treble damages*, seizure of assets, and other extreme measures that were originally intended to counteract drug crimes and organized-crime activities.

This extremely complex piece of legislation accomplished several purposes for Congress and the federal administration. First, since the government was the insurer of all deposits of $100,000 or less, they had no choice but to fund the S&L cleanup. During the 1988 election campaigns, neither the incumbent Congress nor George Bush told the American people how bad the situation was, nor did their challengers—they all had received campaign contributions from the financial-services industry and their PACs. Now, they had to pay the piper, and the $50 billion committed in FIRREA was one hell of a lot more than the public had been told—and one hell of a lot less than the real ultimate cost. FIRREA let them continue to sneak up on the problem while they conditioned the taxpayers, a little at a time, to accept the true enormity of the problem.

Everyone in Washington knew that there would be more requests for funds to cover the cost of the failed S&Ls and banks. That's where the second purpose of FIRREA enters the picture. FIRREA, with its new regulations, enforcement provisions, and civil and criminal penalties, shifted the focus off of Congress and the administration and onto the owners and managers of insured institutions. The government cast itself as a tough regulator and prosecutor who was pitted against the evil forces within the S&L and banking industry.

The new regulations, which unwound Garn-St. Germain, were designed to stop the bleeding by curtailing high-risk investments and by creating tougher capital requirements. Once again, Congress screwed up. Institutions that had been victimized by falling real-estate prices saw their capital eroded by increased reserves for loan losses. These walking-wounded were not able to meet the new capital requirements, especially after they were paid a visit by the regulators who forced additional reserves on them. So, in droves, they joined the ranks of the other failed shops.

FIRREA didn't stop the bleeding. As bigger institutions, with far greater asset levels than earlier failures, fell victim to the new capital requirements, it caused massive hemorrhaging.

The regulators, now armed with unprecedented powers, did become tougher. In fact, they became bullies. They threatened the managers of banks and S&Ls with severe punishment if they did not knuckle under to the regulators' demands. Appraisal losses became commonplace. Defaulted loans, caused by the eroded real-estate collateral values, became evidence of unsafe and unsound practices and, sometimes, criminal violations.

The institutions who survived the ravages of the regulators, and there aren't many of them, decided to get out of the lending business rather than face the penalties threatened by FIRREA. There was less risk in investing in Treasury securities than in taking a chance on making a loan which might not be collected in the future.

The friendly U.S. government facilitated the choice to invest in Treasury securities. Because of the astronomical federal deficit, the federal government has a voracious appetite for credit and is the largest borrower in the market. The government's borrowing habit is so great that by 1991 and 1992, the interest rates it paid on its Treasury securities exceeded the rates that the banks and S&Ls paid on their deposits, often by 300 to 350 basis points. By staying away from lending, and buying these securities, the institutions earned a nice spread and avoided the regulators' goon squads.

All this, of course, added to the existing credit drought. When the Federal Reserve cut interest rates, there was no impact on the recession because there was no stimulation created by the lower rates. The institutions still weren't about to make loans; instead, they simply bought more government securities and enjoyed even better spreads and record profits.

The nation's bankers were scared out of their wits by the regulators' tactics under FIRREA, and they weren't about to start making loans. Nothing good could come from lending. Capital requirements under the new risk-based system would go up; the spreads on loans weren't any better than those that could be achieved just by buying Treasury securities; and you couldn't be threatened with civil or criminal penalties. So, why make loans?

The final pieces in the new get-tough policy were the civil and criminal penalties of FIRREA and the amended RICO. These draconian measures allowed federal lawyers and prosecutors to go after the crooks and scalawags who were, in Congress' new version of history, the real reason the industry had collapsed. The whole problem, the government would have one believe, was that a bunch of thieves had looted the S&Ls of all their assets.

FIRREA allowed the feds to file civil lawsuits against S&L owners, directors, and management, as well as their accountants, lawyers, and consultants, to recover the losses that the institutions had suffered. All the feds needed to file such a suit was the fact that the S&L had failed, losses had resulted, and a somewhat plausible theory of culpability on the part of the targets of the lawsuit—just enough so the suit would not get thrown out on a motion for summary judgment or dismissal.

It has become routine for the feds to sue any officers and directors who are covered by directors' and officers' liability insurance (D&O coverage), as well as all other deep pockets available. The government knows, with almost absolute certainty, that all of the named defendants will settle before trial. They have no choice—the risks of trial are too high. Thus, FIRREA, combined with RICO, gave the feds the means to practice "legal extortion" with impunity.

The criminal penalties are the last piece. Let's say a bank officer makes a loan—a non-recourse loan—to a borrower. The S&L goes belly-up after it's savaged by the regulators. The buyer defaults, and the property is foreclosed. With its customary ineptitude, the RTC sells the property at a loss. The federal prosecutors, using hindsight, can contend that the borrower never intended to repay the loan at the time the loan application was made; the bank officer knew that; the S&L suffered a loss; and the whole transaction was nothing more than an artifice to defraud the S&L. All the prosecutor has to do is convince a grand jury—which the prosecutor controls by deciding what they'll hear and how they'll hear it—that the story is plausible, so they will vote to indict. Under the indictment, the prosecutor can turn this set of facts into several distinct alleged crimes, such as bank fraud, wire fraud, mail fraud (when the loan funds were disbursed), and making a false statement to obtain the loan. Both the borrower and the bank officer can face multiple violations, adding up to potential fines in the millions and a lengthy term in prison.

Now, assume in the circumstances described above that the loan transaction was, in fact, a normal lending transaction. The borrower had every intention of repaying the loan when he applied for the credit. Things just didn't work out when the real-estate market soured. He was unable to repay the loan, and, because of the soft market, he couldn't sell the property. He believed at the time he submitted the loan application that the property had a value equal to or greater than the amount he sought to borrow. Both the borrower and the bank officer have to be able to prove this at trial, or they risk being convicted and facing the stiff penalties.

Now, suppose the prosecutor isn't really interested in the borrower—the fish that he's after is a bank officer, say someone like Charlie Keating. The prosecutor goes to the borrower and, just like Monty Hall, says, "Let's make a deal. You plead guilty to one count and agree to testify against the bank officer, and we'll go easy on you. A light sentence, probably probation, and no fine." Does the borrower have a choice? It's a possible twenty years and everything he owns versus going along with some revisionist history and a plea agreement. What would you choose in those circumstances? As for the bank officer, he's screwed. It's either a trial and huge risks, with a cooperating witness to testify against him, or a plea agreement that's not going to be anywhere near as favorable as the one the borrower received.

The fact is that these extreme penalties have made it impossible for a person to defend himself in a trial before a jury of his peers—even if the person is absolutely without guilt. The potential penalties are simply too great. FIRREA has converted the normal practices of trade and commerce into criminal violations by, for all intents and purposes, denying a person the right to a fair trial. Again, it's legal extortion.

As Congress was contemplating the circumstances it faced in 1989, when FIRREA was in its embryonic stage, it needed something else to divert the public's attention. Congress didn't want the voters to focus on the fact that the legislation it had adopted had turned the S&Ls into shambles. Congress needed a scapegoat. Someone whose neck the whole mess could be hung around.

Congress had already missed the S&L operators in Texas. Jim Wright, the former Speaker of the House whose home state was Texas, shielded them from congressional scrutiny and public display. Besides, Gonzalez, the chairman of the House committee, was also from Texas, and he must have known that you don't trash your own state if you can avoid it. True, there had been books published that painted the Texans as a bunch of crooks, but the spotlight was now off of them. But not to despair, Gonzalez and his committee had found a perfect candidate—Charlie Keating.

Charlie had all of the characteristics that the committee could possibly have hoped for to meet its political needs. He was an outspoken and highly visible opponent of the regulation, or perhaps more precisely the re-regulation, of the thrift industry. He was active politically, and there had been reports that certain senators had interceded with the FHLBB on his behalf—senators who had received campaign contributions from Keating and his associates. There was the controversial removal of the Eleventh District and the, presumably, unprecedented MOU. There was the publicity that had surrounded the leaks which indicated Lincoln may have been a problem association from the very day ACC acquired ownership of it. Lincoln owned the type of assets that Congress now found so objectionable—real estate, junk bonds, hotels, equities, commercial loans, and loans secured by raw land. There had been mention of criminal referrals. Keating lived a flamboyant life-style, and ACC had been portrayed as a company that paid extremely high salaries, owned a fleet of aircraft, and exhibited other signs of being a high-profile organization. There were the bondholders in California, who could be painted as a group of senior citizens who had been taken advantage of and who had lost their life's savings in ACC's collapse. There were rumors linking Keating to people who had been appointed to the Bank Board. Finally, the FHLBB had called Lincoln the costliest failure of any S&L to date.

Everything was there to make grand theater if the committee handled it correctly. Theater that would shift the media spotlight off of Congress and its role in the most expensive fiasco in American history.

Gonzalez had tried, back in 1988, to get information from Danny Wall on what was happening in the Lincoln situation. Because Lincoln was an operating association, Wall refused to supply the requested information, citing the confidentiality provisions in the FHLBB's regulations. But with the conservatorship and the publicity attendant to it, the committee renewed its requests. Initially Wall balked, because, even in conservatorship, Lincoln was still technically an open association. It was clear, however, to Wall and the rest of the FHLBB that Congress could not be put off forever and that, sooner or later, the FHLBB would have to give the committee the information it was seeking.

This was troublesome. There were the issues of why the FHLBB had not acted sooner and why it had agreed to the MOU. There was division within the FHLBB structure—division between the folks in San Francisco and those in Washington. San Francisco said that the seizure of Lincoln was proof that they had been right back in 1987. They said that the only reason Lincoln had stayed open was that the Washington people were soft regulators, unwilling to take strong, assertive action because they were afraid of Keating and his political strength. Washington, on the other hand, was in the process of developing the story that the 1986 exam and the related findings were flawed because of the "inexperience" of the Eleventh-District examiners and mishandling by their supervisors. Added to this schism within the FHLBB was the CDSL, which would probably now maintain that they had been in favor of strong action against Lincoln all along but had deferred to the FHLBB.

Wall had good reason to be worried about Congress. During 1988, the FHLBB disposed of over two hundred S&Ls. In order to make these associations attractive, buyers were given huge tax benefits—primarily the right to offset the accumulated net operating losses of the failed thrift against the otherwise taxable income of the acquirer which had been derived from other sources. Normally net operating losses can only be used to offset the future income that the failed thrift might earn. Without the right to use these net operating losses to offset other income of the acquirer, the losses would, in all likelihood, lapse and produce no benefits. The ability to use these losses was worth billions to the acquirers of these associations. It's hard to tell how many billions were given away because the tax-loss benefits are not included in the figures that the FHLBB reports as the cost of disposing of these associations. In addition, the FHLBB granted the acquirers other inducements, such as income guarantees, for which the true cost will not be determinable for years to come. The public was beginning to understand that the real cost of these S&L dispositions was far greater than the government was reporting. The media was starting to ask embarrassing questions—of both Congress and the administration. So, Wall was on the hot seat, and, if someone had to be sacrificed within the government, he was an ideal candidate.

The schism within the FHLBB structure opened even farther as the result of a May 4, 1989, letter which Patriarca sent to Dochow, with copies to the Board members and many others. The letter contained the following comments:

> During the course of the prior 407(m) investigation of Lincoln, Mr. Hershkowitz of the Office of Enforcement (OE) failed to question a single witness, observing that Lincoln was not a priority because it was not insolvent. He explained his failure to investigate alleged file stuffing by Lincoln by noting such actions had not been proven. As a result of this failure to investigate, Ms. Sobol was detailed, over Ms. Stewart's strenuous objections, to undertake the investigation. Ms. Sobol did so with vigor. When Ms. Sobol's detail ended, Mr. Hershkowitz resumed the lead role . . . and again failed to depose any witnesses. As a result, the 1986 examination was hindered.
>
> In the course of the 1986 examination, Lincoln obstructed the examination by insisting that all requests for information come through its New York litigation counsel. Ms. Stewart negotiated an almost equally obstructive arrangement involving an on-site litigation counsel for Lincoln.
>
> Ms. Stewart then became an outspoken proponent for removing this District's jurisdiction over Lincoln—despite ORPOS's favorable review of our findings and its determination that there was no evidence of misconduct by this District. Ms. Stewart and Mr. Hershkowitz were vocal apologists for Lincoln's misconduct. Ms. Stewart displayed open, personal animus toward this District's supervisory personnel and counsel. Ms. Stewart repeatedly emphasized her fear that Lincoln would sue unless it was transferred to another District. Ms. Stewart even recommended that this District be barred from having a silent observer present when Lincoln addressed the Enforcement Review Committee (ERC) in Washington D.C. Ms. Stewart recommended that this District not be permitted to complete its presentation to the ERC and that this District not be permitted to present its position before the Bank Board.

OE also took a lead role in negotiating the Memorandum of Understanding and related Agreement with Lincoln. These agreements were drafted in a clearly unsatisfactory fashion. The language led to wholly unnecessary restrictions being placed on your examination of Lincoln, placed illusory limitations on Lincoln, prejudiced the Bank Board's authority to take enforcement action or appoint a conservator or receiver for Lincoln, and is the basis for Lincoln's pending suits against the Bank Board and FSLIC.

Patriarca then complained that Stewart and Hershkowitz were not granting San Francisco enough power to conduct its newly returned investigative powers and supervisory controls over Lincoln. Patriarca wanted to bring an injunctive action to gain access to records that ACC refused to produce, and Stewart told him that only OE could bring such an action. He wanted the same authority. Also, he wanted the power to enforce subpoenas that the Eleventh District had asked OE to serve on ACC, but which ACC was essentially ignoring. So, Patriarca recommended that the investigations "be conducted by the Eleventh District under delegated authority using legal counsel, supervisory personnel and other experts of our choosing."

Wall responded with a letter of his own to Patriarca, dated May 18, 1989. It said, in part:

The hostile attack that you chose to make on individuals within the Office of Enforcement is disturbing, smacks of sour grapes, and was done in an inappropriate manner.

By mid-July 1989, Lincoln and ACC were being featured frequently in the press. In April, several different groups of subordinated debenture holders filed class-action lawsuits against ACC, its officers and directors, its auditors, its lawyers, and other defendants.

In various cities in California, the plaintiffs in these actions formed groups, with the direct participation of the attorneys who represented them, and held periodic meetings to discuss their losses and, perhaps more importantly, to attract media attention to and support for their actions against the named defendants. They were successful. The media was very receptive and published numerous articles recounting the plights of these investors and repeated the allegations that they had made against Keating and others.

The government, specifically the RTC and OTS, also filed suits against ACC, certain of its officers and directors, and former officers and directors of Lincoln. Alleging RICO violations, the RTC suit sought actual damages in excess of $1 billion, an amount which could be trebled under RICO. The OTS suit asked for restitution in the millions of dollars. With numbers like these, the suits received a lot of ink in the press. Each article reported one paragraph of new information, followed by dozens of paragraphs that repeated, over and over, from article to article, the allegations contained in the suits.

ACC also filed suits against the FHLBB challenging the conservatorship and alleging that leaks by specific FHLBB personnel had damaged Lincoln. In addition, in connection with various bankruptcy proceedings, Charlie held press conferences and invited the press to meetings where the actions of the FHLBB were assailed. The ACC meetings were publicized, but not as well as the various actions against ACC.

With all this activity, the public, as well as Congress, was clamoring for information from the FHLBB supporting the actions it had taken against Lincoln. The FHLBB needed to refute the claims made by Keating that the FHLBB had been unjustified in seizing the association. The lawyers for the FSLIC and the FHLBB retained Kenneth Leventhal, as an expert witness, to look into the accounting for the various land-sale transactions which O'Connell, who had gotten much of his data from Gene Stelzer of the CDSL, had used as a basis for the conservatorship. During the mid-July period, Leventhal produced a draft report and, before the report was finalized, delivered it to the FHLBB for review and consideration. In an apparent attempt to justify its past actions, the FHLBB released this draft report to the press. Because of the sweeping, accusatory nature of the report, it was immediately reported in newspapers and television newscasts throughout the country.

The Leventhal firm enjoyed a reputation for being experienced in real-estate matters. But prior to their involvement as a consultant to the FHLBB and RTC, which now are a very large source of revenue to the firm, Leventhal was not an experienced auditor of savings and loans. In mid-1989, there were about three thousand S&Ls in the country. On November 14, 1989, Leventhal partners Roger Johnson and Terry Gilbert summarized the firm's experience in auditing S&Ls by responding to questions posed by Congressman Carroll Hubbard, as follows:

HUBBARD: Could I ask Mr. Johnson and Mr. Gilbert this question. How many savings and loans did your firm audit in 1986, 1987, and last year?

JOHNSON: We audited probably six or seven.

HUBBARD: Six or seven during those three years?

JOHNSON: Six or seven continuing audit clients during that time period, some of them being public savings and loans. Once again, our primary practice is in the real estate area.

So, with a representation of six or seven S&Ls out of the three thousand then in existence, the Leventhal firm's industry experience was, for all practical purposes, nil. With respect to real-estate matters, the Leventhal firm did enjoy a national reputation of being expert in such matters. But their expertise was more as tax advisors and consultants than as auditors. In any event, this was the firm used by the FSLIC and FHLBB to provide potential expert opinions on these selected transactions of Lincoln's.

The Leventhal report first identified the transactions that they had been asked to address. There were fifteen transactions in all: ten sales of Hidden Valley land between October 1986 and June 1988; the sale of a property known as Continental Ranch, located in Tucson, to R.A. Homes in September 1986; the sale of an interest in Crowder Water Ranch to Nalley in September 1986; the sale of property in Estrella Phase II to U.S. Home Corporation in February 1987; the sale of property at Cotton Lane and Northern, in Phoenix, to Emerald Homes in September 1987; and, finally, the Wolfswinkle equity kicker in October 1987.

The report listed the procedures that Leventhal performed with respect to these transactions and the documents they utilized. The report stated: "The documents that we considered were obtained principally from the association's records. Additional information was provided to us by the Federal Home Loan Bank (FHLB), the Federal Deposit Insurance Corporation and the California Department of Savings & Loan." Included in those documents were the examination reports and the recommendation for a conservatorship, which told Leventhal precisely which theories its report needed to buttress and support.

The report then contained a section on the limitations of the report and its contents. This section was worded as follows:

> Because the above procedures do not constitute an audit made in accordance with generally accepted auditing standards, we do not express an opinion on any financial information of Lincoln or its affiliates. Moreover, we analyzed only the fifteen specific transactions described in this letter. Certain of the loan files we obtained were incomplete, and we were unable to obtain loan files for certain loans asserted to have been discharged through refinancing. Some of the documents we were provided showed no evidence of the originals having been signed by the issuer or parties thereto. The individuals who represented Lincoln in structuring and executing the fifteen transactions were not available for interview or inquiry, and we had no contact with others who participated in or might have had direct knowledge of the transactions, other potentially related transactions or information, or the parties' intent, such as

borrowers, buyers, sellers, appraisers, attorneys, or former accountants or auditors. Under applicable professional standards, we are precluded from providing you the same level of assurance that we might have provided had we audited Lincoln's financial statements. Had we performed additional procedures, or had we made an audit in accordance with generally accepted auditing standards, other matters may have come to our attention that would have been reported to you. This report relates only to the fifteen transactions to which it is directed and does not extend to any financial statements of Lincoln or its affiliates taken as a whole.

The above paragraph is accountant's jargon that says the persons performing the procedures didn't have access to a lot of information that they needed in order to give an opinion equivalent to what an auditor, such as Arthur Andersen, Arthur Young, or Touche Ross, would render. Moreover, the information they did look at was incomplete and, because certain documents weren't signed, the documents may or may not have been a part of the transactions they were looking at—they may have been nothing more than drafts. And in the very first sentence, they say, "We do not express an opinion on any financial information of Lincoln or its affiliates." In fact, however, after having stated they had an insufficient basis to do so, they did express very strong opinions.

The report then presented an overview of Leventhal's findings as follows.

Based on the procedures we performed, and our knowledge of the real estate and savings and loan industries, we have concluded:
- The transactions should not have been recognized using the full profit accrual method of accounting.
- The substance of the fifteen sales transactions was materially influenced by related transactions between Lincoln and the purchasers.
- Lincoln accounted for the transactions according to their form rather than their substance.
- As a result of reviewing the facts and circumstances surrounding the fifteen transactions, we would question whether the form of any major Lincoln transaction represents its substance.
- Applying generally accepted accounting principles to the substance of the fifteen transactions requires that profits reported by Lincoln be reversed.

The tenor of the report is exemplified by the comment: "We would question whether the form of any major Lincoln transaction represents its substance." The statement is so sweeping in scope that it detracts from the objectivity and validity, if any, of the other findings. Even the FHLBB people, like O'Connell and Smuzynski, who had axes to grind with Lincoln, would not draw such a gross, generalized conclusion after looking at only fifteen transactions out of the thousands that Lincoln entered into between 1986 and 1988, the period during which these isolated transactions occurred.

Given the information to which Leventhal acknowledges it didn't have access, the findings are logically the product of assumptions that Leventhal had to make in order to fill in the gaps in the information that it did have. Its conclusions about substance therefore are, in turn, based largely on assumptions rather than on complete knowledge of the transactions. Without access to *any* of the parties to the transactions, and without the assurance that all of the relevant data was in hand and had been considered, Leventhal must have had to assume what transpired, or, alternatively, it must have relied on what the FHLBB, FSLIC, and their lawyers represented the missing information to be. And, absent the parties to talk to, Leventhal had to interpret the meaning and intent of documents in a vacuum. With all of these assumptions which had to underlie Leventhal's conclusions, the report, nonetheless, condemns, without restraint, all of Lincoln's accounting for all of its transactions.

The report provides a list of some of the things they considered in reaching their conclusions. The list was:

- In every instance, one or more linked transactions provided substantial benefits or concessions to the other party, undercutting the accounting employed by Lincoln.
- A document from Westcontinental Mortgage Investment Corporation provides written evidence of the contrived nature of the transactions.
- Transactions were generally consummated for amounts materially above appraisal values.
- Lincoln, in substance, provided net cash to the purchasers in almost all transactions. The net cash expended by Lincoln to accomplish the "sales" aggregated $217,725,000. Related payments to American Continental Corporation (ACC), Lincoln's parent, under the controversial tax sharing agreement would have reduced Lincoln's funds by an additional $54,108,000.
- The loans which Lincoln provided to purchasers were below market and poorly underwritten, frequently resulting in subsequent modification of loan terms or non-accrual status.
- In no instance does it appear that the subject sales transaction would have occurred were it not for the related linked transactions.
- In general, the substance of the transactions appear to provide Lincoln with no "net" economic benefit.

Again, this list is largely dependent on assumptions that Leventhal necessarily had to make. In the first bullet, Leventhal asserts that there were transactions which were "linked" to the sale transactions. It is true that there were other transactions between Lincoln and the purchasers of land in these fifteen cited transactions. Some of these other transactions occurred on the same day as, or in close proximity to, the land-sale transaction. However, to assert that the transactions were linked logically requires one to have knowledge of the intent of both the buyer and the seller. The transactions can be linked only if one was dependent on the other. If the transactions were independent events, even though they occurred on the same day, they wouldn't be linked as Leventhal asserts. The interdependence of the transactions would have to be evidenced either in the transaction documents or by the intent of the parties. That is, there should be evidence, other than mere timing, that the parties would not have entered into one transaction had it not been for the other. In this case, Leventhal appears to have assumed that the sale would not have occurred had it not been for the other transaction, but that's an assumption and not necessarily fact.

The reference to the document from Westcontinental Mortgage Investment Corporation refers to a letter, which was attached to the Leventhal report, from Westcontinental to E.C. Garcia and Company, Inc., a customer of Lincoln. The letter states, in part: "We are convinced that all we can do is report as if the corporation were not the true/beneficial owner, but merely the nominal title holder, which is consistent with the facts and reality of the situation. Correspondingly, it seems that you should have, and report, the real tax burdens and benefits arising from this property."

The letter indicates, as have oral statements made by the Westcontinental and Garcia people, that Westcontinental was a nominee for Garcia in the transaction. Apparently, for whatever reasons, Garcia didn't want the property and related debt on its books. This is an issue between Garcia and Westcontinental. Yet, Leventhal asserts that Lincoln "contrived" the transaction. Based solely on this letter, that's a great leap. Moreover, Leventhal goes farther and says that, based only on a letter between two parties who aren't related to Lincoln, it is evidence that *all* the transactions are "contrived."

The report cites that Lincoln paid out cash aggregating $217,750,000 in connection with these transactions. This aggregate amount is for all the transactions that Leventhal has assumed are linked to the fifteen sale transactions. These other transactions include loans and purchases of land and other assets. Many of these other transactions were with affiliates of the buyer and not the buyer.

Also, Leventhal does not indicate anywhere in its report that it made any independent investigation into the circumstances surrounding the tax-sharing agreement; nonetheless, it buys into the FHLBB's conclusion that the payments under this agreement were directly connected to, and were the motive behind, the land sales.

The final conclusion of the report was stated as follows:

Lincoln's parent company (ACC) is publicly held. Management of any publicly held company will, out of concern for compensation and stock market value, have an interest in maximizing profits. But there are rules of the game, and Lincoln's and ACC's management violated these egregiously. They were squeezed by capital requirements, and the direct investment and "loans to one borrower" rules. Lincoln's earnings had declined. ACC was starved for cash and the tax allocation pipeline from Lincoln could not flow unless profits were reported by Lincoln. Accordingly, in order to boost earnings, Lincoln entered into non-economic transactions and turned to accounting gimmickry.

Lincoln went to great lengths to insure that the form of the fifteen transactions we analyzed complied with the "cookbook rules" in order to attempt to justify the reporting of profits on each sale. However, the accounting treatment Lincoln accorded these transactions ignored the overriding accounting principle that substance rules over form. As a result, we believe that as of December 31, 1988, adjustments totaling $135,269,000 are required to reverse previously reported pre-tax accounting gains.

The other parties to these transactions were also motivated to consummate deals with Lincoln. Lincoln provided incentives to these other parties in various ways, including:

- Providing net cash to the other party through linked transactions. Real estate companies are generally "cash poor." Lincoln was "cash rich" because it could raise federally insured funds.
- Purchasing and selling real estate in linked transactions at inflated prices, in effect trading "two one-million dollar cats for a two-million dollar dog."
- Solving the other party's problems, e.g., release of guarantees, extension of loan terms, etc.
- Insuring that the other party had no risk in the transaction, i.e., nothing to lose.

Seldom in our experience as accountants have we encountered a more egregious example of the misapplication of generally accepted accounting principles. This Association was made to function as an engine designed to funnel insured deposits to its parent in tax allocation payments and dividends. To do this, it had to generate reported earnings by making loans or other transfers of cash or property to facilitate sham sales of land. It created profits by making loans. Many of the loans were bad. Lincoln was manufacturing profits by giving its money away.

Now, I submit that that's a mouthful for someone who said: "Because the above procedures do not constitute an audit made in accordance with generally accepted auditing standards, we do not express an opinion on any financial information of Lincoln or its affiliates." I have to believe that before they used the language that they did in the conclusion quoted above, some lawyer must have pounded on them with a vengeance.

There's not a hint in the report that Leventhal ever analyzed ACC's cash flow or read the tax-sharing agreement. Yet, without any qualifications, Leventhal asserts that "ACC was starved for cash" and the "tax allocation pipeline from Lincoln could not flow" and "this Association was made to function as an engine designed to funnel insured deposits to its parent in tax allocation payments and dividends." Without looking at ACC's records, what factual foundation could Leventhal possibly have had for these statements?

Leventhal also asserts that Lincoln was "squeezed" by the "loan to one borrower" rules, but there was never a single violation of these rules ever cited in any of the examination reports. So, how was Lincoln squeezed by them?

Leventhal asserts that in the so-called linked transactions, Lincoln purchased real estate at "inflated prices." But there were no appraisals or other data supporting such a conclusion, and Leventhal does not point to any such evidence. This appears to be nothing more than pure conjecture.

All this after stating, in no uncertain terms, "This report relates only to the fifteen transactions to which it is directed and does not extend to any financial statements of Lincoln or its affiliates taken as a whole." Maybe Leventhal forgot to read its own limitations? Or could it be that they couldn't resist the pressure of a headlock that a lawyer might have applied? Or, with a practice which specialized in real estate, and with the real-estate market having gone south along with many of their real-estate clients, could it be they just needed the money that the FSLIC and FHLBB must have waved in front of them?

I suspect, under cross examination, any good attorney could have caused the Leventhal people to choke on the language and assumptions used in this report. But for this report to serve the needs of the FSLIC and the FHLBB, they didn't have to appear in a courtroom. When it was released to the press, reporters gobbled it up, and ACC, Lincoln, and Keating, not to mention ACC's auditors, were buried in an avalanche of adverse stories.

Because it served the purpose of supporting the theory that ACC and Lincoln were bad guys who cooked their books, the congressional committee treated the Leventhal report as the Gospel. Lawyers for civil plaintiffs picked it up and, after cleaning up the language, used the same assumptions and theories to amend the complaints they had already filed. By the time the experts for the defendants could rebut Leventhal, it was too late. Even though it was nothing more than assumption and opinion, this report had been quoted so many times, by people who didn't bother to challenge it, that it was regarded as truth and fact. Once again, leaks worked to the advantage of the FHLBB and severely damaged ACC and Keating.

The stage was now set for the congressional hearings. The public had been prepped by the press, who had been given the complaints filed by the various plaintiffs opposing ACC and Keating, as well as the leaked Leventhal report, to view Keating as the villain who single-handedly destroyed an entire industry.

Nineteen

Keating and Wall Cast as Scapegoats

The hearings of the House Committee on Banking, Finance and Urban Affairs started on October 12, 1989, when the committee met to approve the issuance of subpoenas to various individuals for the production of documents and appearance as witnesses before the committee. The opening statement of Chairman Gonzalez introduced the intent—at least as it was to be portrayed to the public—of the hearings when it said, in part:

> . . . [W]e already know that in Lincoln we have on our hands a case that will cost the savings and loan insurance fund at least $2 billion. On top of that, thousands of individual citizens who bought securities issued by American Continental Corporation—the parent of Lincoln—stand to lose hundreds of millions of dollars.
>
> This Committee, under its clear assignment and jurisdiction from the House, is required to determine what went wrong within the regulatory agencies and what administrative and legislative remedies must be adopted to ensure that these events do not recur and that the public's insurance funds are fully protected. To make these determinations, we must develop the facts as completely as possible. . . .

The opening statement alluded to the fact that additional legislation or changes in administrative practices were the expected outcome of the hearings. Since FIRREA, the most sweeping regulatory legislation in decades, had been passed and signed into law just a few short months before the hearings started, the stated intent of the hearings was at best disingenuous. No new legislation was required. FIRREA was comprehensive and addressed every conceivable problem presented by the Lincoln case.

The real intent of these hearings was much simpler. They were a stage play. A play featuring a plot acted out by a carefully selected cast of actors. The director was Henry Gonzalez. The audience was the

American, tax-paying public, who were being asked to accept the revisionist history presented in this melodrama.

The first day of actual hearings was October 17, 1989. These hearings received wide attention from the media, both print and electronic. The hallway leading into the hearing room was crowded with the equipment and personnel of various news services. Many stations, particularly those associated with the Public Broadcasting Service, carried the hearings live. Attendance was so great that overflow rooms, with piped-in audio coverage, had to be set up to accommodate the crowd.

The hearing room, which was the stage for this drama, was imposing. The committee members sat in several tiers of raised seating with the chairman in the middle of the uppermost level, which placed him eight to ten feet above floor level. The table for the witnesses was at floor level and was set back about ten feet or so from the first tier of committee members, who were also slightly elevated above floor level. As a result, a witness had to look up to see any of the committee members. In the space between the witness and the committee, still photographers were permitted to lie or kneel on the floor directly in front of the witness. Television cameras were aligned on either side of the witness table. To the rear of the witness, about three or four feet away, was the gallery, which had seating for over two hundred people.

Among the first witnesses called before the committee was William Seidman, then chairman of the FDIC. Again, in a brief opening statement, Gonzalez set the tone for the day, and, this time, he was more blunt about what the agenda was shaping up to be when he said, in part:

> The sad fact about this failure is that the warning signals were there and the stop signs posted in time to prevent much of the loss to the insurance fund. But, the Federal Home Loan Bank Board, instead waved the association through the stop signals and let it continue racing down the fast lane until it crashed, taking the public's money with it.
>
> In May 1987—after a wrenching 16-month examination of Lincoln—the Federal Home Loan Bank of San Francisco came down hard, recommending that the institution be placed in conservatorship or receivership, or placed under a binding cease and desist order.
>
> What happens? The Federal Home Loan Bank Board orders the messenger—the Federal Home Loan Bank of San Francisco—shot, removed from further examination and supervision of Lincoln. Meanwhile, the owner of the institution—Charles Keating—meets privately with the new Federal Home Loan Bank Chairman, Danny Wall, and his enforcement staff—without the

supervisory personnel from the San Francisco Bank.

The upshot: no conservatorship, no receivership, no cease and desist. The Board in Washington finally does summon up the courage to execute a "memorandum of understanding" with Mr. Keating—a memorandum heavy on "understanding" and light on enforcement.

Faced with the embarrassment of an examination that minced few words, the Federal Home Loan Bank Board decided that Lincoln deserved a "second chance"—a second examination that would exclude those harsh critics coming out of the San Francisco Bank. There was even talk of a "third chance," shifting Lincoln to another bank district for examination and supervision in future years.

While this shuffling of paper and responsibility went on at the Home Loan Bank Board in Washington, Lincoln continued to run up losses, all to be picked up eventually by the insurance fund and the taxpayers.

Finally, in April of this year, Chairman Wall threw in the towel, stated the obvious, and placed Lincoln in conservatorship—almost twenty-four months and two billion dollars of losses after the action had been recommended by the San Francisco Bank.

A two-billion dollar mistake surely requires a full explanation even in the secret world of the Home Loan Bank Board. The answers vary about why the "cops on the beat" were pulled off in the middle of the night.

We're told that "bad feelings" had developed between the San Francisco Bank and Lincoln.

In another instance, we're told that Mr. Keating's private auditors disagreed with the San Francisco Bank's examiners.

Now we hear that some creative souls may have a new version suggesting that the Home Loan Bank Board ordered a "second chance" examination only because it wanted to be more thorough in examining Lincoln's parent holding company—American Continental.

The mystery of the second chance exam continues to grow, new explanations notwithstanding. Hopefully, when we complete these hearings we will have some answers that will meet a credibility test or, at least, a $2 billion test.

The job of cleaning up this mess and trying to save a few dollars for the insurance fund has fallen to FDIC Chairman Bill Seidman, our witness this morning. Unfortunately, Chairman Seidman did not have authority over the regulation of Lincoln. He did not enter the picture officially until after the wreck.

Danny Wall had the wreckage towed in and said "Here Bill, it's all yours . . . You write the check . . . We've done our job . . ."

In characteristic fashion, Mr. Seidman has moved vigorously to save what he could out of the wreckage and to file legal actions to recover the maximum for the insurance fund and the taxpayers. I am pleased with the hard-nosed, no nonsense approach taken in the conservatorship and receivership. . . .

With a mixture of fact, revisionist history, and outright distortion, Gonzalez established the story line for the stage play that Congress was going to present to the American public during the hearing. Keating was a bad guy. Wall was a lax regulator and was making up excuses for such laxity. The San Francisco people were the good "cops on the beat" who, if only Washington had listened, would have prevented a $2-billion loss. And Bill Seidman was the messiah who would end all the problems and save the taxpayers. Later, anyone who sided with Keating and Wall would also be labeled bad guys, and all who were against them would be the good guys. Simple theater.

In Seidman's opening statement to the committee, he described a lawsuit that the RTC had filed on September 15, 1989, against Keating and other officers and directors. Portions of his description are:

The RTC's complaint alleges that the former management of Lincoln contributed significantly to its insolvency by structuring sham transactions which enabled them to siphon cash out of Lincoln for their personal benefit.

Lincoln relied upon high-cost brokered deposits to sustain rapid growth. Investments focused largely on high-risk assets with uncertain earning power, such as raw land or other speculative investments such as corporate equities and junk bonds.

Certain of those investments were used by Lincoln's management to structure certain inside transactions which were reported as though they created large profits. However, when the transactions were properly analyzed, gains reported by Lincoln were illusory and had to be reversed.

We believe that linked transactions were instituted where certain parties received benefits to enable Lincoln to report sham profits. As a result of their improper inflation of Lincoln's and ACC's books, the insiders of Lincoln's former management were able to fund excessive salaries and dividends from ACC and reap fraudulent profits on the sale of ACC stock. . . .

We believe that the schemes used by the defendants involved both intentional fraudulent misdeeds and negligent activity. Elaborate misrepresentations, including sophisticated accounting abuses, were used to deceive the public about the true nature of the business being funded by Lincoln's depositors.

The deception employed numerous false statements constituting wire fraud, mail fraud, bank fraud and securities fraud. Because the defendants employed a pattern of such activity in furtherance of their fraudulent schemes, the RTC has sought additional relief under the antiracketeering laws of Arizona and the United States. This would entitle the RTC to treble damages as an additional remedy designed to deter future misconduct by others, and to provide a more adequate remedy for the overall losses which are anticipated.

With these remarks and, of course, the lawsuits themselves, Seidman provided the foundation for the second theme of the hearings—Lincoln had been destroyed by fraud. The charges by the RTC were the same issues contained in the examination reports, but now they were dressed up as fraud. Interestingly, even though these issues were surfaced by the FHLBB examiners, Seidman and the RTC took credit for asserting all of these allegations, as if they were discovered only after the RTC took control of the conservatorship.

Prior to these hearings, ACC had filed suit against the government alleging that the seizure of Lincoln was improper; as such, ACC was seeking substantial damage payments. If ACC prevailed in its claim that the government was at fault, it would establish a precedent that all the other ravaged associations could follow. Thus, it became imperative that Keating and ACC be stopped and their legal actions against the government quashed. Otherwise, the government, especially the agency which Seidman headed, could face billions of dollars in claims for damages from the former owners and managers of seized thrifts. So, the government went on the offensive. It leaked the Leventhal report; it filed suit against Keating and others, using RICO to claim extortionate damages; it held these hearings; and it turned loose its dogs—the FBI and prosecutors. It was all necessary to crush Keating's ability to establish legal claims against the government and its agents.

Aside from casting Keating as a crook, Seidman presented the committee with an interesting exhibit. The managers installed by the FDIC had been creating all kinds of reserves against loans, investments, and real estate. The exhibit presented Lincoln's balance sheet as of February 28, 1989, as adjusted for all these reserves. The exhibit reflects a cumulative loss of $766 million, which is a far cry from the $2 billion plus that keeps being bandied about as the loss on Lincoln's demise.

Now, one should focus on the fact that Seidman was appearing before Congress on October 17, 1989—six months after the government had taken control over Lincoln. The feds had had this entire period of time to ferret out any and all losses in Lincoln's assets, including those caused by routine fluctuations in interest rates as well as those which could be expected to be produced by the liquidation of assets. One would expect, so as to avoid future criticism, that the exhibit which Seidman presented to the committee would reflect the absolute, worst-case scenario. It would take into account all possible losses. With all this in mind, the projected loss is $766 million. Why does the committee claim Lincoln's losses will exceed $2 billion? Where does the other $1.2 billion come from? Could it be that it's a hedge against the cost of the RTC's expected ineffective sale of assets?

If Lincoln's losses were only $766 million—the same number the government used a few months later in court testimony—Lincoln was a far cry from the worst S&L failure in history. Moreover, one has to believe that included in the $766 million were the effects of the disastrous decisions that the FHLBB's managers had made during the six-month period— decisions that cost hundreds of millions of dollars in losses.

The government could not let this number stand, especially in these hearings. Lincoln had to be portrayed as a $2-billion failure, and Gonzalez knew this. Otherwise, Lincoln was just another failure out of the thousands that had occurred across the country. And Keating wouldn't look like such a great villain. Nothing special. No theater. So, the committee continued to use the fictitious $2-billion number. It had to in order to preserve its desperately needed scapegoat.

One other point should be made about the use of reserves and write-downs in value of a seized thrift's assets. In a recent book which Seidman authored (*Full Faith and Credit*, Times Books, 1993), he described a dispute that the FDIC had had with the General Accounting Office. In the passage, Seidman wrote: "Any accountant can break any company with paper entries merely by debiting (reducing) net worth and crediting (adding) a loss for a future disaster." Seidman was describing the exact tactic that the FHLBB and the FDIC used to justify their inappropriate seizures of and subsequent lawsuits against S&Ls, such as Lincoln. They sent their agents out, with pens in hand, to create paper losses where no true losses existed. The paper losses reduced the S&L's net worth below its required capital, providing the basis for the seizure. Seidman's comment in his book shows that the regulators knew precisely what they were doing when they used this tactic.

The second full day of hearings was October 26, 1989. The "panel" for the day included Bill Black, Mike Patriarca, and Commissioner Crawford. If there were any question that the committee was setting up Wall and Keating, the fact that this was the second panel, coupled with Chairman Gonzalez' opening remarks for the day, should have erased the doubt. The chairman's remarks, in part, were:

> Before us today are some of the battle-scarred veterans of the Lincoln wars— key players in what has become one of the strangest—I'd say bizarre—and most alarming chapters in the history of financial regulation.
> Two key factors weighed heavily against these West Coast regulators:
> First, Lincoln operated as a renegade institution that considered itself above regulation. Publicly insured institutions across this Nation accept willingly the need for examination, and are responsive to the regulator's routine requests for data. Without this, the system doesn't work, and the

industry generally accepts this fact.

But in the eyes of the management of Lincoln, examiners and supervisors were the enemy to be fought at every turn with whatever weapon was within reach. Attack, not cooperation, was the order of the day. Every issue became a donnybrook with wave after wave of law firms thrown into the battle.

In the world of Charles Keating, it was the examiners, not Lincoln that were to be examined.

Mr. Keating's efforts ultimately would have collapsed in a mile-high stack of lawyer's bills had it not been for the second factor—the chief Federal regulator in Washington, DC, who willingly cut the legs out from under his regulatory troops in the midst of the battle. After knocking unsuccessfully on the courthouse doors, Mr. Keating found an open door at the Federal Home Loan Bank Board.

Faced with the fact that Mr. Keating didn't like his examiners, Federal Home Loan Bank Board Chairman, Danny Wall, had an easy answer: banish them to Siberia, give Mr. Keating a second chance with a new more pleasant team.

The decision to pull the regulators out of Lincoln sent a blast of cold wind throughout the entire regulatory system coast to coast. Riding on that wind was the message: "Go slow, the people at the top won't support you when the big guys complain."

With those remarks, which were appropriate for the theater Gonzalez was directing—fiction based loosely on fact—the California people were given a green light to unload on Wall, Keating, and anyone aligned with them. Gonzalez had already anointed them heroes and nobody was going to take exception to the role in which he had cast them.

Crawford went first. While he shot a few arrows at Keating, he was droll and didn't really follow Gonzalez' lead of launching an all-out attack. Patriarca and Black were not as constrained. Sharing Gonzalez' disregard for the complete truth, these two were completely at home. The signal was clear—they were free to distort the past as much as they wanted to with complete impunity. They were also more than willing to don the mantle of heroes and embellish their roles and importance in this drama. Patriarca preceded Black, and his remarks followed the chairman's script to a tee. Some of his opening statement was as follows:

The story of Lincoln unfortunately is sadly familiar. Fraud, insider abuse, risk taking beyond all bounds with insured deposits that went unchecked by the board of directors and outside auditors until the losses were truly extraordinary. Unfortunately, even the regulators have some blame to share in the Lincoln debacle.

The plot, sadly enough, has been rerun in recent years with absolutely numbing frequency, but in other ways, the Lincoln story does have its unique aspects. Chief among these perhaps is the incredible arsenal of hired guns that

Lincoln hired to lend it respectability. Individuals, firms and officials who should have known better fell all over themselves to sell their reputation in furtherance of the Lincoln cause. In both numbers and prestige the Lincoln arsenal was truly a formidable force. It covered many arenas. . . .

Finally, the Lincoln case has its unique aspects on the regulatory front as well. As you know, the Bank Board removed our jurisdiction to exam and supervise Lincoln. This was a mistake. Not because it embarrassed me and my San Francisco colleagues in the national spotlight, but because it called into question the whole organization's willingness as a vigorous regulator. . . .

Patriarca then gave himself some oblique compliments and self-administered pats on the back. He spent quite a bit of time rationalizing why San Francisco had approved the tax-sharing agreement; why they hadn't conducted a holding-company exam; why their case for a conservatorship or receivership had been strong; why it had taken so long to finish the exam and issue a report; and why they had approved ACC's debt budget. Everything was laid at someone else's doorstep. He came across as a sincere guy who had absolutely no axe to grind with Washington, because "the Office of Enforcement was entitled to its opinion, and the Bank Board was entitled to rely on its opinion and to reject ours." A slightly different tone from that of his May 4 letter, when he'd ripped the skin off OE. But he hadn't been on television then.

The facts indicate that Patriarca was driven to attack Lincoln because he wanted to establish a reputation within the FHLBB structure as a tough regulator. When he was rebuked by Dochow and the ERC, he was not only "embarrassed," he was enraged. Washington had stepped on his considerable ego, as it had also done to Black's. The tone of virtually every piece of correspondence that Patriarca sent to Washington regarding Lincoln and Keating indicates that this was clearly the case. So, his remarks to this committee obviously don't reflect his real motivations and attitudes toward Lincoln and the Washington-based regulators.

After Patriarca's opening statement, Black presented his opening remarks. Where Patriarca was somewhat diplomatic, Black assailed the people in Washington while, at the same time, describing his actions and those of his colleagues in heroic terms. Some of the remarks in his opening statement were:

Thrift regulators find heroic action to be a losing proposition careerwise, a form of professional suicide. They know that attempting to close a horde of zombie thrifts might provoke personally ruinous flows of contrary political pressure focused through Congress. Congressional pressure for forbearance can be compared with a marshall's having to worry about his gun backfiring or being shot in the back by an alleged colleague in the midst of a gunfight.

Well, clearly we were shot in the back by the Bank Board as we battled to protect the taxpayers in the Lincoln matter.

The thrust of Black's and Patriarca's testimony, in addition to excoriating Wall and the others in Washington, was to make targets of Charlie and me, as we were the only ACC people scheduled to testify and, thus, the only ones who might contradict their distorted and untruthful version of the past. If we were discredited, our remarks, if any, would lose their validity. In my particular case, they were still harboring animus because of their meeting with the five senators in 1987 and the letter that I had written in response to the specific questions the senators had asked of me. Black got to me early in his remarks by saying:

I want to acknowledge that of course there were contrary predictions about the fate of Lincoln, from Lincoln's paid experts. Mr. Atchison, then the lead partner on Arthur Young's audit of Lincoln Savings, and soon to be on American Continental's extraordinarily generous payroll at almost a million dollars a year as a senior officer, wrote Senator DeConcini on March 17, 1987, that Lincoln was a quote, "strong and viable financial entity," unquote.

In answers to questions by committee members, Black and Patriarca reinforced this theme. Here are some of their comments:

BY PATRIARCA: And they [the senators] were telling us on the basis of a letter they received from Mr. Atchison from the Arthur Young accounting firm, that our examination was extraordinarily adversarial, and this was a strong company. And I was fairly surprised that we were the ones doing the examination and they were the ones who knew the condition.

BY BLACK: And in addition to Mr. Atchison, who was their partner on the audit, who gives this extraordinary letter of advocacy that is completely contrary to the theory of independence for accountants. . . .

BY BLACK: The Atchison letter to the Senators. The Atchison letter to the Senators is not like any letter I have seen from an accountant ever about an audit of an institution. It is clearly an advocacy piece. It goes well beyond accounting issues into things, you know, totally beyond his ken about how an examination should be run by Federal authorities. . . .

Now, if one tells a story enough times without contradiction, people begin to believe that it is true. That's what happened here. Patriarca and Black had, in front of the national press, tarnished my spotless reputation. An undeserved spotlight was turned on me during these hearings by self-serving and deceitful people—congressmen included.

Charlie fared far worse. The testimony didn't generally single him out by name, but the inferences were always there. The image created is summed up by the comments of Congressman Schumer when he said:

If you took any one of the 20 or 25 actions of Keating that you have documented, you might say, "well, maybe there's an explanation for it." But when you add them all up, every single time he had the opportunity to pervert or destroy the system to take advantage of people, to maximize his profits regardless of the law, he did it. And you know, he ends up being—he just angers me, I guess. He's a financial pirate. You could call him the black beard of finance. And I just hope he is brought to justice because the fact that he hasn't been, the fact that he is still able to run certain parts of that empire can make one's blood boil.

It should be noted that Schumer, who describes himself as a lawyer, reached this conclusion midway through the second day of the hearings. He said: "But I feel, I bet just about everyone in this room—with the exception of those, I guess, who are retainer for Mr. Keating—I shudder to think how many there are—would like to stand up and applaud you for the work you have done and the grief you have undergone to do what you did."

Schumer's comments were echoed by others on the committee, including the chairman in his opening statements and in his remarks throughout the proceedings.

Now, if one believes these hearings were intended to be an objective determination of the facts underlying the Lincoln situation, conducted by impartial and unbiased government officials, the fact that these people had reached such conclusions shortly after the hearings started, and before the bulk of the testimony was presented, should expel those beliefs. These people—Schumer, Gonzalez, and others on the committee—had decided the outcome of this kangaroo-court charade before the first witness ever appeared.

The characterizations of Charlie and me were picked up by both the written and electronic media. Patriarca and Black appeared on television shows and were quoted in newspapers and magazines, each time continuing to pervert the truth for their own self-aggrandizement. While already prominent, Charlie became exactly what the committee had intended—a symbol of what was wrong with the S&L industry—an image the committee would continue to reinforce.

We weren't the only ones on whom Black and Patriarca spewed their venom. The Washington regulators, particularly Rosemary Stewart, whom Black obviously despised, were also vilified. Typical of their comments were the following:

BLACK: Lincoln kept on threatening suit, because it found out that threats worked and frankly, I think what we all know is cowardness [*sic*] breeds bullies.

Chairman Wall's instructions to Mr. Dochow to achieve a "peaceful resolution" with Lincoln assured this outcome. I mean peaceful meant no litigation and they were going to litigate unless they got what they wanted so a peaceful resolution meant they won and the only thing that remained, frankly, was to negotiate the terms of surrender for the Bank Board. Lincoln got the veto right over, as I said, who could negotiate, who could exam it, and ultimately over who could supervise it. No other institution in America; bank, savings and loan, credit union, has ever obtained this to our knowledge.

Lincoln was permitted to enter into an unprecedented memorandum of understanding and was given a notorious side letter about criminal and SEC referrals with the Bank Board, something that I characterized today under oath as the worst so-called enforcement document in history. In the field, the MOU was known as Rosemary's Baby, after Rosemary Stewart, the Office of Enforcement Director who purportedly was negotiator for the Bank Board on this. . . .

There are two conclusions to draw from the Lincoln debacle. First, it need not have happened and it would not have happened if the Bank Board had shown any backbone. Second, future Lincolns can still happen because the same folks are still in charge of regulating thrifts. . . .

. . . [B]asically Rosemary Stewart bears very considerable personal animus. She does so with regard to former Chairman Gray, because former Chairman Gray was about to move her aside on the grounds of what he perceived to be incompetence. . . .

Black and Patriarca made a mistake in using their untrue statements to tar and feather Stewart, because she would call them on their distortions of the truth when she testified later. It was an uphill battle for her. The committee had already declared these people heroes—in front of the press—and they didn't want to backpedal and ruin their perfect script of the new version of Lincoln's history.

The third day of the hearings featured some of the more junior state and federal regulators, including Barabolak, Jim Clark, Robert Concannon, who was an examiner from Boston, Gozdanovich, Jack Meek, David Riley, who was an examiner from Atlanta, Newsome, and Stelzer. The themes for this day were to show that the 1988 exam, under Steve Scott's direction, had started out as a whitewash and that Washington had gone easy on Lincoln. The committee also wanted to smear the Senate a little bit more.

Once again, Gonzalez laid out the script with his opening statement, as these portions of his remarks show:

As both majority and minority staff director of the Senate Banking Committee during the 1980's, Danny Wall should have been in a position to know that Lincoln was not the leading candidate for a savings and loan merit badge.

When he sat down at his desk as the new chief of the Federal Home Loan Bank Board on July 1, 1987, the regulatory reports about Charles Keating and Lincoln should not have come as a great surprise, yet he took the reckless course of ignoring the evidence, shutting out the people who had examined the institution, and embarking on a series of ex parte meetings with Lincoln officials, concluding with a weak-kneed Memorandum of Understanding that he failed to enforce while $2 billion of public moneys went down the drain.

This Nation has had its share of regulatory scandals, but the unprecedented actions taken in the Wall-Keating affair will have a special historical niche. . . .

Again, was this a fair and impartial hearing? In these remarks, after only two days of testimony, the judge, Gonzalez, had rendered the verdict. The "Keating-Wall affair will have a special historical niche." He had already condemned both men. The verdict was reached solely on the basis of San Francisco's assertions, even though Gonzalez' very own statements prove that he was clearly aware that San Francisco and Washington disagreed over the facts of the Lincoln situation, as of course did Keating.

Gonzalez didn't care what these other points of view were. He liked the picture painted by San Francisco, because it suited his political purposes. If Keating, Wall, and others were destroyed in the process, so what? Gonzalez had his own political agenda, and the hell with Keating, Wall, and the others. They were expendable, especially if their demise would get the monkey off the back of Congress.

The comments by the various witnesses followed the chairman's lead as they, without regard for facts or the truth, painted a bleak picture of the FHLBB and ACC. Some of the more pertinent comments they made were:

NEWSOME: By the end of my stay in Phoenix in early November 1988, the phrases "whitewash" and "cover-up" were almost standing jokes in Phoenix relating to the Lincoln loan exam among State and Federal examiners on-site. Mr. Scott, the designated examiner in charge of Lincoln for the Bank Board, advised me shortly after I arrived in Phoenix that the total loan loss classifications aggregated less than $10 million.

I responded at that time to him with words to the effect of, "What about the Hotel Pontchartrain's $20 million unsecured loan? It is obviously a loss." He indicated it was only doubtful, which would not require specific loss reserves. I was immediately concerned about the possibility of a whitewash, as the Hotel Pontchartrain appeared a loss the day it was funded, and had deteriorated since, and was probably the most flagrant self-dealing regulatory violation I had ever seen. . . .

BARABOLAK: When unable to draw dividends from Lincoln, ACC siphoned $94 million of improper tax payments from Lincoln, payments based on fictitious income. When this source was cut off, ACC turned to the public through the avenue of subdebt sales and, late in our examination, sales of $500,000 to $700,000 a day provided the life blood of ACC's continuing existence. . . .

. . . Perhaps most disconcerting was Mr. Keating's threats that the FSLIC would lose more than $2 billion if Lincoln were taken out of his hands. It appeared that he was really admitting that Lincoln was a valueless asset. . . .

. . . ACC employed an army of lawyers and accountants to structure transactions in such a way as to provide appearances of profitability and to keep the regulators at bay. However, the questions cannot be avoided. What were the proceeds of the tax payments from Lincoln and the funds from small investors? What was it used for?

First, ACC and its employees' stock ownership plan bought back ACC shares from its owners. Mr. Keating proved right in his predictions that Lincoln was a worthless asset. However, before the stock value dropped to zero, he and his family members were able to sell their shares back to ACC at generous prices.

Since buyers and sellers were often one and the same, cash found an easy route from ACC treasury to insider's pockets.

Two, ACC personnel traveled to Europe, the Bahamas, and other ports of call ostensibly for investment advice. These high overhead expenses did not improve profits. Trading losses totaled $10 million in 1987 at the ACC level, $25 million in 1988, and about $13 million in the first two months of 1989.

Furthermore, losses may not have been as great—may have been greater had securities profits not been diverted from Lincoln.

Number three. Employees earned six, sometimes seven figure salaries, exorbitant rewards, considering the company's nonperformance. Consultants around the world profited. ACC maintained a fleet of five aircraft and owned its own hanger. Gifts and political contributions were generous, the largest being a $400,000 contribution to the Center for Participation in Democracy. The contribution was acknowledged in a letter from Kim Cranston, Senator Cranston's son, to ACC's Jim Grogan, who is Senator Glenn's former aide. . . .

The opening statements from these people were characteristic of previous testimony. They expressed suspicion about events and investments, such as the foreign investments, about which they had only partial data and almost no true knowledge or understanding. They distorted the facts they did have to fit the story they wanted to tell. They never offered any of the information which had been given to them by Lincoln or its attorneys that presented Lincoln's version of the transactions and the appropriateness of same. So, the committee and the press were presented with a very one-sided and slanted picture. A picture that suited the committee's purposes very well.

The deceit is most evident in the comments regarding the ESOP stock purchases. The testimony implied that these purchases had occurred in 1988, when Barabolak said, "before the stock value dropped to zero, he and his family were able to sell their shares back to ACC at generous prices." The fact is that the ESOP purchased the shares in 1985. Moreover, Charlie and his family owned millions of shares of ACC stock at the time ACC filed for bankruptcy. They didn't sell back their shares as implied. They suffered a huge loss. Had Barabolak been more truthful, the impression formed by the committee and the press might have been dramatically different.

There were many other half-truths and outright lies. For example, Barabolak said that the overseas trips were made "ostensibly" to obtain investment advice—implying that there was another, perhaps sinister, purpose for these trips. Yet, all the evidence he had supported the fact that these trips were, indeed, for legitimate business purposes. Meek also tried to raise the aura of wrongdoing by pointing to the business which Lincoln conducted with foreign persons. He said it was "mysterious." It wasn't mysterious and he knew it. He was playing to the cameras, enjoying the limelight, and, in the process, smearing Lincoln and ACC with innuendo.

The testimony also disclosed a distrust of other regulators and a paranoia about potential criminal behavior that might have been humorous had it not been for the circumstances. The references to potential criminal activities were spread freely to anyone who had disagreed with these people, including other regulators and prominent politicians. Here is a sampling of those references:

NEWSOME: In terms of what was going on in this examination, there were unusual aspects in terms of Senators and Representatives—or particularly Senators, as I recall—that were, according to the newspapers, using influence to direct things.

Frankly, when we saw a large amount of money going to something [Center for Participation in Democracy] that we were not sure what it was, that had the names of people [Kim Cranston and Senator Cranston] on it, we felt obligated to get it to people [FBI] who could either do something with it or bury it.

NEWSOME: Our threshold of findings being sent to the SEC, Department of Corporations of the FBI, on this institution was very low.

The following were questions to Newsome and Meek from Congressman Neal:

NEAL: I am not quite clear about one thing. Is it your opinion that there has been criminal activity here, criminal activity in terms of attempts to defraud the savings and loan fund, or taxpayers? Or how would you characterize it?

NEWSOME: It sure smells like it. There is so much evidence of indication of it in terms of intent and all that stuff—we are not criminal people as far as investigator types, but it sure looks like it to me.

MEEK: I think there is overwhelming evidence to indicate probable criminal activity.

NEAL: Have criminal charges been filed?

MEEK: I prepared a criminal referral and sent the criminal referral to Washington D.C., where they did a final review, and it was filed with the Justice Department.

NEAL: Against whom? Mr. Keating?

MEEK: Among others.

NEAL: Do you know the status of that now?

MEEK: I understand there is a very active criminal investigation being conducted by the FBI in both Phoenix and Los Angeles.

NEAL: Does it sound to you like there is any criminal activity on the part of the Federal regulators?

STELZER: We think it should be looked into. We think the possibility is certainly there.

NEWSOME: There are a lot of things that do not make sense. I mean, obviously, here. When you find out the answers and go up the ladder, maybe you will find out there was.

These guys also really unloaded on Steve Scott as the following shows:

STELZER: I spoke with Mr. Scott [about Hidden Valley]. I don't remember at what point in my investigation that I spoke with him. I found him just totally uninterested. I sort of gave up speaking with him because of his attitude.

Frankly, it was like he worked for the Lincoln Public Relations Department. . . .

NEWSOME: I think the Federal people in Arizona on the holding company level and the California people in Arizona and the California in Irvine—I think that we all felt that we didn't believe what ORA or Mr. Scott felt or said to us, that these people [Lincoln's people] were creative and that they should stay.

I think we commonly felt that the sooner they got out of the industry, the sooner we could figure out how big the hit to FSLIC was, but there was—I think that is how we—our thought processes worked. . . .

MEEK: I would say that it was reasonably apparent to me that Mr. Scott was biased in favor of the Lincoln officers and the ACC officers.

Riley also chimed in with comments indicating that he thought that Scott was "overly optimistic" about Lincoln and Lincoln's management, and he went on for some length about how he had come to that conclusion. There was certainly no reluctance by any of the examiners, except for Gozdanovich, to dump on the person to whom they had reported during the examination. They all appeared to want to make themselves look good to the committee at Scott's expense.

The attitudes expressed by these people should have frightened the committee members, but they didn't. Here were examiners in the employ of both the state and federal governments who were willing, at the drop of a hat, to label anyone who disagreed with them as biased or, worse, potentially guilty of criminal activity. Moreover, they were more than willing to make these claims about other people in front of a national television audience and the nation's press. For those who lived through the 1950s, it should have revived memories of the McCarthy hearings.

If there is any question that these hearings were carefully staged to cast Keating and Wall in the most adverse light possible, consider the witnesses who appeared during these first three days. Not one witness was supportive of either Wall or Keating. Because witnesses met with the committee's staff and submitted information prior to their actual appearance, the committee knew what each witness would say in his testimony. Yet, there was no attempt to schedule witnesses in such a fashion so that balance would be achieved in the story being presented to the public. Day after day, the press was full of the negative testimony offered by these initial witnesses. Nor was it going to get any better—the next scheduled witness was Ed Gray.

Had the committee possessed even a small grain of fairness, it would have called witnesses such Steve Scott, Arthur Andersen's personnel, Touche Ross' people, the Kaye Scholer attorneys, or other persons who could refute the so-called evidence presented by the examiners and other government personnel. But that didn't happen. Most of the potential witnesses who could have given Lincoln's perspective weren't even scheduled to appear. This was a setup from start to finish—and every person on this committee had to know it.

When the fourth day of these hearings, November 7, 1989, opened, some of the committee members apparently started to understand that they were engaged in a carefully orchestrated piece of theater and not in proceedings aimed at disclosing the truth. Before the day's witnesses were called, several members asked the chairman what was going on and why certain witnesses were seemingly being either shuffled around on the schedule or canceled. Others were concerned that some of the previous witnesses perhaps were doing more than simply reporting facts. Some of the comments made by these committee members were:

CONGRESSMAN HUBBARD: But you haven't heard yet from Danny Wall or his assistants. Yet you seem to criticize him on every public statement. Why don't you just have him come in and testify? He has had to call in reporters one at a time to try to get his message out to the public, rather than be the victim of these continuing hearings which chastise him. Why don't you just bring him in? Why don't you let him testify today since you are so anxious to find out why he "gambled so heavily in the face of so much evidence"?

CONGRESSWOMAN OAKAR: . . . [T]hese hearings are extremely important, and I believe, Mr. Chairman, that the committee has an obligation to seek the truth and conduct its proceedings in a fair and judicious manner.

Obviously, with the failing of Lincoln, there was a $2 billion loss to ultimately the taxpayers. Unfortunately, Mr. Chairman, some witnesses in their zeal to get their story out to the committee, in my opinion, wittingly or unwittingly from time to time may have gone beyond merely reciting the facts as they know them to perhaps attempt to put their own spin on the issues that are raised.

In so doing, a number of individual names, and I am talking about staff, not necessarily the Senators, because they can come and defend themselves, and personally, I hope that they do, but, Mr. Chairman, when you get to individual names of staffs have been mentioned not necessarily in a complimentary manner, whose reputation may have been tainted by innuendo or guilt by association. . . .

The chairman offered explanations in answer to these comments but, in reality, had no desire to change the way things had been going. Given his series of opening statements, the witnesses, so far, had been telling stories which fit his script perfectly.

The first witness on this day was former FHLBB Chairman Ed Gray. His appearance and the manner in which the committee treated him show, indeed, that politics makes for strange bedfellows. When Gray was FHLBB chairman, his attempts to re-regulate the S&L industry were opposed by over 25 members of this committee, when they joined more than 220 congressmen in signing a resolution opposing the direct-investment rules. Now, with Wall under attack, the committee was about to cloak Gray in the robes of a hero. This was probably very hard to do, because not only had they opposed his policies but, by many accounts, he was insufferable even under normal circumstances. In the role the committee was about to cast him in, Gray would make them make amends for their failure to pay homage to him in the past.

Gray's testimony was one of the clearest examples of the revisionist form of history that took place in these hearings. Like other witnesses, he assassinated the character of numerous people with rumor, hearsay, half-truths, and, perhaps, outright falsehoods. He painted himself as a noble warrior who had battled in solitary against legions of evil forces as he sought to protect the country from ruin. In so doing, he conveniently forgot to accept responsibility for the fact that hundreds of S&Ls failed during his tenure on the FHLBB and acted like the phenomena had absolutely nothing to do with any of the policies that he had supported or had enacted. It was all someone else's fault. To hear him tell it, he was as pure as the driven snow.

Some of the characteristic comments from his testimony were:

My regulatory policy, and my philosophy in the proper role of thrifts ran counter to Lincoln's philosophy. Charles Keating was used to getting his own way, and I stood in the way as his regulator by virtue of the safety and soundness regulations we were pursuing at the Bank Board. Mr. Keating undertook a vigorous campaign to halt our regulatory policy.

Lincoln hired no less than Allen [*sic*] Greenspan, then a powerful economist in the private sector, a top member of the President's Economic Policy Advisory Board, a man who has become Chairman of the Federal Reserve Board, to represent Lincoln and its interests before the Bank Board, the Executive Branch and Congress.

Mr. Greenspan made a plea to Lincoln's supervisory agent in early 1984, immediately after the Bank Board had adopted its direct investment regulation to free Lincoln from the regulation. Mr. Greenspan, citing the need for Lincoln to make sizable amounts of direct investment—and I would call them risky investments—claimed that Lincoln was "financially strong" and that it presented—to use Mr. Greenspan's words, "No foreseeable risk to the Federal Savings and Loan Insurance Corp. . . ."

These comments confirmed, as Lincoln had always believed, that Gray, in fact, did resent Lincoln's opposition to his policies. He especially resented the fact that Lincoln used consultants, such as Alan Greenspan, to buttress its arguments against his proposed regulations. Gray's remarks also demonstrate that, contrary to what he told the five senators, Gray knew a great deal about Lincoln and its affairs.

In answers to questions, he continued to smear, using rumor and hearsay, others who had opposed him. For example, after Gonzalez prompted him with a question, he took a shot at Senator DeConcini. Gonzalez' basic question and his response were:

GONZALEZ: What about the story that there was a trade out between the Senator from Arizona [DeConcini] and Mr. Regan, the Chief of Staff, on the matter of the vote on the Contras?

GRAY: Well, it has been very difficult to determine exactly what happened, what led to this appointment [Henkel], but I will say that one of my fellow regulators, since I have been gone, told me that he understood that the appointment had been made in return for a vote by Senator DeConcini on the Contra vote, the Contra funding, but I can't verify that.

Gray was skating along in fine fashion with his mishmash of character assassinations until it was Congressman Hubbard's turn to ask questions. In his opening remarks and in a written statement that he had submitted to the committee, Gray had described the meeting which he attended on April 2, 1987, with Senators DeConcini, McCain, Glenn, and Cranston regarding Lincoln. Gray's account of this meeting, which asserted that the senators had acted improperly, was soundly refuted by all four senators. For example, in a letter to Gray, DeConcini wrote: "There is little relationship between the meeting you described and the one we had. Your recollection of the meeting is so distorted as to bear no resemblance to fact." All of the others wrote letters which echoed DeConcini's comments.

Hubbard, apparently upset by Gray's tactics, began a recitation of Gray's own misdeeds while he was on the FHLBB. He talked about the expense-report abuses; the excessive costs that Gray had incurred in decorating his office; and the favors he had accepted from the S&L industry. The recitation was followed by this exchange:

HUBBARD: Did you send us a letter in December 1986—us meaning the House and Senate Banking Committees—indicating that you did have flawed judgment?

GRAY: Absolutely. Listen, let me say we had—.

HUBBARD: Your testimony may be flawed too, Mr. Gray.

The rest of Gray's testimony dealt with accusations that he leveled against the senators and the administration. Most of the committee didn't buy his story. In the end, Gray admitted that he had no evidence that any senators had ever accepted anything from Keating in exchange for an improper action on their part. Curiously, while the committee was willing to defend other members of government against Gray's slanted testimony, they were inclined to believe his assertion that Keating had somehow engineered a massive web of influence within Washington. It would seem that if Gray wasn't truthful about some events, he may not have been truthful about anything.

The next witness called by the committee was former FHLBB member Lee Henkel. One has to believe that the reason for Henkel's appearance was to demonstrate that Keating had influenced his appointment to the FHLBB and that Charlie had helped frame the proposal which Henkel had submitted to change the direct-investment regulations. The committee struck out on both counts. Henkel was an impressive witness. In no-nonsense fashion, he described his appointment to the Bank Board and debunked any idea that Keating had played a major role, if any role at all, in the process. He also clearly stated that the proposed change in the regulation had been his idea and his alone. He had not talked to Keating or anyone else at Lincoln or ACC about the proposal.

He also distinguished himself by confining his testimony to what he personally knew. He explained, in detail, his own actions and did not try to cast any unfavorable light on any other person. He did not engage in speculation. He answered questions in a straightforward manner and never gilded the lily. He was, in my opinion, the first truthful witness to appear before the committee. He had no hidden agenda and wasn't out to put any particular spin on the events as he knew them. Once the committee figured out that they weren't going to be able to embarrass him, or anyone else, his testimony ended rather quickly. There was also one other feature which set Henkel apart from the preceding witnesses—he wasn't adverse to either Lincoln or Keating. Henkel was the first neutral witness called by the committee.

The next witness was Larry Taggart, the former California commissioner of the Department of Savings and Loan. The purpose for calling Taggart was to lay blame on his shoulders for allowing Lincoln to invest in the level of direct investments that it had and to point out the permissive nature of state-chartered S&Ls. Taggart began by laying out, in a matter-of-fact manner, his dealings with Lincoln while he was the commissioner. In his opening remarks, he also made some observations and posed some questions which threatened the course along which Gonzalez was so carefully steering the hearings. These comments, which came at the end of his opening statement, were:

For several years, Lincoln's profitability and return on assets was very impressive, and their performance positioned them among the few top leaders in the industry. American Continental, as well, became publicized as one of the most active and promising stocks to buy.

In light of the achievements and apparent success during those years, you have to ask yourself why. Why did the Federal and State regulators spend 3 1/2 years examining Lincoln to find something wrong? Why was Lincoln seized even though the regulators couldn't write down sufficient assets to make it insolvent? Why wasn't ample time and cooperation granted to enable Lincoln to be sold when the regulators clearly wanted to remove existing management?

It's a shame that what was once a small skirmish between the regulators and Lincoln evolved into a major confrontation, a battle which because of the past years will cost massive amounts of money to resolve.

The irony of the whole matter is what might have been different if both parties had put down their weapons and the regulators had reached out their hands to assist and help rather than assume such an adversarial role. . . .

This was not what Gonzalez wanted to hear. He immediately tried to present a case to show that there had been a conflict of interest between Taggart, as commissioner, and Lincoln. He pointed to Taggart's ownership in a company called TCSF and the fact that, after Taggart left state government, Lincoln purchased a 10-percent interest in the company. Gonzalez pointed to a registration statement filed by TCSF which indicated that Taggart was an officer of the company while he was still the commissioner. Taggart explained that the registration statement was in error.

Congressman Lehman joined in with Gonzalez and, quoting newspaper articles, challenged Taggart's assertions that the registration statement was wrong and that he had had no role in TCSF until after he left state government. Congressman Parris then joined the fray, also quoting from newspaper articles. The three congressmen badgered Taggart and treated him as no other witness had been treated.

Congressman McDermott then took a different approach. His questions and Taggart's responses were:

McDERMOTT: . . . I read your statement here it says why did the Federal Government regulators spend 3 1/2 years examining Lincoln to find something wrong. Do you think they didn't find something wrong?

TAGGART: That is a very good question. A typical examination would take anywhere from 1 1/2 to 3 months of an association of that magnitude. If there were problems it might take a longer period of time. When Lincoln started to get examined, I think it was 1985–1986. I just happened to mention to them, I said, if they are here longer than 3 or 4 weeks you have got a problem.

Oh, no, there is no problem, no, no, I don't think we are going to have a problem.

Sure enough, it went on for months and months and months. It is very, very unusual for an association to be examined for 3, 3 1/2 years. One, it is extreme disruption to the operation. There are very few associations in this country that can ever withstand that kind of pressure to be examined for 3 years. It totally disrupts everything.

Number two, there was even a comment that was made in the paper in Phoenix, or I believe it was one of the supervisors in the Federal home loan bank made, "Yes, we haven't found anything yet." That just happened recently, "We haven't found anything yet, but we know when we get in there we are going to find something."

McDermott: Then it is your testimony that this was some kind of witch hunt that they got into, and by God, they were going to find something, no matter how long it took, and that really the regulators brought down the institution?

Taggart: Yes sir.

McDermott: There was nothing wrong financially, it was very sound business practice that Mr. Keating had carried on, everything he did was perfectly good, acceptable business practice, safe and sound business and all those things?

Taggart: I can only comment probably up to the end of 1985, beginning of 1986. Beyond that, I really can't comment.

McDermott: So that is your conclusion?

Taggart: Yes. I tried to make a point in January in San Francisco [at an earlier committee meeting], and it didn't hit. If you take a look at the losses in this country and take a look at the solutions of the industry, putting aside the problems, look at the solutions, most of the losses that are perceived, $250 billion or $50 billion, or whatever figure you want to pick, are created with the stroke of a pen.

Examiners go in and they mark assets to market, they say, here is a $50 million hit, here is a $25 million hit. You have to ask yourself what if they didn't have to take these losses, what if nobody wrote these assets down at this time? Would the depositors complain? No. Would Congress complain? No. Would the regulators complain? No. The only time you ever have to liquidate assets in a savings and loan association is when you have a run on the bank. Have we had any runs in this country? No. Why are they liquidating assets? I don't know.

You have to ask yourselves, it is a very deep rooted question.

McDermott: [with deep sarcasm] Did you ever think that maybe you got out of that job just in time?

Taggart: No. Actually, I wish I had stayed in, to tell the truth. I probably would have caused havoc. Most of the losses that are created are created with the stroke of a pen. Somebody's idea that the asset isn't worth as much as it was. I believe in writing off carrying costs because we go through economic cycles every 3 to 5 to 7 years, so you write off the carrying costs. You don't write off the asset.

McDERMOTT: Your conclusion is that this problem that we have been discussing here for weeks was created by zealous regulators going in and saying—looking at the numbers, using some kind of strange accounting principles, and saying we have to write this stuff down because it doesn't really exist?

TAGGART: Yes sir. When they attacked the Phoenician—I think it was about 2 1/2 years ago—they attempted to write it down $60 million, and I think Lincoln sold off half of it for $200 million.

The regulators said, heck, there is another $60 million we have lost that we can't write down. They kept trying to write down assets to make Lincoln insolvent, and they couldn't get there, so they finally threw up their arms a year, year and a half ago, and said the heck with it, we will just take them anyway.

McDermott was intent on discrediting Taggart because he was taking a position contrary to the committee's view of the Lincoln situation and the story that they were trying to feed the public. McDermott, and the rest of the committee, failed to grasp the significance of what Taggart was telling them. It was the most important concept discussed in the entire hearing.

The Achilles' heel of a bank or savings and loan association is liquidity—the ability to pay depositors when they demand their money—not its capital. Savings and loans can operate for an indefinite period of time, often many years, with capital deficiencies. The FHLBB's ill-conceived MCP program proved this point. For example, Security Savings of Phoenix operated as an MCP shop for several years. Security's total assets, at that time, were around $1 billion, and, before the feds decided to liquidate it, its capital deficit had grown to several hundred million dollars as well. Yet through it all, Security met the needs of its depositors and was never confronted with a fatal run on the deposits.

McDermott was also derisive of Taggart's economic background, but his attack only exhibited his own economic ignorance, especially when you consider for whom he worked—the U.S. government. The federal government is, perhaps, the best example of how an entity can operate without capital if it has liquidity. The U.S. government has an accumulated deficit—the equivalency of negative capital for a business enterprise—of about $4 trillion. It has more debt than any other entity in the entire world. Yet, because it can print money and borrow, it can pay its bills and continue operations. If the government were blocked from borrowing—that is, if it had to pay all of its obligations out of its current revenues and accumulated capital, which, as stated, is a huge negative number—it would fold over-night.

Taggart's point is also proven by the literally thousands of unregu-lated companies who experience major operating losses, resulting in capital deficiencies. They can continue operating as long as they have cash to pay their bills when they come due. When the cash runs low, many seek protection from creditors under the various chapters of the Federal Bankruptcy Code, often Chapter 11. In bankruptcy, these companies continue to operate while their debts are placed on hold. During bank-ruptcy, they can restructure their debt by modifying repayment terms, and, often, they are able to secure new funds. If the bankrupt company can continue to operate and return to profitability, it can survive and emerge from bankruptcy as a viable entity—and many do just that.

This is particularly true if the bankrupt company's problem is the consequence of isolated transactions or assets, rather than a fundamental flaw, which cannot be eradicated in a relatively short period of time. I contend, as I believe Taggart was trying to explain, that the majority of the S&Ls which have been closed, including Lincoln, were closed because of real or perceived losses on isolated assets. The regulators wrote these isolated assets down, producing a capital failure. The capital failure was then used to seize the institution and to conduct a wholesale liquidation. This was absolutely unnecessary.

The capital standards are at best an illusory form of protection for the insurance fund. There is *no* bank or S&L in the United States, whether it meets its capital requirement or not—none—that can be liquidated at anything but a loss. The simple fact is that in a liquidation, assets of banks and S&Ls will bring cash realization prices of 80 percent or less of their aggregate book value, especially if the liquidation is forced and rapid, as is the modus operandi of the RTC. No S&L has capital equal to 20 percent of its total assets. Most have capital positions of 6 percent of assets or less—far below what would be required to assure against losses on liquidation. The use of a capital-based standard is an illus ion of protec-tion—a myth.

What Taggart was trying to convey to the committee was that the write-downs forced by the regulators, and the capital reductions resulting from these write-downs, were meaningless to the S&L's ability to survive. If the S&L had liquidity, and was able to operate some profitable lines of business, it could survive. The rub is that once a S&L failed its meaningless capital test—a test which kept changing as the Congress and regulators constantly fiddled with the rules—the regulators either seized it or prohib-ited it from pursuing any profitable business. The feds blindly applied a cookie-cutter approach to the industry without any real economic analysis. This cookie-cutter approach says, "If an association fails its capital test, close it and liquidate it. Don't get caught up in deciding whether, if given time, it can survive." This cookie-cutter approach has been used, in knee-

jerk fashion, by an army of economically naïve and intellectually challenged people to destroy, without valid cause, hundreds of associations
who never should have been closed and liquidated.

Considering the extent to which interest rates declined in the 1991–
1993 period, and with the resurgence of real-estate prices in many markets,
the vast majority of the closed S&Ls would have recovered. The fact is that
banks and the remaining S&Ls earned record profits in 1992 and 1993 and
are continuing to do so in 1994. The seized S&Ls would have enjoyed
these same profits, covering losses from bad loans, and they would have,
in all likelihood, avoided the horrendous losses suffered by the inept RTC.
The expensive burden placed on the shoulders of the American taxpayers
was unnecessary. If Congress had simply understood what Taggart was
trying to say, billions could have been saved.

Gonzalez, following McDermott, picked up the attack on Taggart and
tried to discredit him further, so the press and others would not take
Taggart's testimony seriously. The key questions and answers were:

GONZALEZ: You seem to think there was no real legitimate crisis in the thrift
industry.

TAGGART: There is a crisis. It is how it was caused and how it all came about, how
it was fabricated.

GONZALEZ: In other words, if we eliminated all examiners, the crisis would have
been averted?

TAGGART: No, that is not correct, sir. You still need examiners, they will need to
monitor the association as much or more so than they are doing today. It is a
matter of whether you are going to go in and really write down the assets.
Where that direction comes from—it comes from Washington—to go in and
write down those assets.

When Gonzalez was unable to shake Taggart's view of what had
happened in the industry, he returned to the TCSF registration statement,
still trying to make it look like Taggart had a conflict of interest while he
was state commissioner—an issue which was irrelevant to the stated
purpose of these hearings and was being used simply to discredit the
witness.

The assault on Taggart was then turned over to Congressman Kanjorski,
who used sarcasm and ridicule to try to shake Taggart. Kanjorski returned
to McDermott's line of questioning. The key questions and answers were:

KANJORSKI: . . . You seem to have still indicated to Mr. McDermott when he was
examining you that you really think our whole problem in the United States
today is in damn dumb examiners out there with sharp pencils. Is that the cure?

Is that the cure? Do we call Mr. Bush and say, just break those pencil points, and we won't have a problem?

TAGGART: I don't characterize them as dumb, sir. I think they were highly qualified. I think they are misdirected. That is my own opinion, that they are misdirected.

KANJORSKI: How do you figure when a Lincoln Savings has a $3.5 billion in assets or something to that extent, and the U.S. Government has to shove in $2.4 billion, is that just an eraser or pencil error?

TAGGART: No, sir. The savings and loans had to maintain a minimum net worth of 3 percent for a number of years. Now, that that has been erased—the core capital of the association—it is not difficult to send an appraiser into any association in this country, or examiner, and write down the assets more than 3 percent. I have been involved in a lot of associations. That is not difficult to put every association under water. It is a matter of balance.

Kanjorski continued to browbeat Taggart with a series of inane questions which simply demonstrated that Kanjorski had no clue about Lincoln's true status or any basic understanding of economics or finance.

The committee didn't listen to Taggart, nor did they want the American public to, because the horse was already out of the barn. The government had already unnecessarily ruined an industry and confiscated billions of dollars of assets, which they later squandered, sticking the taxpayers with ruinous losses. Had they understood the concepts that Taggart described to them, it could have been averted. We've all paid dearly for the government's abject ignorance.

I was the next witness scheduled to appear on this fourth day of hearings. I had been in Washington for two days trying to decide whether I would testify to the committee or not. The decision was not an easy one, as there were a number of factors to consider.

First, I knew that criminal referrals had been made by the FHLBB people. I knew that the FBI and the Department of Justice, who I believed were under tremendous political pressure to find fault—criminal fault— in connection with the failure of Lincoln and ACC, were conducting active investigations. I had already been visited by the FBI on matters pertaining to ACC—matters which were not central to these hearings. I believed that all of the officers of ACC and Lincoln, myself included, were, at the time, subject to scrutiny by these federal agencies.

While I knew that my conduct had never been inappropriate and had not been remotely in violation of any law, I also knew from the testimony of previous witnesses who had appeared before this committee that many untruthful statements had been made. I was therefore concerned about creating a record which could be used by federal agencies to lodge a false case against me. I was concerned that these agencies would compare what I said against the untruthful statements made by others to assert that I had made false statements while under oath. In short, I did not believe that it was wise to provide any evidence which could be used by the federal government, in any context, until the direction and focus of the investigations were much clearer than they were at this point in time.

Second, I had followed these hearings and concluded they were nothing more than a politically motivated circus to cover up the failed policies and legislation of Congress. I looked at the witness list and the order of appearances and concluded that Gonzalez had stacked the deck. As I watched prior witnesses on television, the committee's biases were painfully obvious. FIRREA, the most sweeping piece of legislation ever passed concerning S&Ls, had been signed into law, and no new bills were pending. So, the purpose of the hearings was not to frame new legislation. Nor was this a judicial proceeding geared to elicit credible evidence concerning the failure of Lincoln. It was simply a kangaroo court convened to try Keating, Wall, and others whose views were contrary to those held by Gonzalez and his colleagues.

Third, I knew that telling all the facts about Lincoln and ACC, as I knew them, would take, at a minimum, two to three complete days. Here, because Ed Gray had babbled incessantly for hours earlier in the day, I was scheduled to appear after 7:00 P.M. There was not sufficient time to present the facts surrounding the events that had transpired over a period of three years.

Fourth, I knew that the working papers documenting the audits of Lincoln performed by Arthur Young, which I had participated in, consisted of several hundreds of thousands of pages. I had not seen the working papers for a couple of years. If the committee asked specific questions about specific transactions, I was not prepared to answer those questions without first having refreshed my memory. And I knew from seeing earlier testimony, and from knowing that the Kenneth Leventhal report was floating around, someone on the committee had been primed to ask those specific kinds of questions.

Finally, I had watched the questioning of both Taggart and Henkel. As these were the first two witnesses who were not adverse to Lincoln or ACC, I was curious to see whether they would be accorded the same courtesies shown to the federal and state government personnel who had preceded them. They were not. The committee used newspaper clippings, rumors, and innuendo to try to tarnish their reputations and to discredit them. It proved to me that the playing field was not level—not even close to being level.

I concluded, given the time of day, that the committee's only intent would be to use innuendo and the untruthful statements of prior witnesses, and their own biased interpretations of other materials, to try to destroy my reputation and credibility. I believed that their politically driven motive was to cast anyone who might be supportive of Lincoln or Keating, or who was opposed to the government's handling of the S&L situation, as a villain in the script that they were using to deceive the American public.

So, when I appeared before the committee, even though I abhorred the thought of doing so, I asserted my rights under the Fifth Amendment to the United States Constitution and refused to answer any questions posed by the committee. I decided that this was not the forum in which to tell the Lincoln story as I knew it. I believed that there would be opportunities in the future to present the facts to a truly impartial trier of fact.

This ended the fourth day of hearings.

The fifth day of hearings was November 14, 1989. The first witnesses were several people who had purchased subordinated debentures issued by American Continental. They testified that they thought the investments were safe because they had been purchased in a Lincoln branch. They also indicated that ACC's bond representatives who had sold them the debentures had stated that, essentially, the debentures were as good as an insured CD. They said that they had either been told or had inferred that the debentures were insured. From the testimony, it appears that they formed the belief that the investments were insured primarily because the Lincoln branch had a FSLIC sticker on the door. Each of the witnesses told a story of loss which was poignant and regrettable.

The next witness was Richard Breeden, chairman of the SEC. As had become customary for most of the government personnel appearing before the committee, portions of his testimony would later be challenged by other witnesses. In the context of the entire Lincoln affair, Breeden's testimony was uneventful. When asked questions about the SEC's role, he pointed to the SEC's ongoing investigation or cited legal limitations on the SEC's authority. His testimony was ended after a short period.

The witnesses who followed Breeden were all accountants. Three were from Arthur Young: Bill Gladstone, chairman of Arthur Young, and Janice Vincent and Nancy Matusiak, who had both worked on the audits of ACC and Lincoln. Two were from Kenneth Leventhal: Roger Johnson and Terry Gilbert.

I believe that the strategy of the committee was to present the Leventhal report, which used very strong language in condemning Lincoln's accounting for certain transactions, and then to attack Arthur Young's audits and, by so doing, Lincoln's accounting.

Had the Arthur Young representatives appeared separate from, and prior to, the Leventhal people, they would have been the first witnesses who could have presented a logical explanation for the accounting treatments which Lincoln had afforded its various transactions. As it was, the committee wasn't really interested in obtaining testimony supporting Lincoln's practices. The script called for Lincoln's transactions to be labeled as improper; the committee, therefore, wasn't willing to give Arthur Young a complete and fair hearing.

It was patently unfair to both Arthur Young and Lincoln for the committee to have called Leventhal as a witness. Leventhal did not perform its review of the subject transactions until after Lincoln had been placed into conservatorship. Its work wasn't the basis for any regulatory actions involving Lincoln. Leventhal was, pure and simple, an expert witness who was hired to buttress the RTC's allegations in its lawsuit against ACC. Leventhal could not be viewed as an objective party—they knew that their report had to support the findings of the examiners and the RTC's allegations or it would be viewed as useless. Moreover, their own report clearly indicated that their conclusions were based on incomplete data and limited procedures. If the government could present expert-witness testimony, Lincoln should have been permitted to call experts in its own defense. This was simply another example of the bias inherent in these proceedings.

Bill Gladstone was the first to testify. In his early comments, he addressed the subject of my withdrawal from Arthur Young, as follows:

Our firm first became Lincoln's auditors in October 1986. A great deal of work went into the 1986 and 1987 audits, upon which we expressed opinions. Arthur Young spent over 30,000 hours on the 1987 audit, alone.

As you know, Mr. Chairman, Jack Atchison was the Arthur Young partner in charge of the 1986 and 1987 audits. On February 21, I discussed with you and this committee our knowledge of the circumstances of Mr. Atchison's leaving Arthur Young. Even in view of the subsequent events [ACC's bankruptcy and Lincoln's seizure], we have no reason to believe that Mr. Atchison committed any impropriety while he was a partner at Arthur Young.

Also, I want to assure you, Mr. Chairman, and assure the committee, that there were many other Arthur Young partners and staff persons who participated in these audits.

The conclusions of the audit team were reviewed both on a regional and national level, because of the complex accounting and factual issues involved. Arthur Young applied its best independent professional judgment to these audits.

Gladstone then moved on to address the Leventhal report, which was the central issue with which the committee would confront Arthur Young, by saying:

Lincoln was an institution with over $4 billion of assets. An institution of that size conducts thousands of transactions, many of which could individually be called major. Kenneth Leventhal, at the request of the lawyers for the Federal

Home Loan Bank Board, reviewed just 15 of those transactions that occurred in three different fiscal years, 1986, 1987, and 1988.

Based on this limited review, its report reached sweeping and, we believe, unsupported conclusions. We recognize that different accountants can and do reach different conclusions. When an audit involves complex transactions and requires judgment calls on the accounting for many of those transactions, the difference of opinion may legitimately occur.

We do not share Kenneth Leventhal's confidence that theirs is the only correct application of the 200 pages of accounting principles appended to its report. In fact, we also question any alleged analysis which contains the following extraordinary, gratuitous, and I believe unprofessional statement they have made:

"As a result of reviewing the facts and circumstances surrounding the 15 transactions, we would question whether the form of any major Lincoln transaction represents its substance." That is a very broad, sweeping statement.

Others that examined Lincoln and ACC in 1986 and 1987 did not reach the same sweeping conclusions. While the Federal Home Loan Bank Board received critical comments from the San Francisco bank and others, it did not move to take over Lincoln until April 1989, after American Continental had declared bankruptcy.

The other Arthur Young people then made brief statements to the committee and made it perfectly clear that they were prepared to refute all of Leventhal's conclusions. If the committee wanted to get into the specific accounting issues, they were prepared to offer detailed rebuttals to Leventhal's report—an offer the committee had no intention of accepting.

The next opening statement was by Roger Johnson of the Leventhal firm, with supplemental comments by Terry Gilbert. They essentially repeated the contents of their report. However, Johnson did respond to Gladstone's remarks by saying:

I had hoped to focus on Lincoln, which is what we looked at, and not Arthur Young, which we did not look at. I wanted to be fair to Arthur Young, and I still want to be fair to Arthur Young; but their attack on the professionalism of our report frankly dumbfounds me.

It is tragic. It ignores the significance of what happened here. Lincoln was a debacle, by any measure, and frankly I am shocked by what I have just heard.

Johnson knew that he was playing to a home crowd, and he used it for all it was worth, with the same hyperbole that characterized their report. He and Gilbert also threw in some descriptions of Hidden Valley which were popular with lawyers who were adverse to Lincoln. These descriptions, first by Johnson and then by Gilbert, were:

> They involved barren desert land miles from the population center of Phoenix, and are unlikely to be developed in this century.

> Hidden Valley comprises 8,500 acres of vacant land 35 to 40 miles drive from downtown Phoenix, AZ. The project is next to Lincoln's 9,000-acre Estrella Ranch project. The Estrella Ranch project is just getting underway. Lincoln has reportedly spent $100 million on lakes, parks, boulevards, and other improvements in Estrella. However, nobody lives there yet. Hidden Valley will not be developed until after Estrella.

The descriptions were intended to give the impression that the long development period was somehow unexpected or unusual. Lincoln had always maintained that the Estrella project, including Hidden Valley, was a twenty- to twenty-five-year project. That was no secret and no surprise. Johnson testified, "This was barren desert land. That is the substance that we focused on to arrive at our conclusion." In other words, they concluded that these were sham transactions because the land was not developed. Well, that logic would cause virtually every sale of land in Southern Arizona to be a sham sale because, until the property is developed, all land in the southern half of Arizona is "barren desert land." The cities of Phoenix, Tucson, and Scottsdale were deserts before people started to inhabit them.

The accountants from Arthur Young offered several times to go through the fifteen transactions cited by Leventhal, one by one, and to point out where they felt Leventhal had erred in its analysis. The committee didn't want to do this. The committee was content to use the Leventhal report as evidence that these were phony transactions, so the government's actions in seizing Lincoln remained justified.

Again, the only plausible reason for having Arthur Young as a witness was to try to discredit the audits the firm had performed, so that Lincoln and Keating couldn't use these audits as a defense to counteract the Leventhal report and to condemn the FHLBB's seizure of Lincoln. If Arthur Young pointed out deficiencies in the Leventhal analysis, the committee would have, in effect, provided a forum for destroying the centerpiece of the FHLBB's conservatorship and receivership actions, which were dependent on sustaining the argument that these fifteen transactions were inappropriate. So, once Arthur Young offered to provide detailed rebuttals to the Leventhal report, the committee rapidly brought this segment of the testimony to a close, although not before several of the committee members climbed on their soap boxes to praise the Leventhal analysis and to condemn Arthur Young's audits and audits in general.

The last day of these hearings was held on November 21, 1989, and, according to the script laid out by Gonzalez, this was to be the grand finale, as Wall and Keating would be called to defend themselves against the case the committee had constructed against them.

The first to appear would be Danny Wall, accompanied by Dochow, O'Connell, Smuzynski, and Stewart. But before any of them got a chance to speak, Gonzalez, as was now his practice, made an opening statement that showed that these witnesses faced a losing struggle with the committee. Portions of his opening remarks were:

> With a third of the Nation's savings and loan assets under its regulatory wing, including the biggest of the big, the San Francisco Home Loan Bank viewed Lincoln as a "ticking time bomb" that required early action.
>
> Washington, it appears, looked at Lincoln as another case for the Home Loan Bank Board's traditional medicine of negotiation, accommodation and faith that management would ultimately do the right thing. . . .
>
> As the weeks and months went by, the Bank Board found itself mired deeper in the Keating schemes. In a May 1988 meeting, a troubled Bank Board member, Larry White, described the Board's plight, and I quote: "We've got a high-risk institution and to get out of this situation, we have to follow the words of Charles Keating; that it's a two-word admonition; Trust Me. . . . [A]nd if you want me—Keating—to get us out of this situation, trust me; go with me a little bit longer and I will get us out of this situation."
>
> Even this year, with Lincoln in its final hours, Chairman Wall continued down this "trust Keating" trail. Still trying to avoid conservatorship, Mr. Wall assured his colleagues that Keating would find a buyer. Notes produced by Board Member Roger Martin quote Danny Wall as saying on April 5, and I quote: "Conservatorship is not the only alternative—Keating is skilled enough to produce another acquirer. . . ."
>
> This was 9 days before Lincoln died, and the body was willed to the Federal Government, with no funeral expenses provided.
>
> Clearly, that 23-month, 14-day gap in the regulatory tape—May 1, 1987, until April 14, 1989—is troubling to the Office of Thrift Supervision, the successor to the Home Loan Bank Board.
>
> The Washington regulators now claim they lacked sufficient information to follow San Francisco's recommendation for a Government takeover in 1987. The record suggests otherwise, but taking the Washington regulators' claim at face value, the next question is: Why did they fail to move to a binding cease-and-desist order to halt the outrageous activities at Lincoln? Washington rejected the conservatorship. They passed over the possibility of a cease-

and-desist order and ultimately accepted a negotiated memorandum of understanding that everyone should have known would not be obeyed and could not be enforced. It was the kind of enforcement action that Charlie Keating would probably have been willing to sign 7 days a week. . . .

I appreciate the Washington regulators' desire to defend themselves and to place the best possible light on their actions. Some of the testimony to be presented here today suggests that San Francisco operates an incompetent shop, unable to prepare documentation for enforcements, and that its personnel are illegal leakers of confidential material and promotors of a secret agenda of bias against Lincoln.

These are serious charges and are not dissimilar from those brought in a lawsuit against San Francisco by Charles Keating and Lincoln Savings & Loan.

As mentioned earlier, the San Francisco Bank has a third of the Nation's savings and loans under its supervision. If the charges outlined in some of the testimony before us today are accurate, then the question immediately arises why the San Francisco regulators have been allowed to regulate the other institutions in the 11th District of the Home Loan Bank System. Or is the charge simply that the San Francisco regulators are incompetent and biased in only one case—Lincoln Savings & Loan of Irvine, CA? Just this one? Just this one involving Charles Keating?

To be very frank, this seems to stretch credibility pretty far. . . . [I]t seems to run contrary to basic points made by the Chairman of the Securities and Exchange Commission and the Chairman of the Federal Deposit Insurance Corporation, not to mention statements of Bank Board personnel themselves in support of the San Francisco Bank.

Gonzalez essentially was saying that Wall and his colleagues could testify, but nobody should believe them because the evidence was already against them. He commented on all of the defenses they would present, so their comments would be defused and discredited before they were made. By so doing, he severely diminished the effect of their live testimony on the press and the viewing public. It, like most of his actions, was unfair to these witnesses. They were set up by a hanging judge and his kangaroo court.

The first of the Washington people to speak to the committee was Rosemary Stewart. Aside from Danny Wall, she was the person whom San Francisco had attacked the most and whose reputation had suffered the greatest damage. She didn't waste any time setting the record straight. Prior to her appearance, she had submitted a sixty-page document to the committee detailing forty-five false or misleading statements made previously by Black and Patriarca when they testified. She emphasized that these weren't *all* of the misstatements, but only the most serious, and only those related to the work of the Office of Enforcement, strongly implying there were many more statements by these two people which, at best, shaded the truth. She addressed these misstatements in her opening remarks by saying: "My own work and the work of my office has been called incompetent and unaggressive. The documents that I prepared have been characterized as ineffective and damaging to the Government's interest and the actions of an Enforcement Review Committee on which I sit have been distorted beyond recognition. Each of these allegations is wrong, dead wrong."

A key area of concern was the issue of why a conservatorship had not been pursued in 1987. She addressed this issue as follows:

> We discussed all three grounds for appointment of conservators or receivers. The three grounds at that time were that an institution is insolvent; second, that an institution has demonstrated a substantial dissipation of its assets or earnings due to violations of laws, regulations or unsafe and unsound practices; or, third, that there was an unsafe or unsound condition for the institution to continue operating.
>
> With respect to the first ground, Lincoln was far from insolvent. It was reportedly meeting all of its capital requirements at the time. And the San Francisco office had not even mentioned that ground in its recommendation.
>
> Regarding dissipation of assets, we had received the 1986 exam report. We had reviewed it prior to that meeting [where San Francisco's recommendation was discussed]. And while there were losses identified in that exam report, there was absolutely no effort to tie those losses to the regulatory violations or the unsound practices, which the statutory grounds demand.
>
> Moreover, some of the losses were on assets that had already been sold; other losses represented assets or investments that had not been revalued since the time of the year old exam report. And not only were there very few appraisals, but the appraisals that had been done by our staff did not reflect losses of a level significant enough to conclude dissipation of assets.
>
> I would add that there were no large securities trading losses at that time in relation to Lincoln's level of capital. And Lincoln in fact had made a great deal more money on their securities transactions than they had ever lost by May 1987.
>
> It was the consensus of the meeting at that time that grounds did not exist. . . .
>
> The more recent characterizations of this meeting, or this event as being momentous or "stabbing San Francisco in the back," I believe is the quote, or motivated by political influence are, frankly, nothing but theater.

She also discussed the regulators' attitudes regarding Lincoln, as well as the topic of leaked information, with the following comments:

> There was also at that time what I would characterize as a vendetta attitude by members of our agency with respect to Lincoln, and there was a history of

the leaking of confidential information about Lincoln—leaks that had been going on since the fall of 1986. Never in my 15 years of service have I observed a similar situation of such indiscretion. . . .

She provided other comments regarding the leaks of confidential information.

In her comments, she confirmed what Keating had been asserting for more than two years. There was, in fact, a vendetta to get Lincoln. She also said that she hadn't seen a situation similar to the leaks in "my 15 years of service." Coming from one of the FHLBB's top lawyers, this was compelling evidence that the attacks on Lincoln and ACC were not routine, regulatory activities. They were deliberate attempts to cause harm to Lincoln and Keating.

Stewart then turned to the topic of my appearance before the ERC on March 25, 1988. The regulators, in an attempt to explain why the MOU had been entered into, stated that the comments I had made in this meeting had led them to the decision to opt for the MOU. Of course, the record of their deliberations doesn't mention my remarks at the meeting as a factor; instead, it cites the possibility of legal action by Lincoln as the motivation for entering into the MOU. Her comments in this regard were:

As I said earlier, we didn't know what the financial condition of Lincoln was. I will tell you that I was impressed by the presentation made by Lincoln's independent auditors. The audit partner for Arthur Young came to the committee and told us about a recent review that had been done by Arthur Young of all of the major assets and investments of Lincoln and certified to us that they were the correct financial statements that resulted from it, financial statements that disclosed full compliance with the net worth requirements for Lincoln.

Does that mean the committee believed Arthur Young? No. That we accepted his numbers? No. What it meant was we were looking at a report from an auditor that was brand new, that was reporting on assets and investments that our examiners had not looked at. Contrast that with a year-and-a-half old exam report talking about assets that were sold, assets that were no longer properly valued. . . .

The next real issue that she discussed concerned the possibility of San Francisco conducting the new exam. She said:

It was very clear by that time that San Francisco and Lincoln had such a deteriorated relationship that we would have had World War III had we attempted to get a new exam done by San Francisco. We could not have expected a consent by Lincoln—I think that's clear—to any enforcement document being negotiated or handled by San Francisco. And what we contrasted that with was a two-year proceeding that would have been required to put Lincoln under a cease-and-desist order. A cease-and-desist action had never been rejected in the matter of Lincoln. What was rejected was a long period of litigation to get such an order when we felt we could acquire "control" through other means.

After Stewart completed her opening statement, it was Dochow's turn to address the committee. The most interesting point that he made concerned the cost of not acting earlier to take over Lincoln. He presented some charts which tracked Lincoln against other associations in Arizona to demonstrate that Lincoln was no different from all the rest. His comments were:

I think it is interesting to also look at Lincoln in relation to other thrifts. Lincoln has major operations in the State of Arizona, so I asked staff to look at the Arizona thrift industry's trends during the same time period [1986 to 1989], and that's what the second line shows. It shows that Arizona thrifts during the same time period experienced a steady decline in GAAP capital total assets. Every year, it decreased and, in fact, as an industry, by March 1989, was insolvent 1.6 percent.

So, Lincoln's demise and the trend of the Arizona thrift institutions' decline are very similar. Compared to Arizona banks, the picture is just the opposite. The banks improved their position during the same time period.

Although he didn't intend to do so, Dochow actually demonstrated two points. The point that he wanted to make was that Lincoln was comparable to other thrifts and that the loss in value was market wide and not isolated to Lincoln. Which, of course, should then beg the question: If they were all having the same problem, how was Keating any different from any other operator in Arizona? Dochow was trying to show that the delay hadn't caused losses, the market had. But in so doing, he showed that Lincoln wasn't the maverick everyone was painting it to be.

The second point, which he didn't intend to demonstrate and certainly didn't dwell on, was that there was a difference between thrifts and banks in Arizona. The difference was that they had different regulators. While the FHLBB regulators were ordering appraisals with unrealistically low values for all the thrifts in Arizona, and flushing them all down the toilet with the resultant loss reserves that the regulators demanded, the bank regulators were not demanding the same kinds of appraisal losses. It wasn't a difference in how the institutions operated; it was a difference in how the regulators valued their respective assets. The result was that every thrift, of any size, in Arizona was taken over by the federal government, while no commercial banks were. Other states experienced this same phenomena. There was something wrong—drastically wrong—with how thrifts were regulated. But that problem was not what this committee was focusing on. If they had addressed the real regulatory problems—which were the flawed asset valuation and capital policies of the FHLBB—they would have had to acknowledge that billions had been needlessly wasted by the premature closure of hundreds of institutions.

Danny Wall then made his opening statement. His presentation appeared to have several objectives: to show he was, in fact, a tough regulator and not the pushover the committee had painted him to be; to show his decisions had not been influenced by any politicians; to rebut some of Black's testimony about so-called secret or ex-parte meetings that he had had with Keating; to stand behind the decisions that he had made relative to Lincoln; and to indicate that the industry's problem were a long way from being over.

His first theme dealt with whether he was tough enough as a regulator. He said:

> Many people have said I wasn't tough enough. Some people have said that this was a no-win job. Maybe both have been some people's views. But I would submit to you that I have said to 553 institutions you're out of business. And 553 institutions have been brought down in the time that I've been in the positions of responsibility. Not tough enough?

Again, in defending his own actions, Wall raises the larger issue: If 553 institutions were closed in the little over two years that he had been in office, what were the root causes behind these failures? Were their characteristics the same as or different from Lincoln's? If the grounds for bringing them down were insolvency, substantial dissipation of assets resulting from regulatory violations, or being in an unsound condition to operate—the grounds cited by Rosemary Stewart—how could any of them have been different from Lincoln? From the statistics quoted by Wall, which the committee was obviously already familiar with, it is clear that Lincoln was not an isolated case.

At the same time that all these thrifts were being "brought down" by the FHLBB, and now OTS, the phenomenon was not occurring with commercial banks, which in many states also made real-estate loans. What was the difference between the failure rates of these two types of financial institutions? Could it have been a factor as fundamental as the manner in which each type was regulated? Were the rules more favorable for banks as compared to thrifts? If they really wanted to get to the heart of the matter, these are some of the questions that the committee should have asked. The problem was clearly much deeper than simply casting Keating as a villain.

Wall touched briefly on this issue by stating why he thought the Lincoln case was being focused on by the committee, when he said:

This case has clearly reached a high level of notoriety for, it seems to me, two reasons: alleged political influence by five Senators and on the former Chairman, Mr. Gray. I can't speak to that. I have not met with those five Senators in that setting. I was not there with Chairman Gray at the time.

There is also, of course, the controversy between the San Francisco Federal Home Loan Bank, and now the district office, as well was the Bank Board here in Washington, and now the Office of Thrift Supervision.

Wall then turned to the topic of the meetings between FHLBB personnel, including himself, and Keating and other Lincoln representatives that Black had so harshly criticized. His explanation was:

There have been many pejorative references to that and the other meetings that have been held as being "secret" or "ex parte meetings." I am not a Latin scholar, I can assure you, but ex parte, baloney. Secret, baloney, those were meetings that were participated in by multiple members from the Federal Home Loan Bank Board. No one said or indicated in any way to remain or provide confidence as to what took place at those meetings. Notes were kept, as indeed you have them, and the meetings were participated in by anyone who was in the room. I never asked anyone to suppress the information that was discussed. Secret, ex parte—rubbish.

With respect to why the recommendation of San Francisco was turned down in favor of the MOU, Wall introduced a new twist which had not been discussed before. He said:

On May 5, 1988, we saw the options that have been talked about here as having been put forward by the ERC. I will say again: It should not go unnoticed, none of the five recommended option number three, which was to leave the responsibility with San Francisco. My desire for a new exam was reinforced by the Saratoga action 2 days earlier.

What was Saratoga? It was another institution in the State of California regulated by the same people. They had questioned an earlier San Francisco exam before an administrative law judge, as that proceeding provides. The administrative law judge recommended that we throw the exam out. We did not agree, after we at the Bank Board conducted what ended up being the only adjudicated proceeding in my time at the Bank Board, where we sat to review what the administrative law judge had recommended. We made our finding that, indeed, we felt the exam was sufficient as was necessary in that particular case. It has subsequently been appealed and we have won on that appeal, but it took 4 years from when the first exam was initiated—4 years in that situation.

Why option one? That is the position I took. San Francisco examiners, if they went back in, we were going to have legal delays, and how long, no one knew. Again, a similar situation, albeit a smaller one, but not insignificant in size, took 4 years.

Like Rosemary Stewart, Wall was saying that the primary reason the FHLBB and the ERC had opted for the MOU to resolve the 1986 Lincoln exam was to avoid litigation. First, there was a concern over the suit Lincoln had filed regarding damages it had suffered because of leaks of confidential information. The lawyers working for the FHLBB had to believe that Lincoln had a good case and, if such a case were tried, the FHLBB could expect to be assessed substantial penalties. As a result of the MOU, Lincoln had dismissed the suit. Second, the FHLBB knew that Lincoln would resist, through the courts, any actions it took emanating from the 1986 exam. To avoid a lengthy court battle, which it could very well lose, the FHLBB again saw the MOU as a better alternative. All the other various reasons which other witnesses offered to the committee were, to use Wall's word, baloney.

Before the committee began to question these witnesses, Congressman Wylie made this observation:

Now, there has been some disparity in the testimony here this morning between the testimony that we heard last week from Mr. Black and Mr. Patriarca and Mr. Cirona—I guess it was three weeks ago now. But from this member's observation, the areas of disagreement and disparity are significant enough that someone had perjured themselves, because all of the witnesses have been sworn in.

At this point, there was another bizarre twist in the hearings. When Black and Patriarca appeared, they were praised by the committee. Now, these witnesses were telling the committee that both Black and Patriarca had perjured themselves—repeatedly—and, therefore, their testimony was worthless and without merit.

This was disastrous for Gonzalez. There was a real possibility that his carefully orchestrated theatrical production could blow up in his face. Before each session started, Gonzalez had used his opening remarks to excoriate Wall and Keating. His opening statements were based on previous testimony which was now being called nothing but a pack of lies. He had to do something to counteract the testimony of these Washington people. If the proceedings continued as they were going, the public would see they were a farce, and that was the last thing Gonzalez wanted. So, almost unbelievably, Gonzalez asked Black to sit at the witness table, so he could challenge any of the testimony of the Washington people.

Congressman Ridge saw the patent unfairness of Black being at the witness table, and he remarked to Gonzalez as follows:

> Just a point of clarification or information, if I might, and not doubting or challenging the Chairman's discretion to engage with this witness or this panel in any manner in which you see fit, but as speaking for myself, when we had previous panels testify, I think we could reasonably have assumed that there were going to be people who disagreed with their testimony. We did not call those people whom we thought might disagree with that testimony to the panel to rebut that day, on that occasion, the specifics of that testimony, and I would just like to suggest that if the Chairman is inclined to have these witnesses square off against one another, that perhaps it be done at a later date, so that at least we could give this panel of witnesses the same kind of courtesy and scrutiny, without interruption, as we gave previous panels.

Others joined to support Ridge's objection, and, for a while, Gonzalez backed off and bided his time. Gonzalez stalled by saying that he would take the comments by Ridge and others "under due consideration," but he let Black remain at the witness table.

Within a short time, a question was posed to Black, and, in answering it, he became, by default, an active member of the panel and was free to ravage the other witnesses. This turned the remainder of the day into a three-ring circus.

The questioning of these witnesses continued for several hours, with most of the questions centered on whether the FHLBB had had a basis for appointing a conservator back in 1987. The answers given asserted that insufficient grounds had existed at that time. The witnesses also defended the position they had taken with regard to the MOU. Their testimony was therefore in sharp conflict with that previously given by Black and Patriarca. This process continued until 4:30 P.M., when the witnesses were excused for a few minutes, so that the committee could call Charlie Keating to the witness table.

Charlie's appearance was very brief. On the advice of his counsel, Charlie asserted his rights under the Fifth Amendment not to testify. I have not talked to Charlie about the reasons that led him not to testify, but I assume they paralleled my own. This was a forum that had already decided he was the villain in the story being told. The committee members and government witnesses had characterized him as such with great frequency. Nothing he could say would change the script that Gonzalez had developed. If he testified, he would merely be the target of incessant attacks, rumor, innuendo, slurs, and the political biases of his inquisitors. He was much better off waiting to present his case to an impartial forum—if such a forum could be found, given the campaign in the media to blame the entire thrift industry's collapse on him.

With Charlie's departure from the hearing room, the Washington people, along with Black, resumed their positions at the witness table. The questioning continued for about a hour or so with the Washington regulators parrying, with some success, the inquiries of the committee members. Then, Black set the whole process on its ear. He launched into an extended attack against the entire panel of people from Washington. No one was spared. His diatribe continued, unabated, for many minutes. Then, a concerned and troubled Danny Wall tried to stop Black by interjecting, "I have got to interrupt to correct what is a litany of partial truths and half truths and, in some cases, untruths."

Wall was cut off by Gonzalez, who told Black to proceed. After all, Black was doing exactly what Gonzalez wanted him to do—that's why Gonzalez had him at the table. He was there to discredit the testimony of those who were trying to correct the mishmash of lies which were the basis for the committee's indictment of Wall and Keating.

O'Connell jumped into the fray and contradicted virtually everything Black had said. Wall then added, "I will say that the one thing that troubles me deeply is that I heard one officer of the court, a lawyer, call another officer of the court a liar, and that troubles me deeply."

Black shot back, "I never called anyone a liar. There has been one person who has asserted perjury and that is Ms. Stewart."

Throughout the entire day's proceedings, Black was very animated, waving his hands about, gesturing wildly to drive home his points, and aggressive in his tone of voice. In contrast, the others maintained a calm, professional bearing, and, while at times visibly upset with what was happening, they did not resort to dramatic presentations or the wild oratorical antics that Black used. But it was clear that their patience was wearing thin. Rather than responding to Black's litany of charges at this time, Dochow merely said he wanted a transcript of the hearing, so he could rebut, in writing, the misstatements Black had made.

Stewart was asked if she wanted to respond to Black's accusation about her. She was obviously upset, but, still exhibiting a restrained, professional manner, she replied, "I do believe I have answered each of the matters that Mr. Black covered, except to tell you that I appear here today under subpoena, I take my oath very seriously. . . ."

The entire hearing had disintegrated into a series of mean-spirited attacks. The following sequence occurred at the end of the day, and it demonstrates the unfair and prejudiced attitudes of this committee:

KANJORSKI: Ms. Stewart, so it is very clear, what I am saying is you were so disturbed about the leaks occurring out there, this internal battle that you were having, that you missed the forest for the trees. . . .

STEWART: Sir, that is an absolute falsehood. . . .

KANJORSKI: Now, Ms. Stewart, do not use a word like "falsehood" with me. You may call Mr. Black a perjurer, but I am a member of a Congressional Committee, and I do not commit a falsehood. I am giving you my impression of the testimony. If you do not like it, that is fine. But do not say it is a falsehood.

GONZALEZ: The Chair is compelled at this point, in view of that outburst and in support of Mr. Leach, and the right of a Member to conclude based on testimony presented, that Ms. Stewart, your attack on your current and former agency colleagues—and now added Mr. Kanjorski, not to mention former Chairman Gray—is scathing and unrelentless.

On behalf of the taxpayers of America who will pick up the bill for the savings and loan nightmare, I offer the following thought: How much money could have been saved if you had pursued these high-flying S&L operators who were pillaging the Federal insurance funds with the same intensity? Your performance in that regard is well documented in the committee's hearing record, and no amount of attacking others will absolve you of that record.

In other words, "We like Black's story, even though it may be nothing but a pack of lies, better than yours—so, give up, lady—you can't win on this playing field." So, much for truth and justice.

Two comments made earlier in the day pretty well sum up what this final day of hearings was all about. The first was offered by Congressman LaFalce, who said:

Mr. Wall and members from the Federal Home Loan Bank Board, now OTS, I regret that you are coming before us today, because, since there has been such a long delay from the time our hearings began, I believe you have basically and unfortunately already been tried and convicted in the court of public opinion. The delay in your testimony means that you are here before us to try to reverse the judgment that has already been rendered. Whereas, had you testified earlier, perhaps the media would then have had the evidence with differing interpretations, not necessarily interpretations of past events, so that a more balanced presentation could have been made. But, unfortunately that is history.

Here was at least one committee member who had the honesty to admit publicly that the deck had been stacked against Wall and his Washington colleagues. Wall, himself, was aware that he was being railroaded by Gonzalez and the committee, when he said:

> I think I can speak with some degree of experience. I have never seen a process such has been going on before this Committee today and over the course of time.
>
> I am deeply troubled by what has developed today, in the sense that some have had an opportunity to respond to our testimony and we did not have an opportunity to respond to theirs in a contemporaneous way.
>
> I have indicated previously that I was troubled by the lack of timeliness in my being able to appear and being able to provide the resources that are here, the people who are hands-on involved in the process. I am troubled by it, I am concerned about, and you [Gonzalez] made a point that I certainly hope is the case. You said that you are not sitting in judgment. You said that just a few minutes ago.

If there's any doubt that these were rigged proceedings, one only need consider a few simple questions. What was Bill Black doing in the hearing room on this day? He lived in San Francisco. He wasn't a scheduled witness. He had already testified. So, why was he there? Who told him to be there? Who knew that he would be needed to rebut these people? How did he gain access to the materials that the Washington people gave to the committee, so he could ask the questions and make the counterattacks that he did?

These hearings concluded at 8:22 P.M., November 21, 1989. There were no new legislation, no new regulations, no changes in the regulatory process, and no changes in the way S&Ls operated. But that's not what these hearings were all about. They were nothing more than an expensive effort to place a face on the S&L debacle. That face belonged to Charlie Keating. Sure, Danny Wall, Rosemary Stewart, I, and others were severely and permanently harmed by this farce—the statements made by these congressman and by the witnesses would have been slanderous had they been made outside the confines of the hearing room. We suffered damage which can never be repaired. But Charlie got the worst of it. During the course of these hearings, Charlie was turned into a symbol of everything that had gone wrong in this industry. He was labeled a crook and villain of historic proportions.

As the hearings progressed, Keating's name and face, and the accusations which poured out of this committee, appeared in every major newspaper, magazine, and television news program. The public and the media blindly accepted that he was the cause of the S&L crisis. He was the man who had taken their tax dollars. He was the person who preyed viciously on aged men and women—robbing them of their life's savings to support his own decadent life-style. This committee turned him into one of the most notorious people of this century. They did it because they needed a scapegoat who would allow them to hide their blame, and that of other politicians and bureaucrats, for destroying an industry and a nation's economy.

These hearings were not unique. Throughout history, governments have used proceedings like this to feed propaganda to their citizens. Gonzalez was simply following the same pattern. Now that the U.S. government had defeated Keating and Lincoln, it was fair game to treat them as war criminals—or political prisoners—and to use them as the prime subjects in propaganda-driven proceedings designed to shift the American citizens' attention away from the failed policies of their own government. It's the kind of thing that we've come to expect at the end of any war.

These hearings were successful. They prejudiced the public against Keating and his associates; they therefore had a profound effect on the legal battles that followed.

Twenty

Federal Judge Seals Keating's Fate

Shortly after the government seized Lincoln, ACC filed a lawsuit challenging the conservatorship. In essence, the suit asserted that the FHLBB had had insufficient grounds on which to base a conservatorship action; therefore, it had acted inappropriately in seizing Lincoln. The suit asked for Lincoln to be returned to ACC in essentially the same condition it was in at the time it was seized.

ACC's lawsuit created the first instance in which the government and ACC would meet in a courtroom. Since the regulators had never disclosed to ACC and Lincoln many of the findings that were the bases of the FHLBB's vote for a conservatorship, the suit also created the first opportunity that ACC would have to address and refute these findings. It was the opportunity that Charlie Keating had been waiting for—the chance to confront the FHLBB on neutral turf. Unfortunately for ACC and Keating, it didn't turn out the way that Charlie anticipated.

In retrospect, ACC's lawyers made several strategic errors in handling this suit. The errors resulted in the issuance of a federal judge's opinion that would unfavorably color all of the future court actions in which Keating and ACC would become involved. The suit became a pivotal point in the aftermath of Lincoln's failure. For that reason, the suit and the judge's opinion deserve special attention.

The suit was filed in Washington, giving the FHLBB home-field advantage—strategic error number one. Conventional wisdom dictates that if ACC was asserting that the government had acted inappropriately, the suit should have been filed in a district court in California, where the presence of the federal government was not as strong as it was in Washington. The judges in that venue might not have held previous government positions and might not have viewed the government in the same favorable light that Washington-based judges might.

The judge assigned to the case was Stanley Sporkin—another advantage for the FHLBB and strategic error number two. Prior to his appointment to the federal bench, Sporkin had, for many years, headed up the

SEC's enforcement division. There, he earned the reputation as a hard-nosed regulator who was death on corporations and professionals who crossed his path.

While with the SEC, Sporkin was, in effect, a regulator. Under his direction, the enforcement division was active in bringing actions against corporations for alleged false reporting in annual reports and other public-disclosure documents as well as securities fraud. The SEC has historically held very conservative views on accounting issues—views which support early recognition of potential losses, deferral of income, extensive disclosure, and other positions which many consider to be overly conservative.

The suits filed against ACC by class-action plaintiffs and the RTC alleged that ACC's financial reports and public disclosures contained material omissions and misstatements and that securities laws were violated in the sale of the subordinated debentures—the types of issues Sporkin had a history of asserting in the SEC's actions that he initiated. Moreover, the types of issues which were involved in the conservatorship action were consistent with these suits. There was no way—no way—that Sporkin, with his SEC background, could reasonably be expected to take a position adverse to another regulator.

Perhaps more significantly, Sporkin was in the SEC's enforcement division at the time when Keating entered into a consent decree that concerned matters related to American Financial Corp. Thus, Keating's and ACC's lawyers may have had grounds to disqualify Sporkin from sitting on the bench to hear this suit. It is certainly arguable that, even if Sporkin had not been directly involved in the matter of Keating's consent decree, Sporkin's mere presence at the SEC during that time frame and his experiences at the SEC may have colored his attitudes toward Keating and, thus, prejudiced these proceedings.

And while at the SEC, Sporkin was involved in actions against the audit firms that ACC had employed. He suffered at least one very bitter defeat in those actions.

The third advantage to the FHLBB was the congressional hearings. The thrust of the hearings was that the FHLBB was not only justified in seizing Lincoln, but it should have done so earlier. The hearings received extensive coverage in Washington, and no one in that city wanted the blame for Lincoln's demise to shift off of Keating and back onto the government. Every government witness who appeared before the congressional committee testified that ACC and Keating had dissipated Lincoln's assets and had managed Lincoln in an unsound manner. Again, once could question whether any judge in Washington would take a position contrary to these witnesses from the legislative and executive branches, let alone one with Sporkin's background.

ACC's suit contended that the FHLBB had acted in an arbitrary and capricious manner in placing Lincoln into, first, conservatorship and, later, receivership. ACC asserted that Lincoln had, at all times, been managed and operated on a sound financial basis and that the FHLBB's actions had been unjustified. On the other hand, the FHLBB contended that ACC and Lincoln had engaged in unsafe and unsound practices; as a result, there had been a substantial dissipation of Lincoln's assets.

The FHLBB filed motions for summary judgment seeking dismissal of the suit. Before making a determination, Sporkin held an evidentiary hearing to determine whether the FHLBB had had a reasonable basis for its actions or whether it had acted in an arbitrary and capricious fashion. The FHLBB was allowed to select a few transactions that it felt demonstrated that it had acted with proper justification. Both sides were able to call witnesses and present other evidence, but, as I understand what occurred, the witnesses were not subjected to the same level of direct and cross-examination that would have occurred had this hearing been a full-blown trial.

Sporkin issued a Memorandum Opinion, dated August 22, 1990, on the matter. In the Opinion, he cited several principles of law which guided his decision. First, judicial deference was to be given to the FHLBB's judgment. He was to determine whether the FHLBB's actions had been based on a consideration of relevant factors or whether there had been a clear error in judgment. Second, the standard of review was narrow. In making these points, he stated that "the court is not empowered to substitute its judgment for that of the agency." And, "Notwithstanding this deference, the agency must examine the relevant data and articulate a satisfactory explanation for its action including a rational connection between the facts found and the choice made." Thus, it appears that the FHLBB's burden of proof was not substantial. It merely needed to demonstrate that it had had a rational basis for its actions.

Some of Sporkin's thinking was exhibited when, after discussing the FHLBB's authority and the fact that it was "consistent with the need for effective regulation of the savings and loan industry," he stated:

> This is particularly so where, as here, the accounts of a savings and loan association are insured by the federal government for $100,000 per account. While plaintiff ACC invested some $51 million to purchase Lincoln, the institution's $1 billion in assets came from depositors with federally insured accounts. Thus, by virtue of its insurance of Lincoln's accounts, the federal government's interest in Lincoln is many times that of ACC.

This is the same logic that the FHLBB people always expressed—the government's insurance of depositors' accounts granted the government ownership rights in an association's net assets greater than the rights held by the association's stockholders.

The concept that depositors have an ownership interest in an association's assets is appropriate in the case of a mutual association, as there are no shareholders; thus, the depositors do, in theory, own the net assets of the association. But in a stock association, such as Lincoln, depositors are merely unsecured creditors. As for the government, it has no interest, other than as an insurer or, perhaps, more appropriately, a guarantor. The government's property interest, if any, doesn't kick in until it has to pay depositors, in the event the association is unable to.

In a mutual association, management has no economic stake in the association, except as employees. As such, management is, in effect, an agent for the depositors who hold the ownership rights, to the extent such rights exist, to the association's net assets. In this situation, it is understandable why regulators and others, including judges, refer to the assets as those of the depositors. And perhaps that's where the attitude which seems to be held by federal government personnel originated—since most of the entities they dealt with prior to 1983 were organized as mutual associations.

Since the depositors in mutual associations don't really function as owners, the regulator acts as a surrogate for the depositors and assumes the role of judging management's performance. This can include qualitative assessments of management's performance, such as: Is management making the best economic deals possible; is compensation appropriate; are expenses reasonable; is the investment strategy acceptable; and are investment returns consistent with investment risks? These are questions an owner asks about the quality of management's performance. If the regulator, as the owners' agent, concludes that management is not acting in the best interests of the depositors—the owners—the regulator takes action to remove the management group and to install new managers. This makes sense because the appointment of management is a prerogative of the owner.

However, the concept does not fit in the case of a stock association. In a stock association, stockholders—not depositors—have the prerogatives of ownership. As mentioned, the depositors are nothing more than unsecured creditors. They have no priority claims against any of the assets of the association. The owners—the stockholders—have the right to select, evaluate, retain, or replace management. The owners have the right to deploy and invest the association's assets, consistent with applicable laws, as they see fit. The determination of whether the quality of management's performance is acceptable is a decision for the owners—the shareholders—to make and not the regulators, who have no rights of ownership, direct or indirect, as a surrogate or agent.

Thus, in the case of the stock association, the role of the regulator should be different from what it is in a mutual association. Since the depositors have no ownership rights, the regulator cannot act as a surrogate owner on their behalf. The regulator's role should logically be limited to ascertaining whether the association is in compliance with the rules and regulations covering the insurance of accounts.

The object of deposit insurance is the depositors' accounts. The federal insurer is, in effect, saying to depositors, "If you deposit your money in this institution and, for whatever reason, the institution fails to repay you the amount you deposited; then, up to $100,000 per account, we'll make you whole." The beneficiary of this promise is the depositor—not the S&L or its shareholders.

Now, before the S&L is allowed to make this insurance available to its customers, it has to agree to comply with certain rules and conditions—the Insurance of Accounts Regulations. If it fails to comply with the rules and regulations, the insurer reserves the right to pursue certain remedies. In this case, the remedies appear to be a cease-and-desist order (i.e., stop violating the rules and conditions), cancellation of the insurance, or conservatorship. These are remedies which are, in effect, provided for in the insurance policy. They are not ownership rights or property rights.

The first two remedies—cease and desist and cancellation—make sense to me as a nonlawyer. These are comparable to the actions that any insurer can take. If you are not complying with the terms of a policy, the insurer can tell you to stop violating the policy terms and conditions, or coverage will be canceled. If you continue to violate the policy terms and conditions, cancellation of coverage is the private insurer's ultimate remedy. In this case, the insured party—the depositor—is not the party who has to obey the terms and conditions; instead, it's the S&L who has that obligation. So there is a primary difference between deposit insurance and private casualty or property insurance.

The conservatorship remedy may have merit, especially in the case of mutual associations. If the person who is supposed to comply with the policy terms—the S&L's management—doesn't, then, the insurer may have a legitimate right to remove that management and replace it with management who will follow the rules. This clearly appears to be appropriate in the case of a mutual association, where the appointment of a conservator is simply an extension of the regulator's role as agent for the depositor-owners. The conservator simply becomes replacement management.

The appropriateness of the regulator's right to appoint a conservator, or receiver, doesn't make much sense in the case of a stock association. It is logical for the regulator to have the legitimate right to demand, probably through a court-enforced C&D, that the shareholders oust any managers who violate the rules. But to vest in the regulator the right to usurp all the rights of management—unilaterally—does not seem legitimate.

The issue becomes murky in the case where an association fails to meet its capital requirement and the insurer may be exposed to loss. It seems logical that the insurer should be able to take actions to minimize its potential losses. The issue then becomes: Is the capital requirement, as it was applied on April 14, 1989, a fair measure of the potential loss to the insurer? A loss will accrue to the insurer only if the fair value of all of an association's assets does not exceed the amount of the association's liabilities. The trick lies in how fair value is determined.

The determination of the fair value of the assets has to include all assets. This means those with unrealized gains as well as those with unrealized losses. In the case of Lincoln, and I believe every other association that the regulators have placed in conservatorship, this is not the determination that was made. The regulators posted reserves against assets which had "potential" or "possible" losses based on the premise that the assets would be liquidated. There are several things wrong with this approach.

First, unless the decision has been made to liquidate the association—a decision which is totally inconsistent with the concept of conservatorship—then the premise of valuing assets by using a liquidation approach is inappropriate. The premise should be that the association will remain a going concern and that it will maintain its operations. Thus, long-term projects which are in the midst of development should be valued on the basis of the discounted cash flows which will be produced over the development cycle. Other assets, such as real estate held for sale, should be valued based on a selling period which is reflective of current market conditions, with appropriate deductions for holding costs, and not on a forced-sale basis, such as an all-cash sale within six months, if six months is not prudent given current market conditions and if the association has the ability to arrange or provide financing.

Second, the valuation must include all estimated unrealized gains, not just losses. The objective is to determine whether the insurer will ultimately experience a loss. The unrealized gains are as pertinent to that determination as potential losses are. Again, such a determination should be based on a normal operating cycle and a going-concern concept.

Third, in estimating potential losses, the process should take into account all of the actions the association can take to mitigate against loss. For example, rather than simply assuming that loans which are slow paying or delinquent will be foreclosed, the assumptions should consider the effects of loan modifications which can prevent foreclosure and allow the borrower to meet its obligations. If foreclosure is the only recourse, the collateral should be valued based on the most advantageous means of disposal rather than on immediate forced sale.

Now, assuming one accepts that the failure to meet a capital requirement, as promulgated in a regulation, is a reasonable indication that the
insurer might incur a loss, and assuming the capital requirement has been
determined on a going-concern, fair-value basis, then maybe—maybe—
a conservatorship makes sense for a stock association. It still leaves open
the issue of whether, given the shareholders' inherent property rights, the
regulator should be able unilaterally to appoint a conservator or whether
it's a better public policy to require the regulator to go through a judicial
process, much like a bankruptcy court, before a conservator can be
installed.

If a conservator is appointed, the conservator has the legal obligation
to preserve everyone's property rights, including those of shareholders.
The object of the conservator is to manage the assets of the institution in
such a fashion so as to protect everyone's investment. This means that the
conservator needs to create a business plan which has as its objective the
resumption or continuance of profitable operations. If the conservator
does not aggressively manage the association's operations with the intent
to conduct ongoing and profitable operations, it is inevitable that losses
will accrue. If revenue-generating operations are not pursued, the association will slowly bleed to death because of its fixed costs. If a conservator
does not pursue the production of revenue, then the rights of equity
holders, and probably creditors, are not preserved. The conservator's
mission should be the same as any management's—to preserve and
enhance net asset values.

In Lincoln's case, the conservator had a totally different mission. That
mission was to diminish net asset values to the extent that all ownership
interests—other than the insurer's—were extinguished as rapidly as
possible. It appeared to be an affirmative objective of the conservator to
eliminate the stockholder's, or ACC's, interest as expeditiously as it could.
There is no evidence that the conservator ever entertained the questions:
How can we see that the equity holder realizes as much as possible out of
these assets, and what can we, as the conservator, do to maximize value and
avert loss?

If you follow Sporkin's logic, ACC never had a primary ownership
interest to preserve. He said, in effect, "Hell, they only put in a measly $51
million, and that's nothing compared to the risk that the federal government was insuring." So, he wiped out ACC's property rights from the very
start. It's as if the real owner had always been the government, and the
government had just let ACC use the assets.

Sporkin's comment ignored the simple fact that, at the time ACC
purchased Lincoln, Lincoln's capital was greater than the amount the

regulations required. ACC and Lincoln met all of the requirements that the law and the regulations for the insurance of accounts demanded. So, ACC's capital, under the prevailing law, was not inconsequential, as Sporkin implied it was. Moreover, Sporkin's comment ignored the inherent and fundamental differences between an owner (ACC), a creditor (depositors), and an insurer or guarantor (the government).

Sporkin appeared to concur that Congress had acted properly when it adopted a statute which established that the FHLBB "shall have the exclusive power and jurisdiction to appoint a conservator or receiver." And, again, he cited: "The delegation of such authority is consistent with the need for effective regulation of the savings and loan industry."

By granting these exclusive powers to the regulators, where they can act unilaterally to confiscate assets and extinguish property rights, Congress gave the shaft to thousands of investors who owned stock in seized S&Ls and banks. Shareholders' rights can be erased with the stroke of a pen. If shareholders believe that the regulators have acted improperly, there's effectively no court to which they can appeal, because federal judges, like Sporkin, uphold the regulators' authority. When they do appear before these judges, the burden of proof that the regulators have to meet is minimal. It's a wonder, given the events of the past few years, that anyone is willing to accept the risks of owning stock in a government-insured and regulated institution. Something has to be corrected—either the law itself or how the law is applied.

Here, Sporkin didn't challenge whether the powers granted to the FHLBB might result in the deprivation of the rights of parties who are subjected to their regulation. Instead, his focus was simply on whether the FHLBB had had a rational basis for its actions or if it had acted in an arbitrary and capricious manner. Its power to act was a given.

Thus, the purpose of the evidentiary hearing was limited: Did the FHLBB meet the arbitrary and capricious standard? However, in his Memorandum Opinion, Sporkin went farther than that when he stated: "While this Court is convinced that the Bank Board satisfied the 'arbitrary and capricious' standard, the evidence proffered and received during the hearing satisfied each of the other standards that are used to review an agency action. In short, this Court finds that the Bank Board was fully justified in taking the actions that it did." Another error that ACC and its attorneys made was getting put in the position where Sporkin could come to this opinion on the basis of the limited hearing that was held. Because others, inappropriately, gave this opinion the same weight it would have received had it been based on a bona-fide trial and not an abbreviated hearing.

The first area which Sporkin addressed in his Memorandum Opinion was the tax-sharing payments. Sporkin summarized the issue as follows:

Although ACC concedes that Lincoln on a stand alone basis essentially owed no taxes during the period, it justifies the upstreaming of this $94,000,000 on two bases: First, it states that the tax-sharing agreement was approved by the Board which ACC claims is evidenced by certain correspondence between Sydney Mar, Supervisory Agent of the FHLB-SF, and Andre Neibling [*sic*], Lincoln's Chief Executive Officer. Plaintiffs point to certain additional correspondence between Mr. Mar and Mark Sauter, ACC's corporate counsel, in support of their position. Second, at oral argument plaintiffs took the position that since the Board had adopted no rules or regulations pertaining to tax sharing agreements, the Board could not after the fact declare tax sharing agreements illegal. According to ACC, what the Board should have done if it did not approve of the way ACC was implementing the tax sharing agreement was issue a cease and desist order. Plaintiffs assert that it was impermissible for the Board to have taken the draconian action it did, which was to remove ACC totally from control of Lincoln.

Testimony and documents were offered by both sides in support of their arguments. The most significant factors were not who testified and what they said, but who did not testify and what was left unsaid or unexplained. Both Niebling and Sauter asserted their Fifth Amendment rights and did not testify. Mar was not called as a witness by either side. Consequently, the three people, and perhaps the only people, who knew what had really happened between the time of Lincoln's and ACC's initial request to Mar to approve the tax-sharing agreement and the time when the approval letter was received from Mar did not testify.

It is understandable why Sauter and Niebling didn't testify, but one has to wonder why Mar was not called as a witness. I can see why the FHLBB didn't call him. All he could say was that the letter he sent did approve the agreement, and that wouldn't help the FHLBB's position. But knowing that, one would think that ACC's attorneys would have wanted him to state, under oath, that he had, indeed, approved the agreement and the method for determining the tax payments. Now, if called, he might have said that he had somehow been deceived, as this seems to be the line the FHLBB wants people to believe, but a skilled attorney should have been able to deflate that argument.

It may have been that since this wasn't a complete trial and depositions hadn't been taken, the attorneys were not comfortable calling a potentially adverse witness without knowing what he would say. It may also have been that the rules which Sporkin laid down for the hearing didn't permit the calling of adverse witnesses. Whatever the reason, the absence of testimony from these three people certainly left a woefully incomplete record of what had actually occurred with respect to the approval of the tax-sharing agreement.

The absence of this critical testimony, which Sporkin acknowledged in a footnote to his opinion as being "unfortunate," didn't stop Sporkin from reaching a strongly worded conclusion regarding the issue—a conclusion which would come back to haunt Keating and certain other ACC executives. Sporkin's conclusion was:

> Plaintiffs' position cannot be sustained on either basis. Let us examine both of plaintiffs' points. First, while there was certain correspondence that was exchanged between the parties, it is abundantly clear from the record that the Board was in no way approving plaintiffs' methodology for determining the timing and amounts of the tax sharing payments. This so-called tax sharing agreement was nothing more than a clever but impermissible way of looting Lincoln by upstreaming funds from Lincoln to ACC. This technique was used largely because the Bank Board would not permit Lincoln to pay any dividends to its parent ACC. Second, plaintiffs' contention that the lack of formal rules or regulations permitted the transfer of $94 million from Lincoln to ACC is tantamount to arguing that theft is licensed in the absence of a rule against the precise method utilized to deprive rightful owners of their property.

Either ACC's attorneys did a horrible job of presenting the facts, or Sporkin chose to disregard the facts, or Sporkin misinterpreted the facts. It is crystal clear that Mar approved the tax-sharing agreement, including the methodology for determining the amount and timing of the payments. Even the FHLBB people—O'Connell, Patriarca, Black, Wall, and Stewart—testified, under oath, to Congress that the agreement had been approved. Sure, they contended that ACC used "deceptive" or "cleverly worded" methods to obtain approval. But Mar has never testified that he was deceived, nor has anyone else ever indicated in any testimony, or even in the internal correspondence of the FHLBB, that Mar has ever said that he was deceived—the FHLBB people have just assumed that he was. Nonetheless, they have all conceded that approval was granted. So, if the record in this hearing indicated that no approval was granted to the tax-sharing agreement, that record is dreadfully incomplete.

Second, if Mar did grant approval, as everyone but Sporkin believes he did, then the payments were not "impermissible" as Sporkin concluded. He even has a footnote, earlier in the opinion, which states, "certain transactions are prohibited unless approval is obtained from regulatory officials." That's what ACC and Lincoln did—they obtained prior written approval from the regulatory official who supervised Lincoln. Just what the regulation said they had to do. No payments were made until after such approval was obtained. The agreement, including the methodology, was fully disclosed each year in Lincoln's financial statements, which were filed with the Board. The tax-sharing agreement was never a secret.

Finally, the use of the word "looting" was pejorative and, in my opinion, not supportable by the evidence that Sporkin had before him. ACC and Lincoln have freely admitted to the regulators, from the very start, that ACC received tax payments from Lincoln when no payments were due to the IRS. That's never been a secret, and there is no evidence that anyone ever attempted to hide that fact. The agreement clearly can, and did, allow that result to occur.

The term "looting" implies that ACC and/or its executives intentionally sought to deprive Lincoln permanently of its assets. The evidence clearly indicates that this is not the case at all. ACC's and Lincoln's internal tax accountants were certainly aware, as they discussed at great length with Kyle Klein and others at the FHLBB, that the tax payments resulted from timing differences. It was fully expected that these differences would reverse over time and, in fact, ACC's and Lincoln's internal calculations, as discussed with the FHLBB, indicated that, based on the then-in-process IRS exam and the operating results for 1988, the reversal had already occurred. The $94 million would turn around, and it was not a permanent transfer of funds from Lincoln to ACC—or it would not have been if Lincoln hadn't been seized and its operations terminated. Sporkin's term "looting" simply was not warranted.

Sporkin clearly didn't like the result that the tax-sharing agreement produced, as evidenced by the following:

> Plaintiffs used the concept of tax sharing as a way of dipping into Lincoln's coffers and taking money which under no circumstances were plaintiffs entitled to have. Although ACC owned 100 percent of the stock of Lincoln, this did not give ACC license to strip Lincoln of its funds, particularly because the funds upstreamed emanated from the savings of individual investors which were insured up to $100,000 per account by the Federal Government.

Farther on in the Memorandum Opinion, and in the same vein, he stated: "There is simply no legal justification for these payments. Moreover, since ACC filed for bankruptcy on April 13, 1989, it is unable to repay Lincoln any part of the $94 million ACC received from Lincoln." Then he said later, "While all tax-sharing agreements between a parent and an insured savings and loan association must be closely scrutinized to assure the S&L is not being disadvantaged by its parent, under no circumstances can such agreements be justified other than on the basis of tax accounting principles [as opposed to GAAP]."

Sporkin's sweeping condemnation of the tax-sharing agreement was, in my opinion, not supported by the facts, and some of his comments were, frankly, just claptrap. First, he again brought up the fact that Lincoln's deposits were insured and asserted that payments "emanated" from those funds. Taxes are based on earnings—without earnings there are no taxes. Thus, the more appropriate source from which the payments "emanated" was earnings, not from borrowings, which is what, in essence, deposits are. The significance of the deposits being insured—and the only significance which was directly relevant to the issue at hand—was that the tax-sharing agreement had to be approved by the regulators before it could be adopted. If Lincoln had not been a regulated entity, ACC and Lincoln could have entered into any form of tax sharing they desired—without approval by anyone other than their respective boards of directors.

That's the second issue. Sporkin said there was "simply no legal justification for these payments." Hogwash. First, there was the agreement—a contract—which was approved by both boards of directors. Second, there was the submission of the agreement to Mar for his subsequent written approval. That was the only approval process required by the law and the regulations. The payments were, therefore, "legally justified" by a binding contract which had been approved, as required, by the appropriate regulatory official in full compliance with the law and published regulations.

Third, he stated, "all tax-sharing agreements between a parent and an insured savings and loan association must be closely scrutinized." Well, that might be Sporkin's personal opinion, but the regulations and the law applicable to insured savings and loan associations were absolutely silent on the subject of tax-sharing agreements. The words "tax sharing" cannot be found in the regulations. If the concern for close scrutiny was as strong as Sporkin implied it was, one would certainly expect some mention of the subject in the regulations. The fact is, the FHLBB had no published policy regarding such agreements—none—let alone a requirement that they be "closely scrutinized." Be that as it may, Lincoln and ACC did submit their agreement to the regulators for whatever level of scrutiny they deemed appropriate. And after the regulators "scrutinized" the agreement, they approved it.

Sporkin said that the tax-sharing payments were the result of a "dishonest scheme" but then admitted: "It is not clear from the record how plaintiffs came up with this dishonest scheme." It wasn't clear, because there was no evidence that a "scheme" existed. Everything related to the tax-sharing agreement was done in broad daylight—by the rules.

Finally, Sporkin asserted that "under no circumstances can such agreements be justified other than on the basis of tax accounting principles." Again, that's not what the regulations stated—the regulations were silent on the subject. So was the law. The assertion was Sporkin's personal opinion. He cited no authority for his opinion. No regulation. No case law. No accounting pronouncement. Nothing. But there was justification for the methodology ACC and Lincoln used. That justification was the judgment of the regulator who approved the agreement. And Sporkin had previously cited the law he had to follow in this case: "The Court is not empowered to substitute its judgment for that of the agency."

Sporkin also offered these conclusions on the subject of the tax-sharing payments:

> The entire Board of Directors [of Lincoln], in addition to Keating and the others that controlled Lincoln, must be held strictly accountable for this flat-out dissipation of Lincoln's assets. . . .
>
> It is the finding of this Court that the upstreaming of $94 million from Lincoln to ACC on the basis of a contrived tax sharing agreement was an unsafe and unsound practice that led to a substantial dissipation of Lincoln's assets and by itself fully justified the actions taken by the Bank Board first to impose a conservatorship and later to place Lincoln in receivership. This is particularly so since ACC went into bankruptcy and was not able to repay the funds it had misappropriated from Lincoln.

The fact that ACC had filed for bankruptcy before the seizure of Lincoln was a factor in Sporkin's reasoning. Had ACC not filed until after the FHLBB moved on Lincoln, the bankruptcy might not have been a factor at all, as ACC would merely have been reacting to a situation which was forced upon it. This appears to have been a significant tactical error by ACC's legal advisors.

Using hindsight, ACC gained absolutely nothing by filing for bank-ruptcy protection prior to the seizure of Lincoln. The government eventually gained control of all of Lincoln's subsidiaries. Had ACC waited until after the government had acted against Lincoln, ACC would have been able to argue more forcefully that it was the government's actions that directly caused ACC's bankruptcy.

These last comments also reinforce Sporkin's previous conclusions that the tax-sharing agreement was a deliberate attempt by Keating and ACC to strip Lincoln permanently of its assets. This conclusion can be reached only if one refuses to accept the fact that Mar approved the arrangement and if one ignores the fact that the payments were the product of temporary differences between book and tax accounting which would reverse over time. Also, as Sporkin had conceded earlier, the record which was available to him did not show clearly how the agreement had come about; in the absence of any knowledge about the genesis of the agreement, it would seem unfair, at best, to attribute any pejorative motives to its creation and operation.

As a final observation on the subject of the tax-sharing agreement and Sporkin's comments about it, in theory, I agree with his comment that tax agreements generally should be based on the tax return rather than on book accounting. Under most circumstances, using the actual tax return as the basis for tax payments between related parties produces the most equitable result. Had I been Sydney Mar, I would not have approved the agreement as it was written. But I am not Sydney Mar, and he did approve it. Once Mar, as the supervisory agent, approved the agreement, it didn't matter what methodologies might have been preferable to the one set forth in the agreement.

The tax-sharing agreement played a pivotal role in Sporkin's analysis of the other four issues, or transactions, that the FHLBB presented in support of its actions. Sporkin stated: "The tax sharing agreement was merely the mechanism used to permit the impermissible taking that occurred. What the defendant has next alleged and proven is that the plaintiffs engaged in additional unsafe and unsound practices for the purpose of creating bogus profits in order to justify the remittance of monies from Lincoln to ACC under the tax sharing agreement."

The first of the four issues that Sporkin addressed was the sale of land in Hidden Valley to West Continental Mortgage and Investment Corporation (Wescon). The sale occurred on March 31, 1987, and involved 1,000 acres of land with a total sales price of $14 million. The down payment was $3.5 million, and the remainder of the sales price was represented by a non-recourse note. Lincoln recognized a gain on the sale of approximately $11 million. The FHLBB asserted that the gain resulted in a tax-sharing payment of about $4.4 million from Lincoln to ACC.

Wescon was, as I understand it, introduced to Lincoln by Ernest ("Ernie") Garcia, president of E.C. Garcia & Company. Ernie Garcia was a young, Hispanic businessman from Tucson. In late 1986 and 1987, he was touted by the business press in Arizona as one of the state's up-and-coming business leaders. His company developed, syndicated, and managed a number of multifamily projects in Tucson and Phoenix. Additionally, the company purchased and sold, or was in the process of selling, to a number of different investment partnerships, including Wescon, a large acreage of undeveloped land located south of Tucson near the retirement community of Green Valley. Garcia's company was funded through an investment made in its common stock by a subsidiary of Tucson Electric Power Company (TEP). Garcia also owned a significant interest in a small, commercial bank, Arizona Commerce Bank, and he had previous experience in the investment-brokerage business. By all indications, he was a successful businessman with a promising future ahead of him.

In late 1986 or early 1987, Bruce Dickson, who headed up Lincoln's lending function, contacted Garcia about the possibility of Lincoln supplying E.C. Garcia & Company with its future financing requirements. After discussions between Garcia and Dickson, a loan, which was secured by real property, was made by Lincoln to E.C. Garcia & Company in late January 1987. This was the first of what would be many transactions between the two companies.

During his initial discussions with Dickson, Ernie Garcia discussed two other transactions he wanted to do which required financing. First, he wanted to buy out TEP's interest in his company, and, to do so, he needed about $20 million. Second, he was interested in buying a broker-dealer company located in Phoenix, and, to do so, he needed additional funds, perhaps as much as $30 million. Dickson thought that these were the kinds of loans that Lincoln should make, but the loan amounts were greater than his approval authority, so he introduced Garcia to Charlie and Judy in order to obtain their approval of the transactions.

As I understand the story, when Charlie met with Garcia, Charlie knew that Garcia was in the business of syndicating land to investment partnerships. The primary purpose of the meeting was to discuss the financing to buy the TEP interest, and Charlie, apparently, indicated that the transaction sounded acceptable to him, as long as the financial statements of E.C. Garcia & Company supported the loan amount. Then, Charlie suggested that Garcia consider the purchase and syndication of some of the Hidden Valley land. Garcia apparently said that he would consider such a purchase.

It should be pointed out that this was how Charlie did business. When he sat down with someone, he presented a variety of deals for their consideration, and, if they wanted to present deals to him for his consideration, he listened to the proposals from the other party. He had always done things this way. He was a deal maker. He used every opportunity to present those things that he had to sell which appeared to fit the other party's business. He didn't expect that the other party would necessarily react favorably to all the deals he presented, but he knew, as any deal maker does, if you don't offer something, the other party can't consider it.

In a subsequent meeting, Garcia purportedly told Charlie that his company couldn't buy the Hidden Valley land at that time because he was still marketing the land that his company held south of Tucson. Also, he didn't want the additional debt on his balance sheet. But Garcia added that he did know someone who was interested—Wescon—a party to whom he had sold land before. Garcia apparently said that Wescon would buy the land and syndicate it to others. Wescon itself was not a substantial company. It was represented to be a middleman which only held property very briefly before it was placed into a partnership. Wescon purportedly made its income off of syndication fees and from partnership interests that it retained for putting the deals together for others. Such an arrangement was not uncommon among syndicators.

On March 31, 1987, Lincoln disbursed $20.2 million in loan funds to the account of E.C. Garcia & Company. Of that amount, $19.6 million was wired to TEP to effect the purchase of the stock it held in Garcia's company. The remaining $600,000 was retained by Lincoln as a loan-commitment fee.

On that same day, the Hidden Valley land was sold to Wescon. Later, it turned out that Garcia had loaned Wescon the $3.5 million that Wescon used as its down payment. Wescon's officers have asserted that Wescon was acting as a nominee or accommodation party and that E.C. Garcia & Company was the true purchaser of the land. These Wescon representatives purportedly said that Garcia asked them to buy the land for his company, so he wouldn't have to record it on his balance sheet. Again, Garcia said that he didn't want his other creditors to see the debt, and, because he was still selling the Green Valley land, he didn't want to show additional land as an asset. ACC's personnel have asserted that they later learned that Garcia had provided the down-payment funds to Wescon, but they were not aware of the nominee arrangement between Wescon and Garcia. Moreover, the Hidden Valley land was not reflected in the audited financial statements of E.C. Garcia & Company, which was another indication to those who reviewed those financial statements that Garcia did not have an ownership interest in the property.

In late May 1987, Lincoln made another loan to E.C. Garcia & Company. The loan proceeds were to be used to purchase a Phoenix-based broker-dealer, to refinance certain debt, and to provide working capital. The loan was for $25 million. The loan was secured by the common stock of E.C. Garcia & Company and by the stock of the broker-dealer.

In June 1987, Lincoln purchased, at face value, a series of notes which E.C. Garcia & Company had received from the sale of its Green Valley property. The notes were secured by the property which was sold, and appraisals indicated that the loan-to-value ratios for this collateral were less than 75 percent. Interest rates on the loans were comparable to those charged by Lincoln on the loans which it extended to its customers. The total purchase price paid by Lincoln for these notes was approximately $37 million. A portion of the proceeds from the sale of these notes was used by Garcia to pay off the earlier $20.2-million loan.

At the same time, Garcia bought from Lincoln one-half of Lincoln's interest in the GOSLP partnership for $60 million, paying a cash down payment of $10 million, with the remainder of the purchase price in the form of a note which was secured by the partnership interest. Garcia also purchased Memorex shares from Lincoln for $1 million in cash. Lincoln retained an option that allowed Lincoln to repurchase the Memorex shares, on or before December 31, 1988, for about $4.2 million.

At about the same time, ACC purchased some land in Tucson, with an appraised value, assuming rezoning, of about $8.3 million, from Garcia for $7.4 million. There has been an assertion that Ernie Garcia asked someone at ACC, purportedly Bruce Dickson, to consider buying this land because he needed cash to cover the money he had previously loaned to Wescon. Apparently, this request came after the Wescon sale had occurred and was not discussed at the time of the sale. But where Garcia is concerned, one cannot be certain of what is true and what isn't true, as he appears to have told different stories at different times—and it appears some of those varied stories were told under oath.

On the day following the "Black Monday" stock-market crash in October 1987, Garcia apparently needed to infuse cash into his broker-dealer company to cover market losses. He purportedly asked Lincoln for additional loans. Instead of lending him more money, ACC purchased the Memorex stock for about $2 million, and Lincoln acquired an option to repurchase the GOSLP interest. In March 1988, Lincoln sold the GOSLP option to a subsidiary of the Saudi European Bank, which, in turn, exercised the option, taking Garcia out of the GOSLP deal altogether.

In June 1988, after suffering losses in the broker-dealer, which were attributed to overexpansion and burdensome overhead costs, Garcia was unable to make the payments on Lincoln's loans. Lincoln foreclosed and took over the broker-dealer and received other real estate to settle the loans. Apparently, by this time, Wescon had conveyed, or at least had tried to convey, the Hidden Valley property to Garcia—although, again, the Hidden Valley property was not reflected in Garcia's financial statements. In any event, whether on Garcia's books or Wescon's, the note related to the property went into default.

Ernie Garcia did not testify in the hearing before Sporkin, as he was asserting his rights under the Fifth Amendment. But, earlier, he had been deposed by the SEC, and the transcript of that deposition was entered into the record. I don't know the circumstances leading to that deposition. It may have been in connection with the SEC's investigation of ACC, or it may have been in connection with an investigation of the broker-dealer that Garcia had owned. Some people have said that the SEC was concerned about the possibility of irregularities in the broker-dealer's operations and that law enforcement agencies were investigating those alleged concerns.

Sporkin's conclusions about the Wescon transaction were as follows:

It is clear, and this court finds, that the sole reason for the Wescon transaction was to enable the ACC complex to record an $11 million profit and thus allow ACC to improperly take $4.4 million from Lincoln. ACC justifies its actions by stating that certain arcane accounting provisions allowed it to book the $11 million profit. Indeed a great deal of testimony at the trial was devoted to the propriety of the accounting treatment of this and a number of Lincoln's other profit-recording transactions. If ACC, its accountants and experts are correct, that $11 million can be booked as a profit from this transaction and that ACC was entitled to extract $4.4 million in cash from Lincoln as a result of the transaction, then the system of accounting that exists in the United States is in a sorry state. Here we have a sham transaction from the start with the identity of the real party in interest being shielded from those who must exercise appropriate oversight of the transaction. Because of the use of a straw buyer the accounting audit trail does not disclose all of the salient points associated with the transaction. According to the appraisal obtained by Lincoln, the appraised value of the property was only $9 million, or some $5 million under the designated sales price. The purported buyer was woefully underfinanced and on the basis of its financial statements unable to repay its loan or even service the debt. Since under the terms of the transaction the seller had no recourse against the buyer for the unpaid balance of the debt and since the pay downs on the debt were to be made on a deferred basis, it is clear the seller was not looking for the debt to be repaid in any realistic time frame.

Of particular importance as to this aspect of the transaction was the fact that the actual 25 percent down payment ($3.5 million) emanated from a loan E.C. Garcia made to Wescon. This meant that Wescon had not invested a single dollar of its own money in the transaction. Moreover, when the entire series of transactions between the Garcia and ACC complex of companies is reviewed, it emerges that in fact the money for the down payment actually emanated from Lincoln itself. The Garcia stable of companies was a heavy borrower from Lincoln. Indeed, at about the time of the Wescon transaction approximately $30 million [of which only $20.2 million was ever disbursed] in loans were being finalized between the Garcia companies and Lincoln. It is also clear from the record that E.C. Garcia was not really interested in buying the Hidden Valley parcel, but was doing so because he did not want to jeopardize a loan of over $20 million he was in the process of obtaining from Lincoln that was going to be used in a transaction that was extremely important to Garcia. It is more than a coincidence that this $20 million loan from Lincoln to Garcia was closed on the same day as the $14.5 million sale of property to Wescon was concluded.

The facts in this transaction are not as clear as Sporkin states them to be. It is clear, with hindsight, that Wescon was acting as a nominee for Garcia. Wescon apparently never intended to own the property, although Garcia purportedly asserted to ACC and Lincoln that Wescon was, in fact, the true buyer and that Garcia was merely a lender—making a loan to a customer with whom it had had prior business dealings. Garcia appears not to have told the truth. Garcia also testified to the SEC that he *believed* it was possible that he would not get the $20.2-million loan if he, or Wescon, didn't buy the Hidden Valley property.

What's not clear is whether ACC or Lincoln knew of any of this at the time. Garcia apparently has not said that ACC, Lincoln, or Keating ever made buying the Hidden Valley property a condition of obtaining the $20.2-million loan. Garcia just *thought* that not buying the land would hurt his chances to obtain the loan. If Garcia had told Lincoln that he wasn't interested in the Hidden Valley property and hadn't brought up Wescon as a potential buyer, the loan might have been made anyway. But that's an unknown, because, on his own volition, he did introduce Wescon to the deal. ACC and Lincoln have always represented that the $20.2-million loan and the Hidden Valley sale were separate and independent of each other, and, in the past, Garcia has confirmed that representation.

It's also unclear whether anyone at either ACC or Lincoln knew of the true relationship between Wescon and Garcia. If ACC and Lincoln were unaware of Garcia's behind-the-scenes dealings with Wescon, then the treatment afforded the transaction would not have been improper as Sporkin has concluded. It's not clear from the Memorandum Opinion whether Sporkin was able to determine, or whether he even tried to determine, the extent of ACC's and Lincoln's knowledge of the Garcia/Wescon relationship.

Sporkin indicated that Wescon had a balance sheet which showed a minor net worth. But Wescon had also been a party to a purchase of land in Green Valley where it brought in partners. The purchase required a substantial down payment which came, presumably, from these partners. And that's the situation that Garcia represented was occurring in this transaction—Wescon was going to bring in partners to own the land—which was a normal occurrence among syndicators. If Garcia's representation about syndicating the property had been true, then Wescon's own balance sheet wasn't a significant factor. And as far as Garcia lending the down payment to Wescon, that was not inconsistent with E.C. Garcia's business.

Finally, had Garcia disclosed that it, not Wescon, was the purchaser, and had that fact been known at the time of the transaction, the accounting for the transaction might very well have been the same—at least that was the opinion expressed by the accounting experts who testified on this matter. The use of proceeds from the $20.2-million loan appears clear. The funds were wired to TEP. They were not used as the down payment. The down-payment funds came from other resources of E.C. Garcia. The evidence does not support Sporkin's contention that the down payment emanated from Lincoln via the $20.2-million loan. Thus, it can be argued that the sale was still recordable with full profit recognition.

Garcia's role in the Hidden Valley transaction, and perhaps in the other transactions that he had with Lincoln, is certainly suspect because of the purported misrepresentations that he has made and because of how he used Wescon.

In 1991, Garcia entered a plea of guilty to a federal felony charge concerning this transaction and agreed to cooperate in the government's cases against Keating. Purportedly, not long before he entered this plea, the government had threatened to charge him with more counts which, if he had been tried and found guilty, could have resulted in a long prison sentence.

The second transaction that Sporkin addressed was another sale of Hidden Valley land to Hidden Valley Properties Limited Partnership (HVPLP) in early 1988. I am not familiar with the details of this transaction and, therefore, cannot comment on it.

The third in the series of transactions, or issues, that Sporkin considered involved the Memorex stock. Lincoln acquired this stock in late 1986 in connection with the purchase of some of Memorex' high-yield bonds. Lincoln acquired 79,275 shares at $1 per share or a total price of $79,275. In April 1987, Lincoln asked the FHLB-SF for permission to sell the shares to ACC for a price equal to about $35 per share, to be payable in cash. While the FHLB-SF was considering the transaction, the terms were amended to provide for the sale to be for notes rather than cash. The FHLB-SF wanted a detailed valuation, or appraisal, of the shares before it would grant approval.

As previously mentioned, Lincoln sold the shares to E.C. Garcia in June 1987 for $1 million, or about $12.75 a share. Lincoln retained an option to buy the shares for $4.25 million [Sporkin indicates the option price was only $1.25 million, but documents indicate that this is an erroneous price]. In October, 1987, ACC repurchased the stock from Garcia for $2 million, or about $25 per share. In March and April of 1988, ACC sold the shares for a total price of about $13.3 million, or approximately $168 per share.

One of the central questions asked by Sporkin was: Why did Lincoln relinquish its option at the time that ACC repurchased the stock from Garcia? At least two answers have been given to this question.

First, there was a concern that Lincoln would be severely criticized by the regulators if it repurchased shares at double the original selling price. In this connection, neither ACC nor Lincoln had a detailed appraisal supporting the price paid to Garcia, and neither apparently believed they could get one at that time. They believed that the FHLBB would be critical of Lincoln repurchasing the Memorex shares because of the amount of the purchase price, the absence of an appraisal, and the fact that the shares were considered to be a direct investment.

Second, in exchange for relinquishing the Memorex option, Lincoln obtained the option to repurchase the GOSLP interest, which ACC and Lincoln believed, at the time, was more valuable than the Memorex option.

Both explanations have some validity, although Sporkin stated: "The several proffered explanations given by the plaintiffs for this voluntary act are not credited by the Court." Which is easy to say when one knows the results of the transactions on an after-the-fact basis.

One of Sporkin's primary concerns in reviewing these transactions should have been to determine what ACC's people knew and when they knew it. It is clear from reading the Memorandum Opinion that he relied on hindsight for some of his conclusions. The evidence was that ACC offered to buy the Memorex shares from Lincoln at $35 per share, based on an indication from Drexel that the shares were worth that amount. But apparently that's not what Garcia would pay for the shares—he paid only $12.75 per share. Garcia was to retain any profits between $12.75 per share and about $54 per share—the per-share price in the option held by Lincoln. There is no indication that, in October 1987, ACC or Lincoln had any knowledge that the shares were worth anything near $54 per share and, thus, that the option had any value.

Sporkin addressed the issue of the value of the option by stating: ". . . [T]hat the option had substantial value is demonstrated by what occurred subsequent to ACC's acquisition of the stock. In March and April, 1988, ACC disposed of the Memorex shares for $167.77 a share, for a total sum of $13.3 million." He made such a statement without any indication that he had the slightest idea of whether any events had occurred between October 1987 and March 1988 which might have affected the value of the stock. He appears to have assumed that the value at the time that ACC acquired the shares from Garcia was greater than the price ACC paid—and greater than the option price that Lincoln would have to have paid.

If that's true, why didn't Garcia, who was in the business of buying and selling stock as a broker-dealer, who was desperate for cash because of the stock-market crash, and who could have asked Drexel what the shares were worth, ask for more than $2 million for the shares? Surely, if they were really worth $4.25 million, this person, who was knowledgeable about stocks and who desperately needed cash, would have wanted the maximum value he could get. Sporkin's conclusion makes sense only if you ignore Garcia's circumstances and you don't make any meaningful inquiry into the events and factors which could have impacted the value of the Memorex shares between October 1987 and March 1988.

Not having asked the relevant questions, Sporkin then went on to say:

The Court does not understand why Lincoln's Board of Directors acquiesced in ACC's purchase of the Memorex stock and relinquished its purchase option for no consideration. The Board's members clearly were not acting in Lincoln's best interest when they approved the transaction. Moreover, they took no steps to recapture any of the profits realized by ACC when they ultimately learned how Lincoln had been overreached. Here again is another example of abusive conduct of a holding company toward its wholly-owned banking subsidiary. The way ACC acted toward Lincoln in this and other transactions discussed in this opinion is akin to an adult taking candy from a helpless child.

Based on the apparent shallowness of Sporkin's inquiry into the facts as they existed at the time these transactions were entered into, this is an absurd conclusion. The option ran from Garcia to Lincoln. When ACC purchased the shares from Garcia, the option was automatically extinguished. Lincoln could have purchased the shares for the $2 million which ACC paid. But without an appraisal, how would the regulators, who had already castigated Lincoln for purchasing equity securities in companies whose shares weren't listed on a major stock exchange, have reacted? Lincoln's board did not possess a crystal ball. They could not have known what the shares would be worth six months in the future. Sporkin's conclusion simply doesn't hold water. It appears to be another example of questionable reasoning, the use of hindsight, and grossly pejorative overstatement and hyperbole.

The last set of transactions that Sporkin addressed involved GOSLP, GUAC, and GOIL. The first was GOSLP. As previously mentioned, Lincoln sold one-half of its interest to Garcia on June 30, 1987, for $60 million, payable $10 million down and $50 million in the form of a non-recourse note. In viewing this transaction, Sporkin noted:

> The Court finds that Garcia's $10 million cash payment indirectly came from Lincoln as a result of other transactions between Lincoln and Garcia. Specifically, Lincoln purchased from Garcia a parcel of land for $7 million and certain notes receivable for $37 million. Garcia had purchased the land for only $4 million and Lincoln's $7 million was at Garcia's asking price. The notes, which totaled $37 million, were non-recourse and were sold to Lincoln at par. All of the notes are now in default.

Once again a few pertinent facts were omitted. First, the land was purchased by ACC, not Lincoln, for $7 million and was appraised at $8.3 million when zoned at its highest and best use. Second, all of the notes which were purchased had been originated within the six-month period preceding their purchase. The notes were secured by land with appraised values that were more than 25 percent higher than the amount of the notes. The notes were included as assets, at their undiscounted face amount, in

Garcia's recent, May 1987, financial statements, which were audited by a Big Eight firm that had never performed services for ACC or Lincoln. These were the facts that were available at the time. The fact that the notes later went into default has to be viewed in light of the market conditions which existed later and the fact that the conservator may not have been willing to modify terms, so as to allow the makers of the notes to repay them—factors which could not have been known in June 1987.

In October 1987, Lincoln obtained an option to repurchase the GOSLP interest from Garcia. Lincoln paid $2 million for the option. In March 1988, the option was sold to a subsidiary of the Saudi European Bank for $2.25 million. The Saudi European Bank exercised the option, by paying Garcia $7 million in cash and assuming the $50-million note payable to Lincoln. Saudi European officials have stated that they exercised the option because they expected that Sir James Goldsmith, the general partner of GOSLP, would sell the partnership's assets at a gain and that they would realize a nice profit from the investment.

Sporkin had this view of the transaction:

ACC realized that it would have difficulty sustaining its ability to report a $38 million gain on the GOSLP transaction and retain the $15 million in tax sharing payments it had received from Lincoln because of the reversal of the GOSLP transaction with Garcia. To avoid having to reverse the transaction, Lincoln sold its option to repurchase GOSLP to Lanier, an affiliate of the Saudi European Bank, an entity in which Lincoln held a 10 percent interest.

In September 1988, in order to complete the GOIL transaction (see Chapter Thirteen), Lincoln repurchased the GOSLP interest from Lanier, Saudi European's subsidiary, for a price equal to Lanier's investment plus $2.75 million. At Lanier's request, the $2.5 million was structured as a fee. Sporkin's view of this transaction was:

The terms of the repurchase of the GOSLP interest from Lanier lead this Court to the conclusion that Keating was engaged in a series of "parking" transactions. The reason the interest was parked was to bail Lincoln and ACC out of certain accounting problems they had when Lincoln repurchased the GOSLP interest from Garcia in the same year that Lincoln had sold the interest to Garcia and recognized a $38 million profit.

It is this Court's finding that the transaction with Lanier was spurious from its inception. This is largely proven by the terms of Lincoln's reacquisition of GOSLP from Lanier. The transaction was not at market price. Instead Lincoln re-acquired the interest at Lanier's acquisition cost plus a "fixed fee." According to Lincoln's own evaluation of GOSLP at the time of the transaction, the GOSLP interest was worth $15 million more than Lincoln's cost of reacquisition. Thus it is quite clear that Lanier would not have abandoned the opportunity to make a $15 million profit unless it was a party to a parking transaction on terms that had already been fixed. While ACC denies the existence of a parking transaction, this Court simply does not find the denial by ACC's officials in this regard to be credible in any respect.

Again, Sporkin's conclusion is supportable only if one chooses to disregard certain facts. First, Lincoln, as he so clearly stated, never repurchased the GOSLP interest from Garcia. Documents indicate that Lincoln acquired an option, which it did not exercise. It sold the option to Lanier, which did exercise it.

Second, no Lanier people were called to testify in this abbreviated hearing. However, they were deposed by the SEC and in other actions, and they testified, in no uncertain terms, that their purchase of the option, the exercise of the option, and the subsequent sale of the interest to Lincoln were motivated by their own profit motives. They denied that there was any "parking" or that they were an accommodation party for ACC or Keating. They also confirmed that they wanted the repurchase transaction structured in the form of a fee for their own tax purposes.

Third, the repurchase was made only after ACC had structured the GOIL deal. Had the GOIL deal not occurred, there would have been no motivation for ACC to repurchase the GOSLP interest.

Fourth, Sporkin argued that the GOSLP interest was worth more than Lincoln paid to repurchase it. Later, when it was part of the GOIL deal, he argued that GOIL wasn't worth what Lincoln asserted it was. He can't be right both times and with opposite conclusions.

Sporkin next looked at the GUAC side of the GOIL exchange. He said:

> The Centrust acquisition of GUAC turned out to be another parking transaction. In September 1988, Lincoln reacquired GUAC from Centrust for $36 million, which resulted in Centrust realizing a profit of $6 million for holding the GUAC interest for only 3-4 months. Thus, Lincoln was not only out the $10 million tax sharing payment, but also had to pay from its treasury some $6 million as a "parking fee"' to Centrust for holding GUAC for this brief period. Shortly, after the GUAC common stock was reacquired it along with the GUAC preferred stock was packaged with Lincoln's GOSLP interest and approximately $8.75 million in cash to obtain a 25 percent interest in GOIL.

Here, again, Sporkin chose to disregard facts. First, the GOIL transaction was entered into prior to the settlement of the GUAC profits interest. That's what necessitated settling the profits interest with CenTrust. If the GUAC shares were sold, the contract with CenTrust entitled CenTrust to receive its profits interest, up to a maximum of $36 million in the first year.

They were sold to GOIL. The value attributed to the GOIL transaction by Lincoln, as well as the exchange agreement, required Lincoln to pay CenTrust the maximum amount of $36 million.

Second, the GUAC interest was not "reacquired," nor was any "GUAC common stock reacquired." CenTrust never bought the GUAC common stock. It bought the right to receive 62.5 percent of the profits realized from the common stock. This right was not reacquired; it was settled as required by terms of the contract.

Third, at the time CenTrust acquired the profits interest, there were a number of parties who were actively interested in acquiring GUAC. That's what gave value to the profits interest—the possibility that one of these parties would buy GUAC at a substantial price.

Sporkin never mentioned these factors. Certainly, if one ignores salient facts, the substance of a transaction can be altered. That's what Sporkin did here—he ignored the nature and terms of the profits interest; he ignored the chronology of actual events; and he ignored some events altogether. Is it any wonder that he then found the transactions lacking?

He went through the same faulty process with GOIL. His most pertinent comments dealt with the value of GOIL, which appeared as a footnote to his Memorandum Opinion. He said:

> The true value of GOIL remains to be seen. Keating testified Lincoln's 28,600,000 shares of GOIL constitute a valuable asset. His testimony was supported by an appraisal from Merrill Lynch which placed a value of between $11.30 and $12.40 per share on the GOIL stock. Thus, according to the Merrill Lynch report, the total value of the GOIL stock is between approximately $323 million and $355 million. Whatever GOIL is worth is somewhat beside the point. Its value can only be accurately ascertained when it is finally sold. The booking of profit by Lincoln based upon the acquisition of GOIL through an exchange of GOSLP, GUAC common and preferred stock, and $8.75 million in cash only contributed to a further dissipation of Lincoln's assets. Because Keating elected to recognize a gain on this exchange, Lincoln's potential tax liability was significant. As far as the record shows, no tax payment has yet been made on this transaction because of the revocation of the tax sharing agreement and the collapse of ACC and Lincoln prior to the filing date for the taxable year in question.
>
> It is highly doubtful that the GOIL stock is worth the amount attributed to it. This is for two reasons. First, the GOIL shares are thinly traded and only have a market on two exchanges—the Vancouver and London Stock Exchanges. Although GOIL has substantial holdings in the United States, GOIL stock is not traded in the United States. Second, if the shares carried the value as stated Lincoln certainly would have sold them because $323 million would have gone a long way in restoring Lincoln to a solvent position.

Here Sporkin conceded that the appraisal valued the GOIL stock at between $323 million and $355 million—$125 million to $157 million greater than Lincoln's book value. But then he said, in essence: "Appraisals don't count. Value can only be accurately ascertained when the asset is sold." Remember that, because on the very next page of his opinion, he concluded that Lincoln was insolvent based on *appraisals of its assets*. Now, if an appraisal is not reliable for determining an unrealized gain, how does it become reliable for determining unrealized losses?

He also said the value of the GOIL stock is "somewhat beside the point." Then, one sentence later, he said there was a "dissipation of Lincoln's assets." If the GOIL stock is worth $125 million more than book value, how can there be a dissipation of assets? The value of the stock was definitely not "beside the point"—it was the point! If the GOIL exchange produced the value that the appraisal indicated, how can anyone claim assets have been dissipated? The whole purpose of the GOIL exchange was to obtain greater value for Lincoln, and the appraisals indicate that this was exactly what occurred.

Sporkin also criticized Keating for having "elected to recognize a gain on this exchange" and for increasing "Lincoln's potential tax liability." Keating didn't have anything to do with making an "election." The Internal Revenue Code determines whether a transaction is taxable or not. Under the Code, exchanges of non-like-kind property are taxable. Keating didn't have an option of "electing" to make the transaction nontaxable; it was taxable by its very nature. All of ACC's tax advisors came to this conclusion. One doesn't have to be a tax expert to recognize that there was no "election" available to Lincoln on the transaction—it was not even close to being nontaxable. So, Sporkin can't nail Keating to this cross.

Then Sporkin said, "Lincoln certainly would have sold them [the GOIL shares] because $323 million would have gone a long way in restoring Lincoln to a solvent position." Had Sporkin merely taken the time to read the GOIL Exchange Agreement he would have found the following: "AMCOR hereby agrees that it will not prior to 30 September 1990 directly or indirectly transfer, sell, charge, pledge, offer or otherwise dispose of any of the subscription shares or any interest in the subscription shares. . . ." It's amazing what reading actual documents—often referred to by courts as evidence—can disclose. Facts and verified evidence often answer questions better than unfounded assumptions. And the facts are clear—Lincoln could not have sold the GOIL shares, as Sporkin suggested it should have done, because the GOIL Agreement prohibited such a sale.

Then Sporkin considered the issue of Lincoln's solvency. He stated:

Upon appointment of the conservator on April 14, 1989, the conservator initiated a process of reviewing Lincoln's financial condition. As part of this review an appraisal was made of most of Lincoln's assets. Based upon the testimony produced by the Bank Board and the documents introduced, this Court finds that Lincoln was in fact insolvent as of the date the receiver was appointed. While plaintiffs made some valid points as to the accuracy of certain of the values submitted by the Bank Board's appraisers, Lincoln's deficit was so massive that a few inconsistencies would not have made a material difference to the ultimate amount of the insolvency.

The key question that Sporkin did not address or answer was: How could the FHLBB examination, completed less than six months earlier, not have disclosed the "massive deficit" if, in fact, it existed?

Sporkin claimed that the deficit was based on appraisals, which just one page earlier, he had dismissed by saying, "value can only be accurately ascertained when it [an asset] is finally sold." Yet, when it suited the government's purposes, appraisals were taken, even by Sporkin, as true measures of value. It was impossible—impossible—for the conservator to have appraised "most of Lincoln's assets" by the date of the receivership as Sporkin asserted. *That did not happen.* The reserves against most of Lincoln's assets were, at the time, based on estimates by the FDIC's people and nothing more substantive than estimates.

Sporkin concluded that the Bank Board was justified in appointing the conservator and later a receiver for Lincoln. The Memorandum Opinion was, I believe, long on rhetoric and short on reasoning. The Memorandum Opinion took gratuitous potshots at ACC's and Lincoln's attorneys and accountants and attributed motives to Keating and others which were not supported by the facts that were, or should have been, before him. Unfortunately many people believed this Memorandum Opinion was based on a trial and not on an abbreviated hearing. As a result, more credence was given to it than it deserved.

ACC had good intentions when it filed this lawsuit against the FHLBB. It believed the that FHLBB had placed Lincoln into conservatorship without just cause—and the facts support this belief. ACC wanted to be compensated for the damages it had suffered as a consequence of the FHLBB's unjust actions, so that ACC could fulfill all of its obligations to its creditors, including the holders of its subordinated debentures. But ACC rushed into court too soon—before it had had time to prepare its case adequately.

Keating's lawyers, I believe, made a grave mistake in allowing the evidentiary hearing to proceed as it did. Without having done any real discovery beforehand, they were not able to present all of the evidence which should have been presented. They were not able to produce all of the relevant documents and witnesses to support the propriety of ACC's and

Lincoln's actions. They were not able to secure the internal documents of the FHLBB. Their case was weakened by the fact that many potentially key witnesses were forced into the position of having to assert their Fifth Amendment rights and, thus, were not available to testify.

The evidence presented in this hearing—and the reasoning exhibited in Sporkin's opinion—was full of more holes than a ton of Swiss cheese. But without adequate preparation—depositions, document production, etc.—ACC's lawyers were not able to point out the holes effectively. They should have waited until they had all the evidence they needed—evidence which was abundantly available—before they entered the courtroom. Then, they could have avoided the ambush that the FHLBB and Sporkin set for them.

The rules of the hearing also hampered ACC. There was not the customary rigorous cross-examination of the witnesses called by the opposing party. The FHLBB selected the transactions that it wished to defend; thus, the FHLBB was able to choose those they had the most documentation for and, therefore, those that were the easiest to present in the hearing. And when the FHLBB failed to ask the proper questions or enough questions of a witness, Sporkin filled in the gap by asking questions for them—questions which were obviously intended to buttress the FHLBB's position and to detract from ACC's arguments.

The scope of the hearing ranged far beyond the limited issue under consideration, thereby creating a broader record which could be used in other pending actions, such as the class-action/RTC suits and the FBI's investigation.

Since all the FHLBB had to demonstrate was that "there was a rational connection between the facts found and the choice made," the burden of proof that the FHLBB had to satisfy was not substantial. The FHLBB simply had to show that it had acted rationally and not in an arbitrary and capricious manner. The story might have been different if the FHLBB had had to demonstrate that its findings were correct or if ACC and Lincoln had only had to demonstrate that there was reasonable and rational justification for the transactions which were being criticized and that there were supportable arguments to rebut the FHLBB's findings; then, the issue would have been: who was the more correct—ACC or the FHLBB—in interpreting the propriety of the transactions?

But that wasn't the case. ACC had to show that the FHLBB was arbitrary and capricious, which would seem almost impossible to prove without first having access to the FHLBB's internal documents and to its people in depositions. The discovery process would have given ACC the opportunity to show what the FHLBB knew on April 14, 1989, as opposed to what information it learned later. As it was, the evidence that the FHLBB presented in this hearing may not have been known by it until months after it appointed the conservator. But without discovery, ACC, and Sporkin, had no way of knowing when information came into the FHLBB's possession or when the FHLBB learned the significance of that information.

ACC received no benefit from the suit it filed. But the Memorandum Opinion severely damaged Keating and others. With words like "looting," "skullduggery," "flat-out dissipation of assets," "unsafe and unsound practices," "impermissible taking," "overreaching," and "parking," the Memorandum Opinion was used by others adverse to Keating to embellish his image as a villain and "financial pirate." It also turned up the political heat on various law enforcement agencies to charge Keating with criminal acts. And it gave heart to the various civil plaintiffs.

What ACC's lawyers had viewed as a nonthreatening action to recover ACC's rightful assets became a real turning point in the legal battles facing ACC and Keating. This Memorandum Opinion set the tenor for all of the other proceedings that would follow. It, coupled with the congressional hearings, put Keating into an impossible defensive posture and sealed his fate.

Twenty-One

Legal Extortion

After most business failures, especially those where a company has issued equity or debt securities to the public, litigation usually occurs. Individual security holders or creditors, acting on their own behalf as well as for all similarly situated persons, generally enlist the services of attorneys who specialize in representing such plaintiffs, normally on a contingent-fee basis. Since more than one suit may be filed purporting to represent the same class of similarly situated persons, the attorneys rush to file a complaint in state or federal court in order to be first in line to represent the class.

These actions, known as class-action lawsuits, are the norm where there are large numbers of persons who have purchased securities. It would be a burden on the court system and to each individual to file separate lawsuits with similar allegations. Moreover, the cost of pursuing litigation on an individual basis may far exceed the damages suffered by a single plaintiff; thus, individual actions are economically impractical. So, individuals join together as a class and pursue their claims collectively.

The complaints that are initially filed look like fill-in-the-blanks products. They state why the court in which the action is filed has the proper jurisdiction over the matter and, thus, is the appropriate venue. The plaintiffs are identified, along with a brief description of the securities which the plaintiffs purchased, the date the securities were purchased, the dollar amount of the purchase, and other factors. The named defendants are identified. Reasons asserting why a class action is proper are set forth. The factual allegations about the defendants' wrongful actions are presented. Then, the complaint lists the various counts or causes of action against the various defendants, along with a statement of damages sought by the plaintiffs.

When the complaint is first filed, the allegations are often fairly broad and general. The complaint may cite financial statements, annual and quarterly reports, press releases, and other public disclosures made by the defendants and then alleges, based on events which have occurred, that these documents and disclosures suffer from material omissions and misrepresentations, are false and misleading, are the products of fraud or a conspiracy, or violate the requirements of a specific statute. The allegations raise just enough factual issues to prevent the complaint from being summarily dismissed. This is all that the attorneys want from the initial filing. They want the ability to begin the discovery phase of the litigation where they can secure documents and subpoena witnesses for depositions.

If they can conduct discovery, they believe they can find information which will allow them to augment and expand the allegations through amendments to the initial complaint. In effect, from a layman's viewpoint, the initial complaint grants the plaintiffs' attorneys a license to conduct a fishing expedition through the defendants' documents and records. If the fishing is good, the complaint will become stronger and the plaintiffs' chances of winning or obtaining a favorable settlement improve.

The first complaint in the ACC affair was filed in the United States District Court in Los Angeles, in early April 1989. This suit named ACC, Lincoln, and eight officers and directors as defendants. The second suit was filed a couple of weeks later in a state court in Orange County, California. It named three accounting firms—Arthur Young, Arthur Andersen, and Touche Ross—two law firms—Kaye Scholer and Parker, Milliken, Clark, O'Hara & Samuelian—and sixteen individuals, along with one hundred John and Jane Does, as defendants. Other suits by security-holder plaintiffs were filed later.

Eventually, all of these suits, along with one filed by the RTC, were consolidated, at least for discovery purposes, and were assigned to one federal judge in Tucson, Arizona. Over the next several years, the complaints were amended repeatedly, and new defendants were added. The new defendants included three more law firms—Sidley & Austin; Jones, Day, Reavis & Pogue; and Mariscal, Weeks, McIntyre & Friedlander; several banking entities; a number of corporate borrowers and customers of Lincoln, as well as some of their officers; investment bankers, including Drexel; consultants; and numerous individuals, including the spouses of defendants who lived in community-property states. All told, the list of defendants totaled over ninety companies and individuals.

The discovery phase of these actions would take nearly three years. A document depository was established in Phoenix, and all parties to the litigation were directed to deposit in the depository all of the relevant documents they had been asked to produce pursuant to subpoenas. Any party who wanted to review these documents, or to obtain copies of them, had to visit the depository and view the documents there. Eventually, the total number of documents in the depository was purported to be about thirty-five million.

The documents were contained in boxes or on rolls of microfilm. Each party who deposited documents also submitted an index, but these indices were not very useful. For example, a typical index entry might be "ACC-accounting records." So, the only way that a party to the litigation could know what was in the boxes or on the film was to look at everything and, then, sort out what was relevant and what was not. Consequently, each of the principal litigants was forced to commit a small army of young lawyers and paralegals to the task of going through the massive contents of the depository—a time-consuming and very expensive undertaking for each party.

While the document production and review aspects of this litigation were extensive, the deposition process was staggering. A deposition, in layman's terms, is where a witness is questioned, under oath, by the attorneys for the parties to the litigation. The questions asked and the answers given are recorded by a court reporter. The purpose of the deposition is to learn what the witness knows about the matter being litigated and to determine what the person will testify to at trial. There were about seven hundred depositions taken in connection with this litigation.

Because of the large number of people the various parties sought to depose, witnesses were divided into groups, or tracks. For example, all of the regulators were in one track, while all of the accountants were in another. All told, there were about a half-dozen tracks. On any given day, there could be one witness from each track being deposed—that is, six depositions taking place on the same day. Because witnesses were scattered all over the country, so were the depositions. Thus, depositions could have been going on simultaneously in six different cities. This created a logistical nightmare for the attorneys involved in the litigation. If they wanted someone to attend each deposition, they had to commit six attorneys, or more, to just the deposition phase of discovery. Each plaintiff and each defendant was entitled to have his respective attorneys present at each deposition. As one might imagine, the number of attorneys involved in this matter was unbelievable.

The estimated cost to a principal defendant, such as one of the accounting firms, for the routine discovery phase of the ACC/Lincoln litigation ranged between $25 million to $30 million, in fees alone. The cost to a minor defendant, such as an individual officer, could range from $3 million to $10 million. The out-of-pocket expenses were also staggering, amounting to between $3 million and $4.5 million for a principal defendant. And these weren't all the costs.

In addition to the routine discovery effort, each principal defendant had lead attorneys who were working almost full time on the litigation, primarily doing things that were not directly related to the retrieval of documents and taking of depositions. Their efforts cost a major defendant another $8.5 million in fees and about $500,000 in expenses. Which brings the total for attorneys to between $35 million and $45 million.

Then there are the expert witnesses who are needed if the case goes to trial. In a case like this, each major party required about a dozen experts. An estimated $2.5 million to $5 million per litigant was required to cover the cost of the experts, exhibits, and other direct trial costs.

In total, a major party in this class-action litigation was looking at costs and fees of $40 million to $50 million—and that could be low. For a minor party, the total cost could easily be $5 million or more. In order to defend oneself, a defendant had to have personal resources or insurance coverage sufficient to pay these litigation costs. Many of the named defendants didn't have the necessary resources. It should also be noted that most of the named defendants in this litigation had to defend themselves in numerous other actions emanating from the demise of ACC and Lincoln. So, these costs were, for some, just the tip of the iceberg.

The RTC was a major factor in the civil litigation. It filed suit in the Federal District Court in Arizona on September 15, 1989, naming Keating and other officers and directors as defendants. The RTC also let it be known that it intended to name other defendants later. This complaint alleged RICO violations and sought damages, after trebling, of over $2 billion. The factual allegations were much the same as the findings in the various FHLBB exam reports: direct-investment violations, file stuffing, back-dating documents, tax-sharing payments, the so-called Leventhal transactions, ESOP, Pontchartrain loan, Memorex stock transaction, etc.

The RTC's entry into the fray was, in my opinion, a real boon to the class-action plaintiffs for several reasons. First, it got the government on their side. This certainly added some legitimacy, in the eyes of the media, to their claims and further cast the defendants, particularly Keating, in the role of true villains.

Second, the resources of the government entered the discovery process. The attorneys for the RTC poured through the depository and retrieved documents that all the other plaintiffs needed in the case. Without the RTC's efforts in this regard, one has to believe that the class-action plaintiffs' discovery effort would have been vastly more difficult. Also, the RTC attorneys handled a lot of the questioning in depositions—questioning which served the class-action plaintiffs' needs as much as it served those of the RTC. By cooperating with the RTC, the class-action plaintiffs were, I believe, relieved of tremendous burdens and considerable costs.

Third, the leaking of the Leventhal report, along with the allegations contained in the RTC's complaint itself, supplied other plaintiffs with ammunition to amend their complaints. The amendments included RICO allegations, which dramatically increased the stakes of the game. Without

RICO, the class-action plaintiffs were seeking, in round numbers, about $400 million in damages. The addition of RICO raised the stakes to over $1.2 billion, most of which fell outside the insurance coverage of the defendants.

Fourth, after all complaints were amended, the stakes, in reality, increased to impossible levels. The RTC's allegations and those of the class-action plaintiffs became parallel. If the defendants went to trial in either case and lost, they would almost automatically lose the other case. If, at that time, they weren't defendants in the RTC case, it was an absolute certainty that they would be added. Thus, the real limit of damages that the defendants faced was the combination of both actions, or about $3.2 billion. No defendant could afford to take the risk of going to trial and losing. No matter how strong they thought their defense was, the stakes were simply too high.

Fifth, the RTC was in a position to influence a number of witnesses in this case as well as some of the factual issues. Many of the witnesses and some defendants were borrowers from institutions that the RTC controlled, either through conservatorship or receivership. In addition, the FDIC, which in effect was the RTC's direct relative, controlled every other bank and S&L in the country. The potential hold that the RTC had over people was enormous. The RTC could institute foreclosure, or it could modify loans. It could extend credit, or, wherever the person sought credit, the RTC could cut any credit off completely. If the person cooperated, the treatment might be favorable. If the person didn't cooperate, the consequences could be severe. The RTC never had to voice the existence of this incredible power. It was just there—and everyone knew it.

With other parties, like the accounting and law-firm defendants, the implied threat was a little different. They had other clients who were insured institutions or people who did business with insured institutions. If they didn't settle amicably and on terms acceptable to the government but instead went to trial, all this other business was threatened. Moreover, they could be barred, directly or indirectly, from serving any insured institutions. Thus, losses could extend far beyond the case at hand. This was tremendous leverage for the government.

With respect to factual issues, the way the RTC handled various assets—loans, securities, and real estate—could determine the size of the loss, if any, that the government could claim the defendants had caused. For example, assume that the RTC sold the Phoenician at a lower price than might otherwise have been achieved through better marketing of the property. They could say, "The loss was there when we took control." It would be difficult to prove otherwise, because, by that time, the loss would exist. This was true of any asset that Lincoln held on April 14, 1989. The RTC controlled what happened to the asset.

Sixth, as a governmental entity, the RTC was in a position to act in concert with, or cooperate with, other governmental entities, such as the FBI, the United States Attorneys in various cities, the IRS, OTS, and the SEC, just to name a few. Referrals could be made. Information could be exchanged. Pressure could be applied.

Finally, in most litigation, cost is a factor to both the plaintiff and the defendants. Usually, the litigants have finite resources and must weigh the probable outcomes of the litigation against the costs. That's true for both plaintiffs and defendants. But to the federal government, cost is not a factor. The government will spend millions to pursue a defendant who has little or no resources. The government doesn't care about cost/benefit considerations. If the government's lawyers want to hang a scalp on their tent pole, they'll go after it no matter what the cost. And in this case, there were a number of scalps they dearly wanted—Keating's in particular. So, the normal economics of litigation were no longer operative.

The RTC wasn't the only government force affecting the civil litigation. There were several others, and their effect on many of the defendants and witnesses was equally as important.

Along with the U.S. Attorney's office in Los Angeles, the FBI was conducting an active investigation, pursuant to criminal referrals that the Justice Department had received. They were interviewing scores of people and had classified many as targets of their investigation. If a person was a target, it meant the government was trying to build a case against them. There was also a federal grand jury sitting in Los Angeles which was hearing evidence that would serve as the basis for indicting people who would be charged with federal criminal violations.

The common wisdom among defense attorneys whose clients are either targets or subjects—subjects are people who are under investigation but who have not yet risen to the target level—is to tell the person to assert his or her Fifth Amendment rights and not to testify in any proceeding. If the client's status is unclear, or unknown, caution dictates that the person not testify until his or her status is clarified and an indictment is not a threat.

In this case, many, many people received that advice from their respective attorneys. Consequently, many people who may have had information that could have helped the case of the defendants, including their own case if they were also a named defendant, were not in a position to testify in either the class-action or RTC cases. This stripped the defense attorneys of significant tools they needed to defend their clients. For some defendants, it made it impossible to launch a defense at all.

The possibility of criminal charges had an economic effect as well. The lawyers who defend civil actions do not necessarily defend criminal matters—the knowledge and skills are different in the two fields of law.

So, many defendants had to engage criminal as well as civil attorneys, which further strained already severely taxed financial resources. It also added a number of events and actions in different arenas, making it almost impossible to keep up with everything that was happening. The civil suits were complicated enough, given the broad scope of the discovery efforts, and the added burden of criminal concerns simply drained all of the defendants' resources—financial and otherwise.

The SEC also was conducting an ongoing investigation—which started in 1987 and wasn't concluded until 1994. The SEC periodically demanded documents and sought to interview or depose witnesses. While not in any way diminishing the seriousness of the actions that the SEC can take against a firm or a person, at this point in time, they were more of a constant irritant than anything else. If they were going to do something, other than pile on people who had already been knocked down by another plaintiff or agency, they should have done so in 1987. Any benefits which could be derived from their actions were, by at least early 1990, diminished by the costs they had incurred and would incur.

The OTS also weighed in against Keating and a handful of Lincoln officers and directors. They sought, among other things, restitution for the tax-sharing payments and other so-called asset dissipations. They also added a new wrinkle. They sought to have the assets of the defendants frozen. As a result of this action, the defendants could not use any of their economic resources to hire attorneys to defend themselves. The asset freeze tied up everything the defendants owned, which, by the time of this action, was no longer very much.

There were investigations by the Federal Election Commission into political contributions. The Los Angeles District Attorney and the Attorney General for the State of California were conducting their own criminal investigations into the conduct of some of the defendants. And various state licensing boards in California and Arizona were making inquiries which led to complaints against some defendants.

Faced with extremely adverse press, staggering litigation costs, and, if they went to trial and lost, astronomical damages, all of the defendants were prime targets for what I call "legal extortion." Lawyers for the various plaintiffs knew that if they offered to settle with a defendant at an amount less than or equal to the costs of launching a defense, the defendant would be hard pressed not to accept the deal. So, part of the plaintiffs' strategy was to drive up the costs of discovery and, by asserting RICO charges, to increase the risk of going to trial. This strategy made it economically impossible for most defendants to turn down the proffered settlement. Thus, threats of litigation costs and potential damages were used effectively to extort payments from the defendants and their insurance carriers.

Several defendants, primarily law firms, opted to settle fairly early in the process. The projected costs of launching a competent defense far exceeded the settlement costs they had to pay. These firms were looking at a cost of as much as $40 million for a major law firm, like Kaye Scholer, and well over $10 million for a firm with a lesser role, like Parker Milliken. These numbers presented a situation where it was advantageous to settle early, before any substantial litigation costs were incurred. Parker Milliken took this option and settled for something less than $10 million. Kaye Scholer settled in the $20-million range. And Mariscal Weeks got out for under $5 million. That their decision was largely cost driven demonstrates that legal extortion works.

None of these firms admitted any wrongdoing on their part. The decision to settle was an economic decision and not a decision based on the merits of the plaintiffs' allegations. Such is the status of our legal system. If a defendant proceeds all the way to a trial and a verdict and prevails, the defendant is still out the cost of the defense. If the defendant can settle for an amount which is less than the estimated cost of the defense effort, it makes no economic sense to proceed to trial and defend one's good name. If the system were such that, if the plaintiff did not prevail, the plaintiff would have to reimburse the defendant for all defense costs, the economic equation would be different. If the defendant could recover all defense costs, the settlement decision would then rest on the merits of the plaintiffs' allegations and not economics; then, legal extortion would, in part, be removed from the system.

Under the system as it now stands, it also makes sense for plaintiffs to practice legal extortion to force a few early settlements. If they are successful, they can raise the ante that the remaining defendants will have to pay to avoid litigation costs. This is particularly true in a situation like the ACC/Lincoln litigation, where there were a number of major defendants with the requisite deep pockets and where the discovery effort was so massive. Here, the plaintiffs' lawyers were able to calculate that the total defense costs to the five or six major defendants would, in the aggregate, easily exceed $200 million. If the lesser defendants were included, since most had some insurance, the plaintiffs could anticipate that the legal costs for these lesser parties would aggregate another $50 million. Thus, the stakes required to defend against the complaints were such that the possibility of settlements was high, and the potential settlement amounts, which are a function of the expected defense costs, were equally high.

Aside from the litigation costs, the plaintiffs enjoyed several other advantages conferred upon them by the legal system, facilitating the use of legal extortion. The defendants faced joint-and-several liability. In layman's terms, this means that each defendant is potentially liable for the entire amount of any damages awarded to the plaintiffs. For example, assume there are five defendants, and one has extensive insurance coverage and net assets, while the other four are virtually bankrupt; assume damages are awarded to the plaintiffs in the amount of $500 million; and, finally, assume that the financially well-off defendant is, by far, the least culpable of all of the defendants. Under this set of assumptions, the defendant who has financial resources could end up paying the entire $500 million in damages. That's why it is absolutely necessary for the plaintiffs to have a couple of deep pockets named as defendants—they need at least one party who can pay the damages if they are awarded.

The existence of joint-and-several liability makes the risks unacceptable to a well-heeled defendant, especially if the other defendants are financially weak. Even if the party played a limited role in the situation, and has to defend only a few allegations, he is potentially at risk for all the damages that may be awarded. This is a risk that few defendants are willing to assume—no matter how convinced they are that their defense is strong. No one can be sure how a jury will react, particularly in a case involving complex financial transactions, hundreds of witnesses, and thousands of exhibits. Add to that the fact that the plaintiffs will parade before the jury, as witnesses, scores of elderly and infirm individuals who will say they have lost their life's savings because of the actions of some of the defendants. Even if a defendant is convinced that the evidence will show he was not responsible for causing loss, no one wants to take the risk that the jury will not understand the defense or that it will act out of emotion and not reason. The risks are too high.

If that's not enough economic pressure on the defendant, consider the effect of RICO. Under RICO, damages can be tripled. Because the added damages are considered punitive rather than actual damages, they are, in all likelihood, not covered by insurance; hence, they have to come directly out of the defendant's own pockets. So, in the example above, the potential risk to a defendant increases from $500 million to $1.5 billion, with $1 billion not covered by insurance. There are very few defendants who can absorb a hit of that magnitude and still survive economically.

To add to this very negative equation, those punitive damages probably cannot be extinguished in bankruptcy. So, if they are assessed against a defendant, and the defendant can't pay the damages, they may remain as an obligation for life. That means everything the defendant earns in the future will go to satisfy the obligation. Not only does the defendant lose everything that he, she, or it has, but the loss encompasses everything that he, she, or it will ever have in the future.

Faced with those economic possibilities, the question in the ACC/Lincoln civil litigation was really not one of "if" a given defendant should settle, but "when" and for "how much." The discovery process then became a subtle form of negotiation. If a witness was favorable to the defendant, the settlement price went down a little. If a witness was unfavorable, the price went up. The same was true with document discovery—a document which buttressed the defendant's case reduced the price, and damaging documents increased it. As the trial date neared, the reports of expert witnesses came into play. A strong, compelling expert report helped, and a weak report hurt. The situation was just the reverse with the experts retained by the other side—a weak report helped and a strong expert increased the potential cost of settlement. The lawyers were converted from warriors to negotiators, and legal extortion became the game.

There were also noneconomic factors that added to the dynamics of the situation. One of the most significant was the concurrent criminal investigations. First, as previously stated, many potential witnesses who could have aided the defendants' causes still had to assert their Fifth Amendment rights. This was a factor that the plaintiffs could use if the case went to trial. Even though the Fifth Amendment is there to protect every citizen, and, by asserting this basic constitutional protection a person is not admitting guilt, the public, including lawyers and judges, doesn't necessarily view it that way. Many say, in effect, "If a person asserts the Fifth Amendment, they must be guilty of something or they must have something to hide." That's not the attitude that the framers of the Constitution had in mind when the Fifth Amendment was drafted, but, unfortunately, that's the way it's interpreted by many in our society today. In this case, the plaintiffs were allowed to draw a "negative inference" from the fact that a witness or defendant asserted his or her Fifth Amendment rights—an inference that was, I believe, clearly prejudicial to the person who elected to assert one of the basic rights available to all citizens.

Many witnesses were also visited by the FBI, and some were called before federal grand juries by the Justice Department. Others were interviewed by other governmental agencies such as the RTC or the SEC. Some lawyers for the defendants contended that these actions by the government had the effect of "chilling" the witnesses—forcing them to clam up. They felt witnesses were being intimidated and frightened, and, because of that, their testimony was being affected.

But by far, the worst effect on the civil cases was the fact that criminal charges were brought against some individuals. The most dramatic was the indictment of Charlie Keating, Judy Wischer, Rob Symes, and Ray Fidel on charges of violating the securities laws of the State of California. All four were arrested, placed in handcuffs, and taken to a jail in Los Angeles. When they were arraigned, bails were set at astronomical levels—what one might expect for serial killers or mass murderers—and none could meet bail out of his own resources.

The media had a field day with the arrests of these people. All the major television networks broadcast pictures of them in handcuffs and shackles, being led from vans into the court building. Newspapers and magazines across the country carried pictures of them in prison jumpsuits and chains. Keating had already been described in words and print as a villain and a crook. Now, the media had pictures they could use to embellish further the image they and the politicians had created.

That they had been handcuffed, chained, and photographed was not an accident, nor was it necessary. These were not dangerous people who had ever, in their entire lives, shown any sign that they would physically harm another person. They were not arrested for violent crimes. Nor were they a flight risk. They knew that sooner or later, because of political heat, they were going to be accused of criminal offenses by the state, the federal government, or both. If they were going to flee, they would already have done so.

They were handcuffed and treated this way so they could be photographed and shown on television. That's exactly what the prosecutors wanted. They wanted media attention. They wanted the image of Keating in handcuffs to be burned permanently into the minds of any prospective jurors. They also wanted publicity which would further their own careers and political ambitions. And, finally, they wanted to send a message to the bondholders that the prosecutors were on their side in the fight against Keating and his associates.

In the cases of Keating and Wischer, most of their wealth had been in the form of ACC's stock. When ACC went into bankruptcy, they lost the bulk of their assets. Keating had also made loans to family members who, without the value of their ACC stock, were purportedly unable to repay these loans. As a consequence, Keating presented financial statements showing a significant negative net worth—in effect, he was broke. It took several weeks, and a bail reduction, before friends and family members were able to post assets to support the bail requirements and the four were released from jail.

In short order, Symes and Fidel entered into plea agreements— another form of legal extortion—pleading guilty and agreeing to testify against Keating and Wischer. The trials of Keating and Wischer were severed, and Keating was scheduled to go first. The basic allegations were that investors had been fraudulently induced into purchasing ACC's subordinated debentures and that Keating was, as ACC's CEO, responsible.

There's not much question as to Fidel's and Symes' roles in the debenture-sales program. They ran it. Dariush Razavi, Fidel's primary assistant, outlined the program in a letter to Mark Randall, dated July 26, 1989, which had been presented as evidence in the congressional hearings. The pertinent section of the letter is:

The responsibility for selecting bond representatives and establishing the procedures for marketing, referral and selling ACC bonds at the branch offices rested with Robin S. Symes and Ray C. Fidel, Executive Vice President and Senior Vice President respectively of Lincoln Savings.

The letter provided numerous details of the actions that these two people took in conducting the bond-sales program. However, nowhere in this letter was there any indication that either Keating or Wischer had anything to do with the recruitment, training, or supervision of the people involved in the bond program. That was the bailiwick of Fidel and Symes.

The subordinated-debenture program, including the method of distribution, seems to have been the brainchild of two of ACC's in-house attorneys, David Thompson and Mark Sauter. The registration statements and prospectuses were handled by Kaye Scholer's attorneys, along with ACC's financial staff. Kaye Scholer also reviewed, when they were requested to do so, advertisements and other materials related to the debenture sales. I can never recall seeing or hearing that either Keating or Wischer ever got involved with these aspects of the debentures, except, perhaps, to sign a document at an attorney's request. Nor did they ever appear to have any involvement with the selection, training, or supervision of the bond representatives; instead, they left that to Fidel and Symes. There were times when Keating made complimentary remarks about the success of the program and about Fidel's ability to achieve the sales volume that the program produced. But those were very generalized and broad comments and never, to my recollection, gave any indication that Keating had any real knowledge about the details of the program.

The only instances where he apparently had involvement were when one of the attorneys indicated to him that Fidel was not following the attorneys' instructions. In those few instances, Keating asked Kielty to make sure that Fidel completely followed all of the guidelines the attorneys had established. Keating, himself, didn't get directly involved.

From my observations of his modus operandi, Keating was content to let someone manage an activity without any interference or input from him, as long as the activity or program was, from all indications, operating effectively and producing results. He placed great reliance on attorneys and other managers to implement ideas or to effectuate transactions after the parameters of a deal had been laid out. He didn't show any propensity to get involved with the details of a transaction or activity unless a problem was brought to his attention. And in the case of the debenture-sales program, there is no evidence that Keating was involved in the "how" aspects of the sales.

Judy showed more interest in "how" things got done, but not with respect to the bond program. It simply wasn't her area of responsibility.

I was not present for any of Keating's trial, nor have I read any of the transcripts of the proceeding. But I have discussed the events of the trial with several attorneys who sat in on portions of the trial.

The setting itself was not helpful to Keating. There were a couple of instances where, as he was entering the courtroom, he was accosted by bondholders and was either physically or verbally assaulted. In one instance, a man, who was wearing a wig and who was apparently an "actor" pretending to be a bond purchaser, hit Keating with a device that covered him with white powder. Also, the corridors outside the courtroom were, as I've been told, frequently crowded with bondholders. The jurors, when they arrived, at lunchtime, or at the end of the day, had to pass through this throng of people who were openly hostile toward Keating. The observers said that the constant presence of the bondholders, and the remarks they made, had to have impacted the jurors—and negatively so.

The initial witnesses for the prosecution were bondholders, who apparently testified that they had been induced to buy the debentures through false statements made by bond sales representatives. The general theme, which was the same one used later in the civil cases, was that the bondholder had been the holder of, or was seeking to purchase, a Lincoln certificate of deposit which was covered by FSLIC deposit insurance. They alleged that they were directed to the ACC bonds by Lincoln personnel and that they were told, essentially, that the bonds were a "safe" alternative to a CD and carried a higher yield. Apparently, most testified that they had told the bond representatives that security, rather than income, was their primary concern and that they had sought assurances from the representatives that the bonds were safe and secure. With variations, they alleged that they had been told the bonds were "as safe as an insured CD" and that bond representatives had extolled the virtues of ACC, its various projects and investments, and Keating's and ACC's track records. The witnesses also said that upon entering the Lincoln branch they had been comforted by the FSLIC sign on the door and had "expected" that any bonds or accounts would be FSLIC insured. And of course, they went into great detail about the hardships caused by the loss of their money.

I think it is clear that some percentage of the debenture purchasers were, in fact, the victims of overzealous sales tactics and, perhaps, of misrepresentations by some of the bond representatives. Too many bond-holders have said that was the case for anyone to deny that it happened. However, there is a real question as to how prevalent these irregularities were versus how many complaints were the product of a kind of a "me too" syndrome that may have developed after some of the bondholders talked with lawyers, or other bondholders, and found out that some recovery of loss might be possible.

The real issues were: What was the origin of the misrepresentations;

were they caused simply by the overreaching of zealous bond representatives; were they the product of instructions from Keating; did Keating
know about the misrepresentations; and what role did anyone above Fidel
and Symes, especially Keating, play, if any, in encouraging or condoning
such misrepresentations? Those questions were, or should have been, the
essence of this trial.

As I understand it, the only witnesses who could testify to Keating's
role were Symes and Fidel. No one has told me that any other witnesses had
direct contact or correspondence with Keating, except perhaps seeing him
in attendance at various functions. I am told that the testimony of Symes
and Fidel was of an inferential nature. They apparently did not make any
statements which said that "Charlie Keating told me to say or do this" or
"Charlie Keating knew we were doing thus and so."

Instead, there was a lot of testimony about Charlie's penchant, or
obsession, for neatness. They commented on the fact that he wanted all
desks cleaned off at night; he selected the pictures and furnishings for the
offices in Phoenix; he established dress codes; and, with some projects,
like the Phoenician, he got involved with the details. The inference created
was that anyone who was so detail conscious "must" have known about,
and thus condoned, the details of the bond-sales program.

That doesn't necessarily compute. For example, I know a good
number of people who are very fastidious about their personal grooming
and surroundings but who are oblivious to business details. I know plenty
of others who maintain sloppy offices, piled high with papers, yet who are
obsessed with details. The fact that a person likes a certain order in his or
her personal surroundings doesn't necessarily carry over into other aspects
of his or her behavior.

There was also an allegation that Keating failed to inform the bond
representatives of the seriousness of the FHLBB examination, the exam
findings, and the potential actions which could be taken against Lincoln.
Added to this was the allegation that ACC's financial condition was
deteriorating, and Keating should have informed the bond representatives
and potential bond purchasers about that fact.

The attorneys who advised ACC on disclosure matters were aware of
the status of the FHLBB examination and related matters. I think that
Keating reasonably believed that, if any disclosures were necessary, the
attorneys would inform him of the necessity or they would, themselves,
see that they were made. These were not the kinds of matters that Charlie
got directly involved with because others were responsible for such things.
Moreover, he had no reason to believe that those who were charged with
such matters were not fulfilling their responsibilities and obligations. Not
one bond purchaser testified that he or she had ever contacted Keating
regarding any aspect of the bond program, nor did anyone testify that

Keating had been informed of any problems with the program.

When the program was established, one of the requirements was that a prospective bond purchaser had to submit a form attesting to the fact that he or she had received all of the required disclosure materials. These materials clearly indicated that the bonds were not insured, and the materials also disclosed the risk factors associated with the bonds. Hearing no complaints, Keating had a reasonable right to expect that all purchasers were reasonably informed about the nature of the investment that they were making or had made.

As for ACC's financial condition, the real problem, in Keating's eyes, was that Lincoln had to be sold. If Lincoln were sold, he thought that ACC would be in fine shape and he could get all the refinancing he needed to continue ACC's operations in a profitable manner. He had reason to believe that Lincoln would be sold. First, until it began to fall through a month or so after the deal was signed, he thought the sale to the Spencer Scott Group was viable. Second, he thought that the sale to LSAC would be approved. It appeared that the various concerns which the FHLBB had regarding the proposed sale had been, or were being, addressed, and, until the very end, Dochow's comments indicated that the sale would be approved. That, of course, did not happen. And again, Keating thought that the attorneys were aware of what was happening with these transactions and that, if disclosures were necessary, they would be made.

So, the only people who testified directly about what Keating did or did not do were Fidel and Symes. Lawyers who sat in on portions of the trial told me that the inferential testimony of Fidel and Symes, because of their guilty pleas, could be considered by the jury only if it were corroborated by other witnesses or other evidence. The observers did not think that any corroborating evidence was presented which supported the testimony of these two people. Thus, the circumstantial or inferential evidence against Keating should not have been a factor in the jury's decision.

After the prosecutors finished with their case, the record contained no testimony or other evidence that Keating (1) ever communicated with any bond purchasers, (2) ever told Fidel, Symes, or any bond seller to lie or withhold information, (3) was ever told by anyone that bond purchasers were being lied to or misled, or (4) was told anything whatsoever about what bond sellers had told bond purchasers. Hence, there was no evidence that Keating ever played any direct role in misleading any purchaser of ACC's bonds. And the trial judge acknowledged that there was insufficient evidence to convict Keating of being a "direct perpetrator" in the fraudulent sale of securities—the charge on which he had been indicted.

With no evidence to support the charges in the indictment, the prosecutors and judge adopted a novel theory and changed the charges against Keating to "aiding and abetting" violations of one of the sections of California's securities code—a charge which was not presented to the grand jury and a charge which was different from the one contained in the indictment. Moreover, Keating's lawyers argued that California's criminal laws do not cover any such crime, nor has anyone, other than Keating, ever been charged with and prosecuted for such a crime.

Thus, when the prosecution had finished presenting its case, Keating's lawyers believed that the state had failed to meet its burden of proof and had not demonstrated that Keating had committed any criminal offenses of any kind. Therefore, Keating's lawyers did not believe they had to present a defense, so they didn't—they rested after the prosecution finished with its witnesses.

There were two other factors which may have influenced the decision not to put on a defense. One was money. Keating still faced civil suits by the class-action plaintiffs, the RTC, and OTS. There was a high probability that the SEC would bring a civil suit and that the U.S. Attorney would indict Keating on federal criminal charges. The legal actions, ACC's bankruptcy, his inability to pursue income-producing activities, and the bail requirements had stripped Keating of his economic resources—he asserted that he was broke. He had very limited means to defend himself against all the remaining actions. Thus, it was necessary to husband his resources carefully.

The second reason was the threat of the federal indictment and subsequent trial. He would be much better off in that action if the federal prosecutors didn't have a record of his own testimony to use against him. If he conducted a defense in this state case, he would surely have to testify on his own behalf. Otherwise, the jury would view his failure to testify negatively, even though they were not supposed to. If there were no defense presented, the issue of whether Keating testified or not became moot.

After final arguments by the prosecutors and Keating's lawyers, the case was sent to the jury. Keating faced seventeen counts. The jury, to the surprise of many, returned verdicts of guilty on all seventeen counts. In February 1992, Keating was sentenced to approximately ten years in prison for these counts. At the time, he was almost seventy years old. If he has to serve all ten years, he will be almost eighty upon release. He is now serving his sentence. He remains confident that, on the basis of what he and his lawyers believe were egregious errors by the trial judge, these convictions will eventually be overturned on appeal.

The media attention was very strong against Keating and those associated with him, even prior to his conviction in California. The state criminal trial in California simply intensified the media coverage, and Keating's image went from bad to worse.

In the Phoenix community, and in his hometown of Cincinnati, Keating had been a supporter of numerous charities; he had been considered a solid businessman; he was a strong family man; he was a community leader; he was devout in his religious faith and a supporter of his church; he was respected for his honesty; and many people relied on him. Now he was regarded, by almost everyone, as a crook and an evil person. People who had never met him had strong and vocal negative opinions of him. He became a pariah in the space of two years. From the heights of society, he fell to the depths. People who had tried to get in his good graces two years earlier, now pretended they didn't know him or that they had always disliked or distrusted him.

Keating's fall from grace did not go unnoticed by the other defendants or by those who had been associated with him. Since early 1989, when the negative media coverage started, these people had been subjected to a kind of guilt by association. The press and various governmental agencies attacked people simply because they had worked at or with ACC or Lincoln. The assumption was, if Keating was crooked, so was everyone around him. Consequently, most of the people who had worked in management positions at ACC or Lincoln found themselves tainted, particularly if they were named as a defendant in one of the civil actions. Most were unable to pursue their careers or find meaningful employment, partly because of the taint and partly because they had to spend extensive amounts of time with their attorneys working on their own defense in the various lawsuits. As a result, their economic resources dwindled rapidly. With Keating's conviction, the guilt-by-association attitudes became more widespread and intense.

The federal government stepped up its already active criminal investigation. The grand jury in Los Angeles, which had been sitting for almost two years, called more and more witnesses. People heard, through their lawyers, that they were a subject or target of the investigation. Several were threatened with indictment. Convinced that anyone who had been associated with Charlie Keating was doomed, and potentially facing multiple counts that could lead to lengthy sentences if they were convicted, they had to consider the available alternatives.

Most were out of money and could no longer afford to hire their own lawyers. Which meant, if indicted, they had to rely on a court-appointed attorney for their defense. That didn't offer good prospects for success. The court-appointed attorney would be up against more experienced government prosecutors who had been working on the case for two years, and, because the government could commit legions of people to the case, they would be outgunned as well. Moreover, the Lincoln/ACC case was very complicated. Every transaction involved legal, accounting, regulatory, and business issues. It was unlikely that a court-appointed, criminal-

defense attorney would have the business background to understand fully
and defend these issues.

On the other hand, the government might offer a plea arrangement,
where the person could plead to an act which occurred before mandatory
sentencing guidelines went into effect. With a promise to cooperate in the
government's investigation and prosecution of others, the person could
receive a light sentence—maybe probation. The reality of the situation was
that the government was more than willing to make a deal. It wasn't going
to make or break a prosecutor's career if these people were convicted or
not. Keating was the one they wanted. If they could collect a few scalps
along the way with plea agreements—legal extortion—so much the better.
And they needed a few scalps because of the media and political attention
that had been focused on ACC and Lincoln.

Prior to mid-December 1991, the federal government obtained plea
agreements from Ernie Garcia, Mark Sauter, Bruce Dickson, Fidel, and
Symes. All agreed to cooperate in the investigation and eventual prosecution of others. Their sentences would reflect the level of cooperation they
provided.

In mid-December 1991, the federal government returned indictments
against Charlie Keating, Charles Keating III, Judy Wischer, Bob
Wurzelbacher, and Andy Ligget. The events or acts that these persons
allegedly committed were: a sham profits scheme, a bond-sales scheme,
tax-sharing theft, a Rancho Acacias bailout scheme, and an insider-loan
scheme.

The sham profits scheme involved six transactions: the sale of land,
known as Continental Ranch, to R.A. Homes; the sale of an interest in
Crowder Water Ranch; the Hidden Valley land sale to West Continental
Mortgage; the sale of the GOSLP interest to Garcia; the sale of Hidden
Valley land to HVPLP; and the sale of Hidden Valley land to Gascon
Development. The indictment alleged that these transactions involved the
following elements: the sale of land was at inflated prices; a promise was
made that the purchaser would be reimbursed for the down payment or that
ACC or Lincoln would enter into another transaction favorable to the
purchaser, or that ACC or Lincoln would repurchase the property or
arrange for it to be sold at a profit; the sale triggered tax-sharing payments;
and the sales contract and related documents were fraudulently crafted.

The bond-sales scheme alleged that purchasers were deceived about
the "high degree of risk associated with the bonds, the finances and
prospects of ACC and Lincoln, and the dishonest management of Lincoln
and ACC." Seventeen transactions were used as the basis for the counts
associated with this "bond-sales scheme," resulting in forty-two counts
against each of the individuals. Each transaction was translated into

multiple counts, as was true with all the other transactions in the indictment.

The allegations in the tax-sharing theft related only to Andy Ligget and asserted that certain tax-sharing payments had been made prematurely, thereby providing ACC with interest-free loans to the detriment of Lincoln and the benefit of ACC.

The so-called Rancho Acacias bailout related to a loan participation on a property known as Rancho Acacias which Lincoln sold to the Saudi European Bank (SEB). The indictment alleged that, as part of the sales agreement, "ACC agreed to repurchase the loan participation if SEB so demanded." The indictment further alleged that SEB intended to require ACC to repurchase the loan participation and that Keating and Wischer "promised SEB that, among other things, if SEB released ACC from its obligation to repurchase the loan participation, Lincoln would buy it instead." The allegation then asserted that Keating and Wischer, with others, not only caused Lincoln to buy the loan participation but also gave SEB a "profits participation" entitling SEB to 25 percent of the profits from any sale of the Rancho Acacias property. The indictment asserted that "the profit's participation was not ACC's to give, but rather belonged to Lincoln." It further stated that Lincoln's purchase of the loan participation was "fraudulently" hidden, so as to avoid regulatory challenge.

The insider-loan scheme alleged that, in contemplation of ACC's bankruptcy filing, monies were fraudulently transferred out of ACC for the personal benefit of Keating, Keating III, Wurzelbacher, Wischer, and members of their families. The loans were allegedly made by Medema Homes of Utah, Inc., a subsidiary of ACC, and the indictment alleged: the money for the loans came not from Medema but from ACC; the recipients had no intention of repaying the loans; and Medema was a shell corporation used only to loan money to certain officers and employees of ACC.

The indictments sought forfeiture of any monies or property obtained from the alleged racketeering activities. The amount of forfeiture that the government sought ranged from $265.5 million from Keating and Wischer to $227 million from Ligget.

Each of the defendants faced from sixty-four to approximately seventy-one counts. If the defendants went to trial and lost, they would each face sentences which could range between ten and twenty-five years, plus the economic penalty of forfeiture.

As was the case in the state indictment, each had to go through the bail process all over again. Wischer, Ligget, and Wurzelbacher were able to work this out with the government and avoided any jail time while awaiting bail. Charlie and C-III were not as fortunate. Once again, it took some time before they could meet the bail requirements, so they spent time in jail while friends and family members raised the necessary monies.

Charlie made bail first, after several weeks of incarceration. C-III had to wait a few more weeks before he was released.

Bail is intended to assure that a person will not flee and will appear at trial. It is not supposed to be punitive in nature. In Keating's and Wischer's case, they had made every court appearance they were required to make in the state's earlier case. They had never attempted to avoid prosecution by leaving the country. The federal government knew this before it sought bail in the federal case. Keating and C-III had amply demonstrated they were not flight risks. Nonetheless, bail was set at very high amounts. It was a punitive undertaking by the federal government, deliberately designed to deprive Keating and C-III of their freedom, as well as to humiliate and degrade them by providing more photo opportunities to the media. Arizona's newspapers took great delight in the fact Keating was once again behind bars.

The situation in the criminal case is not unlike that in the civil cases. Going to trial exposes defendants to enormous risks—in this case, the loss of personal freedom as well as severe economic consequences. These risks are so great that a defendant cannot afford to lose; thus, negotiating a plea agreement becomes the only viable alternative.

This is particularly true when the defendant does not have the financial resources to fund a vigorous and competent defense. For example, Judy Wischer did not have the resources to allow her to engage her own attorney and had to have an attorney appointed by the court. That attorney was not provided with the funds to hire investigators or experts to aid in Judy's defense. Contrast this to the U.S. Attorney who would prosecute the case. The U.S. Attorney's office has the FBI at its disposal, can tap into numerous other federal agencies, and has unlimited financial resources. It simply isn't a level playing field.

All of the defendants, except Charlie, were relatively young people—in their thirties or early forties. They all had families, including young children, to support. They all had seen their financial resources disappear. They had to sell their homes and cars. Their bank accounts were depleted. They had substantial civil judgments against them. Because of the pending litigation, including the threat of criminal actions, they had not been able to find meaningful employment which allowed them to maintain a reasonable standard of living. They had not only been destroyed economically; they were emotionally drained. Their families had been under constant stress for nearly three years. Now, they just wanted the legal battles to end so they could go on with their lives.

The decision to enter a guilty plea, especially when a person is convinced that he has not intentionally broken any law and is innocent of the charges asserted against him, is not an easy one to make. The person becomes an admitted felon and sacrifices certain societal rights and privileges. A stigma becomes attached to him that can never be erased. But the alternative of fighting and losing is worse. With the extensive potential penalties they faced, they really had no option. They had no choice but to bend to the legal extortion inherent in the system.

By June of 1992, Wurzelbacher, Ligget, and Wischer had all entered guilty pleas. Wischer and Ligget agreed to cooperate fully with the government in the case against Keating and in other ongoing investigations the government was conducting. Wurzelbacher also agreed to cooperate, except against Keating, his father-in-law.

The day after the federal criminal indictment was returned, the SEC filed a suit against the people who had been indicted and five others, including me. That suit sought injunctive relief against all of the individuals. The SEC also sought an order to require Keating to "disgorge" monies equal to all losses avoided as a result of the conduct alleged in the complaint, as well as civil penalties equal to three times the losses avoided by sales of stock during the five years prior to the date of the complaint.

This suit was stayed until after Keating's federal criminal trial, primarily because the U.S. Attorney didn't want any civil lawyers to get a shot at deposing or cross-examining the witnesses it intended to call against Keating. Nonetheless, before this case went to trial in May 1994, all of the defendants, except for me, had settled with the SEC in an attempt to get all pending litigation behind them.

In May 1994, after a brief trial, the trial judge entered a judgment in my favor on all of the counts contained in the SEC's complaint.

The judge's ruling in the SEC case demonstrates that if a defendant has the opportunity to enter a courtroom, the government's allegations can be proven to be unfounded. This case also shows several other things about the government's lawyers' approach to litigation. First, even if the government has but the scantiest of evidence to support its contentions, the lawyers will continue to attack a defendant. The government's lawyers know that the filing of a complaint damages a defendant's reputation. They know if the defendant doesn't bow to their legal extortion and goes to trial and prevails, the defendant still will be forced to commit hundreds of thousands of dollars to the defense. Thus, even if the government loses, the lawyers accomplish their purpose—they inflict pain, suffering, and hardship on the defendant and get their pound of flesh. Second, the government will spend untold thousands of dollars to inflict this pain, even if the suit doesn't offer the government any chance of recovering its costs of litigation.

This case should make any citizen cringe with fear. If a citizen offends some bureaucrat or regulator, that citizen can find him or herself the target of a vicious and unrelenting attack by prosecutors and other government lawyers, even though there is no credible evidence that the citizen has engaged in any misconduct or wrongdoing.

The criminal indictments and pleas had a chilling effect on the remaining defendants in the class-action lawsuit. There had always been a strong suspicion that the lawyers for the plaintiffs and the government prosecutors had been pretty cozy with each other. If the plaintiffs' lawyers could tell the civil jury that many of ACC's and Lincoln's officers, directors, or customers had entered guilty pleas, had been convicted or were under indictment, it made the job of showing that civil fraud had occurred pretty easy. Conversely, the prosecutors' job was easier if civil judgments had been returned against the defendants for the same transactions which were the basis of the indictment. As for the defendants, they were caught in a squeeze by the two cooperating forces.

As the civil trial was about to start in March 1992, the civil defendants who remained in the case were not in an enviable position. Because of the news coverage of Keating's criminal difficulties, much of which washed over onto anyone who had had any association with him, they had been bombarded with unfavorable press. If matters ever actually went to a jury, they were facing impossible economic risks. The jury was to be drawn from several counties in southeastern Arizona, and one had to assume that most, if not all, of the jurors would have little or no business knowledge, certainly not at the level needed to understand the complexities of the transactions at issue. The jurors also could not be expected to be knowledgeable about or understand the various rules and principles which governed the practice of accountancy or law. The plaintiffs appearing as witnesses would all be elderly or ill and would tell heart-wrenching stories about what the loss of their investment meant to them. The defendants, on the other hand, would be presented as large, fat-cat organizations that could afford to take an economic hit. It wasn't a situation that offered much chance of success to any defendant.

On the first day of the trial, which started in mid-March 1992, Arthur Andersen settled for between $20 million and $30 million. That put pressure on the other defendants. Within a day or so, Arthur Young settled for about $63 million, as did the law firm of Jones, Day, Reavis & Pogue, for about $24 million. Shortly thereafter, the remaining deep pockets, not wanting to be stuck with the whole bag, all settled. That left only a few defendants—Keating, Wolfswinkle, Saudi European, and Continental Southern—and they didn't have any real assets left.

Because he needed to defend himself in various criminal actions, Keating didn't present a defense in the class-action suit. In fact, neither he nor his attorneys made any appearances in court. Thus, the plaintiffs were unopposed when they presented their case against him.

Nonetheless, the case went all the way to the end, and the jury returned a verdict against Keating and the others. The final judgment against Keating was for $1.7 billion—one of the highest awards in U.S. history. Later, the RTC received a judgment against Keating for $4.2 billion, giving Keating the dubious distinction of being the subject of two of the five highest civil judgments ever awarded in this country. These awards were totally out of proportion to any actual damages suffered by any plaintiffs. And they show how badly the scales of justice can be tipped when the government seeks to destroy a person totally.

The verdict in the class-action case was really only symbolic in that there was little hope that anything could be recovered from the defendants. But the verdict did confirm that those who settled were very wise to have done so, because had they stayed in the case, this jury would have returned a verdict against them calling for huge damages.

Just as the class-action lawsuit was nearing its trial date, the OTS dropped a bombshell which sent shivers down the spines of lawyers throughout the country. Early in the game, the law and accounting firms that had not been named as defendants in the RTC suit sought to settle with the RTC, so as to avoid any additional litigation. The RTC had, they assumed, succeeded to any claims that the FHLBB, which was now no longer in existence, may have had against them. After lengthy negotiations, these firms reached multi-million-dollar settlements with the RTC. Understandably, they believed they had satisfied any potential claims the regulators may have had.

Then, OTS entered the picture. OTS threatened to bring suits which would ban the firms from providing future services to any federally insured, depository institution; would ban specific partners from providing services to the institutions; and would seek restitution in the amount of millions of dollars. The firms questioned OTS' ability to bring such actions. When services had been provided to Lincoln, there had been only one regulatory agency that could possibly have had a claim against these firms, and that was the FHLBB, either in its own right or as agent for the FSLIC, which no longer existed either. When the FHLBB went out of existence, the RTC became the receiver for Lincoln; as such, the RTC stepped into the FHLBB's shoes.

The acts which could have given rise to any claims against the firms by the FHLBB occurred before that time, as the firms did not provide any services to Lincoln after the date of the conservatorship. Therefore, any potential injury that the firms may have caused was limited to a single entity, the FHLBB, and, by succession, the RTC. If both the RTC and OTS asserted claims against the firms, there would be, in effect, two parties now claiming injury, instead of the one party in existence at the time the services were rendered. Something didn't smell right. How could the government create, after the fact, another victim by merely bifurcating the FHLBB?

OTS' authority to seek restitution, penalties, and damages against independent contractors, which is what these firms were, was established by FIRREA, and FIRREA did not exist until months after Lincoln was placed into conservatorship. To assert that these firms were liable under FIRREA was to apply the law retroactively. In effect, the firms would be accused of violating laws that did not exist at the time the alleged act occurred. This makes no sense.

Even assuming that the OTS had a legitimate legal right to assert claims against the firms, an assumption which defies logic, the penalties sought should have been limited to the level which could have been claimed by applying the statutes which existed at the time the alleged acts occurred. Civil money penalties would presumably be limited to $1,000 per day. Assuming a firm started providing services from the instant that ACC acquired Lincoln and the penalty applied to every day from that date forward, the claim would cover twenty-two hundred days, or a maximum penalty of $2.2 million. As for restitution, recovery should logically have been limited to the amount of the fees that the firm collected from Lincoln. For a firm like Arthur Young, that would be something around $6 million and for a Kaye Scholer probably $10 million or less. Yet, the monies that the OTS was seeking from the firms was far greater than that. OTS could only create these larger claims if it retroactively applied FIRREA.

As for seeking sanctions against the individual partners, common sense dictates that sanctions should be taken against them only if they acted outside of their authorities and responsibilities as partners. The firm was the independent contractor, not the individual partners. The partners were simply agents of the firm. As long as the individuals did not exceed their authority, the firm should be the only party that the government can look to for recovery or sanctions.

Kaye Scholer apparently challenged OTS' ability to assert liability, especially since it had settled with the RTC. In response to Kaye Scholer's unwillingness to settle and pay over the blackmail money that OTS demanded, OTS filed suit. In so doing, OTS asked the court to freeze the assets of Kaye Scholer and certain of its partners. The court granted the request.

Deprived of access to its assets, the firm might not have been able to operate. Without cash, it couldn't be expected to meet payrolls or pay its vendors. In effect, if it didn't succumb to OTS' demands, it would be out of business and all of its partners and employees would be destroyed economically. One has to wonder how OTS' actions are any different from the situation where a person is accosted on the street by a thug with a gun who says, "Give me all your money or I'll kill you." Kaye Scholer had no choice but to pay OTS the extortion money it demanded and to bow to the sanctions against its partners.

In its actions against Kaye Scholer, the government demonstrated, for all intents and purposes, that the Constitution no longer applies to any person who runs afoul of the banking or thrift regulators. With FIRREA, Congress stripped these people of their inherent rights as citizens of the United States. The courts were not available to them. They could not seek protection from the rogues and thugs in OTS, RTC, and other government agencies, because these agencies had the power effectively to block access to the judiciary. With asset freezes, RICO, FIRREA, mandatory sentences, and joint-and-several liability, no one is immune to their wrath and their extortionate demands. Not even the most respected and prestigious professional firms in the country. The risks and penalties are so severe that the objects of the government's actions are precluded from defending themselves or challenging the constitutionality of the government's actions. They are forced to accept, without resistance, the punishment meted out by power-mad bureaucrats who will destroy anyone who crosses their path, without so much as the blink of an eye.

In November 1992, Ernst & Young, as the successor to Arthur Young and Ernst & Whinney, reached a settlement with the FDIC, RTC, and OTS covering all insured institutions that had failed by the date of the settlement, as well as certain open institutions, which it or its predecessor firms had audited, including Lincoln. The settlement required the firm to pay the agencies the sum of $400 million. In addition, several partners or former partners, including me, consented to, without admitting any wrongdoing, either a cease-and-desist or a prohibition order.

The federal trial of Charlie Keating and his son, C-III, on the criminal charges set forth in the December 1991 indictment started in Los Angeles in the fall of 1992. Charlie was transferred from the correctional facility in San Luis Obispo to Los Angeles. He had lost a considerable amount of weight since the beginning of his incarceration in the state facility— dropping from about 215 pounds down to about 175 pounds—a large decrease for a man who stands six feet, five inches tall. Despite the weight loss, he was reported to be in good spirits and was anxious to defend himself against the charges brought by the government.

As had become the norm in the ACC/Lincoln situation, this case promised to be different from other cases which were previously associated with the S&L industry's collapse. There have been many cases in the thrift and banking industries where individuals have intentionally violated the law in order to obtain personal benefits. Most of the cases involved traditional forms of wrongdoing, such as embezzlement, accepting bribes or kickbacks in exchange for extending credit, making false statements to secure loans, misapplying loan funds, or diverting loan funds for personal use. Often such schemes involved persons and institutions acting in concert. These are the types of acts for which the vast majority of persons have been convicted in connection with failed thrifts and banks.

In this case, the government alleged that transactions, which ACC and Lincoln represented to be routine commercial transactions entered into in the normal course of business, were contrived and lacked any valid business or economic purpose. Underlying the government's allegations was the premise that the transactions entering into these schemes were improperly accounted for on ACC's and Lincoln's books. That is, the accounting entries did not reflect the true nature of the transactions.

These elements—the conversion of commercial transactions into fraudulent artifices and improper accounting—made the case different from other S&L-related cases in the past. They also made the case technically difficult to present to a jury consisting of people who might have limited knowledge of business organizations, economics, appraisal techniques, accounting principles, land values, and other elements which entered into the various transactions. This was the same dilemma that had faced the civil attorneys, for both the plaintiffs and the defendants, in the class-action lawsuits—how does one present the evidence to the jury so they can understand its significance?

In the civil case, the plaintiffs' attorneys had chosen a simple approach. They had presented just enough information on each transaction to create the impression that there was something improper about the transactions per se. They had then referred to persons associated with ACC or Lincoln who had entered guilty pleas in criminal actions or who were asserting their rights under the Fifth Amendment and had painted a picture of an organization seeded with people who were admitted felons or who "must" have something to hide because they were refusing to testify. The plaintiffs' attorneys had then added two more significant elements to their story for the jury.

First, they had presented, as witnesses, several of the bond purchasers. Each was elderly or infirm and each told a story of having been misled by bond representatives. Moreover, each told of the terrible consequences that the loss of their invested money had produced. This painted ACC and Lincoln as heartless organizations whose officers and directors preyed on the elderly and unfortunate.

Second, the plaintiffs' attorneys had put Charlie Keating's life-style on trial. They had talked of corporate jets, trips to Europe, vacation homes in Florida and the Bahamas, an opulent home in Phoenix, luxury automobiles, and so on. They had created an image of Charlie and other ACC executives making phony transactions and selling bonds in order to finance high salaries and stock purchases, so they could support their lavish life-styles.

The plaintiffs' attorneys hadn't tried to prove the technical aspects of the allegations. Instead, they had put on a case of images—images the jury could understand. On the one hand, they had the image of elderly and infirm persons who had lost a great deal of money. On the other hand, they had an image of people who were living lavishly, presumably off of the money the first group had lost. Sandwiched in between had been some evidence which suggested, but didn't necessarily attempt to prove, that ACC's and Lincoln's transactions were improper. Thus, a very technical case had been reduced to a few, relatively basic, emotional issues.

As the federal criminal trial neared its starting date, the federal prosecutors were able to extract plea agreements from a number of people who agreed to cooperate in the case against Keating. This not only provided the prosecutors with needed witnesses, it added the element the civil attorneys had enjoyed—the ability to paint Keating as a person who headed an organization which harbored a number of people who admitted to committing unlawful acts. That's not to say that all of the people who entered into such agreements were guilty—many probably were not. A person who enters into a plea arrangement is not necessarily guilty of the offense to which he has pled.

Based on plea agreements, there appear to be some people involved in the Lincoln/ACC case who did do things they knew were not appropriate and which violated the law.

Ernie Garcia appears to have made intentional misrepresentations in connection with the Wescon transaction. It is very unclear whether anyone at ACC or Lincoln knew that the statements Garcia made were false or that Wescon's role in the transaction was not what it was represented to be.

It appears Ray Fidel and Rob Symes did, in fact, do things in connection with the sale of ACC subordinated debentures which were wrong and which they knew were wrong at the time they did them. However, there is evidence that whenever others within ACC, including Charlie, learned that Fidel and Symes were acting inappropriately, they took steps to insure that the inappropriate activities were halted. Fidel and Symes also apparently did some things others within the ACC management group did not know about. It is logical and understandable that others may not have known of their activities, because Fidel and Symes were in California, and the others were in Arizona. Thus, the primary officers of ACC did not have many occasions, if any, actually to observe the practices that Fidel and Symes approved, encouraged, and conducted.

It also appears that Mark Sauter converted corporate funds to his own use by engaging in false transactions. He has pled to "file stuffing" related charges, but one has to think that the real reason for entering this plea was the subsequent disclosure of his illegal conversion of funds. In addition, it is not certain, I suppose, whether he acted alone or whether he had help in converting the funds to his own use.

I don't know enough about the circumstances or facts surrounding the plea entered by Bruce Dickson to comment much about it. Apparently he admitted wrongdoing in connection with certain transactions involving the Continental Ranch property in Tucson and R.A. Homes. Bruce also was deeply involved in the transactions with Garcia.

With respect to Wischer, Wurzelbacher, and Ligget, the pleas they made appear to have been defensive moves to avoid the severe threat which would be present if they went to trial. They had exhausted their financial resources. They were underrepresented in comparison to the resources which were aligned against them. And they must have felt that with all the adverse publicity attendant to ACC, Lincoln, and Keating, the chances of a successful defense if they were sitting next to Charlie at the defense table were either slim or nonexistent.

This left Charlie and his son, C-III, to face trial in federal court.

C-III, during the time I knew him, was enmeshed in Lincoln's land-development activities. His real interest was in the construction aspects of these projects—designing and building lakes, bridges, and roads. Unlike his father, C-III is not a deal-maker, and, thus, he was less interested in the sales and marketing aspects of the land-development activities. He was uncomfortable in formal business meetings but was right at home on a construction site. Consequently, you were more likely to see C-III wearing a hard hat and work boots than a tailored suit and tie.

C-III was very proud of the Estrella project and appeared to believe firmly that the development efforts in the project, combined with the completion of the interstate highway, created great values in the property and the adjacent property in Hidden Valley. Based on that, he believed that persons buying property in Estrella, or Hidden Valley, would realize profits from their investments.

C-III's beliefs with respect to Hidden Valley rested on a firm foundation. The land-development activities which he directed were responsible for generating annual gross profits of over $70 million a year. He had seen many other projects which started out as "raw desert land" end up as vibrant communities full of satisfied home buyers. Hidden Valley and Estrella were just two more properties where he expected similar results to occur.

As for the tax-sharing agreement, it is highly doubtful that C-III had any understanding of how it worked or how it affected either ACC or Lincoln. C-III was not involved with, nor did he exhibit the slightest interest in, subjects like the tax-sharing agreement, the sale of debentures, accounting issues, or regulatory matters. He focused on development activities—and his interests started and ended there.

As for Charlie, as the trial approached, his prospects didn't look very good. He had been so vilified by politicians and the press that his name had become the symbol for everything that went wrong in the collapse of the S&L industry, as well as for any unethical behavior in the business world in general. The plaintiffs' lawyers and prosecutors, with a cooperative media, cast him as a person who intentionally preyed on the elderly and disabled in order to support his own lavish life-style.

As the civil attorneys had asserted in the class-action case, Charlie did live lavishly. He traveled in private planes, rode in stretch limousines, lived in a mansion-like house, had luxurious vacation homes, enjoyed expensive restaurants, and wore tailored clothing. But he had the means to support this kind of life-style well before ACC acquired Lincoln. He and his family purportedly had had a net worth well in excess of $50 million before he ever heard of Lincoln Savings and Loan. And he had already adopted the life-style he and his family enjoyed before that date as well. So, the acquisition of Lincoln was not the start of the fine life for Charlie Keating.

While the press was correct in reporting that Charlie lived very well, they did not present the other facets of the man. He has a deep concern for others, as is reflected by the generous donations of time and money he has given to various charities. Charlie never turned them down. He supported numerous efforts whose purpose was to feed, shelter, treat, or clothe those who were in need.

Charlie grew up in a home where his father was disabled and unable to work. He appreciated the burden that his mother and other family members had to bear. He understood what it was like to have to struggle to make ends meet and simply to be able to afford the absolute necessities of life. He knew the physical and emotional pain and suffering that his father had to endure. Because of that experience, he empathized with those who coped with hardship. That's why those who know him do not believe that a person with his upbringing and background could ever intentionally cause harm to anyone who is elderly or infirm. Sure, he achieved the good life, but that doesn't mean he ever forgot his past or turned his back on others. That he has been cast as a person who "preyed" on others has been, perhaps, the hardest and cruelest part of this whole mess with which Charlie Keating has had to cope.

In my dealings with Charlie, he expressed a concern that things be done properly. He surrounded himself with lawyers and consultants, not, as the media and his adversaries have asserted, to find ways to circumvent the rules, but to abide by them. When the direct-investment rules were being adopted, he did, in fact, attempt to grandfather the greatest amount of investment possible. He did, in fact, work right up to the last minute to accomplish that goal. But he did so within the rules, as he understood those rules to be. And he relied on the best attorneys available to advise him on those rules and Lincoln's compliance with them.

If Charlie believed that he was in the right, he would pursue his cause until he exhausted all of his options. In the GOIL transaction, he thought that Lincoln should be able to recognize gain. He pursued this to the highest levels of Arthur Young and with other firms. He sent Touche Ross to the FASB and the SEC with the issue. When the options were exhausted and the SEC disagreed with Lincoln's position, he complied with the SEC's answer and did not pursue the matter farther.

With regard to the regulators, he felt that their findings and criticisms regarding Lincoln were incorrect. He directed counsel to document and present Lincoln's position to the regulators thoroughly and to pursue every avenue available within the law and regulations. The regulators have asserted that these actions were obstructive and demonstrated an unwillingness to accept the authority of the FHLBB and the CDSL.

The regulators used every tool available to them in their examination and regulation of Lincoln. They engaged appraisers, outside attorneys, accountants, and consultants, even when the use of such resources was inconsistent with the regulations. They illegally leaked confidential information. They referred to and used other agencies. They gathered information from other associations. If the regulators could go to these extremes, why was it improper for Lincoln to avail itself of the administrative processes provided in the regulations? Why was it improper to defend positions aggressively that Lincoln believed were correct and to contest actions and findings that it believed were incorrect? Had ACC and Lincoln acquiesced to adjustments proposed by the regulators—adjustments management legitimately believed were wrong—management would have been negligent and would have failed to live up to its responsibilities to its shareholders.

Keating has been accused of entering into so-called linked transactions to induce customers to buy land or other assets from Lincoln. Clearly, Lincoln did enter into multiple transactions with the same party and had done so for several years. In 1985, an Arthur Andersen partner asked Keating about this practice in connection with a series of transactions with Southmark Corporation, and he was told that "None of the transactions was inter-related." Further, Charlie told him, "ACC had developed a good relationship with Southmark Corporation and felt comfortable doing business with them" and added, "all the transactions were conducted on an arm's-length basis, and there were no trade-offs between deals."

Keating believed that it was best to do business with people whom ACC knew and trusted, rather than with people they did not know. He felt this reduced risk. Charlie would sit down with customers and present several deals to them, and, if they had something they wanted to sell or they had a lending transaction they were interested in, he would listen to their presentations. If a deal was good, he'd do it. If wasn't good, he wouldn't. He consistently represented that every transaction stood on its own, and none was a trade-off for another. And this appears to be, in fact, how he thought about these deals and transactions. Now, the other party may not have separated the transactions, but it appears that Keating did.

There were also allegations that certain properties were sold at prices which exceeded their fair values. Supporting these allegations are appraisals which Lincoln apparently obtained and did not show to auditors. The claim was made that the existence of the lower appraised value of the property sold would have affected how Lincoln or ACC accounted for the sale transaction. But even if the claims about the appraisal values were true, it doesn't necessarily follow that Lincoln's accounting for the sale transactions would have changed.

The primary issue to Lincoln was the value of the consideration it received in these transactions and not the value of the property it surrendered in the transaction. Gain or loss is determined by comparing the fair value of the assets Lincoln received to the cost of the assets it surrendered. To my knowledge, no one has questioned the value of the assets that Lincoln received—including the regulators, Kenneth Leventhal, or the prosecutors. It is also my understanding that the values of the assets, at the time they were received, were supported by appraisals.

It's also logical in a business transaction for the buyer to determine the value of the property being purchased. The buyer may or may not rely on an appraisal in making the determination. Most land developers and home builders believe they can determine the value of a given piece of property to their business better than most appraisers. In Lincoln's case, after the regulators asked Lincoln to obtain appraisals for all property acquisitions, Lincoln apparently did so. It's my understanding that these appraisals supported the values which Lincoln ascribed to the acquired properties. Nonetheless, in many cases, Lincoln's personnel believed that the property was worth more than the appraisals indicated. This is because Lincoln expected to enhance value by zoning, planning, annexation, and development efforts. It did not intend to sell the property in its "as is" condition—the condition on which most appraisals are based.

That was the whole basis of Lincoln's land-development activities—to create added value. Lincoln did not view land as a commodity which was to be held in its "as is" condition for later sale. Had it done so, its profits would have been dependent on an increase in the property's speculative value—a value driven largely by inflation—rather than development. Charlie's belief was that value had to be created, it didn't just happen. Thus, Lincoln's development activities focused on building attractive amenities, such as lakes or parks, or improving access to major public facilities, such as through airports or interstate highways. This was the significant difference between how Charlie and the regulators viewed a given piece of ground. The regulators saw it as it was, and Charlie saw it for what it could become. This is the difference between a bureaucrat and an entrepreneur.

As for the property Lincoln sold, the determination of value was a function of what the buyer was going to do with it, combined with the value-added effects that the development of adjacent or nearby land might have. It wasn't Lincoln's duty to make this determination for the buyer—that was the buyer's responsibility.

As for the appraisals related to the land which Lincoln sold, their primary use was to determine the appropriateness of Lincoln's carrying value of the unsold property Lincoln held—not the appropriateness of the price paid by the buyer. Of course, there may have been questions as to why a buyer paid an amount substantially greater than the appraisal value. The answers to those questions would depend on the buyer's plans for the property and other factors which Lincoln may or may not have been aware of at the time of the sale. These may have been questions that the regulators would have asked, but the answers may not have had any effect whatsoever on Lincoln's accounting for the transactions.

The regulators and the prosecutors also used Charlie's own words to allege that he thought that Lincoln's and ACC's financial health was worse than what was disclosed to the public. Charlie is a spontaneous person who often speaks without thinking how his words may be misinterpreted by others. He is also prone to use hyperbole in order to drive his point home. He has said in front of regulators, and others, words to the effect that, "If you do that, you'll bankrupt me." He never thought those words would be taken literally. They were an exaggeration intended to say, "Hey, this is important."

Keating is a person who is at his best in one-on-one or small-group settings. There he is relaxed and comfortable. He is, perhaps, at his worst in front of a large group (more than a dozen or so people) or when he's in the spotlight. There he forces things and tries to make too strong an impression. In the group meetings with the regulators, he said some dramatic things to make a point, and the regulators took him literally. These gaffes have come back to haunt him, as adverse parties have asserted that these comments reflected Charlie's true view of things. They did not. He says and does things on the spot—spontaneously—and then wonders, "Why did I do that?"

As the trial was about to start, these were some of the things that one would expect the prosecutors to use against Charlie Keating—his life-style, his public image, his pursuit of an issue to the very end, his deal making, his fight with the regulators, spontaneous remarks, and exaggerated statements taken out of context and interpreted literally. Additionally, one would expect these factors to be reinforced by witnesses who were compelled to cooperate with the government in order to preserve themselves. Their testimony could be expected to be added to by witnesses who had always been hostile to Keating and by some who were less than truthful. All this would be placed within the framework of a bankrupt ACC and a failed Lincoln.

I did not attend any portion of the trial of Charlie and C-III. But I have talked to several people, including attorneys, who observed portions of the trial or who appeared as witnesses. I have also read the press reports, which were surprisingly brief and sporadic. From these accounts, the trial ran true to form.

The initial witnesses included Judy Wischer, Ernie Garcia, and Bruce Dickson. Later in the trial, other people who had entered pleas also appeared as witnesses. All testified pursuant to their agreements with the prosecutors. Not surprisingly, their direct testimony tended to support the version of events as alleged by the prosecution. After all, they had met with the prosecutors—as many as several times a week for several months—and their recollections of events and transactions had been refreshed, challenged, hammered, and bent, until the prosecutors were satisfied that they were "cooperating."

On cross-examination, their stories came under attack, and a myriad of inconsistencies were disclosed between earlier testimony and statements and the stories they offered in this trial. The defense pointed out that the earlier testimony was made when the people were not faced with the loss of their personal freedom and, therefore, not subject to any form of coercion. In this trial, the stakes were high for all these witnesses, as their future depended on the degree to which they "cooperated" with the prosecution. The question raised was: Under the circumstances, was their testimony credible?

It should be noted that defense attorneys asked each of the witnesses who had entered into plea agreements whether the government had given them any promise of leniency in exchange for their testimony. All asserted that no promises had been made. Were their statements true? To answer the question, consider the fact that the only people who entered into plea agreements who were sentenced to any prison time were Bob Wurzelbacher and Andy Ligget—the only two who did not testify against Keating and C-III. All of the others, including Judy Wischer, received probation.

Now, consider some of the people who were granted probation. The evidence clearly shows that if any bond purchasers were lied to or misled, the people who were responsible for seeing that such misrepresentations did not occur were Fidel and Symes. They recruited, instructed, and supervised the bond sales force, not Keating. They admitted that they violated laws, but Keating did not—he maintains that he is innocent of any such violations. The trial judge in the state case acknowledged that there was no evidence supporting the allegation that Keating had had any direct participation in the bond sales, but the judge made no such finding with respect to Fidel and Symes. Yet, Keating was sentenced to ten years in prison, while Fidel and Symes don't have to serve a single day in prison.

The evidence shows that Garcia made misrepresentations to ACC, Lincoln, and their auditors regarding the Wescon transaction. Garcia was the recipient of millions of dollars of loan proceeds and received additional millions for the assets he sold to Lincoln. If Keating participated in sham transactions with Garcia, then Garcia must have participated in sham transactions with Keating; therefore, Garcia was equally guilty of any transgressions. Yet, Garcia received no jail time, while Keating did. Nor was Garcia required to pay the government millions of dollars in restitution.

Sauter allegedly stole about $1.5 million from Lincoln in a garden-variety embezzlement scheme. He pled guilty to violating the law. Yet, he didn't receive any jail time, nor did he have to make any huge restitution payments.

With respect to Judy Wischer, who was the prosecutors' star witness against Charlie and C-III, I have no reason to believe, in spite of her plea agreement, that she ever committed any criminal act. Her testimony came after over one thousand hours of meetings and "cooperation" with the government. She is reported to have made over fifty trips from Phoenix to Los Angeles and Washington to meet with government lawyers. Who knows what effect the intense questioning by the prosecutors, coupled with the threat of incarceration and the possible loss of custody of her children, may have had on Judy's recollections and interpretations of events. Certainly, those recollections and interpretations were different when offered as testimony in this trial from what they had previously been.

One thing is certain, however. The case against Keating was dependent on Judy's testimony. The *Los Angeles Times*, on October 25, 1994, reported that, when Judy was sentenced, the federal judge said, "I really don't think the case could have been prosecuted without you. I thought that when I was listening to your testimony."

Judy had pled guilty to two bank-fraud charges and one securities-fraud charge, far more serious offenses than those to which either Ligget or Wurzelbacher had entered guilty pleas. She faced up to fifteen years in prison. But, after her cooperation, she received three years probation, whereas both Ligget and Wurzelbacher, neither of whom testified against Keating, received jail time. Again, perhaps, legal extortion worked to the government's advantage and against Keating.

The same could be said of many of the others who entered guilty pleas.

The situation has to lead one to conclude that the government wasn't really interested in punishing people who broke the law; instead, the government's sole interest was in exacting its revenge on Charlie Keating, even if it meant letting admitted felons walk away scot-free.

A few of the witnesses were former borrowers and purchasers of land from Lincoln. At the time of Lincoln's seizure, these people owed Lincoln millions of dollars. Somehow, after the RTC took over, these people were able to satisfy their debts to Lincoln. Which is strange. Prior to the seizure, they didn't have the funds to pay the debts, and, after the RTC took control of Lincoln, the properties securing the debts were sold by the RTC at huge losses. So, one certainly has to wonder how these witnesses were absolved of their debt. Could wiping out the debt have been a trade-off for their willingness to "cooperate" with the government by testifying against Keating and C-III?

Certain of these witnesses testified that Keating made oral promises to them that, if they didn't realize a significant profit on the land that they purchased from Lincoln, Lincoln would make them whole by buying the land back, presumably at a higher price than they were paying. They also testified that other oral promises were made to them regarding the land they were buying. Now, all of these people were experienced with real estate, and some had law backgrounds. Surely, they knew that oral promises made in connection with the purchase or sale of real estate are neither binding nor enforceable. Surely, they were aware that the last clause in all the contracts Lincoln entered into contained words to the effect that, "this agreement contains the entire understanding between the parties with respect to the subject matter hereof and supersedes all prior written and oral negotiations and agreements between them regarding the subject matter hereof." So, surely, they knew that any comments made during the course of negotiations which were not reduced to writing, and which did not amend or supplement the purchase contract, were nothing more than "salesman's talk"—statements, commitments, promises, or whatever that were totally superseded by the written contract and therefore had absolutely no force or effect on the transaction whatsoever. Unfortunately, jurors who are not experienced in real-estate matters or who do not have law backgrounds may not have understood that the so-called oral promises described by these witnesses were, for all intents and purposes, meaningless.

Witnesses who had not been subjected to the prosecutors' tactics or who had not seen their debts miraculously disappear testified that the purchases that they made from Lincoln were not shams, as the government asserted, but, in fact, were legitimate business transactions.

With respect to the allegation that the accounting for these transactions was improper, an auditor was called by the government, and, as I understand, she testified that, based on the facts known by the auditors,

Lincoln's accounting for the subject transactions was not improper. She also stated, in effect, that had the auditors known all of the facts asserted by the prosecution, including the oral promises and appraisals which Lincoln allegedly withheld from the auditors, the accounting results might not have changed at all.

Much of the government's case was based on the allegation that the accounting for the transactions was improper, thereby allowing Keating to channel tax-sharing payments improperly from Lincoln to ACC. Moreover, the accounting for transactions ran to the heart of the allegation that ACC's financial statements and the prospectuses related to the subordinated debentures contained material misrepresentations and omissions. Yet, not one auditor from any of the firms which served as ACC's auditors testified that the accounting for any transaction was improper. No prosecution experts testified that the accounting was inappropriate. No accounting firm ever testified that it had knowledge that it was intentionally lied to or misled by Keating or C-III. No tax expert testified that the tax-sharing agreement was inappropriate or that the payments made pursuant to it were improper. No auditor or expert testified that the disclosures in ACC's financial statements or prospectuses were materially deficient. So, where was the evidence, the proof, that anything was improper with respect to the questioned transactions? It certainly was never presented in this trial.

The defense called expert witnesses who, I'm told, testified that the values of the properties cited in the indictment which were sold by Lincoln were not inflated; rather, the prices were consistent with similar properties in the areas in which they were located.

When Charlie took the witness stand in his own defense, he testified that all of the criticized transactions were, to the best of his knowledge and belief, proper. He said that they were not contrived or sham transactions but, rather, had been entered into on an arm's-length basis after appropriate negotiations. He denied that the various transactions were linked or dependent on one another. He refuted the testimony of the witnesses who had testified pursuant to plea arrangements with the government.

Now, when one questions whether Keating's claim that the transactions were valid is true or not, one has to ask: If the transactions were shams, why weren't any of the other parties to the transactions indicted and tried? If, as the government asserted, the transactions were fraudulent, the other parties received monies from Lincoln in a fraudulent manner. Some of the parties received millions of dollars on loans which later went into default. Why, then, were none of these borrowers or purchasers prosecuted? There are several possible answers to the question. First, the government wanted Keating's scalp so much that it was willing to overlook the transgressions of the other parties if they would testify against Keating—and tell the jury the story that the government wanted them to tell. Second, the government may not have believed that they could force these people to surrender to extortionate tactics and thus would have had to prove their claims against them in court. If the government hauled them into court and lost, the government's case against Keating would be totally destroyed. Finally, if the government indicted them, they would assert their Fifth Amendment rights and refuse to testify. Without the stories they told, none of the government's allegations against Keating would stand up, because all of the written documents related to the transactions indicated that every transaction was proper. Whatever the answer, none was indicted or prosecuted, with the possible exception of Garcia, who submitted to a plea arrangement.

Charlie has always maintained, and a plethora of facts support his contentions, that the troubles of Lincoln and ACC were largely, if not totally, the product of his long-running dispute with the regulators. He has contended that the failure of Lincoln resulted from regulatory abuse— illegal leaks; improper interpretation and application of the regulations and the law; personal animus by several key regulators; and a disregard for the true facts surrounding Lincoln and ACC. However, the role of the regulators could not be presented by the defense in this trial. At the start of the trial, the judge ruled that no claims could be asserted about the regulators and their actions, except in response to contentions made by the prosecutors.

Given the available record of the regulators' activities, the prosecutors would have been crazy to allow their conduct to be examined by the defense in this trial. If it had been, the picture presented to the jury would have placed the conduct of the entire federal government into question. A new victim—other than bondholders—would have been introduced to the jury: Charlie Keating! Once again, the government was able to suppress and cover up its own contribution to this debacle.

Keating's defense was further inhibited by the fact that many people who could have offered testimony regarding the allegations in the indictment were still being told that they were "targets" or "subjects" of ongoing criminal investigations. Now, this was late 1992, and any possible criminal offenses would have been committed prior to April 14, 1989. Government agents had poured over millions of documents, had access to hundreds of depositions, and had conducted hundreds of interviews during the three years following Lincoln's seizure. Surely, if there were any evidence of wrongdoing, the government would have found it by late 1992, and indictments would have been obtained. There was no valid reason— none—that people should have remained "targets" or "subjects" at this late date. The reason they were targets or subjects is simple: the government didn't want them to testify. In fact, Keating's attorneys attempted to obtain grants of immunity, so that some of these people could testify. But the government declined to grant them immunity. This was further proof of the unfair tactics involved in this trial.

Unable to make a case based purely on the factual allegations in the indictment, the prosecution reverted to the strategy of the civil lawyers for the class-action plaintiffs and put Charlie's life-style on trial. One of the areas criticized was a house in Florida which was owned by ACC. The house was large, luxurious, and quite expensive. While it did contain a room which served as an office—complete with word-processing equipment, fax machine, copier, and other office equipment—the house was primarily used by the Keating family, and others, as a vacation facility or for personal business.

Immediately after ACC purchased the Florida house, the house was extensively remodeled. After the remodeling, when the house became habitable, ACC obtained an appraisal of its fair rental value. Each year, Charlie Keating was required to report the fair rental value of the house as income—added compensation—on his personal income-tax return. This was the procedure recommended by ACC's attorneys prior to the purchase of the house.

The prosecutors also questioned the use of ACC's corporate aircraft, particularly trips that Charlie and his family members took to Europe. Charlie and various family members did take a number of trips to Europe. Some of the trips were in connection with the transactions with Sir James Goldsmith and the KIO—trips which greatly benefited ACC and Lincoln. Other trips involved investments in foreign equity securities or consultations with ACC's consultant on commodity trading and with other consultants.

But the trips that the prosecutors derided most were trips when Charlie, Mary Elaine, and his daughters visited various hotels in Europe. Mary Elaine and several of the daughters did almost all the interior-design work, including the purchasing of furniture and artwork, for the Phoenician. They also played a central role in determining the style of the various restaurants in the Phoenician as well as the type of food which would be offered. The purpose of these trips was to visit the finer hotels in Europe in order to obtain ideas that would benefit the Phoenician. Their efforts resulted in a resort which reflects a style reminiscent of the finest hotels in Europe—a style which sets the Phoenician apart from its competitors and has earned the Phoenician critical acclaim. Moreover, any portion of these trips which was considered to be of a personal nature was reflected as additional compensation in the person's annual reported taxable earnings from ACC.

As a last-ditch attack, the prosecutors questioned Charlie's purchase of two barbecue grills. The purchase was made well after ACC had filed for bankruptcy and was paid for by personal funds. The purchase also occurred after Charlie had indicated he was broke and in dire financial straits. The prosecution apparently offered no evidence that there was anything illegal about this purchase. Had they, every owner of a barbecue grill in American better run for cover. Rather, they implied this was evidence that, in spite of ACC's bankruptcy, Charlie Keating was still living a life of luxury. When I read and heard about this ploy, I viewed it as evidence of how bankrupt the criminal justice system in this country has become—you can be prosecuted because your life-style, or wealth, is inconsistent with what a prosecutor believes is appropriate.

So, as the case neared the point where it would be presented to the jury, just before Christmas 1992, the key issues became, in large part, the same images that the civil attorneys had created several months earlier. Elderly and infirm investors who lost money by purchasing ACC's bonds were contrasted with a man who lived a lavish life-style. Images which would play to a jury's emotions rather than reason.

The jury received its instructions and began deliberations on December 28, 1992. On January 6, 1993, the jury reached its verdict. Charlie was found guilty of all seventy-three counts against him, and C-III, even though very little of the testimony offered in court was directed toward him, was found guilty on sixty-four counts with which he was charged in the indictment.

In July 1993, Charlie was sentenced to a little over twelve years, to be served concurrently with his state sentence. C-III was sentenced to eight years. In both cases, the sentences imposed by the judge exceeded the recommended guidelines because of the "harm inflicted on the community."

The war was over.

Charlie Keating is now labeled a criminal. The government succeeded in completely destroying him. The government won the war—which had lasted for nearly nine years—and Charlie lost.

Most of the people left in the wake of the Lincoln Savings War have suffered terrible losses. The debenture purchasers and other class-action plaintiffs, even after the settlements paid and judgments won, will lose a significant portion of the money they invested. The professional defendants suffered devastating blows to their reputations and paid millions in their settlements with the class-action plaintiffs and various governmental entities. The other civil defendants are, for the most part, bankrupt. Many of the people who were objects of criminal indictments, or threatened indictments, are not only ruined financially, but they are also either admitted or convicted felons; as such, their names are forever tarnished. Several politicians and regulators were publicly criticized and scorned. Citizens of Arizona have seen their property values destroyed as the RTC unloaded, and continues to unload, the assets of Lincoln and the other thrift failures. Taxpayers have been stuck with a massive bill to clean up the mess.

There are a few winners. The regulators gained enormous power, and, as they continue systematically to terrorize the thrift and banking industries, their jobs are secure. Lawyers for both the defendants and the plaintiffs walked away with millions and millions of dollars and are actively in search of new financial carrion on which to feed. Congress and several administrations have been able to avoid responsibility for their ruinous legislation and policies by pinning the blame on a few scapegoats. Prosecutors have gained a few more scalps for their lodge poles, advancing their careers and enhancing their political futures. Finally, the bottom-fishers are in seventh heaven as they continue to scoop up the bargains which fall from the lap of the RTC.

This saga started out as a philosophical dispute between an entrepreneur and some regulators. It ended as an unmitigated disaster. Taxpayers will feel the effects of this debacle, and others like it, for years to come.

Epilogue

Has the Truth Been Told?

In the days following the government's seizure of Lincoln Savings, Charlie Keating's primary goal was to appear before an impartial court where the truth about the Lincoln Savings War could be told. And he did appear in several courtrooms—Sporkin's court, the state court in Los Angeles County, and the federal court in Los Angeles—and his appeals of various cases may bring him into other courtrooms in the future. Unfortunately, however, Charlie is learning what most of us who have been involved in this conflict have already learned—the business of courtrooms and trials is not about truth or, for that matter, justice. It is about winning and losing.

The prosecution or plaintiff's attorneys, as the case may be—the offense—has but one objective: to present to the jury information designed to prove that the allegations against the defendant are valid under the law, and, therefore, a verdict should be returned in favor of the offense. The sole objective of the defendant's lawyers—the defense—is to counteract all of the arguments served up by the offense in order to show that the information offered by the other side lacks merit, and, therefore, the opposition has failed to meets its burden of proof, thereby requiring a verdict in favor of the defense. Thus, a trial is nothing more than a contest between two opposing groups of attorneys. The team that presents its case in the most persuasive fashion wins, and the other side loses.

Because of the circumstances surrounding Lincoln's seizure, state and federal prosecutors had to assert and prove that there was criminality on the part of some of the participants in the Lincoln War. The public had heard the words of the regulators who appeared before Congress—Black, Patriarca, Barabolak, Newsome, Meek, Stelzer, O'Connell, and Smuzynski. The words were "fraud," "wrongdoing," "looting," "illegal," and "criminality."

These words had originated with a group of regulators who delved into areas far outside the boundaries of their knowledge and experience and who misinterpreted, ignored, and distorted data and facts, causing them to label all that they did not understand as fraudulent or improper.

The words were repeated in civil complaints filed by plaintiffs who sought, by any means, to recover money they had lost and by federal agencies who tried to justify the actions that they had taken in closing another institution that should not have been closed. They were legitimized by a federal judge who held an abbreviated hearing and who issued an opinion that was short on facts and logic but long on colorful and exaggerated language. They were printed in newspapers and aired in television and radio broadcasts throughout the country.

The words were uttered at a time when taxpayers were being told that they were stuck with a massive bill to clean up the failed S&L industry. The taxpayers demanded explanations of why and how the whole mess had happened.

Out of political expediency, the words were readily embraced, echoed, and endorsed by the members of a congressional committee who were desperately searching for a scapegoat and plausible explanation that would absolve them of their culpability in the demise of an industry and the destruction of the economy. With a scapegoat, the politicians hoped to avoid the taxpayers' wrath, so they could get reelected—a politician's primary goal in life.

So, government prosecutors were forced into the position of asserting that criminal conduct had occurred. They needed scalps—as many as they could get—to satisfy their political bosses.

The prosecutors turned loose the dogs—the investigatory agencies. In order to obtain information that would allow them to construct a case, the government agents demanded documents and intimidated, threatened, and interrogated people. Focusing on the transactions that the regulators and their hired guns had already used to rationalize and justify the government's actions in destroying ACC and Lincoln, the agents hammered and bent information so it would conform to a series of themes that converted routine, commercial transactions into arguable acts of criminal conduct. The government's themes were developed with, picked up on by, and shared with attorneys for civil plaintiffs, who incorporated the themes into their strategy for the civil trials, thereby allowing both the criminal prosecutors and the civil attorneys to conduct a coordinated attack against the defendants.

Then, the tactics of "legal extortion" were employed on both the civil and criminal litigation fronts to pound as many defendants as possible into submission.

Civil attorneys, utilizing RICO statutes and taking full advantage of the inherent inequities of joint-and-several liability, threatened civil defendants with extortionate levels of punitive damages. These potential damages, when combined with the effects of staggering litigation costs, federal and state indictments of some of the defendants, asset freezes and seizures, the possibility of being put out of business, and the silencing of potential witnesses through the use of thinly veiled threats of indictment, rapidly brought the civil defendants to their knees. The defendants had no reasonable alternative but to settle with the plaintiffs and fork over the blackmail money.

On the criminal front, the legal extortion took a different form. The government used a carrot-and-stick approach with borrowers and customers by saying to them, "Cooperate—i.e., give us damaging testimony against our targets—and your loans and debts will be resolved amicably, credit will be made available, and we won't pursue you. Don't cooperate, and your projects will be foreclosed, credit will disappear, civil suits will be filed, and we'll lock you up and throw away the key." With particularly vulnerable individuals, the legal extortion was less subtle, as the government said, "We have indicted you or will indict you on multiple counts. If you cooperate, we'll let you cop a plea to a single offense, and we will go easy on sentencing you. If you don't cooperate, we will pursue you as vigorously as we can, using all the resources and power of the government, and, in the end, we'll nail you. We'll take all your assets, put you in jail for a long time, and see that you never earn a decent living again." Most people took the government's deal.

There was also a legion of people who were condemned to limbo-land. They'd been investigated and subtly threatened but not charged with anything. The government wanted these people merely to stay on the sidelines—not to screw up the civil or criminal cases. So, they were left as targets, subjects, or in an unknown status, never officially cleared or charged. As such, they were advised by their attorneys to remain silent by asserting their Fifth Amendment rights.

Professional firms, primarily accountants and lawyers, who could have aided Keating by debunking some of the government's theories and allegations, were also kept out of the game. They had paid the extortionate demands of the RTC, OTS, and the FDIC, but the government still held powerful weapons in reserve. For example, the SEC, which, through the use of various sanctions, had the ability effectively to deny the firms the ability to conduct their practices. If the firms assisted Keating by testifying for the defense, it's logical to assume that these weapons would be employed—either as threats or as tools of destruction. So, the firms were removed from the game—they couldn't hurt the prosecution or assist the defense.

Then, the prosecutors were aided by the courts. Keating believed that to defend himself adequately, he needed to show that it was the government—not he—who was responsible for all the losses. He consistently maintained that he was the victim of the government's actions and policies—regulators operating with improper motives and outside the boundaries of the law; overzealous and misguided bureaucrats; failed public policies; illegal leaks; improper re-regulation; improper interpretation and application of existing laws; and so on. He maintained that, were it not for the government's actions, Lincoln would have survived and prospered; ACC's creditors would not have suffered losses; and no acts of wrongdoing ever would have been alleged. He asserted that he was accused of crimes simply because the government had to justify and cover up its own actions. And he has stated that if he could present the evidence of the government's culpability, any jury would find in his favor.

Keating may be right.

The government's role in this whole affair has been reprehensible. With the express intent to inflict harm on Lincoln and ACC, government agents leaked information to the press. They willfully and knowingly breached agreements and contracts. They distorted and misapplied the laws and regulations they were charged with upholding. They disregarded information which detracted from their own agenda. They intentionally gave their superiors incomplete and purposefully distorted information. They repeatedly stepped out of the bounds of their legal mandate. And, under oath, they repeatedly perjured themselves.

While the conduct of the government's agents was reprehensible, the actions of the policymakers—Congress and several White House administrations—was unconscionable. They enacted the legislation that enabled and encouraged S&Ls to expand and diversify—increased deposit insurance limits, Garn-St. Germain, and the 1981 tax bill, among others. They passed the 1986 tax bill which destroyed real-estate values and the collateral held by insured institutions. After the S&Ls were fully committed to diversification, they remained silent while the regulators changed all the rules in midstream, condemning hundreds of thrifts to certain death. While regulators went across the country and unnecessarily closed institution after institution, the politicians sat idly and watched the losses mount. They covered up and lied to the public about the nature and depth of the problems in the industry. They purposefully, deliberately, and deceitfully vilified people in order to hide their own culpability. They allowed government liquidators—FADA, FDIC, and RTC—to squander billions of dollars. And while all this was happening, they lined their pockets with campaign contributions from the very people they would condemn and destroy.

As anyone who has dealt with the bureaucracy in Washington can attest, the halls of government are full of people who take almost orgasmic delight in driving spears into the chests of citizens. The bigger, wealthier, and more powerful the citizen they impale, the greater the high they receive. They render harm to citizens for one simple reason: because they can. It's raw power that they can and most certainly do exercise whenever they want—and against whomever they choose. Their actions lead one to conclude that each year more damage is done to the American citizenry by their own government than by all the other forces on earth combined. And in the Lincoln Savings War, there were some truly vicious bastards who exercised the immense power of their governmental positions with total impunity.

That's, in part, what Keating wanted a jury to see.

But in each case, the judge denied Keating the ability to show the jury—through documents and witnesses—the role that the government had played in the charges alleged against him.

The judge's function in the game is that of a referee—an impartial person who sees that the playing field is even and that both sides observe the rules in presenting their cases to the jury. But, as any sports fan knows, referees can and do have an effect on the outcome of the game—a good or bad call can have a dramatic impact on the fortunes of the contestants. Here, the calls by the judges stripped Keating of his primary game plan.

Nor was the playing field even. In both criminal trials, the prosecutors had the advantage of witnesses who had been thoroughly subjected to the process of legal extortion. They had entered guilty pleas which required cooperation with the prosecution. Hence, was their testimony truthful, or was it merely a convenient story, crafted with the help of government agents, that was told to aid the government's case and to protect their own skins? As for Keating's potential witnesses, they were either eliminated by the judges' rulings that limited comment on the government's role or were people who, because of extortionate threats, found it necessary to remain silently on the sidelines.

Under such circumstances, did the truth come out in these legal proceedings?

The government says it did. The government says that the jury heard all of the relevant evidence and, on the basis of that evidence, concluded that Keating violated the law and is a criminal who deserves to be incarcerated.

On the other hand, Keating maintains that, because of the uneven playing field, the truth has not been told. He maintains his innocence.

Today, Charlie Keating sits in a prison cell hoping that the day will come when the American public will learn the full story of the Lincoln Savings War. He believes that could occur when various appellate courts review the proceedings of the state and federal criminal trials. That may or may not turn out to be the case. The focus of the lower courts wasn't on truth, so why should truth enter into the deliberations of any higher court? Nevertheless, Keating and his lawyers remain hopeful.

As Keating awaits the appeals, those who know him believe that he sees himself, not as a criminal, but as a political prisoner of an unfair government. Keating might be right.

History is replete with instances where individuals have been accused and convicted of crimes simply to meet the propaganda needs of a government in trouble. Why should this government be any different?

Only when the whole story comes out—and that may never occur—will the truth be known.

Until then, we will each have our own views of Keating and his role in the S&L industry's demise—views that we will form on the basis of what we see, hear, and read. There are many sides to the story and many versions of the story. Some represent truth, others don't.

Based on all that I have seen, read, and heard since I first got involved in this War, the story presented in this book is truthful. But you be the judge of that.

Characters

AMERICAN CONTINENTAL CORPORATION
Charles H. ("Charlie") Keating, Jr., Chairman of the Board and CEO
Judy J. Wischer, President
Robert J. ("Bob") Kielty, Executive Vice-President and General Counsel
Andrew F. ("Andy") Ligget, Chief Financial Officer
Timothy ("Kruck") Kruckeberg, Assistant to Judy Wischer

LINCOLN SAVINGS AND LOAN ASSOCIATION
Andre A. ("Andy") Niebling, various positions
William ("Bill") Hinz, Chairman for a brief period in 1987–1988
Robin S. ("Rob") Symes, various positions
Ray C. Fidel, various positions
James Grogan, General Counsel
Mark Sauter, General Counsel
David Thompson, General Counsel
Ronald Stoll, General Counsel
Virginia ("Ginger") Novak, General Counsel
Scott Siebels, General Counsel
Bruce Dickson, Lending
Randy Conte, Loan Administration
Sheldon ("Shelly") Weiner, Investments
James ("Jim") Upchurch, Investments
Charles H. ("C-III") Keating III, Land Development, Charlie's son
Robert M. ("Wurz") Wurzelbacher, Jr., Commercial Properties, Charlie's son-in-law
Robert Hubbard, Insurance, Charlie's son-in-law
Joe Sanicola, Regulatory Accountant

OTHER KEATING FAMILY MEMBERS
Mary Elaine Keating, Charlie's wife
Kathy Hubbard, daughter
Mary Hall, daughter
Gary Hall, M.D., son-in-law, an ophthalmologist
Beth Wurzelbacher, daughter
Elaine Boland, daughter
Brad Boland, Lincoln's Commercial Properties, son-in-law
Maureen Mulhern, daughter
Thomas Mulhern, Lincoln's Land Development, son-in-law

FEDERAL HOME LOAN BANK BOARD
Edwin Gray, Chairman until June 1987
M. Danny Wall, Chairman following Gray
Lawrence White, member
Roger Martin, member
Lee H. Henkel, Jr., briefly a member and a customer of Lincoln Savings

FEDERAL HOME LOAN BANK BOARD—STAFF
Darrel Dochow, Director of Office of Regulatory Policy, Oversight and Supervision (ORPOS) [subsequently ORA and now Office of Thrift Supervision (OTS)]
Rosemary Stewart, Office of Enforcement
Stephen Hershkowitz, Office of Enforcement
Jordan Luke, General Counsel
William Robertson, Director of Office of Regulatory Activities (ORA)
John Price, ORA
George Barclay, Dallas, member of Enforcement Review Committee (ERC)
Karl Hoyle, member ERC
Alvin Smuzynski, ORPOS
Kevin O'Connell, ORPOS
Carol Larson, Accounting Fellow
Kyle Klein, Tax Accountant
Julie Williams, Legal

FEDERAL HOME LOAN BANK OF SAN FRANCISCO
James Cirona, President
Michael Patriarca, Director, Agency Group
William Black, General Counsel
C.A. Deardorff, Agency Group, Deputy Director
B.J. Davis, Supervisory
Sonja Rodriguez, Staff
Sidney Mar, Lincoln's Principal Supervisory Agent in 1986

FEDERAL HOME LOAN BANK OF SAN FRANCISCO—
1986 EXAMINATION TEAM
Richard Sanchez, Supervisory Agent
Del Fassett, Los Angeles Office
Joe Kotrys, Examiner-in-Charge
Robert Dove, Kotrys' Supervisor in Los Angeles
Dennis Fitzgerald, Examiner
Glen Sanders, Appraiser

FEDERAL HOME LOAN BANK BOARD—
1988 EXAMINATION TEAM
Steve Scott, in charge of Lincoln exam
James Clark, Investment area
Charles ("Chuck") Gozdanovich, Lending and Real Estate areas
Steve Rohrs, Operations areas
Alex Barabolak, in charge of ACC holding-company exam
John ("Jack") Meek, Examiner
Robert Concannon, Examiner
David Riley, Examiner

CALIFORNIA DEPARTMENT OF SAVINGS AND LOAN (CDSL)
William Crawford, Commissioner
Lawrence Taggart, former Commissioner preceding Crawford
William Davis, Deputy
Wallace Sumimoto, Supervisor
Harvey Shames, Supervisor
Tommy Mar, Senior Examiner
Eugene Stelzer, Examiner
Richard Newsome, Examiner
Gerald Castillo, Examiner

PILLSBURY, MADISON & SUTRO
Alan Litman
Bruce Ericson

KENNETH LEVENTHAL & COMPANY
Roger Johnson
Terry Gilbert

KAYE, SCHOLER, FIERMAN, HAYS & HANDLER
Peter Fishbein
Lynn Toby Fisher
Karen Katzman

ARTHUR YOUNG & COMPANY
William Gladstone
Janice Vincent
Nancy Matusiak

TOUCHE ROSS
Jerry Mayer
Fred Martin

SIDLEY & AUSTIN
Margery Waxman

OTHERS IN GOVERNMENT
Donald Regan, Secretary of the Treasury and Reagan's Chief of Staff
David Stockman, Director of OMB
Stanley Sporkin, Federal Judge
William Seidman, FDIC
William Isaac, FDIC
Richard Breeden, SEC
Henry Gonzalez, Chairman, House of Representatives, Committee
on Banking, Finance and Urban Affairs
Senator Donald Riegle
Senator Dennis DeConcini
Senator John Glenn
Senator Alan Cranston
Senator John McCain

LINCOLN'S CUSTOMERS AND BUSINESS ASSOCIATES
Ernest ("Ernie") Garcia, borrower
Conley Wolfswinkle, borrower

Neil Gascon, borrower
James C.V. Nalley, borrower and purchaser of assets
Sir James Goldsmith, partner in ventures
R.A. Homes, borrower
Julius Trump
Eddie Trump

POTENTIAL BUYERS OF LINCOLN
Spencer Scott
Ernest Leff
Herman Rappaport
James Fail
John Rousselot

U.S. LEAGUE OF SAVINGS INSTITUTIONS
William O'Connell

OTHERS
Alan Greenspan, consultant to Lincoln
Professor George Benston, consultant to Lincoln

Abbreviations

AA: Arthur Andersen & Co.
ADC: acquisition, development, and construction
ACC: American Continental Corporation
AFL: American Founders Life Insurance Company
AICPA: American Institute of Certified Public Accountants
AMCC: see ACC
APB: Accounting Principles Board
ARM: adjustable-rate mortgage
BIF: Bank Insurance Fund
C&D: cease and desist
C&L: Coopers & Lybrand
CAP: Central Arizona Project
CDSL: California Department of Savings and Loan
CEBA: Competitive Equality Banking Act of 1987
CEO: chief executive officer
CH: Crescent Hotels
CHC: Continental Homes Corporation
CHGM: Crescent Hotel Group of Michigan
CMO: Collateralized Mortgage Obligation
CPA: Certified Public Accountant
CRA: Community Reinvestment Act
CZ: Crown Zellerbach
D&O coverage: directors' and officers' liability insurance
DSL: Department of Savings and Loan
ERC: Enforcement Review Committee (FHLBB)
ESIP: Employee Stock Incentive Plan
ESOP: Employee Stock Ownership Plan
FADA: Federal Asset Disposition Association
FASB: Financial Accounting Standards Board
FDIC: Federal Deposit Insurance Corporation
FHA: Federal Housing Act

FHLB: Federal Home Loan Bank
FHLB-SF: Federal Home Loan Bank of San Francisco
FHLBB: Federal Home Loan Bank Board
FHLMC: Federal Home Loan Mortgage Corporation
FIRREA: Financial Institutions Reform, Recovery, and Enforcement Act
   of 1989
FNMA: Federal National Mortgage Association
FRESOP notes: Floating Rate Employee Stock Ownership Plan notes
FSLIC: Federal Savings and Loan Insurance Corporation
GAAP: generally accepted accounting principles
GSE: government-sponsored enterprise
GNMA: Government National Mortgage Association
GOIL: General Oriental Investments Limited
GOSLP: General Oriental Securities Limited Partnership
GUAC: Grand Union Acquisition Corporation
HPLP: Hotel Pontchartrain Limited Partnership
HVPLP: Hidden Valley Properties Limited Partnership
IRS: Internal Revenue Service
KIO: Kuwait Investment Office
LSAC: Lincoln Savings Acquisition Corporation
MAI: Member of Appraisal Institute
MCP: Management Consignment Program
MDC: M.D.C. Holdings, Inc.
MLCM: Merrill Lynch Capital Markets
MOU: Memorandum of Understanding
NOW Accounts: negotiable order of withdrawal accounts
NRLP: National Realty Limited Partnership
OE: Office of Enforcement
OMB: Office of Management and Budget
ORA: Office of Regulatory Activities
ORPOS: Office of Regulatory Policy, Oversight and Supervision
OTS: Office of Thrift Supervision
PAC: Political Action Committee
PSA: Principal Supervisory Agent
RA: R.A. Homes, Inc.
RAP: regulatory accounting principles
RICO: Racketeer Influenced and Corrupt Organizations Act
RTC: Resolution Trust Corporation
REVCO: Revco D.S., Inc.
S&L: savings and loan association
SAIF: Savings Association Insurance Fund
SEB: Saudi European Bank
SEC: Securities and Exchange Commission

SFAS: Financial Accounting Standards Board Statement
SFR ARM: Single-family, adjustable-rate mortgage
TCSF: TCS Financial, Inc.
TEP: Tucson Electric Power Company
Wescon: West Continental Mortgage and Investment Corporation
WGI: Wolfswinkle Group, Inc.